KT-475-483

THE RISE AND FALL OF AMERICAN GROWTH

The Princeton Economic History of the Western World

Joel Mokyr, Series Editor

A list of titles in this series appears at the back of the book.

THE RISE AND FALL OF AMERICAN GROWTH

THE U.S. STANDARD OF LIVING SINCE THE CIVIL WAR

ROBERT J. GORDON

Princeton University Press
Princeton and Oxford

Published by Princeton University Press, 41 William Street, Princeton, New Jersey 08540
In the United Kingdom: Princeton University Press, 6 Oxford Street, Woodstock, Oxfordshire OX20 1TW

press.princeton.edu

Jacket image: "Construction of a Dam," by William Gropper. Oil on canvas, 1939.
Jacket design: Faceout Studio, Kara Davison

Library of Congress Cataloging-in-Publication Data

Gordon, Robert J., author.
The rise and fall of American growth : the U.S. standard of living since the Civil War / Robert J. Gordon.
pages cm. — (The Princeton economic history of the Western world)
Includes bibliographical references and index.
ISBN 978-0-691-14772-7 (hardcover : alk. paper) — ISBN 0-691-14772-8 (hardcover : alk. paper)
1. Cost and standard of living—United States—History. 2. United States—Economic conditions—1865–1918. 3. United States—Economic conditions—1918–1945. 4. United States—Economic conditions—1945- I. Title.
HD6983.G69 2016
339.4'20973—dc23 2015027560

British Library Cataloging-in-Publication Data is available

This book has been composed in Minion Pro

Printed on acid-free paper. ∞

Printed in the United States of America

10 9 8 7 6 5 4 3 2 1

For Julie, who knows our love is here to stay

CONTENTS

PREFACE

This is a book about the rise and fall of American economic growth since the Civil War. It has long been recognized that economic growth is not steady or continuous. There was no economic growth over the eight centuries between the fall of the Roman Empire and the Middle Ages. Historical research has shown that real output per person in Britain between 1300 and 1700 barely doubled in four centuries, in contrast to the experience of Americans in the twentieth century who enjoyed a doubling every 32 years. Research conducted half a century ago concluded that American growth was steady but relatively slow until 1920, when it began to take off. Scholars struggled for decades to identify the factors that caused productivity growth to decline significantly after 1970. What has been missing is a comprehensive and unified explanation of why productivity growth was so fast between 1920 and 1970 and so slow thereafter. This book contributes to resolving one of the most fundamental questions about American economic history.

The central idea that American economic growth has varied systematically over time, rising to a peak in the mid-twentieth century and then falling, in a sense represents a rebellion against the models of "steady-state growth" that have dominated thinking about the growth process since the mid-1950s. My interest in the mid-century growth peak can be traced back to my 1965 summer job at age 24 after completion of my first year of graduate school in economics at MIT. One of our projects was to research the issue of corporate "tax shifting," that is, the question whether business firms escaped the burden of the corporation income tax by passing it along to customers in the form of higher prices. The technique was to compare prices and profits in the 1920s, when the corporate tax rate was low, to the 1950s, when the tax rate was much higher. While the existing literature supported the idea of shifting through higher prices, because before-tax profit rates per unit of capital were substantially higher in the 1950s than in the 1920s, there was no corresponding increase in the ratio of profits to sales. This discrepancy was caused by the sharp jump in the ratio of sales to corporate capital between the 1920s and 1950s.

During that summer, economists interested in growth were just beginning to digest John Kendrick's magisterial 1961 book *Productivity Trends in the United States* that presented for the first time a consistent set of annual data on output and inputs back to 1889. The Kendrick data showed that the sharp jump in output relative to capital between the 1920s and the 1950s characterized the entire economy, not just the corporate sector. This appeared to conflict with our MIT classroom growth models that were characterized by a long-run constancy in the ratio of output to capital. Recognizing this potential contradiction between theory and fact, I wrote home to my economist parents on August 26, 1965, "I am fascinated by this because the rise in [the ratio of output to capital] must have been for technological, structural ('real') reasons."[1]

My summer research on tax shifting led to a term paper that was accepted for publication in the *American Economic Review.* My PhD dissertation was on the puzzle of the jump in the output-capital ratio between the 1920s and 1950s, which is the counterpart of the rapid rise of productivity growth in the middle of the twentieth century that forms a central topic of this book. While much of the thesis contributed little to a solution, the most important chapter discovered that a substantial part of the capital input that produced output during and after World War II was missing from the data, because all the factories and equipment that were built during the war to produce tanks, airplanes, and weapons by private firms like General Motors or Ford were paid for by the government and were not recorded in the data on private capital input.

In the late 1990s I returned to twentieth century growth history with a paper written for a conference in Groningen, the Netherlands, in honor of Angus Maddison, the famous compiler and creator of growth statistics. Published in 2000, the paper's title, "Interpreting the 'One Big Wave' in U.S. Long-term Productivity Growth," called attention to the mid-century peak in the U.S. growth process. At the same time there was clear evidence that the long post-1972 slump in U.S. productivity growth was over, at least temporarily, as the annual growth rate of labor productivity soared in the late 1990s. I was skeptical, however, that the inventions of the computer age would turn out to be as important for long-run economic growth as electricity, the internal combustion engine, and the other "great inventions" of the late nineteenth century.

My skepticism took the form of an article, also published in 2000, titled "Does the 'New Economy' Measure Up to the Great Inventions of the Past?" That paper pulled together the many dimensions of invention in the late nineteenth century and compared them systematically to the dot.com revolution of the 1990s. Thus was born Part I of this book with its analysis of how the great inventions changed everyday life. The overall theme of the book represents a merger of the two papers, the first on the "One Big Wave" and the second on the "Great Inventions."

The book connects with two different strands of literature. One is the long tradition of economic history of explaining accelerations and decelerations of economic growth. The other is the more recent writing of the "techno-optimists," who think that robots and artificial intelligence are currently bringing the American economy to the cusp of a historic acceleration of productivity growth to rates never experienced before. Chapter 17 places techno-optimism in perspective by arguing that the main benefits of digitalization for productivity growth have already occurred during the temporary productivity growth revival of 1996–2004. Chapter 18 points in a different direction as it finds additional sources of slowing growth in a group of headwinds—inequality, education, demography, and fiscal—that are in the process of reducing growth in median real disposable income well below the growth rate of productivity.

Writing began in the summer of 2011. For the chapters in Part I, I knew relatively little and had to start from scratch, aided by a series of undergraduate research assistants (RAs). The first RA was hired soon after the book project was conceived in 2007, and, through the final updating in charts in the summer of 2015, a total of 15 Northwestern undergraduate RAs worked on the project. Their names and those of many others who made this book possible are contained in the separate acknowledgments section at the end of the book.

For the chapters in Part I on 1870–1940 the sources were primarily library books that formed large stacks on tables in my Northwestern and home offices. The most interesting books were written not by economists but rather by historians and nonacademic authors. My favorite book of economic history is James Cronon's *Nature's Metropolis: Chicago and the Great West,* which I devoured as soon as it was published in 1991. Two of the most fruitful sources in writing the early chapters were Thomas Schlereth's *Victorian America: Transformations in Everyday Life, 1876–1913* and Ann Greene's *Horses at Work: Harnessing Power in Industrial America.*

The task of writing the post-1940 chapters of Part II was easier. There was less need to rely on books because articles were plentiful. Now I was on my home turf because I had previously written much that was relevant to postwar advances in the standard of living. One of my current classes is a freshman seminar titled "Did Economics Win the Two World Wars?" which has provided the opportunity over 15 years to read extensively on the economics of the home front during World War II. This background helped lead me to the conclusion of Chapter 16, that the Great Depression and World War II taken together constitute the major explanation of the sharp jump in total factor productivity that occurred between the 1920s and 1950s.

When it came time to write about the improving postwar quality of clothing, houses, household appliances, TV sets, and automobiles, I returned to my previous role as a critic of conventional measures of price indexes. Many of the estimates in Chapters 10 through12 of changes in quality come from my 1990 book, *The Measurement of Durable Goods Prices.* The core arguments of Chapters 17 and 18 were developed first in a 2012 working paper on the "end of growth," in its 2014 sequel paper, and in innumerable speeches and debates with the "techno-optimists."

The resulting book combines economics and history in a unique blend. The book differs from most on economic history in its close examination of the small details of everyday life and work, both inside and outside of the home. It is not like most histories of the evolution of home life or working conditions, for it interprets the details within the broader context of the analysis of economic growth. More than 120 graphs and tables provide new transformations and arrangements of the data. The analysis contributes a joint interpretation of both the rapid pace of economic growth in the central decades of the twentieth century and of the post-1970 growth slowdown that continues to this day.

The book is a readable flashback to another age when life and work were risky, dull, tedious, dangerous, and often either too hot or too cold in an era that lacked not just air conditioning but also central heating. The book is not just about numbers and trends and growth rates going up and down but also about individual sweat and tears, about the drudgery of doing laundry in the era before running water and the washing machine, where the only tools were the scrub board and the outdoor clothes line. This is a book about the drama of a revolutionary century when, through a set of miracles, economic growth accelerated, the modern world was created, and then after that creation the potential for future inventions having a similar impact on everyday life of necessity was inevitably diminished. The implications for the future of U.S. and world economic growth could not be more profound.

Robert J. Gordon
Evanston, Illinois
August 2015

THE RISE AND FALL OF AMERICAN GROWTH

Chapter I

INTRODUCTION

The Ascent and Descent of Growth

> The century after the Civil War was to be an Age of Revolution—of countless, little-noticed revolutions, which occurred not in the halls of legislatures or on battlefields or on the barricades but in homes and farms and factories and schools and stores, across the landscape and in the air—so little noticed because they came so swiftly, because they touched Americans everywhere and every day. Not merely the continent but human experience itself, the very meaning of community, of time and space, of present and future, was being revised again and again, a new democratic world was being invented and was being discovered by Americans wherever they lived.
>
> —Daniel J. Boorstin, 1973

THE SPECIAL CENTURY

The century of revolution in the United States after the Civil War was economic, not political, freeing households from an unremitting daily grind of painful manual labor, household drudgery, darkness, isolation, and early death. Only one hundred years later, daily life had changed beyond recognition. Manual outdoor jobs were replaced by work in air-conditioned environments, housework was increasingly performed by electric appliances, darkness was replaced by light, and isolation was replaced not just by travel, but also by color television images bringing the world into the living room. Most important, a newborn infant could expect to live not to age forty-five, but to age seventy-two. The economic revolution of 1870 to 1970 was unique in human history, unrepeatable because so many of its achievements could happen only once.

This book is based on an important idea having innumerable implications: Economic growth is not a steady process that creates economic advance at a regular pace, century after century. Instead, progress occurs much more rapidly in some times than in others. There was virtually no economic growth for millennia until 1770, only slow growth in the transition century before 1870, remarkably rapid growth in the century ending in 1970, and slower growth since then. Our central thesis is that *some inventions are more important than others,* and that the revolutionary century after the Civil War was made possible by a unique clustering, in the late nineteenth century, of what we will call the "Great Inventions."

This leads directly to the second big idea: that economic growth since 1970 has been simultaneously dazzling and disappointing. This paradox is resolved when we recognize that advances since 1970 have tended to be channeled into a narrow sphere of human activity having to do with entertainment, communications, and the collection and processing of information. For the rest of what humans care about—food, clothing, shelter, transportation, health, and working conditions both inside and outside the home—progress slowed down after 1970, both qualitatively and quantitatively. Our best measure of the pace of innovation and technical progress is total factor productivity (hereafter TFP), a measure of how quickly output is growing relative to the growth of labor and capital inputs. TFP grew after 1970 at barely a third the rate achieved between 1920 and 1970. The third big idea follows directly from the second. Our chronicle of the rise in the American standard of living over the past 150 years rests heavily on the history of innovations, great and small alike. However, any consideration of U.S. economic progress in the future must look beyond innovation to contemplate the headwinds that are blowing like a gale to slow down the vessel of progress. Chief among these headwinds is the rise of inequality that since 1970 has steadily directed an ever larger share of the fruits of the American growth machine to the top of the income distribution.

Our starting point, that a single hundred-year period, the "special century," was more important to economic progress than have been all other centuries, represents a rebellion against the theory of economic growth as it has evolved over the last sixty years. Growth theory features an economy operating in a "steady state" in which a continuing inflow of new ideas and technologies creates opportunities for investment. But articles on growth theory rarely mention that the model does not apply to most of human existence. According to the great historian of economic growth, Angus Maddison, the annual rate of growth in the Western world from AD 1 to AD 1820 was a mere 0.06 percent per year, or 6 percent per century.[1] As succinctly stated by economic commentator Steven Landsburg,

> Modern humans first emerged about 100,000 years ago. For the next 99,800 years or so, nothing happened. Well, not quite nothing. There were wars, political intrigue, the invention of agriculture—but none of that stuff had much effect on the quality of people's lives. Almost everyone lived on the modern equivalent of $400 to $600 a year, just above the subsistence level.... Then—just a couple of hundred years ago—people started getting richer. And richer and richer still.[2]

This book adopts the "special century" approach to economic growth, holding that economic growth witnessed a singular interval of rapid growth that will not be repeated—the designation of the century between 1870 and 1970 as the special epoch applies only to the United States, the nation which has carved out the technological frontier for all developed nations since the Civil War. This book's focus on the United States, however, does not deny that other nations also made stupendous progress, that western Europe and Japan largely caught up to the United States in the second half of the twentieth century, and that China and other emerging nations are now well on their way in the catch-up process to the techniques and amenities enjoyed by the developed world.

Our first order of business is to identify those aspects of the post-1870 economic revolution that made it unique and impossible to repeat. We are so used to the essential comforts of everyday life, of being clean and warm, that we can easily forget how recently those comforts were achieved. In 1870, farm and urban working-class family members bathed in a large tub in the kitchen, often the only heated room in the home, after carrying cold water in pails from the outside and warming it over the open-hearth fireplace. All that carrying and heating of water was such a nuisance that baths were not a daily or even weekly event; some people bathed as seldom as once per month. Similarly, heat in every room was a distant dream—yet became a daily possibility in a few decades, between 1890 and 1940.

Progress did not suddenly begin in 1870. Rather, that year marks the start of our saga, for the Civil War provides a sharp historical marker separating the antebellum and postbellum ages. A tale of economic progress needs numbers to document that progress, and the raw data of economics became much more adequate with the first Census of Manufacturing, carried out in 1869, a year that coincidentally brought the nation together when the transcontinental railroad was joined at Promontory Summit in Utah.

Our starting point in 1870 should not be taken to diminish the progress that had been made in the previous half century. A newborn child in 1820 entered a world that was almost medieval: a dim world lit by candlelight, in which folk remedies treated health problems and in which travel was no faster than that possible by hoof or sail. Three great inventions of that half century—the railroad, steamship, and telegraph—set the stage for more rapid progress after 1870. The Civil War itself showcased these inventions when northern trains sped Yankee troops to the front and steamships blockaded supplies to the south from Britain, hastening southern defeat. And no longer was news delayed by days or weeks. Half a century earlier, the Battle of New Orleans had been fought on January 8, 1815, three weeks after the Treaty of Ghent was signed to end the War of 1812. Before development of the telegraph and undersea cable, news traveled very slowly. But during the Civil War, the daily newspapers carried dispatches announcing the outcomes of battles mere hours after they occurred.

The flood of inventions that followed the Civil War utterly transformed life, transferring human attention and energy from the mundane to soaring skyscrapers and airplanes. What makes the period 1870–1970 so special is that these inventions cannot be repeated. When electricity made it possible to create light with the flick of a switch instead of the strike of a match, the process of creating light was changed forever. When the electric elevator allowed buildings to extend vertically instead of horizontally, the very nature of land use was changed, and urban density was created. When small electric machines attached to the floor or held in the hand replaced huge and heavy steam boilers that transmitted power by leather or rubber belts, the scope for replacing human labor with machines broadened beyond recognition. And so it was with motor vehicles replacing horses as the primary form of intra-urban transportation; no longer did society have to allocate a quarter of its agricultural land to support the feeding of the horses or maintain a sizable labor force for removing their waste. Transportation among all the Great Inventions is noteworthy for achieving 100 percent of its potential increase in speed in little more than a century, from the first primitive railroads replacing the stagecoach in the 1830s to the Boeing 707 flying near the speed of sound in 1958.

Households in the late nineteenth century spent half their family budgets on food, and the transition of the food supply from medieval to modern also occurred during the special century. The Mason jar, invented in 1859 by John Landis Mason, made it possible to preserve food at home. The first canned meats were fed to Northern troops during the Civil War, and during the late nineteenth century a vast array of branded processed foods, from Kellogg's corn flakes and Borden's condensed milk to Jell-O, entered American homes. The last step to the modern era, the invention of a method for freezing food, was achieved by Clarence Birdseye in 1916, though his invention had to wait for decades to become practical at home until in the 1950s the electric refrigerator had finally progressed enough to be able to maintain a zero temperature in its freezer compartment. In 1870, shoes and men's clothing were purchased from stores, but women's clothing was made at home by mothers and daughters. The sewing machine had only recently reached the mass market and "held out the impossible promise that one of the great drudge pastimes of domestic life could actually be made exciting and fun."[3] By the 1920s, most female clothing was purchased from retail outlets that did not exist in 1870—namely, the great urban department stores and, for rural customers, the mail-order catalogs.

Some measures of progress are subjective, but lengthened life expectancy and the conquest of infant mortality are solid quantitative indicators of the advances made over the special century in the realms of medicine and public health. Public waterworks not only revolutionized the daily routine of the housewife but also protected every family against waterborne diseases. The development of anesthetics in the late nineteenth century made the gruesome pain of amputations a thing of the past, and the invention of antiseptic surgery cleaned up the squalor of the nineteenth-century hospital. X-rays, antibiotics, and modern treatments for cancer were all invented and implemented in the special century.

What made the century so unique is not only the magnitude of its transitions, but also the speed with which they were completed. Though not a single household was wired for electricity in 1880, nearly 100 percent of U.S. urban homes were wired by 1940, and in the same time interval the percentage of urban homes with clean running piped water and sewer pipes for waste disposal had reached 94 percent. More than 80 percent of urban homes in 1940 had interior flush toilets, 73 percent had gas for heating and cooking, 58 percent had central heating, and 56 percent had mechanical refrigerators.[4] In short, the 1870 house was isolated from the rest of the world, but 1940 houses were "networked," most having the five connections of electricity, gas, telephone, water, and sewer.

The networked house, together with modern appliances, changed the nature of housework. The long days previously devoted to doing laundry on a scrub board, hanging clothes outside to dry, making and mending clothing, and baking and preserving food had now transitioned into fewer hours of housework. Hours released from housework were now available for women to participate in market work. The improvement in working conditions for men was even more profound. In 1870, more than half of men were engaged in farming, either as proprietors or as farm laborers. Their hours were long and hard; they were exposed to heat in the summer and cold in the winter, and the fruits of their labor were at the mercy of droughts, floods, and infestations of insects. Working-class jobs in the city required sixty hours of work per week—ten hours per day, including Saturdays. More than half of teenage boys were engaged in child labor, and male heads of households worked until they were disabled or dead. But by 1970, the whole concept of time had changed, including the introduction of blocks of time that were barely known a century earlier, including the two-day weekend and retirement.

Thanks to all these irreversible changes, the overarching transition in the half century after the Civil War was from an agrarian society of loosely linked small towns to an increasingly urban and industrial society with stronger private and governmental institutions and an increasingly diverse population. Milestones on the one-way road from a rural society to an urban one are marked off by the urban percentage of the population, defined as those living in organized governmental units with a population of 2,500 or more. The percent of the nation classified as urban grew from 24.9 percent in 1870 to 73.7 percent in 1970.[5]

There is no greater example of the importance of the inventions of the special century than the aftermath of Hurricane Sandy, a freakishly powerful storm that devastated much of New York City and the seacoast of New Jersey in late October 2012. Floods have been common throughout human history, but interaction between the weather and the Great Inventions had not previously occurred on such a scale. Sandy pushed many of its victims back to the nineteenth century. Residents of New York City below Thirty-Fourth Street learned what it was like to lose the elevators that routinely had carried them to and from their apartments. Not only was vertical movement impeded, but the loss of the subways to flooding, along with the electrical blackout, eliminated the primary means of horizontal movement as well. Anyone who had no power also lost such modern inventions as electric lighting, air-conditioning and fans to ventilate dwelling spaces, and refrigerators and freezers to keep food from spoiling. Many residents had no heat, no hot food, and even no running water. Those living in New Jersey were often unable to find gasoline needed for commuting, because gas station pumps could not function without electricity. Moreover, communication was shut off after batteries were drained on laptops and mobile phones.

SINCE 1970: A NARROWER PALETTE OF PROGRESS COMBINES WITH DIMINISHING RETURNS

Designating 1870–1970 the "special century" implies that the years since 1970 have been less special. First, the technological advance started to show its age. With a few notable exceptions, the pace of innovation since 1970 has not been as broad or as deep as that spurred by the inventions of the special century. Second, after 1970, rising inequality meant that the fruits of innovation were no longer shared equally: though those at the top of the income distribution continued to prosper, a shrinking share of the growing economic pie made its way to the Americans in the middle and bottom of the income distribution.

The special century was special not only because everyday life changed completely, but also because it changed in so many dimensions, including those associated with electricity, the internal combustion engine, health, working conditions, and the networking of the home. Progress after 1970 continued but focused more narrowly on entertainment, communication, and information technology, in which areas progress did not arrive with a great and sudden burst as had the by-products of the Great Inventions. Instead, changes have been evolutionary and continuous. For instance, the advent of television in the late 1940s and early 1950s caused attendance in motion picture theaters to plummet as television sets became ubiquitous—but movies did not disappear. Instead, they increasingly became a central element of television programming, especially after cable television opened up hundreds of channels that needed programs for viewers to watch. Similarly, television did not make radio obsolete but rather shifted the radio's role from a central piece of living room furniture into a small and portable device, most often listened to in the car. Nothing appeared to make television obsolete; instead, the technical aspects of TV became ever better, with huge, flat, high-definition color screens becoming standard.

Communication was dominated by the landline telephone for more than a century from its 1876 invention to the 1983 breakup of the Bell telephone monopoly. Since then mobile telephones have prompted an increasing share of households to abandon use of landline telephones. Information technology and the communication it enables have seen much faster progress after 1970 than before. The transition from the mainframe computer of the 1960s and 1970s to the isolated personal computer of the 1980s to the web-enabled PC of the 1990s to smartphones and tablets of recent years represents the fastest transition of all—but, again, this is relevant only to a limited sphere of human experience. Total business and household spending on all electronic entertainment, communications, and information technology (including purchases of TV and audio equipment and cell phone service plans) amounted in 2014 to only about 7 percent of gross domestic product (GDP).

Outside the sphere of entertainment, communications, and information technology, progress was much slower after 1970. Frozen food having long since arrived, the major changes in food availability have entailed much greater variety, especially of ethnic food specialties and out-of-season and organic produce. There has been no appreciable change in clothing other than in styles and countries of origin, whereas imports of clothing have caused an almost complete shutdown of the domestic U.S. apparel industry. By 1970, the kitchen was fully equipped with large and small electric appliances, and the microwave oven was the only post-1970 home appliance to have a significant impact. Motor vehicles in 2015 accomplish the same basic role of transporting people and cargo as they did in 1970, albeit with greater convenience and safety. Air travel today is even less comfortable than it was in 1970, with seating configurations becoming ever tighter and long security lines making the departure process more time-consuming and stressful.

American achievements after 1970 have been matched by most developed nations, but in one important regard Americans fell significantly behind, struggling with the enormous cost and inefficiency of the nation's health-care system. Compared to Canada, Japan, or any nation in western Europe, the United States combines by far the most expensive system with the shortest life expectancy. Progress in medicine has also slowed after 1970 compared to the enormous advances made between 1940 and 1970, which witnessed the invention of antibiotics, the development of procedures for treating and preventing coronary artery disease, and the discovery of radiation and chemotherapy, still used as standard treatments for cancer.

THE STANDARD OF LIVING AND ITS MEASUREMENT

The most accessible definition of the standard of living is the ratio of real GDP (that is, the total production of goods and services adjusted for price inflation) per member of the population, or "real GDP per person." The use of this measure of the standard of living is easily explained by the reliability of population data for most countries and the widespread standardization of methodology for measuring real GDP. Comparisons of nations often rank countries by their level of real GDP per person, and it has become conventional to discuss the "convergence" of poor nations to the living standard of rich countries using the criterion of the growth rate of their real GDP per person.

This book shows that there are two important reasons why real GDP per person greatly understates the improvement in the standard of living for any country, and particularly for the United States, in the special century. First, GDP omits many dimensions of the quality of life that matter to people. This occurs by design rather than being a flaw in the concept of GDP, because GDP is a measure of goods and services exchanged in markets and is not intended to include the value of nonmarket activities that matter to people. Second, the growth of GDP, even on its own terms as a measure of market activity, is systematically understated, for price indexes used to convert current-dollar spending into constant inflation-adjusted "real" dollars overstate price increases. We begin in this section by broadening the concept of the standard of living beyond real GDP, next turns to the sources of price index bias, and concludes with examples of major aspects of human activity that are either omitted from GDP or greatly understated in their importance.

The standard of living is defined with reference to Gary Becker's theory of time allocation.[6] Utility is created for the household by combining market-purchased goods and services with time. Added household equipment, such as TV sets, and technological change, such as the improvement in the quality of TV-set pictures, increase the marginal product of home time devoted to household production and leisure. For instance, the degree of enjoyment provided by an hour of leisure spent watching a TV set in 1955 is greater than that provided by an hour listening to the radio in the same living room in 1935. The addition of an automatic washing machine and dryer makes the time devoted to household production more valuable than it was when the laundry was done with a scrub board and an outdoor clothesline.

The Becker framework is broadened by adding a third element, the decrease in the household's welfare created by the disutility of the market work that must be performed to obtain money to buy market goods and services. For instance, if a particular quantity of goods and services that in 1900 could be purchased using the income earned from sixty hours of work can be bought in 1940 using the income earned from forty hours of work, then the subtraction for the disutility of work is smaller in 1940 than it was in 1900. The interpretation of shorter work hours has a long history in the sources of growth literature, going back to Edward Denison, who argued that people would produce more per hour when the work week was shortened from sixty to forty hours, simply because fatigue made those extra work hours relatively unproductive.[7]

Improvements taking the form of a decreased disutility of work need not involve a reduction of hours, but rather may involve a decrease in the physical difficulty of work and in the discomfort involved in the nature of a work—for example, working in the intense heat of a steel mill. Consider the greatly diminished disutility of a farmer who now plants his field in an air-conditioned and GPS-equipped tractor, contrasting it with the 1870 farmer guiding a plow behind a horse or mule. This approach interprets the improvement in the standard of living by viewing members of each household both as consumers and as workers.

The greatly increased quality of work includes the shift from the physical strain and danger of manual blue-collar work to air-conditioned work in offices, hotels, and retail stores. It includes such improvements of quality as increased flexibility and control over one's own work hours, a contrast to the highly regimented nature of assembly work in the heyday of manufacturing. Likewise, the "quality of youth" has been improved by the end of child labor and the advance of educational attainment, captured by the sharp contrast between the children of 1900 guiding mules in dark and dangerous coal mines and the pampered teenagers of 2015 texting, tweeting, and playing games on multiple electronic gadgets.

Thus, by including home production, the value of leisure time, and the decreased unpleasantness of work, our concept of the standard of living goes beyond changes in the quantity and quality of goods and services purchased on the market. Yet even those items included in GDP are subject to error because of flaws in the price indexes used to convert current-dollar spending into constant inflation-adjusted dollars. This conversion requires a set of price indexes to translate, say, 1965 spending by consumers on gasoline from the current 1965 price paid of $0.30 per gallon to the price that would have been paid for the same gasoline in the 2009 base year of $3.00 per gallon. In this example, because the price of gasoline increased by a factor of ten between 1965 and 2009, the 1965 spending on gasoline of $20 billion in current 1965 prices would be converted into $200 billion in base-year 2009 prices. The summing up of all the goods and services purchased in 1965 as valued in 2009 prices yields the total of real GDP in 1965 and in every other year.

But not all products are like gasoline, a commodity that maintains a constant quality over the decades. When a new product is introduced—say, the room air conditioner—there is no allowance for the improvement in consumer welfare of being able to sleep on a hot summer night in a cool bedroom. The available price indexes tell us what happens to the price of the air conditioner once it is being sold, but nothing about its fundamental value. Even worse, new products typically experience a sharp decline in price in their early years as manufacturers ramp up production to achieve economies of scale, yet the official indexes have consistently been introduced many years after the new product was available for sale. For instance, the room air conditioner was first sold in 1951 but was not included in the official price index until 1967; the videocassette recorder (VCR) was first sold in 1978 but was not included in the price index until 1987.

One of the most important product introductions was the Model T Ford, which went on sale in 1908 at an initial price of $950. Over the next fifteen years, Henry Ford's introduction of the assembly-line method of manufacturing to the production of automobiles brought an astonishing reduction in price to $269 in 1923 (see table 5–2). The number of current dollars spent on Model T Fords represented more than three times the real GDP in 1923 as in 1908, a fact entirely missed in the GDP statistics, because there was no price index for cars at all until 1935.

Thus price indexes miss the welfare benefits of new products and the welfare-boosting effect of the price reductions early in the lives of new products. In addition, there is "quality bias" in the measurement of the quality of existing goods. In any given month, most models of TV sets are the same as those sold in the previous month, and the price index captures any month-to-month price change in existing models. However, this ignores the constant introduction of new models offering larger screens or higher-definition picture with little change in price. Consumers flock to the new models and stop buying the old models, but the price index makes no allowance for the improvement in the ratio of quality to price.[8] Improvements in the fuel efficiency of automobiles and the energy efficiency of home appliances, such as room air conditioners and clothes dryers are particularly significant sources of quality bias in the official price indexes.

Price indexes also miss the benefit to consumers of new types of retail outlets. For example, Walmart usually charges lower prices for food than does a traditional supermarket.[9] There are two price indexes—one for eggs at the supermarket, and another for eggs at Walmart. Because consumers' ability to purchase identical eggs for, say, 20 percent less is never recorded as a reduction in price, increases in GDP are missed, for the price indexes overstate how much consumers are actually paying for eggs. This "outlet substitution bias" has caused large amounts of real GDP to be missed again and again, first when department stores replaced small specialty merchants, again when mail-order catalogs competed with small country general stores, again when food began to be sold in supermarkets, again when Walmart offered food for lower prices than conventional supermarkets, and most recently when Internet sales offered wider variety and lower prices than traditional outlets.

Many sources of the higher standard of living are not included in GDP at all, starting with the enormous advance in the quality of housing represented by the replacement of outhouses by indoor plumbing and the replacement of wood fires and potbelly stoves by central heating. The invention of the antibiotic penicillin might save thousands of lives, each of great value, but the GDP statistics would record only the expenses of the labor and equipment used in its discovery and production. Other similar examples include Pasteur's germ theory of disease and the attendant emphasis on soap and cleanliness, the development of urban sanitation infrastructure that made indoor plumbing possible, and the realization in the late nineteenth century that some food being sold was tainted, adulterated, or diluted.

A final dimension of improvement is the indirect effect of increased life expectancy in providing leisure and locational choice after retirement from work. In earlier eras, workers often died before the age of retirement or had no financial resources enabling them to enjoy retirement, leaving them confined as dependents in the dwellings of their children. Now most people outlive the date of retirement, often with enough financial resources to move to a sunny retirement community offering golf, pools, card games, and Facebook contact with children and grandchildren.

Some improvements in the quality of housing involved inventions, particularly electrification. But others did not—the transition from tenements to suburban single-family homes largely resulted from the positive income elasticity of housing square feet, as well as from the development of credit institutions that allowed working-class families to buy their own homes. Higher incomes also spilled over to affect other types of purchases that did not necessarily require innovations, including public expenditures on clean water and education.

This distinction between innovation-driven and income-driven progress should be qualified: The demand for residential space required transportation innovations to make suburbs possible, while clean water depended on filtration and chlorination technology. The coexistence of industries experiencing rapid productivity growth (e.g., manufacturing) and those with little or no productivity growth (e.g., house-building or education) is summarized by the paradigm of "Baumol's disease," in which the relative price of the innovation-intensive industries, e.g., the production of computers, declines over time while the relative price of the noninnovative industries, e.g., the playing of a string quartet, increases over time. Baumol's disease can be cured in some instances, exemplified by how the inventions of phonograph records, tapes, CDs, and MP3s have allowed a single performance of a string quartet to be heard by millions. But some parts of economic activity still exhibit Baumol's disease without technological relief for rising relative costs, including seats for live performances, college tuition, and medical care expenses.

This theme of mismeasurement interacts with the designation of the one hundred years between 1870 and 1970 as the "special century." Measurement errors are greatest in the early years, both in the scope of the standard of living and in the extent of price index bias. Clearly the welfare benefits to consumers in the categories of life entirely omitted from GDP were greatest long ago: the transition from the scrub board to the automatic washing machine was a more important contributor to consumer welfare than the shift from manual to electronic washing machine controls or from a twelve-pound tub to an eighteen-pound tub. The most important unmeasured benefit of all, the extension of life expectancy, occurred much more rapidly from 1890 to 1950 than afterward. Price index bias was also greater in the early years of the special century. Nothing in the history of price index bias compares with the omission of automobile prices from the official price indexes over the entire period from 1900 to 1935. Price indexes themselves have been subject to continuous improvements: the price indexes of 2015 are better than those of 1995, which are themselves better than those of 1975 or 1955.

THE IRREGULAR ADVANCE OF THE LIVING STANDARD AND PRODUCTIVITY

Most of our attempt to broaden the concept of the standard of living is qualitative, for the concepts of improved consumer welfare in response to innovation and technological change cannot be measured precisely. Nevertheless, it is important that we comprehend the important message contained in the historical record for the standard concepts. Shown in figure 1–1 are the basic data

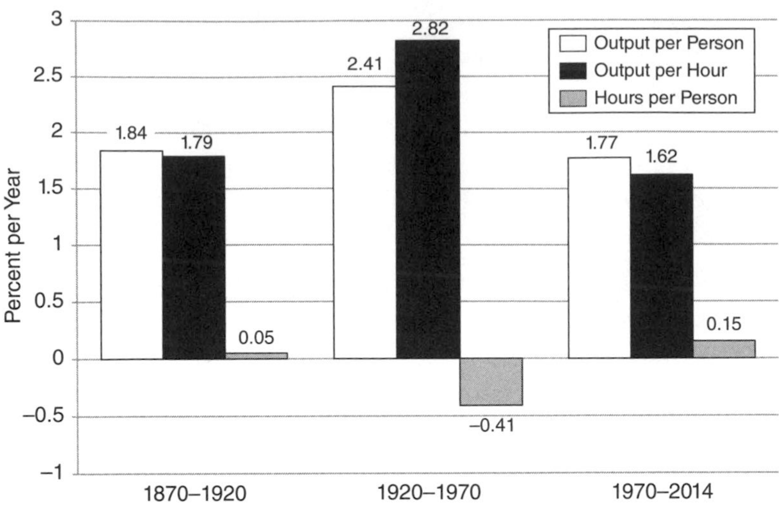

Figure 1–1. Annualized Growth Rate of Output per Person, Output per Hour, and Hours per Person, 1870–2014
Source: See Data Appendix.

for the standard of living, productivity, and hours worked per person covering the post-1870 period, divided at 1920 and 1970. Shown for each of the three periods are three bars, each depicting the average annual growth rate over the respective interval. The left (white) bar in each group of three shows the growth rate of per-person real GDP, the middle (black) bar growth in real GDP per hour (i.e., labor productivity), and the third (gray) bar growth in hours worked per person.

There are two striking aspects to this historical record. The first is the symmetry of the graph: the first and last periods are almost identical in the height of each bar, but the middle period (1920–70) is quite different. Output per person growth is substantially higher in the middle period, and productivity growth is much higher—2.8 percent per year compared to 1.8 percent in the first period and 1.7 percent in the last period. The much greater excess of productivity growth over output per person in the middle period, compared to that in the first and last periods, reflects the sharp decline in hours worked per person between 1920 and 1970. This raises a question: why did hours worked per person decline so rapidly in the middle interval? And a second question arises as well: did rapid productivity growth cause hours to decline, or did the decline in hours worked per person rather in some way contribute to relatively rapid productivity growth?

The decline in hours worked per person from 1920 to 1970 reflects numerous factors that all point in the same direction. First was the long-run decline in hours of work per week for production workers, which by 1920 had already declined from sixty to fifty-two hours per week. Second was the influence of New Deal legislation, both in reducing hours directly and also in empowering labor unions that fought for and achieved the eight-hour workday and forty-hour work week by the end of the 1930s. An unrelated factor was the baby boom of 1947 to 1964, which increased the child population (0–16) relative to the working-age population (16–64) and thus reduced the ratio of hours worked to the total population. The reverse feedback from productivity growth to shrinking hours reflects the standard view in labor economics that as real income rises, individuals choose not to spend all their extra income on market goods and services, but rather consume a portion of it in the form of extra leisure—that is to say, by working fewer hours.

The change in hours worked per person in the first period (1870–1920) was negligible and presumably reflects modest declines in the work week for urban working-class employees, offset by the effects of shifting employment from farms to cities, where working hours were longer and more regimented. The slight increase in hours worked per person after 1970 mixes two quite different trends. In the first portion of the interval, roughly between 1970 and 1995, hours worked per person rose as a reflection of the movement of women from housework into market employment. Then, after 1996, hours worked per person fell as a result of a steady decline in the labor force participation rate of prime-age males and of young people. After 2008, these labor force dropouts were joined by the retirement of the older members of the baby boom generation.

Why did labor productivity grow so much more quickly between 1920 and 1970 than before or after? We can divide the sources of the growth in labor productivity into three components, as shown in figure 1–2. The time intervals are the same as before, except that the absence of some data series requires that we choose 1890 rather than 1870 as our start date. Each bar is divided into three parts. The top section, displayed in white, is the contribution to productivity growth of rising educational attainment; these are the widely accepted estimates of Claudia Goldin and Lawrence Katz.[10] The middle section, shaded in gray, displays the effect of the steadily rising amount of capital input per worker hour; a continuing source of rising labor productivity is the larger quantity of capital, of increasingly better quality, with which each worker is equipped.[11] The

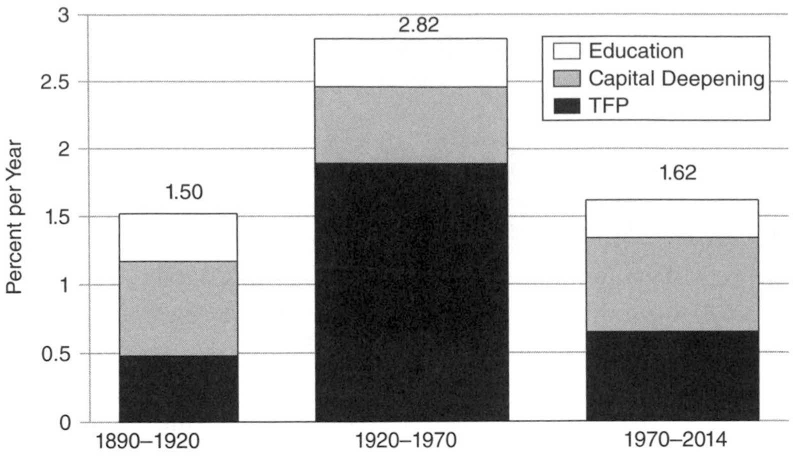

Figure 1–2. Average Annual Growth Rates of Output per Hour and Its Components, Selected Intervals, 1890–2014
Source: See Data Appendix.

effect of a rising ratio of capital input to labor hours is usually called "capital deepening."

What remains after deducting the contributions of education and capital deepening is the growth of total factor productivity (TFP), often called "Solow's residual" after the most prominent inventor of growth theory and growth accounting, Robert M. Solow. This measure is the best proxy available for the underlying effect of innovation and technological change on economic growth. And the results are surprising. Because the contributions of education and capital deepening were roughly the same in each of the three intervals, all the faster growth of labor productivity in the middle period is the result of more rapid innovation and technological change. I have previously called attention to this aspect of American economic history as "one big wave."[12]

The margin of superiority of TFP growth in the 1920–70 interval is stunning, being almost *triple* the growth rate registered in the two other periods.[13] To take another perspective, note that the fifty years 1920–70 represent 40 percent of the 124-year period from 1890 to 2014. If each year or decade were equally important, then the five decades starting in 1920 would have accounted for 40 percent of the cumulative TFP growth since 1890. But instead the post-1920 half century accounted for fully 66 percent of the cumulative TFP growth.

Our previous designation of the whole century 1870–1970 as "special" appears to conflict with the behavior of TFP growth as summarized in figure 1–2. Apparently only the second half of the special century exhibited TFP growth that was substantially above average. We can state this puzzle in two symmetric ways: Why was TFP growth so slow before 1920? Why was it so fast during the fifty years after 1920?

The leading hypothesis is that of Paul David, who provided a now well-known analogy between the evolution of electric machinery and of the electronic computer.[14] In 1987, Robert Solow quipped, "We can see the computer age everywhere but in the productivity statistics."[15] David responded, in effect: "Just wait"—suggesting that the previous example of the electric dynamo and other electric machinery implied that a long gestation period could intervene between a major invention and its payoff in productivity growth. David counted almost four decades between Thomas Edison's opening in 1882 of the Pearl Street power plant in Lower Manhattan and the subsequent upsurge of productivity growth in the early 1920s associated with the electrification of manufacturing. He attributed the delayed implementation of electricity in manufacturing not just to the time needed to invent and perfect the machinery, but also to a sharp decline in the price of electricity itself.

David's analogy turned out to be prophetic, for only a few years after his 1990 article, the growth rate of aggregate U.S. productivity soared in 1996–2004 to roughly double its rate in 1972–96. However, the analogy broke down after 2004, when growth in labor productivity returned, after its eight-year surge, to the slow rates of 1972–96, despite the proliferation of flat-screen desktop computers, laptops, and smartphones in the decade after 2004. By way of contrast, in the 1920s, electricity's stimulation of industrial efficiency lasted much longer than eight years. Productivity growth soared in the late 1930s and into the 1940s, creating the remarkable average 1920–70 growth rate displayed in figure 1–2.

It is appealing to explain David's dynamo/computer analogy's failure to hold true longer than eight years by concluding that the electricity revolution was more important than the computer revolution. Moreover, the productivity upsurge after 1920 did not rely only on electricity, but also on the internal combustion engine. It is not surprising that motor vehicles had little impact on labor productivity or TFP growth before 1920, for they had come into existence only a short time before. There were only 8,000 registered motor vehicles in 1900, yet there were 26.8 million just three decades later, when the ratio of motor vehicles to the number of U.S. households had reached 89.2 percent. Productivity in the aggregate economy depends in part on how quickly workers, including truck drivers and delivery personnel, can move from place to place. Just as the thousands of elevators installed in the building boom of the 1920s facilitated vertical travel and urban density, so the growing number of automobiles and trucks speeded horizontal movement on the farm and in the city.

WHY DID GROWTH PEAK IN THE MIDDLE OF THE TWENTIETH CENTURY?

Though the central task of this book is to extend our understanding of economic growth beyond the scope of GDP, one aspect of the record of U.S. real GDP growth nevertheless cries for explanation. Why, as shown in figure 1–2, was TFP growth so much more rapid during 1920–70 than before or since? An explanation is provided in chapter 16, which considers alternative explanations for the puzzle of the "Great Leap Forward." As shown in figure 16–5, the superior growth record of 1920–70 comes to an even more prominent peak at the middle of the twentieth century when TFP growth over 1890–2014 is split up into twelve separate decades. Why did TFP grow so rapidly midcentury?

The surprising answer of chapter 16 is that both the Great Depression and World War II directly contributed to the Great Leap. Had there been no Great Depression, there would probably have been no New Deal, with its NIRA and Wagner Act that promoted unionization and that both directly and indirectly contributed to a sharp rise in real wages and a shrinkage in average weekly hours. In turn, both higher real wages and shorter hours helped boost productivity growth—higher real wages by promoting substitution from labor to capital during 1937–41 and shorter hours by reducing fatigue and improving efficiency.

Less speculative is the productivity-enhancing learning by doing that occurred during the high-pressure economy of World War II. Production miracles during 1941–45 taught firms and workers how to operate more efficiently, and the lessons of the wartime production miracle were not lost after the war: productivity continued to increase from 1945 to 1950. In addition to the increased efficiency of existing plant and equipment, the federal government financed an entire new part of the manufacturing sector, with newly built plants and newly purchased productive equipment. Chapter 16 shows the staggering amount of this new capital equipment installed during the war—its acquisition cost in real terms was equal to fully half the stock of privately owned equipment that had existed in 1941 and was more modern, and hence more productive, than the old equipment.

The productive efficiency of the new capital installed during 1937–41, as well as during the war itself, brings us full circle to Paul David's explanation of the long lag between the first electric generating plant in 1882 and the electrification of industry that centered on the period 1919–29. His focus on the 1920s as the breakthrough decade misses the fact that the full force of the expansion of modern equipment, not just in manufacturing, but also in the rest of the economy, was centered in the years 1929–50. Economists are so distracted by the unprecedented slump in output during the depressed years of the 1930s that they forget how much innovation occurred in that decade. Alex Field is responsible for the revival of interest in 1930s innovation, and the present book provides evidence of rapid progress during that decade in many dimensions, including radio, the quality of motion pictures, and a sharp jump in the quality of motor vehicles.[16]

SETTING THE LIMITS: THE SCOPE AND RESULTS OF THIS BOOK

Scope. The subject of this book is the standard of living in the United States, the country that has expanded the frontier of technology, innovation, and labor productivity since 1870. Where the United States has led, the major nations of western Europe have followed, with Japan a laggard until after World War II. Both world wars greatly delayed implementation of the Great Inventions of the late nineteenth century in Europe and Japan, so much so that in 1950 the level of labor productivity in western Europe was only half that in the United States. When Europe caught up in the years the French call "les trentes glorieuses" (1945–75), Europeans were chasing the frontier carved out by the United States decades earlier. In fact, it has been claimed that the percentage of the French population having access to electricity and an automobile in 1948 was roughly equal to that of the United States in 1912.

Not only is this book limited to the American experience between 1870 and 2014, but it is also limited to the viewpoint of the household in its twin roles as consumer and worker. Many of the traditional topics of American economic history fall outside its purview, including financial booms and crashes, the rise of the trusts and ensuing antitrust legislation, the Progressive Era, and the struggles of labor unions. Our interest in Prohibition is not in its adoption or abolition, but rather its role in causing U.S. consumption of food and drink to be substantially understated in the data for the 1920s.

A book of such vast scope must be selective, so there is little room here for much detail, if any, about regional differences. The details of farm life reflect the typical farms of the Midwest and the Great Plains in the late nineteenth century, taking only a sideways glance at the plight of southern sharecroppers. Only once do rural southern farmers receive attention, and even then only in tables showing how far behind they were in 1940 in obtaining the modern conveniences of electricity, running water, and indoor bathrooms, compared to urban dwellers, among whom conversion to the modern world was almost complete.

Approach. This book intends to create a quantitative and qualitative record of the changes in the American standard of living that so greatly increased consumer welfare, especially during the special century, 1870–1970. It focuses on the aspects of improvements of human life that are missing from GDP altogether. For instance, real GDP calculates food consumption by adding the constant-dollar cost of beef, pork, potatoes, and onions while placing no value on the shift from the boring 1870s meal of "hogs 'n hominy" to the much more varied diet of the 1920s. Chapter 3, which covers the evolution of food and clothing, combines the quantitative record of what Americans actually ate with the stories of inventors and their inventions of processed food, from Underwood's deviled ham to Kellogg's corn flakes. The treatment of clothing focuses on the effect of the sewing machine in easing the burden of women, gradually shifting from the making of clothing at home to market-purchased clothing. We care not only about what families ate and wore, but also about where they bought it, so chapter 3 includes the dazzling arrival of the great urban department stores, often the first buildings fully outfitted with electric lights, and the utter transformation of rural purchases made possible by the mail-order catalogs of Montgomery Ward and Richard Sears.

Subsequent chapters trace the improvements that are omitted from GDP across the many dimensions of the home and its equipment, public and personal transformation, information, communication, entertainment, and public health and medicine and, in the most novel part of the book, treat in detail of improvements in working conditions for adult males on the job, adult women in the home, and youth during the gradual transition from child labor to schooling.

Inventions and Inventors. The major inventions of the late nineteenth century were the creations of individual inventors rather than large corporations. We go behind the scenes to Thomas Edison's laboratory in Menlo Park, New Jersey, where on the epochal night of October 10, 1879, a particular variety of cotton filament finally made possible an electric light bulb that would last not just for an hour but for days and weeks. We also visit Karl Benz's lab, where, just ten weeks after Edison's discovery, he took the last step in developing a reliable internal combustion engine.

Although this book is about the United States, many of the inventions were made by foreigners in their own lands or by foreigners who had recently transplanted to America. Among the many foreigners who deserve credit for key elements of the Great Inventions are transplanted Scotsman Alexander Graham Bell for the telephone, Frenchmen Louis Pasteur for the germ theory of disease and Louis Lumière for the motion picture, Englishmen Joseph Lister for antiseptic surgery and David Hughes for early wireless experiments, and Germans Karl Benz for the internal combustion engine and Heinrich Hertz for key inventions that made possible the 1896 wireless patents of the recent Italian immigrant Guglielmo Marconi. The role of foreign inventors in the late nineteenth century was distinctly more important than it was one hundred years later, when the personal computer and Internet revolution was led almost uniformly by Americans, including Paul Allen, Bill Gates, Steve Jobs, Jeff Bezos, Larry Page, and Mark Zuckerberg. Among the pioneering giants of the Internet age, Sergei Brin (co-founder of Google) is one of the few to have been born abroad.

Organization. The book proper begins with chapter 2, on living conditions in 1870. Part I includes eight chapters (chapters 2–9) on the revolutionary advances in the standard of living through 1940, a dividing year chosen both because it is halfway between 1870 and 2010 and because 1940 marks the year of the first Census of Housing, with its detailed quantitative measures of housing and its equipment. Part II (chapters 10–15) extends the narrative from 1940 to the present day, and its chapters are organized to give less attention to food, clothing, and other aspects of life that changed slowly and to place more emphasis on the rapid changes that occurred in the spheres of entertainment, communication, and information technology. Part III begins in chapter 16 with an attempt to explain "the Great Leap Forward," assessing reasons why labor productivity and TFP grew so much more rapidly from 1920 to 1970 than before or after. Then chapter 17 compares changes in the pace of innovation since 1970 with that likely to occur in the next quarter century. Part III concludes with chapter 18, on the headwinds that are slowing U.S. economic growth below the pace that otherwise would be made possible by technological advance. The book closes with a short postscript chapter proposing a menu of directions for policy that might be helpful tacks against the headwinds.

The Rise and Fall of Growth in the Standard of Living. The subsequent chapters trace out a distinct sense of ascent and subsequent descent in the growth rate of the standard of living, labor productivity, and TFP. The historical record displayed in figures 1–1 and 1–2 provides the quantitative part of this record. A major theme is that real GDP understates the true growth in the standard of living and that many new inventions that made possible the achievements of the special century through 1970 were beyond anyone's imagination. Along every dimension in the chapters of part I, we find aspects of life being improved in ways not included in GDP—for example, take the transition from the country store to the Sears catalog, which greatly improved well-being by substantially increasing consumer choice and reducing prices. The chapters of part II (except for chapter 12, on entertainment and communication, and chapter 13, on information technology) have a different character. They all cover progress from 1940 until today but typically find that progress was rapid from 1940 to 1970 but slowed thereafter. Maintaining growth at the pace of the years before 1970 proved to be beyond the realm of possibility. Nevertheless, progress has continued after 1970, albeit at a slower pace, and often in realms receiving little attention in part I, evident, for instance, in the rapid decline in automobile fatality rates and an airline fatality rate that has been virtually zero for close to a decade[17] Likewise, fatalities by homicide have declined in almost every city since 1990.

The new element in part III is the headwinds—inequality, education, demography, and debt repayment—that are buffeting the U.S. economy and pushing down the growth rate of the real disposable income of the bottom 99 percent of the income distribution to little above zero. The outlook for future growth in the U.S. standard of living is not promising, and this book ends by doubting that the standard of living of today's youths will double that of their parents, unlike the standard of living of each previous generation of Americans back to the late nineteenth century.

The Past and the Future. This book's sober ending requires a distinction between the past and the future. The past is a matter of record, the future a matter for speculation. We know that the growth rate of labor productivity since 1970 has been disappointing, as shown in figures 1–1 and 1–2, and the growth rate of TFP since 1970 is barely a third of the rate achieved between 1920 and 1970. It is also evident that the modest growth rate of average per-person real GDP has not been shared equally. Moreover, the population is aging, educational attainment is flagging, and the slowing of growth creates a feedback loop requiring higher tax rates and/or lower transfer payments.

Knowing what we do about the recent past, what can we extrapolate to the future? We cannot predict every new invention; indeed, even for those on the horizon, such as driverless cars and legions of small robots, we can debate their likely effect and importance. But there is much that we can predict. For instance, the baby boom generation is currently aged between fifty and sixty-eight, so we can predict with reasonable accuracy the effect of its members' retirement within a percentage point or two, depending on how many of them will work until later ages than past generations. If American high school students regularly rank poorly in international tests of reading, math, and science, then a sudden spike in scores to levels previously unseen may be considered improbable. If the stock market continues to advance, we know that inequality will increase, for capital gains on equities accrue disproportionately to the top income brackets.

This book's predictions that future growth will be slower than in the past are strongly resisted by a group of commentators whom I collectively call the "techno-optimists." They tend to ignore both the slow productivity growth of the past decade, as well as the force of the headwinds. Instead, they predict a future of spectacularly faster productivity growth based on an exponential increase in the capabilities of artificial intelligence. Another group of economists dismisses pessimism out of hand. The economic historian Deirdre McCloskey writes, for instance, that "pessimism has consistently been a poor guide to the modern economic world. We are gigantically richer in body and spirit than we were two centuries ago." [18] Whereas McCloskey has room in her toolkit for only one rate of growth spanning the past two centuries, this book provides three separate growth rates over the past 150 years, divided at 1920 and 1970. Yes, we are "gigantically" ahead of where our counterparts were in 1870, but our progress has slowed, and we face headwinds that are stronger barriers to continued growth than were faced by our ancestors a century or two ago.

Part I

1870–1940—THE GREAT INVENTIONS CREATE A REVOLUTION INSIDE AND OUTSIDE THE HOME

Chapter 2

THE STARTING POINT

Life and Work in 1870

> The best business you can go into you will find on your father's farm or in his workshop. If you have no family or friends to aid you, and no prospect opened to you there, turn your face to the great West, and there build up a home and fortune.
>
> —Horace Greeley, 1846

INTRODUCTION

This history of the standard of living in the United States begins in 1870, when the standard of living was low by today's standards but hardly primitive. The United States in 1870 was not a medieval agricultural society as had been western Europe in the 1600s but rather had already enjoyed, adapted, and advanced many of the fruits of the British-led First Industrial Revolution of the late eighteenth century. By 1870, the United States had reached 74 percent of British and 128 percent of German per-capita income.[1]

Americans were perceived, both by themselves and by Europeans, as having particular talent in mechanical engineering. Their image as country bumpkins in the eyes of Europeans was erased at the London Crystal Palace exhibition of 1851, when British and foreign observers were shocked and impressed not just by the advanced tools displayed by the Americans, but, more important, by their apparently new method of manufacture:

> Americans [were thought to be] little more than amiable backwoodsmen not yet ready for unsupervised outings on the world stage. So when the displays were erected it came as something of a surprise that

> the American section was an outpost of wizardry and wonder. Nearly all the American machines did things that the world earnestly wished machines to do—stamp out nails, cut stone, mold candles—but with a neatness, dispatch, and tireless reliability that left other nations blinking.... Cyrus McCormick displayed a reaper that could do the work of 40 men.... Most exciting of all was Samuel Colt's repeat-action revolver, which was not only marvelously lethal but made from interchangeable parts, a method of manufacture so distinctive that it became known as the American system.[2]

The upper classes of Britain and Europe viewed America with trepidation. One did not need multiplication tables to infer that with rapid population growth resulting from its high birth rate and unfettered immigration, the United States would soon have a population greater than that of any European nation. Indeed, the population of the United States surpassed that of the United Kingdom (including the whole of Ireland) in 1857 and that of newly united Germany in 1873.[3] A more serious challenge for the Europeans was the set of manufacturing skills that the United States steadily developed in the mid-nineteenth century, as exemplified by the 1851 Crystal Palace reaction.

The two most famous European observers of America in the nineteenth century were Alexis de Tocqueville and James Bryce. Because Tocqueville's two volumes of *Democracy in America* were published in 1835 and 1840, they describe an earlier era than the America of 1870 examined in this chapter. More relevant, then, is Bryce's *The American Commonwealth*, a work of evocative historical description, comparison, and analysis, based on the author's five trips to America in the 1870s and 1880s, in which Bryce painstakingly reproduced the travels of Tocqueville.[4]

The Bryce narrative poses a central challenge for this chapter: was the American standard of living in 1870 pathetic and pitiable, or was it surprisingly agreeable and pleasant? Much of the available descriptive literature on living conditions of 1870 portrays a dismal existence of week-long household drudgery for housewives and dangerous, backbreaking working conditions for husbands. Life was short, large families were crammed together in small living spaces, much food and clothing was home-produced, and such marketed goods as could be afforded were mainly raw food and dry goods—for example, fabrics for making clothes at home.

But Bryce saw American life not from the perspective of contemporary well-off Americans pitying the poor or of later generations looking back after decades of progress, but with the acute eye of an English professor of history and law. To him, the American standard of living was high, not low, and his many explicit comparisons with England and the European continent reveal that the majority of Americans were better off than their European counterparts. After dismissing the astonishment of upper-class Europeans at any suggestion that life in America, "where refinements were just beginning to appear," could be any better than in Europe, he provided his core rebuttal:

> In Europe, if an observer takes his eye off his own class . . ., he will perceive that by far the greater number lead very laborious lives. . . . In England the lot of the labourer has been hitherto a hard one, incessant field toil, with rheumatism at fifty and the workhouse at the end of the vista. . . . In Connecticut and Massachusetts the operatives in many a manufacturing town lead a life far easier, far more brightened by intellectual culture and by amusements, than that of the clerks and shopkeepers of England or France.[5]

The essential core of his observation, that the life of the American working class was better than that of counterparts in England and France, cannot be dismissed. Indeed, living conditions for a substantial share of Americans living in small towns and rural areas were actually much better than in Europe. The dismal urban conditions applied only to certain large eastern cities and may have been better than the standard among the lower classes in European cities of similar size. However, we must be cautious not to paint too glowing an image of the 75 percent of Americans living in rural areas, because 26 percent of the 1870 U.S. population lived in the states of the old Confederacy and, as we shall see, their living conditions were dismal in 1870 and had deteriorated significantly from their state in 1860 because of Civil War destruction. Bryce could retain his optimistic assessment in part because he traveled in the north and west, but, apparently, little—if at all—in the south.

The America of 1870 cannot be assessed without a firm grasp of the percentage distribution of the population—50 percent northern and western rural, 25 percent largely rural southern, and 25 percent urban, mainly in the north and Midwest. As the urban percentage began its inexorable rise decade after decade, living conditions for many rural-to-urban migrants deteriorated, and the ranks of city dwellers were swelled by immigrants who never experienced rural life at all, at least within the United States. Just as the country-to-town migration in Britain reduced the standard of living of the average worker during

1800–1830, so the urbanization of America after 1870 also reduced the average standard of living of working-class Americans.[6]

THE GOLDEN SPIKE AS A SYMBOL OF AMERICA IN 1870

A quintessential symbol of the American advance and future promise is captured by the 1869 hammering of the golden spike that united the transcontinental railway. This story combines the British invention of the railroad, rapidly adapted to the much larger land mass of the United States, with the American invention of the telegraph.[7] The event happened at noon on May 10, 1869, at Promontory Summit, Utah. That moment was a pivotal episode in world history as Leland Stanford pounded a golden spike with a silver hammer and in an instant ended the isolation of California and the Great West from the eastern half of the United States.

Just as important, symbolizing the revolutionary increase in the speed of communication achieved by the 1844 invention of the telegraph and first 1858 undersea ocean telegraphic cable, the famous message "DONE!" was transmitted within a second to the entire United States, Canada, and the United Kingdom.[8] This was the first time that news of an epochal event had been greeted with such celebration by so many people at the same time:

> Across the nation, bells pealed. Even the venerable Liberty Bell in Philadelphia was rung. Then came the boom of cannons, 220 of them in San Francisco…, a hundred in Washington, D. C., countless fired off elsewhere. It was said that more cannons were fired in celebration than ever took part in the Battle of Gettysburg.… A correspondent in Chicago caught exactly the spirit that had brought the whole country together. The festivity… "was free from the atmosphere of warlike energy and the suggestions of suffering, danger, and death which threw their oppressive shadow over the celebrations of our victories during the war for the Union."[9]

The joining together of the nation through a transcontinental railroad and instantaneous telegraphic communication together symbolize how much the American standard of living had improved by 1870. After millennia in which the life of rural farmers remained little changed since the days of ancient Rome, the First Industrial Revolution had begun to spread its bounty in many directions before 1870, particularly in the form of steam engines, cotton gins, railroads, steamships, telegraphic communications, and rudimentary agricultural machinery that greatly eased the burden of human labor on the farm. If the beginning of the First Industrial Revolution dates to 1750, the pace of its improvement in living standards was relatively slow, as documented in numerous histories, including that of Joel Mokyr.[10] The year 1870 is chosen for the starting date of this book not just because a wide variety of economic data are available only back to 1870, but also because the pace of advance picked up markedly in the three decades after 1870.

All the fruits of the Great Inventions of the Second Industrial Revolution, many of them never included in statistics on GDP, were yet to come in 1870. In that year, light was obtained from candles, whale oil, and town gas, and most motive power in manufacturing came from steam engines, water wheels, and horses. An ever-expanding network of passenger and freight railroads provided intercity transportation, but train speeds were barely one-third those achieved by 1940, and transport within the city and between small towns depended largely on horses; most people lived close enough to factories to walk to work.[11]

COUNTING AMERICANS IN 1870: NATIVE-BORN, FOREIGN-BORN, AND FERTILE

The U.S. population reached almost exactly 40 million people in the year 1870. The most distinctive aspect of U.S. demography was the rapid rate of population growth, which from the founding of the Republic in 1790 to the eve of the Civil War in 1860 had averaged 3.0 percent per year, an unprecedented rate that implied a doubling of the population every twenty-three years.[12] After 1860, the population growth rate slowed to 2.3 percent during 1860–1890, 1.9 percent during 1890–1910, and 1.4 percent during 1910–1930. Nevertheless, these rates were high compared to the developed countries of western Europe, where population growth rates during 1870–1913 were 1.2 percent per annum for Germany, 0.9 for the U. K., and a mere 0.2 for France.

As early as 1798, Thomas Malthus commented on the high fertility and large family sizes in the United States, which he attributed to the extreme cheapness of farm land:

> And on account of the extreme cheapness of good land a capital could not be more advantageously employed than in agriculture.... The

consequence of these favorable circumstances united was a rapidity of increase probably without parallel in history. Throughout all of the northern colonies, the population was found to double in twenty-five years.[13]

Table 2–1 places several aspects of American demography in 1870 into perspective by providing the same data for 1940 and 2010. The top section highlights not only the rapid growth of the population in the years adjacent to 1870, but also the large average household size and the relatively high percentage of married couple households. By 2010, persons per household had declined by half, from 5.3 to 2.6, and the percentage of adults in married couple households had declined from 80.6 percent to 48.4 percent. Seven-eighths of the 1870 population was white and the remaining eighth black, with virtually no representation of other races. The 1940 population was even more homogenous, with nearly 90 percent white and most of the remainder black, in sharp contrast to the 15 percent in 2010 made up of races other than white or black (primarily Hispanic and Asian, but also people reporting being of two races).

An important difference between 1870 and 2010 was in the age distribution. The percentage of the population below the age of 25 was an amazing 59 percent in 1870, contrasted with 43 percent in 1940 and 34 percent in 2010. Shares above age 25 were by definition much lower in 1870, both for the 25–64 and 65+ age groups. It is notable that only 3.0 percent of the 1870 population was 65 years old or older, as compared to 6.8 and 13.0 percent in 1940 and 2010, respectively.

Also shown in the same section of table 2–1 is that almost 14 percent of the 1870 population was foreign-born, and almost all of these were from Europe. In contrast, nearly 9 percent of the 1940 population and 12 percent of the 2010 population were foreign-born; whereas the 1940 foreign-born population was heavily European, almost all the 2010 foreign-born population originated from outside of Europe, more than half from Latin America and most of the rest from Asia.

The next section of table 2–1 presents data on labor force participation by age and sex and suggests several important differences in 1870 compared with recent years. Teenage males aged 16–19 had a participation rate of 76 percent in 1870, compared to 51 percent in 1940 and a much lower 40 percent in 2010, reflecting child labor, the low educational attainment in 1870 and also, to some degree, the ongoing impact of the 2007–9 recession on youth

Table 2–1. Demographic Dimensions 1870, 1940, and 2010

	1870	1940	2010
Total Population (millions)	39.9	132.0	308.7
Average annual growth rate in adjacent 5 years	2.7	1.1	1.0
Total number of households (millions)	7.5	34.9	116.7
Persons per household	5.3	3.7	2.6
Married couple households as percent of all	80.6	76.3	48.4
Percentage breakdown			
White	87.1	89.8	72.4
Black	12.7	9.8	12.6
Other	0.2	0.4	15.0
Age 0–24	59.4	43.2	34.0
Age 25–64	37.6	50.0	53.0
Age 65+	3.0	6.8	13.0
Percent of population foreign born	13.9	8.8	11.9
Percent of population foreign born from Europe	13.7	8.7	1.4
Percent of population foreign born from non-Europe	0.2	0.1	10.5
Labor force participation rates			
for selected sex and age groups[a]			
Male 16–19	76.1	50.8	40.1
Male 40–49 or 35–44	97.6	92.9	92.2
Male 60–64	94.5	81.3	59.9
Female 16–19	29.0	27.8	40.2
Female 40–49 or 35–44	21.1	24.6	76.1
Female 60–64	8.1	15.2	48.7
Birth, death, and immigration rates			
Birth rate per 1,000	41.6	19.4	14.3
Death rate per 1,000	23.1	10.7	8.0
Net Immigration rate per 1,000	9.2	0.4	3.7
Total fertility rate			
White	4.6	2.2	2.1
Black	7.7	2.8	2.2

(*Continued*)

Table 2–1. (*Continued*)

	1870	1940	2010
Infant mortality rate per 1,000, white	175.5	43.2	6.8
Life expectancy at birth, white	45.2	64.2	77.9
Life expectancy at age 60, male	14.4	15	20.9
Life expectancy at age 60, female	15.3	16.9	23.9

Sources: 1870 and 1940, HSUS, various tables.
2010 sources. Foreign born population by country of origin from *U. S. Census Bureau, Foreign-Born Population of the United States, Current Population Survey, March 2009*
http://www.census.gov/population/www/socdemo/foreign/cps2009.html
Most other 2010 data are taken from U. S. Department of Commerce, *Statistical Abstract of the United States: 2011.*
Some of the data listed in the 2010 column refer to the most recent available year, sometimes 2007, 2008, or 2009.
Notes: a. Age groups are 40–49 and 60–69 for 1870 and 1940, but are 35–44 and 60–64 for 2010.
Rates for the earlier years refer to the decade prior to the year, e.g., 1861–70 for the first column labelled "1870."

participation. In contrast, many fewer females than males participated in the labor force in 1870, implying that most young girls were neither in school nor at work and instead were available to help their mothers with housework. A rough caricature of the life of youth in 1870 is that male teenagers on the farm were farm laborers, doing the basic work of farming as instructed by their fathers. Both rural and urban teenage females helped their mothers with the household drudgery that dominated the weekly activities of farmers and of the urban working class.

Labor force participation of prime-age males was a near-universal 98 percent in 1870, compared to a substantially lower 93 percent in 1940 and 92 percent in 2010. Female prime-age participation changed in the opposite direction, rising from 21 percent in 1870 and 25 percent in 1940 to 76 percent by 2010. The data suggest that older men worked more in 1870 than recently, whereas older women worked much less. In fact, as we shall see, contemporary sources suggest that men "worked until they dropped"—until they could no longer work due to disability or death—and thus that the concept of retirement for men did not exist. In the absence of old-age pensions and Social Security, men had to keep working to support their families.

The bottom section of table 2–1 chronicles a decline in both birth and death rates. By today's standards, fertility rates in 1870 were astonishing (4.6 for whites and 7.7 for blacks) and substantially exceeded the peak fertility rate of 3.7 reached at the height of the postwar baby boom in 1957–58. The fertility rate of white mothers in 1870 was twice as high as in 1940 or 2010. For black mothers, this rate was nearly three times as high in 1870 as in 2010. However, by 1870, the white fertility rate of 4.6 had already declined substantially from the rate of 7.0 recorded in 1790.[14] Many of these babies died in their first year, and the steady decline of infant mortality helps explain why life expectancy at birth increased from 1870 to 2010 by 33 years even as life expectancy at age 60 increased by much less—6.5 years for males and 8.6 years for females.

A picture emerges of a young, rapidly growing population, with most households consisting of married couples living together while having lots of babies, some of whom died during or soon after childbirth. Families were large, and households headed by single males or females (whether never married, widowed, or divorced) were quite rare. The relatively rapid growth rate of population was spurred by a combination of a very high fertility rate together with a rapid rate of immigration.

Michael Haines has estimated that natural increase accounted for half of U.S. population growth between 1790 and 1920, in the sense that the natural increase of those present in 1790 would have led to a population of 52 million in 1920, in contrast to the actual 1920 population of 106 million.[15] Immigration and the fertility of the immigrants who arrived after 1790 accounts for the remaining half of population growth. From roughly 1850 on, foreign-born households had a higher fertility rate than native-born, partly because of early marriage ages and a higher percentage of marriages.

Where did Americans live in 1870? About 35 percent lived in New England and the Middle Atlantic states—that is, between Maine and Washington, DC. Another 35 percent lived in the east and west north central states, which included both West Virginia and Kentucky. Another 26 percent lived in the eleven states of the old Confederacy. This left only about 4 percent in the vastness of the Mountain and Pacific states. Exactly a quarter of the total population was classified as "urban" in 1870.[16] Most of the urban population lived in the northeast portion of the nation, east of the Appalachians and north of Virginia.[17]

The relatively large share of the east and west north central states reflected both the ongoing phenomenon of east-to-west internal migration during the nineteenth century coupled with immigrants' preference for living in the northeast and north central states. Immigrants flocked to climates with which they were familiar, which helps explain why so many Scandinavians wound up in Minnesota. Immigrants had an aversion to the old Confederacy states, where the percentage of foreign-born was less than one-third of the percentage in the northern states.[18] No matter which direction they went, except south, immigrant settlers could find people who spoke their language and who shared their geographic and cultural roots. A Swedish immigrant inadvertently confirmed how chain migration patterns were shaping the ethnic makeup of rural America when he related, "West of us there live nothing but Swedes for a distance of about sixteen miles. East and south and north of us lives a mixed population of Americans, Germans, and Bohemians, Negroes, and Mexicans, so it is certainly a strange mixture."[19]

CONSUMER SPENDING: HOW COULD SO MANY LIVE ON SO LITTLE?

Consumption expenditures in 1870 were about 76 percent of GDP. Multiplying this ratio by the per-capita GDP estimate cited at the beginning of this chapter yields implied consumption expenditures per capita of $2,808 in 2010 prices. Most contemporary American households would be incredulous that people could have kept body and soul together for only $54 per week in today's prices, including food, clothing, and shelter.

If we link together price indexes from the most reputable sources, the ratio of average consumer prices in 1870 to those in 2010 is 7 percent. This means that per-person consumption in the current prices of 1870 was $3.80 per week, or $197 per year. Because the average household had five members in 1870, the implied average household consumption was $983 per year. Our main contemporary reference to assess this $983 number is the 1874–75 budget study by the Massachusetts Bureau of Labor Statistics (hereafter MBLS). This survey of 397 wage-earner families reports an average consumption level of $738. The survey included only wage earners, of whom roughly half were skilled. Excluded were salaried employees, professionals, and proprietors, so allowing for higher incomes in the excluded groups, it is quite possible that average consumption per household was close to the $983 number derived indirectly from macroeconomic time series.[20]

How could the families of 1870 have lived on so little? The answer is the same as for most societies that are relatively primitive by our standards—consumer spending went almost entirely for the three necessities of food, clothing, and shelter, with virtually nothing left over for discretionary items. Robert Gallman found that in 1869, 51.9 percent of consumer expenditures were for perishable goods, 15.7 percent for semi-durable goods, 9.3 percent for durable goods, and the remaining 24.1 percent for services, mainly rent.[21] The first column in table 2–2 displays these Gallman numbers for the four major categories of consumer expenditures.

More detail can be provided about the composition of expenditures within these groups and is also displayed in the first column of table 2–2. The shares for the detailed categories are calculated by multiplying Gallman's share for a major category—e.g., semi-durable goods—by the shares within those categories reported in William Shaw's compilation of data on commodity flows.[22] About 87 percent of perishable spending was for food and the remainder for tobacco products, drugs, printed material, and fuel/lighting products. Spending on semi-durables was divided into rough thirds for manufactured clothing, shoes/boots, and fabrics and other dry goods destined to be made into clothing. A tiny share remained for toys, games, and sporting goods.

In the durable goods category, about half of spending was on furniture, cooking apparatus, floor coverings, and other household furnishings. The next largest categories were jewelry, watches, and horse-drawn vehicles. The remainder was scattered across chinaware, utensils, musical instruments, luggage, and burial monuments and tombstones. No information is available for the distribution of the 24.1 percent share of services between rent and other services.

Table 2–2 also provides consumer expenditure shares for 1940 and 2013. Some categories are combined to match the subcategories in the 1869 data. Comparing the expenditures from 1869 to 1940 and 2013, we find stunning differences. The share of food for "off-premises" (mainly home) consumption declined from 44.3 percent in 1869 to 22.3 in 1940, then even further, to 7.6, by 2013. The residual perishable category, mainly heating/lighting fuel, likewise declined from 7.6 percent to 1.6 percent between 1869 and 2013.

The overall share of semi-durables has remained roughly constant over the last 140 years, but the composition has completely changed. The shares of clothing, footwear, and dry goods plummeted from 14.9 percent in 1869 to 10.1 percent in 1940 and 3.1 percent in 2013, and about two-thirds of 2013 semi-durable spending was on categories that did not exist in 1869. The share of durable goods increased modestly between 1869 and 2013, but there was virtually

Table 2–2. Consumer Expenditures by Category, Percent Shares, 1869, 1940, and 2013

	1869	1940	2013
Perishable goods	51.9	28.2	9.2
Food, alcohol for off-premises consumption	44.3	22.3	7.6
Tobacco, printed material, heating/lighting fuel	7.6	5.9	1.6
Semi-durable goods	15.7	17.3	13.4
Clothing and footwear	9.9	10.1	3.1
Dry goods for making clothing at home	5.0	0.0	0.0
House furnishings, toys, games, sports equipment	0.8	0.8	1.2
Not invented yet, including motor vehicle fuels, pharmaceuticals, recreational items, and housing supplies	0.0	6.3	9.1
Durable goods	9.3	11.5	10.9
Furniture, floor coverings, house furnishings	4.5	2.8	1.4
Glassware, tableware	0.9	0.7	0.4
Sporting equipment, guns, ammunition	0.0	0.3	0.5
Books, musical instruments, luggage	0.9	0.8	0.6
Jewelry and watches	1.5	0.6	0.7
Horse-drawn vehicles	1.3	0.0	0.0
Not invented yet, including motor vehicles, appliances, video and IT equipment, recreational vehicles, therapeutic appliances, telephone equipment	0.0	6.3	7.3
Services	24.1	43.1	66.5
Rent including imputed rent on owner-occupied dwellings		13.2	15.5
Food services and accommodations		6.2	6.2
Contributions		1.5	2.7
Not invented or not purchased	0.0	22.2	42.1
Household utilities		2.7	2.7
Health Care		3.1	16.7
Transportation Services		2.7	2.9
Recreation Services		2.2	3.8
Financial services		3.4	7.2
Other services (communication, education, professional, personal care, household maintenance)		8.1	8.8

Table 2–2. (*Continued*)

	1869	1940	2013
Summary			
Share of spending on categories that existed in 1869	100.0	65.2	41.5
Share of spending on other categories	0.0	34.8	58.5

Sources: 1869. Major categories from Gallman (2000, Table 1.10, p. 30), allocated into subcategories with data from Shaw (1947, Table II-1, pp. 108–52).
1940, 2013. NIPA Table 2.4.5.

complete turnover in the types of durables away from traditional goods such as furniture, household furnishings, jewelry, and horse-drawn vehicles toward goods invented or largely developed after 1869. These included motor vehicles, electric appliances, and a vast array of computing, communications, and entertainment equipment.

The change in services was even more dramatic, expanding from 24.1 percent in 1869 to 66.5 percent in 2013. By 2013, the combined share of tenant rent and owner-occupied equivalent rent had declined from about 24 percent to 15.5 percent. Perhaps the most interesting finding in table 2–2 is that in 1940, more than one-third of the consumer budget went toward goods and services that did not even exist in 1869. By 2013, spending for these post-1869 goods and services made up nearly 60 percent of total consumer spending. Table 2–2 teaches us that the invention of new services has been, if anything, more important than the invention of new goods. The most important of these new services, health care, played a partial role in achieving the major improvement in life expectancy already displayed in table 2–1.

FOOD: WHAT THEY ATE AND WHERE THEY BOUGHT IT

What did Americans eat? The most important single fact about food consumption in 1870 was the dominance of home production in a mostly rural nation. Because diets were tied to what farmers could raise on their own land, they were monotonous. Lack of means of preservation made salted and smoked pork the dominant meat. Pork was popular in all regions, not just because it could be easily preserved, but because pigs needed little attention and could be allowed to roam freely, eating acorns and other vegetation in forests. Likewise, corn was easy to grow almost everywhere, and the ubiquity and cheapness of cornmeal made products baked from corn the dominant starch, along with corn derivatives such as hominy or bread made from a mixture of corn and wheat flour.

> "Hog 'n' hominy" still was the chief fare in the southern and western communities not yet serviced by railroads. According to Frederick Law Olmsted, who traveled during the 1850s throughout the South, southern planters subsisted mainly on bacon, corn pone, and coffee sweetened with molasses.[23]

In northern climates, the summer season brought a welcome variety of fresh vegetables. Because leafy vegetables spoiled, plantings were dominated by types that could be stored or preserved, including turnips, pumpkins, and beans. In the south, few vegetables other than corn were eaten in the summer because of spoilage caused by heat and humidity. Though white or "Irish" potatoes were a staple in the north, in the southern states they matured too early and could not be stored in the hot climate, forcing southerners to rely on the sweet potato, which did not mature until autumn. Although vegetables were home-grown on farms and in urban back yards during the summer, only root vegetables and dry beans were available in the winter. Fruits were largely missing from the American diet of 1870, except for apples, which could be stored for several months. Fresh fruit was little eaten, because it spoiled rapidly, and much of what was available was made into cider and brandy. Fruit from trees could be made into jam and preserves, but in newly settled areas, fruit was scarce, for fruit trees took years to mature.[24]

Chocolate, tea, and particularly coffee were the beverages of choice almost everywhere. "The coffeepot could almost stand beside the six-shooter or the covered wagon as a symbol of the Old West."[25] Iced tea had become common in eastern cities by 1870. Milk and water were also consumed in large quantities, but there were continuing problems with impure water and diluted milk (we take up this issue in chapter 3).

Even in 1870, Americans ate relatively well compared to Europeans. Available data for 1870 estimate a total of 3,029 daily calories per capita in the United States, as compared to about 2,500 in the UK for the same period.[26] A Swedish immigrant is recorded as exclaiming that "even the greatest gourmet" in his native Sweden "would be amazed" at the bountiful supply and variety of foods in America. [27] The English novelist Anthony Trollope "found the United

States to be one of the few countries in the world where meat was eaten two or three times daily."[28]

Doubtless the American diet provided plenty of calories, and evidence of malnutrition was limited to individuals or families living in poverty, mainly in large cities. Yet immigrants had to adjust to the monotony of food available on the frontier and missed many of their traditional foodstuffs. Because most European immigrants had lived closer to the sea in Europe than in America, they missed fish. In particular, the Swedes missed salt herring, and those from central Europe missed "really good sweet–sour rye bread."[29]

Closely related to food consumption was another perishable commodity, tobacco. Production of manufactured cigarettes was only thirteen per capita in 1870. In that year, brand names were few, as exclusive trademarks date from federal legislation passed in 1881. A mere 120 trademarks existed in 1870, as compared to more than 10,000 registered in the year 1906 alone.[30] The first trademark of all, adorned with a flaming mustachioed devil, was granted in 1867 for Underwood's deviled turkey and deviled ham. [31]

Preservation of food was primitive in 1870. Although the icebox had been invented in the 1860s, it did not become common until the 1880s. Also missing in 1870 was the refrigerated rail car (invented in 1871), which in the last part of the century greatly expanded the variety of available food items, including chilled Midwestern beef sent to the urban northeast and California-grown lettuce sent everywhere. Before the development of centralized slaughterhouses and refrigerated railcars, beef reached the city "on the hoof," shipped live from the west in slow trains. The starved cattle were virtually dead on arrival. Harper's Weekly complained in 1869, "The city people are in constant danger of buying unwholesome meat; the dealers are unscrupulous, and the public uneducated." Meat or fowl for sale were hung on racks or placed on market counters and according to the New York Council of Hygiene in 1869 "undergo spontaneous deterioration... becoming absolutely poisonous." Another contemporary 1872 source complained of cartloads of decayed fruit such as bruised oranges and rotten bananas.[32]

Kitchen equipment in 1870 did not yet reflect the many advances of the late nineteenth century. The kitchen sink was made of wood with a grooved wooden drainboard; iron and porcelain sinks were still in the future. Wood and coal remained the principal fuels for cooking. Gas stoves had been invented but were considered dangerous, and indeed there were numerous reports of explosions. Because most cooking, particularly in farm households, was done on the hearth rather than in enclosed stoves, preparing food was time-consuming, and food was cooked with the intention of serving leftovers from most of the cooked items. If a typical cornmeal pudding was served for dinner, its remnants might be sliced, fried, and served with milk or molasses for the next day's breakfast. When a meat stew was served at the midday meal, supper might consist of cold meat and potatoes saved from the stew. The gradual increase in the urban fraction of the population diminished the importance of the hot midday meal, for the husband had to be sent off to his work with simple food, including sandwiches made from leftover meat and dessert consisting of leftover pie.[33]

In 1870, the words "processed" and "purchased" were only marginally relevant to a population that was 75 percent rural. Most Americans lived on farms in 1870 and produced much of their food and clothing at home. Typical frontier farmers raised livestock for meat, grew potatoes and other vegetables, and, when geography was favorable, grew wheat for flour. But they still needed a cash income to purchase sugar, coffee, spices, and other basic foodstuffs that could not be produced on the farm, and they also needed enough cash income to buy clothing, or at least fabric to make homemade clothing, as well as cooking utensils and the most basic of farm implements.[34]

The standard source of both food and dry goods (e.g., fabrics for making clothes) was the closest country store. It was customary for the counters and shelves along the store's right side to hold dry goods and for those on the left to hold groceries, tobacco, and patent medicines. The colorful packaging of consumer goods was still in the future, so in the country store of 1870, goods were displayed primarily in bulk in barrels, jars, bins, and sacks. Customers had to wait while their orders were filled by clerks who spooned out and weighed the coffee, tea, sugar, and other bulk products.[35]

Home production and the country store were supplemented by small specialized urban markets in the large cities, as well as street vendors selling a variety of items. The rural equivalent of the street vendor was the itinerant peddler who traveled from town to town, sometimes bringing unusual goods that the country store did not stock. Both in the country and the city, most goods were sold on credit. Fixed prices were rare until the development of the department and chain stores later in the nineteenth century. The time-consuming process of waiting while individual orders were sold from bulk containers was prolonged by the need to haggle over price. It was not uncommon for higher prices to be charged to those of higher status and economic position.

CLOTHING MADE WITH FABRIC, NEEDLE, AND THREAD

Soon after 1870, a marketing revolution changed how clothing was sold, with the simultaneous development, between 1875 and 1910, of the large urban department store and the mail-order catalog, as described in chapter 3. But in 1870, the production and distribution of clothing was much more primitive. In both the city and the countryside, women and their daughters spent much of their time making clothing for themselves. A smaller share of boys' and men's clothing was made at home and a larger share bought at urban shops and rural general stores. Most rural adults had just one or two sets of everyday clothing—shirts and pants for men and simple dresses for women. Depending on income, the adults might have a set of better clothing for church or social occasions. The younger children were clothed with hand-me-downs. "Modern standards of cleanliness did not apply. Working clothes were washed at most once per week and were filthy after days of hard labor in dirty surroundings." [36]

The portion of clothing that was purchased on the market rather than home-made was greater for middle- and upper-class families. For wealthy families, clothes were made to order in exclusive shops in the large cities or even ordered from Europe (as did Scarlett O'Hara in an early 1860–61 segment of the movie *Gone with the Wind*). But even for the middle class, clothing for women was primarily made at home. "Families who had money hired seamstresses to help with clothing, but only rarely to do the whole task; usually a seamstress fashioned and cut the dresses, leaving the actual needlework to the women of the family."[37]

Thus the 1870 clothing shopper did not yet benefit from the main innovations of the department store, including fixed and low prices, a money-back guarantee, and much greater variety. A central topic in chapter 3 is the innovations that occurred after 1870, which were distant dreams, or unimagined progress, for farm families and urban households alike in 1870.

FOR MOST, THE ROOF OVERHEAD WAS NOT A TENEMENT

More than for food and clothing, any discussion of housing conditions in 1870 must make a central distinction between the 75 percent of the population classified as rural and the remaining 25 percent classified as urban. Many contemporary accounts of wretched living conditions of urban working-class households, most notably that by the reformer Jacob Riis, refer to New York City tenements. However, these were not typical of living conditions among the urban working class in other cities. In seventeen of the twenty-five largest American cities in 1890, multifamily dwellings made up less than 5 percent of the housing stock.[38] Urban workers were much more likely to live in simple single-family cottages than in multifamily walk-up tenements. In addition, urban conditions differed substantially from the housing owned by the average American farm household.

A continuing theme of this chapter is what the households of 1870 "did without"—that is, those major sources of improved living standards that were invented and developed over the subsequent seven decades, between 1870 and 1940. The share of homes that had electricity in 1870 was exactly zero. The share of central heating and indoor plumbing was very close to zero. For instance, the hot water radiator was invented only in the late 1850s, implying that there was little central heating in 1870.[39]

The lack of central heating meant that a fuel, whether wood or coal, had to be hauled into the dwelling unit and the ashes removed. Despite all the work that this hauling entailed, the dwellings of 1870 remained cold in the winter. "Rags stuffed into cracks provided the only insulation. Most rooms were hotter near the ceiling, floors almost universally chilly."[40] In 1870, tight, well-built wood- or coal-burning heating stoves had not been perfected, and because the fire typically burned out overnight, most people woke up cold in unheated bedrooms. The lack of electricity meant that any chores or reading done after dark required a device with a flame, whether a set of candles, a kerosene lamp (invented in 1855), or a lamp fueled by town gas (available in some cities since the 1820s, but typically too expensive for the working class). From today's perspective, an essential characteristic of the 1870 dwelling was its dimness after dark.

Open fires for heating and open-flame gas or oil lamps for illumination created the constant danger of fire in the America of 1870 and, indeed, during the entire nineteenth century. Sparks could set wooden buildings ablaze, and the oil in lanterns could be spilled. Indeed, an oil lantern kicked over by Mrs. O'Leary's cow was the often cited (and often disputed) source of the Great Chicago Fire of 1871. Although the development after 1870 of the enclosed stove for heating reduced fires related to home heating, lightning remained a source of fire danger throughout the century.

In 1870, dwellings of all types, for all classes and in all regions, lacked not only electricity and central heating, but also running water, bathrooms, and indoor flush toilets. Sources date the invention of the first plunger-type water closet to 1875, implying that in 1870 urban dwellers relied on "chamber pots and open windows and backyards to dispose of their waste in addition to the universal outdoor privy."[41] Only in the decade of the 1870s was knowledge developed about the design of drainage and venting procedures for toilets, particularly to prevent sewer gases from backing up into the home.[42] Virtually unknown in rural America, plumbing was only slightly more common in larger cities: "the United States Commissioner of Labor's 1893 report found that 53 percent of New York's families, 70 percent of Philadelphia's, 73 percent of Chicago's, and 88 percent of Baltimore's had access to only an outside privy."[43] The percentages in those cities must have been even higher in 1870.

These aspects of "what was missing" characterized most 1870 dwellings. But there were differences between farm and city and across regions. Farmhouses in the established regions of the north, which in 1870 meant from Minnesota, Iowa, and Missouri eastward, were quite substantial even by modern standards. Starkly different from the ill-ventilated urban tenements with their "dark" (windowless) rooms, farmhouses usually were constructed with two stories and had from four to eight rooms with windows that brought ample light into each room. Rural farm homes usually included spacious porches rimming the first floor. These houses were sometimes built by the original settlers who first occupied the land and sometimes, particularly after 1870, by contractors. The first floor consisted of a kitchen, a parlor, and sometimes a dining room. There would usually be three bedrooms on the second floor—one for the parents, one for the male children, and one for the female children.[44]

These farmhouses would have seemed unbelievably spacious to working-class households in the nation's rapidly growing cities. Historians have long believed that the dismal conditions of the urban working class contributed to an overall decline in the overall average living standard, as the nation shifted from a rural-urban ratio of 75-25 in 1870 to 60-40 in 1900 and 43-57 in 1940. Urbanization and industrialization squeezed large families into small apartments. In working-class Pittsburgh as late as 1910, most lower-class families in the city had to obtain their water from outside spigots or a communal tap.[45] In Pittsburgh in 1870, "the average blue-collar family of 5.1 people was crowded 1.25 to a room."[46] The high ratio of people to rooms reflected not only the high birth rate and large family sizes, but also the need in many families to obtain extra income by housing a lodger.

A negative evaluation is provided by Frank Streightoff:

> In most large cities, and in many smaller ones, the more poorly recompensed laborers inhabit tenements. They pay exorbitant rents for dark

or dingy rooms lacking in proper toilet and bathing facilities. High rentals make it necessary to accommodate boarders and lodgers, thus fearfully overcrowding the small apartments.... Workmen can no longer generally own their homes—thus they lose the steadying effect of proprietorship, they have less incentive to thrift, and they are less likely to be such reliable citizens as of old.[47]

This quotation refers to the period 1900–1910, by which time the share of urban workers living in tenements was greater than it had been in 1870. A boon to the living standard of any household in a detached building was an outdoor yard, no matter how small. This was particularly true in the smaller towns and cities, where residential lots were larger. "A seed-store proprietor who had lived in Muncie, Indiana since the Civil War estimated that 75–80 percent of the town's families gardened in 1890."[48]

PARLORS AND SERVANTS: LIFE AT THE TOP

Though most of the discussion of housing and living conditions in this chapter appropriately applies to rural farmers and the urban working class, we must recognize that there was a substantial urban middle class and a small but very prosperous urban upper class in 1870. The most obvious evidence of the middle class is archeological, in the sense that we can walk down streets in most of the older cities and inner suburbs of the urban northeast and north central states and view the houses of the middle class of that day. There are many examples of 1870-era middle-class houses in every city of the northeast, from Cambridge, Massachusetts, to Washington, DC. Block after block of architecturally significant houses can be viewed on house tours in Charleston, South Carolina, and Savannah, Georgia. And these houses were built to last: there are currently many such houses for sale, built in 1870–75 in states ranging from Maine to Arkansas to California and in between, now easily viewable online.[49]

Who had enough money in 1870 to purchase these houses, which cost roughly $3,000 to $10,000 to build in the nominal dollars of that time? We can gain some perspective from the occupational distribution of 1870 discussed below, in which 8 percent of households were classified as managers, professionals, or proprietors. People in these occupational groups were the initial occupants of the iconic nineteenth-century brownstones of New York City and the substantial Italianate and Queen Anne houses built in cities and towns throughout the northern tier of states.

One proposed definition of the middle class in the late nineteenth century encompassed any household that kept a servant.[50] Table 2–3, later this chapter, shows that in 1870, 7.8 percent of the members of the workforce were classified as "domestic service workers." Assuming that almost all these worked outside the farm sector, roughly 15 percent of nonfarm families employed a service worker. By this reckoning, the 1870 share of the middle class could plausibly be fixed at roughly 15 percent, with the remaining 85 percent the working class.

Most of the descriptive literature on the middle-class home of the late nineteenth century refers to the period after 1875. From the perspective of 1870, virtually all the progress of the late nineteenth century was still in the future—gas fires would become common in the 1880s and gas cookers in the 1890s, and the electric light bulb would become available only in the 1880s. Middle-class houses built in 1870 may look impressive from the outside as we walk by them today, but inside, as originally constructed, they lacked all the amenities that began to change the world in the late nineteenth century.

RAILS, HORSES, AND DUST: THE MOVEMENT OF GOODS AND PEOPLE

The 1869 ceremony of the golden spike, already described, tied together a sprawling nation that could now travel from Boston to San Francisco by rail, albeit slowly by today's standards. Yet long-distance travel was too expensive for most, making local transit of greater concern. Within cities in 1870, horse-drawn trolleys and carriages still dominated, as they would for the subsequent two decades. Poor roads, slow horse-drawn carriages and carts, and a lack of communication isolated the rural family in 1870. Even assuming that the household owned a horse, making trips into town feasible by carriage, the roads barely existed and were pitted with ruts and pools of mud after rains. Travel speeds were extremely slow. Though newspapers could afford to send telegraph dispatches across the country by 1870, neither the telegraph nor mail service reached the western farmers of 1870. Rural Free Delivery was still two decades in the future.

However, enormous progress in the distribution of mail was under way in the years immediately before and after 1870. George Armstrong began in 1864 to establish the moveable railway post office cars that greatly accelerated the distribution of mail. Passenger trains that ran at relatively high speeds were equipped with postal cars carrying postal clerks, sorting the mail as the train sped along. At the end of each line, mail, already sorted, would be handed over to connecting trains going in different directions. Armstrong, who died in 1871, had lived long enough to see his system of railroad postal cars established throughout the nation.[51]

For all the accolades accorded the railroads by commentators in the late nineteenth century, and for all the enormous progress that they enabled, the transportation revolution enabled by the steam engine was incomplete. Steam railroads did cross the country by 1870, but this did not help the urban worker in the daily task of transportation from home to factory or office. For intra-urban transportation in 1870, the horse was the central actor in the drama, as *The Nation* reminded its readers in an 1872 article:

> We have come almost totally to overlook the fact that our dependence on the horse has grown almost *pari passu* with our dependence on steam. We have opened up great lines of steam communications all over the country, but they have to be fed with goods and passengers by horses. We have covered the ocean with great steamers, but they can neither load nor discharge their cargoes without horses.[52]

Towns and cities were entirely dependent on horses for transportation, construction, and distribution. In the geographically compact city of Boston in 1870, 250,000 citizens shared the streets with 50,000 horses. The density of horses in Boston was roughly 700 per square mile. In New York City in 1867, horses killed four pedestrians per week. The importance of the horse became apparent when in the fall of 1872 horses in cities throughout the northeast caught a virulent strain of horse flu and could not be used for work:

> City life came to a standstill… Streetcar companies suspended service, undelivered freight accumulated at wharves and railroad depots, consumers lacked milk, ice, and groceries, saloons lacked beer, work halted at construction sites, brickyards, and factories, and city governments curtailed fire protection and garbage collection.[53]

A full century after James Watt's steam engine, why were cities so dependent on horses rather than steam-powered devices? Disadvantages of steam engines within the narrow confines of cities included the ever-present danger of fires started by sparks, their acrid black smoke, their deafening noise, and their heavy weight, which cracked street pavements.

LEISURE, FROM NEWSPAPERS TO SALOONS

By 1870, the American invention of the telegraph had announced the joining together of the transcontinental railway, had in 1861 made the Pony Express obsolete, and had allowed local print newspapers to report the events of national and world affairs on the day that they happened, including daily chronicles of carnage in the Civil War. The great surge of popular journalism in the late nineteenth century had not yet arrived, and in 1870 relatively few people read newspapers. In 1870, there were 574 newspapers having a combined circulation of 2.6 million, numbers that would grow by factors of four and ten, respectively, between 1870 and 1909. Furthermore, in 1870 the telephone, phonograph, motion picture, and radio had not yet been invented.

In working-class households there was little entertainment in 1870. And what entertainment there was consisted mainly of the male head of household drinking with friends in the local saloon. Females were not invited and were accustomed to their secondary rank within the family, remaining at home to take care of the children and the household chores while the male was out drinking. "The saloon as a leisure space clearly distinct from home thus gave workers a more comfortable and appealing place to spend their leisure time. Thus, few women went to saloons, as it offered social entertainment almost exclusively for men."[54]

Remarkably few other leisure time activities were available. Urban families traveled to nearby municipal fairgrounds and parks. Rural families, constrained by horse transportation, had almost nowhere to go. Vacation time was almost unknown. Farmers had time away from work in the winter, but it could hardly be described as leisure when they struggled to keep their livestock from dying in the severely harsh winter conditions of the Midwest. The relatively small urban middle class began to earn vacation time but, because of primitive transportation, had few places to visit beyond local parks and attractions.

A notable early source of working-class entertainment was the Coney Island amusement park in Brooklyn, New York, which began attracting holiday visitors in the 1830s and was already connected with central New York City by streetcar by the 1860s.[55] Other major amusement parks that provided inexpensive entertainment for the working class, such as Chicago's Riverview, which opened in 1904, are treated in subsequent chapters. In 1870, major-league sports were still to come.

DEATH FROM DIET, DISEASE, AND CONTAMINATION

Life expectancy at birth was only 45 years in 1870, contrasted with 78 years recently. This change is much greater than the improvement of life expectancy at age 65, reflecting the precipitous decline of infant mortality, which in 1870 was 176 per thousand. Kleinberg attributes high infant mortality to poor living conditions, particularly poor sanitation, and places special emphasis on the lack of contamination protection in milk distribution: "The quality of milk could be a critical factor in infant mortality, for the tendency toward early weaning grew during these years."[56]

Most American births in 1870 took place at home, aided by a midwife or perhaps by other women from the neighborhood. Deaths were common not only in the first year of birth, but also during childhood and adolescence. There was no effective treatment for most diseases. "Besides intermittent epidemics of yellow fever, cholera, and small pox, there was the ever-present influenza, pneumonia, typhus, scarlet fever, measles, whooping cough, and, above all, tuberculosis."[57] Industrial accidents were a frequent cause of death for male heads of households.

A distinctive feature of the medical profession in 1870 was the lack of licensing, which was gradually introduced state by state after 1870. There was no system to screen out physicians who had little education or who had trained at inferior institutions. Medicine was divided into warring camps by differing philosophies of medical practice. Particularly popular in the northeastern cities in 1870 was homeopathic medicine, which was based on the beliefs that diseases could be cured by drugs that, when given to a healthy person, produced the same symptoms as the disease to be treated; that the effect of drugs was greatest when administered in extremely small doses; and that nearly all diseases were the result of a suppressed itch, or "psora." The opposing school of "eclectic" medicine was based on herbal medicine and opposition to excessive drugging and bleeding.

In 1870, America was on the cusp of a wave of medical reform described in chapter 7, which began with the appointment of Charles Eliot as president of Harvard in 1869 and the death in 1873 of Johns Hopkins, a Baltimore merchant, who gave an enormous gift, by the standards of the time, to establish a new hospital and university. The state of the medical profession in 1870 is best described by a contemporary comment of Eliot's: "The ignorance and general incompetency of the average graduate of American Medical Schools, at the time when he receives the degree which turns him loose upon the community, is something horrible to contemplate."[58]

In 1870, the United States was primarily an agrarian nation, but urbanization was proceeding rapidly and brought with it a host of public health problems. Part of the problem was diet. Heavy on meat and starch, and light on fruits and vegetables, the typical 1870 diet resulted in calcium deficiency, rickets, pellagra, scurvy, and constipation. A further health toll was levied by hard physical labor and the ongoing impact of dwelling conditions that were usually too hot or too cold, poorly ventilated, smoky from coal and wood fires and gas or oil lighting, and insect-ridden. Though window screening had been invented around the time of the Civil War, it was not recognized in 1870 as a potential solution to the problem of insects. As windows and doors were left open for ventilation in the summer, insects (which have been described as the "national bird of the nineteenth century") flew freely between human and animal waste outside and food on the table. Water was infected as well, leading to an outbreak of typhoid fever almost every summer.[59]

By 1880, only one-third of urban households were equipped with water closets. However, prior to the development of urban sewer waste systems, these water closets drained into "existing privy vaults and cesspools."[60] The two decades preceding 1870 witnessed the first development of "combined sewers," which handled storm water and waste together. However, many of these sewers, including in Chicago and New York City, emptied into rivers with no filtration. In 1873, the president of the New York Board of Health declared that the "rivers [were] great natural purifiers."[61] Though it is true that flowing water gradually purifies human waste through a process called "oxidation," the process did not happen quickly enough to prevent both cholera and typhoid fever from becoming virulent waterborne diseases.[62] The first instance of filtration of water in the United States occurred between 1870 and 1872, but widespread adoption of water filtration did not occur until the early twentieth century.

Part of the improvement in the standard of living after 1870 occurred with the gradual replacement of horses by vehicles powered by the internal combustion engine. As already seen, urban life in 1870 was dominated by the omnipresent horse, and this, too, had a health aspect. The average horse produced twenty to fifty pounds of manure and a gallon of urine daily, applied without restraint to stables and streets. The daily amount of manure worked out to between five and ten tons per square mile.[63] Carcasses of dead horses often lay in the streets for days, creating a public health menace.

However bad the state of health in the northern and western states, it was much worse in the south. Southerners during the Civil War suffered from substandard nutritional intake and a lack of basic sanitation, making them more prone to illness after the war. Peacetime mortality rates increased in the south between 1860 and 1870. Matters were made worse by an epidemic of hookworm disease, its physical symptoms anemia and a loss of energy. "In the course of a few summers a healthy family may become pale and puny; once industrious, they become languid and backward in work; once prosperous, they fall into debt; once proud, property-owning people, they are reduced to tenancy and poverty."[64]

In the warm humid climate, many southern cities were more prone to epidemics than their northern counterparts. In September 1873, yellow fever, cholera, and smallpox struck Memphis simultaneously; of 7,000 people who caught yellow fever, 2,000 died. More than half of the 40,000 inhabitants temporarily left the city. "Memphis had virtually no sewers outside its business district, and filth from open gutters accumulated in adjacent bayous."[65]

WORK: HOT AND DIRTY FOR MEN AND DRUDGERY FOR THEIR WIVES

This book is about not just the standard of living from the viewpoint of the consumer, but also the quality of working conditions both outside and inside the home. Table 2–3 displays the distribution of occupations for 1870, 1940, and 2009. Details are provided for twelve occupational groups and are aggregated into four major groups. The most important fact about 1870 was the dominant role of agriculture in American life: 46 percent of the work force was engaged in farming, including both farmers and farm laborers. Blue-collar occupations predominated in the nonfarm sector, divided roughly in thirds among craftsmen, operatives, and laborers. Service work was relatively less important, and the majority of service workers were domestic servants. The remaining 8 percent of occupations were the core of the middle and upper classes—managers, professionals, and business proprietors.

We will return in subsequent chapters to the enormous change in the occupational distribution between 1870 and 2010. Farming has almost disappeared as an occupation, the share of blue-collar work has declined by one-third, and

Table 2–3. Distribution of Occupations 1870, 1940, and 2009

	1870	1940	2009
Farmers and Farm Laborers	46.0	17.3	1.1
Farmers	26.5	11.0	0.5
Farm Laborers	19.5	6.3	0.6
Blue-Collar Occupations	33.5	38.7	19.9
Craft Workers	11.4	11.5	8.3
Operatives	12.7	18.0	10.2
Laborers	9.4	9.2	1.4
Service Occupations	12.6	28.1	41.4
Clerical Workers	1.1	10.4	12.1
Sales Workers	2.3	6.2	11.6
Domestic Service Workers	7.8	4.4	0.6
Other Service Workers	1.4	7.1	17.1
Managers, Professionals, and Proprietors	8.0	15.1	37.6
Managers and Officials	1.6	3.7	14.4
Professionals	3.0	7.1	20.5
Proprietors	3.4	4.3	2.7
Total[a]	100.1	99.2	100.0

Sources: 1870 and 1940: HSUS Series Ba1033-Ba1046

2009: *Statistical Abstract of the United States: 2011,* Table 605 for self-employed plus Table 615 for employees.

Notes: a. The 1870 total is greater than 100 due to rounding. The 1940 total is less than 100 due to the addition of an "Unclassified" labor category.

there has been an explosion of the share of service occupations as well as of managers and professionals. The share of professionals today is about the same as that of farm laborers in 1870, implying a tremendous change in working conditions along all dimensions, including physical difficulty, exposure to the elements, risk of injury or death, and educational qualifications.[66] Throughout this book, we trace the gradual transition from unpleasant to pleasant work. If we describe farming, blue-collar work, and domestic service as unpleasant, then 87 percent of jobs in 1870 were unpleasant. In 1940, this percentage was 60.4 percent, and by 2009, it had declined to only 21.6 percent.

These changes in American occupations were not all monotonic, however. For example, blue-collar workers actually increased as a percentage of the work force from 33.5 percent in 1870 to 38.7 percent in 1940, before plunging to 19.9 percent in 2009. Though managers and professionals have risen from less than 5 percent to more than a third of the work force, proprietors have actually decreased from a peak of 4.3 percent in 1940 to 2.7 percent in 2009. Agriculture, thanks to technological advances, has required the efforts of a constantly decreasing portion of the work force, from nearly half of all workers in 1870 to 17 percent in 1940 and only 1 percent in 2009. Work for farmers in 1870 combined backbreaking physical labor reliant on animal power before the invention of self-propelled farm machinery, together with exposure to extreme heat in the summer and cold in the winter, and the climate became more extreme as farmers moved west from the Atlantic seaboard to settle the Midwest and Great Plains states. Plowing a field with a horse or mule in 1870 was a much tougher job than guiding an air-conditioned 2010 tractor equipped with a host of electronic gadgets.

Farmers not only raised crops but also were responsible for every other detail of settlement that would allow their families to live on an isolated patch of earth. Many farmers got their start thanks to the Homestead Act of 1862, registering the free land they had claimed at a nearby federal land office. If the farmer had purchased the land from a railroad, an agent of that railroad would usually assist him with the details. Frequently men traveled to their western destinations by themselves, leaving family and children behind only to bring them out later after the legality of land ownership had been established and an initial structure built.[67]

In 1870, many migrants were venturing west of the fertile fields of Iowa and Missouri into the unknown climate of the Dakotas, Nebraska, Kansas, and Oklahoma. New settlers, particularly from more benign European climates, were not prepared for the extremes that they found in the Great Plains, now known as Tornado Alley, an area of mercilessly cold winters and hot summers. In some summers, hot weather was accompanied by a drought, with dire consequences such as occurred in the Dust Bowl summers of 1934–36. But the extremes of the climate were not the only impediments to the survival of the farmer's family or of crucial farm animals. The hazards of prairie fire, hail, drought, and grasshoppers also afflicted farm production in the 1870s, causing large losses of income to those who had staked their claim in this fertile but fragile terrain.[68] A combination of lack of knowledge and the availability of free land tempted settlers to venture into this area of risky weather.

How large were farms in 1870? How many people worked on them, and how much did they produce? There were 2.66 million farms, having an average of 154 acres and producing an average of $874, in current dollars, per year. The median number of acres was roughly ninety, indicating considerable dispersion in the size of farms. The average farm had $100 worth of farm implements and provided work for 2.2 farmers and farm laborers.

When we combine the occupational data in table 2–3 with the agricultural aggregates, it appears that there were 1.25 farmers per farm, plus an average of an additional single farm laborer. The data also indicate that not all farms were occupied by their owners. In 1870, for the United States as a whole, 75 percent of farms were operated by full or part owners and the remaining 25 percent by tenants. In the south, the figures were 64 percent and 36 percent, respectively, indicating the greater importance of tenant sharecropping in the southern states.[69]

The apparent current-dollar cash income of $960 can be contrasted with the $770 average income of the sample families in the MBLS survey of urban working-class families. This difference is particularly striking because the urban working class families spent more than half of their incomes on food, much of which would have been grown at home by farm families. Thus it appears that on average, farmers were substantially better off than urban working class families, who (as estimated above) comprised roughly 85 percent of urban households.

As primitive as 1870 farm work seems in our perspective, conditions in that year had advanced substantially from those of fifty years before. The 1834 invention of the reaper greatly reduced the amount of labor and time needed to harvest wheat. Horses were used for other tasks, including walking on treadmills that ran machines to compress hay into bundles and to thresh wheat.[70] Scores of inventors struggled to develop self-propelled farm machines, but none was successful before 1873, so we take up this aspect of progress in subsequent chapters.

In comparison to farmers who settled the frontier in the Great Plains states, farmers in the southern states suffered from even hotter and more humid summers but at least were spared the rigors of extreme winter cold and blizzards. Although largely freed from snow and bitter cold, they were victims of excessive rain and an absence of paved roads. "Their mules and horses floundered in mud up to their bellies and the axles of their vehicles dragged ground."[71]

Southern agriculture took decades to recover from the Civil War. Not only was there wartime destruction to cope with, but the competitive position of the southern cotton industry had declined in relation to those of newly emerging producers in other parts of the world, including Egypt and India. Observers also blamed the problems of southern farmers on high tariffs that raised the prices of imported machinery and consumer goods, exorbitant railroad rates (a common complaint in all regions), and tight credit, the result of ongoing deflation that pushed up real interest rates.[72] A more controversial diagnosis of the drop in per-capita income was the Fogel–Engerman argument that the plantation system was more efficient than uncoordinated production by individual farmers; after the slaves were freed, they no longer produced as much as they had under a system of harsh physical control.[73] A broader diagnosis of inefficiency is offered by Lawrence Larsen: "The South entered the 1880s with an agricultural system unsuited to the needs of a free market. Land barons and country merchants presided over a fragmented economy in which sharecropping stifled individual enterprise."[74]

One of the most remarkable aspects of urban working-class life in 1870 was the sharp separation of the roles of men and women. The male household head was responsible for earning the income needed to support the family. Any teenage sons were pressed into work activities to provide extra household income. Women and daughters were expected to stay at home and keep the household running by a repetitive set of weekly chores involving washing, ironing, hauling water, cleaning, and cooking.

Working-class men interviewed in 1871 were vocal about the harsh working conditions of the "wage system." There was no room for complaint or discontent: "There is no redress here, no appeal; the by-word is if you don't like it, get out.... There is intimidation, cruelty, and dishonesty."[75] As had occurred a few decades earlier in England, skilled craftsmen resented the incursion of the machine and, with it, the regimentation of factory life.

Was there mobility between classes? Sons of laborers did frequently move up to become craftsmen or operatives, but almost all of them stayed within the ranks of manual workers, not having the education or other attributes to qualify for middle-class occupations. "The white collar and laboring worlds were clearly separated. One entered the white collar group only after having received considerable schooling, and one entered it directly."[76] "Three quarters of [laborers] attained no occupational mobility after a decade in the community, and nearly 70 percent were still common laborers after two decades."[77]

Working-class households in 1870 urban America are portrayed as constantly on the move, relocating from one city to another when they found themselves unable to achieve a decent standard of living in their original location. In contrast, landowners tended to stay in one location. This had not just economic but also political implications. "Though working-class people usually did not stay very long in the city, a prosperous and relatively stable group of community leaders existed. Consequently a small sector of the population shared a highly developed sense of community and controlled local politics."[78]

The variety of occupations in 1870 and the density of urban life can be illustrated by the composition of establishments in a single block of downtown Philadelphia. There were five stables and two livery operations, a Baptist church, the Knapp Barrel Organ Factory, a brick pressing shop, steam laundry, blacksmith and carpentry shop, wheelwright and machine shop, locksmith, confectionary, Chinese laundry, a cigar factory, school and meeting room.[79] Many job classifications that were important in 1870, from horse breeders to livery stable owners, vanished with the obsolescence of the urban horse. Among the many unpleasant occupations of 1870 were workers for city or private companies that had the malodorous task of removing horse manure.

The most physically demanding chore involved water in an era before running water was available for urban working class families, much less for rural families. According to one calculation made in 1886, "a typical North Carolina housewife had to carry water 8 to 10 times each day. Washing, boiling, and rinsing a single load of laundry used about 50 gallons of water. Over the course of a year she walked 148 miles toting water and carried more than thirty-six tons of water."[80] Not only was the water carried in, but dirty water had to be carried out, not to mention the unpleasant task of emptying chamberpots.

But that was not all the carrying that needed to be done. In 1870, the gas or electric stove had not been invented, so all cooking involved wood or coal. Fresh wood and/or coal had to be carried into the house—and spent ashes carried out.[81] "Paper and kindling had to be set inside the stove, dampers and flues had to be carefully adjusted, and a fire lit. Since there were no thermostats to regulate the stove's temperature, a woman had to keep an eye on the contraption all day long.... Keeping a fire burning all day required 50 pounds each day of coal or wood."[82]

There was no hired help for the household. A Norwegian immigrant on the frontier complained, "Here the mistress must do all the work that the cook, the maid, and the housekeeper would do in an upper-class family at home. Moreover, she must do it as those three together do it in Norway."[83] This sentiment is notable for its apples-to-oranges comparison of an immigrant farm family with an "upper-class family" back home in Norway. Presumably, working-class housewives in Norway in 1870 were required to perform similar chores to those carried out on the farm by Midwestern Norwegian immigrants.

YOUTH, CHILD LABOR, AND SCHOOLING

Persons younger than 25 made up 60 percent of the population of 1870, and their lives were very different from those of contemporary youth. Schooling in 1870 was generally limited to elementary school, with few young people extending their education beyond age 12, and even then often dependent on parental willingness to pay for private schooling. Labor-force participation was high for males aged 16–19. The difference between male and female teenagers should be underlined, with 1870 participation rates for ages 16–19 at 76.1 percent for male teenagers but only 29 percent for females. Furthermore, female participation was relatively short-lived and was terminated by the first pregnancy, whereas male participation was continuous from age 15, or even age 12, to the end of the working life.

High labor force participation of male teenagers was a matter of necessity. The nuclear family had to provide all the labor needed to raise the crops and maintain the household. Male teenagers worked with their fathers in the fields, and female teenagers helped their mothers with the unending household chores (charts showing the evolution of child labor after 1870 are presented in chapter 8). In 1870, the United States was still an agricultural society, and the school year was timed to allow a long summer break for farm children to help their fathers in crop nurturing and harvesting.[84] Albert Fishlow compared educational practices in the United States with those in the major relatively rich European nations and concluded that U.S. education was "comparable." Native-born Americans were largely literate by 1870, and the remaining cases of illiteracy involved immigrants to the northern states or former black slaves in the south.

Though there was virtually no participation in secondary or higher public education in 1870, elementary education was well developed. Elementary schools emphasized numerous measures that would help blend together the multilingual children of a society having a high population of foreign-born immigrants. Most notably, there was an "emphasis on order, efficiency, and regular attendance and punctuality by the students."[85] What were then called "common schools"—that is, elementary schools—had developed during 1840–1870. "It seems that school enrollment was almost universal for children ages 10 to 14 by 1860."[86] Literacy was significantly higher for males than females in 1870, and both school attendance and literacy lagged significantly behind in the southern states.

There were overwhelming problems faced in the education of blacks in the southern states. There had been no schools for them under slavery, and plantation owners had protected their control of slaves by making sure that the latter were uneducated and illiterate. After the Civil War, in much of the south, it was considered unacceptable for southern whites to teach southern blacks, so teachers had to be imported from the north. “By 1868, countless missionary organizations, teachers, and government and military officials had migrated to Mississippi intent upon educating, uplifting, and protecting former slaves.”[87] Educational efforts, often organized through black churches, emphasized the most rudimentary reading and writing skills at a level far below that of the nearby white population.

Just as the youth share of the population was very large in 1870, so the population share of those 65 and older was a very small 3.0 percent. Viewed from the perspective of today’s golf-playing retirees living in their gated communities, the life of the aged was quite miserable in 1870. There was no Social Security program, so male heads of households had to support their families as they aged. But they were mainly farmers or manual laborers, and their productive capacity declined with age. Farmers could rely increasingly on their sons, if they had sons, but the urban working class was not so lucky. “Earning power declined dramatically after the age of 50, . . . and the skilled wage worker entered old age with bleak prospects.”[88] Kleinberg concurs that the manual workers “no longer had the physical strength or agility required by the mill owners.”[89]

CONCLUSION: MODERN AMERICA AT DAWN

The typical 1870 household faced not just stark limitations on the quantities of consumer goods that it could afford, but also the difficulty of the work effort by both males and housewives required to earn the income to buy these goods. The greatest hardship was the unrelenting toil of the rural and urban housewife, who not only had to carry out the daily physical task of moving clean and dirty water, coal, wood, and ashes, but also had to expend further labor making food and clothing that future generations would be prosperous enough to purchase ready-made.

Many of the aspects of life in 1870 that stand out from our perspective as uniquely unpleasant are not recognized by GDP at all. The litany of previously unmeasured deficiencies in the 1870 standard of living, all provided in subsequent generations, is endless. Processed food was largely unavailable, and fresh meat was unsafe, so the diet was a monotonous succession of salted pork and starchy foods. Unless home-grown, fruit was all but unavailable except during the summer months, and vegetables available in the winter were limited to a few root vegetables that could be stored. Clothing was crude and, for most women, home-made, and the labor needed to create clothing before the invention of the sewing machine created a further burden for the rural and urban housewife.

Dwelling units in 1870 universally lacked indoor plumbing, running water, waste disposal, electricity, telephone, and central heating. Although middle-class and upper-class families built homes in cities and nearby suburbs that today constitute cities' historic districts, farmers and members of the urban working class faced much more difficult living conditions. Although many farmers in 1870 had detached farmhouses of six or more rooms, this amount of space was rare for urban residents. Some farmers lived in primitive sod houses and one-room shacks. The absence of window screens in 1870 exposed families everywhere to flies and other insects. The preconditions for disease were present not just in overcrowded urban slum districts, but also on every farm.

Every family in the United States in 1870 was directly or indirectly dependent on the horse. Steam power propelled the railroads and some factories, but in 1870 there was virtually no steam farm machinery nor steam intra-urban transportation. Horses were the dominant source of propulsion, from rural plows and threshing machines to intra-urban transportation, distribution, and construction. The consequences of dependence on the horse in 1870 involved negative externalities unrecognized by GDP, including manure and urine distributed on the streets and the cost of the unlucky laborers assigned to clean up the tons of horse waste, not to mention the diversion of a substantial part of agricultural production to feed the ubiquitous horses, in 1870 numbering 8.6 million, or roughly one horse for every five people.

For the 75 percent of the American population classified as "rural," the overwhelming impression from today's perspective is isolation. In 1870, there not only were no telephones, but also was no rural postal service. Many settlers had gone to the limits of the frontier of the Great Plains to encounter extreme weather conditions that daunted even the weather-hardened Scandinavians and Eastern Europeans who settled there.

GDP data ignore the daily burden of the rural and urban housewife. Within a few decades, many of these tasks would be swept away by innovation, but in 1870, they were front and center. This toil occurred amid a household that could see the vicissitudes of the weather destroy the crop that was a rural family's only income or, in the urban America of 1870, for which a macroeconomic event could cause urban employment opportunities to vanish, as occurred in 1873 and the following years of depression.

The year 1870 represented modern America at dawn. Over the subsequent six decades, every aspect of life experienced a revolution. By 1929, urban America was electrified and almost every urban dwelling was networked, connected to the outside world with electricity, natural gas, telephone, clean running water, and sewers. By 1929, the horse had almost vanished from urban streets, and the ratio of motor vehicles to the number of households reached 90 percent. By 1929, the household could enjoy entertainment options that were beyond the 1870 imagination, including phonograph music, radio, and motion pictures exhibited in ornate movie palaces. By 1929, infant mortality had been almost conquered, and hospitals and the practice of medicine had achieved their current form of licensing and professionalism. By 1929, workdays were shorter, a smaller proportion of men worked in manual jobs, and electric appliances had begun to lighten the everyday chores of home production.

This epochal transformation began slowly, and its pace picked up after 1900 as electrification and the motor vehicle spread rapidly. But within the first decade after 1870, the foundations of the modern age had been laid. Electric light, the first reliable internal combustion engine, and wireless transmission were all invented within the same three-month period at the end of 1879. Within the same decade, the telephone and phonograph were also invented. The Second Industrial Revolution was on its way to changing the world beyond recognition.

Chapter 3

WHAT THEY ATE AND WORE AND WHERE THEY BOUGHT IT

> With lack of hygienic standards, the established purveyors in the slum districts—from street vendor to corner grocer—sold food that would not today be considered fit for human consumption.
>
> —Otto Bettmann, 1974, p. 109

INTRODUCTION: THE NECESSITIES

The three necessities of life are food, clothing, and shelter. The evolution of the standard of living between 1870 and 1940 with respect to the first two is considered in this chapter, whereas the next chapter treats the evolution of the quantity and quality of shelter, including the role of electrification, indoor plumbing, and central heating in revolutionizing life within the home. In contrast to the changes chronicled in the next chapter, those treated here are evolutionary rather than revolutionary.

More important than changes in what people ate and wore was a set of epochal changes in how their food and clothing were produced and where they were purchased. As America steadily became more urban and as real incomes rose, the share of food and clothing produced at home declined sharply, freeing some of the time previously engaged in household production. New types of processed food were invented, and many of today's name brands became commonplace in the last three decades of the nineteenth century.

The initial food and drug legislation in 1906 began the long process of ridding the food supply chain of rotten meat, diluted milk, and intentional measurement errors. With urbanization came the convenience of the chain store, which allowed shoppers to purchase most of their food requirements in one location instead of several smaller specialty stores. The transition of clothing from home production to market purchases was accelerated by two late nineteenth-century inventions: the large urban department store and the mail-order catalog. Department stores in the large cities, starting with Wanamaker's in Philadelphia in 1876, not only greatly increased the variety of items available, but also lowered prices through their efficient organization.

The mail-order catalogs, notably that of Montgomery Ward starting in 1872 and that of Richard Sears and Alvah Roebuck starting in 1894, ended the isolation of rural America and made visible in printed pages the ongoing explosion of variety in American-made manufactured goods, including older goods that were becoming steadily cheaper, such as nails and hammers, as well as newly invented goods like bicycles and sewing machines.

The chapter begins with budget studies to identify the evolution of the share of household consumption spending on food, clothing, and other categories, and then examines evidence of shifts in the broad categories of food consumed. Treated next are innovations in food production, food marketing, food quality and safety. The implications of food consumption for nutrition are then examined through the lens of biometric studies of adult height and other physical characteristics.

The treatment of clothing is briefer. A central theme is the shift from home-produced clothing, particularly for women and children, to market-purchased clothing made available in abundance by mail-order catalogs and urban department stores. The chapter concludes by assessing the numerous reasons why conventional data on prices and output understate the contribution of food and clothing to the growth in the American standard of living.

THE SURPRISING PERSISTENCE OF SPENDING ON FOOD

The record of U.S. food consumption in the nineteenth and twentieth centuries implies a startling conclusion: calories of food consumption hardly changed over the past 200 years, at least up until the past three decades. Figure 3–1 plots average calories consumed per person for each decade between 1800 and 2011. For the decades before 1980, there were wiggles up and down but little overall change:—consumption was 2,950 calories in 1800 and 3,200 in 1980. The subsequent discussion of other measures of food consumption should be viewed from the perspective of relatively constant calorie intake.

Food is the most basic of the three necessities (food, clothing, and shelter). When people are poor, most of their household budget is spent on food. Then,

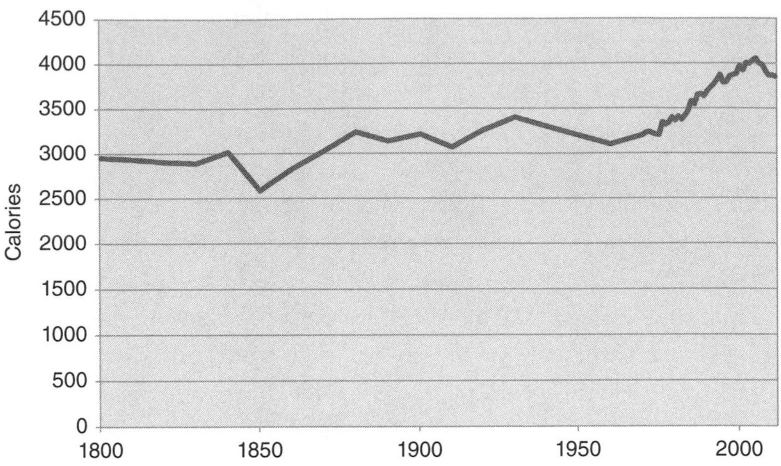

Figure 3–1. Daily Caloric Availability per Person, 1800–2011
Sources: Floud et al. (2011) Table 6.6, Food and Agriculture Organization's Food Balance Sheet ratio-linked forward after 1970.

as their incomes rise, they can afford to spend more on clothing, shelter, and other goods and services that add to the pleasure of life but that are not necessities, including on personal care, such as for purchased haircuts and entertainment items such as movie theater admissions.

The first known budget study for the United States was conducted by the Massachusetts Bureau of Labor (MBLS) in 1874–75. Inspired in part by the MBLS study, the newly formed U.S. Bureau of Labor (BLS) undertook large-scale studies for 1888–91, 1901, 1917–19, and 1935–36, the results of which are summarized in table 3–1.[1] We use the Consumer Price Index (CPI) to convert the nominal numbers on total expenditures into real terms.[2] The resulting levels of real total expenditures per household are shown on the bottom line of the table in 1901 prices. The annual growth rate of real household consumption between the midpoint of 1888–91 and 1901 was 1.99 percent per year, followed by much slower annual growth rates of 1.06 percent between 1901 and 1917–19 and then 0.95 percent between 1917–19 and 1935–36.

Because consumer spending increased from one survey to the next, we would expect the percentage spent on food gradually to decline. But this is not what is shown in table 3–1. In the first three columns, spanning the years 1888 to 1919, there was virtually no change in the expenditure shares across categories, and particularly no shrinkage in the expenditure share of food, which

Table 3–1. Four Consumer Budget Studies, 1888–1936

	Workers in Nine Cities in U.S., 1888–91	**Working Families in 1901**	**Urban Familes in 1917–19**	**Consumption expenditures of urban families, 1935–36**
	(1)	(2)	(3)	(4)
Sample Size	2562	11156	12896	14469
Average Family Size	3.9	4.0	4.9	3.6
Income before Taxes	573	651	1505	N.A.
Expenditures				
Total	534	618	1352	1463
Food	219	266	556	508
Clothing	82	80	238	160
Rent	80	112	224	259
Fuel	32	35	74	108
Sundries	121	124	260	428
Percent Expenditures				
Food	41.0	43.0	41.1	34.7
Clothing	15.4	12.9	17.6	10.9
Rent	15.0	18.1	16.6	17.7
Fuel	6.0	5.7	5.5	7.4
Sundries	22.7	20.1	19.2	29.3
Total Expenditures in Prices of 1901	491.6	618.0	739.7	873.6

Sources: Columns (1)-(3) from HSUS Cd465-Cd502. Column (4) from HSUS Cd540-557.
Note: "Rent" in column (3) includes "household operation."

varied only between 41.0 and 43.0 percent. With so much of the consumer budget dedicated to food and no change in total calories consumed, there is little room in this interval for a major improvement in the standard of living, unless it occurs in the variety and types of food consumed. Clothing and rent round out the traditional three necessities, and fuel for heat and light qualifies as a fourth necessity. The total share of spending on the three categories of clothing, rent, and fuel was relatively stable across the four surveys and summed to 36.4 percent, 36.7 percent, 39.7 percent, and 36.0 percent, respectively.

It was only in the 1935–36 survey that food consumption declined below 40 percent. This made room for an increase in the miscellaneous "sundries" category from 19.2 percent in 1917–19 to 29.3 percent in 1935–36. What were these items? They included spending on insurance, medical care, tobacco, haircuts, meals away from home, furniture, union dues, church contributions, and public transit fares.[3]

WHAT PEOPLE ATE: ADDING VARIETY TO A BORING DIET

The best source of changes in the consumption of particular foods is the USDA time series of apparent consumption of food.[4] We are presented in table 3–2 with a cosmic sweep of data on the consumption of specific types of food over 140 years. The top section of the table records the consumption of various types of meat and immediately poses a puzzle. Meat consumption declined from 1870 to 1900, with lower pork consumption more than offsetting increased beef consumption. Then, after 1900, meat consumption of both beef and pork declined precipitously. By 1929, total meat consumption had declined by one-third from 1870, beef had declined by a quarter, and pork by fully half. Consumption of lamb, mutton, chicken, and turkey taken together did not grow at all between 1870 and 1929 and thus did not offset the declines of beef and pork consumption.

Which food types replaced the decline in meat consumption? Categories registering increases included fats and oils, fruit, milk products, eggs, sugar, and coffee, whereas flour and cereal products declined in importance. The decline in pork consumption was part of the antidote to the boredom of the American diet already described in chapter 2. As processed foods were invented and became popular, households found more satisfying ingredients and could vary their meals. The 1870 breakfast of pork and grain mush by the 1920s was replaced by corn flakes and other packaged cereals and citrus fruit juice.

Although the variety of the diet improved after 1870 in the north and west, the southern diet, based on pork, corn, and game, remained the same for decades. Previously prosperous planters were now impoverished, and only a small upper class carried on the tradition of fine southern cuisine that had been practiced in plantation kitchens before the Civil War. By one estimate, southerners ate twice as much pork as northerners in the last third of the nineteenth century. A doctor from Georgia, commenting on the high rate of southern pork consumption in 1860, wrote, "The United States of America might properly be called the Great Hog Eating Confederacy or the Republic of Porkdom."[5]

Table 3–2. Apparent per Person Consumption of Foods, 1800–1940 (in pounds per person, except eggs)

	1800	1870	1900	1929	1940
Meat	212	212	190	130.7	141.2
Beef and veal	74	62	78	45.0	50.1
Pork	123	131	83	64.8	68.3
Lamb and mutton	1	3	6	5.0	5.9
Chicken and turkey[1]	15	17	22	16.0	16.9
Fats and oils				48.7	50.1
Butter		11	20	17.6	17.0
Margerine			1	2.9	2.4
Lard			13	12.7	14.4
Other fats and oils				15.5	16.3
Fruits[2]	80	73	219	193.7	202.2
Vegetables[3]	334	220	273	319.9	291.1
Total Milk Equivalent[4]	509	472	750	811.9	818.2
Milk and Cream			253	300.3	305.7
Cheese		4	4	5.9	7.9
Frozen Dairy			0.3	10.2	11.7
Eggs (numbers)	72	102	255	324.3	309.2
Sugar and sweeteners[5]		35	65	112.7	108.4
Flour and Cereal Products		334	317	236	199
Coffee		6	10	10.2	13.0
Total			1366	1368	1330

Sources: 1929–1940 USDA ERS Food Availability Data System, HSUS (1960) G552-584, HSUS (1975) G881-915. 1800-1900 *The Changing Body: Health, Nutrition, and Human Development in the Western World since 1700* (Floud et al), SAUS, "Farm Gross Product and Gross Investment in the Nineteenth Century" from *Trends in the American Economy in the Nineteenth Century* (Towne and Rasmussen).

Notes: 1. 1800–1900 does not include turkey, which was a small fraction of total poultry.

2. Fruits includes HSUS Melon category. Conversion factor of 40 lbs per bushel of fruit was used for 1800–1900 data.

3. Includes corn for human consumption and potatoes. 1800-1900 data assumes truck crops solds for the same price per bushel as peas and beans. Peas, beans, and truck crops estimated at 40 lbs per bushel.

4. Includes butter, listed under Fats and oils.

5. 1800–1900 only counts sugars. For comparison, sugar consumption in 1929 was 97 pounds per person.

North or south, critics of the typical diet singled out the American addiction to the frying pan:

> Flour fried in fat is one of our delights. Dough-nuts, pancakes, fritters, are samples of what we do with good wheat flour. Fried ham, fried eggs, fried liver, fried steak, fried fish, fried oysters, fried potatoes, and last, not least, fried hash await us at morning, noon, and night.[6]

Even before the development of refrigerated rail cars in the 1880s, the urban diet by the 1850s benefited from the reach of unrefrigerated rail transport. Upstate New York supplied northeastern cities with fresh milk, vegetable farms surrounding the big cities provided vegetables in the summer, and even fruit came from as far away as Florida and California.

The Lynds' detailed survey of life in Muncie, Indiana, distinguishes between the "winter diet" and the "summer diet" in the 1890s.[7] In the winter, the main foods eaten were meat, macaroni, potatoes, turnips, cole slaw, and cake or pie for dessert. Preserved pickles were used for flavoring. A common complaint was "spring sickness" resulting from a lack of green vegetables over the winter. Vegetable gardens were almost universal in this medium-sized city, in which almost everyone, even the working class, lived in single-family structures. A major change between the 1890s and 1920s was the increasing availability of fresh vegetables in the winter as a result of refrigerated railroad cars and in-home iceboxes.

Just as in Muncie, in most medium-sized cities and towns, the population lived in single-family dwellings and usually had access to garden plots to grow their own vegetables. It is possible that the USDA data displayed in table 3–2 misses a substantial portion of the increase in urban consumption of vegetables made possible by these garden plots. There was a stark difference between food consumption on the farm and among the poorer classes in the growing cities. Farmers were not entirely self-sufficient and sold their surplus of preserved pork, grains, and vegetables to acquire sugar, coffee, shoes, and crude farm implements. Urban dwellers required cash income for all their food, and the macroeconomic depressions of the 1870s and 1890s created a large underclass of people who avoided starvation only by consuming meager rations provided by soup kitchens. Undernourishment caused deteriorating health, aggravated in the larger cities by crowded living quarters incorporating minimal light and ventilation.

Another view of changes in food consumption after 1909 is shown in table 3–3, which measures food intake in three ways: by food consumed, by pounds of food consumed, and by daily number of calories consumed. The "food consumed" index is weighted by food prices per pound and rises if there is a shift, for instance, from one pound of low-valued food, such as potatoes, to one pound of high-valued food, such as steak. It is evident from this table that there was hardly any change in food consumption between 1909 and 1940, as measured by food consumed, pounds of food consumed, or daily number of calories consumed, which register annual growth rates, respectively, of 0.22 percent, –0.21 percent, and –0.18 percent per year.

We can calculate the unit value of food consumed if we divide "food consumed" in the first column of table 3–3 by the pounds of food in the second column. There was remarkably little increase in the unit value between 1909 and 1929. Instead, the main increases occurred after 1929. The bottom section of the table shows that there was an increase in the unit value at an annual rate of 0.40 percent per year between 1909 and 1940 and a slightly more rapid 0.51 percent per year between 1940 and 1970.

Table 3–3. U.S.D.A. Indexes of Food Consumption, 1909–1970 (1967=100)

	Food Consumed	Pounds of Food	Daily Calories	Unit Value (Consumption per Pound)
1909	85	113	109	78
1919	84	107	106	79
1929	87	110	106	82
1940	91	106	103	88
1950	95	105	100	95
1970	103	101	100	103
2006			122	
Annual Growth Rates				
1909–40	0.22	–0.21	–0.18	0.40
1940–70	0.41	–0.16	–0.10	0.51
1970–2006			0.55	

Source: HSUS series Bd559-567, USDA Economic Research Service.

Throughout the late nineteenth and early twentieth centuries, immigrants bought an increasing variety of foods. Among the upper classes, French cooks were prized, and cookbooks were full of French-inspired recipes. More relevant for the working and middle classes was the influence of German cooking, especially in cities populated by German immigrants, including Cincinnati, St. Louis, and Milwaukee. The Germans brought new ways of cooking pork, new types of sausages, sauerbraten, and sauerkraut, not to mention German traditions such as Christmas cookies and Christmas trees. By 1900, the Nuremberg custom of serving sausages with a piece of bread had made its transition to the American hot dog in a bun, said to have been first sold at Coney Island. Italian immigrants brought ubiquitous restaurants and showed native Americans many new ways of cooking and saucing pasta, already familiar as macaroni since the early nineteenth century.

In the late nineteenth century, the use of ice to cool railroad cars and in iceboxes was described as "refrigeration" long before the invention of the mechanical refrigerator. Though few homes had iceboxes in 1870, they became common in the south during the 1870s and 1880s and in the north a decade afterward. Large northern cities used more than five times as much ice in 1914 as they had in 1880.[8] Ice was delivered by horse-drawn wagons well into the twentieth century; wintertime deliveries from the coal wagon were replaced between May and October by deliveries from the ice wagon. As early as 1879, the U.S. census found that ice consumption in large cities amounted to two-thirds of a ton per person per year.

Food processing and refrigerated shipping brought an increased variety of fruits and vegetables, and by 1903, California growers had developed a lettuce called "Iceberg" that remained fresh as it crossed the country.[9] At the same time, the use of iceboxes continued to spread. In a 1907 New York City expenditure survey, "refrigerators" were present in 81 percent of the families earning $800 per year or less and in 90 percent of the higher-income households. However, this definition of *refrigerator* hardly equates to our use today: "In some cases it is reported that the ice is kept in a tub; in some cases an ice-box is reported, which is often hardly better than the tub, but in the majority of cases the refrigerator serves as a place for keeping perishable food as well as for keeping the ice itself."[10]

Refrigeration was able to reduce the price of many perishable items, reduce seasonal fluctuations in prices, increase the shelf life of many items, and ultimately increase nutrition and the stature of individuals. We return to the issue of stature below. For now, we quote the conclusion of Craig, Goodwin, and Grennes on the benefits of premechanical refrigeration:

> The upturn in nutrition and adult stature coincided with the adoption of mechanical refrigeration in the storage and shipping of perishable commodities. Refrigeration contributed significantly to the spatial and temporal integration of the U.S. economy in the late nineteenth century. The estimated impact of refrigeration on calorie and protein intake was in the neighborhood of 0.75 and 1.25%, respectively. As much as one-half of the improvement in nutrition in the 1890s might have been directly attributable to refrigeration.[11]

Just as patterns of food consumption changed over the decades, so did those of alcoholic drinks. German immigrants drank more beer than native-born Americans, and Italians drank more wine. But we must be careful in our interpretation of data concerning aggregate food and drink consumption, such as those provided by Stanley Lebergott, who for most products has created the best available data on consumer spending by category over the three decades between 1900 and 1930. Unfortunately, Lebergott takes the word "prohibition" literally, and he records the share of alcohol consumption in total food consumption as being 15 percent in 1914 yet exactly zero from 1920 to 1930.[12] Lebergott appears to ignore Clark Warburton's important book on the economic effects of Prohibition, in which Warburton sifts through a wide variety of data to determine how much alcohol was actually consumed, and at what prices, during the Prohibition years of 1920–32.[13]

Data on consumption of alcohol by volume understate the effect on nominal expenditures, because Prohibition pushed up prices. Warburton concludes that alcohol consumption in 1929 was $5 billion, fully 5 percent of 1929 GDP.[14] This was higher than Lebergott's estimate of 4 percent of GDP in pre-Prohibition 1914.[15] Thus we reach the ironic conclusion that far from eliminating spending on alcoholic drinks, Prohibition actually raised the share of GDP devoted to spending on alcohol.

FROM CORN FLAKES TO CATSUP: THE RISE OF PROCESSED FOODS

The first three decades after 1870 witnessed enormous growth in manufactured (i.e., processed) food. Starting from a diet dominated by basic unprocessed food products, there was substantial growth in consumption of canned and dried fruits and vegetables; processed butter, cheese, and margarine; processed flour, hominy, grits, oatmeal, and breakfast food; refined sugar; macaroni and noodles; pickles, preserves, and sauces; bottled mineral and soda water; and the large category of processed meats, including fresh and cured meat, such as sausages.[16]

Before the 1880s, grain was converted into flour in neighborhood or regional mills. The gradual transition from home production to market purchases included bread. In 1850, commercial bakeries produced less than 10 percent of the bread consumed in the United States, and by 1900, this ratio had increased only to 25 percent.[17] Bread and other baked goods had been manufactured for centuries, but the share of marketed baked goods grew only when households could afford to switch from baking at home. A 1929 survey of farm women in upstate New York reports that about half baked all or most of their own bread. By the 1920s, "taste and preference were more common reasons than cost."[18]

The processing of food greatly accelerated after 1870 but had existed for centuries. Crackers dated back to the eighteenth century and had long been a staple of the larder of naval ships. Large commercial cracker bakeries expanded in the 1850s to satisfy the demand for the sale of crackers in barrels, a staple of country stores.[19] The process of canning had been invented as far back as 1809 by Frenchman Nicholas Appert, who developed a process for vacuum-packed hermetically sealed jars for food. Although the Appert system was maintained as a French state secret for years, by the 1830s, two Englishmen who had recently arrived in America succeeded in duplicating Appert's technique. One of these was William Underwood, who led the switch from glass jars to tin cans, perfected in the 1840s, and who would soon become famous for America's first registered trademark, granted in 1867 to his Underwood's deviled ham and turkey.[20]

Another of the earliest entrepreneurs of canned food was Gail Borden, whose entrepreneurial career was worthy of his contemporary, Horatio Alger: "According to legend, he had been shocked by the Donner Party disaster,"[21] in which a group of pioneers snowbound in 1846 in the Sierra Nevada resorted to cannibalism for survival. Borden was determined to perfect a method for reducing or "condensing" food so that it would provide nourishment in a relatively small package. The invention which made his name and fortune was condensed milk, which he patented in 1856. Soon the Civil War would provide a ready market for his canned nourishment among the northern troops and sealed his success as an early pioneer of canned food.

Many American men had their first experience of canned food as Union soldiers during the Civil War. Some of their favorites included not only Borden's condensed milk and Underwood's deviled ham, but also canned pork and beans provided by the Indianapolis-based Van Camp Company. Another early branded product, still in use today, was Lea and Perrin's Worcestershire sauce.[22] Although isolated examples of canned fruits, vegetables, and seafood had appeared, production in 1870 amounted to less than one can per person per year.[23] Home preserving did not take off until after 1900, despite the introduction of the Mason jar in 1859, because of the perceived difficulty of the techniques and the relatively high price of the sugar needed for preserving.[24]

Canned foods were slow to be accepted in the eastern parts of the country because of expense, worry about contamination, and housewifely pride in "putting up" one's own food and admiring the rows and rows of Mason jars with their colorful contents. It was in the frontier west that canned goods first reached widespread acceptance, primarily because they were the only way of introducing variety into an otherwise monotonous diet. An 1865 comment extolled the role of canned goods in the west:

> Few New England housekeepers present such a variety of excellent vegetables and fruits as we found everywhere here, at every hotel and station meal, and at every private dinner and supper. Corn, tomatoes, and beans, pine-apple, strawberry, cherry and peach, with oysters and lobsters are the most common... Families buy [the cans] in cases of two dozen each. And every back yard is near knee deep in old tin cans.[25]

The years 1869–1900 witnessed the development of nationwide brands produced by firms that became much larger than those started in the Civil War era. These included Swift and Armour for meat, as well as General Mills and Pillsbury for flour. Although H. J. Heinz had developed his "57 varieties" by 1900, there is no evidence of spending on canned vegetables or condiments in the detailed food listing included in the 1907 New York City budget study cited above, nor in the listing of food quantities in table 3–1. The iconic Coca-Cola brand was invented in 1886, but it remained a soda fountain drink until its first bottling plant was established in 1899, so most of its growth occurred after 1900.[26] The same goes for prepared foods such as Jell-O, invented in the 1890s.[27]

Other firms that had become established by 1900 included Campbell's Soups, Quaker Oats, and Libby's canned meats. Particularly successful immediately after their invention in 1894 were cold breakfast cereals, of which the first, Kellogg's corn flakes, was accidentally produced by Dr. J. Harvey Kellogg, a physician at a sanitarium. Soon competition emerged with the 1897 introduction of Post Grape-Nuts, invented by C. W. Post, who was a former sanitarium patient of Dr. Kellogg.[28] Cold cereals were a convenient and labor-saving alternative to hot mush. The interval between 1890 and 1920 marks the transition, thanks to mass production and industrial economies of scale, from expensive brand-name products available only to the middle class and rich to mass market acceptance by working-class households. By 1900, the American food-processing industry already accounted for 20 percent of manufacturing output. In 1910, more than 3 billion cans of food were manufactured, or thirty-three cans per person per year.[29]

The broad reach of individual entrepreneurs extended even to what we would now call junk food. Two brothers, Frederick and Louis Rueckheim, began as humble street vendors who sold an improbable mixture of popcorn, molasses, and peanuts at the Chicago World's Fair of 1893 and by 1896 had perfected their recipe, obtaining the trademark for "Cracker Jack," which was soon advertised and available across the nation. In 1905, Frank Epperson, age 11, accidentally left a powdered-soda drink outside overnight with the stirring stick inside; he awoke to find a delicious frozen concoction on a stick and for some reason waited until 1923 to patent his discovery as "Epsicles." His children had another name, and it stuck: Pop's 'sicles. Soon afterward, in 1928, Walter Diemer developed the first bubble gum, which he named Dubble Bubble.[30]

The next transition beyond canned food was the wide variety of frozen fish, meat, vegetables, fruit, and prepared dishes that have become common in the postwar years. The frozen food industry was still in its infancy in 1929. Its entrepreneurial genius, Clarence Birdseye, had made his essential discovery of how to capture flavor in frozen foods on a trip to the forbidding climate of Labrador in 1912, where he observed how the local Inuits preserved frozen fish. After the inevitable tinkering, he was ready to launch his line of frozen foods in the 1920s, although initially progress was slow because iceboxes could not maintain frozen food at a sufficiently low temperature and mechanical refrigerators were slow to become common in households because of their expense. The spread of frozen food would have to wait for postwar America, when, by 1950, refrigerators would be sufficiently advanced to feature substantial frozen food compartments.[31]

Which manufactured and preprocessed foods were consumed in 1900? The New York City household budget study provides precise quantities of foods purchased in six sample households, and here we summarize expenditures in a household having the income closest to the average of the sample as a whole.[32] The father (male income-earner) was a shipping clerk making $760 per year, to which was added $104 from a lodger. There was a wife, a boy of 12, and a girl of 3. The budget was enough to provide the father with 3,685 calories per day at a cost of thirty-five cents per day, and amounts consumed by the wife and children are converted into "man-equivalents."

Weekly food expenditure was $7.04, or $1.01 per day, which includes thirty-five cents for the father and sixty-six cents for the other three members of the family combined. From today's perspective, the family's 10.5 pounds of meat consumed weekly (beef, corned beef, mutton, and chicken) seems almost extravagant. Divided by the four members of the family, this comes out to 136.5 pounds per person per year, somewhat below the national average of 190 pounds recorded for the year 1900 in table 3–2. Added to all that meat in the family's weekly diet were two pounds of fish and a can of salmon. Weekly dairy consumption included one pound each of butter and cheese, 16 eggs, and 21 quarts of milk. Cereal included 7 loaves of bread, 49 rolls, 2 boxes of crackers, 3.5 pounds of flour, and 1 box of breakfast food. Many various vegetables were consumed, but quantities are not specified for all of them. Examples include 4 quarts of potatoes and 1.5 pounds of apples. The diet included oranges, bananas, carrots, and unspecified other fresh vegetables. Finally is the consumption of 0.5 pound each of tea and coffee, 3.5 pounds of sugar, unspecified spices, a pint of whisky, and an unspecified quantity of wine.[33]

One of the most extreme examples of low-priced food concerns the free lunches that were available at local saloons throughout urban America at the turn of the century. The urban working-class male could obtain enough free food for a filling lunch at saloons for the price of a five-cent beer. A typical saloon meal might consist of some rye bread, baked beans, cheese, sausage, sauerkraut, and dill pickles. The low price of the beer/food package deal was made possible by subsidies from the liquor industry, which bought food in volume for the saloon keepers.

By the 1920s, the American diet had made most of its transition from the "hogs 'n' hominy" monotony of 1870 to the more varied diet typically consumed today. Breakfasts by 1920 consisted of citrus fruit, dry cereal and milk, or eggs and toast, followed by a light lunch of a sandwich, soup, and/or salad and a dinner consisting of meat or another entrée served with potato and vegetable side dishes and perhaps a light dessert such as Jell-O or ice cream.[34] Dinner entrees no longer consisted simply of roasted or fried meat but were influenced by immigrants from Italy, Germany, and Eastern Europe, who often cooked one-dish meals with multiple ingredients, such as stews, goulashes, or Italian pasta dishes containing tomatoes, olives, sausages, and other ingredients.[35] The immigrant tradition of consuming smaller quantities of meat mixed with other ingredients such as pasta, potatoes, and vegetables may play an important role in explaining the overall decline in meat consumption that occurred between 1900 and 1929 in table 3–2.

Another dimension of progress was in the increased variety of restaurants along with the rising incomes that led an ever larger share of the population, especially in cities, to escape their cramped living quarters. The rapid expansion of restaurants in the late nineteenth century ranged from upscale hotel dining rooms serving ten-course meals cooked by French chefs to more accessible and inexpensive ethnic restaurants, especially Chinese, German, and Italian. Soda fountains appeared in Woolworth's and other chain stores, and ice cream (which had been invented much earlier, in the 1810s and 1820s) continued its growing popularity. My own city of Evanston, Illinois, lays (a contested) claim to the invention of the ice cream sundae in 1890.[36]

The automobile brought with it a transformation in food consumption that we usually associate with the 1950s and 1960s. By the 1920s, major highways were lined with drive-ins of varying degrees of rustic or metallic modern appearance, sometimes with female servers in uniform. Howard Johnson's nationwide chain of orange-roofed Georgian-style restaurants with its uninspired food was established in 1925. The first White Castle hamburger chain restaurant opened in 1921.[37]

FROM GENERAL STORE TO SUPERMARKET: HOW FOOD WAS SOLD

Our image of food retailing in 1870 is framed by the 75/25 division of the nation between rural and urban residents. In farm households, most food was produced on the farm, and a trip to the local general store was both time-consuming and a special occasion. The entire family would come along and spend its surplus of marketed food in trade for shoes, men's clothing, and fabrics for the women to use in making their own clothes. Prices were determined by haggling, and credit was the normal means of payment, with bills settled monthly or even less frequently if weather, insects, or other factors made local farming conditions difficult. Local general stores were often monopolies, more so in the very smallest towns and less so as town size increased.

The end of the Civil War transformed commerce in the rural south. Before the war, many transactions consisted of large purchases by plantation owners from wholesale merchants. During the war, popular consumer goods had been unavailable. The end of the war brought a rush of country merchants eager to provide credit to an impoverished clientele. Farm families, both black and white, purchased as much as they could, up to the credit limit set by the merchants.

> When the war ended, these customers were again ready buyers. Most southerners were without money, but as a result of lien laws recently passed by the state legislatures, they were able to purchase astounding amounts of merchandise. Everywhere there was an anxiety to buy new goods, even if buying meant going hopelessly into debt.... Where there had been one store before the war, there were now ten. A flush postwar market had created thousands of outlets.[38]

In densely occupied cities, housewives walked to nearby merchants. The larger the city, the more likely it was to have one or more centralized markets offering a cross-section of sellers ranging from farmers who lived nearby to merchants selling specialized food and nonfood items. By 1860, Boston and St. Louis had ten of these large markets apiece, and San Francisco had five. The range of articles included not only a wide variety of food transported over substantial distances by rail, but also household products such as brooms and baskets. In these markets, prices were set by bargaining, as in the rural general stores, but payment was in cash, reflecting the absence of the continuity of the relationship between the buyer and seller. Foreign observers approvingly reported on the "almost endless variety of the choicest articles of food—meat, poultry, fish, vegetables, and fruits from all parts."[39]

There was a sharp dichotomy in the mid-nineteenth century between the variety of food available to rural and urban residents. Within each city, the middle and upper classes could afford a more varied diet than working-class households. There was also a dichotomy in the prices paid, as rural families were often victims to price gouging by local monopoly country stores, whereas there was competition within the large urban markets between merchants, not to mention further competition between the markets themselves and ubiquitous street peddlers. Peddlers were in effect daily deliverymen, selling dairy products, baked goods, meats, or produce. They also sold ice, coal, and firewood and bought rags, scrap metal, and recyclable trash.[40]

At the beginning of the twentieth century, roughly one-third of Americans lived in small towns having fewer than 2,500 inhabitants, where town residents were free of the monopoly of the country store. These towns were large enough to have specialized merchants in a number of categories, including groceries, meats, and produce. Nonfood shops included those selling harnesses, paint, bicycles, guns, books, and either female or male apparel.[41] A description of a walk along Main Street of a small town in Texas evoked these reactions:

> He liked the smells here: the moth balls of textiles, the paint and grease of farm implements, the earthiness of vegetables, the leather of saddles, the food smells, making an unmistakable alloy of their own.[42]

Arriving in this retail milieu was one of the primary marketing innovations of 1870–1900, the chain food store. The A&P chain was originally founded in 1859 under a different name and renamed the Great Atlantic and Pacific Tea Company in 1869.[43] By 1876, the firm had sixty-seven stores. Its period of most rapid expansion began in 1912. Around this time, A&P, which had previously provided delivery and credit, made the switch to cash and carry in the numerous relatively small new stores that it opened. Soon "chain store" and "cash and carry" became synonymous.

After the 1859 founding of A&P, other major chain food stores were founded, including the ancestors of the Grand Union (1872) and Kroger (1882) chains. Volume buying by the chains allowed them to undercut the prices of local merchants, and anti–chain store activists protested just as today's anti-Walmart activists protest, and for the same reasons, including the threat to small independent merchants. A difference in the late nineteenth-century opposition to chain stores is that it did not involve labor unions, whereas today's resistance to Walmart in some cities is led by unions, which protest the steadfastly nonunion makeup of the Walmart workforce.

This transition to the new world of chain stores came to fruition in the 1920s. The leading national chain stores had 7,500 outlets by 1920, a number that quadrupled to 30,000 by 1930, of which 15,000 were operated by A&P.

The chain stores tended to stock standardized national brands and had poor selections of locally grown produce, meats, and cheeses, which allowed specialty independent green grocers, butchers, and bakery shops to survive. Chain stores were very small by today's standards and mainly stocked groceries; customers lined up and waited while clerks fetched items from shelves behind them. Though lower prices were the main factor explaining the rise of the chain food store, other contributory factors included larger and more attractive stores, better locations, fresher merchandise, wider assortments, and use of advertising. Chain stores could obtain volume discounts not just for merchandise but also for equipment, and they were better capitalized and thus able to borrow money more cheaply, so they could stay in business at a lower profit margin.[44] However, just because new forms of food merchandizing were being developed does not imply that all working-class shoppers flocked to them; some continued to patronize more expensive neighborhood stores rather than buy from larger retail chains.

Peter Shergold postulates that neighborhood stores were not only more personal and welcoming, but also allowed workers to purchase items on credit. However, because workingmen usually patronized neighborhood stores, they had to pay a substantial premium for foodstuffs because of the inefficiency of small stores.[45] Small-town merchants had a small inventory and slow turnover that required them to price goods higher than merchants in larger towns. It has been estimated that their practice of extending credit raised their cost of doing business by roughly 10 percent.[46] "In effect, therefore, the persons who paid most for their foodstuffs were the group least able to afford it."[47] One of the benefits of the automobile that will be treated in chapter 5 was the freedom it gave to farmers and small-town residents to escape the monopoly grip of the local merchant and travel to the nearest large town or small city.

Advertising developed in part as a result of mass production; likewise, it was said that advertising made mass production possible.[48] Firms decided that there was a limit to attracting customers through lower prices, and they tried the alternative strategy of increasing volume by brand-centric advertising. Although advertising began in the late nineteenth century with the development of the first branded products, its true explosion came in the 1920s, when it became increasingly tied to the newly invented radio.

Butter, that everyday and commonplace product, provides an example of how mass marketers reacted to the 1906 Pure Foods Act and used it to their advantage to promote regional and national brands. Wrappers on butter in response to the new regulation provided a way for individual creameries to establish their identities. This replaced the previous practice by which individual farmers would imprint their cubes of butter with wooden stamps. One author laments the passage from individually flavored to standardized butter: "This label is a haunting reminder of how butter devolved from a luxury product with the nuanced flavors of *terroir* to the standardized and relatively anonymous-tasting product we know today."[49]

The marketing revolution for food that extended from 1870 to 1940 and beyond raises the likelihood that the increase in the standard of living has been understated. The history of the A&P chain of food stores in the early twentieth century dramatizes the extent to which prices were lower in chain stores than in small mom and pop stores. Critics charged that A&P's prices were "too low" and alleged that the source of the low prices was large-scale deals from wholesalers and the development of in-house brands that eliminated the middleman. But the critics were complaining not about A&P, but instead, unknowingly, about economic development in a capitalist system, which allows the most efficient operators to replace small, inefficient, and sometimes incompetent country merchants and small family-owned urban stores.[50] The reason the growth in the standard of living has been understated is that the Consumer Price Index (CPI) recorded price changes for each type of merchant separately and did not compare prices between types of merchants. Thus if the price of a box of Kellogg's corn flakes remained fixed at twenty cents in March and April in a traditional store and was seventeen cents in a nearby A&P store newly opened in April, the price would be treated as fixed. This error in the CPI is called "outlet substitution bias" and has continued in the past three decades as Walmart has opened stores that charge less for groceries than traditional supermarkets do.

Fortunately, we can quantify the extent to which chain stores reduced food prices, thanks to a survey that provides a price comparison between neighborhood stores (which would typically be patronized by working people) and chain stores in Pittsburgh in 1911. This survey was conducted over several years by the University of Pittsburgh.[51] From the data we can calculate the log percent price reduction in chain stores compared to neighborhood stores, and this amounts to an unweighted average of –21.3 percent over forty-five separately listed food items. To determine whether outliers are skewing the results, we can recalculate this price difference excluding the ten smallest and largest discrepancies—and the resulting mean of twenty-five food items is an even larger –23.5 percent. The chain store discounts appear to be larger for meat items—roughly –35 percent—and about –15 percent for staples such as sugar, flour, and canned fruits and vegetables.

This evidence suggests that outlet substitution bias in the CPI occurring with the arrival of the chain stores in 1911 may have been quantitatively as significant as the arrival of Walmart in the 1980s and 1990s.[52] In both cases, consumers were able to buy food items for substantially less, yet the CPI and its predecessor price indexes track only price changes in a given type of outlet without counting as price changes the decrease in prices when a new more efficient type of retail trade emerges as the result of innovation.

STAY AWAY FROM THE MILK AND THE MEAT: A JUNGLE OF DISEASE AND CONTAMINATION

The previous section demonstrates that well before even 10 percent of American homes had electricity or an automobile, the foundations of the nationwide food manufacturing, distribution, and trademark system had been laid. However, throughout the 1870–1940 period and beyond, American households faced the risk of contaminated or adulterated food. Mary Ronald, editor of an 1897 cookbook, warned mothers that milk was a disease carrier and advised that all milk be boiled before being served to children.[53] Kleinberg devotes considerable attention to the possible role of milk contamination as a factor helping to explain the rise in the infant mortality rate from 17.1 percent in 1875 to 20.3 percent in 1900:

> Impure water supplies, impure milk, and, and inadequate waste removal all contributed significantly to infantile diarrhea. . . . Almost all U.S. cities exhibited increased infant mortality during the hottest months, a pattern that disappeared only when rising standards of living resulted in the widespread ownership of iceboxes, when public health campaigns cleaned up milk and water supplies.[54]

The first pasteurized milk was introduced in Pittsburgh in 1907, and in 1913 the U.S. Department of Agriculture condemned a railroad for transporting milk in unrefrigerated containers. During previous decades large distant milk producers had driven out of business more than 700 dairymen who lived near Pittsburgh. Doctors blamed mothers for feeding babies bottled milk rather than breast milk and sometimes listed the cause of an infant death as "bottle feeding."[55]

Henderson provides a detailed study of the milk problem in 1906, a time before the development of pasteurization, when it was not uncommon in periods of milk shortage to "stretch" the milk by an infusion of water.[56] The same year was also a landmark, for it was then that the first program of cow testing and regulation began. Soon afterward, cows were regularly tested for disease and quality of feed, and milk became pasteurized. By the decade spanning 1910–19, milk was sold in sealed glass bottles (invented in 1886), though daily delivery was necessary to compensate for the absence of adequate refrigeration in the home.

Bettmann provides a rich trove of anecdotes and illustrations that suggest the range of dangers of contamination in the 1870–1900 era. Milk was not only contaminated but also diluted; dealers merely required "a water pump to boost two quarts of milk to a gallon." To remove the color and odor of milk from diseased cattle, dealers "added molasses, chalk, or plaster of Paris." In 1902, the New York City Health Commission tested 3,970 milk samples and found that 52.8 percent were adulterated. Even bread was not above suspicion. New York City bakers in the 1880s stretched and preserved their dough with doses of alum and copper. "Customers were continually enraged to discover chunks of foreign matter in their loaves, such as oven ash and grit from the baker's machinery."[57]

Worse yet were standard practices in the meat industry. The most famous protest against these conditions was Upton Sinclair's famous 1906 *The Jungle*, an account of the grisly conditions of production and employment in the Chicago meat-packing industry. He described unsanitary conditions in the making of sausages and even implied that occasionally a worker fell into a vat and became part of the product. To disguise the smell of rotten meat and other food spoilage, food producers used additives to enhance the flavor, smell, and/or color of food products. Some of the acids used to preserve beef turned out to be harmful to health.[58]

Despite the immediate response to *The Jungle* in the development of food safety regulations, there were a longer-lived effects of Sinclair's muckraking. The immediate response to the campaign inspired by the book was a halving of meat consumption. Even in the late 1920s, meat packers were still struggling to boost meat sales back to anything approaching their pre-1906 heyday, as shown in table 3–2. This was not only because of the lingering effects of *The Jungle*, but also because of the higher costs incurred by federal government inspection of all beef carcasses or products that entered into interstate commerce.[59] More generally, the new regulations furthered the speed of consolidation of food processing into a few large companies, for smaller companies could not afford to comply with the new laws.[60]

Several main conclusions emerge from our previous discussion of food that are relevant to the issues of safety and contamination. Safety was gradually improved as the result of the refrigeration of freight cars and the introduction of iceboxes in the home, the development of new canning and bottling technology, the beginning of a system of nationwide brand names for processed food, and the spread of chain food stores that reduced prices by purchasing in volume and introducing standardized methods that the local general merchant could not match. However safe many food products may have been, the scandals in the early twentieth century surrounding the safety of milk and meat had long-lasting effects, especially on the quantity of meat consumed and on its cost of distribution.

A GENERATION OF MIDGETS: WHY DID PEOPLE GROW SHORTER?

As a complement to the data presented thus far on quantities of food measured by inflation-adjusted value, by weight, and by caloric intake, we now turn to indirect evidence about food consumption drawn from biometric studies of stature and its relationship to nutrition and health. Richard Steckel provides a short survey of the literature on the relationship between human stature and both health and economic issues.[61] Growth charts by age were originally used to establish a standard for normal growth from infancy to the teenage years. Studies have traced differences in height to nutrition, public health and sanitation, exposure to diseases, and the nature of physical work and exposure to hazards.

There is a strong relationship between income and health, but it exhibits diminishing returns to higher income. After people transition from malnourishment to an adequate diet, they do not become taller, no matter how rich they are. The relationship between income and height extends beyond the provision of food to also include the ability to afford health care, as well as better housing conditions affordable to those who earn a higher income. Because deprivation stunts growth whereas extreme affluence does not increase height, the average height of a given population declines with greater income inequality.

Much of the biometric literature concerns differences across nations, while here we are interested in the evolution of stature in the United States over time. The most stunning result is that the adult height of native-born American males declined by more than 3 percent, from 68.3 inches for birth year 1830 to 66.6 inches for birth year 1890, after which there was a spurt to 69.6 inches in birth year 1940, with little change after that.[62] Why did height decline in an era when economic growth was so rapid and progress occurred along so many dimensions, including average per-capita food consumption?

The puzzle deepens when we plot male adult height by birth cohort against per-capita calories of food intake, as in figure 3–2. Though the overall slope of the line is positive, the observations for the entire period 1860–1920 are below the regression line, whereas those for the entire period 1930–80 are above the line. Some aspect of American economic growth other than population-wide malnutrition must have caused heights to shrink after 1840 and to recover only slowly during 1890–1920.

The explanations briefly listed by Steckel include rising food prices, growing inequality, damage from the Civil War, and the possible spread of diseases through urbanization and the proximity of children in the public schools that created the possibility of faster contagion.[63] We postpone discussion of health-related causes until chapter 7. Damage from the Civil War seems a dubious explanation considering that more than half the 1830–1890 decline in height had already occurred by 1860. The chronology of food prices is also no explanation, for food prices were lower in 1890 than in 1830 and then shot up in 1915–20, when height was rising most rapidly.[64]

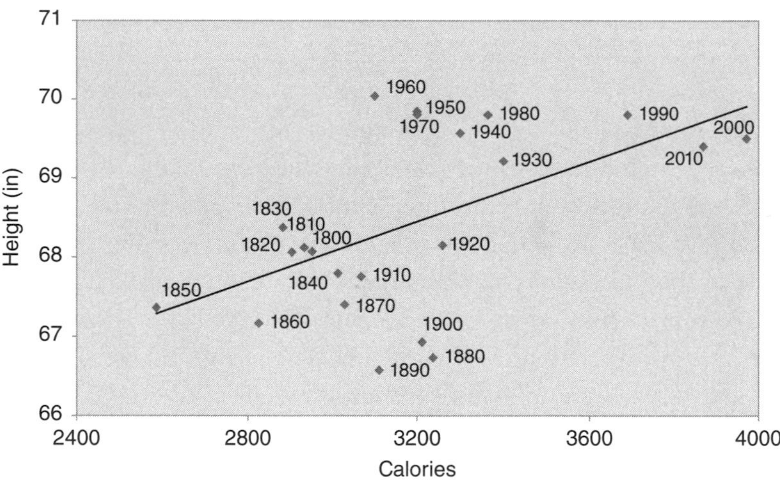

Figure 3–2. Daily Caloric Avaliability and Average Male Height, 1800–2010
Source: Floud et al. (2011) Table 6.6 and 6.10, CDC Vital Health Statistics after 1970. Caloric data after 1970 from Figure 3-1.

Despite the claim by some that population growth outran food production between 1800 and 1860, and that this contributed to the 1830–1890 decline in height, the food production data does not support their claim.[65] We have already examined the rise of per-capita food consumption in the nineteenth century in table 3–2. Clearly, American food production was sufficient to sustain a growing population. Based on the same scatter plot of height and caloric intake reproduced in figure 3–2, we conclude that food consumption cannot be the cause of shrinking height, and we instead point to the determinants of health and particularly those of infant mortality. The best evidence that non-food aspects of health were responsible for the decline in height is that infant mortality worsened as height was decreasing between 1830 and 1890.

PUT DOWN THE NEEDLE AND THREAD: THE RISE OF MARKET-PURCHASED CLOTHING

The issues that arise in the development of clothing and apparel consumption are less complex than those for food. The most important development in the interval 1870–1940 was the transition from home-produced to market-purchased apparel. In 1870, except for the upper-class women who could afford to hire a dressmaker or buy designer fashions, most women made their own clothes, as well as a substantial fraction of their children's garments and at least some of their husband's clothes. Each woman was expected to sew; indeed, such skills were indispensable throughout most of the nineteenth century. Dry goods and notions accounted for as large a share of the family budget as did purchased clothing in 1870, and only thereafter did the relative shares tilt increasingly away from dry goods and home production toward purchased clothing.

Thanks to the expense of purchased clothing and the time needed to make home-produced apparel, most rural families made do with limited wardrobes. Men typically had one or two sets of sturdy everyday items and women a few simple one-piece dresses. Some but not all rural families had a single set of clothing for special occasions, such as church or funerals. Children were clothed in hand-me-downs within the family or from relatives and friends. By modern standards, clothing was typically dirty thanks to the arduous labor of home laundry. Outerwear often went unwashed or uncleaned for months.[66]

Though farmwomen and working-class urban wives made simple dresses and frocks, middle-class women were under substantial pressure to make well-tailored outfits; they had to cut and sew their own clothes if they were to be respectably dressed, because there was no affordable alternative to doing it oneself. In 1844, the *Ladies' Hand Book* declared that "the female who is utterly regardless of her appearance may be safely pronounced deficient in some of the more important qualities which the term 'good character' invariably implies." As middle-class fashions evolved after 1850 toward close-fitting garments with bouffant skirts and tight waists, women increasingly used paper patterns sold by specialized merchants or available in pattern magazines, but these were not sized, leaving sizing to a particular female's form a matter of guessing and experimentation.[67]

This historical record of the transition from dry goods to market-purchased apparel is summarized in figure 3–3. Dollars of expenditure per year per person are divided among three categories: dry goods and notions,[68] clothing and personal furnishings, and shoes and other footwear. Total spending in the constant prices of 1913 grew from $11 in 1869 to $21 in 1899 and $30.50 in 1929. Notice that there was little growth between 1869 and 1899 in the dry goods and shoe categories—and that almost all the growth occurred in the clothing category. Then, between 1899 and 1929, spending on dry goods and shoes actually declined, whereas clothing expenditures more than accounted for the growth in total spending, as would be expected from the shift from clothing

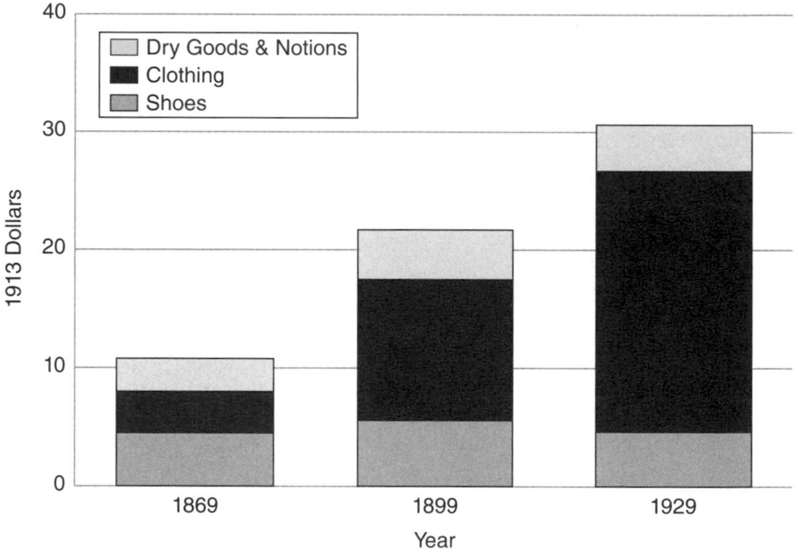

Figure 3–3. Value of Dry Goods, Clothing, and Shoes, per Person in 1913 prices, 1869–1929

made at home to clothing bought from stores and catalogs. The arrival of immigrants from Eastern Europe after 1890 promoted the purchase of ready-made clothing, for many of the new arrivals were tailors. The development of

> machine-made clothing for the masses . . . was wrought by pale, undersized, poverty-stricken east-European tailors in New York who toiled incredible hours in dark, stinking workshop-apartments, or in fire-dangerous, dirty lofts, working with the fury and persistence of a people intent not only upon earning a living but also upon demonstrating their right to live.[69]

The readily available archives of the Sears Roebuck catalog provide evidence of changes in female fashions.[70] The catalog in 1902 displayed page after page of "cloth and silk jackets, tailor-made suits, wash skirts, walking skirts, silk skirts, under-skirts, silk waists, and ladies wrappers," all of which uniformly exhibited tight, even pinched waists with broad shoulders, loose-fitting tops, and flared or puffed out skirts.[71] These fashions shared in common the tight waists but allowed for looser tops than the fashions typical of the 1870–90 period.[72] Shortly after 1902, a new fad in women's clothing was the shirtwaist, a blouse that fit tight at the waist but that was fit looser on top, an American innovation "sniffed at" by "haughty" Parisian dressmakers. Only five of these were listed in the Sears 1902 catalog (at prices between $0.50 and $1.65), yet by 1905 the catalog listed no less than 150 models made from every conceivable type of domestic and foreign fabric. By 1919, this style had completely disappeared.[73]

Before 1890, virtually all skirts were floor-length. The popularity of the bicycle first induced women to take the risk of wearing "walking skirts" that were less than floor length. This transition to shorter skirts occurred slowly over the two decades between 1890 and 1910. Perhaps one-third of the skirts illustrated in the 1902 catalog are "street skirts" shorter than floor-length skirts by perhaps eight to ten inches.[74] It was only after World War I that skirt lengths began to shorten and by 1926 rose above the knees. And the catalog's skirts cautiously followed this fashion and evolved in the late 1920s, looking very different than they had in 1902. By 1927, the pinched waist was entirely missing. Dresses were boxy, hanging straight down from the shoulders with no waists at all, a loose band around the hips, pleated skirts, and skirt lengths barely covering the knee. The boyish figure had become the fashion and the "boyish bob" the accompanying hair fashion.[75]

Not only did women's fashions evolve steadily, but they also became more important as a focus of retail commerce. In 1902 the opening pages of the Sears catalog were devoted to pocket watches and watchmaker's tools, reflecting Richard Sears's origins in the watch-making business. But by 1925, women's clothing had taken over the opening pages.[76] In the 1927 edition, fully 163 pages at the beginning of the book (compared to fifty-three pages toward the end of the 1902 book) were devoted to women's and children's apparel of all types, from fur coats to "apron frocks" to bridal wreaths.

FROM GENERAL STORE TO GRANDEUR: THE URBAN DEPARTMENT STORE

In the America of 1870, local merchants had local monopolies, and their customers had little ability to compare prices. Thus there was constant tension between the rural customers and the merchants, for there were few guidelines for judging whether a price was fair.

> It was "dog eat dog"—"tit for tat." Our cottons were sold for wool, our wool and cotton for silk and linen; in fact nearly everything was different from what it represented... Each party expected to be cheated, if it was possible... the "tricks of the trade" were numerous.[77]

This was not so much of a problem for standardized food products such as butter and grain, for newspaper market reports provided some basic information on prices. But manufactured goods were not standardized and were susceptible to few benchmarks. National advertising did not begin to bring information about alternative goods and their prices until the end of the nineteenth century. In this environment, we can understand why mail-order catalogs were such a salvation for rural customers.[78]

Peddlers and itinerant merchants were not only omnipresent in cities but also traveled to small towns and farms selling a wide variety of specialized merchandise. Sometimes called "jobbers," these intermediaries played the role of wholesalers and solved the problem for the country store proprietors about what to sell. For instance, jobbers were quick to follow up on F. W. Woolworth's concept of the five- and ten-cent store and provided country merchants with cartons of mixed goods, such as "crochet hooks, wash basins, baby bibs, watch keys, and harmonicas."[79]

The year 1870 was on the cusp of a revolution in the merchandizing of clothing. The modern American department store found its roots in Bouçicaut's Bon Marché in Paris, which by 1862 had developed into a grand emporium. Here originated many of the innovations that were part of the American counterparts from their beginnings: fixed prices with no haggling, a money-back guarantee, a philosophy of low prices and high volume instead of the reverse and a welcome to customers to browse without any moral obligation to buy.[80] The development of the American imitators of Bon Marché was centered in the period 1870–1910, and their effect of lowering prices, much as had the chain food stores, created an improvement in the standard of living that was missed in the statistics on consumer prices and total inflation-adjusted consumer expenditures.

The literature on the early department stores emphasizes their palatial, luxurious amenities modeled on their French ancestors. Long before electrification entered the working-class American home, electricity was adopted for lighting and other functions in the department stores. Electric elevators, electric light, and electric fans encouraged customers to visit the upper floors, helping management improve use of space and personnel. Electricity-powered pneumatic tube systems allowed centralized cashiers to provide receipts and make change. During this period, stores operated on a cash-only policy that allowed them to pay their suppliers rapidly, and they made most of their profits on discounts from suppliers.[81]

These temples of merchandise became the prime sightseeing destinations of their cities, not least in the case of Marshall Field's landmark State Street building, completed in 1907, with its Tiffany glass ceiling, both the first and the largest ceiling built of Tiffany's unique iridescent art glass—containing 1.6 million pieces. With the large investment required to build these urban palaces, the owners needed to find a way to draw the shoppers to the upper floors. Marshall Field had an entire floor of restaurants and cafes on its seventh floor, sometimes with live musical performers, to draw shoppers upward on the newfangled elevators. It and other major urban department stores attracted their prime female customers with reading and writing lounges. There were also post offices, beauty salons, nurseries, meeting rooms, and repair services.[82]

> Shopping in these stores became an adventure in high art. Department stores became museums in which a status hierarchy of objects placed works of art at the top and encouraged the customers continuously to try and raise their standards.[83]

The pleasures provided by the owners of the department stores were augmented by the attraction of the new method of buying for urban housewives. Previously women had to haggle with storeowners and could not even see all the store's merchandise, some of which was hidden behind the scenes (partly for lack of space). Department stores had everything on display at a fixed price, and women (at least in large cities which had more than one such store) enjoyed their newfound ability to compare prices charged by different merchants.[84]

Most of the department stores remained single-store operations during the 1870–1940 interval. In 1929 R. H. Macy sold almost $100 million in its single 34th Street Herald Square store, with no suburban stores until the early postwar years. The first chain store devoted to clothing and dry goods was J. C. Penney, established in the unlikely location of a twenty-five- by forty-five-foot space in Kemmerer, Wyoming, in 1902.[85] Steady growth allowed the chain to reach fourteen stores by 1910, 312 by 1920, and 1,023 by 1929. Sears started later, supplementing its catalog operation by opening retail stores starting in 1925. By 1929 it had 319 stores, far behind Penney's, and in that year 60 percent of its sales were still obtained from its catalogs.

The large and elegant central city department stores were not the only innovation in nonfood retailing during this period. Woolworth's variety store chain began with a single store in 1879 and was so successful that by 1911 there were 318 stores and enough financial backing for the proprietor to build New York's Woolworth Building, the tallest building in the world between its completion in 1913 and 1930. Three decades later, Walgreen's drug store chain started as a single small store in 1909 but by 1920 had nineteen stores; by 1929, it had 397. The variety and drug store chains contributed directly to the rise in the American standard of living, just as did the mail-order catalogs, by providing a nationwide outlet for many types of specialized goods that might not otherwise have been produced at all. They made possible economies of scale and mass production in goods as diverse as notions and needles, doll furniture to pens, stationery, and writing equipment.

YOUR MONEY BACK WITH NO QUESTIONS ASKED: THE MAIL-ORDER CATALOG

The benefits brought by the large department stores to urban dwellers were accompanied by equal or larger benefits to the majority rural population by the mail-order catalog firms, primarily those of Montgomery Ward and Sears

Roebuck. Ward issued his first catalog in 1872, whereas Sears issued his first multi-hundred-page catalog in 1894 after dabbling in the mail-order sale of watches over the previous decade.[86]

Coming two decades before Sears, Aaron Montgomery Ward deserves the credit for revolutionizing rural commerce. He knew that rural customers needed an alternative to the tension-filled dealings with country merchants and peddlers. Thus his philosophy was based on honesty and his genius for converting each transaction into a risk-free proposition. Customers flocked to an alternative world of money-back guarantees and the acceptance of returns with no questions asked. Thus catalogs did more than lower prices; they also increased the quality of each transaction. Because higher productivity of leisure time raises well-being, the catalogs raised the standard of living beyond the measurable price reductions they offered.

It is no accident that both Sears and Ward's were located in Chicago, because by then that city had established itself as the national railway hub, offering unmatched access to all parts of the country. Sears surpassed Ward's sales around 1900 by expanding into nearly every product line in existence.[87] By then Sears was fulfilling 100,000 orders per day. The 1902 Sears catalog contained 1,162 pages. By then Sears sold the full range of semi-durable goods, from elaborate hats to wigs to corsets to fur coats, as well as durable goods, from bicycles to banjoes to central-heating furnaces to guns. The only important category of goods not sold in the catalog was food, except for tea and coffee.

The success of the catalogs in penetrating rural America owes a great debt to the introduction of Rural Free Delivery, which began in the early 1890s and was fully implemented by 1901. Catalogs instructed their customers that they could "just give the letter and money to the mail carrier, and he will get the money order at the post office and mail it in the letter for you."[88] Parcel post service came along in 1913 and cut the cost of shipping of the catalogs, which by then were already well established despite the need to charge for shipping. Then gradually the spread of automobiles through rural America made it possible for farm families to venture farther for their purchases, and the growth of chain stores, including retail stores established by Sears itself starting in 1925, began to siphon off some of the custom for the catalogs.

Nevertheless, the role of the catalogs in bringing the modern age to rural America cannot be overstated. From isolation and dependence on the local general store monopolist, each farm family now had the cornucopia of manufactured goods available at a glance in the catalogs. The explosive growth of circulation of the Sears catalog attests to its growing influence—catalogs went to 3.6 percent of American households in 1902, 15.2 percent in 1908, and 25.7 in 1928.[89]

> For the rural American, the change was crucial. Now he was lifted out of the narrow community of those he saw and knew, and put in continual touch with a larger world of persons and events and things read about but unheard and unseen.[90]

CONCLUSION: COULD SOME OF AMERICAN GROWTH BE MISSED BY THE STATISTICS?

Food consumption advanced slowly along the dimension of variety but not in terms of quantity, for calories consumed were actually fewer in the 1920s than in the 1870s. Clothing changed little in quantity or quality; instead the change was in the quality of work life for housewives, who by 1929 bought most of their clothes rather than making them out of economic necessity. Price reductions in marketed clothing, accomplished both through manufacturing efficiency and the evolution of mail-order catalogs and department stores, together with higher household incomes, made it possible for women to buy rather than sew clothing.

The slow growth in food and clothing consumption may be no paradox; declining expenditures on these traditional necessities may have been a voluntary decision by households to make room in their budgets for purchases made possible by the new inventions. But there are good reasons to believe that the growth of food and clothing consumption were understated as the result of price index bias, in particular thanks to a failure to take account of lower prices obtained by consumers as they switched from high-priced country and neighborhood stores to chain stores for their food purchases. We have calculated that food prices of chain stores in 1911 were more than 22 percent lower than prices in traditional outlets, indicating a potential food price index bias of perhaps –1 percent per year over the first quarter of the twentieth century, when chain stores became dominant. A similar bias may have occurred in clothing prices thanks to the lower prices made available by the urban department store and by the mail-order catalog.

But in addition to price index bias for food and clothing, there is a broader and perhaps more important reason why existing measures of real consumption per capita may understate the improvement in the standard of living. The benefits of the Great Inventions, from ridding the streets of manure to eliminating the hauling of water by urban and rural housewives to providing electricity for light, transport, and consumer appliances, have largely been excluded from GDP and thus hidden from view. We turn in the next chapter to topics that involved far greater transformations of the living standard than food and clothing—namely, the quantity and quality of housing, including the effects of the big four dimensions of improved quality—electrification, running water, indoor plumbing, and central heating.

Chapter 4

THE AMERICAN HOME: FROM DARK AND ISOLATED TO BRIGHT AND NETWORKED

> During the last two decades of the 19th century, business executives, city leaders, and engineers in many parts of the world began to direct installation of trolley, water, sewer, and telephone as well as gas and electric networks.
>
> —Rose (1995), p. 2

INTRODUCTION: HOUSING

Unlike the slow, incremental 1870–1940 advance of food and clothing examined in the last chapter, the changes in household shelter and its equipment treated in this chapter were revolutionary. American farmers replaced primitive farmhouses, including the mud huts and log cabins of the frontier, with more solid and substantial farm dwellings. Urban apartment dwellers moved from fetid, dark tenements to modern apartment blocks and high-rises where individual apartments were reached by elevators. Most American households on farms or in small towns, and even most urban dwellers, lived not in tenements or apartments, but in single-family detached homes, throughout this seventy-year interval.

By 1940, fully 57 percent of Americans lived in cities having 2,500 or more inhabitants, a percentage that had more than doubled from 1870. A single word summarizes the interior revolution achieved in urban America during this period: *networked*. Within a few decades, urban American homes became networked in a substantial transformation that could never be repeated. Instead of relying on candles and kerosene carried into the home, each home was connected to the electricity network that provided electric light and an ever growing variety of electric home appliances.[1] Instead of relying on privies and outhouses and cesspools, each home was gradually connected to two more networks, one bringing in a supply of clean running water and the other taking waste out into sewers. Houses of the rich after 1880 and of the working class after 1910 were increasingly supplied with central heating. As of 1940, most central heating was provided by furnaces burning coal or fuel oil, both of which arrived by delivery truck rather than automatically through a pipe. But even in 1940, the nation was well on the way to its current network of connections to reliable and silent natural gas. Another network, that of telephones, also grew rapidly after 1890 (and is treated in chapter 6).

Networking inherently implies equality. Everyone, rich and poor, is plugged into the same electric, water, sewer, gas, and telephone network. The poor may only be able to afford to hook up years after the rich, but eventually they receive the same access. Compare that to 1870, when the rich had servants to do the hauling and carrying of water, coal, and wood that was necessary before the arrival of networks, whereas the working and middle classes had to do the brute-force physical labor themselves. Although initially the water delivered to middle- and upper-class neighborhoods may have been cleaner than that delivered to working-class neighborhoods, any such inequality had largely disappeared in urban America by 1929.

The networking transformation of urban America happened very quickly by the standards of any age, whether before 1870 or after 1940. As we shall see, 77 percent of the dwelling units in existence in the United States in 1940 were constructed after 1900, and most of these were initially constructed incorporating the new technologies of electricity, water, and sewer connections. By 1940 in urban America, electricity was universal, the percentage of homes with washing machines and electric refrigerators had reached 40 percent, and telephone connections, running water, private bathrooms with modern plumbing fixtures, and central heating had become commonplace.

Although it took longer for small-town and farmland America to catch up, by 1940 most of the transition to the modern age had already occurred. Another transition that could happen only once was that from a nation that was almost entirely rural, in 1800, to one that by 1940 was 56 percent urban.[2] It was much easier to deliver the modern conveniences to urban America than to the outlying farms and small towns, simply because the housing units were much closer together. These "economies of density" provide an important explanation for why modern conveniences came first to the cities; then to medium-sized towns, counted as urban; then to small towns having fewer than 2,500 inhabitants, counted as rural; and finally to farms, which were usually at least a half-mile apart.[3]

The chapter turns first to the size, location, and external environment of American housing. We dissect a multidimensional mosaic, distinguishing between farms, small towns, and cities; between single-family houses, tenements, and apartments; and between city and suburb; and we recognize the particularly poor conditions throughout the American south, especially in rural areas.[4] In 1940, virtually no southern farmer had access to any of the modern conveniences that had become common in urban areas.

The middle part of the chapter traces the evolution of light within homes, including Edison's great invention of 1879, and the magnitude and timing of the spread of water and sewers. Each development is interpreted from the point of view of consumers: When did the transformations happen? What difference did they make to everyday life? How far had they extended by 1940?

By maintaining the perspective of changes in the standard of living as viewed by the consumer, we omit most topics related to urban planning, urban politics, and the regulation of electric utilities. The spread of the city is treated in chapter 5, in which the development of the city is viewed as a corollary of a succession of transportation innovations that steadily increased the distance that was feasible to travel between the home and the workplace. Decisions that encouraged urban sprawl after World War II are reserved for chapter 10, on housing after 1940. Another deliberate omission from this chapter is the effect of the business cycle. The ease or difficulty of finding jobs varied across recession intervals and across decades, and the decline in the standard of living during the Great Depression stands out. But the Great Depression did not cause housing units to become unplugged from the electricity, water, and sewer networks; the appliances purchased before 1929 still worked to improve the standard of living; and the decade of the 1930s witnessed a sharp increase in the diffusion of electric refrigerators and washing machines.

A core theme of this book is that many of the great inventions could happen only once. In the seven decades between 1870 and 1940, the urban dwelling was utterly transformed from a primitive state hard to imagine (as described in chapter 2) to a level, in 1940, surprisingly similar to the way we live today. The core of the housing revolution was the equipping of newly built housing units, and the retrofitting of previously built units, with the modern conveniences made possible by networks. The life-changing implications of the revolution, especially in liberating American women, is a central aspect of the increase in the standard of living between 1870 and 1940 and has been largely neglected by the official data on GDP per person.

WHERE AMERICANS LIVED: THE GREAT URBAN TRANSITION

Popular images of housing in the late nineteenth century are heavily influenced by social reformers such as the Danish immigrant newspaper reporter Jacob Riis, whose squalid description of working-class life in New York City in *How the Other Half Lives* might convey the impression that the bottom half of the income distribution in 1890 lived in crowded, small, poorly ventilated apartments from which windows looked out on stinking air shafts and in which a good portion of the rooms had no windows at all.[5] Indeed, in 1890, fully two-thirds of New York City's inhabitants in 1890 lived in tenements, defined as any building having three or more apartments in the same structure. The tenement law passed in 1867 called only for one water closet per every twenty people and for sewers "only if possible." But these regulations were poorly enforced.[6]

Because the share of rural America remained greater than 50 percent until 1920, Riis's title, *How the Other Half Lives*, greatly exaggerates the misery of the working class for the nation taken as a whole. The rural half of residences in 1920 consisted of single-dwelling detached structures surrounded by open space, not crowded multifamily tenements. New York City, however important as a port of entry for immigrants, represented only a small portion of the American urban population. Indeed, the tenement buildings depicted by Riis, with details provided in Robert Chapin's 1909 survey, were concentrated in the Lower East Side of Manhattan, and multifamily dwelling units in most other American cities rarely contained more than two or three units, nor were higher than three stories.[7]

Our perspective on the heterogeneity of housing begins in table 4–1. The first impression is of rapid growth. The population more than tripled over our 1870–1940 interval, and the number of households grew almost fivefold. Indeed, it is striking that the number of households and the number of dwelling units so closely coincided, suggesting a small role for vacation homes or other second dwellings. Average household size declined during 1870–1940 from 5.0 persons to 3.7 persons. This shrinkage in average household size reflected a declining birth rate and resulted in less crowded living conditions.

Table 4–1. Population, Households, and Occupied Dwellings by Urban, Rural Nonfarm, and Farm, 1870–1990

	(Numbers in millions)				Shares of Population (percent)		
	Population, Total in Households	Number of Households	Number of Occupied Dwellings	Population per Household	Urban	Rural Nonfarm	Rural Farm
	(1)	(2)	(3)	(4)	(5)	(6)	(7)
1870	37.0	7.5		5.0	23.2	38.6	38.2
1880	48.2	9.8		4.9	26.3	33.8	40.0
1890	59.4	12.5	12.7	4.7	32.9	29.6	37.6
1900	70.3	16.0	16.0	4.4	37.3	27.3	35.4
1910	87.3	20.0	20.3	4.4	46.3	18.8	34.9
1920	101.3	24.1	24.4	4.2	51.4	18.5	30.1
1930	118.4	29.8	29.9	4.0	56.2	18.9	24.9
1940	127.6	34.9	34.9	3.7	56.5	20.3	23.2
1950	145.0	42.9	42.8	3.4	59.0	25.7	15.3
1960	174.4	53.0	53.0	3.3	64.4	26.9	8.7
1970	197.5	63.6	63.4	3.1	67.7	27.5	4.8
1980	220.5	80.4	80.4	2.7	68.0	29.3	2.7
1990	240.9	91.9	91.9	2.6	69.3	28.8	1.9
2000	267.9	103.1	103.2	2.6	70.2	28.0	1.8
2010	300.8	115.7	109.2	2.6	71.7	26.6	1.7

Sources:

(1) US Census and HSUS series Ae85, which is missing values for 1890 and 1930. These were obtained by interpolating the ratio of total population (Ae7) to population in households between the adjoining decades.

(2) HSUS series Ae79, US Census

(3) HSUS series Dc660, US Census

(4) (1)/(2)

(5) HSUS series Aa728/Aa716, US Census. Urban definition changed in 1950; ratio-linked after 1950 to pre-1950 definition. Urban percentage available from Aa728 back to 1880; 1870 share ratio-linked at 1880 from Haines, (2000, Table 4.2, p. 156).

(6) 100 percent minus (5) minus (7)

(7) HSUS series Ae81/Ae79 before 1910, series Da2 1910–1990. Before 1910 refers to households instead of population. Definition of a farm changes in 1980. Farm operator data from the Census of Agriculture, ratio adjusted, used after 1990.

The most important aspects of table 4–1 are the division of housing by type of location. The urban share more than doubled, from 23.2 percent in 1870 to 56.5 in 1940. The share of farm dwellings dropped by almost half, from 38.2 percent to 23.2 percent, over the same interval. The share of rural nonfarm dwellings (i.e., in small towns) likewise decreased, shrinking from 38.6 percent to 20.3 percent. Surprisingly, though, the portion of the U.S. population in these villages and small towns increased during the postwar period to regain its 1890 share by 1980, whereas the share of the population living on farms withered away to almost nothing.[8]

When were dwellings constructed during the 1870–1940 interval? Table 4–2 shows statistics on dwelling units in 1940, including their age and location. Although not surprising in the context of rapid population growth, it is still striking that there was an almost complete turnover of the American housing stock between 1880 and 1940. Of the dwellings that existed in 1940, only 7.3 percent were built before 1880.

Thus the description of primitive housing conditions provided in chapter 2 for 1870 applies to only a small minority of dwellings in which people lived in 1940. Even for farm dwellings, 89 percent were built after 1880. Our image of today's antebellum historic districts in Charleston, South Carolina, and Savannah, Georgia, greatly overstates the importance of old dwellings in the south, where 96 percent of dwellings occupied in 1940 were built after 1880. Table 4–2 in the bottom row gives the median age of housing in 1940 as 25.4 years. The median date of construction was 1910 in the north, 1919 in the south, and 1922 in the west. Most dwelling units, at least in urban areas, were built after cities had been wired for electricity and had developed the urban sanitation infrastructure of running water and sewer pipes.

How rapidly was the housing stock replaced by tearing down old structures and replacing them with the new? If we take the units constructed before 1880 from table 4–2 and boost the total by the percentage not reporting the construction year, we obtain a total of 2.7 million dwellings that existed in 1940 that had been built before 1880. This compares with a source reporting that in 1880 there were 6.1 million dwelling units.[9] Thus at least half of the units in existence in 1880 had disappeared by 1940.

After 1880, the importance of multifamily buildings increased, but not nearly as much as the tenement critics would imply. Over the four decades 1900–1939 fully 53 percent of newly constructed urban dwellings consisted of single-family structures. A surprising aspect of the prevalence of single-family

Table 4–2. Dwelling Units in 1940 by Year of Construction, Type, and Location, pre-1859 to 1939

	Millions of Dwelling Units by Year Built	Percentage Distribution					
		Urban	Rural Nonfarm	Rural Farm	North	South	West
Total Dwelling Units	37.33	57.9	21.6	20.5	58.7	29.1	12.2
Reporting Year Built	34.66	91.4	94.0	96.0	91.2	95.0	95.6
1859 or earlier	1.01	1.9	3.4	5.1	4.1	1.8	0.2
1860–1879	1.54	4.1	4.0	5.8	6.3	2.3	0.8
1880–1889	1.95	5.8	4.5	6.3	7.7	3.0	2.1
1890–1899	3.56	11.3	7.7	10.4	13.1	6.8	5.4
1900–1909	6.12	18.9	14.0	18.0	18.6	17.0	14.7
1910–1919	6.45	19.2	16.1	19.6	17.1	20.7	20.7
1920–1929	8.52	27.8	23.3	17.2	22.4	25.9	31.2
1930–1939	5.53	11.1	27.0	17.6	11.1	22.3	24.7
Not Reporting Year Built	2.66	8.6	6.0	4.0	8.8	5.0	4.4
Median Age (Years)	25.4	26.1	20.2	28.1	30.2	21.1	18.3

Source: U. S. Census Bureau, *U. S. Census of Housing: 1940,* Table 5, p. 12

detached structures is that most of them were rented.[10] A further 19 percent were two-family dwellings. Occupants of these duplex units, with one apartment on the first floor and another on the second floor, had as much light and air for each room as did occupants of single-family dwellings, and they often had access to a yard and garden. The remaining 29 percent of urban dwellings built between 1900 and 1939 were structures containing three or more dwelling units. But most of these were not tenements. Three-unit wooden "triple-deckers" built in the early decades of the century are still ubiquitous through the city of Boston. The triple-decker has all the characteristics of a duplex, with full exposure to light and air, with the disadvantages of more stair-climbing for those in the top unit and less access per household to a yard or garden. At the other end of the scale were large multistory elevator buildings, which were a substantial part of the 1920s residential construction boom and which still line the areas surrounding New York's Park and Fifth Avenues, Chicago's Lake Shore Drive, and streets at the center of other upscale multifamily residential neighborhoods.

EVOLUTION OF HOUSING UNITS: FEWER ROOMS, EVEN FEWER PEOPLE

An assessment of living conditions requires a dynamic view that takes account of changes over the life cycle and over time. In the first stage of their life cycle, children in working-class families lived in bedrooms that were crowded with two or three children per room. In the next stage of life before marriage, teenagers and young adults may by choice have left their families and lived temporarily in boarding houses or dormitories. Then they may have moved into small apartments after marriage. Crowding increased during the two decades when the children were home and then decreased as children grew up and moved away. Empty nesters did not necessarily move back into small apartments but may have continued to live in their dwellings, tending the gardens of their mainly single-family detached houses.

Beyond the life cycle, over time the standard of living was improving at each stage of life. Working-class children had a better chance of arriving at middle-class status as education improved and as the available jobs shifted from backbreaking, tedious, or menial tasks to more pleasant sales, service, and white-collar work. Children born in Franklin Roosevelt's birth year, 1882, may have arrived with their immigrant parents in the great wave of immigration of the 1880s, lived in crowded immigrant working-class quarters of large cities in their childhood, and had their own children born around 1910 into homes equipped with electric light and running water and arrived at in automobiles. The parents born in 1882 and children born in 1910 would together have witnessed the revolution that brought a new world of consumer products, safety, and convenience by the 1920s. The children of 1910 were likely to have completed high school; some would have gone to college. Their own children, born around 1940, would have grown up in the 1950s surrounded by consumer appliances, television, recorded music, and access to cars.[11]

Yet another aspect of dynamism that was peculiarly American concerned intercity and interstate mobility. The constant and endless flow of domestic migration, in addition to that of international immigration, meant that "the United States was not only a nation of immigrants, but a nation of migrants." Boston's estimated 1890 population of 450,000 was actually smaller than the 600,000 people who had entered the city in the preceding decade and the 500,000 people who had departed. In the *Middletown* studies of Muncie, Indiana, between 1893 and 1898, some 35 percent of Muncie families moved; between 1920 and 1924, this proportion rose to 57 percent.[12]

As the share of the population in urban dwellings grew and as that in farm dwellings declined, the most notable change in housing quality was the increase in density and the decline in exterior space that is inherent in an urban environment. Did the amount of interior space per dwelling increase with the standard of living, as would be expected if "space" is a normal good? Though the number of rooms per dwelling unit decreased, this was entirely because of the shrinkage in average household size between 1870 and 1940 from 5.0 persons to 3.7 persons (see table 4–1). The number of rooms per dwelling unit decreased more slowly, so the number of rooms per person in the unit increased by about 10 percent.[13] However, an alternative source claims that the number of rooms per person increased by 35 percent between 1910 and 1940.[14] Either way, this increase in space per person was one component of an increasing standard of living.

There is some evidence that houses became smaller and more efficient between 1910 and 1930. One possible cause of the decline in resources invested per dwelling unit was a reduction in "dead space"—stairways, corridors, and unusable corners in the "typical frame house of the past."[15] Another indication that the move toward smaller houses was real and not a statistical illusion was a widespread rejection, further described later, of overly ornate and elaborate Victorian upper-middle-class houses. By the turn of the century, a shift had begun to simplified floor plans that reduced or eliminated large entry halls and multiple formal parlor rooms, culminating in the explosion of bungalow housing in the period 1910–1930.

URBAN HOUSING: TENEMENTS DWARFED BY SINGLE-FAMILY STRUCTURES

The period between 1900 and World War I was known as the "reform era," and many complaints were published concerning the poor quality of housing for the working class. Detailed investigations were carried out to document the conditions of working-class living in Boston, New York, Washington, Chicago, Pittsburgh, and many other cities.[16] "The same conditions meet us everywhere—lot overcrowding and room overcrowding, dark rooms and inadequately lighted rooms, lack of water, lack of sanitary conveniences, dilapidation, excessive fire risks, basement and cellar dwellings."[17]

The most important single piece of quantitative evidence on New York City working-class housing comes from a detailed 1907 survey of 400 families reported by Robert Chapin, who found that on average, five people lived in three rooms.[18] Moreover, 60 percent of these households reported that at least one of their rooms was "dark" (i.e., windowless). Dark rooms are treated by contemporary observers as nearly ubiquitous: "The number of interior rooms in old houses, without windows to the outer air, is incredible to those who have not studied the subject. New York City had over 350,000 of such rooms in 1901 . . . and then there are millions of rooms, only a little better, whose windows look out on dark, narrow courts and passage ways, sometimes mere cracks between two walls."[19]

A more vivid account describes living conditions in New York City tenement slum areas: "Among the indignities they were forced to suffer were vile privies; dirt-filled sinks, slop oozing down stairwells; children urinating on the walls, dangerously dilapidated stairs; plumbing pipes pockmarked with holes that emitted sewer gases so virulent they were flammable."[20] Though initially, as already noted, the word "tenement" simply meant any multifamily structure that contained three or more dwelling units, the meaning of the word shifted after the Civil War to mean "slum housing"[21] Many of the "old-law" tenements were built with the "dumbbell" design, with the side units extending from the street to the back of the lot, and the middle units recessed in the center to provide a small air shaft. This design allowed the accommodation of twenty or more families on a small lot, usually twenty-five feet wide by 100 feet deep. The structures were five, six, or seven stories tall, and each floor had four apartments containing a total of fourteen rooms. The airshaft was typically five feet wide and sixty feet deep. The airshafts invited the tossing of garbage, which in turn made vile odors pervasive, especially in summer, when the windows were opened. Finally the dumbbell design was banned by a 1901 legislative reform that introduced the "new-law tenements."[22]

Yet even contemporary critics recognized that the housing conditions in New York City were uniquely bad: "workers in New York were housed worse than any other city in the civilized world."[23] Further evidence can be provided that New York City was a special case. Though half of all New Yorkers lived in buildings with six or more families in 1885, this was true of only 1 percent of the residents of Philadelphia. Structures housing two or three families made up about half of the housing stock of Chicago and Boston at the same time.[24] Immigrants in other cities typically lived in one-story and two-story structures, not in tall brick buildings. "High-rise tenements did not become commonplace in [Chicago's] slums."[25] Another authority agrees that Chicago "had few large-scale tenements like New York's," adding that "a desire to prevent the construction of such tenements as well as a concern for the housing conditions of the city's poor people living in smaller tenements explains the housing activity in Chicago."[26]

HOUSING DENSITY: EXPANSION THROUGH THE STREETCAR

By the standards of Europe, whether exhibited in the narrow, terraced residences in England or the multifamily apartment blocks in continental Europe, the open space of the American Midwestern cities was a revelation. In his classic *The American Commonwealth*, James Bryce found

> in cities like Cleveland or Chicago…miles on miles of suburb filled with neat wooden houses, each with its tiny garden plot, owned by the shop assistants and handicraftsmen who return on the horse cars in the evening from their work.…The impression which this comfort and plenty makes is heightened by the brilliance and keenness of the air, by the look of freshness and cleanness which even the cities wear. The fog and soot-flakes of an English town, as well as its squalor, are wanting; you are in a new world, and a world which knows the sun.[27]

Bryce was viewing the American city of the mid-1880s in contrast with crowded and sooty English cities of the same era. Others noted the lower density of American cities than in Europe. Adna Weber in 1899 calculated that the population density of fifteen American cities was twenty-two persons per acre as compared to 158 for thirteen German cities.

Gradually, between 1840 and 1870, the suburban ideal became based on the virtues of separation rather than physical connections between adjacent dwellings. "The lawn was a barrier—a kind of verdant moat separating the household from the threats and temptations of the city."[28] As the outskirts of cities were developed after 1870, property covenants often required that houses be set back a certain distance from the street and sidewalk. The change in the appearance of the urban space was described by Lewis Mumford: "Rows of buildings no longer served as continuous walls, bounding streets that formed a closed corridor: the building, divorced from its close association with the street, was embosomed in the landscape and deliberately absorbed by it."[29] The feasibility of large lawn areas surrounding houses was facilitated by the invention, in the 1860s, of the lightweight lawnmower.

These newly built areas, two or three miles from the city center, were made possible by horse-drawn streetcars and from the beginning were called "streetcar suburbs." Observers noted that the new streetcars could "'enable everyone to have a suburban [home].'"[30] Because they were the first step in the upgrading of living conditions for the working class, they were also called "the zone of emergence."[31] Even in the late nineteenth century, developers in places such as Chicago were building streetcar suburbs on large tracts of land and selling them on installment plans, and some developers had interlocking financial relationships with the developers of streetcar lines, for houses in the new developments could not be sold unless they could be reached by streetcar.[32]

What Bryce was observing in Chicago is called by architectural historians the "workingman's cottage."[33] These were one-story structures containing four to six rooms, plainly built, featuring little or no ornamentation. Though some deteriorated or were replaced by crowded multifamily living units, many others survived and were improved with electricity and plumbing in the early years of the twentieth century. Cottage neighborhoods provided housing for the great wave of southern and central Europeans who arrived during these years, who in many Midwestern cities such as Chicago, Detroit, Cleveland, and Milwaukee lived in conditions much better than those offered by the New York City tenements. A substantial fraction of these cottages were owned by the families that occupied them, and they only gradually added modern conveniences as their owners could afford the installation cost.

In Chicago, the typical lot size for worker cottages in the late nineteenth century was twenty-five by 125 feet.[34] A one-story, four-room worker's cottage in Chicago could be built in 1886 for $600, and a two-story dwelling with a fireplace could be built for about $1,300.[35] Independent evidence suggests that working-class residential dwellings could be built for $1 per square foot during the entire period between 1880 and 1905.[36] These cottages did not initially incorporate bathrooms or central heating. After the coal or wood-fired enclosed stove was invented in the 1870s and 1880s, such stoves became the dominant form of heating, and bedrooms were typically cold in the winter without separate heating. First appearing in the 1860s, many of these dwellings had basements that provided additional living space and that sometimes, by providing rentable basement rooms, allowed families to attract boarders and add enough income to afford homeownership.

Lodging, or the rental of space for overnight sleeping quarters, was a much more common practice than implied by the number of lodging houses. Many working-class women were trapped at home by their large numbers of children. In 1870, a woman who had five children could be expected to raise the children over twenty to twenty-two years, until the youngest child had reached age 16 (assuming that the children had been born soon after one another). If this woman had her first child at age 23, she would not have been able to enter the labor force until age 45 or older. One of the few ways that women could supplement their income was taking in lodgers, and lodging was very common in urban America between 1870 and 1920. Chapin's 1907 survey reports that about one-third of the families in the survey took in lodgers and from their fees raised their family income by between 10 percent and 15 percent.[37]

Some accounts of boarders suggest a single boarder occupying a bed in a corner of the kitchen or in some other inconspicuous space, but others report as many as six to twelve persons squeezing into small houses containing only a few rooms.[38] Some immigrant families rented out beds on double shifts, so that workers on different schedules shared the same bed. Agreements with boarders included complex arrangements for services provided by the housewife, including food preparation and laundry. The first column in table 4–3 provides a comprehensive time series of the percentage of urban households having boarders; this fell by half from 23 percent to 11 percent between 1900 and 1930 and then temporarily increased in 1940 as a result of depressed economic conditions in

Table 4–3. Boarders, Congestion, and Home Ownership, 1900–1970

	Percent Shares			Ratio
	Boarders of Urban Households	**Home Ownership, All Households**	**Home Ownership, Urban Households**	**Persons Per Room, All Households**
	(1)	(2)	(3)	(4)
1900	23	47	37	
1910	17	46	38	1.13
1920		46	41	
1930	11	48	46	
1940	14	44	41	0.74
1950		55	53	0.68
1960	4	62	58	0.60
1970	2	63	58	0.62

Source: Lebergott (1976), Tables 3, 6, and 7, pp. 252–59.

the 1930s. But by 1960, the practice had virtually disappeared, except in unusual situations—for instance, in large houses located close to college campuses that provided rooming for college students.[39]

In the late nineteenth century, the newer Midwestern cities such as Milwaukee had no older and inferior housing stock to be turned over to recently arrived working-class immigrants, so new housing was built not just for middle-class families, but also for immigrants. One area in the city's poorest district contained newly built homes built for Polish immigrants. A house that Clifford Clark describes as "typical" was on a "deep" lot with thirty feet of frontage.[40] The house, built in the 1890s, was one and a half stories, with an outer dimension of twenty-two by forty feet, indicating a total area of about 1,250 square feet. The family consisted of the husband, wife, and six children. A second-generation German iron molder, described as having climbed the "next step up the social ladder," lived in a two-story structure.

Though the single-family detached dwellings occupied by the working class may have been small, the typical middle-class house of the late nineteenth century was comparable in size to some of today's suburban single-family units. Custom-built houses designed by architects competed with lower-cost mail-order "plan books" long before Sears Roebuck began selling mail-order complete houses in the early twentieth century. The typical house had two stories, with four rooms on each story. Details on room sizes provided with some of the plans suggest that typical houses contained roughly 1,000 to 1,500 square feet.[41] Elaborate ornamentation was quite common, and its cost had been greatly reduced as manufacturers learned to replace skilled craftsmen with modern machines. "Instead of stone carvers who chiseled the cornices, there was a machine that stamped out cheap tin imitations. Instead of wood-carvers, a hydraulic press squeezed wood into intricate carved shapes."[42]

About 10 percent of residents of major cities in the 1880s owned substantial homes large enough to require the services of at least one servant. Many of these houses were in the streetcar suburbs, which were laid out between 1850 and 1900. Suburban housing from the start was designed to house different classes and income levels in the same area so that workmen, retail merchants, and household servants would be able to tend to the needs of middle and upper-class families. "Unlike post-World War II suburbs, which are relatively homogenous socioeconomically, those of the tracked city [streetcar suburbs] were not restricted to a single economic class."[43] Early maps of these suburbs, such as of Hinsdale and Evanston, Illinois, show that they were divided up into a diverse set of lot sizes, with frontages ranging from thirty to as much as 200 feet, in contrast to narrower lots prevalent in the inner city.[44] Most of these late nineteenth-century houses still exist, having benefited from continuous reequipping and improvements.[45] A stark difference between development in 1870–1900 and after 1900 was the diversity of styles and sizes of housing within a given community.

THE BUNGALOW MOVEMENT: SYMBOL OF CHANGE

Some accounts of changes in American urban housing over the 1870–1930 period paint a picture in which the large Victorian house of 1880–1900 was replaced by the much smaller and simpler bungalow house built between 1910 and 1930.[46] However, the reality is more complex. The bungalow dwelling represented the first stage of a multistep process by which the pre-1900 working class became the broad middle class of the 1950s and beyond. The efficiency of the bungalow design coincided with a steady increase in real income. Innovations that reduced the real cost of residential structures allowed working-class families to move from small and flimsy cottages and crowded tenement rental dwellings to solid homes that they could afford to buy on the installment plan. The emphasis on the bungalow in this chapter represents its central role in the democratization of owner-occupied housing in the early twentieth century, when automobiles were also simultaneously creating a radical transformation in the freedom of movement for many families.

The bungalow was initially developed in the Los Angeles area but had spread to Chicago by 1905, where it led the transition of working-class families to the modern age and modern conveniences.[47] In the words of one author, "the more prosperous segment of the working class became the primary beneficiaries of the new [bungalow] construction in the 1920s."[48] Bungalow construction still dominates Chicago's enormous "bungalow belt," which spreads across roughly one-third of the 225 square miles within Chicago's city limits.[49] Some 80,000 bungalow houses were built between 1910 and 1930, and an additional 20,000 units were built in adjacent suburbs. "The bungalow became the ubiquitous house in Chicago's first market for modern housing, the basic building block in a city of neighborhoods. By combining affordable artistry and affordable comfort so successfully, it also proved to be one of the city's most significant contributions to 20th-century architecture."[50]

"The bungalow represented the antithesis of the Victorian home, simple, informal, and efficient."[51] The standard bungalow had just one story, but many added additional bedrooms on the second floor by piercing the roofline with low, flat dormers. Exterior materials were favored that required no maintenance, including redwood in California, brick in Chicago, stone in New England, and adobe in Arizona. A typical bungalow had 1,000 to 1,200 square feet on the first floor and another 300 or 400 feet of extra bedrooms on the second floor.[52] Chicago bungalows were built with "generous windows, a full basement, and include[d] the modern amenities of central heat, electric service, and indoor plumbing."[53]

Because Chicago was such a large city and was growing so quickly between 1900 and 1930, the particular features of its bungalow belt are of great interest in providing a leading example of the nationwide progress achieved during this era that was duplicated in other large and medium-sized cities. Reflecting the arrival of the automobile age, all bungalows were built with garages in the back, and every block was bisected by a service alley through which cars entered and from which garbage was collected. Poles for electric and telephone wires were all hidden away in the alleys, giving the Chicago streetscape a neat, clean look, featuring landscaped parkways between the paved sidewalk and the street, with trees planted in the parkways.[54]

The floor plan on the first floor represented a radical change from the standard Victorian house. Anticipating the postwar family room that was often integrated with the kitchen as a single room, the bungalow often merged the living room and dining room into one larger common space adjacent to the kitchen. The Victorian entry hall had been eliminated, and entry was often directly into the combined living room and dining room. While bungalows with their twenty-five- or thirty-foot lots strike us today as unacceptably small, they are deceptive from the outside. Their popularity doubtless resulted from their extremely low cost, sometimes as little as $1 per square foot, excluding the cost of the land.[55] The feasibility of building a bungalow at such a low price was fostered by the aggressive sales by Sears Roebuck and others of a complete set of prefabricated materials that were sent to the building location, requiring only the assembly of the materials.

Even after the post–World War I inflation, Sears offered all the components of a Chicago-style bungalow for between $750 and $2,000, to which the purchaser would need to add the cost of acquiring the land and the labor to put together the Sears-provided material.[56] Sears publicity bragged that one of its houses could be converted from a stack of precut materials to a finished house in 352 carpenter-hours.[57] The use of standardized plans and prefabricated materials in bungalow building represented the culmination of a long process of innovations in construction dating back to the mid-nineteenth century that brought access to single-family homeownership to a substantial share of the population. Daniel Sichel has shown that the real price of nails dropped by a factor of ten between 1830 and 1930.[58] Together with the development of thin-cut lumber for "balloon frame construction," cheaper nails greatly reduced the real price of construction per square foot compared to the previous technology of homes crafted out of local materials by skilled carpenters.

Despite the common size and tightly spaced arrangement of bungalows in a city such as Chicago, builders achieved a variety of appearance by using many sizes and shapes of windows, different colors of brick, and decorative limestone elements for window frames, caps for staircases, and stone window boxes for summer flowers. Interior elements were upscale in comparison to many subdivisions built after 1945; features included built-in furniture and cabinets, a fireplace, and hardwood floors. Interior mass-produced wooden furniture was part of the standard equipment of bungalows before they were purchased, including "built-in bookcases, window seats, mantels, china closets, breakfast benches, dressing tables, and radiator enclosures."[59] The wide variety of decorative elements provided by masons and the woodworking industry was supplemented by the capital-intensive mass production of plumbing, heating, and kitchen equipment.[60]

BETWEEN METROPOLIS AND FARM: SMALL TOWNS AND MEDIUM-SIZED CITIES

Most of our attention has been devoted to large urban areas. What about the "middle," the medium-sized cities in which so many Americans lived in the 1920s? Numerous details of housing conditions are contained in Robert and Helen Lynd's classic 1929 survey report on Muncie, Indiana, a city of 38,000 people living in 9,200 dwelling units, or 4.13 per unit, very close to the 4.0 ratio of population to occupied dwellings recorded for 1930 in table 4–1.

In Muncie, 86 percent of the housing units were single-family, "each standing on a separate patch of ground," and 10 percent were in two-family units. Only 1 percent were in apartments. One-third of working-class families interviewed and 80 percent of "business-class" families lived in single-family homes that had two stories of space within a single dwelling unit. In contrast to the lot frontages of twenty-five to thirty feet common in Chicago, Muncie lot frontages were forty feet. Ages of homes were similar to those in the 1940 census data presented in table 4–2, which recorded that 72 percent of existing homes in 1929 were built between 1900 and 1929. The need for driveways and garages to accommodate automobiles had reduced the size of yards and gardens; gardens were further squeezed by a tendency to shrink lot sizes on blocks developed in the 1920s compared to those developed in the 1880s.[61]

The Lynds distinguish between the homes of the "poorer working man" and "the working man with more money." The differences involve behavior, furnishings, and equipment more than house size. When the poorer working man arrives home, he "walks up the frequently unpaved street, turns in at a bare yard littered with a rusty velocipede or worn-out automobile tires, opens a sagging door . . . from this room the whole house is visible—the kitchen with table and floor swarming with flies and often strewn with bread crusts, orange skins, torn papers, and lumps of coal and wood."[62] In contrast, the better-off member of the working class walks in past "geraniums in window boxes . . . the sewing machine stands in the living room or dining room, and the ironing board with its neat piles of clothes stretches across one corner of the kitchen."[63] The array of dwellings ranges across the classes from "mean and cluttered" to the "spacious and restful."

There was no sharp distinction between middle-class and working-class housing in early twentieth-century small towns. The small town street grid initially set up all lot sizes to be the same. The upper classes escaped this discipline only by combining several lots. Because both the middle and working classes lived in single-family dwellings, the quality distinctions were subtle. "The chances of living next door to someone substantially richer or poorer than oneself was high in the American small town in the early 20th century. The idea of small-town social equality was encouraged by residential mixing."[64] All residents of small towns experienced much lower densities than the crowded urban tenement conditions described by Riis, Edith Wood, and other social reformers. By definition, the countryside surrounded the small town and was a short walk away for the gentry and working class alike. Almost every family had a garden that produced vegetables in the summer. "Strawberries came in May; peas and new potatoes followed; then string beans, beets, turnips, carrots, sweet corn, tomatoes, and the full tide of summer's fruits."[65]

The sturdy single-family farm dwellings of the north and west contrasted with greatly inferior conditions in the south. A survey carried out in North Carolina in the mid-1920s described the "cabins" in which most black tenant farmers lived. There were one to three rooms in the black dwellings, whereas those for whites averaged four rooms. There was no plaster or other covering on the walls, and in place of window glass was a simple opening with no sash. Some window openings were protected by shutters to keep the rain water from coming in. About one-quarter of the families had four people or more per bedroom.[66] Despite the advances in housing quality for many Americans, deep regional divides still existed.

CHANGES IN RURAL FARM HOUSING: THE LIMIT OF MODERN CONVENIENCES

James Bryce's admiration for the individual worker cottages on the suburban-like streets of Midwestern cities was understated compared to his rhapsodic view of life on the American farm.[67] "All over the wide West, from Lake Ontario to the Upper Missouri, one travels past farms of two to three hundred acres, in every one of which there is a spacious farmhouse among orchards and meadows. . . ."[68]

Just as the unvarying street grid defined the spatial relationships in cities from New York, Philadelphia, and Washington, D.C., westward, so the grid applied to the dividing lines between farms in the Northwest Territories beyond the Appalachians. The "200 to 300"–acre farms that Bryce observed in the north and central states resulted from an unvarying division of the empty territory of the Northwest Territories and the Louisiana Purchase into square-mile portions of 640 acres. Half a square mile came out at 320 acres, similar to the farm sizes that Bryce observed. But historical statistics place the median size of the American farm as less than half that size—153 acres in 1870, 147 acres in 1900, and 157 acres in 1930, still substantial from Bryce's European perspective.[69]

In light of Frederick Jackson Turner's much-discussed 1893 hypothesis of the closing of the frontier, it is somewhat surprising to note, as shown in table 4–2, that substantially more than two-thirds of American farm dwellings in existence in 1940 were built after 1900. Many of the newly constructed farmhouses were replacements for the sod huts and log cabins that immigrant farmers initially built to shelter their families from winter in the northern and western plains. "These primitive structures more closely resembled sheds than solid, comfortable houses."[70] The quality of farmhouses steadily improved during 1870–1940, at least outside the south.

The two-story single-family detached farmhouses were similar to single-family detached dwellings built in small towns and all but the largest cities in the late nineteenth century, including the standard upper-working-class homes of Muncie, Indiana, as portrayed by the Lynds.[71] The first floor consisted of a kitchen, a parlor or sitting room, and perhaps a dining room. The second floor usually included three bedrooms—one for the parents, one for the male children, and another for the female children. Heating transitioned from the open-hearth fireplace to the enclosed iron stove/boiler between 1870 and 1900.

The period of farm prosperity from 1900 to 1920 was accompanied by improvements in farm dwellings. Partly thanks to the ease of buying through the Wards and Sears catalogues, farm families purchased furniture, fabrics, and kitchen devices. The age-old problem of carrying water was partly solved by linking a cistern to the kitchen with a hand pump, thus reducing the burden of the endless female task of carrying water into and out of the house. As these primitive pumps were being added, so were window screens and screened doors, ridding farmhouse interiors of flying insects.

Yet the farmers of America lagged increasingly behind their urban fellow citizens, in part because the modern conveniences were so slow to arrive. Relatively few farmers had access to electricity, running water, and indoor plumbing by 1940. Indeed, the 1920s were a period of depression, both economically and emotionally, in America's farmland. Farmers were restless with the feeling that they had been bypassed by modern progress, an unease captured by the World War I popular song "How Ya Gonna Keep 'Em Down on the Farm (After They've Seen Paree)?"[72] The cities of the 1920s were full of excitement and popular culture, whereas on the farm "economic distress, population decline, and psychological doubt and despair seemed to sap the lifeblood of the countryside." A farmer from Tennessee captured this unease with the memorable contrast: "The greatest thing on earth is to have the love of God in your heart, and the next greatest thing is to have electricity in your house."[73] This accords with a primary theme of this chapter—that the modern conveniences made urban dwellers more equal but made urban and rural life ever more different.

THE SURGE OF ONE-TIME-ONLY CHANGES: CREATING THE MODERN DWELLING, 1870–1940

The revolution that remade the American dwelling and the American standard of living occurred during a relatively small slice of human history, mainly between 1910 and 1940. Viewed from the perspective of millennia of economic stagnation, the networked modern conveniences arrived in a rush, from virtual invisibility in 1910 urban America to near pervasiveness in 1940. This section provides an overview of the percentage of housing units equipped with each of

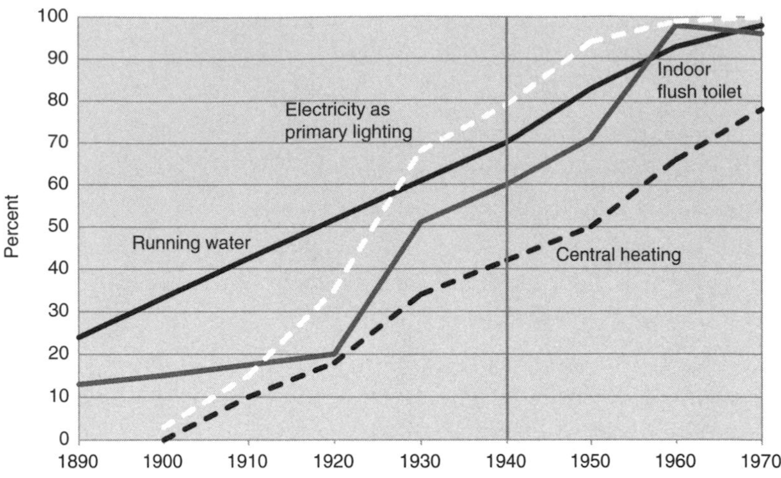

Figure 4–1. Diffusion of Modern Conveniences, 1890–1970
Source: Lebergott (1976), pp. 260–88.

the following in each decade between 1890 and 1970: running water, indoor flush toilets, central heating, electricity as the primary lighting source, washing machines, and mechanical refrigerators. For comparison and perspective, we also plot the diffusion of the automobile (otherwise treated in chapter 5) and of the radio (chapter 6).

All the diffusion percentages in figures 4–1 and 4–2 are taken from the same work, which in turn goes into considerable detail about the most consistent sources.[74] The percentages are divided into two diagrams for visual clarity, with the built-in equipment of the house in figure 4–1 and the appliances, together with the automobile, plotted in figure 4–2. Starting in 1900, the modern conveniences had barely tiptoed onto the stage. Running water had reached one-third of dwelling units, whereas indoor flush toilets were present in about 15 percent of homes. The two figures indicate that all the plotted lines exceeded 40 percent by 1940. Electricity and the automobile explode upward from near 0 percent in 1900 to 1930, when electricity had reached 68 percent, automobiles had reached 60 percent, and indoor toilets had reached 50 percent. Despite depressed economic conditions in the 1930s and wartime production prohibitions in World War II, the interval 1930 to 1950 reflected the most rapid adoption of the mechanical refrigerator and central heating.

By 1970, the diffusion rates had clustered into two groups. Automobiles, washing machines, and central heating reached a plateau of about 80 percent

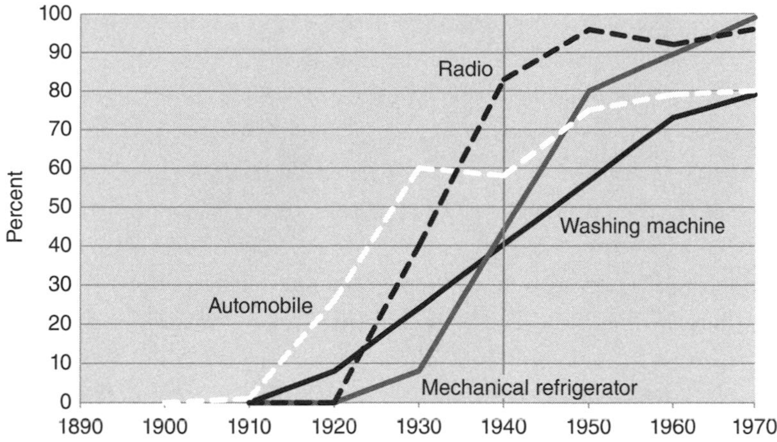

Figure 4–2. Diffusion of Modern Appliances and Automobiles, 1890–1970
Source: Lebergott (1976), pp. 260–88.

coverage. Some families in dense urban environments such as New York City chose not to have cars and instead relied on public transit. Some apartment dwellers did not have room for washing machines and chose to rely on the nearby Laundromat. And central heating was not necessary in some warm areas of the south and southwest. Otherwise, all the other plotted lines reached 96 percent to 100 percent by 1970. A revolution had occurred in seventy years, much of it in forty years. This transformation of the quality of the dwelling unit was fundamental and could happen only once. Today's houses and apartments are much more similar to those of 1940 than those of 1940 are to their predecessors of 1900.

THE MIRACLE OF ELECTRIFICATION: LIGHTING AND EARLY APPLIANCES THROUGH 1940

Electrification's effect was universal and revolutionary, although it took fifty years to reach most urban homes and even longer to change life in farm and rural nonfarm dwellings. As with plumbing, running water, and central heating, the rich obtained the modern conveniences before the middle class or the poor, city dwellers before small towns and farms, and the northern and western states before the south. In a mere fifty years, the residential United States underwent a transformation from the home production of heat and light by household members who chopped wood, hauled coal, and tended kerosene lamps to a new era of gas and electricity, purchased as commodities and arriving automatically at the dwelling unit without having to be physically carried.[75] When electricity arrived, gone was the darkness, not to mention the air pollution emitted by candles, wax lamps, and gas lamps as well as the "care and feeding" of kerosene lamps, which included filling, emptying, and wick-trimming. That said, however, the arrival of electricity moved the pollution from the inside of the home to the outside, for the generation of electricity from coal-fired plants sent carbon emissions into the atmosphere.

From today's perspective, an essential characteristic of the 1870 dwelling was its dimness after dark. The light emitted by a single candle at a distance of one foot at a given angle defines the lumen, and a single wax candle emits about thirteen lumens, whereas a 100-watt filament bulb emits about 1,200 lumens. None of the sources of illumination available in 1870 produced more than six to eight candle-hours, or roughly eighty to 100 lumens. Thus a single state-of-the-art lamp burning town gas, whale oil, or kerosene emitted light between one-twelfth and one-fifteenth the intensity of a single 100-watt light bulb.[76]

Before electric light was invented in 1879, illumination inside the home at night required that a fuel be burned, producing not just a flame but also some degree of odor and smoke. In 1870, kerosene lamps were a relatively recent invention (having been introduced in the 1850s), and many homes still used candles and whale oil lamps. Kerosene was prized for its clear flame and illumination power, burning as brightly as ten candles. Compared to whale oil, kerosene was less dangerous, having a higher flash point, having a lighter weight, and selling for a tenth the price.[77] "The discovery of petroleum in Pennsylvania gave kerosene to the world, and life to the few remaining whales."[78] The main drawback of kerosene was the need for constant cleaning of lamps to maintain brightness and also maintain safety.

Town gas, a by-product of turning bituminous coal into coke, had been used in England since the early years of the nineteenth century. Its first use for illumination was in the cotton spinning plants of northern England, where during the dark half of the year lighting was necessary to support the long work day. Gas lamps had a brighter and whiter flame than oil lamps and candles, but the light flickered and the lamps gave off through the burning process emissions of ammonia, sulfur, carbon dioxide, and water. Furthermore, gas lamps consumed oxygen, causing breathing problems for people in poorly ventilated rooms. Their discharges and consumption of oxygen were less a problem outdoors than inside, so they became the standard form of street lighting, dazzling visitors to Paris in the 1820s and New York City in the 1830s.

In most cities, only the wealthiest neighborhoods benefited from gas light. Though gas pipes were not extended to the poorer neighborhoods, the gasworks were nonetheless located there, with "their furnaces belching a dense, foul smoke that permeated everything with a sulfurous stench. The gasworks contaminated nearby soils and subsoils with ammonia and sulfur, polluted water supplies, and drove the surrounding area into decline."[79] Gas explosions were frequent enough to make the gas supply unreliable. Many homes used a mix of gas and oil lamps, preferring to keep gas and its odor out of personal spaces such as bedrooms.[80] Such lamps, along with open fires for heating, posed a substantial fire risk for households of the nineteenth century.

Thomas Edison did not invent the electric light, but he was responsible for making it commercially viable in the United States, partly because he combined a practical electric lamp with the development of electric power generation, starting with the Pearl Street station in New York City in 1882.[81] Edison's unique contribution was his solution of the double problem of inventing an efficient light bulb that could be manufactured in bulk while also establishing electric generating stations to bring power into the individual home.

Compared with the international celebration of the golden spike in 1869 (see chapter 2), the moment when electric light became commercially viable was a much quieter affair. Throughout 1879, Edison's laboratory in Menlo Park, New Jersey, had been focused on the search for the best material for the filament in the electric light bulb. Finally, it all came together, on the night of October 22, 1879:

> At 1:30 in the morning, Batchelor and Jehl, watched by Edison, began on the ninth fiber, a plain carbonized cotton-thread filament . . . set up in a vacuum glass bulb. They attached the batteries, and the bulb's soft incandescent glow lit up the dark laboratory, the bottles lining the shelves reflecting its gleam. As had many another experimental model, the bulb glowed bright. But this time, the lamp still shone hour after hour through that night. The morning came and went, and still the cotton-thread filament radiated its incandescent light. Lunchtime passed and the carbonized cotton fiber still glowed. At 4:00 pm the glass bulb cracked and the light went out. Fourteen and a half hours![82]

Few, if any inventions, have been more enthusiastically welcomed than electric light. Throughout the winter of 1879–1880, thousands traveled to

Menlo Park to see the "light of the future," including farmers whose houses would never be electrified in their lifetimes. Travelers on the nearby Pennsylvania Railroad could see the brilliant lights glowing in the Edison offices. The news was announced to the world on December 21, 1879, with a full-page story in the *New York Herald*, opened by this dramatic and long-winded headline: EDISON'S LIGHT—THE GREAT INVENTOR'S TRIUMPH IN ELECTRIC ILLUMINATION—A SCRAP OF PAPER—IT MAKES A LIGHT, WITHOUT GAS OR FLAME, CHEAPER THAN OIL—SUCCESS IN A COTTON THREAD.[83] On New Year's Eve of 1879, 3,000 people converged by train, carriage, and farm wagon on the Edison laboratory to witness the brilliant display, a planned laboratory open house of dazzling modernity to launch the new decade.

The contrast with all preceding forms of light was an unambiguous and stark improvement, one of the greatest in the history of invention. Part of Edison's Menlo Park demonstrations for investors and New York City politicians was a display of 300 outdoor lights that he turned off and then on in instantaneous unison. This was one of the most surprising aspects of electric light—the ability to turn it on and off with a click, without gas lights' need for individual lighting and snuffing:

> Here was a little click that meant light was contained in a glass vacuum and need never again be linked with a flame or coaxed forth and adjusted; light that did not waver, tip, drip, stink, or consume oxygen and would not spontaneously ignite cloth dust in factories or hay in the mow. A child could be left alone with it.[84]

The initial electric lamps were about three times brighter than the brightest kerosene lamps, but by 1920, improvements in the metal filaments made them ten times brighter than kerosene and about 100 times brighter than a candle.[85] Electric lights are an example of a technology that had a great burst of innovation early, in this case 1880–1920, and then stood still afterwards. Although the fluorescent bulb had come to dominate lighting in commercial and industrial settings by 1950, virtually nothing changed in home illumination from 1920 until the development of the compact fluorescent bulb after 1990. Nothing in the past hundred years matches the sharp distinction between creating light with a flame and creating it with electricity, although some argue that the replacement of the horse by the motor vehicle was an even more fundamental invention (this is the central theme of chapter 5).

William Nordhaus made a heroic and convincing attempt to calculate the price of light over the centuries.[86] An efficient kerosene lamp of 1875–85 produced a lumen of light at about a tenth the cost of a tallow candle from 1800. By another metric, $20 per year would light a house for three hours in the evening with the light emitted by five candles, or 5,500 candle hours per year. Advances in town gas and kerosene lamps by 1890 (before electricity) would allow the same $20 to purchase 73,000 candle hours per year.

The initial Edison electric light bulb was priced about equal to the best kerosene lamp, and this price dropped by a factor of six by 1920. Taking into account that by 1920 the electric light was ten times more powerful than a kerosene lamp, the same $20 would purchase 4.4 million candle hours per year. Filament incandescent bulbs cost about the same per lumen in 1990 as in 1920 in nominal terms, but in real terms, their cost was much lower, by another factor of eight. None of this decline in prices has been heretofore captured by official price indexes, and the consumer surplus captured by this decline in prices is one of many reasons to consider the growth of real income per capita during 1890–1940 substantially understated. Note that these price comparisons are all based on the *quantity* of light emitted by a device, so all the price declines are understated thanks to the improvement in the *quality* of light. All those improvements in quality—no more odors, no need to clean lamp chimneys, no more danger of fires, no more flickering—are completely missed not only by traditional measures of the cost of living, but also by Nordhaus's creative attempts to link together the prices per lumen of candles, fuel lamps, and electric light bulbs.[87]

Only 3 percent of American homes had electric service in 1900. By 1912, three decades after Edison's Pearl Street power station opened, only 16 percent of American homes were connected to a central power station.[88] The annual output of electric power per capita doubled every seven years from 1902 to 1915 and doubled every six years from 1915 to 1929.[89] This power was supplied not just for light and appliances within the home, but also for manufacturing, retailing, and electric railways and streetcars. Rapid growth in the consumption of electric power was stimulated by a reduction in its nominal price from 16.2 cents to 6.3 cents per kilowatt-hour between 1902 and 1929, which converts to an inflation-adjusted price decline of 81 percent in just twenty-seven years, or 6.0 percent per year.[90]

Table 4–4 supplements figure 4–1 by contrasting for the year 1940 the stark differences between the extent of electrification in urban America and

Table 4–4. Percentages of Housing with Modern Conveniences, by Location and Type, 1940

		Percentage Distribution				
		United States				Southern US
		Total	Urban	Rural Nonfarm	Rural Farm	Rural Farm
Lighting	Electric	78.7	95.8	77.8	31.3	16.4
	Kerosene or Gasoline	20.2	3.8	20.9	65.7	80.7
	Other	1.1	0.4	1.3	3.0	2.9
Refrigeration	Mechanical	44.1	56.0	38.7	14.9	9.6
	Ice	27.1	31.6	23.0	17.9	19.5
	None or other	28.8	12.4	38.3	67.1	70.9
Cooking fuel	Wood	23.6	6.0	28.6	69.5	83.9
	Gas	48.8	73.0	24.0	3.8	2.4
	Other	27.6	20.9	47.5	26.7	13.7
Water Supply	Running Water	69.9	93.5	55.9	17.8	8.5
	Other	24.9	5.8	36.0	67.4	72.2
	None	5.1	0.6	8.1	14.8	19.3
Toilet facilities	Flush - Exclusive	59.7	83.0	43.2	11.2	4.7
	Outside or Privy	32.2	8.6	51.2	78.9	80.1
	None or Other	8.1	8.4	5.6	9.9	15.2
Bathtub or Shower	Exclusive	56.2	77.5	40.8	11.8	5.4
	None or shared	43.8	22.5	59.2	88.2	94.6
Central heating	Total	41.8	57.9	27.0	10.1	1.3
	None	58.2	42.1	73.0	89.9	98.7

Source: Author's tabulations from 1940 U. S. Census of Housing, Tables 7, 7a, 7b, 8, 9b, 10a, and 12a

electrification at the other extreme—farms, especially farms in the south. Table 4–4 shows that light was provided by electricity in 96 percent of dwellings in urban areas, in 78 percent in small towns, and in 31 percent on farms in general, but only 16 percent of farms in the south. More than sixty years after Edison's successful experiment to develop the electric light bulb, 80 percent of southern farm families used kerosene or other fuels for lighting.

The epochal transition from dirty and difficult housework to the modern electric kitchen of the 1950s was just under way in 1917. In that year, General

Electric summed up the appeal of electric appliances as "electric servants, dependable for the muscle part of the washing, ironing, cleaning, and sewing. They could do all your cooking—without matches, without soot, without coal, without argument—in a cool kitchen."[91] Electric household appliances were quickly invented but were slow to reach the average household. Adoption was initially held back by the flimsy electric wiring initially installed in houses, sufficient only to supply light. The heavier electric drain of stoves, refrigerators, washing machines, and irons required rewiring and faced the obstacle that during 1900–1920 there was as yet no standardization of electric plugs and electric outlets. In fact, there was not even standardization on today's alternating current, for some electric companies offered direct current as late as the 1930s. Moreover, voltage varied.[92]

Washing machines had developed substantially by 1940, reaching 40 percent of homes in that year. Two models of electric wringer washing machines were offered in the 1928 Sears Roebuck catalog at prices of $79 and $92. This can be compared to median family income in Muncie, Indiana, in 1925, as cited earlier, of $1,450, equal to $28 per week. Thus the least expensive washing machine cost the equivalent of about three weeks of income.[93] Gradually, as washing machines were hooked up to running water and waste pipes, the multiple tasks involved in doing the weekly laundry became centralized in the basement, which was also the location of the furnace or boiler once central heating arrived.

Electric refrigerators initially made slower progress, being expensive at a time when iceboxes were ubiquitous and ice delivery reliable and cheap. There were virtually no mechanical refrigerators until 1920, and they were in only 8 percent of dwelling units in 1930; as late as 1928, the Sears catalog referred to the icebox as a "refrigerator." But then the percentage of households that had refrigerators soared to 44 percent in 1940. This explosion of use in the 1930s, despite the Great Depression, reflected how the refrigerator was initially much more expensive than the washing machine, $775 in 1919 and $568 by 1926. Sales skyrocketed during the 1930s, from 1 million sold in the entire decade of 1919–29 to 2.5 million by 1932 and 6 million by 1941. The timing of the price reduction can be linked to the first electric refrigerator offered in the 1931 Sears catalog for between $137 and $205.[94] As shown in table 4–4, the percentage usage of mechanical refrigerators in 1940 ranged from 56 percent in urban America to only 10 percent on southern farms.[95]

The appliance most enthusiastically adopted besides the electric light was the electric iron. First sold in 1893, electric irons eliminated the need continually to heat or reheat the heavy iron on a gas or wood stove; the temperature was hard to adjust, and scorching of clothes was common. The primitiveness of flat irons that needed to be independently heated was one of the reasons, in addition to the absence of washing machines, why home laundry was so time-consuming and tedious. As with most appliances, however, key improvements had to wait for decades; in the case of the electric iron, the automatic thermostat was introduced only in 1927; before then, the iron was either on or off. The 1928 Sears catalog displays four different models of irons ranging in price from $1.98 to $4.95, although none of the descriptions mentions any kind of temperature control, and only the more expensive models had on/off switches.[96] Using the Muncie median income level, an iron could be bought for less than one day's income.

By 1940, 79 percent of Americans had electric light, and nearly as many had electric irons. Another popular electric appliance was the vacuum cleaner, which could be purchased for about one week's income.[97] Nevertheless, the electrification of the American home was rudimentary in 1929; electricity consumption in 1929 was enough to power three 100-watt electric bulbs for five hours per day, with no power left over for any other use. The annual growth rate of residential electricity consumption roughly doubled in every decade from 1910 to 1960.[98]

The variety of consumer appliances available in 1929 is provided by research carried out by Chicago's electric company, showing that more than 80 percent of residents of all classes by then had an electric iron and vacuum cleaner. Next with 53 percent was the radio. The only other appliances with usage greater than 30 percent were the toaster and washing machine (37 percent and 36 percent). Appliances with usage by between 10 percent and 30 percent of Chicagoans in 1929 were the percolator (16 percent), refrigerator (10 percent), fan (10 percent), and electric heater (10 percent).[99]

Contemporary accounts focused not on these percentages but on the revolution of electricity itself. The daily cycle of natural light and darkness no longer dictated the activities in which household members could participate. Because electric light was so much brighter than kerosene or gas lamps, a wider variety of activities became possible in the dark hours of the day, particularly in the winter. Household electrification, both through lighting and appliances, radically changed the daily lives of millions of Americans.

THE WATER FLOWS IN AND OUT: THE GREATEST REVOLUTION OF ALL?

The "modern conveniences" of running water and indoor toilets took a long time to become commonplace. In the 1890s, these conveniences were "known to only a few of the very wealthy."[100] Most houses in the 1890s, from densely packed urban tenements to single-family farmhouses, lacked running water. Conditions were worst for tenement dwellers:

> Tenants had to go out into the hallway to use water closets or into an exterior courtyard to use privies. Going outside one's private quarters was more than inconvenient; it was degrading when residents in two or more households had to share a single water closet. People unable to wait to relieve themselves resorted to the nearest private corner or vacant lot.[101]

The greatest curse of the rural and urban housewife was the need to carry fresh water into the house and dirty water out of the house. Even in the early twentieth century, working-class housewives had to haul water from hydrants in the street, a task little different from centuries when farm housewives had brought water from the nearest creek or well. All the water for cooking, dishwashing, bathing, laundry, and housecleaning had to be carried in—and then hauled back out after use.

The pace of infrastructure investment mattered; networks had to arrive to make the modern conveniences possible. Just as electric light could not be purchased for the home until an electric company had brought electric wires to the neighborhood, so households could not simply go out and buy running water. They had to wait until municipal waterworks extended piping to their area. Considering that the earliest municipal waterworks was built in Philadelphia in 1801, progress was extremely slow until about 1870. "Most communities drank their own sewage or that of their neighbors upstream. Typhoid fever and dysentery became endemic, and urban mortality rates were shockingly high."[102] But then an upsurge in the number of municipal waterworks occurred, from 244 in 1870 to 9,850 in 1924.[103] The initial impetus was to improve public health by eliminating waterborne diseases rather than to eliminate the housewife's burden of hauling water in and out. Additional motivations included firefighting, street cleaning, and manufacturing. By the turn of the century, most cities had sewers, but water was treated, purified, and filtered only after 1900.[104]

Sources date the invention of the first plunger-type water closet to 1875, implying that in 1870 urban dwellers relied on "chamber pots and open windows and backyards to dispose of their waste" in addition to the universal outdoor privy.[105] Only in the 1870s was knowledge developed about the design of drainage and venting procedures for toilets, particularly to prevent sewer gases from backing up into the home.[106] Before 1870, the relatively small number of dwellings that had indoor plumbing fixtures obtained the water so used from privately owned wells or from cisterns delivered into the house by a system of shoddy pipes and pumps. Waste was delivered to cesspools, so neither the water nor the waste had any connection to the outside world.[107] Even mansions and luxury country houses may have been equipped with modern plumbing fixtures, but without sewer connections, they were plagued with "the ooze of the cesspool" that penetrated the foundation wall, and settling of the foundation cracked pipes and allowed sewer gasses to permeate the house's interior air.

The development of municipal waterworks created an unexpected problem: the increased amount of water entering the house had to exit the house, and increased wastewater quantities had nowhere to go before the development of urban sewer systems. So serious had this situation become in Boston that in 1844 an ordinance was passed prohibiting the taking of baths without a doctor's order. The urgency felt to develop a wastewater sewer system reflected the public demand to end the need for repeated cleaning of privy vaults and cesspools.[108] The rapidly increasing availability of public water supplies during 1870–1900 linked household plumbing into a network of water and waste pipes that eventually extended over entire cities. The nationwide percentage for private indoor toilets was between 10 percent and 20 percent until 1920, after which the percentage jumped to 50 percent in 1930 and 60 percent in 1940.[109]

There was no running water in Muncie, Indiana, before 1885. By 1890, "there were not over two dozen complete bathrooms in the entire city."[110] Water was pumped to the back door or kitchen from a well or cistern. For roughly 95 percent of families in 1890, "taking a bath" meant lugging a heavy wooden or tin tub into a bedroom or, more usually, the warm kitchen and filling it half full of water from the pump, heated on the kitchen stove. By 1925, running water had reached 75 percent of Muncie's dwellings, and two-thirds had sewer connections. At that point, all new houses, except the very cheapest, had bathrooms, and older houses were installing them.[111]

Simultaneous with the extension of urban water infrastructure was the entrepreneurial effort to develop affordable and reliable modern plumbing fixtures. The plumbing supply industry struggled to mass-produce plumbing fixtures that worked properly and did not leak; this was achieved only after

1915.[112] There was rapid change at the turn of the century. Though the Sears catalog included only sinks among the plumbing fixtures it offered in 1897, by 1908 it offered several full sets of bathroom equipment, including a clawfoot bathtub, a porcelain-enameled sink, and a toilet that today would be considered an elegant antique with its "golden oak" tank and seat. The entire three-part outfit cost only $43.80, equal to about three weeks' working-class income at the time, and had a shipping weight of 480 pounds.[113]

Table 4–4 shows that private flush toilets and private bathrooms reached fewer homes in 1940 than did running water itself. Nationwide 60 percent of families had private flush toilets, leaving the remaining 40 percent either sharing toilets or still mired in the previous century, relying on outside toilets, privies, or no privy at all. Just as for electricity and running water, these percentages were much higher in urban America and much lower in small towns and on farms. The percentage with private flush toilets in 1940 ranged from 83 percent for urban dwellings to 5 percent for southern farms, and for private bathtubs, they ranged from 78 percent for urban families to 5 percent for southern farms.

By 1940, the American bathroom had reached its standard form, which has been little changed until today, including a recessed tub, tiled floors and walls, a single-unit toilet, an enameled sink, and a medicine chest. The gradual diffusion of running water, indoor plumbing, and private bathrooms brought with it another less tangible luxury, personal privacy. Both rural and urban families in the late nineteenth century spent most of their time in the kitchen, where the heat source was located. Not only did they cook and eat there, but they bathed, washed, and socialized there, and bathing (albeit infrequent by today's standards) became a public event. The rapid growth in private bathrooms allowed for a new sense of personal privacy in American households unknown to earlier generations.

HEATING: FROM THE HEARTH TO CENTRAL HEATING

As we have seen, at the dawn of the 1870–1940 era, most heat came from the open hearth of the fireplace, whether in farmhouses or urban dwellings. Though cast-iron heaters and kitchen ranges had been invented as early as the 1840s, they were a significant source of heat only beginning in the 1870s and 1880s. However, this central source of heating for the kitchen and main living area did little to heat the bedrooms. Throughout the northern United States, bedrooms were almost as cold as the outside until well into the twentieth century, though homeowners carried to bed with them warmed iron ingots or ceramic "bed bricks" from the kitchen stove.

Anecdotes trace the first efforts to install residential central heating systems back to the early 1840s, but an initial obstacle had to be overcome. Steam boilers had a tendency to explode, and Mark Twain in *Life on the Mississippi* reported, only partly in jest, that people boarding a riverboat in St. Louis had only a 50–50 chance of making it to New Orleans. In the middle of the nineteenth century there were four boiler explosions per week, and as late as 1888 there were 246 boiler explosions in a single year.[114] A source reports that for every three explosions, two people were killed.[115] Nevertheless, the first steam systems with room radiators were installed in a few locations in the 1850s and 1860s.[116] Safety problems were gradually solved by the establishment of a standard of low pressures to replace the high pressures that had previously caused the boiler explosions, as well as improvements in pipe design and venting.

The widespread use of steam, hot-water, and hot-air central heating systems began in the 1880s, initially in large homes built for the upper classes.[117] This innovation trickled down to middle-class and working-class homes in the half century after 1880. By 1925, 48 percent of houses in Zanesville, Ohio, were heated by central furnaces.[118] This is consistent with 58 percent of urban homes having central heating in 1940, as shown in table 4–4.

That table also shows that central heating was much less common in small towns and on farms. In 1940, only 1 percent of southern farms had central heating, a finding that reflects both the mildness of the southern climate and that very few southern farms had any modern conveniences at all. Of urban homes having central heating, more than three-quarters used coal or coke as fuel, implying that coal had to be delivered and ashes removed, as well as that air pollution was much more common than today, when natural gas dominates as the nation's main fuel for central heating.

One side effect of central heating is that it allowed windows to become larger. A Muncie, Indiana, "building expert" estimated that houses built during 1915–29 had "50 percent more glass surface than in 1890" because "more heat can be secured within."[119] Central heating also contributed to the process by which the cellar turned into an occupied basement. In the late nineteenth century, cellars were ill-ventilated holes in the ground with stone walls and a floor of dirt used only for storage. But the advent of the central heating boiler or furnace was accompanied to the building out of basement to larger spaces that had cement walls and floors.

CONCLUSION: THE TRANSFORMATION OF HOUSING

The transition from farm to city during the 1870–1940 interval is sometimes portrayed as a shift from open spaces and single-family farmhouses to crowded tenement apartments featuring windowless rooms and limited light entering through fetid garbage-strewn airshafts. We have seen that this view is simplistic and inaccurate. Most urban dwellings were not tenements but were structures containing one or two dwellings having open air outside and usually a small yard. Farm dwellings in 1870 were not all classic two-story Midwestern farmhouses but included primitive log cabins, mud huts, and primitive shacks in the south.

Urban dwellers in both 1870 and 1940 lived mainly in detached dwellings, and the primitive working-class cottages of the late nineteenth century were supplemented after 1905 with the modern urban bungalow. These new dwelling types could be purchased for between one and two years' income and from the beginning incorporated the modern conveniences of electricity connections, running water, at least one indoor bathroom, and central heating. Although these bungalows, most of which remain in today's central-city urban landscape, may look crowded together on their narrow lots, they represented a revolutionary leap from primitive to modern housing.

An overall change in life after 1870 was a switch, particularly in urban America, from dependence on self-carried water and fuel to dependence on networks. The new networks of telephone lines, water mains and sewers, and power cables did not just appear suddenly. They were gradually built and expanded from urban cores to areas having less population density. A need was perceived, and a combination of government infrastructure agencies and private capital made meeting it possible. The gradual transition to network connections accompanied two other basic changes in daily life as practiced for millennia. In 1870, the dependence on the open hearth and absence of secondary heating sources made most of the dwelling the same temperature as the outside. The goal of providing an interior year-long temperature of 70 °F occurred in two steps through the gradual diffusion of central heating in the first half of the twentieth century and of air conditioning in the second half.

Can a value be placed on the transition to the networked house? The answer lies in studies of the relationship between house prices or rents and the presence or absence of particular attributes such as indoor bathrooms or central heating. The presence of a full bathroom compared to none raises the rent by 82 percent.

The value of central heating compared to the fireplace kitchen raises the rent by 28 percent. There are no separate studies of electricity, for it became universal so rapidly, but its value must have been as large as that of central heating. Multiplying together these improvements implies that the perceived quality of housing units tripled as a result of the introduction of electricity, plumbing, and central heating between 1870 and the early postwar years.[120] The enormous value of the inventions examined in this chapter may be greater than those of any other chapter in part I of this book, with the possible exception of the value of the conquest of infant mortality discussed in chapter 7.

The role of individual entrepreneurs in achieving the networked house revolution is quite different than for food and clothing as discussed in the previous chapter, where the long list of familiar entrepreneurial names included food processors such as Pillsbury and Borden, and marketing innovators included Marshall Field, Rowland Macy, Aaron Montgomery Ward, and Richard Sears. Housing, by contrast, lacks "big names" except in the invention of electric light by Edison and the role of Westinghouse in the development of electric power. Most of the developments that made possible the networked house of urban America in 1929 were achieved by anonymous and decentralized innovations in home appliances, bathroom fixtures, toilets, and furnaces, not to mention the hundreds of municipal officials who approved and financed the evolution of urban sanitation infrastructure.

The revolutionary transformation of the American dwelling unit illustrates a major theme of the book—these were inventions that could happen only once. Although the diffusion of the modern conveniences took until 1929 to reach most of urban America and considerably longer to reach small towns and farms, after homes were equipped with these conveniences, the transformation was complete. Continuous economic growth required a continuous stream of new inventions. But consumer electric appliances had mostly been invented by 1940, and it was only a matter of time before most households would be equipped with them. With the exception of air conditioning, no post-1940 invention made anything like the quantum leap of change in everyday life—from physical hauling to flipping switches and turning faucet handles—as did the inventions discussed in this chapter.

Chapter 5

MOTORS OVERTAKE HORSES AND RAIL: INVENTIONS AND INCREMENTAL IMPROVEMENTS

> My heart was pounding. I turned the crank. The engine started to go "put put put," and the music of the future sounded with regular rhythm. We listened to it run for a full hour, fascinated, never tiring of the single tone of its song. The longer it played its note, the more sorrow and anxiety it conjured away from the heart.
>
> —Karl Benz, 1879, as quoted by Smil (2005, p. 99)

INTRODUCTION: TRANSPORTATION TAKES GIANT STRIDES FORWARD

Since the beginning of human history, the speed of travel had been limited by "hoof and sail." From the 1820s, steam power ended this tyranny of slowness, as the rapid development of railroads and steamship travel made the world smaller and, by reducing transport costs, created an upsurge in long-stagnant economic growth as well as new forms of commerce and communication. By our starting date of 1870, the United States had built a 60,000-mile network of rail transport and was connected by steamships to every continent. The completion of the transcontinental railway with the "golden spike" ceremony at Promontory Summit, Utah, on May 10, 1869, was heralded in chapter 2 as creating a dividing line in the history of American living standards.

The treatment of transportation in this chapter further develops the main themes of the book. The Great Inventions of the late nineteenth century created an utter transformation in both the rural and urban standard of living that could happen only once, though the transition after each of the Great Inventions was not instantaneous but rather spread out over many years. As demonstrated in chapter 4, the role of electricity, running water, sewer pipes, and central heating in bringing the "modern conveniences" to American dwelling units required the five decades from 1880 to 1930 to transform urban life, whereas most of the parallel conversion in rural American farm and nonfarm households still had not occurred by 1940 and awaited postwar peacetime prosperity.

The transition to higher speed, flexibility, and comfort in transportation was both slower and faster than that of the home conveniences. Just as chapter 4 treated multiple dimensions in housing across rural farm, rural nonfarm, urban, regional, and social class differences, so this chapter distinguishes separate dimensions of the transportation revolution. Intercity long-distance travel evolved slowly and was dominated by the steam railroad throughout 1870–1940, whereas intracity transport experienced a steady and relatively rapid transformation from horse omnibuses in the 1850s and 1860s through horse-drawn streetcars, cable cars, electrified streetcars, and rapid transit taking the form both of elevated and subway structures. By 1904, the electrified express trains of the New York City subway were traveling at forty miles per hour, more than ten times more quickly than the three miles per hour of the horse omnibuses only four decades earlier.[1]

But nothing in the millennia of human history, at least until the 1950–55 spread of television sets into the American home, rivals the speed with which automobile ownership spread in a mere two decades between 1910 and 1930 to the majority of American households. The invention and diffusion of the internal combustion engine utterly transformed the streets of the American city and town in those twenty years from rutted and pitted quagmires of mud, clogged with animal waste, to paved roads along which motor vehicles cruised just as they do today. And the transformation of urban streets is matched by the profound significance of the motor vehicle for the 30 percent of Americans who lived on farms in 1910. Though home-oriented modern conveniences were adapted much more rapidly in urban than in rural America, the automobile was accepted on the farm with unqualified enthusiasm even more rapidly than in the cities.

This chapter provides not just a chronicle of the measures of performance by which each new invention surpassed its predecessor, but also a tale of continuous incremental improvement of each new mode of transportation after its initial commercial introduction. Layer by layer, the comfort, speed, and safety of the passenger train ride in the 1930s was improved multifold from what superficially might seem to be the same mode of transportation in 1870. Layer by layer, the power, comfort, convenience, and speed of the automobile were improved multifold from its initial introduction in 1900 to its near-final form four decades later. Surface street public transport increased in speed and comfort layer by layer through successive improvements, particularly between 1860 and 1900. Each invention could happen only once, but the full working out of all the incremental improvements of these inventions required decades.

Starting in the 1840s and 1850s, the steam railroad made the stagecoach, canal boat, and paddle-wheel river steamboat obsolete almost as quickly as the rails were laid.[2] But except for commuter lines to suburban enclaves for the relatively rich, steam railroads never penetrated the internal passenger transportation needs of the city or solved the farmer's problem of transportation between the farm and the nearest train depot. Instead, urban and rural America before 1900 were subject to the tyranny of the horse. The horse was not only inefficient, eating up one-quarter of the nation's grain output, but also a source of urban pollution, disease, and occupational misery for the workers unlucky enough to have jobs in horse waste removal.[3]

Two transportation revolutions happened almost simultaneously. The urban public transportation transition began within a decade of Edison's epochal commercialization of the electric power generating station and distribution network. The transition from horse-drawn streetcars to electrified streetcars was fully complete in the United States between 1890 and 1902. New York's steam-powered elevated trains extended the length of Manhattan by 1880, Chicago's electrified elevated train structures were largely complete by 1897, and the first line in New York's farflung electrified subway system opened in 1904.

The second and simultaneous motor vehicle revolution began with the invention in Germany of a workable internal combustion engine in 1879, a mere ten weeks after Edison's successful electric light experiment. Initially attached to carriage-like vehicles, the internal combustion engine's promise for motor transportation required another decade in which to develop reliable mechanisms to transfer engine power through a transmission device to the wheels. In 1900, there were only 8,000 motor cars registered in the United States, but the number skyrocketed to 468,000 in 1910, 9 million in 1920, and 23 million in 1929. Most astonishing, the total power created by automobiles exceeded that of all farm animals as early as 1910.[4] A basic difference between the railroad and motor vehicle, viewed as fundamental inventions in the history of transportation, is that the railroad did not replace the horse but rather raised the demand for horses by extending civilization into hitherto unreachable parts of the country, whereas the motor vehicle directly replaced the horse and led to its disappearance as a prime mover.

This chapter views the transportation revolution of 1870–1940 from the point of view of consumer welfare, focusing on how the invention and development of new forms of transportation altered the nature of cities, the pattern of residential development, the relationship between the farm and the small town, and made possible new forms of work and recreation while greatly reducing rural isolation. These changes resulted from not just the initial effects of each invention, but also the ensuing dramatic improvements in speed and other quality attributes in subsequent decades. The speed of intercity railroad travel almost tripled between 1870 and 1940, whereas the development of a nationwide network of paved roads likewise increased the speed of automobile travel by a factor of at least five between 1905 and 1929.

The chapter is organized in terms of the chronological order of the invention, starting with the interurban railroads that were already substantially developed by 1870, followed by the role of horses in both the urban and rural economies. We document the transition from horse-drawn omnibuses and streetcars to electrified streetcars and rapid transit. Our treatment of the automobile, truck, and bus revolutions includes technological developments and quality changes that mattered to consumers, including complementary inventions such as highways, suburbs, supermarkets, and leisure travel, each of which shifted the demand curve for motor vehicles to the right and thus raised the consumer surplus associated with the initial invention.[5]

To limit the scope and length of the chapter, no attention is devoted to transatlantic steamships.[6] Riverboats and canal boats are also excluded, for they were largely obsolete for passenger travel by our starting date of 1870. Air travel had only begun in our terminal year of 1940, so the treatment of the evolution of airline passenger travel is reserved for chapter 11 in part II of the book.[7]

THE INTERURBAN STEAM RAILROAD: INITIAL PRIME MOVER OF ECONOMIC DEVELOPMENT

The American railroad network expanded so rapidly from 1840 to 1900 that any description of railroad travel or the benefits of railroads must specify exactly which year is being discussed. A map of railroad tracks for 1861 displays dense coverage of the Union states between Maine and Wisconsin, at least three mainline routes between New York and Chicago, but only a tentative entry into eastern Iowa and Missouri and nothing west of that. Railroad tracks were also sparse in the Confederate states.[8]

Perhaps Abraham Lincoln lacked knowledge of direct service between Chicago and New York when he traveled to give his epochal Cooper's Union speech in New York City on February 27, 1860.[9] He traveled by a circuitous route from Springfield, Illinois by way of Fort Wayne, Pittsburgh, and other intermediate stops. In contrast to the 825 miles between the two cities as the crow flies, Lincoln's journey extended over 1,200 miles and required five trains, two ferries, four days, three nights, and endless delays.[10] As a further example, train travel from Washington to New York in 1860 was not just a train trip but also a horse trip, requiring four separate train rides, three ferry rides, and seven separate horse rides between the trains and ferries.[11] The 31,000 miles of railroad completed in 1860 were not well connected, particularly because the gauge (width between the two rails of the track) was different in the south, in the north, and in Canada.

The nationwide adoption of standard gauge facilitated interline transfers of equipment that allowed passengers the convenience of traveling longer distances without the need to remove their luggage from trains or to wait for connecting trains on platforms or in drafty train stations. Even before gauge was standardized, the railroad network expanded rapidly. Railroad mileage is displayed in figure 5–1. Though few railroads were built during the Civil War, total mileage increased by a factor of five between 1870 and 1900. Nearly twenty new miles of track a day, on average, were built for thirty years. In contrast to the single transcontinental line from Omaha to Sacramento linked together in the historic 1869 ceremony, by 1893 there were seven transcontinental lines, of which three were relatively close together, traversing Kansas and Nebraska, and two were quite close together in their paths through the sparsely populated Dakotas and Montana.[12] The building of the transcontinental railroads is a tale of ambitious entrepreneurs, leverage and shady finance, and repeated business failures that twice contributed to financial panics that dragged the nation's economy into major depressions.[13] A common theme in commentaries on the late nineteenth-century railroad industry is "overbuilding," and indeed, by 1900 there were no less than six different railroad lines available to transport passengers from Chicago to Minneapolis or Omaha.[14]

Data on passenger-miles of railroad traffic are shown in figure 5–2. Excepting the extraordinary peak of traffic in World War II, the busiest decade for passenger traffic was 1911–20, whose average annual traffic of 38.1 billion passenger miles is dwarfed by the U.S. airline industry's 850 billion passenger miles in 2014.[15] Thus the average person in the 1911–20 decade traveled only

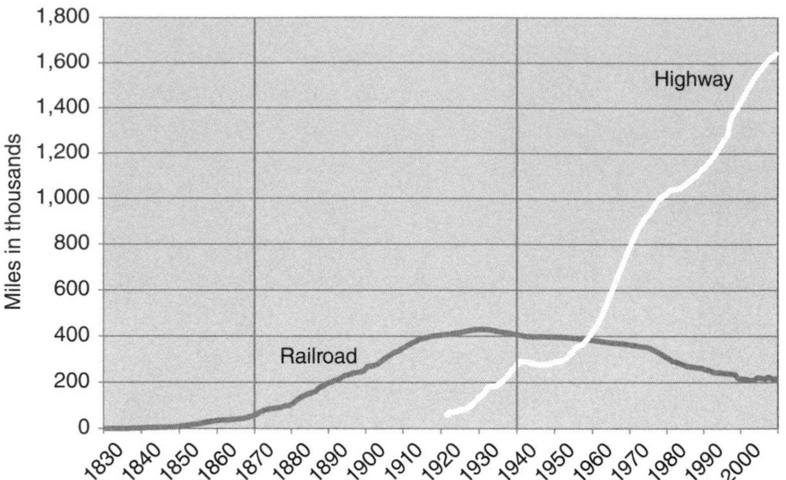

Figure 5–1. Total Railroad Track Operated and Paved Highway Mileage, 1830–2009

Sources: HSUS series Df213 and 214, Df 876, and Df931, SAUS, Fraumeni Highway Capital Stock data, and BEA Fixed Assets.

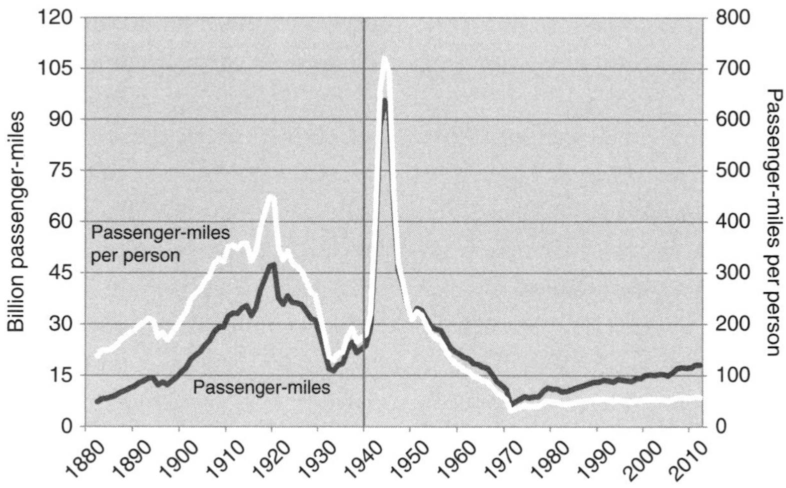

Figure 5–2. Railroad Passenger-Miles and Passenger-Miles Per Person, 1880–2012

Sources: HSUS series Df903, Df950, and Aa7, National Transportation Statistics Table 1-40.

379 miles by rail, whereas the average person in 2010 traveled 2,571 miles by air. After fluctuations caused by the Great Depression and World War II, rail passenger traffic per person experienced a steady decline in the postwar years and by 1958 had declined below the level of 1882.

The expansion of railroads in the central states in the 1850s and 1860s brought many benefits besides the sheer speed of the railroad when compared to horse or water transport.[16] The railroad routes were not constrained by the pre-existing locations of rivers but could be built in straight paths from city to city. The previous regime of canal and river boat traffic always required horse-drawn transport to reach the final destination, so the railroad eliminated the mud bogs that afflicted horse-drawn travel in the rainy seasons. Most important was the elimination of winter's effects in suspending commerce from December to April as the Midwestern rivers froze from St. Louis north, making the vast river network inaccessible to shipping commerce for those five months each year.

Abraham Lincoln was several years late in appreciating the introduction of rapid rail service between New York and Chicago, for 1852 marked the first year when travel from New York to Chicago was reduced from two weeks to less than two days.[17] However, the benefits of train travel went far beyond speed. Reliability was also a novelty, for previous travel modes, including canal and river transportation and horse-drawn coaches, could be delayed for hours or even days by "weather, accidents, or other hazards."[18] Not only did railroads change by an order of magnitude the speed of surface travel, but the ability to harness hundreds of horsepower in a single locomotive meant that much heavier loads in long trains could be transported, greatly reducing the cost of transport of both passengers and freight, all the more so when the value of time saving was taken into account.

James Cronon provides a classic contrast of the life of an Iowa merchant named Burroughs before and after the arrival of the Chicago and Rock Island line at the Mississippi River in 1854.[19] His pre-railroad business combined retail and wholesale trade in groceries, dry goods, and hardware, purchasing raw farm products directly from farmers, including sacks of grain, preserved meat, and a variety of fresh vegetables. Everything he bought or sold was received or shipped by river boat, but this could happen only for six or seven months per year, because the rivers froze for the rest of each year. Most of his time was spent trying to obtain information on the potential availability of buyers up and down the river, but news could travel only at the speed of a steamboat or horse.

The establishment of the first railroad between Chicago and Iowa in 1854 did not mean effortless connections to the east coast and New York. Only in 1870 did Commodore Vanderbilt, through agreements with other railroads that he did not own, establish the first through-train service between New York City and Chicago. By the early 1870s, the railroad and telegraph had utterly changed the life of Burroughs and merchants everywhere. News arrived hourly by telegraph and daily by railroad. Gone were the high costs not just of transport, but also of all the credit that had to be granted during the frozen six months when farm products could not be exported or finished goods imported from the east. In fact, Burroughs's business ultimately failed when his role of well-capitalized merchant charging high markups for credit, risk, and inventory storage gave way to the easier post-railroad conditions that allowed the entry of many merchants who did not require large amounts of capital and who could charge lower prices.

The arrival of the railroad and its elimination of seasonal travel restrictions was a gradual process. By subsequent standards, the technology of the first transcontinental railroad, joining the Central Pacific from Sacramento to Utah and the Union Pacific from Utah to Omaha, was primitive. The early locomotives could barely pull loads on the steep tracks that climbed over the Sierra Nevada of California, and winter snow and ice both there and on the Great Plains shut down the transcontinental route entirely for a month or more in the early years of the 1870s.[20]

As seen by the average household, the railroad had profound effects both on the farm and in the cities. Even before the Civil War, benefits for city dwellers began to appear—being able to travel to cities several hundred miles away to explore business opportunities, to consider moving, or to visit friends and relatives. As the 1860 Abraham Lincoln story indicates, railroads were often short-haul routes between nearby cities without reliable connections over long distances; but by 1870, long-distance travel became a practical option.

Far more important than the opportunity to travel was the role of the railroad in freight delivery. Steady supply by railroads reduced the volatility of prices previously caused by frozen rivers and slow horse transportation, and this in turn reduced the cost of goods and increased their variety. The quality and variety of food began to improve with the invention, in the 1880s, of the refrigerated railroad car. These early cars were not cooled mechanically but had slots for blocks of ice, which made possible the widespread distribution of fresh fruit and vegetables from California and refrigerated fresh-cut meat from the

Midwest. The refrigerated car made the beef industry much more efficient and eliminated the death marches in which herds of cattle had been driven on the hoof to large cities. Food quality and variety improved decade by decade, and contamination declined in tandem.

As the produce and meat flowed from the agricultural regions and stockyards, the abundance of modern manufactured goods traveled by rail freight cars from the industrial cities to the small towns and farms. As early as 1869, mail sorting cars on passenger trains were introduced, and by the end of the nineteenth century, these had reduced mail delivery times to one or two days within a given region of the country. Rural Free Delivery, introduced in 1892, and U.S. Mail Parcel Post service, introduced in 1913, greatly facilitated the meteoric rise of the mail-order catalog, which relied on the rail-driven mail to deliver catalogs to farmers and small town residents and orders from these customers back to the central catalog warehouses in Chicago.[21]

The growth of railroads and their influence on the standard of living is synonymous with Chicago's emergence as the world's fastest-growing city between 1870 and 1930. Cronon's (1991) account provides a fruitful organizing structure for the welfare benefits of railroads in the late nineteenth century. Railroads improved the standard of living of most Americans along many dimensions, and most of these can be illustrated with traffic flows into and out of Chicago. Because of the water barrier of Lake Michigan, every passenger or load of freight bound for Wisconsin, Minnesota, Iowa, or anywhere north or northwest had to travel through Chicago. By 1905, about 14 percent of the *world's* railway mileage passed through Chicago.[22]

In addition to its role in funneling to market fresh produce from California and fresh meat from the Chicago stockyards, Chicago was also central in the building of the new territories in the Great Plains, as lumber merchants floated wood logs from Wisconsin forests to Chicago sawmills that created the cut lumber that was then sent by rail to build the houses, barns, retail buildings, and grain elevators of the Great West. By 1889, the 400-square-mile Chicago switching district, twice the size of the Chicago city limits, served 5,000 industries, 160 freight yards, and seventy-six freight stations. By the turn of the century, 650 freight trains arrived in or left Chicago daily on thirty railroads.[23]

Throughout the small towns of America, the railroad depot became the center from which the business district and, beyond it, the residential area radiated. The depot contained the telegraph office with its possibilities of instant communication to distant locations. Trips that would rarely have been contemplated before the arrival of the railroad network became commonplace for countless passengers:

> Through the railroad depot came newlyweds departing on honeymoon trips, school classes off to the city, young men departing for war. There arrived traveling salesmen with valises filled with samples, wives returning from shopping excursions loaded down with bundles, and coffins of the deceased returned home for burial.[24]

We tend to think of rail travel as a standard commodity that remained the same between the time the rails were laid down in the late nineteenth century until the time after World War II, when passenger rail travel shriveled and died, at least in the United States. However, an examination of railroad timetables tells a surprising story about speed, which improved steadily from 1870 to 1940. Improvements came from mergers, interconnections, better switching, roller bearings, and eventually, in the 1930s, the conversion from inefficient steam locomotives to diesel–electric propulsion and air-conditioned passenger cars.

In the pre-computer age, planning rail trips relied heavily on *The Official Guide of the Railways*, which dates back to 1868. The guide provides a unique window on a world that no longer exists, at least within the United States, of an extremely dense railroad network that connected almost every city and town, no matter how small.[25] As an example of this density, the local train between Portland and Bangor, Maine, in 1900 made thirty-two stops along its 135-mile route (one stop every 4.2 miles) and required five hours to do so, for an average speed of twenty-seven miles per hour.

Table 5–1 displays for 1870, 1900, and 1940 distances, elapsed times, and speeds on a variety of different routes, arranged from shorter distances on the top to longer distances at the bottom of the table.[26] For each route, the elapsed time of the fastest train is listed, along with the slowest train providing direct service.[27] In 1870, the speeds were less than twenty-five miles per hour and in 1900 no faster than forty miles per hour, even on the fastest luxury express trains. Surprisingly, the average speed on the Santa Fe's limited-stop train from Chicago to Los Angeles in 1900, twenty-seven miles per hour, was barely faster than on the local from Portland to Bangor![28] Although these speeds seem slow in retrospect, they seemed like rocket travel to those whose previous options included canal travel at four miles per hour or stagecoaches at five to six miles per hour. In fact, the fastest horse travel that ever occurred over long distance

Table 5–1. Comparison of Times and Speeds on Selected Railroad Routes, 1870, 1900 and 1940

			1870		1900		1940		1870–1940	1900–1940
Railroad Company	Route	Mileage	Elapsed Time	Speed	Elapsed Time	Speed	Elapsed Time	Speed	Percent Change in Speed	
Maine Central	Portland-Bangor	135	5:58	22.6	4:00	36.0	3:20	40.5	58.4	11.9
					5:00	27.0	4:20	31.2		14.4
Wabash[1]	Chicago - St. Louis	286	13:50	20.7	7:51	36.4	5:15	54.5	96.9	40.2
					10:00	29.0	7:35	37.7		26.3
Pennsylvania	New York - Chicago	908	37:05[2]	24.5[2]	24:05	37.7	16:00	56.8	84.0	40.9
					27:50	32.6	17:00	53.4		49.3
NY Central	New York - Chicago	961	38:30	25.0	24:00	40.0	16:00	60.1	87.8	40.5
					25:00	38.4	20:00	48.1		22.3
Burlington	Chicago - Denver	1034			27:30	37.6	16:00	64.6		54.2
					33:10	31.2	20:20	50.9		49.0
Santa Fe	Chicago - Los Angeles	2227			83:00	26.8	39:45	56.0		73.6
							49:49	44.7		

Source: Official Guide of the Railways and Steam Naviation Lines of the United States, Puerto Rico, Canada, Mexico, and Cuba. Issues of Sept. 1900 and Sept. 1940 Selected data for September, 1870, taken from *Traveler's Official Railway Guide.*

Notes: Percentage changes in column (8) are calculated using natural logs.

1. Chicago-St. Louis 1870 data for St. Louis, Vandalia, and Terre Haute railway.

2. indicates 1880 not 1870.

was at nine miles per hour, achieved by the Pony Express, with frequent changes of horses and express riders who were recruited to be as lightweight as today's horseracing jockeys.[29]

Speeds increased markedly by 1940, both because new diesel equipment could travel faster and because prestige services were introduced that had fewer stops than before. The fastest of the routes shown was the Denver Zephyr, introduced in 1934, which traveled the 1,034 miles from Chicago to Denver, making twelve stops, at an average speed of 64.6 miles per hour. Almost as fast was the celebrated extra-fare Twentieth-Century Limited of the New York Central, covering 961 miles from New York to Chicago in sixteen hours. The route between Chicago and Los Angeles witnessed a doubling of speed, from twenty-seven miles per hour in 1900 to fifty-six miles per hour on the much-advertised Santa Fe "Super Chief" in 1940. Nevertheless, even in 1940, speeds and elapsed times fell far short of today's Japanese bullet trains and high-speed European rail.

Table 5–1, by featuring the fastest trains between selected destinations, distorts the world of rail travel in the 1870–1940 period. Travel was much slower for those who were traveling not between major cities but between small towns not on the same train line. Travel times in the year 1900 from one county seat to another, if they did not happen to be located on the same train line, usually involved origin-to-destination speeds of less than ten miles per hour.[30] Furthermore, the elapsed times for 1940 were also irrelevant for most travelers. There were supplemental charges for sleeping berths and even for individual trains such as the Twentieth Century Limited or Super Chief. The speeds attained were much slower on the ordinary trains that most passengers could afford. This suggests a little-discussed reason why air travel became so popular so rapidly after World War II—most air travel took the passenger from origin to destination either nonstop or with one or two stops along the way, in contrast to the multiple and frequent stops inherent in passenger rail travel.

The timetables reveal the Achilles' heel of rail travel that made it so vulnerable to competition from air travel after World War II. The fabled Super Chief ran only two days per week rather than daily. More important for movie stars and others who wanted the fastest route from New York to Los Angeles, the fastest New York to Chicago trains of both the New York Central and Pennsylvania Railroads arrived in Chicago at 8 a.m., whereas the Super Chief did not depart Chicago (from another station) until 7:15 p.m. This delay was taken for granted and led to booming business for Chicago merchants as well as for hotels, which rented rooms by the hour.

Leisure travel by rail was still dominant in the 1920s despite the emergence of the automobile, because roads for automobile travel remained primitive and the automobiles themselves were unreliable. Railroads advertised their ability to take people to multiple national parks on a single summer vacation and attracted schoolteachers and college students, some of whom worked in summer jobs at the parks. Passengers desperate to escape Prohibition in the 1920s could take advantage of the combined Havana Special train and steamboat service, which attracted thousands for weekends of drinking and gambling. Railroads also made it possible for families to establish summer homes on the shore in New England, Long Island, or New Jersey, as well as for fathers to maintain their weekday jobs while commuting to join their families on the shore on the weekends.

The railroads reached ever more remote destinations, provided more elaborate and comfortable train stations, and offered ever more through-train service with fewer transfers. But equally or more important from the passenger's viewpoint was the steady increase in comfort inside the train. In the late nineteenth century, immigrants were shipped west in filthy boxcars attached to freight or cattle trains. Wooden benches were the only place to sit, and the air was foul with the smell of food and tobacco. Robert Louis Stevenson in an 1879 essay offered a description of what he called "Noah's Ark on wheels." The immigrant cars on the Union Pacific

> are only remarkable for their extreme plainness... and for the usual inefficacy of the lamps, which often went out and shed but a dying glimmer even while they burned. The benches are too short for anything but a young child.... On the approach of night the boards are laid from bench to bench, making a couch wide enough for two, and long enough for a man of the middle height.[31]

So bad were conditions of travel in the 1870s that Lucius Beebe lamented "the American public rode to dusty destinies in regimented discomfort."[32] Train schedules were guesses more than guarantees, and connections were often missed, particularly in winter. "The old wood-burning locomotives belched cinders that pattered overhead like a hailstorm, and their smoke and steam engulfed the train until, at journey's end, the traveler found himself begrimed like a man who has worked all day at a blacksmith's."[33] American rail travel was less private than in Europe, where trains were divided up into enclosed compartments, typically seating six passengers.

Another danger of railroad travel in the 1870s and 1880s was the reliance on kerosene lighting and unreliable "cannonball" stoves used for heating. These made the frequent crashes much worse, as the wooden cars often telescoped (one car riding up over the next) and then burned. These perils were gradually eased after the introduction on the railroads of steam heating in 1881 and electric light in 1892.[34] A notable further step ahead in railroad comfort occurred in the 1930s, when the first overnight train with air conditioning was introduced in 1931.[35]

The introduction in the late 1860s of Pullman sleeping cars, which were attached to the long-distance passenger trains of every American railroad, was another major improvement. By 1925, Pullman cars accounted for one-third of the passenger miles carried by U.S. railroads and were served by 25,000 employees, most of whom were Pullman porters, the majority of whose income was received from tips.[36] From the point of view of passengers, the porters converted long-distance railroad travel into a civilized and comfortable mode of transportation. Porter duties included carrying baggage from the platform to the compartment, making up beds with fresh linens, showing passengers how to adjust heating (and later air-conditioning) controls, and satisfying a wide variety of passenger requests.[37] The Pullman cars continued to provide a standard level of comfort well into the period after World War II, when long-distance passenger rail travel was made functionally obsolete by the commercial airlines. The transition to diesel and electric-powered "streamliner" trains began with the Burlington's *Zephyr* in 1934; it combined air conditioning, reduced noise, faster speed, a better ride, and the elimination of smoke and cinders. The diesel engine produced four times as much work out of a pound of fuel as did the steam engine.[38]

Whether in primitive conditions in the 1870s, the more comfortable Pullman cars introduced in the late nineteenth century, or the sleek streamliners of the late 1930s, the epochal transformation of American life by the railroad went far beyond passenger comfort or safety. Its influence is conveyed by the conclusion to Holbrook's comprehensive history of the American railroad:

> The Classic Iron Horse spanned the continent in less than a man's lifetime, bound it with arteries that carried the blood of life into its most remote and inaccessible parts—that tamed its wildness, softened its savagery, and civilized its places and people as nothing else could have done. All of this was done so quickly that the world of reflective men has not yet ceased to marvel. This is what the Iron Horse did for America.[39]

THE COMMUTER RAILROAD, THE EMERGING SUBURBS, AND THE HORSE-DEPENDENT CITY

Before the Civil War, transportation within cities was so slow that housing could spread only a few miles from centers of employment. Rich employers lived quite close to their working-class employees; indeed, both walked to work. The "walking city" of the early nineteenth century was unlikely to be more than three miles in diameter, a distance that could be walked across in about an hour. This began to change with the arrival of the railroad, which provided to the rich and upper middle class an escape route from the teeming city. Starting in the 1850s, commuter railroads were established that followed the main intercity railroad corridors. Now the city began to appear not as a circle but as a star, its points representing the new suburbs established along the rail lines extending out from the city.[40]

Because the early commuter railroads were propelled by steam engines, they shared the discomfort of smoke and cinders, hazards that could be alleviated only by closing all the windows and suffocating on hot summer days. But fast steam-powered commuter rail service was a futuristic world apart from the conditions of public transit within the city in the late nineteenth century, where until 1890 the horse was the dominant prime mover of intracity passenger and freight transportation. Steam engines could not be used on city streets because of fear of fires started by sparks, deafening noise, thick smoke, and heavy weight that shook foundations and cracked street pavements. The main mode of transportation in Philadelphia between 1850 and 1880 was still walking for 80 percent of residents.[41] Movement about the city by any means other than walking depended on the horse.

Horse-drawn carriages for hire served as the nineteenth-century equivalent of the modern taxicab. Urban transit, whether the provider was privately owned or a public agency, had three characteristics that differentiated it from the taxi—reasonable price, fixed schedules, and predetermined routes. The earliest urban transit vehicle was the horse-drawn omnibus, a natural evolution of the stagecoach, which was approved for service initially in Paris in 1828 and London in 1832.[42] Omnibus service grew rapidly after its 1833 introduction in New York City and by 1853 the entrepreneur Jacob Sharp, soon to initiate streetcar service, counted 3,100 omnibuses passing Chambers Street on Broadway within thirteen hours, which translated into one every fifteen seconds.[43] Service spread rapidly in the 1840s and 1850s to most other large and medium-sized cities in the Northeast and Midwest.

The omnibus was expensive to run, for rutted and muddy streets created so much friction that three horses were typically required to haul a bus occupied by ten passengers. "It could take crews of men working with ropes and planks two days to rescue an omnibus that had slipped on the planking and into the quagmire" (Young, 1998, p. 36). The *New York Herald* opined in 1864, "Modern martyrdom may be succinctly described as riding in a New York omnibus."[44] Even in New York City there were few paved roads north of Forty-Second Street; "Beyond that was only a dreary waste of unpaved and ungraded streets with a scattering of squatters' shanties. Even in the built-up area there were many unpaved streets where passengers struggled through the mud to reach the horse-cars and omnibuses."[45]

The condition of New York City streets was one of several reasons why Rudyard Kipling concluded in 1892 about the city that "the more one studied it, the more grotesquely bad it grew." On the streets:

> Gullies, holes, ruts, cobble-stones awry, kerbstones rising from two to six inches above the level of the slatternly pavement; tram-lines from two to three inches above street level; building materials scattered half across the street; lime, boards, cut stone, and ash barrels generally and generously everywhere; wheeled traffic taking its chances, dray versus brougham, at cross roads; . . . and, lastly, a generous scatter of filth and more mixed stinks than the winter wind can carry away. . . . In any other land they would be held to represent slovenliness, sordidness, and want of capacity.[46]

Competition among drivers of competing companies led to collisions involving omnibuses, pedestrians, and horse-drawn wagons hauling merchandise. In 1853, a Philadelphia newspaper complained: "A ferocious spirit appears to have taken possession of the drivers, which defies law and delights in destruction."[47] As a result of the high ratio of horses to passengers, fares were high, typically twelve cents per ride in New York City at a time when working-class men earned only $1 per day. As a result, ridership mainly consisted of the upper middle class.

A substantial advance was achieved with the conversion in the 1840s and 1850s to horse-drawn street railways, which forced the omnibus off the streets in many cities. The new so-called horsecars combined the "low cost, flexibility, and safety of animal power with the efficiency, smoothness, and all-weather capability of a rail right-of-way."[48] Reduced friction enabled a pair of horses to pull thirty to forty passengers in a vehicle that had more inside room, an easier exit, and more effective brakes than the typical omnibus.[49] Average speeds doubled from three to six miles per hour.[50] Average fares for a single ride dropped from twelve cents to five cents.

Horsecars also introduced transit innovations that persist to this day, including a flat fare independent of distance, and multiple-ride books of tickets sold to commuters at a discount.[51] Still, only 17 percent of employed persons regularly rode the horsecars from home to work because of the expense. The apogee of the horse-drawn streetcar occurred in the 1880s, when more than 100,000 horses nationwide were engaged in pulling 18,000 streetcars on 3,000 miles of track.[52] More than any other development in transportation, the horse-drawn streetcars made possible the separation of residence and workplace, a major change in the arrangement of cities that occurred primarily in the last half of the nineteenth century.

Though horsecars were an advance over the horse-drawn omnibus, the conditions faced by passengers were primitive by modern standards. The cars were without heat or light, and "crews put a foot of hay or straw on the floor in winter to help riders keep their feet warm."[53] Initial attempts to place heaters under the floors were rejected after a number of fires resulted.[54] Furthermore, as American cities grew and a gridlock of intersecting horsecar lines developed in cities like Chicago, criticism focused on the inherent defects of the horse itself as a machine of propulsion. Horses dropped thousands of tons of manure and gallons of urine on city streets; died in service, leaving 7,000 horse carcasses to be carried away each year in Chicago alone; and carried diseases transmissible to humans.

> The smell of manure heaps and the clouds of flies they attracted were some of the most objectionable nuisances stables created. The nuisance was especially bad in the summer.... On New York's Liberty Street there was a manure heap seven feet high. New York streets...were often covered with layers of manure.[55]

REPLACING THE HORSE: CABLE CARS, ELECTRIFIED STREETCARS, AND RAPID TRANSIT

The search for a replacement of the horse preoccupied individual entrepreneurs and city planners in the last half of the nineteenth century. The most obvious solution was the steam railroad, but we have already seen that this was not suitable for use on city streets. An initial replacement for the horse-drawn streetcars was the cable car, where the motive power came from a steam boiler that generated the power to pull the cables though grooves under the street. Cable cars are always associated with San Francisco, where they began service in 1873 as a response to the difficulty of horses in pulling loads up the steep San Francisco hills.[56]

In fact, the largest cable car system in the late nineteenth century was established in Chicago in 1882, and the motivation was not hills but the desire to draw longer trains with larger loads than was possible with horses.[57] Also the cable car could travel at nine to ten miles per hour, almost double the speed of a horse-drawn streetcar.[58] At its peak, the Chicago system extended over eighty-six miles of cable tracks and was powered by thirteen large steam engines; it played a major role in extending the residential reach of the city. It was estimated at the time to have "removed from a street the voidings of two or three thousand horses."[59]

The peak of the cable car's role occurred on October 23, 1893, when on a single day the Chicago cable car system hauled 700,000 people to and from the Columbian Exposition.[60] Over their brief fifteen-year hegemony in Chicago, cable cars accelerated the outward reach of the city; whenever a cable line replaced a horsecar line, property values increased by 30 percent to 100 percent.[61] But the cable cars did not last long. They had disappeared from the streets of most cities by 1900 and from Chicago by 1906, and they remain to this day only in the single city of San Francisco, where they are primarily a tourist attraction.

Just as the cable network in Chicago and elsewhere was expanding rapidly in the 1880s, the far more efficient option of electric traction became feasible. The central entrepreneur who guided the electric revolution was Frank J. Sprague, an Englishman who, after briefly working for Thomas Edison, was lured to Richmond, Virginia, to devise a system of electric streetcars capable of climbing that city's hills. It was Sprague who perfected the distribution of power from central stations via overhead wires to flexible "trolleys" that would move back and forth to maintain their grip on the overhead wire and maintain a continuous flow of electric power to the motor installed underneath the streetcar platform. After Sprague demonstrated his system's success with so-called trolley cars, the rush was on to electrify the streetcars of America.[62] Within two years of the implementation of Sprague's successful Richmond system, more than 200 electrified streetcar systems were operating across the country. Between

1895 and 1930, the vast majority of urban transit passengers were carried on electric streetcars, and even in 1940, the motorized bus had not yet caught up in its passenger share.

The total of electrified trackage recorded by the first national census of streetcars in 1890 was already 1,260 miles, or roughly 17 percent of the total trackage of the streetcar industry (including horse-drawn, cable-drawn, and electrified). By 1902, total trackage had tripled, and the share that was electrified had exploded to 98 percent of the total. The era of the trolley car had begun. Because electric power was brought into each streetcar by its overhead trolley, power was available not just for traction, but also to provide electric interior lighting and heat. By 1902, nearly 5 billion passengers annually rode the streetcars, compared to 2 billion in 1890.[63]

Despite the efficiency of electricity-powered streetcars, they were still subject to urban congestion, for they all operated at street level along with horse-drawn delivery wagons, private carriages, and horse-drawn taxis. Many photos of downtown Chicago in the 1890–1910 era display complete gridlock, and in one photo fourteen streetcars are visible on a single city block.[64] The convergence of streetcar lines into the center of each city's downtown core made possible the primacy of the urban department store, which tended to be located near the hub of the trolley lines. This central streetcar hub of the city, whether State Street in Chicago or Herald Square in Manhattan, not only brought customers to the grand department stores such as Marshall Field's and Macy's, but also was "surrounded by new skyscrapers made possible by structural steel, the elevator, electric light, ventilation systems, and telephone networks."[65]

The solution to congestion in densely packed U.S. cities emerged from London, where the Metropolitan Railway underground line opened its service with steam engine propulsion in 1863. By definition, an underground or overhead "elevated" service could bypass all traffic congestion on the surface. New York's elevated trains predated electricity and by 1876 with steam propulsion were running forty trains a day from the Battery to Fifty-Ninth Street, and by 1880, four elevated lines had reached the northern tip of Manhattan.[66] Chicago's elevated trains followed sixteen years later when elevated tracks opened for service in 1892, intended to allow small steam engines to bring visitors to the 1893 Columbian Exposition. For the 1893 fair itself, a three-mile elevated loop circled the fairgrounds, the first to be propelled by electric motors located under the carriages, which drew power from an adjacent third rail.[67]

While these elevated tracks were demolished immediately after the fair, by 1896 pre-existing elevated lines powered by steam had been converted to electric traction using third-rail power. The very same Frank Sprague who had invented the overhead trolley system for electric streetcars was instrumental in the development of the "multiple-unit" system of propulsion for rapid transit elevated and underground trains, which used no locomotive but rather electric motors underneath multiple interconnected passenger cars, allowing rapid stopping and starting. The most important aspect of this innovation was that although some cars had motors and some did not, all the cars with motors could be controlled by a single motorman. Automatic closure of the doors came later; early elevated and subway trains had one conductor for every two cars to open and close the doors manually.[68]

Just as horsecars were an improvement over the early omnibus, so elevated trains were an improvement over the horsecar and, for speed, over the electric streetcar. Yet just as horsecars suffered from the inherent defects of the horse, the elevated trains also had their disadvantages. The elevated structures blocked out the sun and sky and darkened the streets below, and the constant passing of trains on overhead rails created an incessant and unpleasant barrage of noise.

Since the opening of the London underground in 1863, American inventors had attempted to gain public support for an underground system. Finally the first underground system opened—not in New York but under Tremont Street in Boston, in 1897. Along its four tracks could travel 400 streetcars an hour, double the capacity of the surface street before the subway was built. In its first year, it carried 50 million passengers along its length of less than two miles.[69] As predicted by its promoters, it immediately reduced congestion in the city streets above. "The effect was like that when a barrier is removed from the channel of a clogged river," wrote the *Boston Daily Globe* soon after the opening.[70]

The first New York City subway line opened in 1904 and was a more ambitious project, extending fifteen miles from city hall to the northern limits of the city. Built from the beginning with four tracks, its express trains traveled at forty miles per hour between stops, much more quickly than streetcars and also more quickly than the competing elevated lines, which were limited to twelve miles per hour.[71] By 1940, the New York City subways and remaining elevated trains facilitated 3 billion of the 5 billion annual journeys on public transit in that city, and as of 1940, it was still possible to ride a subway train all the way from Coney Island to the Bronx for a mere five cents.[72]

No discussion of public transit during 1870–1940 is complete without a separate treatment of the "interurbans," which combined the faster speeds of steam railroads in carrying passengers between adjacent cities with the flexibility of the electric motor. Interurbans had two advantages over the steam railroad. First, their routes combined surface travel within the city with high-speed travel between cities; second, their electric traction was much cheaper to operate than a steam locomotive. The first lines were established soon after the invention of the trolley car, in 1891 between Minneapolis and St. Paul, and by 1905, the interurbans were ubiquitous. In that year the Pacific Electric interurban connected forty-two cities and towns in the Los Angeles area. By 1910, all but 187 of the miles between Chicago and New York City were connected by a host of different but interconnecting interurban lines.[73]

By 1925, public transit in the United States had reached its peak of 383 annual rides per person in cities of 25,000 in population or more, not including those who traveled on steam railroads and the interurbans. The streetcars had an 85 percent share of transit ridership in 1922, which fell to 50 percent by 1940. The share of rapid transit (elevated and subways) was barely changed, whereas the combined shares of the motor bus and trolley coach jumped from 3 percent to 36 percent.[74] Except for the years of World War II, when tires and gasoline were rationed, public transit would never again attain the peak ridership reached between 1913 and 1923. The gradual decline of transit was largely but not entirely owing to the availability of ever cheaper and better automobiles. Also contributing to the decline was a cost squeeze, for many public transit franchises were forced by contract to charge a nominal fixed fare of five cents, which made many operations uneconomic after the general price level rose by 74 percent between 1913 and 1923, another example of the standard economic indictment of price controls. By the end of World War I, one-third of all transit companies were bankrupt.

THE AUTOMOBILE ARRIVES: ITS IMMEDIATE BENEFITS

Few inventions in human history have equaled the internal combustion engine in their effects. Inventors had experimented for much of the previous century attempting to develop a self-propelled engine based on coal-produced gas. By 1876, Nicolaus Otto had developed a four-stroke compression engine, but it did not develop enough power to be suitable for transportation. In one of the greatest coincidences in the history of technology, the successful trial of a two-stroke engine by Karl Benz on New Year's Eve of 1879 occurred just ten weeks after Edison's epochal success in developing the electric light bulb on October 22 (see the epigraph opening this chapter).

By 1886, Benz had developed a four-stroke successor to the original engine and mounted it on a three-wheel chassis, the very first horseless carriage. But unlike Edison's discovery, which illuminated department stores and powered streetcars within its first few years, the internal combustion engine took longer to make a noticeable dent in everyday activities. And also unlike Edison's made-in-America discoveries, most of the seminal inventions of the internal combustion engine and the motor car were made in Europe, particularly in Germany, during the late nineteenth century.

Just as the railroads required a series of technical improvements between 1830 and 1850, so the automobile benefited from a sequence of developments before its emergence around 1910 as a dominant form of transportation and a driving force in the leap to supremacy of America's standard of living. Over the period 1890–1910, a host of challenges were surmounted that seem mundane today but that were crucial to the future of the motorcar industry. Steering was achieved by linking the two front wheels with a rod so that they moved in unison. The engine was moved from under the carriage-like seat to the front of the vehicle, which provided room for ever larger engines. Spark plugs, carburetors, transmissions, and self-starters were invented and gradually improved. Solutions to many mundane problems had already been solved during the 1890s by the mass production of the bicycle, including the development of cold-rolled steel, accurately machined gears, ball and needle bearings, and pneumatic tires; between 1887 and 1894, twenty-four U.S. patents were issued for the rubber tire and the crucial problem of its adherence to a metal wheel.[75]

By 1906, Wilhelm Maybach had developed a six-cylinder engine that approximated the power of today's four-cylinder compact cars such as the Honda Civic. Such was the speed of invention that an approximate (albeit clumsy and heavy) replica of today's modern cars could have been produced within a mere two decades after the invention of the internal combustion engine. This is a classic example of a theme of this book—that many inventions are one-time-only events subject to a long succession of subsequent incremental improvements.

Historians have long recognized that "the automobile is European by birth, American by adoption."[76] It is ironic that the development of the automobile as an inexpensive vehicle for mass transportation was dominated by Americans, particularly Henry Ford and other pioneers, yet the early development of the internal combustion engine and the automobile was dominated by Germans: Benz, Otto, Daimler, and Maybach, with a French role for Peugeot and Levassor. The shift of automobile innovation from Germany to the United States in the 1900–1910 decade reflected not only the retirement or death of the leading German entrepreneurs at that time, but also the frenetic attempts by American entrepreneurs to copy the technical advances that had been achieved by Mercedes and other German automakers.[77]

The automobile took off slowly at the beginning, with just 8,000 U.S. registrations in 1900 and 78,000 in 1905.[78] Travel was difficult for longer than the shortest distances; a Vermont doctor and his chauffeur were the first to succeed in driving a car across the country from San Francisco to New York, but it took them sixty-three days.[79] The slow initial adoption of the automobile is consistent with a 1906 survey by the Minneapolis city engineer's department, which counted vehicles in ten different twenty-four-hour periods. "Mean daily figures were 2,722 horse-drawn vehicles (fully two-thirds trotting), less than 3 horse riders, 786 bicyclists, and only 183 automobiles."[80]

The minimal number of individual horse riders reflected the high initial and maintenance cost of horses. But the transition was extremely rapid. By 1917, a similar survey in Pittsburgh counted twice as many motor-powered vehicles as horse-drawn, and by 1927, "the downtown had begun to look, sound, and smell like the downtown of today; almost fifty times as many gasoline powered as horse-drawn vehicles entered."[81] The small town of Oregon, Illinois, was apparently further ahead than Pittsburgh when a similar count in 1916 registered a greater than five to one advantage of motorized vehicles over horse-drawn, 1,171 to 215.[82]

The automobile was instantly superior to the horse-drawn carriage and replaced horse-drawn vehicles as soon as horse owners could afford to buy the new "horseless carriages." The limitations of the horse went beyond its piles of manure. Horses could pull vehicles only at around six miles per hour and had a range of no more than twenty-five miles before a given horse became exhausted and had to be replaced.[83] The early development of the automobile exhibits several parallels to that of electricity. Both of these "great inventions" faced initial competition—electricity for lighting had to compete with coal gas, electrified streetcars had to compete with horsecars, interurban electrified trains had to compete with steam trains, and even electric elevators had initial competition from pneumatic elevators. In the same way, motor transport had to overcome competition from electric streetcars and interurban trains, not to mention steam-powered long-distance trains. Before internal-combustion technology became dominant after 1905, it had to compete with attempts to develop competing steam-powered or electric-powered motor vehicles.

Much of the enthusiastic transition away from urban mass transit to automobiles reflected the inherent flexibility of the internal combustion engine—it could take you directly from your origin point to your destination with no need to walk to a streetcar stop, board a streetcar, often change to another streetcar line (which required more waiting), and then walk to your final destination. Whether it was faster didn't matter, for it eliminated the need to wait for streetcars and, particularly, to haul packages, which instead could be placed on the back seat of the motorcar. "The twentieth-century urban ridership despised fixed rail transit."[84] The dream of freedom and country living made possible by the automobile was evident to an observer as early as 1904:

> Imagine a healthier race of workingmen who, in the late afternoon, glide away in their own comfortable vehicles to their little farms or houses in the country or by the sea twenty or thirty miles distant! They will be healthier, happier, more intelligent, and self-respecting citizens because of the chance to live among the meadows and flowers of the country instead of in crowded city streets.[85]

THE FIRST DECADES OF THE AUTOMOBILE: PRICES PLUMMET AS QUALITY TAKES OFF

In its first decade, the automobile was owned mainly by the wealthy, who could choose from a cornucopia of designs, each manufactured in small quantities. Table 5–2 traces the epochal progress in reducing the price and raising the quality of automobiles during the 1906–40 interval. The left column provides data on the best-selling car of 1903–5, the Oldsmobile curved-dash runabout, and the rows below provide the price of the lowest-priced model together with basic specifications. The next rows below the line provide alternative measures of quality and quality-adjusted price, including weight divided by horsepower, price divided by weight, a quality index based on a weighted average of horsepower and weight, and a quality-adjusted price index.[86] The bottom section of the table compares both raw prices and quality-adjusted prices to personal disposable income per person as a measure of the affordability of automobiles over this interval of nearly four decades.

Table 5–2. Specifications, Prices, Quality Adjustments, and Disposable Income for Selected Best-Selling Auto Models, 1906–1940

Year	1906	1910	1923	1928	1934	1940
Make	Oldsmobile	Ford	Ford	Ford	Chevrolet	Chevrolet
Model	Model B	Model T	Model T	Model A	Std. Series DC	Master 85
Body Type	Standard Runabout	Touring	2-dr. Runabout	2-dr. Standard	2-dr. Coach	2-dr. Sedan
	(1)	(2)	(3)	(4)	(5)	(6)
Price ($)	650	950	269	480	580	659
Weight (lb)	700	1200	1390	2050	2995	2865
Horsepower (HP)	7	22	20	40	60	85
Revolutions per minute (rpm)	600	1600	1600	2200	3000	3400
Cu. in. displacement	95.5	176.7	176.7	200.5	181	216.5
Length (wheelbase, in.)		100	100	103.5	112	113
Weight/HP	100	55	70	51	50	34
Price/weight	0.93	0.79	0.19	0.23	0.19	0.23
Quality index	100	132	137	179	232	248
Quality-adjusted price	650	722	196	268	250	266
Nominal disposable income (NDI) per capita	263	301	623	643	418	582
Price/NDI per capita	2.47	3.16	0.43	0.75	1.39	1.13
Quality-adjusted price/NDI per capita	2.47	2.40	0.31	0.42	0.60	0.46

Sources: Kimes and Clark (1996). NDI after 1929 from NIPA table 2.1. NDI before 1929 from HSUS 1965 series F9.

The automobile revolution began in earnest with the appearance of Henry Ford's Model T, which began production in late 1908 and continued in production until 1927. The second column of table 5–2 lists the introductory Model T of 1909–10, which was introduced at a price of $950. The genius of Ford's design combined several elements. The car had relatively high horsepower (22 horsepower) for its weight (1,200 pounds), its gear torque allowed it to pull itself through mud that would have stranded heavier vehicles, its unique two-pedal planetary transmission eliminated the need to shift gears, and it was simple and easy to service by farmers, who had ready access to parts through mail-order catalogs. It was "sturdy, reliable, and easy to drive by the standards of the time."[87]

At least superficially, the quality measures in the middle rows of table 5–2 do not provide evidence of a quantum leap for the Model T. Though its ratio of weight to horsepower improved radically and its quality index was 32 percent higher, its price was also higher, making its quality-adjusted price actually higher than that of the 1906 Oldsmobile. But this ignores the unique ability of the Model T's design to handle dirt roads, a feature that endeared it to the nation's farmers and that helped account for its overwhelming success. And before long, its price declined far below that of any other automobile even as its quality continued to improve. Whereas previous cars had been unable to push the weight-to-horsepower ratio below 80-1, Ford's lightweight design achieved a new frontier at 55-1, as shown in table 5–2. The efficiency of the light weight and high-power design was demonstrated when in 1909 a Model T "defeated a stable of heavier, pricier touring automobiles in a 4,100-mile race from New York to Seattle."[88]

Ford's special place in U.S. entrepreneurial history went beyond design, for it was his production innovations that allowed him to reduce the price by so much. At his famous Highland Park factory, which opened on January 1, 1910, he adopted vertical integration, including the making of most parts in house. By 1913, the moving assembly line made mass production a reality, breaking up the labor processes into repetitive motions as the cars slowly moved past each worker performing his task. Also by 1913, Ford had established a network of almost 7,000 dealers and reached small towns having as few as 2,000 inhabitants; 65 percent of Ford dealers were in rural areas.[89] After the Model T became ubiquitous, its unique network of dealers and service stations selling tires, batteries, spare parts, and the cars themselves created the same sort of networking advantage that Apple and Android enjoy today in their smartphone duopoly.

The differences between the quality attributes of the Model T and any post-1925 car are as night and day. The driver of the Model T

> [c]limbs in by the right-hand door for there is no left-hand door... sets the spark and throttle levers... then he gets out to crank. Seizing the

crank in his right hand carefully he slips his left forefinger through a loop of wire that controls the choke. He pulls the lop of wire, he revolves the crank mightily, and as the engine at last roars, he leaps to the trembling running board, leans in, and moves the spark and throttle.[90]

The quality of the Model T did not stand still just because it maintained the same model number designation for twenty years. Even as the price declined, accessories that were once available only at extra expense became standard by 1915, including headlights, windshields, a top, a horn, and a speedometer.[91] Electric starters had begun to replace the hand crank and were universal by 1921.[92] Today one is puzzled at the automobile advertisements from the 1910–25 period, almost all of which display topless vehicles without permanent covers.[93] Only 10 percent of cars were covered with canvas or metal roofs in 1919, but closed-top vehicles rapidly took over, including closed-top versions of the Model T, and comprised 43 percent of automobile sales in 1924 and 85 percent in 1927. Throughout the era when the Ford lacked widely desired accessories, a giant after-market developed to sell new steel fenders for safety and streamlined style, as well as tops, radiator hoods, and mundane items such as a gas gauge.[94] By the early 1920s, the Sears catalog offered 5,000 different accessory items for the Model T.[95]

Mass production kept the price of the Model T much lower than that of most competing cars, and its price in both nominal and real terms continued to decline throughout its two-decade production run, during which 15 million Model T Fords were produced. In fact, by 1914, the Model T had taken over 46 percent of the U.S. market for new automobiles, rising to almost 55 percent in its peak year of 1923, when 1.8 million were produced and sold.[96] Table 5–2 compares the 1910 and 1923 Model T's in adjacent columns. There was little change in specification except for an increase in weight owing to the conversion of previously optional features to standard equipment. The big change was the sharp drop in price from $950 to $269 for a car that was heavier and better in almost every dimension. The ratio of price to weight fell by 76 percent and the quality-adjusted price by 73 percent.

However after 1923, the sales of the Model T began to decline, for twenty years of innovation had made it possible for competing firms, especially General Motors, to build faster, more powerful, and more comfortable vehicles. Partially meeting the demands of its critics, Ford's replacement for the Model T, called the Model A, included many features previously lacking, including shock absorbers, a windshield wiper, combination tail lights and brake lights, bumpers, and an instrument panel featuring a speedometer, oil and gas gauges.[97] The 1928 Ford Model A boosted the quality index from 137 to 179, though it also resulted in an increase in the quality-adjusted price from $196 to $268, in part because of many improvements that went beyond horsepower and weight.

Table 5–2 displays data for two other models that were leading sellers, the 1934 and 1940 Chevrolets. The latter model had eighty-five horsepower, within striking distance of today's compact cars, and a quality index, compared to the 1906 Oldsmobile, of 248. The price-to-weight ratio was only slightly higher than that of the 1923 Model T, despite myriad improvements beyond higher weight, and the quality-adjusted price was about the same as that of the 1928 Model A Ford. The 1940 Chevrolet was a modern car in its ability to travel as fast as road quality would allow, even if it lacked the automatic transmission, air conditioning, and other amenities now standard on all cars. It represented a quantum leap in quality not only from the 1906 Oldsmobile runabout, but also from the Model T.[98]

Figure 5–3 summarizes the behavior of automobile prices for the top-selling models listed in table 5–2. The white line shows the raw unadjusted price, which traces the decline in the Model T price from 1910 to 1923 followed by the increase in price of the Model A Ford and the two Chevrolets. But

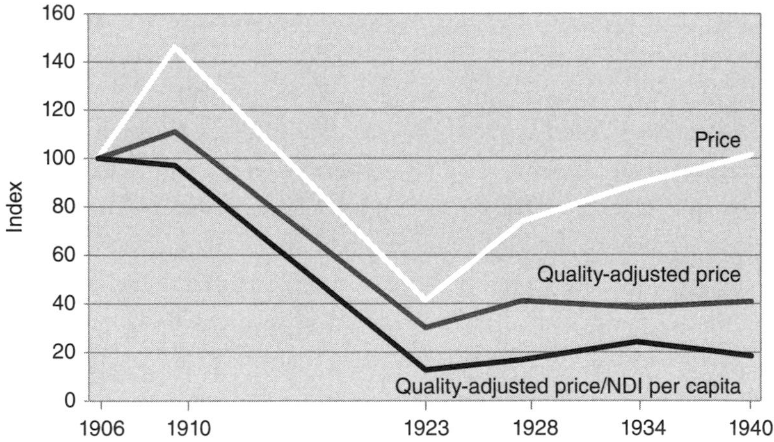

Figure 5–3. Prices of Selected Automobile Models, with or without Quality Adjustment, and Relative to Nominal Disposable Income per Capita, 1906–1940

Sources: See table 5–2.

all this increase in price after 1923 was offset by higher quality, so the quality-adjusted price remains unchanged after 1923. Finally, the black line shows an even greater decline in the ratio of the quality-adjusted price to nominal disposable income per person, demonstrating that much of the rapid adoption of the automobile between 1910 and 1929 reflected a substitution response to a rapid decline in price relative to income.

AUTOMOBILES AND PAVED ROADS: CHICKEN AND EGG

The most important hindrance to the development of motor transport was the lack of paved roads. The revolutionary 1901 Mercedes, commonly called the "first modern automobile," sold in the United States at the price of $12,450 in an era when the average annual income was less than $1,000, and it could cruise at a speed of fifty miles per hour, faster than the elapsed railroad times for 1900 shown in table 5–1. But it could only reach that speed on roads that were smoothly paved.[99] European cars, including those imported to the United States, placed the chassis close to the road to increase stability during rapid cornering. But these European cars were almost useless on American roads, which were described in 1903 as "simply two deep ruts, with a stony ridge in the middle on which the car bottom will drag."[100]

The first few years of the twentieth century saw political gridlock about paving rural roads, in part because of the free-rider problem. Residents of one county worried that if their county paved its roads, residents of an adjacent county would take advantage of them without paving its own.[101] The attire of the average country automobile driver reflected the condition of the roads: "Sheets and hats were worn and travel bags were wrapped in blankets to keep out the dust... extreme cold, snow, rain, and dryness made travel unpleasant as well as unpredictable. Flat tires and blowouts were common."[102]

However, some authors suggest that road building came earlier and made possible the automobile, a contrast to the usual view that the development of the automobile spurred road building. One impetus for road building was the craze for the bicycle in the 1890s, with its encouragement of individual freedom to explore. Another impetus to the development of better roads was the introduction by the U.S. Postal Service of Rural Free Delivery, starting in 1899, and rural parcel delivery, starting in 1913. RFD was an important source of pressure for road improvements, for the post office refused to deliver mail unless roads were of a certain minimum quality. "If good roads were necessary for RFD, then farmers agitated for good roads."[103] Thus the public outcry for good roads antedated the automobile: "Though the people promoting good roads wanted to improve recreation and rural culture, they had to center their efforts on horses and work."[104]

America's 2 million miles of roads in 1904 were largely dirt tracks connecting farms to towns. "If all the hard-surfaced roads in the nation had been laid end to end in 1900, they would not have stretched from New York to Boston."[105] In the entire state of Illinois in 1900, there were only twenty-six miles of surfaced rural roads.[106] A full census of roads as of December, 31, 1914 tallied up a total of 29,000 miles of "good roads" and 257,000 miles of "surfaced roads"—which usually meant gravel.[107]

Figure 5–1, introduced above to display railroad mileage, also exhibits the history of the development of fully paved highway mileage. The Federal Aid Road Act of 1916 began federal support of road construction, and continuous records of American highway mileage are available back to 1923. In the early 1920s, improved highway mileage was barely 20 percent of railroad mileage, but the rapid growth (particularly in the interstate highway construction era of 1956 to 1975) left railroad mileage in the dust. The measure of highway mileage here is weighted by capital expenditure and thus counts a four-lane interstate highway with interchanges as having twice or more the mileage of a two-lane paved rural road of equal length.[108]

The development of roads did not just involve added mileage of paved roads. Other innovations came early. The technology of road building steadily improved between 1900 and 1930 and included the development of asphalt and concrete as durable road surfaces.[109] Numbered highways began in Wisconsin in 1918, the white center line in the middle of the highway dates back to Michigan in 1911, the stop sign was first used in Detroit in 1915, and the modern three-color electric traffic signal was fully developed between 1910 and 1920. The first road atlas, once much more necessary than today to report to drivers on the improved and unimproved conditions of specific routes, was introduced in 1926.[110] In that same year, a uniform route numbering system was introduced, ranging from the designation of the Atlantic Coast Highway as U.S. 1, its Pacific Coast counterparts as U.S. 99 and 101, the Lincoln Highway as U.S. 30, and the old National Road (first developed from Maryland to Ohio in the 1830s) as U.S. 40.

Nevertheless, unpaved highways continued to be a hazard throughout the 1920s. A U.S. map for 1926 that distinguishes between paved and unpaved highways looks almost identical to a map of the U.S. railroad system in 1861;

there were virtually no paved roads west of the Mississippi river except along the Pacific coast.[111] On these unpaved roads, just as mud was a hazard from fall through winter and spring, so dust was a constant nuisance in the summer.

Nevertheless, the federal aid program during the 1920s and 1930s rapidly covered the nation with a network of two-lane paved highways that allowed drivers to travel from coast to coast on designated major routes without encountering a stretch of rutted unpaved road. The 1930s witnessed the construction of multilane engineering marvels, including the George Washington, Golden Gate, and Bay Bridges, as well as the beginning of multilane limited-access turnpikes, including the Merritt Parkway in southern Connecticut and the first section of the Pennsylvania Turnpike. These anticipated, and in some cases became part of, the postwar Interstate Highway System.[112] As of 1940, a map of the principal routes of the U.S. highway system looks virtually identical to a map of today's Interstate Highway System, except that most of the roads were two-lane with intersections rather than featuring limited access.[113]

AUTOMOBILES REPLACE THE HORSE AND PUBLIC TRANSIT

Despite the overnight conversion from horsecars to electrified streetcars in the 1890s, the national population of horses grew by 25 percent in the 1890s, for horses remained the primary means of power in both urban commerce and rural agriculture. The continued role of horses despite the invention of steam railroads and urban electric streetcars reflected a technological complementarity. Steam railroads and urban electric streetcars had the same limitation—fixed rails. As the economy grew, it was still dependent on the horse for the flexible travel to any final destination, a role that would be supplanted by motor transport starting in 1900. The inconvenience, filth, and disease caused by horses was everywhere to be seen:

> Horses were ubiquitous in the urban landscape: standing, walking, trotting, sometimes shying, starting, falling, rearing, plunging, or bolting. They were large beings with which to share space…the smells of manure, sweat, and horsehair mingled with other urban smells of garbage, human waste, and industrial production. Horses contributed to the symphony of urban noise—hooves clattering and scrapping on the streets, wagons rattling and banging, wheels creaking, harnesses jingling, horses whinnying, neighing, groaning, and bugling.[114]

Within a decade the electric streetcar had replaced the horsecar. It took longer for the automobile to replace public transit, but the initial threat of the automobile to the established fixed-rail regime was already widespread by 1910 in the form of the "jitneys," unlicensed taxicabs which operated in a free-for-all to cruise the routes of the streetcars and pick up passengers, especially those loaded with packages. The streetcar operators were particularly irked to see that the jitneys paid no taxes and faced no regulations.[115]

The first motor bus arrived on New York's 5th Avenue in 1905, but the development of the motor bus was surprisingly slow. The initial bus designs were converted trucks, with a center of gravity high off the ground. The first motor bus approximating modern design was introduced by the Fageol brothers in Oakland, California, in 1920 in the form of the "Fageol Safety Coach." Its platform and seats were close to the ground, requiring only one or two steps for entry. Springs were designed for passenger comfort, previously unnecessary in the trucks from which earlier buses were adopted.[116]

Though the motor bus was slow to appear, its adoption was rapid after 1920. The benefits over streetcars lay not only in the obvious lack of need to build expensive tracks and the ability of a bus to travel anywhere in newly developed residential areas, but also in mechanical advantages. The motor bus could accelerate and stop more quickly than the streetcar, and the replacement of the streetcar's steel wheels with rubber tires greatly increased rider comfort and reduced vibration and noise.

As intercity roads were gradually improved between 1910 and 1930, pioneers from all walks of life developed the intercity bus business. By the mid-1920s, technology had evolved to produce buses that had 100-horsepower engines, that could seat thirty passengers, and that included heating and ventilating systems, interior baggage racks, and, in some cases, toilet facilities. The bus had such advantages of routing flexibility and operating costs over the steam railroad that railroad companies began to operate their own bus fleets in place of thinly traveled branch lines. The first coast-to-coast bus service in 1928 made 132 stops and covered the distance from Los Angeles to New York in five days, fourteen hours.[117] By the end of the 1930s, despite many bankruptcies of small bus lines during the Great Depression, intercity bus travel was well established, accounting for 28 percent of intercity passenger traffic.[118]

Most citizens in 1900 did not have a mode of transportation that allowed them to move from a specific origin to a specific destination; they were slaves of the fixed rail system both of the intercity steam railroads and of the intracity electric streetcars. Horses were too expensive and inconvenient for ordinary citizens to maintain. Most homes would not have enough space for a horse or the means to keep it fed, so people walked to a livery stable, rented a horse, and rode or drove with it to a destination. But then the horse would need to be left at that destination, perhaps for many hours, until the time to return.

The inanimate motor vehicle solved many problems: it could be kept near the home, driven anywhere, and then turned off and locked at the destination, with no need for further food or maintenance. Many urban residents who could not handle the expense, stabling space, or maintenance needs of a horse bought automobiles in the early years of 1900–1915. "Automobiles also provided an increasingly protected, private space, an extension of the private home, which surrounded people, even as they traveled farther and faster than ever before."[119]

The freedom to explore and to be released from the fixed train and streetcar schedules played a role in the decline of public transportation. "Deliberate urban policy, in the form of street surfacing, encouraged automobile and truck traffic. The grim picture of decline usually painted is only a small portion of the story of urban transportation. Cities and the people in them to a large extent chose their forms of transportation."[120] Because ridership stagnated and then started to decline, few street railways were able to raise capital to extend their lines to new housing developments.

A vicious circle began, augmented by Henry Ford's success in reducing automobile prices even as rising transit worker wages and stagnating transit system productivity put upward pressure on fares. In real terms adjusted for overall inflation, between 1912 and 1930, the cost of motor vehicle operation declined by 78 percent and the cost of automobile purchase declined by 63 percent, but the cost of the average transit fare declined by only 6 percent.[121] Streetcar systems were particularly vulnerable in middle-sized cities that did not have a commuter rail station or other central node to concentrate traffic, and in these cities, automobiles could circulate freely without motor vehicle congestion. Because the transit lines were privately owned, they had no choice but to respond to declining ridership by cutting service. Fewer routes and longer waiting times further reduced the appeal of transit compared to that of the automobile.

Figure 5–4 plots motor vehicle registrations per household, also shown separately for automobiles and trucks, for the period 1900–2012. This chart in absolute numbers minimizes the rapidity of the spread of automobiles in

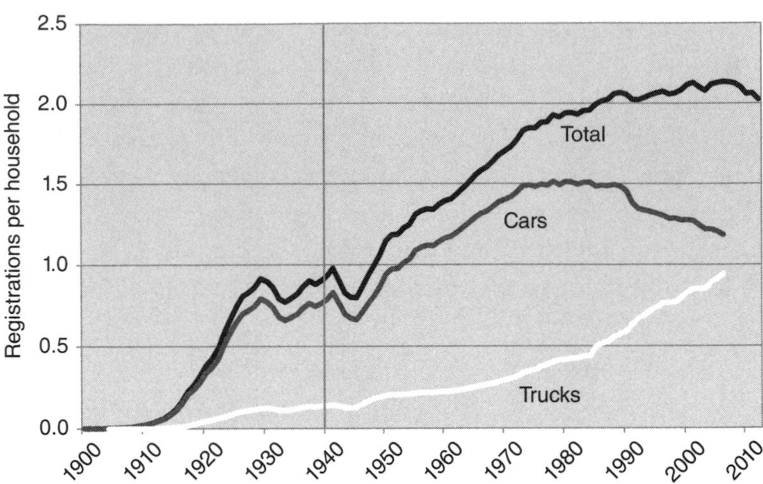

Figure 5–4. Registrations per Household by Vehicle Type, 1900–2012
Source: HSUS series Df339-342 and Ae2, SAUS, National Transportation Statistics Table 1-11. Vehicle classification changed in 2006, so categorical data after 2006 are not comparable to the earlier data.

the era before World War II. When expressed as a percentage of the number of households, motor vehicle registrations exploded from 0.1 in 1900 to 2.3 in 1910 to 38.3 in 1920 to 89.8 in 1930 and to 93.0 in 1940. Thus by 1930 there were almost as many motor vehicles as households in the United States, and an astonishing 78 percent of the world's automobiles were registered in the United States.[122]

Figure 5–5 provides a separate comparison of railroad passenger miles per person, copied from figure 5–2, with motor vehicle miles. As shown by the log scale, the rate of growth of vehicle miles dwarfs anything achieved by the railroads after 1880; indeed, vehicle miles surpassed railroad passenger miles during World War I. The surge of railroad patronage and simultaneous decline in automobile travel during World War II had the same cause, the rationing of gasoline and rubber tires, and after the war, vehicle miles continued their relentless rise while railroad passenger miles drifted inexorably lower.

The United States was unique in its immediate acceptance of automobiles at a rate that we can attribute in part to Henry Ford's genius at producing durable but inexpensive vehicles, as well as to the minimal cost of World War I to the United States in contrast to the substantial economic cost of that war and its aftermath for the most prosperous nations in Europe. That the United States

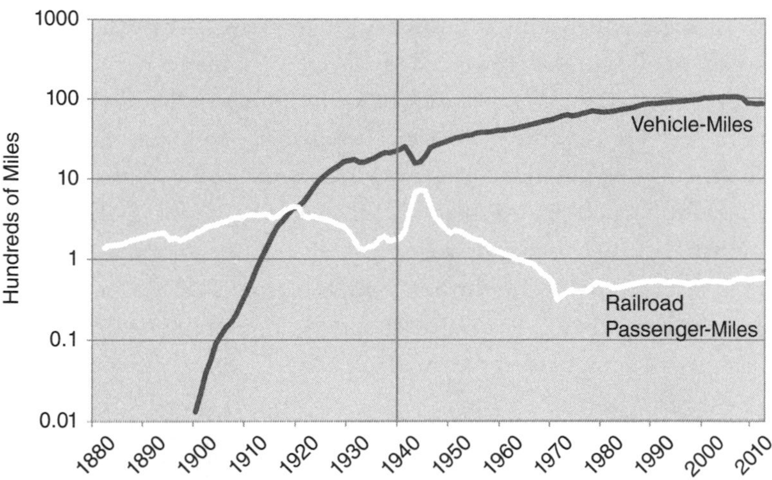

Figure 5–5. Vehicle-Miles per Person and Railroad Passenger-Miles per Person, 1882–2012

Sources: Federal Highway Administration Table VM-201, NTS Table 1-40, HSUS series Df413-415, Df903, Df950, and Aa7.

could produce 6 million internal combustion engines in 1929 alone goes a long way toward explaining how the United States produced so many motor-powered vehicles, including aircraft, during World War II.

AUTOMOBILES TRANSFORM LIFE ON FARMS AND IN SMALL TOWNS

In a nation in which 35 percent of the population still lived on farms in 1900, and in which more than 85 percent of horses were on the farm rather than in the city, very high on the list of benefits of the automobile was its promise to end the plague of rural isolation.[123] The quality of rural life on farms and even in small towns was fundamentally handicapped by the obstacles of time and distance. Poor transportation kept farmers from social gatherings with those beyond a radius of a few miles reachable by horse and buggy, in contrast to urban residents, who needed to travel only from house to house or block to block for their interpersonal contact. "Social contacts were few and commonly limited within a radius of a few miles; the educational facilities were meager and the opportunity to bargain in the sale of farm products or the purchase of supplies was almost absent. All this has been revolutionized by motor vehicles."[124]

It may seem unbelievable from today's perspective, but the appearance of the first automobile in each town and small city was a major event. The *Oregon Republican* reported the arrival of each new automobile in that Illinois city over the entire 1900–1910 decade.[125] Farmers' immediate enthusiasm for the automobile went beyond the end of rural isolation and the ability of the motor vehicle to perform farm tasks. Automobiles changed the meaning of leisure time for farm families; the Sunday drive quickly developed into a rural institution, including visits to friends and the new ability to go beyond the local village for recreation, culture, church events, and shopping. The common interest of farmers in improved rural roads brought them actively into the political process, many for the first time.[126]

The speed of transformation of farm transportation was one of the fastest of any invention in American history and, indeed, rivals the speed of diffusion of the Internet after 1995. By 1924, the 6.5 million U.S. farms were equipped with 4.2 million automobiles, 370,000 trucks, and 450,000 tractors. The equivalent figure for vehicles owned in 1909 would have been close to zero, so this transformation took place in a mere fifteen years. By 1926, fully 93 percent of farmers in Iowa had automobiles, a higher percentage than in urban America.[127]

The automobile changed the look of small towns. Downtown streets were widened and surfaced with all-weather pavement. Horse-related merchants such as liveries and harness, carriage, and blacksmith shops were replaced by automobile showrooms or repair shops, and "horse accessories" were removed from streets, including hitching posts and watering troughs. Painted parking stripes appeared on downtown streets, and signs slowly arrived to regulate parking and signals to regulate traffic. The previously clear delineation between the central business and residential districts became increasingly blurred as the space-consuming by-products of the automobile age expanded, including parking lots, automobile dealerships, repair shops, and service stations.

And the disruption of business occurred in the countryside as well as in the city; among the casualties of the new independence of farmers were the crossroads general store and many small independent local banks.[128] The smaller the town, the greater the threat to local merchants as the automobile allowed farmers and local small-town residents to drive to the nearest large town or small city. Previous loyalties to the local merchants were frayed as the circumference of feasible travel expanded. The automobile "seemed designed to loosen ties and dangle the horizon before the unsettled."[129] Another victim of the automobile revolution was the one-room schoolhouse, as students could now be transported by motor bus to larger consolidated school districts.

BROADER EFFECTS OF THE TRANSITION TO MOTOR CARS

Three factors help explain the automobile's rapid acceptance. First, it was viewed as a necessity by farmers and was purchased enthusiastically as soon as the Model T brought a tough and practical vehicle within the price range feasible for a farmer. Second, the spread of automobiles in the 1920s was greatly facilitated by the development of consumer credit. By 1926, fully 75 percent of new automobiles were financed "on time." Though installment credit had previously been sporadically available for expensive purchases such as pianos and sewing machines, the popularity of automobile credit soon made it routine for households to finance electric appliances in the same way.[130]

But by far the most important reason for the rapid diffusion of automobile ownership through 1929 was the rapid decline in prices, an achievement largely brought about by Ford's Model T and unmatched in any other nation. As shown in the bottom section of table 5–2, the ratio of the purchase price of a Model T to nominal personal disposable income per person declined from 3.16 in 1910 to 0.43 in 1923. That is, by 1923, a new Model T cost only 43 percent of annual disposable income per person, which for a family of four meant only 11 percent of total family income. Because most new automobile purchases in the 1920s were paid for using installment credit, the annual burden could be 5 percent or less of annual income, making the automobile affordable for all but the poorest of the nation's households.

Many contemporary quotations indirectly explain the rapid adoption of the motor car by the simple fact that it was viewed as a more important and vital invention than even the indoor bathroom. One Indiana farm housewife is reported to have said in 1925, "You can't go into town in a bathtub." Another mother of nine children remarked, "We'd rather do without clothes than to give up the car; we don't have no fancy clothes when we have the car to pay for." The Lynds, in their detailed 1929 study of Muncie, Indiana (which was cited frequently in chapter 4), reported that they surveyed twenty-six "particularly run-down houses" and discovered, to their surprise, that only five of these homes had bathtubs, but all twenty-six had automobiles.[131]

The unceasing routine of traveling by streetcar from home to factory and home to the central business district for shopping was replaced by automobile trips to multiple destinations: work, shopping in different neighborhoods, visits to relatives, weekend drives to the country or evening drives on sultry evenings to escape the heat. The central locus of courtship moved from the parlor or back porch swing to the back seat of the family automobile.[132] The arrival of the automobile in all but the lowest-income families created new opportunities not just for the middle-class, but even for working-class families. Workers who benefited from paid vacations could now drive hundreds of miles to visit relatives or see attractions. In some areas, new attractions were built specifically for travelers arriving by automobile that were not accessible by transit or railroad. For instance, by 1929, Robert Moses had built the Southern State Parkway on Long Island, which took automobile travelers to Jones Beach, with its six miles of waterfront and its 23,000 parking spaces for their cars.[133]

Before 1920, there was no commerce along the highways between one city or town and the next. Novelist Eudora Welty captured the staccato alternation of open countryside and discrete town borders, with nothing in between, in memories of a childhood trip taken in 1917 or 1918:

> My father would drive sizing up the towns, inspecting the hotel in each, deciding where we could safely spend the night. Towns little or big had beginnings and ends, they reached to an edge and stopped, where the country began again, as though they hadn't happened. They were intact and to themselves. You could see a town lying ahead in its whole, as definitely formed as a plate on a table.[134]

Highway construction became a boom industry and changed the nature of highways. No longer were they simply a route to travel from town to town, but they became a location of commerce as entrepreneurs developed new kinds of roadside businesses, from gas stations to automobile dealerships and repair shops, to roadside restaurants. "People living along American roads began to realize that the waxing throng was really a motorized river of gold flowing past their doors and that they would be wise to try to scoop up some of it."[135]

But where could the traveler stay? Hotels were located inside cities, not along the road, and they were too formal. Beginning in the late 1920s, private operators began to provide pay camps equipped with grocery stores and gasoline stations. The precursor of the motel started in the late 1920s when camp operators began to add tiny cabins; eventually the cabins were linked together with a common roof and became the motel. An early example is provided in the classic 1934 movie, *It Happened One Night*, when Clark Gable and Claudette Colbert share a motel room, discretely draping a blanket on a line to divide the small room into zones of semiprivacy.

By the late 1920s, the aesthetic consequences of the highway revolution were becoming apparent. The view from the road, which once had been limited to more or less picturesque countryside, now consisted of a garish and unregulated hodgepodge of brightly painted hastily erected buildings and tall signs, often electrified. A 1928 description captured the early days of roadside commerce:

> Every few hundred yards there is a... filling station, half a dozen colored pumps before it. In connection with the stations and between them are huts carrying the sign "Hot Dogs." Where there is neither hut nor filling station there are huge hoardings covered with posters.[136]

Although the flimsy initial roadside structures were often owned and operated by farmers or businessmen from nearby towns, soon a more ambitious group of entrepreneurs began to put together national networks of roadside outlets. The White Castle hamburger chain began in 1921 when Edgar Ingram and Walter Anderson opened a small restaurant in Wichita, Kansas. Howard Johnson's 1925 drug-store soda fountain in Quincy, Massachusetts, began a chain of roadside restaurants that by 1939 had 132 franchised outlets and in the 1950s and 1960s had a dominant market position, with about 1,000 outlets.[137] Harland Sanders developed his famous chicken recipe in 1930 at "Sanders' Servistation" in Corbin, Kentucky; J. F. McCullough founded what became Dairy Queen in Kankakee, Illinois, in 1938.[138]

The victory of the motor vehicle was not without controversy. Government policies encouraged urban sprawl and undermined the financial viability of urban transit and passenger railways. Even before World War II, public policy was skewed in favor of the automobile by building streets and highways with public funds while leaving urban transit and the interurban electric railways to operate as self-sufficient private companies. Many of the early roads were built by issuing bonds on which the interest was paid by local property taxes, so the automobile owner and transit rider paid equally to build a road system that made the automobile ever more attractive than transit. The spread of residential dispersion and the ubiquity of the automobile gradually eliminated common features of pre-1920 street life. Disappearing from American streets gradually over the years before 1940 and beyond were street vendors, delivery boys, the casual walk, the accidental encounter, the corner drugstore, the local café, the neighborhood store, sidewalk displays, and even the sidewalks themselves. Along with these things, a subtle weave of human relations disappeared.[139]

CONCLUSION: A REVOLUTION THAT COULD HAPPEN ONLY ONCE

This and the previous chapter represent the core of the argument in this book. The extent of change created by the modern conveniences to the American home, together with the transportation revolution made possible by the internal combustion engine, radically improved the standard of living through a series of changes that could happen only once. Together, these inventions fostered a transition from a largely rural to a largely urban society, inherently a change that could happen only once, as the urban percentage could not exceed 100 percent.

This chapter has portrayed the epochal change in transportation along at least three dimensions between 1870 and 1940. The first involves the steam-powered intercity railroad, which in 1860 consisted of an ill-coordinated patchwork of lines, almost entirely east of Iowa, that did not provide continuous long-distance travel. In contrast, the typical railroad speeds of twenty to twenty-five miles per hour in 1870 had nearly tripled by 1940, at least on the premium extra-fare express lines, and railroad travel was continuous across bridges and through underground tunnels. Progress included not just multifold increases in speed, but also multidimensional increases in travel comfort, culminating in the near-universal installation of air conditioning in express trains by 1940.

The second dimension is intracity transit, which in 1870 consisted entirely of horse-drawn omnibuses traveling at three miles per hour and horse-drawn streetcars moving at no more than twice that speed. After the brief rule, at least in a few cities, of the cable car, the electric streetcar arrived as if overnight and by 1902 had almost completely replaced its horse-drawn predecessors. Soon the largest cities overcame the street congestions of electric streetcars by building extensive elevated and underground electrified rapid transit, and electric interurban trains provided a relatively high-speed alternative to steam railroads for short distances between major cities. As in the case of steam-powered intercity rail, the 1870–1940 era witnessed major improvements in transit comfort, as omnibuses bouncing over rutted and unpaved urban streets were replaced with smooth rides along streetcar and rapid transit tracks and as electricity brought heat and light to transit vehicles.

The third and most important dimension is the motor vehicle, which revolutionized city and farm life between 1910 and 1930. Flimsy, expensive, low-powered, uncomfortable automobiles, uncovered and exposed to the elements, were soon replaced by the Model T Ford, which was relatively powerful and sturdy and which gradually offered its purchasers conveniences such as covered tops and electric starters. By 1940, automobile bodies were streamlined and enclosed, transmissions and suspensions were greatly improved, and engines were sufficiently powerful to travel at the maximum feasible speed on a newly emerging nationwide network of paved highways.

Thanks to Henry Ford's genius in reducing the purchase price of a sturdy, long- lasting motor vehicle to one-quarter or less of annual household income in the 1920s, there was an almost instant transition in just a few years to a new world in which by 1926 fully 93 percent of farmers in Iowa and other northern states owned their own automobile or motor truck. Banished was rural isolation, replaced by the freedom of farm families in their motor vehicles to roam far and wide in search of the best prices for their produce and the goods they wished to buy, as well as of the recreation and amusements from which they had long been cordoned off by the short traveling radius of the horse-drawn buggy and cart.

Taken together, these three separate dimensions of the 1870–1940 transportation revolution changed the scale, dimensions, and texture of the city. It was the *combination* of electricity and automobile that transformed the city. The electric elevator created a vertical complex of office buildings, hotels, and apartment houses in the central business district, with spatial density particularly high in cities such as New York and Chicago that already had well-developed commuter railway networks. But even as the city became more dense in the center, it became less dense in the periphery. In contrast to the city of 1890, with its compact size limited by the range of the horsecar and commuter rail lines, the automobile and motor trucks allowed the city of 1940 to spread without concern for lost community.

The development of residential suburbs was nothing new: the early railroad suburbs traced their origins back to the 1850s. But these belts of railroad suburbs left large stretches of undeveloped land between the rail lines, and these began to be filled in during the 1920s not just by residential development, but also by new shopping districts that dispersed retail activity beyond the central business district. The pace of suburbanization was interrupted by the Great Depression and World War II but began in earnest again in the late 1940s.

The three dimensions of transportation improvements had different effects on the most notable aspect of transportation in 1870, its dependence on the horse. Somewhat surprisingly, the steam railroad was not a substitute for the horse, but rather a complement to it. By opening up vast new lands for agriculture, railroads increased the demand for agricultural horses. Though railroads expanded the extent of the national market, their mobility was limited by where their tracks had been laid. Only horses could "provide short-distance hauling to and from the railroads and between points not on the railroads . . . horses made the railroads useful in the first place."[140]

In contrast, both electrified urban transit, including streetcars and rapid transit trains, were substitutes for the horse, as was the automobile. We have cited counts of street traffic in cities that indicate that horse-drawn vehicles were dominant in 1905 but had largely disappeared by 1917. That short period of transition for urban streets is one of the most rapid in the history of invention. By 1929, horses had largely disappeared from urban America, though the replacement of the horse by farm machinery was not complete until the late 1950s.

This chapter on transportation during 1870–1940 provides solid evidence for three of the central themes of the book. First, the three dimensions of transportation inventions as classified above unalterably changed the daily life of every member of every family, whether on farms, in small towns, or in cities. Second, most of the benefits to individuals came not within a decade of the initial invention, but over subsequent decades as subsidiary and complementary subinventions and incremental improvements became manifest. Third, taken together, the initial inventions and subsequent complementary improvements could happen only once.

The transition of America from a rural to an urban society that occurred between 1870 and 1940 inherently could happen only once. The increase of elapsed intercity train speeds from twenty-five miles per hour or slower in 1870 to sixty miles per hour or faster in 1940 could happen only once, and after World War II, the transition from piston to jet planes could happen only once. The retirement of horses and their attendant street waste and disease could happen only once. The increased speed of urban public transit within forty years from three to forty miles per hour could happen only once. The transition of automobiles from flimsy open carriage-like runabouts with engines of seven horsepower in 1906 to streamlined enclosed cars having eighty-five to 100 horsepower by 1940 could happen only once, although many postwar improvements in automobile comfort, convenience, performance, and safety lay ahead beyond 1940.

In 1940, most of the future potential of commercial aviation still lay in the future. But the achievements of the great transportation revolution were in place and were complex and multidimensional:

> The benefits of automobility were overwhelmingly more obvious: an antiseptic city, the end of rural isolation, improved roads, better medical care, consolidated schools, expanded recreational opportunities, the decentralization of business and residential patterns, a suburban real estate boom, and the creation of a standardized middle-class national culture.[141]

The year 1940 is a particularly inappropriate place to split this book, because it neglects the advances in commercial air travel, small and fragmentary in the 1930s by today's standards, but representing the cusp of a postwar revolution that within eighteen years of 1940 would produce a single product, the Boeing 707, that traveled at 0.85 of the speed of sound and that bound the world closer together for passenger travel than anything previously invented over centuries and millennia. The passenger transportation revolution was not over in 1940, but, as we shall see in chapter 11, it was largely over by 1970.

Chapter 6

FROM TELEGRAPH TO TALKIES: INFORMATION, COMMUNICATION, AND ENTERTAINMENT

> When Charlie Chaplin was eight, he performed in three large music halls an evening. Ten years later, in 1915, each night he could be seen in thousands of halls across the world. The remarkable transformation of spectating into a non-rival setting where Chaplin could be watched in many places simultaneously was made possible by motion pictures. They industrialized entertainment by automating it, standardizing it, and making it tradable.
>
> —Bakker (2012), p. 1036

INTRODUCTION

The year 1870 has been called the dawn of the "age of mass communication." Everything involving information, communication, and entertainment utterly changed from 1870 to 1940. A nation bereft of information in 1870 soon benefited from the growth in newspapers as technology cheapened the price of paper and printing almost as dramatically as the Internet reduced the cost of communication in the 1990s. Soon everyone read newspapers, from the lowest working-class families to the richest tycoons. The circulation of mass-market magazines exploded, as did the circulation of books through sales and the proliferation of free public libraries. Though the telegraph was invented before 1870, its epochal improvement in the speed of communication had its main effect after 1870 as information from world news to financial markets and grain prices was instantly communicated. From 1876, the telephone surpassed the telegraph by introducing instantaneous two-way communication.

There was no entertainment available to the average family in 1870, except for a few traveling musicians or circus performers or in-home board or card games. The phonograph broadened the audience for professional performances, and after 1900, millions could hear a Caruso aria or a Gershwin song. But nothing in history swept across the country faster than the sensation of radio. No longer did the most humble family need to buy records to hear music; it was all free on a radio that by 1930 could be purchased for less than $20.

Though radio was a sensation, it was the visual images and superstars of motion pictures that galvanized popular culture, especially in the dismal years of the 1930s when the gleaming visions of the silver screen distracted the entire population from the grim reality of a failed economy. The quality of phonographs and radio sound reproduction improved steadily, but nothing compares to the advance of motion pictures, especially in the last fifteen years of the 1870–1940 period covered by this chapter. A 1924 movie was silent, with intertitles and accompaniment by a piano or organ in the theater, but in a mere fifteen years, two of the greatest movies of all time appeared almost simultaneously in 1939 with full color, music, and sound: *The Wizard of Oz* and *Gone with the Wind.* Those two movies' appearance in 1939, close to the 1940 borderline between parts I and II of this book, creates a symbolic bookend to the progress between 1870 and 1940. No other era in human history changed the life of ordinary citizens so rapidly in so many different dimensions, including the realm of information, communication, and entertainment.

The central themes of previous chapters can be summarized in a few words, such as "variety" for food and clothing, "networking" for the arrival of the modern conveniences in the home, and "revolutionary change followed by incremental improvement" for the successive phases of the transportation revolution. In this chapter, the first theme is again networking, for the telephone and, later, the radio by 1940 had connected the home to the outside world. Indeed, with remarkable foresight Alexander Graham Bell, on the very night of his first successful telephone experiment in 1876, predicted that his invention would join the network of utilities connected to each home "just like water or gas."

A second theme in this chapter is "multiplication" as the successive phases of innovation in entertainment allowed a given performance to be viewed by ever larger audiences. The curse of "Baumol's disease"—that productivity in labor-intensive industries cannot grow because the four players in a string quartet cannot play any faster or to any larger audiences—was revoked as early as the 1890s by the invention of the phonograph. Actors whose efforts had previously been limited by the size of a theater audience by 1910 were appearing before millions in silent movies. By the 1930s, Jack Benny, Rochester, Don Wilson, and their compatriots on weekly radio programs, relying only on a few jokes and sound effects, could entertain millions without the need for cameras, scenery, or props.

A third theme is that the evolution of information and communication technology made business firms and workers more productive while the development of new entertainment media raised the value of leisure time, as in the Becker framework introduced in chapter 1. Families indicated which ways of spending their leisure time were most valuable to them by shifting from pianos and card playing in the 1890s to motion pictures after 1910 and to radio after 1920.

NEWSPAPERS AND MAGAZINES: A WHOLE LOT OF READING GOING ON

Literacy was advanced by 1870. Census data for that year indicate, as shown in table 6–1, that fully 80 percent of the total population and 88.5 percent of the white population claimed to be literate. The total American literacy rate was held back by the aftermath of slavery; in 1870, only 20.1 percent of the black population could read. The high literacy rate of the white population, in contrast, reflected nearly universal elementary education. For the total population, elementary school enrollment as a percentage of the population aged 5–13 in

Table 6–1. Literacy Rates by Race and Location of Birth, 1870–1940

	Total	White			Black and Other
		Total	Native Born	Foreign Born	
1870	80.0	88.5	--	--	20.1
1880	83.0	90.6	91.3	87.9	30.0
1890	86.7	92.3	93.8	86.9	43.2
1900	89.3	91.8	95.2	87.1	55.5
1910	92.3	95.0	97.0	87.3	69.5
1920	94.0	96.0	98.0	86.9	77.0
1930	95.7	97.0	98.2	89.2	81.6
1940	97.1	98.0	98.9	91.0	88.5

Source: HSUS series Bc793-797

1870 was 81 percent, implying a percentage close to 90 percent for the white population.[1] The black literacy rate improved steadily after 1880 and reached 88.5 percent by 1940. The American white literacy rate in 1870 was substantially in excess of the 76.9 percent British literacy rate in the same year.[2]

What did Americans read in the last three decades of the nineteenth century? Throughout the long century between 1870 and the commercialization of the web browser around 1995, the reading choices were limited to books, newspapers, and periodicals. There are no available data on the numbers of copies of books sold; as John Tebbel writes, "The fact is that no entirely satisfactory figures were kept... inconsistencies and confusion abound in the [book publishing] industry's record keeping."[3] However, at least we can track changes in the number of books published. Roughly 2,000 books were published annually in 1880, a figure that expanded greatly to 11,300 by 1940.

Much of this increase reflected the rapid growth of population. Figure 6–1 displays decade averages to compare the spread of books, newspapers, and periodicals; each point plotted refers to the subsequent decade, so the 1880 point for books provides an average for 1880–89 and indicates that 0.36 books were published per 1,000 households in that decade. Book publishing per thousand households peaked in the 1910 decade at 0.50, fell to 0.24 in the 1940 decade, and then

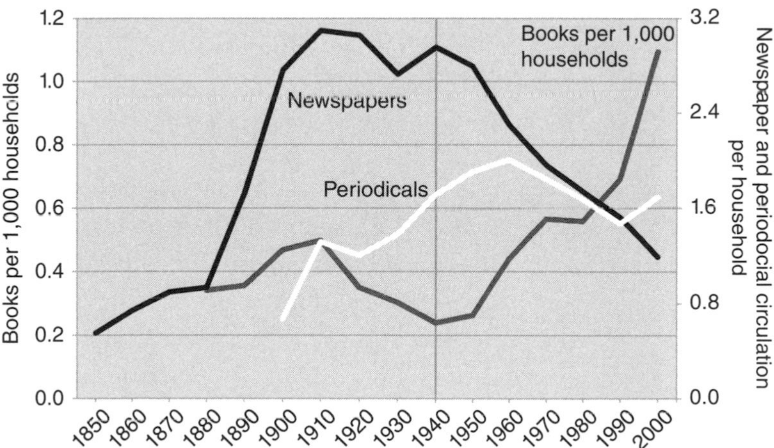

Figure 6–1. Book Publications, Newspaper Circulation, and Periodical Circulation Per Household, by Decade, 1850–2009

Sources: HSUS series Dg225, Dg254, Dg256, Dg266, and Ae2; SAUS tables 1129, 1134, 1135. Each year refers to the average over the following decade (e.g. 2000 refers to the average over 2000–2009).

advanced to new highs in the 1970s and beyond. The surge in book publishing after 1950 conflicts with widespread predictions in the early postwar years that television would mean the death knell of book reading as a leisure activity.

At the turn of the century, fiction was the dominant form of book, with more than 2,200 new works of fiction published in 1901, and the romantic novel was by far the most popular form of fiction. Biography and history took second and third place. In 1901, fifteen novels achieved sales of 100,000 copies or more, typically priced at $1.00 to $1.50 per book, and these novels were also widely circulated by public libraries, of which there were more than 1,700 in 1900.[4] The appetite for reading continually increased as the percentage of 14- to 17-year-olds attending high school increased from 6 percent in 1890 to 41 percent in 1928.

Newspapers were already well established by the nineteenth century. In England, they originated at the beginning of the seventeenth century, and the first American newspaper was established in Boston in 1695. Unlike the British press, which was restricted by content rules imposed by the church and the government, the American press was uninhibited from the start. Also free of the taxes that limited the ability of the British press to reduce prices, the American penny press spread rapidly in the 1820s and 1830s. In 1829, the ratio of newspapers printed per person was nine times higher in Pennsylvania than in the British Isles, the price of the newspaper was a fifth, and the price of an advertisement was a thirtieth. The low prices of American newspapers and their advertisements were made possible by the invention of the steam-powered press in 1813, and by the 1830s, presses had been developed that could print 4,000 copies per hour.[5]

Daily, Sunday, and weekly newspaper circulation increased from 7 million in 1870 to 39 million in 1900 and 96 million in 1940. Even on a per-household basis, as shown in figure 6–1, this growth was impressive, tripling from 0.90 in the 1870 decade to more than 3.0 between 1910 and 1930. The fact that the average household, including the lowest stratum, purchased 3.1 different newspapers is one of the most surprising in this chapter.[6] The fastest growth occurred in 1870–1900, by which time newspapers had become firmly established as the main source of information and entertainment for a growing population.[7] Color presses were introduced in the 1890s and were first used to produce color comics and supplements.[8] By the early twentieth century, newspapers had extended their content far beyond the news itself and added "gossip columns, travel and leisure advice, color comics, and sporting results."[9]

The interval from 1880 to 1905 was the age of "yellow journalism," likely named after the "Yellow Kid" comic strip character popular at the time. Metropolitan newspapers were locked in circulation wars in which success depended on publishing ever more sensational and sometimes sordid stories featuring "violence, sex, catastrophe, and mayhem." The most famous circulation battle was in the late 1890s, between Joseph Pulitzer's *New York World* and William Randolph Hearst's *New York Journal*. Hearst was eager to stoke the flames of conflict between Spain and the United States over Cuba and sent Frederick Remington the photographer, who could find no signs of war. In a famous exchange of cables, Hearst responded to Remington, "You provide the pictures; I'll provide the war."[10]

The mass-circulation national magazine was a creation of the 1880s and 1890s. Unlike newspapers, for which the circulation area was limited by the need to provide time-sensitive news to a particular metropolitan area, the features contained in magazines could reach readers at a more leisurely pace. Hence magazines were national almost from the beginning in the mid-nineteenth century, and among those with the highest circulations late in the century were *McClure's*, *Collier's*, the *Saturday Evening Post*, and the *Ladies' Home Journal*.

By the 1920s, the sedate general-interest periodicals had been joined by the more scurrilous sex and confession magazines. "The publishers of sex adventure magazines...learned to a nicety the gentle art of arousing the reader without arousing the censor." *True Story* was founded in 1919 and had a circulation of almost 2 million by 1926, "a record of rapid growth probably unparalleled in magazine publishing."[11] Henry Luce invented a novel style of news and feature summaries in his new *Time* magazine founded in 1923 and then, in 1937, launched *Life*, which featured stunning action photos facilitated by continuous improvements in photographic equipment and long-distance transmission. By the 1930s, newspapers and magazines had matured into their modern form; they experienced little further change until the arrival of cable news networks in the 1980s and the fragmentation of news delivery made possible by the arrival of web browsers in the 1990s.

THE TELEGRAPH SPEEDS UP COMMERCE, TRANSPORT, AND JOURNALISM

Crowning many previous attempts to develop a telegraph system, dating back into the eighteenth century, the first patent for the electromagnetic telegraph was granted to William Cooke and Charles Wheatstone in England in 1837.

At about the same time, Samuel F. B. Morse had heard about experiments in Europe and by 1838 had developed his own version, complete with his own Morse code. Six more years were necessary to find a way of sending the signal over a substantial distance.[12] The commercially viable telegraph age began on May 24, 1844, with the famous message "What hath God wrought?" sent by Morse from the U.S. Capitol building in Washington, D.C., to a railroad depot in Baltimore.[13] Until then, the speed of travel of news had been limited to that of the foot, horse, sail, or, more recently, rail.

Morse's system was the breakthrough that mattered. Within only two years, there were nine telegraph companies, whose 2,000 miles of wire stretched all the way from Portland, Maine, to Chicago and New Orleans.[14] The telegraph network was ubiquitous in the east by 1855, the transcontinental telegraph debuted in late 1861, and after an abortive start in the late 1850s, a working undersea cable linking Britain and America was laid in 1866. Contemporary observers recognized the importance of the telegraph almost immediately. As early as 1847, the telegraph was seen as "facilitating Human Intercourse and producing Harmony among Men and Nations." In the late 1860s, a writer anticipated "when the missing links shall have been completed of the great chain that will bring all civilized nations into instantaneous communication with each other . . . breaking down the barriers of evil prejudice and custom . . ." At the same time another optimistically suggested that "whenever science achieves a victory, a rivet is loosened from the chains of the oppressed."[15]

Though the cost of sending a telegram was initially too high for the telegraph to gain widespread usage by private households, it was immediately viewed as essential by three industries—finance, railroads, and newspapers. The telegraph could transmit prices of commodity and financial asset data, thus reducing or eliminating the role of arbitrage for traders who had particularly good or bad access to information. By squeezing margins, news provided by telegraph began to eliminate wholesalers and middlemen who had depended on differential access to information. A domestic financial transaction could be ordered and confirmed by 1890 in less than two minutes. Before the undersea cable, the six-week delay for a round-trip crossing from New York to London could lead to inefficient purchase and sale decisions for commodities and other goods, implying that the welfare benefits of the telegraph and cable included not just financial markets, but also the real sector of the economy.[16]

The telegraph became an essential tool to railroads in controlling the flow of passenger and freight trains. Perhaps the most measurable social benefit of the telegraph in the late nineteenth century was to allow the major railroads to operate single-track lines rather than the double-track lines common in Britain. The telegraph could signal ahead of the arrival of a train and the need to shunt a train traveling in the opposite direction onto a side spur. Alexander Field estimates a social benefit of about $1 billion, as of 1890, that the telegraph contributed to freeing the railroads from the need to build double-tracked lines, an amount that translates to about 7 percent of 1890 nominal GDP.[17]

The telegraph and railroad working together created a single integrated market for the entire nation east of the Mississippi River by the 1870s. The nationwide marketplace used the railroads to bring goods from manufacturers to wholesalers and retailers, and the telegraph was instrumental in hastening the transition from an economy of small, mainly single-function firms operating in local and regional markets, to large national multifunctional firms. The telegraph and the railroad together made it possible for the rapidly developing large urban department store to stock a myriad of items and manage inventory levels.

For years after the transcontinental telegraph line, the mail remained important in the transmission of news. Telegraph service was very expensive and was reserved for only brief summaries of the most important news. The mails remained the main source of communication for longer stories that were less timely and involved editorial opinion. Almost immediately after the first telegraph lines were built, the Associated Press was founded in 1846 by a group of New York newspapers that wanted to share the expense of covering the Mexican–American war and quickly grew into a nationwide association sharing news gathered from its member newspapers and its own employees. The Associated Press and the Western Union telegraph company developed together as monopolies, one of information and the other of communication. In 1875, Western Union, with its network of telegraph wires and offices that reached even the smallest towns and villages could be described as "the only American corporation of truly nationwide scope."[18]

THE POSTAL SERVICE COMES TO EVERY FARMER'S MAILBOX

The early growth of the U.S. Postal Service began long before our starting date of 1870, in fact almost a century earlier with the appointment of Benjamin Franklin as postmaster general by the Continental Congress in July 1775.[19] A sharp drop in postal rates made possible by the railroad had already occurred by 1870.

The rate to send a half-ounce letter more than 500 miles was twenty-five cents between 1792 and 1845, then dropped to ten cents and, after 1851, to three cents to send a letter as far as 3,000 miles.[20]

Lesser known than most of the many revolutions in the late nineteenth century was that involving mail. In 1890, the population was nearly 76 million, but only 19 million received mail at their door delivered by the U.S. Postal Service. For the remaining 57 million in small towns and on farms, there was no delivery. Farmers would have to hitch up their carriages and drive down rutted and muddy dirt roads to the nearest village large enough to have a post office. They then had to wait in lines to receive their mail from the local mail clerk. Then, like an overnight miracle, Rural Free Delivery (hereafter RFD) suddenly arrived. The benefits of RFD that raised the standard of living of millions of farmers are well described:

> For the first time in their lives they could have the news of the world every day except Sunday..... They would know when to sell their crops to the best advantage.... Important letters that sometimes meant dollars and cents to them... would no longer lie two or three days in the post office because there had been no way of knowing they were there. And the time they would save! A man could cultivate an extra acre of corn or haul a couple of loads of hay in the time he had formerly spent going to the post office.[21]

Implementing the RFD system took about a decade starting in 1901. There were numerous difficulties including the recruiting of thousands of men to ride horses to deliver the mail, not to mention the mundane task of designing the rural mailbox to be of the correct size and shape to be sanctioned by the federal government. Once it began, RFD was highly successful. The traveling rural mail carrier became the local handyman and errand boy for his patrons. Soon the automobile revolution replaced his sturdy horse with a Model T Ford as the delivery vehicle. On his route, he served as a deputy postmaster, selling stamps, postcards, and envelopes and accepting registered letters and money orders. His duties multiplied in 1913, when Parcel Post was extended to the RFD network. Throughout the 1890–1915 period, when RFD became universal, political pressure was generated for better roads, supporting the view that better roads made the automobile possible as much as the automobile created the demand for rural roads.

"NUMBER, PLEASE" AS THE TELEPHONE ARRIVES

Like the 1879 invention of electric light discussed in chapter 4 or the nearly simultaneous invention of the internal combustion engine summarized in chapter 5, the invention of the telephone had been preceded by several decades of speculation and experimentation. But the gestation period for the telephone was shorter; its 1876 invention occurred only twenty-two years after Philip Reis's idea, in 1854, that a flexible plate vibrating in response to air pressure changes created by the human voice could open and close an electric circuit.[22] Further progress was limited by the inability to provide the variable pitch and tone of the human voice rather than the simple on-off alternation created by the telegraphic switch. The turning point awaited an inventor who had a deep understanding of the processes of speech and hearing.

Alexander Graham Bell was not a professional inventor. His expertise was in human speech, not electricity or mechanics. His grandfather was a Shakespearean actor who eventually founded a well-known school of elocution in London that specialized in curing stammering, and his father was a professor of elocution who developed a new method of teaching the deaf to speak.[23] The son began his career in their footsteps in 1873 as a professor of "vocal physiology" at Boston University but became distracted by his interest in trying to develop a "harmonic telegraph" that could transmit several messages at once on a single telegraph wire.

In early 1876 Bell filed what has been called the most valuable patent application in history for a speaking telephone, only hours before a competing patent was filed by rival inventor Elisha Gray. At that time, neither had achieved a functional telephone, so these patents were speculations about future success. This dramatic event, measured in two hours, has been called "the best-known instance of nearly simultaneous independent filing in the history of patenting."[24] Bell's breakthrough came only one month after the patent application and was achieved by "by gradually increasing and diminishing the resistance of the circuit" in contrast to steady intermittent signals. Success was achieved in Boston on March 10, 1876, with the famous message sent between adjoining rooms as Bell spoke into the primitive transmitter while his assistant waited in the next room "Mr. Watson, come here—I want to see you." So sure was Bell that he had achieved a great invention that he wrote to his father that same night, "I feel that I have at last struck the solution of a great problem—and the day is coming when telegraph wires will be laid on to houses just like water or gas—and friends converse with each other without leaving home."[25]

Just as early automobiles did not work very well, the earliest telephone instruments were clumsy to use and produced indistinct sounds that were barely audible behind static. The transmitter and receiver were the same piece of equipment. One spoke into it loudly and, when finished, removed the instrument from the mouth and shifted it to the ear to hear the response. Nevertheless, Bell's device worked well enough to be introduced to the world at the Philadelphia Centennial Exposition in June 1876. Bell had achieved what men had long attempted, a device to send a human voice over a wire. In fact, it seems odd in retrospect that the telegraph and telephone were developed before Edison's electric light and power station—this was made possible by electric batteries, which had been introduced as early as the 1830s.[26]

Within a year, telephone service had begun in the nation's largest cities, in an environment then dominated by the telegraph, its forest of telegraph poles and wires, and its small army of uniformed boys who "scurried through the streets delivering messages." A publicity circular aimed at telegraph customers noted the advantages of the telephone: (1) "No skilled operator is required, but direct communication may be had by speech," (2) "Communication is much more rapid," and (3) "No expense is required either for its operation, maintenance, or repair." All that was required was a leasing fee—$20 per year for home use and $40 per year for business use.[27]

There were 250,000 telephones in use by 1893 and more than 6 million by 1907.[28] But telephones along with electricity widened the divide in living standards between rural and urban America. In between large urban areas and individual farm houses were medium-sized towns such as Muncie, Indiana, as extensively surveyed and described in the Lynds' *Middletown*. Although the first telephones appeared in Middletown in the early 1880s, it took many decades for them to reach majority status in the town's households. In 1924, roughly half of Middletown houses had telephones. This is a strikingly slow diffusion of an invention almost fifty years later, compared to the radio in the two decades after 1920, television after 1946, or the Internet after 1990.

Figure 6–2 shows how the telephone dwarfed the telegraph industry almost immediately after its invention. Telegraph messages per household per year jumped from one to four between 1867 and 1878 but never exceeded eight. Already by 1880, the telephone was used for ten conversations per household per year, a total that reached 125 in 1899 and 800 in 1929. The further growth

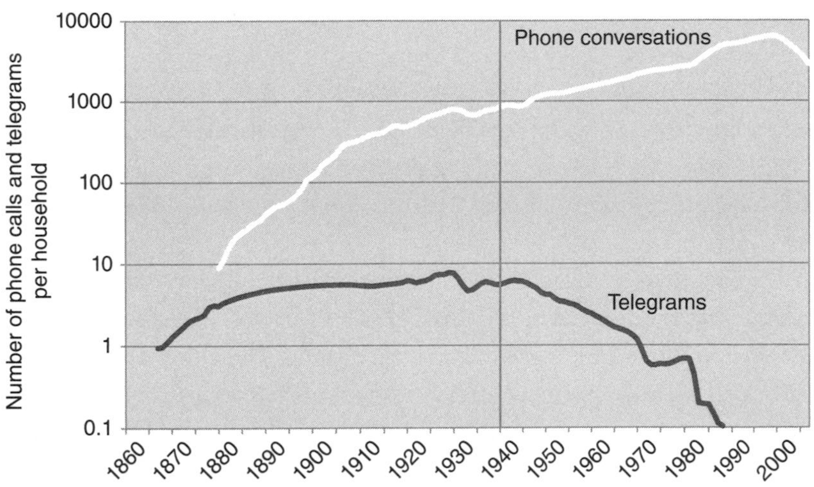

Figure 6–2. Number of Annual Phone Conversations and Telegrams Per Household, Two Year Moving Average, 1867–2007

Sources: HSUS series Dg8, Dg9, Dg51, Dg52, and Ae2 before 1982, FCC *Trends in Telephone Service* (2010) after 1986. Data interpolated between 1982 and 1986.

in phone calls per household to 2,440 in recent years is explained by the fact that the ratio of telephones to households rose from 40 percent to 160 percent between 1929 and 1985 (see figure 6–4, later this chapter).

The telephone switchboard was developed almost immediately and could connect fifty to 100 lines as an operator plugged the metal tip of a cord into a jack to establish the connection. The rotary dial phone and automatic switch were invented and patented as early as 1892 but were not introduced into service by AT&T until 1919, being "resisted by Bell leadership."[29] Progress was also slow in extending the reach of the telephone across the nation. The first long-distance calls between New York and Chicago did not occur until 1892, nor the first between New York and San Francisco until 1915. That thirty-nine-year gap between the initial invention and transcontinental service was more than twice as long as the seventeen-year gap between the 1844 invention of the telegraph and the 1861 completion of the transcontinental telegraph.

The varying growth rate of subscribers is evident in figure 6–4, later this chapter. Growth accelerated between 1893 and 1908 after the expiration of the original Bell patents with the emergence of independent companies. In the fifteen years after 1894, price competition pushed the annual rates for Bell residential service down by two-thirds.[30] By 1907, the independent companies accounted for almost half the telephones in the United States, but five years later, the Bell companies controlled 85 percent of the telephones either directly or through sublicense agreements. At this point, "AT&T had effectively subdued competition in the rest of the country."[31] As the Bell companies bought up their competition, prices stopped declining, and the growth of subscribers visibly slowed between 1920 and 1929, followed by the cessation of growth during the Depression decade of the 1930s.

The telephone was essential for business before it became a part of everyday American life for households. Among the first adopters of the telephone were police departments. Telephone boxes connected to fire stations were common by the 1880s. The distinction between initial business use of the telephone and the delayed adoption for personal use was blurred as customers asked to use the telephones of local merchants for personal calls. A Chicago druggist reported in 1888 about "a young lady who called to inform her fiancé that she no longer intended to marry him."[32]

The great expansion of telephone service to the household brought multidimensional benefits that have never entered the GDP statistics. The telephone saved lives by allowing those suffering from illness or injury to summon help. It joined with the invention of the electric elevator in making multistory high-rise office and apartment buildings possible. It made living alone possible and contributed to the breakup of multigenerational households—a mixed blessing, as was also brought by the telephone's role in diminishing, if not extinguishing, the ancient art of letter writing.[33]

The central role of the telephone operator in the early decades led to previously unanticipated uses for the telephone:

> The operator many times gets the request, "Please ring my bell at 6 o'clock tomorrow morning"; 5,000 times every day in Chicago she is asked the time of day; election and prizefight results, football and baseball scores are asked for and repeated.[34]

Likewise, the rural operator became an information center for the local community, helping locate missing children and providing warning of floods and fires. In rural areas, most phones were on the "party line" in which two, four, or more households shared the same line. Just as would be true today for multiple extension telephones within the same home, when the instrument was picked up on a party line, one often heard an ongoing conversation. In those days before radio soap operas, listening to neighbors talk on the party line became a standard form of rural entertainment.

One major limitation of the 1940 phone network was the price of long-distance phone calls. Figure 6–3 shows telephone rates for three-minute calls between New York, London, and San Francisco. Though rates had dropped significantly by 1940, a three-minute call to San Francisco from New York was $46 in 2005 dollars, and the same call to London was a lofty $242. Rates remained persistently high into the later twentieth century. A three-minute call to San Francisco did not drop below $10 until 1966, and the London rate finally fell below $10 in 1981. Such prices kept the usefulness of the phone network primarily on the local level.

The telephone was a uniquely American innovation. Not only was it invented in the United States, albeit by a transplanted Scotsman, but also its spread and usage far exceeded that in other countries. The number of telephones per person in 1900 was four times more than in England, six times more than in Germany, and twenty times more than in France. There were as many telephones in New York state as in all Europe. The main reason why the Bell monopoly was tolerated by the U.S. government antitrust authorities was that telephone usage was far ahead of other countries. Foreign telephone companies

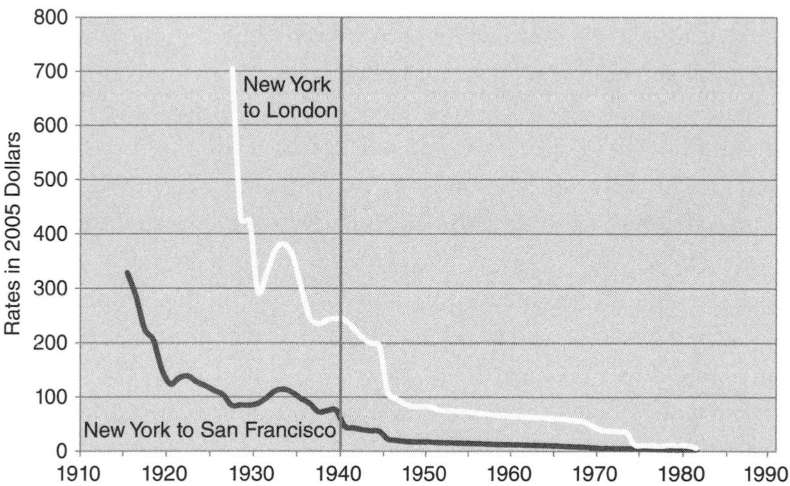

Figure 6–3. Telephone Rates for 3-minute, Daytime Telephone Calls between New York, London, and San Francisco, 1915–1981

Sources: HSUS series Dg59, Dg60, and Gordon (2012a) Appendix Table A-1.

were also monopolies but were owned by the government, and they typically set such low rates that there were insufficient funds to build the network and, often, long waiting lists for telephone service.[35] The government-imposed breakup of the Bell system would wait another half-century, until 1983.

THE PHONOGRAPH: THE FIRST STEP IN CURING BAUMOL'S DISEASE

Baumol's cost disease was originally proposed using the example of a Mozart string quartet.[36] Any performance of the quartet would always require four players, thus precluding any productivity gains. But in the economy as a whole productivity increases, and wage rates increase roughly at the same rate.[37] Thus, to prevent chamber music players from defecting into other lines of work paying higher wages, their wages must increase as well, thus requiring price increases for classical music concerts. This "cost disease" afflicts not just classical music, but also education, health care, and any industry in which productivity gains are limited, right down to the lowly neighborhood barbershop.

Even though Baumol was writing in 1967, the constraints imposed by his disease were already loosened as long ago as July 1877, when Thomas Edison invented the phonograph. In few other inventions was there a longer time gap between the low quality of the product in the initial attempt to convert music and speech into a reproducible form and the ultimately superb quality of the product—consider the contrast between Edison's initial piece of tin foil and today's music reproduction on digital audio players.[38]

Though the telephone was in commercial use within a year of its initial invention, Edison's 1877 discovery, in which he recited and then reproduced "Mary Has a Little Lamb," was not ready for prime time. The tin-foil recording medium was flimsy. Even though Edison laid claim to the invention, in part by transporting it in 1878 to a demonstration for then President Rutherford Hayes, the design and production of a mass consumer product eluded him. Edison did not originally intend the phonograph to be used for entertainment and rather viewed it as a business device, an early ancestor of the Dictaphone; he referred to it as the "talking machine." An early *New York Times* editorial treated the main usefulness of the recording machine as a device to store forever the speeches of current politicians.[39]

Edison himself was better at prophesying than at mechanical perfection. In an 1878 article, he predicted that phonographs would allow books to be read to the blind, to teach children to speak correctly, to create singing dolls, to transfer a musical performance from one moment in time to another, and the preservation of the voices of previous generations of family members. Edison's imagination soared in predicting that the "phonographic clock will tell you the hour of the day; call you to lunch; send your lover home at ten."[40]

Even though Edison soon began to record on wax cylinders, these turned out to be too soft and fragile and were difficult to manufacture and ship in large quantities. By 1884, critics wrote that "the failure of the phonograph did much to destroy the popularity of Mr. Edison." Edison was furious that a competing technology called the "Graphophone," backed in part by his rival Bell, was produced by "pirates attempting to steal my invention."[41] Only in 1888 did Edison introduce his "Perfected Phonograph," but it was far from perfect, as mechanical parts were prone to malfunction, and the internal battery was unreliable.

The early phonographs relied not on electricity, but rather on a crank or foot treadle. Both Edison's phonograph and the competing Graphophone technology were soon eclipsed by Emile Berliner, who perfected, by 1888, a better method based on a flat disc, which initially revolved at about 70 rpm.[42] Berliner invented the main technical feature of recorded discs, in which the groove in the disc both records laterally and propels the stylus.[43] The word "record" was in common use by the mid-1890s. Berliner's invention eventually was sold and became the Victor Talking Machine Company, which eventually merged in 1929 with RCA to become RCA Victor, the world's largest recording company. Its famous trademark, the dog Nipper listening to a gramophone, was borrowed by Berliner from a French painting and was promptly registered as a trademark in 1900 as "His Master's Voice" and later the abbreviation "HMV." The machines made by the Victor Talking Machine Company were advertised as "Victrolas," and this name came to be used generically to refer to any type of record player, particularly the floor models that were enclosed in hardwood casing carved to match other pieces of furniture.

The first phonographs appeared in the 1890s not in homes, but as coin-slot machines in soda fountains and saloons. For a nickel, patrons could hear renditions of military marches by John Philip Sousa or folk ballads written by Steven Foster. The growth in home ownership of phonographs after 1900 helped promote new types of music, including the "dance craze" of 1910–15, when record companies advertised their "authentic dance tempo" records in popular magazines such as the *Saturday Evening Post*.[44]

Though the phonograph for the first time brought professionally performed music into the home, so did the player piano, which was invented at about the same time and which became widely sold around the turn of the century. From today's perspective, we might have expected the newly born player piano industry to have been eclipsed by phonographs that could reproduce the voices of singers and many musical instruments, not just the piano. But the player piano in 1900–1905 competed not with today's fidelity of sound reproduction, but rather with the primitive phonographs of that era, with their spring-loaded cranks, poor acoustical reproduction, and breakable shellac records. The piano for decades had been a central component of "cultural capital" in which young women were expected to take piano lessons and become proficient.[45]

Phonographs allowed ordinary people for the first time to hear music properly performed by professionals. At a moment's notice, music could be produced that went far beyond piano playing, including bands, orchestra, and both popular and classical voices. Enrico Caruso, who made 490 commercially released recordings between 1902 and 1920, became one of the best-known personalities of his era.[46] Whatever the flaws of the early phonographs, the initial encounter of an ordinary person with a recording device represented a moving experience that utterly changed the availability of music and voices.

The initial pace of introduction of the phonograph into the American home was limited by competition with the piano, and expenditures for records were an alternative use of limited family budgets that could otherwise purchase sheet music and piano lessons. The phonograph did not create instant obsolescence for the piano, and indeed the Census of Manufactures shows that more pianos than phonographs were produced in 1899, 1904, and 1909.[47] The piano was a major expenditure. Consider these prices in the context of a nominal average personal disposable income per household in 1910 of $1,240.[48] Whereas the 1902 Sears, Roebuck catalog lists home organs for as little as $27, the single piano shown, an upright with a carved mahogany and walnut cabinet, cost $98 plus delivery, and its 800-pound weight imposed substantial additional freight charges.

The same 1902 Sears catalog devoted four pages to a wide variety of phonographs ranging in price from $20 to $120. Two disc-based models were offered at $20 and $40. A selection of prose from the catalog tells us much not just about the disc player, but also about the art of catalog writing in 1902, revealing only at the end that this phonograph was propelled not by electricity, but by winding up a spring-loaded motor:

> [It] is the most beautiful instrument, massive in proportion and handsome in appearance. The mechanism is contained in a handsomely designed

quarter-sawed highly polished oak cabinet....The mechanism of the machine is well nigh perfect...assuring spring and reliable action, and running three of the large 10-inch concert records with each winding.[49]

Not only was the power for early phonographs based on winding and springs, but the recording itself was acoustic, collected by the phonograph's horn rather than by an electrical microphone. A singer had to stand close and put his or her face into the horn, and only some instruments in an orchestra could be heard at all. It was not until 1925 that the technology of microphones and vacuum tubes had progressed far enough to achieve accurate music reproduction on records. Until 1948, all records were recorded live, from beginning to end, with no editing. Any flaw or error either would be present on the recording or would require another performance to eliminate the flaw.

A series of innovations in the mid-1920s made previous phonographs obsolete. The wind-up spring drive was replaced by an electric motor; the sound for the records themselves began to be created using a microphone and vacuum tubes rather than the acoustic horn, and record changers were introduced that allowed an entire symphony to be heard without the need manually to change records every three minutes. By the late 1920s, the floor-standing cabinet phonograph had been made obsolete and was replaced by a radio/phonograph combination unit that used the radio's amplifier to produce the sound from the phonograph, thus replacing the acoustical horn not just for recording, but also for listening.

How rapidly did household use of the phonograph grow in comparison with the telephone and the radio? Figure 6–4 compares the number of phonographs per household with the number of residential telephones per household.[50] The race between the telephone and phonograph was surprisingly close. Note that fully fifty years elapsed between the nearly simultaneous invention of the telephone and phonograph and the date when they were present in half of American homes.

Figure 6–4 also contrasts the very different pattern of telephone and radio use in the 1930s, when the percentage of households that had telephones declined from 45 percent in 1929 to 33 percent in 1933. Because telephones were rented rather than bought outright, phones simply disappeared from homes in which the Depression had slashed incomes so much that the telephone bill could not be paid. In contrast, radios were purchased, and radio ownership soared throughout the 1930s, from 35 percent in 1929 to 82 percent in 1940. When Franklin Roosevelt gave his "Day of Infamy" speech the day after the

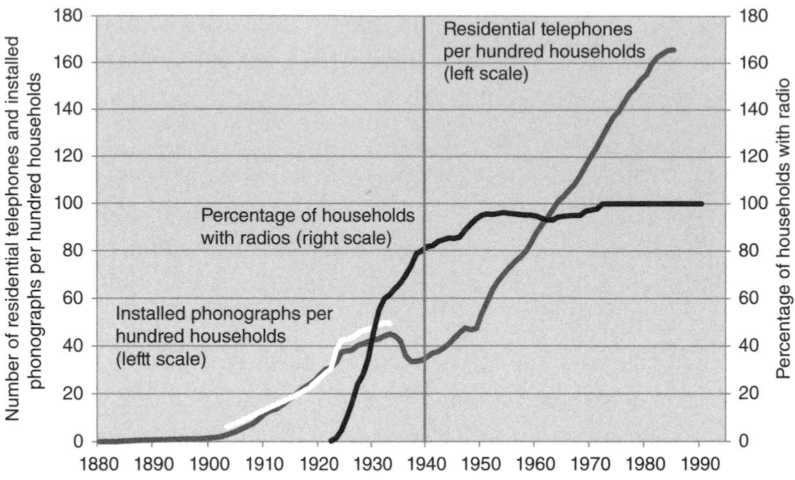

Figure 6–4. Diffusion of telephones, radios, and phonographs by household, 1880–1990

Sources: HSUS series Ae2, Dg46 ratio-linked backwards at 1920 with Dg48, and Dg128, HSUS 1958 P231.

Pearl Harbor attack, almost the entire nation was equipped to listen to him in their own homes. In contrast, telephone usage in the household did not exceed 50 percent until 1953.

Electricity, motor vehicles, public transit, and public sanitation infrastructure changed American life, particularly in cities, virtually overnight between 1890 and 1929. The telephone and the phonograph were part of this epochal set of changes. Telephone lines linked at least half of total households and most of those in urban areas, adding further connections to the "networked house" already hooked up to the outside world with electric, gas, water, and sewer lines. The telephone allowed people to talk to each other without leaving the house, and phonographs replaced amateur music with professionally performed music, displaced performances across months or years of time, and represented the first of many inventions that cured "Baumol's disease."

RADIO BRINGS THE WORLD INTO ALMOST EVERY HOME

Radio spread across the nation like wildfire, so rapidly that more than 80 percent of American homes had at least one radio within twenty years of the launch of the first commercial radio station in 1920. The speed of radio's arrival exceeded that of electricity, the motor vehicle, the telephone, or the phonograph, and it is easy to see why. Unlike the acoustic phonograph, the radio arrived as a fully electric device and indeed, with its vacuum tubes, constituted the first phase of the electronics revolution that dominated the postwar years. After the radio was purchased, all the entertainment it provided was free, with no need to buy records or player piano rolls. And its ability to provide instantaneous news reports put it into competition with the daily newspaper.

Transmission of messages through the air rather than via wire long antedated the introduction of commercial radio. As with most of the great inventions of the late nineteenth century associated with particular names such as Edison or Bell, the discoveries of lesser-known predecessors extend back decades earlier. Although in 1896 Guglielmo Marconi obtained the first patent for wireless telegraphy, more than three decades earlier, in 1864, James Clark Maxwell first presented his theory of electromagnetic waves. The earliest experiments that transmitted and received waves were carried out in London by David Edward Hughes in December 1879, the same month when Karl Benz developed the first workable internal combustion engine and two months after Edison's first electric light. A newspaper article in 1899 summed up Hughes's unappreciated role: "the 1879 experiments were virtually a discovery of Hertzian waves before Hertz, of the coherer before Branly, and of wireless telegraphy before Marconi and others."[51]

What Marconi achieved was to become the first person to send wireless signals over significant distances. Though numerous other inventors had come close to his particular combination of components originally invented by others, he was the entrepreneur who put the ingredients together and at age 22 filed the first patents in 1896, in both the United Kingdom and the United States. His first public 1896 demonstration sent a clear signal over almost two miles in the United Kingdom, and by 1901 he had sent a signal across the Atlantic. Almost immediately, the British navy adopted wireless telegraphy, and the role of wireless in the 1912 *Titanic* disaster, when several nearby ships did not have their receivers turned on, has become an iconic part of popular culture.

The implementation of commercial radio required a whole series of additional inventions between 1900 and 1920 to transmit voice and music instead of just Morse code. Among these was the 1907 vacuum tube, which was central to electronics until the transistor emerged after 1947. Though the generators, antennas, amplifiers, and receivers were ready to create commercial radio as early as 1913, World War I intervened and required a postponement.[52]

By election night 1920, the planets were aligned, the technology was in place, and the world's first commercial radio station went on the air—not in London, not in New York, but in Pittsburgh. The electrical magnate George Westinghouse, whose AC current had triumphed over Edison's DC, saw great potential for his company to sell radio sets, but currently there was nothing for them to listen to except for sporadic and unpredictable speech and music transmitted by ham radio operators on unknown frequencies. Westinghouse worked with a local ham operator, Frank Conrad, and built a small shack on the roof of a Westinghouse building. At precisely 6:00 p.m. on election night, November 2, 1920, KDKA's announcer Leo Rosenberg spoke the first words ever heard on commercial radio and humbly asked at the end, in effect, "Is anyone listening out there?"

> This is KDKA of the Westinghouse Electric and Manufacturing Company in East Pittsburgh, Pennsylvania. We shall now broadcast the election returns. We are receiving these returns through the cooperation and by special arrangement with the Pittsburgh Post and Sun. We'd appreciate it if anyone hearing this broadcast would communicate with us as we are very anxious to know how far the broadcast is reaching and how it is being received.[53]

Immediately after the KDKA inaugural evening, interest in radio exploded throughout the nation. At night, KDKA could be heard throughout the eastern states. In 1921, the station went from one "first" to another as it broadcast the first Presidential inaugural address, the first sporting event, the first play-by-play baseball broadcast, and the first football game broadcast. Initially the audiences for these broadcasts were small, because it took time for manufacturing plants and distribution networks to be set up to sell receivers widely.

Then, in the winter of 1921–22, the commercial potential of radio arrived as the floodgates were opened. The word "radio" quickly replaced "wireless telephony." A San Francisco newspaper described the simultaneous discovery by millions of Americans that "[t]here is radio music in the air, every night, everywhere. Anybody can hear it at home on a receiving set, which any boy can put up in an hour." By the end of 1923, there were 556 radio stations, and sales of radio receivers soared from $60 million in 1922 to $843 million in 1929.[54]

We have already examined the diffusion of the telephone and phonograph in figure 6–4. Also shown in the same chart is that 46 percent of American families had radios by 1930 and fully 80 percent by 1940. No single event in the history of invention before 1940 brought about a more striking egalitarianism of a particular product, news and entertainment that could be enjoyed equally by the richest baron or poorest street cleaner.[55] The stunning impact of radio was summarized in late 1922, before most families had receivers, in this contrast between listening to the radio and being in a theater:

> [Now] we are assembled again in KDKA's unlimited theater, where rear seats are hundreds of miles from the stage and where the audience, all occupying private boxes, can come late or leave early without embarrassing the speaker or annoying the rest of the audience.[56]

It could be argued that the radio defined the first half of the twentieth century as much as the automobile did. Though the phonograph had brought professionally performed music into the home, now the whole package of news, music, information, and advertising was available every day and evening. "The first modern mass medium, radio made America into a land of listeners, entertaining and educating, angering and delighting, and joining every age and class into a common culture."[57]

Everything provided by the radio was free after the receiving set had been purchased. In 1927, Sears sold tabletop radios for as little as $24.95 and offered them on the installment plan at $4 down and $4 per month ($25 was less than 2 percent of a typical working-class household income in the 1920s). Just as floor-model phonographs had become available two decades earlier housed in elaborately carved wooden cabinets, cabinet radios were listed in the 1927 Sears catalog at prices ranging from $50 to $100.[58]

Among the broader effects of radio was the transformation of immediacy and intimacy. Listeners could hear events as they occurred, including the vocal reaction of the Parisian crowds to Lindbergh's 1927 flight, without waiting for a dry newspaper account the next day. Immediacy was joined by intimacy. Both describe the effects of Roosevelt's galvanizing first fireside chat of March 12, 1933, when he spoke to each listener as if he or she were there at FDR's side, starting with the explanation that the banking system relies on confidence and assuring the nation that it would be safe to place deposits in the banks when they reopened in the following week.

Even before the first commercial radio broadcast in 1920, General Electric (GE) had established the Radio Corporation of America.[59] RCA became the symbol of the new radio era, and its stock was referred to simply as "Radio." The spectacular rise and fall of its stock became an icon of the 1920s stock market boom and bust; its stock price rose by a factor of 100 between 1924 and the 1929 peak and then lost almost all its value by 1931.[60]

As early as 1922, the need was seen for linking together radio stations so that they could share the same programming. Network radio as we know it arrived in 1926 with the formation of the National Broadcasting Company (NBC) as an enterprise jointly owned by RCA, GE, and Westinghouse. Before the formation of NBC, there had been two groups of stations, one centered around New York's WEAF (now WNBC) and the other around WJZ (now WABC). These became two separate networks known as NBC Red and NBC Blue, which later in 1943 became ABC. By the time of Lindbergh's flight in June, 1927, the NBC Red network had linked together with telephone lines fifty stations in twenty-four states.[61]

The spreading influence of the networks was intertwined with the development of the large clear-channel stations, each of which was the only station on its frequency, and each of which could be heard for long distances at night.[62] By the early 1930s, almost all evening programming came from the networks, so rural listeners in Iowa would hear the same programming whether they tuned in to WCCO in Minneapolis or KMOX in St. Louis. For the 47 percent of Americans who in 1925 lived on farms and in small rural towns, the radio was a blessing:

> When they say "The Radio" they don't mean a cabinet, an electrical phenomenon, or a man in the studio; they refer to a pervading and somewhat godlike presence which has come into their lives and homes.[63]

Rural areas differed from urban America by adopting the motor vehicle and the telephone in larger percentages than electricity and radio by 1929. But during the 1930s, that changed as radio sets declined in price. Electricity had not yet arrived in rural America because of the high cost of building the distribution network. Nevertheless, the rural use of radios became almost universal in the 1930s, thanks in part to the development of efficient battery-powered sets.

The central role of radio during the 1930s is supported by a survey finding that "Americans would rather sell their refrigerators, bath tubs, telephones, and beds to make rent payments, than to part with the radio box that connected to the world."[64] As radio shifted toward a financial system based on advertising commercials, so programming shifted away from educational features and classical music to popular music and comedy/variety shows, often starring those who had been displaced from vaudeville. At its peak in 1933, the daily *Amos 'n' Andy* show earned its two black-faced comedic stars an annual income of $100,000, higher than that of the presidents of NBC, RCA, or the United States.[65] The commercials that financed this extravagance were for widely distributed packaged goods that were consumed across the entire nation, including cigarettes, toothpaste, coffee, and laxatives.

Comedian George Burns recalls the *Amos 'n' Andy* show in his autobiographical memories of the effect of radio on his previous career as a vaudeville comedian:

> Then radio came in. For the first time people didn't have to leave their homes to be entertained. The performers came into their house. I knew that vaudeville was finished when theaters began advertising that their shows would be halted for 15 minutes so that the audience could listen to "Amos 'n' Andy." . . . It's impossible to explain the impact that radio had on the world to anyone who didn't live through that time.[66]

In part, the growing popularity of radio reflected the continuing decline in the prices of receivers and improvements in their quality, a familiar theme from the postwar electronic age. But an equally important stimulus to receiver sales was the increased quality and variety of programming. Cabinet radios became the central piece of furniture in American households and served to join parents and children alike together to listen to comedy and variety shows, the latest news, drama, and even the newly developed "soap operas." "The radio . . . offered the compensations of fantasy to lonely people with deadening jobs or loveless lives, to people who were deprived or emotionally starved."[67]

The commercialization of radio in the 1930s was intertwined with the pervasiveness of its advertising. Unlike a magazine, in which a page could be flipped, radio advertisements could not be escaped, particularly because most people sat around a console radio and would have to get up from their chairs to turn down the volume. Advertising was, indirectly, the reason why the radio invaded the American household so much more quickly than did the phonograph or telephone, for advertising allowed the content to be free. Listeners in the 1930s were rarely reminded that the Great Depression was occurring:

> Dance bands played happy music, and Jack Benny would have worried about money in the best of times. In this apparent paradox, perhaps, lay radio's ultimate appeal. Real life in the 1930s was hard enough to bear. When people clicked their radios on, they were seeking not reality but escape. Radio brought relief, with a message from our sponsor.[68]

The establishment in 1934 of the Federal Communications Commission threatened broadcasters with a new era of regulation to force them to broadcast more cultural and public service programming instead of so much light comedy and music financed by the sponsorship of commercial advertising. Responding before any significant regulation occurred, Sarnoff hired Arturo Toscanini to create an entire orchestra and conduct it, and the NBC Symphony was given its own separate studio in the RCA building, now known as "30 Rock." Starting on Christmas night 1937, the NBC orchestra continued until 1954.

The public service component of broadcasting turned in the late 1930s to the threat of war. An epochal moment in the history of news broadcasting occurred on the night of the Anschluss, the German takeover of Austria, on March 13, 1938. On that night was born "CBS World News Tonight," which still broadcasts nightly even today, and which then achieved the first transatlantic shortwave radio link between Robert Trout in New York and correspondents from London, Paris, Berlin, Vienna, and Washington. Notably, the broadcast featured the network broadcasting debut of Edward R. Murrow, reporting that evening from Vienna in a colloquial and informal style notably different than the other contributors.[69]

In the gloomy Depression years the downtrodden masses looked to sources of inspiration, to the Horatio Algers who by effort and luck could lift themselves from poverty to success. By 1937, "all of these new social and technological forces were converging.... The new machine of fame stood waiting. All it needed was the subject itself."[70] And that subject turned out to be a horse named Seabiscuit. The rise of this small, crooked-legged horse from obscurity fascinated the nation, and Seabiscuit has been called, at least by the standard of popular interest, the biggest single news event of 1938. The match race between Seabiscuit and War Admiral in June 1938 has been called not only the greatest match race of all time, but also the most-listened-to radio broadcast in history up to that time, with 40 million listeners in a population of 129 million. "FDR was so absorbed in the broadcast that he kept a roomful of advisors waiting. He would not emerge until the race was over."[71]

Fewer than sixty years separated the earliest wireless experiments from the mature radio industry of 1938. In 1879, David Edward Hughes succeeded in sending a wireless signal over a distance of a few hundred meters in London, and by 1938, network radio had gained the ability to connect correspondents on different continents in live and instantaneous communication, as in the inaugural CBS World News Tonight broadcast, and the enormous audience for the Seabiscuit race demonstrated radio's ability to focus the nation's attention on a single event. Only three years later, an even larger audience would listen to FDR's condemnation of the "Day of Infamy" as the United States declared war on Japan.

THE MOTION PICTURE FROM THE NICKELODEON TO *GONE WITH THE WIND*

The history of the motion picture begins with the still photo, going back to Aristotle's first observations about the laws of optics around 330 BC and to the invention of the pinhole camera *(camera obscura)* by an Arab around AD 1000. Until the 1820s, however, there was no way to preserve the images that emerged from the pinhole. The daguerreotype, invented in 1839 by Louis Daguerre, was the first process that allowed a permanent image to be created, and soon afterward, in 1841, the Englishman Henry Fox Talbot developed a method for making a negative from which multiple positive prints could be made. However, these early processes were clumsy and relied on wet plate negatives that had to be developed quickly after the photograph was taken, in practice requiring the photographer to carry a darkroom along with him. Only in 1879 was the dry plate negative invented, making possible handheld cameras, and finally, in 1889, George Eastman invented film and, with it, the modern era of photography.[72]

The initial development of motion pictures focused on the creation of motion and the achievement of a projected image on a wall. Already Edison had been left behind in the development of the phonograph by clinging to the cylinder instead of adopting the flat record disc. In the same way, he failed in the early 1890s to create a motion picture product that was more than a novelty. His "kinetoscope" of 1894, which was a cabinet into which the viewer squinted to see a small moving image, suffered from its inherent limitations: The image was very small, and the film loop had a viewing duration of only twenty seconds, though it was soon extended to ninety seconds. Edison failed to see the commercial potential of motion pictures as anything other than a tool of education.[73] In the end, the problem of passing sufficient light through the film to illuminate a large screen was solved by Thomas Armant, who devised a projector in which bright pictures and smooth action were achieved by stopping each frame as it passed by the projection lamp.

Because Armant did not have sufficient funds or reputation to commercialize his project, he reached an agreement to share the profits with Edison for the newly christened Vitascope. Its debut in 1896 included "Uncle Sam knocking a diminutive bully, John Bull, to his knees, street scenes from New York, and the first medium range close-up of a kiss.... the audience fairly shrieked and howled approval.'"[74] Thus thanks to his wealth and fame, Edison received credit for the motion picture, even though he played virtually no part in its invention.

Still photographs were originally viewed through home instruments called "stereoscopes" and in public penny arcades, which also provided access to phonographs, fortune-telling machines, and sometimes slot machines. As with vaudeville, penny arcades were not available in rural areas and tended to flourish in dense urban neighborhoods, where families could participate for a few pennies without having to spend scarce cash on public transportation. Around 1905, penny arcades began to create separate sections in the back for the projection of motion pictures on a wall or screen; because admission to the motion picture cost five cents rather than a penny, such operations quickly became known as "nickelodeons."

Soon nickelodeons emerged from the back room of the penny arcade and became separate buildings. By 1908, there were more than 200 nickelodeons in Manhattan alone and at least 8,000 nationwide, attracting 4 million customers per day. The standard design was twenty feet wide and eighty feet long, with wooden chairs or benches for seating. A basic technological limitation was the projection mechanism that halted the film at each frame. These stops and starts made the screen pulse with an eye-straining "flicker" effect, which led to the new expression "going to the flicks."[75] At the front, behind a railing, was the enclave of the piano player who accompanied the silent features. Though the interiors might be plain, increasingly the exteriors featured giant arches and extensive decoration in themes ranging from Moorish to Gothic to Beaux Arts, often decorated with dragons, faces, or statuary. Every theater was studded with lightbulbs, leading to the description of each city's theater district as the "Great White Way."

From our perspective, it is hard to imagine the excitement that these early film shows evoked, but many of the viewers had never traveled or had a chance to see places more than a few miles from their homes. For the first time, a person might see what a moving elephant looked like or gain a first view of a beach on the Atlantic or Pacific oceans. In one early nickelodeon feature, when a train pulling into a station came straight toward the camera, several customers in the front rows panicked and ran out.[76]

The transition from nickelodeons to movie palaces began as early as 1911 with the opening of Detroit's Columbia Theater, which was equipped not only with 1,000 seats, but also with the first movie pipe organ. The few years before America's 1917 entry into World War I were the most frenetic period of theater building as the small and simple nickelodeons were replaced by mammoth theaters in the center of every city and similar but smaller theaters in the residential neighborhoods. The ornate decoration of the palaces included "carved niches, the cloistered arcades, the depthless mirrors, and the great sweeping staircases.... [W]atch the eyes of the child as it enters the portals of our great theaters and treads the pathway into fairyland."[77] The exotic architecture included themes inspired by Babylon, Granada, and the Riviera.

The new movie palaces provided a social leveling, as the working-class customers, for a mere seven cents, were able to enter palaces that would have inspired upper-class barons and lords. "They offered a gilded mansion for the weekly invasion of those who lived in stuffy apartments, or a gorgeous canopy to spread over a cramped and limited life."[78] In October 1921, a *Chicago Tribune* report on a theater opening gushed that "for sheer splendor, expensiveness, and display, the Chicago Theater sets a world's record."[79]

The decade of 1910 to 1920 witnessed a complete transition from very short features in nickelodeons to full-length features in large theaters. Despite its crude racism and glorification of the Ku Klux Klan, D. W. Griffin's *The Birth of a Nation* pioneered many movie techniques, including close-ups, rapid editing, and fade-outs. The swift rise of weekly moviegoing brought with it the star system, and by 1915 Charlie Chaplin and Mary Pickford were familiar names, and their fame from film appearances was magnified by newspaper and periodical profiles.

By 1922, nationwide weekly movie attendance had reached 40 million per week, or roughly 36 percent of the population. This implies that the entire population, from babies to elderly grandmothers, were going to the movies more than once every three weeks. This number is particularly impressive considering that the nation in 1920 was still half rural; thus the frequency of moviegoing must have been close to once per week in urban America. A 1919 study of Toledo, Ohio, tallied a weekly attendance of 316,000 in a population of 243,000: Movie attendance per person had reached 130 percent!

The Toledo study provides valuable insight into the motion picture industry in 1919. The prices of movie attendance ranged from seven to fifty-five cents, with an average of fifteen cents. Another source suggests that in 1913 movie tickets averaged a mere seven cents.[80] The average movie show lasted roughly 2.3 hours and consisted of "news review, treatise of titles from magazines, an educational reel, clown comedy, and finally the feature film."[81] Newsreels were common during the silent film era, and the first all-news theater opened in New York City in 1909. Audiences who had previously learned of the news from dry newspaper accounts were now captivated by their vivid new view of real events.

In Toledo and across the nation, the largest theaters had live organ performances to accompany the feature film. The studios distributed "cue sheets" of suggested music, but the organist or pianist had full license to improvise, so *The Birth of a Nation* could sound quite different in Toledo from how it sounded in, say, Seattle. In a 1922 essay, an organist cited examples of the pieces of classical music that were ready to accompany any scene: For instance, a movie scene with rapidly rushing water could be accompanied by "Prelude to the Deluge" by Saint-Saens. Organists and pianists played their accompaniment over and over for multiple daily performances, so their performances could sound improvised but were the result of intensive homework.[82]

A surprising aspect of film history is that the industry became so large even before the talking picture was invented. Another surprise is that the marriage of motion pictures with sound took so long, considering that sound motion pictures had been a goal of Edison's as early as 1890. The problems bedeviled inventors through the 1920s, including the core problem of achieving synchronization of voice and picture, and the awkward fact that sound amplification in 1925 was unable to match the space dimensions of a modern motion picture theater. The American Lee de Forest invented the technique of sound-on-film in which the sound track is photographically recorded on the side of the strip of motion picture film. With the sound is physically adjacent to the picture on the film strip, perfect synchronization is automatic.

Though sound-enhanced newsreels of Lindbergh's flight had been shown in theaters as early as May, 1927, a few more months were required for the sensational premier of the first "talkie," Al Jolson in the *Jazz Singer*. The large profits made by Warner Bros. from the first talkie, followed by three more in 1928, convinced the other studio owners that they needed to convert immediately to sound. The conversion occurred almost overnight, and by 1930, movie advertisements carried the reassuring logo "100% talking."[83] The transition from silent to sound movies occurred very fast and created obsolescence not just in mechanical equipment and jobs for pianists and organists, but in the previous stars. As famously satirized in the 1952 movie *Singing in the Rain*, some stars of the silent era had screechy and unattractive voices and were passed over for a new generation of movie stars.

As shown in figure 6–5, during 1929–33, the worst years of the economy's collapse, weekly movie attendance per person declined from 73 percent to 48 percent. But then there was a rapid recovery to 68 percent in 1936–37, and the ratio remained above 60 percent consistently from 1935 to 1948 before

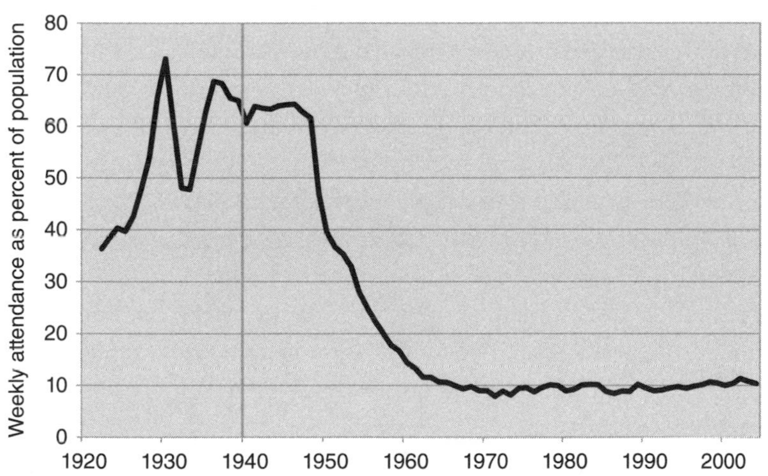

Figure 6–5. Weekly Motion Picture Attendance as a Percentange of Total US Population, 1922–2004

Sources: HSUS series Aa7, Dh388 before 1950, *International Motion Picture Almanac* (2006) ratio linked forward after 1950.

plummeting to 10 percent in the 1960s and thereafter as television became the main form of entertainment. The continued popularity of movies through the late 1940s reflected a different business model than radio, whose provided content was free after the receiver was purchased. A movie show could be purchased without any initial investment, and first-run movies at downtown palaces fell in price during 1929–33 from fifty cents to twenty-five cents, and second runs in neighborhood theaters from a quarter to a dime.[84] At twenty-five cents per admission, a person could attend fifty annual movie shows for $12.50, or 2.4 percent of 1936 nominal disposable personal income per capita of $525.[85] Audiences in the 1930s came to expect their admission to purchase a double feature, and the array of choices was endless, from gangster films, westerns, and screwball comedies to musical epics with choreography by Busby Berkeley or the light-footed dancing of Fred Astaire and Ginger Rogers. Fantasy, horror, and science fiction rounded out the list, with Dracula, Frankenstein, and King Kong evoking screams from millions of moviegoers.

Four of the top ten movies of the twentieth century, as ranked by the American Film Institute in 1998, were made in the four years between 1939 and 1942. Two of these, *Citizen Kane* (1941) and *Casablanca* (1942) lie slightly after the 1940 dividing line between parts I and II of this book. But the other two provide a demonstration as clear as day and night of the progress of the sound motion picture over the decade since *The Jazz Singer*. The *Wizard of Oz*, with its unprecedented mix of sepia-toned monochrome in the early sequences followed by vivid color afterward, not only enchanted movie viewers in 1939, but became even more familiar to postwar audiences thanks to its annual rebroadcast on CBS television starting in 1956.[86] The movie made Judy Garland a star and earned two Academy Awards for the classic score by Harold Arlen and Yip Harberg. How the nation must have gasped with wonder and delight when Dorothy emerged intact after the monochrome tornado, which had dumped her house on top of the Wicked Witch of the East, and wandered out into the Technicolor paradise of Oz, turning to her canine friend with the line that would echo through the rest of the century: "Toto, I have a feeling we're not in Kansas anymore."[87]

Even though The *Wizard of Oz* is as familiar to us today, thanks to its postwar TV rebroadcasts, as is *Gone with the Wind*, the latter film was a much greater sensation for Americans in 1939. Margaret Mitchell's epic novel had been a best-seller in 1936, and the nation's attention was riveted for two years in the search for the actress to play Scarlett O'Hara:

> Fan magazines breathlessly reported on anything even remotely associated with the project, and MGM went so far as to replicate the portico of Tara, Scarlett's family home, for a gala opening night.... All the hoopla paid off: *Gone with the Wind* was an immediate, enduring hit.... [It] wraps up the 1930s in grand style.... [F]or sheer entertainment—the real reason people attend the movies—it stands as the champion of the decade.[88]

CONCLUSION: FROM PREHISTORY TO THE MODERN ERA IN SEVENTY YEARS

If we view this book as setting out a contest between improvements in the standard of living before and after 1940, then surely this chapter would provide the weakest evidence of advance before 1940 compared to the other chapters in part I. What could compete with the revolutions in chapter 3 for food production, variety, and distribution and the shift from homemade to store-bought apparel; or in chapter 4 the emergence over 1870–1940 in the networked home with its connections to electricity, gas, water, and sewer, together with the development of enclosed furnaces, stoves, and all the other consumer appliances; or in chapter 5 the evolution from primitive horse-drawn omnibuses to the rapid transit of elevated trains and subways, as well as the epochal shift from the urban pollution of horses to much faster, more efficient, and cleaner motor vehicles?

Compared to such fundamental progress, it might seem that this chapter's topic of information, communication, and entertainment might pale into insignificance compared to postwar developments. After all, so much that we take for granted today was missing in 1940, when even the most primitive early nine-inch black-and-white television sets were still in the future, not to mention color television and later cable television with its hundreds of channels; music played on long-playing discs, tapes, compact discs, and digital audio players; and information gathered on the Internet and viewed on ever smaller and more convenient desktops, laptops, smartphones, and tablets.[89] Yet one can argue that the effect on American culture and society of the progress before 1940 made more difference than that which has occurred since 1940.

During the 1870–1940 interval, isolation was replaced by communication. So many aspects of human existence that did not exist in 1870 became possible, from phoning a neighbor to borrow a cup of sugar to an anguished plea by a farmer to request emergency assistance to the availability on phonograph records of the world's classical and popular music to the radio revolution that made news and entertainment live, immediate, and free and, finally, to the motion picture with its extraordinary emergence as the dominant form of entertainment.

As we lament the passing of print media today in the face of Internet competition, it is easy to lose sight of how dominant the print media were after 1870 but not before. The readership of books, magazines, and newspapers exploded after 1870. This supports the theme in this book that economic growth, though simmering in the wings before 1870, came onstage and became the driving fact in human existence in the century after 1870. It was not just the effect of technology in creating rapid reductions in the price of paper and printing technology, but also the contribution of almost universal literacy (except for the former slaves in the south). And this quantum leap in the amount of reading in the population was fueled not just by advances in the private sector, but also by the government provision of free public libraries.

Before 1844, the speed of communication was limited to that made possible by the railroad, horse, and sailing ship. In the history of technology spanning millennia, there had never been so radical an increase in the speed of communication as that made possible by the 1844 invention of the telegraph. By 1870, there was a long line of inventors waiting to take the next step by converting the dot-dash of the telegraph code to the human voice sent over a telephone. By a narrow margin, Alexander Graham Bell achieved the first patent, and for that reason, during the twentieth century, the telephone network of AT&T was known as the "Bell System." Telephones arrived in the American home relatively slowly over the five decades between 1876 and 1926, but it became the dominant form of communication during that interval.

The innovations that created modern entertainment started with the phonograph. Before its arrival, there was no way that most families outside of the largest cities could hear professional renditions of classical or popular music. The slow development of the phonograph contrasted with the instant acceptance of radio. Unlike the phonograph, which imposed a cost to buy recordings, radio offered its multiple forms of content, from news to comedy to music, for free. Though there is supposed to be "no such thing as a free lunch," radio almost achieved that impossibility, especially in the 1930s when radio set prices fell below $20. No longer did the most humble family need to buy records to hear music; it was all free on the radio.

A contemporary reader might join me in being surprised at the early chronology of motion pictures and the rapidity of its transition to a major industry.

The nickelodeon suddenly emerged in 1906–7, and by 1911 the grand movie palaces were being built, with terra cotta decoration and full-length silent features to attract customers. Throughout the first three decades of the twentieth century, the quality of every aspect of entertainment improved, and by 1928 the era of the talking motion picture had begun.

How far had we come? Starting from nothing but isolation in 1870, within seventy years, the nation was brought together. No fewer than 40 million people, fully a third of the population, listened to the 1938 radio Match Race between Sea Biscuit and War Admiral. Millions witnessed that magical moment when Dorothy emerged from sepia into color with the iconic words "Toto, I've a feeling we're not in Kansas anymore."[90]

Perhaps no greater symbol of the arrival of mass entertainment is a little-known journey taken by David O. Selznick, producer of *Gone with the Wind*, two months before that movie's 1939 release. The theater owner had been contacted, he had agreed, and the producers showed up in Santa Barbara with a big surprise for the audience. An announcement came over the public address system—that they would not be seeing either of the double features scheduled for that night.

> The theater manager told the audience it was about to see a "very special" picture, and that no one would be allowed to leave once it had started. Guards were posted in the lobby throughout the screening. When the main title came on the screen, there were excited gasps and cheers. Many people rose to their feet and applauded, as they did at the end, three hours and forty-five minutes later without intermission. Selznick was moved to tears by the enthusiasm.[91]

The audience left the theater that night with a sense of privilege that they had chanced upon something so special that it would instantly make them famous among their friends and about which they would be able to brag to their grandchildren many years hence.[92]

None of that could have happened in 1870. Yet in 1939, everything seemed possible. Radio and the motion picture had reached the pinnacle of their achievement, but television was still to come, vividly demonstrated at the 1939–40 New York World fair. Was the modern world of 1940 more distant from 1870 than today's entertainment in 2015 is from that of 1940? We will revisit that question in chapter 12.

Chapter 7

NASTY, BRUTISH, AND SHORT: ILLNESS AND EARLY DEATH

> Outstanding among these consequences is the virtual eradication or the effective control in many areas of communicable diseases spread by water, milk, and food, or transmitted by insects, rodents, and man himself, so that in countries like the United States once-dreaded diseases, such as yellow fever, typhoid fever, diphtheria, and malaria, are a thing of the past.
>
> —George Rosen, 1958

INTRODUCTION

Previous chapters have traced the role of major inventions and their complementary follow-up innovations in raising the standard of living by providing new types of products and services that increased consumer welfare, raised the value of hours spent in leisure-time activities, and reduced the drudgery and tedium of home production. This chapter examines another dimension of improvement—the set of developments that made possible increasing life expectancy, thus raising the number of years over which the new products and uses of time could be enjoyed. During the 1870–1940 interval covered in part I of this book, life expectancy improved at all ages but most rapidly at birth, because these years witnessed the near eradication of infant mortality. By several estimates, the value of reduced mortality, particularly of infants, was as great as the value of all the growth over the same period in market-purchased goods and services.

Predictions of future economic progress from our current vantage point place major emphasis on continuing advances made possible by medical research, including the decoding of the genome and research using stem cells. It is often assumed that medical advances have moved at a faster pace since the invention of antibiotics in the 1930s and 1940s, the development from the 1970s of techniques of radiation and chemotherapy to fight cancer, and the advent of electronic devices such as the CT and MRI scans to improve diagnoses of many diseases. Many readers will be surprised to learn that the annual rate of improvement in life expectancy was *twice as fast in the first half of the twentieth century as in the last half.* In the words of David Cutler and Grant Miller, "together with the late 19th century, no other documented period in American history [as 1900–1940] witnessed such rapidly falling mortality rates."[1]

How was that epochal improvement in life outcomes achieved? This chapter pulls together the many explanations. These include the development of urban sanitation infrastructure, including running water and separate sewer pipes, that were part of the "networking" of the American home that took place between 1870 and 1929 (as discussed in chapter 4). A contribution was made by Louis Pasteur's germ theory of disease, which fostered public awareness about the dangers inherent in swarming insects and pools of stagnant water. The internal combustion engine deserves its share of credit for removing the urban horse and its prodigious and unrestrained outpouring of manure and urine onto city streets. Window screens, invented in the 1870s, contributed by creating a barrier in farmhouses to prevent insects from commuting back and forth between animal waste and the family dinner table. Government action at the local level built urban sanitation infrastructure and, at the national level, created the Food and Drug Administration.

No period illustrates better than 1870–1940 that health and longevity depend on more than expenditures on doctors and hospitals. This theme is common today as analysts speculate how much of the relatively low ranking of U.S. life expectancy in the world league tables results from factors that emerge from outside of the health industry sector, including obesity and smoking. Nevertheless, the role of the health care sector gradually became more important over time. The great achievement between 1870 and 1940 was the rapid reduction in the mortality rate of infants and children. In contrast, life expectancy at age 60 increased more rapidly after 1940 than before.

This book views the household from the perspective of Gary Becker's economic theory of time.[2] Households purchase market-produced goods and services and then combine them with their own time to produce the ultimate object that produces utility—for example, a home-cooked meal or an hour listening to the radio. Thus within the utility function is a household production function in which goods, services, and time are inputs. Joel Mokyr and Rebecca Stein broaden this interpretation to apply to health. For them, the household production function produces not just enjoyment, but also good health as consumers purchase items such as soap or aspirin. Items such as tobacco can subtract from health. The same good can produce both enjoyment and bad health, including too much food, which produces obesity, and cigarette smoking, which produces lung cancer. In their interpretation, a significant part of the decline in mortality in the early twentieth century resulted from improved knowledge about health at the level of the individual household.[3]

There is no dispute that however the improvements in life expectancy are achieved, they are of great value. The studies we examine agree that the values are stunning even if the experts may differ on whether health advances at any given time would raise estimates of per-capita GDP growth by 50 percent or 100 percent. The value of reducing infant mortality is greater than of improving the life expectancy of a 65-year-old, and this implies that improvements in health contributed a larger addition to household welfare before 1940 than after. Improvements in the standard of living are measured not just by changes in life expectancy, but also by QALYs, or quality-adjusted life years, which attempt to convert into a quantitative measure the results of medical interventions.[4]

The central task of this chapter is not just to explain the rapid increase in life expectancy from 1870 to 1940, but also to identify aspects of change that improved the quality of life beyond the reduction in mortality. The first step is to quantify progress along the dimensions of life expectancy at different ages, death rates, and causes of death. The next sections search for the causes of improvement. Possible candidates include progress made outside the health sector, including diet, nutrition, running water and sewers, food and drug regulation, and a reduction in both industrial accidents and violence. Within the health sector, we credit the early pharmaceuticals, starting with aspirin and advances in medical technology, including the early X-ray machines. We ask "what did doctors and hospitals do?" in those early years when drugs were few and medical knowledge was primitive. The transformation of health care can be dated to the same fifty-year period between 1890 and 1940 when so much else was revolutionized in the American standard of living, as hospitals joined other new institutions, such as the hotel, the factory, the club, the opera, the symphony, the theater, the high school, and the university, in taking roughly their modern-day form.

NEVER MATCHED BEFORE OR SINCE: DIMENSIONS OF IMPROVEMENT, 1870–1940

There was no improvement in either mortality rates or life expectancy before 1870, and in most data series, there was no improvement before 1890. In 1870–79, male life expectancy at age 20 was identical to that in 1750–79, and that for females was actually lower.[5] The central fact in the improvement of life expectancy was the decline of infant mortality, as shown in figure 7–1. The rate of 215 per 1,000 births for 1880 was unchanged from rates in the range of 200 to 250 reported as far back as Tudor England.[6] There was no improvement between 1850 and 1880, followed by a steep decline from 1890 to 1950 and then a much slower rate of decline after 1950. The historic decline in infant mortality centered in the six-decade period of 1890–1950 is one of the most important single facts in the history of American economic growth. Out of every 1,000 births, the number of lives saved by improvements from 1880 to 1950 was 188, and the additional number saved from 1950 to 2010 was a mere twenty-one.

That life expectancy did not begin its historic ascent until 1890 is consistent with substantial evidence that conditions deteriorated before that year. Robert Higgs concludes, "There is little evidence that mortality in the mid-nineteenth century countryside was markedly lower than it had

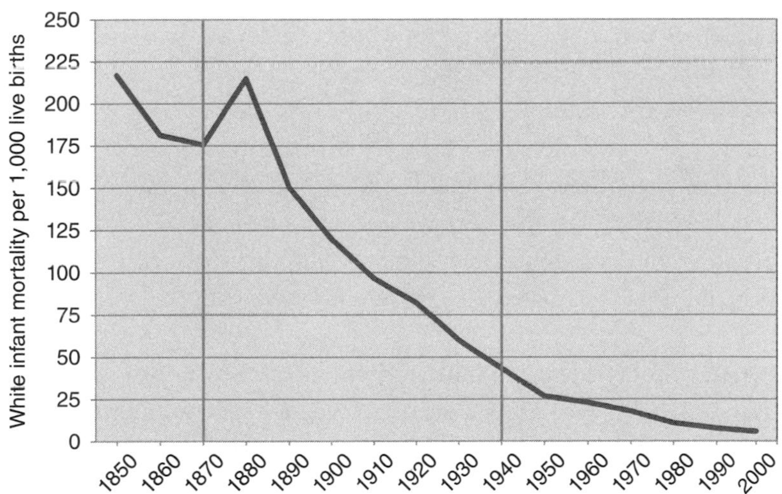

Figure 7–1. White Infant Mortality, 1850–2000

Source: HSUS series Ab9.

been a century earlier."[7] Roderick Floud, Robert Fogel, and their coauthors document that life expectancy at age 10 declined steadily between 1790 and 1850, remained on a plateau until 1880, and only then began to improve. Life expectancy at birth also stagnated between 1850 and 1880, only to march steadily higher after that year.[8] Consistent with this view of a late-century takeoff is evidence compiled by the same authors on human heights, which indicate a steady decline between those born in the 1830 decade to those born in the 1890 decade, followed by a steady increase that was at its most rapid between 1890 and 1930.[9] There is separate evidence that life expectancy in Massachusetts improved more during the thirty years 1890–1920 than in the entire century before 1890.[10]

Historical studies have consistently found higher mortality rates and lower life expectancy in urban areas than in rural areas.[11] Food consumed on farms was fresher, whereas food was often contaminated by the time it reached urban consumers. Contagious diseases spread faster when people lived closer together in cities, the effect of standing water in breeding disease-carrying insects was greater than on farms, and the airless, poorly ventilated and often windowless rooms in tightly packed urban tenements contributed to illness and death. By one estimate, life expectancy at birth in 1900 was 46.0 years for white rural males and 39.1 years for white urban males, with the rural/urban differential about half that for white females. "Urbanization moved people from lower to higher mortality regimes, exacting a price for the increased economic opportunity of the city."[12] The very industrialization of the late nineteenth century made air and water pollution greater threats than before:

> Earth was scarred by mining pits and railway tracks; air was fouled and darkened by factory soot; water was polluted by industrial wastes or ran unchecked down eroded mountains once covered by forests. Americans became imperialists within their own nation.[13]

Figure 7–2 highlights the quite different rates of improvement in life expectancy at birth, with life expectancy at higher ages ranging up to age 70. The chart shows the point of inflection at 1950, after which life expectancy at birth radically slowed from its previous rate of ascent. But life expectancy viewed from each older age improves much less, and this is the direct corollary to the conquest of infant mortality as part of overall life expectancy

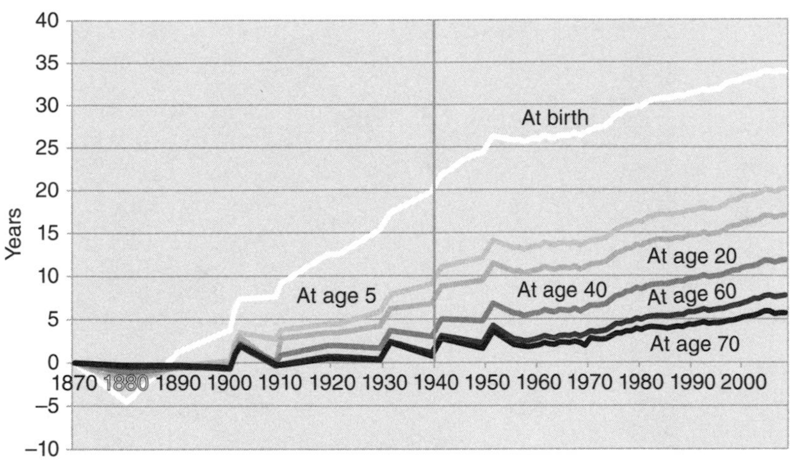

Figure 7–2. Years of Additional Life Expectancy Compared to the Year 1870, at Various Ages by Year, 1870–2008

Sources: HSUS series Ab656-667, 2002 SAUS no. 93, 2003 SAUS no. 107, 2004–2005 SAUS no. 94, 2006 SAUS no. 98, 2007 SAUS table 100, 2008 SAUS table 101, 2009 SAUS table 103, 2010 SAUS table 105, 2011 SAUS table 105, and 2012 SAUS table 107.

improvement. Whereas life expectancy at birth increased at twice the rate during 1890–1950 as during 1950–98 (0.32 years of annual improvement versus 0.15 years), the relationship was reversed for life expectancy at age 70 (0.03 versus 0.05 years annually for the two intervals).[14] After Americans "made it" through childhood, their life expectancy did not increase radically over time. We are reminded of one of the most bizarre coincidences of American history: both John Adams and Thomas Jefferson died on July 4, 1826, on the exact fiftieth anniversary of the Declaration of Independence, Adams at the grand old age of 90 and Jefferson aged 83. Though infant mortality was shockingly high by modern standards, Americans who survived early childhood, even in the eighteenth century, had the potential to live as long as Jefferson and Adams.

Another way of dramatizing the role of infant mortality in contributing to the increase of life expectancy is to plot survival rates. Of 100 people born, how many survived to each age, from age 1 to age 80? Three sets of survival rates are plotted in figure 7–3, those for 1870, 1940, and 1997. The lower 1870 line clearly shows the devastating role of infant mortality in reducing survival by age 5 to 75 percent, as compared to 94 percent in 1940 and 99 percent in 1997. Also shown is that half of the 1870 group were dead by

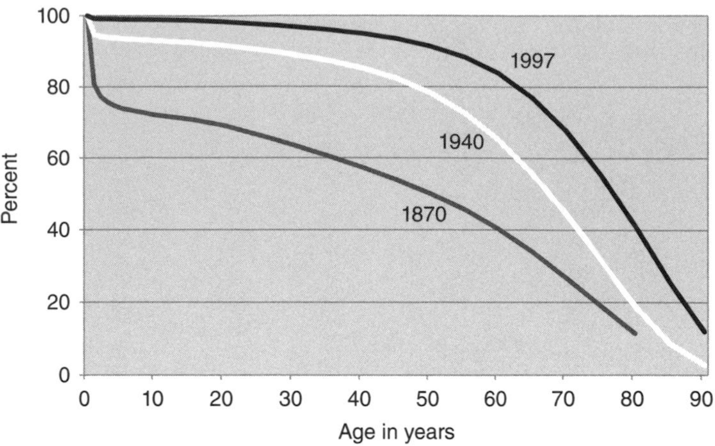

Figure 7–3. Survival Rate by Age in 1870, 1940, and 1997
Source: HSUS series Ab706-728.

age 50, whereas the 50 percent survival rate did not occur until age 67 in the 1940 group and not until age 77 in the 1997 group. Kevin Murphy and Robert Topel have captured this dramatic improvement with a simple factual comparison: "In 1900, nearly 18 percent of males born in the United States died before their first birthday; today, cumulative mortality does not reach 18 percent until age *62.*"[15]

Mortality was consistently lower in the northern states than in the south, and it was also lower for southern whites than nonwhites. The lingering effects of slavery and of post–Civil War poverty and discrimination resulted in 1900 life expectancies at birth for both nonwhite males and nonwhite females that were sixteen to seventeen years shorter than for their white equivalents. By 1940, this difference had narrowed markedly. Life expectancy at birth for white males had increased from 48 to 63 between 1900 and 1940 and for nonwhite miles from 33 to 52, for a reduction in the gap from fifteen to eleven years, still very substantial. For females, the gap declined over the same period from sixteen years to twelve years.[16] One reason for the shorter life expectancy of nonwhites was the explicit Jim Crow policy of denying nonwhite areas of cities and nonwhite rural areas the modern improvements of running water and sanitary sewage disposal provided to whites.[17]

Other chapters have emphasized the unprecedented pace of change in the living conditions of Americans in the decades after 1870. The same appears to be true for the mortality rate of the 75 percent of Americans classified as "rural" in 1870. In the forty years 1870–1910, the rural death rate declined by between 30 percent and 40 percent. As stated by Robert Higgs,

> In a half century after 1870 nothing less than a vital revolution occurred in the American countryside. It is highly unlikely that a long-term mortality decline of this proportion could ever have occurred in American history before 1870.[18]

WATER COMETH AND SEWERS TAKETH AWAY: A CENTRAL SOURCE OF MORTALITY IMPROVEMENT

Douglas Ewbank and Robert Preston highlight the central issue about declining mortality. "Death is a biological event and all influences must ultimately affect mortality from biological variables." Their analysis of the decline of infant mortality is equally concise: "The dominant biological variables affecting infant and child mortality in the United States a century ago … are exposure to infectious diseases and human responses to that exposure."[19] Even before the formal development of the Pasteur theory of disease and the related discoveries of treatments for specific infectious diseases, there was a widespread belief that cities were unhealthy places. Authors in 1858 described an urban world that was condemned to poor health and death:

> The crowded narrow tenements to which avarice drives poverty, in filthy streets and noisome courts, become perennial sources of deadly miasmata that may be wafted to the neighboring mansions of wealth and refinement, to cause sickness and mourning there, and when once the breadth of pestilence becomes epidemic in any city, commerce and trade are driven to more salubrious marts.[20]

During the pre-1940 era, improvements in medical care by doctors and hospitals played a relatively small role in the decline of mortality rates and the accompanying increases in life expectancy at birth. Higgs concludes that "changes in medical practice during the period 1870–1920 could, at best, have contributed only negligibly to the decline in the rural crude death rate."[21] The most outspoken proponents of this view are John and Sonja McKinlay, who plot a figure similar to figure 7–4, which we have updated from their 1972 termination date to 2009. Our updated version plots the overall mortality rate, as well as the rate minus the contribution of eight infectious diseases.

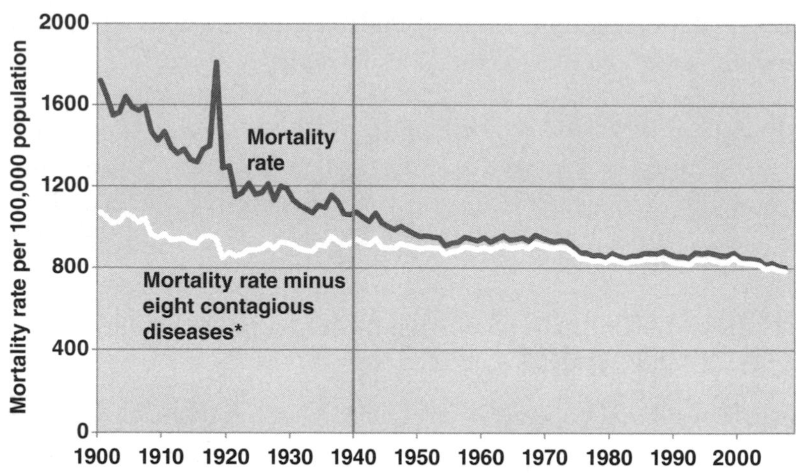

Figure 7–4. Mortality Rate as Percentage of GNP, 1900–2009

Sources: HSUS series Bd46 and Ab929-943, 2002 SAUS no. 101, 2003 SAUS no. 116, 2006 SAUS no. 107, and 2012 SAUS tables 120 and 134.

The first conclusion is that more than 37 percent of deaths in 1900 were caused by infectious diseases, but by 1955, this had declined to less than 5 percent and to only 2 percent by 2009.[22] In contrast, over the same period, the percentage of deaths caused by three chronic conditions (heart disease, strokes, and cancer) increased from 7 percent to 60 percent. The second conclusion is that almost all of the decline in the infectious mortality rate had been achieved by 1955, which is before the share in GDP of medical care spending began its inexorable rise from 4 percent in the mid-1950s to 17 percent by 2010. A central question of this chapter is whether the chief causes of the decline in mortality before 1940 had anything to do with drugs, doctors, and hospitals—and, if not, what set of factors caused the decline.

Before that question is addressed, note should be made of the sharp spike in figure 7–4 in deaths from infectious diseases that occurred in 1918–19, interrupting the otherwise relatively smooth decline. Fully 675,000 Americans died in the Spanish flu pandemic of 1918–19, a relatively small fraction of the estimated global mortality toll of 20 million to 50 million, which far exceeded fatalities caused by World War I. The precise cause of the pandemic was never determined, the study of viruses being in its infancy at the time. It was not until 1933 that the influenza A virus was isolated and not until 1944 that the first influenza vaccine was introduced.[23] The "Spanish" nickname for the pandemic came about because wartime censors limited reporting to preserve public morale, and the wartime neutrality of Spain meant that much of the influenza news came from that country, leading to belief that Spain had been the origin of the event.

Leaving aside the 1918–19 flu pandemic, the conquest of infectious diseases proceeded gradually over the first half of the twentieth century. The McKinlays compare the timing of the decline in mortality from each infectious disease with the introduction of the medical intervention designed to treat that ailment—for instance, penicillin and other vaccines. Their finding is striking: that most of the decline in mortality from the major diseases, particularly tuberculosis and influenza, had already occurred before the introduction of the medical intervention. Their conclusion is that "3.5 percent probably represents a reasonable upper-limit estimate of the total contribution of medical measures to the decline in mortality in the United States since 1900."[24]

Edward Meeker agrees with the McKinlays that the main drivers of the decline in the death rate, which for him begins around 1885, were the taming of the infectious diseases. Meeker rejects as causes either improvements in medical practice or genetic changes in the virulence of disease organisms. Instead, his searchlight beams in on the crucial improvements in public health, such as the urban sanitation infrastructure, largely consisting of filtered central water supplies and sanitary sewers, as were emphasized in chapter 4 as part of the development of the "networked home" in urban America between 1870 and 1940. Meeker provides data on the sharp decline in the incidence of typhus in twenty American cities after a filtered water supply was introduced.[25] The importance of a pure water supply was not a new idea: "From time immemorial the human race had recognized that, if health was to be maintained, such bodily wastes as urine and feces must be kept rigidly separated from food and drink."[26]

The importance of water piped under pressure to homes and businesses is often neglected in the history of the Great Inventions. Chapter 4 focused on the role of water in creating the "networked house" and the associated reduction of the drudgery of the water-carrying by housewives, who were previously forced to carry literally tons of water per year in their function as a beast of burden to provide the family's water supply. In this section, we link the provision of running water and sanitary sewage systems to the decline in mortality rates in the first half of the twentieth century. Beyond personal convenience and health, there are further uses of widely available running water that may be overlooked or forgotten, and they suggest the reasons why towns competed to achieve a fully distributed water supply:

> Perhaps the most important public use of a water supply is the extinguishing of fires ... other important public uses are in street sprinkling and sewer flushing, in furnishing water for public buildings, and for drinking and ornamental fountains. ... [A]ll the benefits accruing from a good water supply act indirectly to increase the desirability of a town for many purposes and to enhance the value of the property therein.[27]

The years 1890 to 1940 were the period when the spread of filtered running water and sanitary sewer pipes reached its fastest pace. The percentage of urban households supplied with filtered water grew slowly at first, from 0.3 percent in 1880 to 1.5 percent in 1890 and 6.3 percent in 1900. But then came the great rush of construction of waterworks, bringing the urban percentage up to 25 percent by 1910 and to 42 percent by 1925.[28] According to the first Census of Housing (see table 4–4), by 1940, fully 93 percent of urban households had running water, and 83 percent had sole use of an indoor toilet. The great increase of running filtered water availability in urban America, from 25 percent in 1910 to 93 percent in 1940, contradicts the claim by Mokyr and Stein that "by 1914 [running water] was basically universal." Without agreeing with their timing, we concur with these authors' conclusion that "it was finally water that conquered us by transforming the world and becoming part of our daily life."[29]

Higgs contrasts the central role of water, sewers, and public health initiatives in urban America with the lack of these improvements in rural America:

> The rural population continued to obtain its water supplies from traditional sources—shallow wells, springs, and cisterns in most cases. Milk escaped pasteurization. And the privy continued to provide the same primitive means of human waste disposal. In short, the public health movement that triumphed in the larger American cities between 1890 and 1920 almost completely by-passed the countryside.[30]

In fact the initial motivation in rural settings for a supply of running water was protection against fires, with no concern for the purity of the water. The rural population depended on wells and rivers well after the 1940 census that certified the ubiquity of running water in urban America.

Historians attribute the spread of water and sewer infrastructure not to any technological revolution but to a changing set of priorities, including the discovery that several diseases were spread by unsanitary water, as well as to the increasing wealth that allowed the investment to be financed and to the example of Europe, which was well ahead, having substantial infrastructure completed by 1875.[31] Another impetus was the Memphis yellow fever epidemic of 1878, which killed 10 percent of that city's population. Though soon thereafter the cause was identified as mosquitos, the cause in 1878 was unknown even as the effects were universal, including jaundice and the failure of the liver and kidneys, and "victims literally turned yellow and died in agony."[32]

Early municipal water systems were not a panacea and did not prevent many types of waterborne diseases, as animal waste deposited on the streets was pushed by street cleaners into drains and ultimately into municipal water supplies. Sewers for many cities either on rivers or on the Great Lakes emptied into bodies of water that were the source of drinking water. It was one thing for families to change their attitude toward the disease-preventing virtues of cleanliness in the late nineteenth century. It was another to achieve it, and here the transition to running hot and cold water and the indoor bathroom became central. The perceived cost of taking a shower today is trivial—two or three minutes of standing under running hot water with soap in hand. It was far different before indoor plumbing, when a bath was taken in a large metal container after a tedious process of carrying water into the home and heating it.[33]

The primary goal of the public health movement of the late nineteenth century was to create universal clean water supplies and sewage systems. In fact, clean water technologies have been labeled as "likely the most important public health intervention of the twentieth century."[34] Empirical research based on a comparison of cities in 1890 and 1900 shows that the extent of construction of waterworks, measured by miles of waterworks per person and per acre, have a significant negative correlation not just with infant mortality, but also with adult mortality. During this period, 80 percent of the decline in the total mortality rate is accounted for by four categories: diarrheal diseases, typhoid, tuberculosis, and diphtheria.

Cutler and Miller date the major advance of chlorination to the years between 1906 and 1918 and of filtration to 1906 to 1922.[35] This coincides with the extremely rapid decline in the death rate from typhoid fever, a primarily waterborne disease, by a factor of five between 1900 and 1920.[36] Before 1910, "water was 'ample,' [but] it was hardly pure." Home filters "had been available since the mid-1850s but did not become common items in the home until the 1870s."[37]

These authors estimate that clean water filtration and chlorination systems explain half of the overall reduction in mortality between 1900 and 1936, as well as 75 percent of the decline in infant mortality and 67 percent of the decline in child mortality.

PASTEUR'S GERM THEORY AND THE TRANSITION FROM ADULTERATION TO REGULATION

Even the Cutler–Miller results leave room for a complementary set of additional explanations of the reduction in mortality before 1940 beyond the rapid diffusion of urban sanitation infrastructure. There were other goals of the public health movement besides clean water and sewers, including "general street cleaning, improvements in slum housing, inspections of food and milk, use of quarantine and disinfection practices, and the distribution of diphtheria antitoxin."[38] A set of scientific discoveries together have been called the "Pasteur Revolution," in which during 1880–1900 "pathogenic organisms were discovered at the average rate of one a year."[39] Experiments in the latter decades of the nineteenth century identified the bacterial causes of numerous diseases, a scientific revolution that occurred with amazing speed.[40]

Although much of the initial research had been carried out in Germany, by 1900, the United States became a leader in the implementation of preventive measures against germ disease. Public health laboratories containing a diagnostic bacteriological laboratory had been established in most states and cities. A laboratory established in New York City in 1892 within two years had developed the first diphtheria antitoxin, and within two decades an effective vaccination program had been developed that led to a reduction in the death rate from 785 per 100,000 in 1894 to only 1.1 per 100,000 in 1950. A major cause of death had been completely wiped out within sixty years. Soon research extended to the bacterial causes of "tuberculosis, dysentery, pneumonia, typhoid fever, scarlet fever, and the role of milk in disease."[41]

Not only did the arrival of clean running water help conquer waterborne diseases, but it also improved the cleanliness of the home and of the family itself. When water had to be hand-carried into the house, baths with recycled water were, at best, a Saturday-night luxury. Gradually the washtub was replaced by full adult-sized bathtubs that could be easily filled with water, although that water had to be heated on the stove until the apartment building or house was equipped with an automatic water heater.[42]

Among the supplementary explanations was the effect of the Pasteur theory on the behavior of parents, especially mothers. Mokyr and Stein develop a production–function approach to the understanding of declining mortality, which combines the external effects of the environment to the household's own choices in combining market-purchased goods and services and household time into the achievement of health outcomes. In this framework, changes in the external environment include the availability of clean water and sanitary sewers, as well as the reduction of animal waste on the streets as a cleaner environment was achieved by the transition from horses to motor vehicles. Changes in the quality of market-purchased food, including the reduction in contamination and adulteration, would be included in the environment external to the household.

Another aspect of the late nineteenth-century environment was air pollution. Chicago's concentration of industrial plants led to the description "the smoke has a peculiar aggressive individuality." Rudyard Kipling was blunt about Chicago when he said, "Having seen it I desire urgently never to see it again. Its air is dirt." The largest stockyards in the world added "a pungent flavor to Chicago's air." In Kansas City, the confusion and stench of patrolling hogs were so penetrating that Oscar Wilde observed, "They made granite eyes weep." New York City was not immune from the observation that

> no dumping ground, no sewer, no vault contains more filth or in greater variety than does the air in certain parts of New York City during the long season of drought. No barrier can shut it out, no social distinction can save us from it; no domestic cleanliness, no private sanitary measures can substitute a pure atmosphere for a foul one.[43]

Within the household's set of choices are improved knowledge about the relationship between purchased goods and uses of time and better health outcomes. This would include shifting purchases to buying more soap and disinfectants to minimize the presence of germs and infections, as well as keeping babies as far away as possible from other family members suffering from any infectious disease. Though the health advantages of breastfeeding had long been known, the practice had new appeal as a means of insulating the baby from infection caused by impure milk and water. Mokyr and Stein emphasize the role of learning and public education in creating these behavioral changes that hastened the decline of infant mortality.[44]

Food spoilage and adulteration was not an ancient problem suddenly addressed after 1890, but rather a new problem created by industrialization itself. Before 1870, when Americans mainly lived on farms and in small towns, much of the food was either grown at home or purchased from neighbors. Each household could take steps to protect itself from spoilage and contamination. But as America urbanized, more of the food was produced in factories and shipped long distances in a world in which mechanical refrigeration had not yet been invented. Avarice and greed by food manufacturers combined with new chemical processes that could accomplish the adulteration and disguise the results with coloring agents. Consumers were helpless, for most food items were subject to adulteration. Only by purchasing alternative brands, tasting them, and observing the results could consumers begin to make an informed choice, because so few unadulterated products were available. About milk adulteration, a cynic once remarked "a water shortage would put the milkman out of business ... all [dealers] required was a water pump to boost two quarts of milk to a gallon ... to improve the color of milk from diseased cattle they frequently added molasses, chalk, or plaster of Paris."[45] The dangers posed by market-purchased milk were significant because of adulteration with polluted water. "As late as 1900 the nation's milk supply was seriously contaminated with tuberculosis, typhoid, scarlet fever, diphtheria, and streptococcal germs."[46]

Even beer and alcoholic drinks were adulterated. A retired brewer in Rochester, New York revealed that "salicylic acid, quassia wood, tannin, glycerine, and grape sugar" were added to his firm's beer during its processing. A retired liquor manufacturer in New York City told a reporter, "A man stands about as good a chance of being struck by lightning as of buying pure brandy in New York."[47] Anticipating Upton Sinclair's unsettling exposé of the Chicago stockyards in 1906, the New York Council of Hygiene reported in 1869 that foods hung on racks or placed on counters "undergo spontaneous deterioration becoming absolutely poisonous."[48] In the early 1880s, little progress had been made:

> Much of New York City's meat supply ... reached the stockyards afoot through labyrinths of residential streets, strewing manure and trailing clouds of dust and flies. The remainder came from diseased cows fed on distillery swill in the city's notoriously filthy dairies .... Children reveled and played downstream in ditches which drained the slaughterhouses.[49]

Progress was gradually made in the 1880s and 1890s to clean up these foul conditions, an achievement of one of the first political movements in American history led by women. The New York's Ladies' Protective Health Association (LPHA), established in 1884, was soon joined by similar organizations in a nationwide reform movement to force slaughterhouse owners to make drastic reforms, and this political pressure was resisted fiercely by lobbying and political contributions by the owners, who were eventually defeated by the influence of public opinion on legislation. The grand climax of the fight between the reformers and the abusive profit-oriented suppliers of adulteration and contamination came suddenly. In February 1906, Upton Sinclair's *The Jungle* was published. A semifictionalized account of health and working conditions in the Chicago stockyards, *The Jungle* was intended by Sinclair to be "the *Uncle Tom's Cabin* of the labor movement."[50] Barely twenty years after the revelations of conditions in New York by the LPHA, the details about Chicago were even more sickening; the meat, "without being washed, ... was pushed from room to room in rotten box carts, all the while collecting dirt, splinters, floor filth, and the expectoration of tubercular and other diseased workers."[51]

The book became an instant bestseller, and because it accused federal meat inspectors of taking bribes, it immediately caught the attention of President Theodore Roosevelt, who launched an investigation. The in-person inspection by top federal officials, including the U.S. Commissioner of Labor, reported back that conditions were nearly as bad as Sinclair had depicted. The brief interval between the discovery of the abuse and the proposal of its cure may have set a record for speed in the history of U.S. regulation, as the political remedy came within a few weeks. After the release of the government report and the shocked commentary of the nation's newspapers in early June 1906, "trade in lard, sausage, and canned goods came almost to a standstill. ... Restaurants reported a vast decline in business."[52] Almost instantly by June 30, Congress had passed, and Roosevelt had signed into law, the Pure Food and Drug Act, which established the ancestor of today's Food and Drug Administration.[53] Newspapers and other publications hailed the act as "the most important piece of legislation ever passed by Congress."[54]

Commentators trace the epochal legislation back at least two decades. But Sinclair's book was clearly the catalyst that made the legislation possible sooner rather than later:

> Sinclair's novel "struck such a chord" because it "confirmed and publicized what people already knew or suspected" about commercialized

> food and drugs. *The Jungle* was "merely the final, spectacular, fictionalized climax" to the "long agitation" by "patient investigators"—women's organizations, food chemists, journalists, and other reformers and altruists.[55]

During the years after passage of the act, progress was slow, as inspectors had to be hired and trained, and food manufacturers did everything they could to delay the act's full implementation. States and local governments gradually passed their own legislation and implemented rules and inspections. The widespread acceptance of the Pasteur germ theory of disease led to an increased emphasis on cleanliness at every stage of food production, from slaughterhouses to every other type of food producer, retailer, restaurant, and saloon. The scope of disease prevention broadened to include control of insects, replacement of open buckets with modern sanitary water fountains, and banning of spitting in public.

PHARMACIES AND THE TAMING OF THE "WILD WEST" OF DRUG DISTRIBUTION

Our image of drug purchases during the late nineteenth century is one of a Wild West frontier in which customers could obtain any kind of drug freely over the counter without the intervention of a doctor's prescription. Pharmacies were virtually unregulated before 1870. "Drug adulteration was reputedly so common that doctors customarily prescribed excessive dosages on the assumption that the medication's strength had been substantially reduced."[56] The ready availability of drugs from pharmacies elevated the position of pharmacists relative to doctors. Pharmacies sold three different classes of drugs to consumers. The first group consisted of the reputable drugs that are recognized even today as having a valid therapeutic benefit, including not just aspirin but morphine, quinine, and diphtheria antitoxin. The second group consisted of the patent medicines that were heavily advertised to provide miracle cures yet that contained little more than colored water and alcohol. The third group included the narcotics other than morphine that are largely banned today but that were widely available in 1900, such as opium, cocaine, and heroin. There was some overlap between the second and third group, for some patent medicines included opium as an ingredient.

By the 1880s, Chinese immigrants, originally recruited to build the first transcontinental railway, had established Chinese enclaves in San Francisco and elsewhere and set up opium dens, spreading addiction to the native population. Not just opium and its derivatives but also cocaine were common treatments over the 1880–1930 interval for treating pain, easing sleep, reducing coughs, and curing other medical ailments.[57] Because drugs did not require prescriptions, the pharmacist had an exalted position and was expected to diagnose the customers' ailments. Few druggists could resist the temptation to sell to the customer the most profitable drugs that they resold or created on their own by combining ingredients. The most potent emerging competition for the pharmacists was the availability of many drugs, particularly patent medicines, at lower cost through mail-order catalogs.

In this chaotic world so unfamiliar to us today, any drug that could be obtained with a doctor's prescription could also be obtained without a prescription. But doctors' prescriptions provided a promotional value to pharmacists, even though they could dispense the same drugs without prescriptions. When a patient arrived with a prominent doctor's prescription for a particular drug, pharmacists could advertise that particular medicine as a cure-all that had been endorsed by Dr. Famous. And yet, because they had no monopoly on the writing of prescriptions, doctors could sell drugs directly to patients in their offices, add to their incomes as doctors, and thus undermine the business of pharmacists. There was also a symbiotic relationship in the late nineteenth century between newspapers and drug companies. The drugs were widely advertised in newspapers, and in appreciative return, the newspapers suppressed coverage of any dangers or side effects created by use of the drugs.[58]

In the 1880s and 1890s, the Woman's Christian Temperance Union (WCTU), better known for its fight against alcohol, became the leading organization that crusaded against addictive drugs of all types. One of its pamphlets in 1898 claimed that the United States seemed "to be radically becoming a nation of cocaine fiends" and that physicians were "careless, selfish, unprincipled, or unobservant."[59] The 1906 Pure Food and Drug Act took the first steps to regulate drug marketing. Any product containing alcohol, morphine, cocaine, heroin, or cannabis had to be explicitly labeled but was not prohibited. From 1914 to the 1930s, additional legislation and enforcement effectively banned all these drugs, including alcohol, under the Prohibition legislation in force between 1920 and 1933.

Before 1940, there were not many effective drugs, and those that were marketed dealt with surface symptoms without effectiveness in curing underlying conditions. In that era, pharmacists actually compounded the ingredients of drugs, instead of merely reselling drugs manufactured by large pharmaceutical firms. Trial and error by consumers had more effect on purchase decisions than any influence of government regulation.[60] The rate of discovery of effective pharmaceutical drugs increased rapidly after the 1935 discovery of sulfonamide drugs and penicillin during World War II. Because most of the effects of this acceleration were felt after 1940, it is treated in chapter 14.

The regulatory environment was radically changed by the successor to the 1906 food and drug legislation, which was passed in 1938 after years of debate. The first important change was the requirement that the FDA approve the introduction of newly developed drugs. The second was perhaps even more radical, requiring doctors' prescriptions for many commonly used drugs. This utterly changed from the previous world, in which drug companies had no reason to advertise to doctors, to a new world in which doctors were showered in advertisements, traveling drug salespeople, and abundant samples. The modern world of drug regulation and the new distinction between the rights of pharmacists and doctors to determine the availability of drugs began in 1938, conveniently close to our 1940 transition year from part I to part II of this book, and the 1938 legislation still serves as the foundations of FDA regulation today.

WHAT DID DOCTORS DO?

The period 1850–1930 witnessed the "consolidation of professional authority" of doctors, as their own ignorance and refusal to learn from scientific discoveries yielded to a consensus practice of modern medicine.[61] If national accounts were available in detail for the late nineteenth century, the medical care industry would be almost invisible. Most medical care did not even take place in the market economy, but rather at home and across households as neighbors helped neighbors. Indeed, in 1929, total expenditures on health care of all types amounted to only 2.3 percent of GDP, compared to 16.6 percent in 2013.[62]

Perspective on the limited role of the formal medical sector is provided by the fact that 75 percent of the American population was rural in 1870, living on farms or in small towns having population of less than 2,500. Farms were far apart, and the small towns were far apart from each other. Many rural towns were too small to support a doctor of their own, and the high cost of transportation put a natural limit on the availability of medical care achieved through doctors' house calls. Doctor fees included not just a basic charge for a home visit, but also a per-mile charge to compensate the doctor for his trip by buggy to the farm patient. One doctor complained about the endless travel, claiming that he spent "half of his life in the mud and the other half in the dust."[63]

In the absence of doctors, most rural areas had midwives to deliver babies and women, usually unpaid, who specialized in tending the sick. "Most pioneers' first response to sickness was to employ folk remedies and tender loving care."[64] The local general store provided staples of frontier medicine such as opium tincture for pain. Another popular drug for the relief of physical and mental pain was whiskey. "For indigestion, a solution of rhubarb bitters or cayenne pepper mixed with whiskey was rubbed into the abdomen, often combined with whiskey and water taken internally."[65]

As motor vehicles replaced horse-drawn buggies, and as people grouped together closer in cities, the reduced cost of transportation brought more market-produced services into reach. "Getting a haircut, visiting a prostitute, and consulting a doctor all became, on the average, less expensive because of the reduced costs of time." Perhaps no other profession than the medical doctors embraced the automobile so enthusiastically. "Besides making house calls in one-half the time," wrote a physician from Oklahoma, "there is something about the auto that is infatuating, and the more you ride the more you want to ride."[66]

Medical care provides an example of the consumer benefits of the invention of the telephone. Before the telephone reached the farm, extra travel was required by a relative or friend of the patient who had to go and fetch the doctor in person. In many cases, the doctor could not be found because he was out on another call, and the emissary would have to wait or frantically try to find out where the doctor had traveled. The telephone was essential in the organization of office visits, allowing patients to phone in advance for appointments and allowing the doctor to become more efficient by packing his schedule with prearranged rather than unexpected visits by patients.

In 1870, there were virtually no specialist surgeons. One surgeon said in 1876 that it was "safe to affirm that there is not a medical man on this continent who devotes himself exclusively to the practice of surgery."[67] Seemingly insurmountable problems held back the development of surgery, including patient pain resulting from the absence of reliable anesthetics and the high death rate caused by postoperative sepsis, caused in part by unsterile procedures and the lack of antiseptics. The presence of many patients who had open wounds in large wards led to cross-infection from one patient to another. This is an example of the deterioration of health caused by urbanization, because city hospitals were much more crowded, and were much more likely to have large wards, than rural private homes.

Throughout the 1870–1940 period, activities shifted from home production to market purchases. Medical care also made a transition from home self-sufficiency to house calls by itinerant doctors to office visits and, finally, to hospital treatment. During this period, the most basic common tools of doctors were developed, including the stethoscope, ophthalmoscope, and laryngoscope. The prototype of contemporary blood pressure instruments, involving the pumping of air into a rubber bag wrapped around the upper arm, was developed by an Italian physician in 1896 only a few months after Wilhelm Röntgen's discovery of the properties of X-rays and the first use of an X-ray machine. Soon thereafter, in 1901, a Dutch physiologist invented the electrocardiogram, which began to be widely used in the 1920s.[68]

We can erect signposts to measure progress of the medical profession in 1876, 1901, and 1926. The situation in 1901 was little better than described above for the decade of the 1870s. Doctors were still engaged in destructive debates about homeopathy and other types of unconventional quack medicine. They felt assaulted by pharmacists who provided free medical advice and who used their prescriptions to become self-promoting prescribers of particular drugs "recommended by Dr. X." They faced competition from too many doctors, many of whom had been produced by disreputable, profit-making medical schools lacking in standards.[69]

The problems perceived in 1926 were very different from those in 1876 and 1901. Doctors had become a respected profession earning a substantial income; disreputable medical schools had been closed, reducing competition from improperly trained doctors; licensing laws had restricted competition from pharmacists and inadequately trained physicians. The medical profession had "turned hospitals, drug manufacturers, and public health from threats to its position into bulwarks of support. … In short, it had helped shape the medical system so that its structure supported professional sovereignty instead of undermining it."[70]

But problems remained. At the top of the list was the maldistribution of doctors, who were abandoning rural communities faster than those small towns and farms were shrinking as a share of the national population. Furthermore, thanks to an improvement in the standards of medical schools after 1900, fewer doctors per capita had made their way through medical school, so the generation of doctors educated under the lax standards of the 1890s was starting to die out. Thus for the roughly half of the population that was still classified as rural in 1926, medical knowledge may have been abundant, but the medical practitioners to apply the knowledge were increasingly absent, a situation described at the time as ranging "from serious to desperate."[71]

Figure 7–5 displays the number of doctors per 10,000 people from 1850 to 2009, as well as the number of hospital beds per 10,000 people from 1910 to 2009. Reflecting the retirement of doctors who were trained before the tightening of professional standards, the ratio for doctors declined from a peak of 17.6 in the 1850s to 12.5 in 1929. The ratio was roughly constant, at 13.3, between 1940 and 1959 and then increased to 16.9 in 1970, 25.6 in 1990, and 31.6 in 2009. The inexorable upward creep of the physicians ratio evident in figure 7–5 reflects the growing number of specialties and the increased relative income of doctors that was in turn a partial cause of the unrelenting increase in medical care expenses that began after 1955 and that is discussed in chapter 14.

The history of hospital beds per 10,000 people shows a modest inverse relationship with the physician ratio. The development of antiseptics and anesthesia in the late nineteenth century made hospitals a more acceptable place to go for medical cures. The hospital beds ratio exhibits a doubling from forty-seven in 1910 to ninety-three in 1940, followed by a temporary bulge

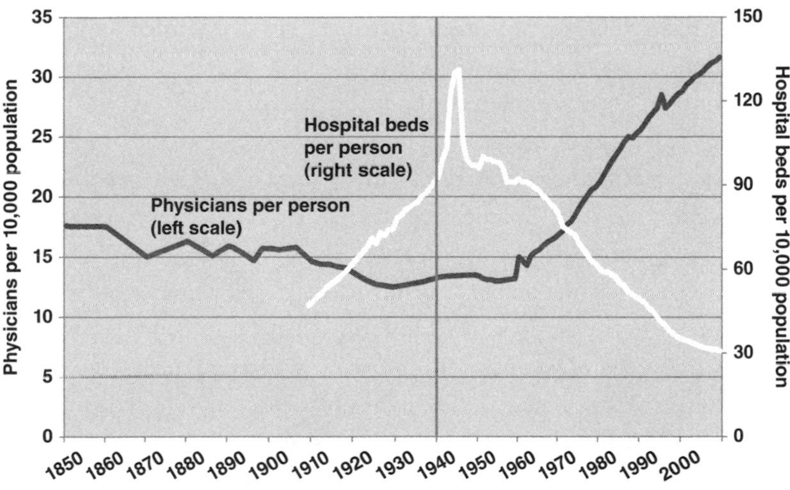

Figure 7–5. Physicians and Hospital Beds per Person, 1850–2009

Sources: HSUS series Bd242, Bd134, and Bd120, 2002 SAUS no. 153, and 2012 SAUS tables 160 and 172.

during World War II when additional beds were temporarily needed to treat the wounded. The beds ratio declined in the postwar years thanks to the declining role of hospitals in long-term care (some of which was transferred to nursing homes and mental health facilities); increased efficacy of treatment, which made shorter stays possible; and the increased relative price of hospital care, which led patients to seek other types of medical care.

THE HOSPITAL: FROM A "CESSPOOL FOR THE INDIGENT" TO CURING DISEASE

In some ways, the large urban hospital of 1870 was more akin to modern-day nursing homes than to today's large teaching and research hospitals. Between 1870 and 1920, the hospital was transformed from an asylum for the poor into something resembling the modern hospital as its numbers multiplied from only 120 in 1873 to 6,000 by 1920.[72] The reputation of hospitals was gradually changed from "repositories of filth and infection" to clean places where advanced medical care was practiced.[73] But in the 1870s and 1880s, the hospital was little changed from the previous century, regarded as a dumping ground for the lower classes and impoverished immigrants, a place where a patient was likely to fall victim to sepsis. An 1872 visitor to Bellevue Hospital in New York reported, "The loathsome smell sickened me. The condition of the beds and patients was unspeakable. The one nurse slept in the bathroom and the tub was filled with filthy rubbish."[74] In fact, postoperative sepsis infection caused the death of almost half of patients undergoing major surgery. "A common report by surgeons was: operation successful but the patient died."[75]

The development of antisepsis or "antiseptics" created a major reduction in postoperative deaths and amputations during the 1870–1900 period. The central discoveries in the development of antiseptics were achieved soon after the Civil War by Joseph Lister, a surgeon at Glasgow Royal Infirmary, and in 1879 Listerine mouthwash was named after him, a brand still widely sold today. Lister realized that airborne germs could cause putrefaction in wounds, and he concluded that the germs on the wound had to be destroyed during the operation itself, choosing carbolic acid as his initial antiseptic. This proved insufficient, and over the next few decades, new methods of sterilization were developed for the surgeon's hands, instruments, gloves, and clothing.[76] The central role of infection in hospital deaths is symbolized by the 1881 death of President Garfield by an assassin's bullet; expert doctors were said to have probed for the bullet using their fingers and unsterilized instruments, and Garfield's death from secondary infection followed soon after.[77]

The hospital in that period was not central to the practice of medicine, and in the middle and upper classes, sickness was endured at home in the presence of traveling doctors. Even victims of railroad, streetcar, and horse cart accidents were largely taken to their homes rather than to hospitals.[78] Summarizing the contemporary attitude toward hospitals, a columnist in the *Boston Evening Transcript* wrote in 1888:

> There is something about this all-pervading presence of Sickness, with a large S, this atmosphere of death, either just expected or just escaped, and all of this amiable perfunctoriness of nursing and medical attendance, that is simply horrible. The hospital … gives only sickness to think about morning, noon, and night.[79]

In that era, hospitals were supported not by financial contributions from the poor or the government, but rather by voluntary philanthropy of the wealthy and sponsorship by religious orders and ethnic associations. Doctors whose main income came from private practice worked almost gratis in hospitals to gain experience and knowledge of difficult cases that they might not see in their rounds of in-home visits. A major problem for hospitals in the late nineteenth century was that although they might be reviled by the middle and upper classes, the free food and bed and care that they offered were very attractive to poor people, and policies had to be established, and often changed, regarding the maximum length of a hospital stay. Free patients stayed an average of five weeks in the late 1870s.[80]

The small role of the late nineteenth-century hospital for childbirth was consistent with its minimal role in health defined more broadly. "Nineteenth-century maternity hospitals were urban asylums for the poor, homeless, or working-class married women who could not deliver at home but who doctors and philanthropists believed deserved medical treatment." Though in 1900 only 5 percent of American women delivered their babies in hospitals, the gradual conquest of in-hospital puerperal fever slowly changed the public's perception of hospitals as a place to give birth. By 1921, more than half the births in many major U.S. cities took place in hospitals as women came to view hospital births as safer and as procedures were developed (such as the caesarean section, which occurred first in 1894) that could not be performed at home. By 1939, half of all women and 75 percent of urban women were delivering in hospitals, and by 1960, the percentage for all women had reached 95 percent. As Rose Kennedy is said to have remarked, the "fashion changed."[81]

An early step in the transformation of hospitals was achieved by the formation of the first nursing schools in the 1870s; previously nursing had been considered to be at the same low level of social status as household cleaning women. The number of nursing training schools grew from three in 1873 to 432 by 1900 and 1,129 by 1910.[82] By the early twentieth century, the development of medical technology began to attract patients from the more comfortable income classes, both because antiseptics and increased cleanliness had made hospitals less fearsome and because hospitals could now perform surgical and other procedures that could not be done at home. By the 1920s, the occupational distribution of patients in hospitals was similar to the population as a whole.

> Where only twenty or thirty years before there had been noise, dirt, and disarray, there was now [by 1910] control and organization: the rustle of the nurse's uniform, the bell of the telegraph, the rattle of the hydraulic elevator, the hiss of steam, the murmured ritual of the operating room. Digitalis, quinine, and mercury gave promise of relief to patients, while morphine, opium, cocaine, and sulfonal reduced the noisy manifestations of pain ... the fetid smell of festering wounds had been banished with antiseptics and unrelenting cleanliness.[83]

Doctors performing services in hospitals billed the patient an extra fee beyond the hospital's own charges while continuing to donate time to care for the indigent, and a greater load of poor patients would cause a doctor to raise fees for paying patients to compensate for his time. Hospitals began to organize their beds into "first-class and steerage," reserving private or semiprivate rooms for the paying patients and "charity wards" for the nonpaying indigent. Further segregation separated black from white patients and victims of venereal diseases from otherwise similar patients who suffered from other types of ailments.[84]

Hospital finance began to change toward the modern American system based on health insurance, which began in the first decade of the twentieth century in the form of workers' compensation for industrial accidents. Encouraged by President Theodore Roosevelt, workers' compensation paid the cost of care for injured workers by levies on firms, and by 1919 a majority of states had such systems. By modern standards, hospital care was still extremely cheap, with a room rate (excluding hospital and doctor charges for procedures) of $10 *per week* common in the decade before World War I.[85] After adjusting for inflation, the room rate comes out at $170 *per week* in 2013 dollars. The cost of a birth, including hospital room rates, fees for doctors and nurses, and extra hospital charges, could amount to between $50 and $300 in current prices by 1923. Part of this surge in hospital rates was a result of the economy-wide doubling of the price level that occurred during World War I. In New York City by 1920, hospital rooms had reached $5 per day.[86]

The shift to childbirth in hospitals had two desirable side effects. It is no coincidence that the period of rapid decline of infant mortality between 1890 and 1950 coincided with the nearly complete shift from home births to hospital maternity wards. The second effect was the substitution effect of the relatively high cost of hospital care, which changed household decision-making in the direction of having fewer children, thus lowering the birth date. Midwives had been a much less expensive choice than hospital care and continued to be preferred by immigrant women, but by the 1930s, they were no longer an option. As elderly midwives retired or died, a new generation failed to replace them, both because there were other better-paying option for native-born women and because the inflow of young foreign midwives had been cut off by the restrictive Immigration Acts of 1921 and 1924.[87]

The 1920s were the heyday of the construction of hospitals, and the inflation-adjusted spending on hospital construction would not exceed the rate of the late 1920s until the mid-1950s. The consumer standard of living was boosted not just by the decline in both infant and adult mortality, but also by the increase in comfort made possible by the newly constructed hospitals. Privacy was a new commodity of great value, and new hospitals in 1928 devoted 46 percent of their beds to private rooms, 23 percent to semiprivate rooms, 21 percent to small wards, and only 7 percent to large wards.[88] The lack of privacy in wards, and the difficulty of having private time to talk to visitors, added to the determination of middle- and upper-income patients to pay for the best, the private room, which reinforced the social segregation within the hospital that had developed since the late nineteenth century.

By 1926, 6,800 institutions were classified as hospitals within the United States. Of these, 44 percent maintained clinical laboratories, and 41 percent had X-ray departments. About 28 percent of these hospitals were owned by federal, state, or local government, and the remaining 72 percent were divided among church-run, individually or partnership-owned, and independent (i.e., nonprofit) institutions.

MEDICAL RESEARCH, MEDICAL SCHOOLS, AND THE TRANSFORMATION OF MEDICAL KNOWLEDGE

Medical knowledge advanced slowly but steadily before 1940. The elements of surgery and the use of ether as an anesthetic were developed before the Civil War, and research on the use of anesthesia, including ether, chloroform, and even cocaine, continued after the Civil War. In the late nineteenth century, techniques were developed to use anesthesia in surgery, to remove gallstones, and to treat appendicitis, heart murmurs, and liver disease. Louis Pasteur, Joseph Lister, and Robert Koch have been described as "the remarkable trio who transformed modern medicine."[89] Although individuals such as Pasteur and Koch often get credit for individual cures, progress was a team effort as scientists from the United States and several European countries replicated and improved on the early experiments.

Though some doctors welcomed these new discoveries, others did not and were often hostile to the germ theory of disease. It was not unusual "for well-known physicians to get up and leave the hall when medical papers were being read which emphasized the germ theory of disease. They wanted to express their contemptuous scorn for such theories and refused to listen to them."[90] Because of warring factions and different philosophies of medical science, the history of medical schools in the nineteenth century is "a tale of schisms, conspiracies, and coups, often destroying the institutions in the process."[91] Part of the deep divisionresulted from widespread acceptance of homeopathy, not just skepticism about the germ theory.[92]

Other reasons for the hostility was a widespread suspicion of science, a refusal to believe that widespread epidemics could be caused by nearly invisible microorganisms, and the threat to physicians' expertise in prescribing the palliative drugs available at the time. Nevertheless, the development of vaccines gradually converted the doubters, and the first benefits from the germ theory came from an increased emphasis on cleanliness and sterilization, as well as the spreading of knowledge about what true sterilization required in doctors' offices and hospitals. Homeopathic medical theories were increasingly rejected, and homeopathic medical schools had almost disappeared by 1920.

The state of medical and scientific knowledge includes the condition of medical schools. There were only sixty medical schools in 1870, and all but the best had a short and shoddy program of instruction. A medical degree could be earned in two years of eighteen weeks each. The schools were weak to nonexistent on the basic disciplines of anatomy and physiology and also lacked clinical training. What they taught was the middle slice of a modern medical school, the how-to techniques of medical diagnosis and procedure. For most medical schools, there were no admissions requirements, and no grades were given in courses. In contrast were the high standards of the Johns Hopkins Hospital and John Hopkins Medical School, founded, respectively, in 1889 and 1893.[93]

In the late nineteenth century medical education was dominated by for-profit "diploma mills" that "turned out nothing more than warm bodies with diplomas." In addition, many "pretenders" displayed invalid medical certificates. By the end of the nineteenth century, a "degree" in medicine could be obtained for between $5 and $10, its cost depending on the quality of the paper on which the diploma was printed. "These certificates were not too expensive even for the most poverty-stricken quack."[94]

One of the great milestones in the history of American medicine was the publication of the Flexner report in 1910, a report that the American Medical Association, which realized that it could not enter such controversial territory directly, had commissioned to be carried out by the prestigious Carnegie Foundation for the Advancement of Teaching. The young educator Abraham Flexner visited all of the nation's medical schools and was welcomed by each, the institution thinking that the visit might be an inspection in advance of a Carnegie financial contribution. But invitations expecting a financial gift were shocked later to learn that the report questioned the necessity of their very existence.

Flexner's report complained, "The professor … lectures to ill prepared students for one hour a few times weekly … private quizmasters drill hundreds of students in memorizing minute details that they would be unable to navigate if the objects were before them."[95] Flexner devastated the claims of legitimacy of the private for-profit schools, showing that "touted laboratories … consisted of a few vagrant test tubes squirreled away in a cigar box; corpses reeked because of the failure to use disinfectant in the dissecting rooms. Libraries had no books; alleged faculty members were busily occupied in private practice."

Flexner's recommendations administered a guillotine to much of American medical education—the top schools, such as Johns Hopkins and Harvard, should be strengthened, a few of the best medical schools should aspire to top status, and the rest of the medical school industry should be shut down.[96] And indeed many did shut down, and with a lag, this reduced the number of doctors per person, as we saw in figure 7–5.

HOW DID PATIENTS PAY FOR MEDICAL CARE?

In the earlier era lasting until 1910 or 1920, medical costs were not an important issue. Most medical service was dispensed by doctors making house calls, and the doctor's charge for a home visit was often very low by any subsequent standard, with an extra charge for mileage traveled. The interval 1905–20 was the heyday of the itinerant doctor traveling in his new automobile. Especially in rural America, doctors provided whatever service they could in the home and did not send patients to hospitals, in part because the latter were few and far between.

By the 1920s, the majority of doctors were organized into individual practices, charging fees for service on a patient-by-patient basis and without any formal salaried connection with a hospital.[97] House calls continued, and it was estimated that in 1925, two-thirds of patients disabled by illness were being treated in their homes by doctors and the remainder inside hospitals. Cooperation between primary doctors and specialists was uncoordinated and primitive, the very opposite of the goal of today's health care with electronic medical records covering all aspects of a patient's care. Patients could drop in to a specialist's office without any contact with or referral from a primary physician, and they had to pay out of pocket for that specialist's service.[98]

The cost of medical treatment rose inexorably after 1910. Part of the cause was the reform of medical schools, which raised the cost of going to medical school and hence caused doctors' charges to rise to create sufficient incentives to attract students to medical schools. Licensing of doctors created a quasi-monopoly that boosted physician charges. The rise of the American hospital after 1900 brought with it new financial problems for patients. An increasing fraction of medical ailments were treated using X-rays and other modern equipment. As infectious diseases were conquered, the remaining set of health problems increasingly required access to specialists. Costs to patients increased because specialists charged more than general practitioners, because hospitals were increasingly used as a replacement for house calls in patients' homes, and because the charge for cure of a particular ailment increasingly required payment to multiple providers:

> In some instances there may be eight or ten separate charges—one each from the family physician and several specialists, one or more for laboratory tests, another from the hospital for room and board, one or more from nurses, still another for nurses' board, and extra charges for the anesthetics, operating room, and medicine.[99]

How, then, did patients pay for this increasingly complex medical system? In some cases, doctors were willing to adjust their fees by charging more to the rich and less to the poor, but they faced a basic handicap in that they had no independent method of verifying their patients' family income. A contemporary source listed seven different ways in which patients responded to the high costs of medical care in the mid-1920s: (1) free dispensaries and clinics; (2) generously provided free care provided by the family physician; (3) willingness to pay the doctor's bill as a matter of pride; (4) available but inadequate medical insurance provided by fraternal orders and some trade unions, as well as workmen compensation and commercial providers; (5) avoidance of treatment by poor people, contributing to their higher death rates; (6) patronization of quack doctors and other nonprofessionals; and (7) self-treatment with potions and patent medicines.[100] To the extent that commercial health insurance was available, it suffered from all the abuses of modern health insurance, including "cream-skimming" to find the healthiest patients, age limitations to avoid insuring the old, medical exams to detect pre-existing conditions, and a reluctance to insure the lower classes, who were predicted to have greater exposure to infectious diseases and other ailments.

Notably absent from the list of seven was any comprehensive form of health insurance, which had been part of Theodore Roosevelt's Progressive Party platform in the 1912 Presidential election campaign. The platform promised "protection of home life against the hazards of sickness, irregular employment, and old age through the adoption of a system of social insurance adapted to American use."[101] Roosevelt's loss to Woodrow Wilson in that election was followed by five years of legislative struggle between advocates of universal health care and an unlikely set of opponents, including doctors, pharmacists, employers, and even labor unions.

The proponents suggested as their model the comprehensive social insurance programs initiated by Germany in 1883, the United Kingdom in 1911, and in many other European countries in between. As with the European plans, the Roosevelt idea was not just to cover medical costs, but also to alleviate poverty by compensating income lost as a result of illness. A contemporary survey of 4,500 workers in a Chicago working-class neighborhood revealed that over the previous year, one in four had lost at least one week's wages because of sickness, and for this subgroup, 13.6 percent of annual income was lost.[102] Noting the failure of even a single state to introduce health insurance, a proponent in 1917 lamented

> We are still so far from considering illness as anything beyond a private misfortune against which each individual and each family should

protect itself, as best it may, that Germany's heroic method of attacking it as a national evil through government machinery seems to us to belong almost to another planet.[103]

The early forms of health insurance, often called "sickness funds," date back to the 1890s and became more common during the Progressive Era of 1900–1920. A 1917 estimate for three industrial states indicated that fully a third of the nonagricultural workforce had some form of health insurance, consisting of sickness funds established by fraternal organizations, firms, unions, as well as privately purchased insurance. Nationwide coverage reached perhaps half of the one-third estimate taking lower coverage of farmers, farm workers, and nonagricultural workers in the southern states into account.[104]

Increasing average costs during the 1920s were only part of the problem of financing medical care, for the increasing capability of hospitals to treat complex diseases greatly increased the *variability* of charges. Though illnesses that required hospitalization were still relatively uncommon, members of the middle class unlucky enough to suffer from prolonged hospital stays could expect to receive bills equal to a third or half their annual income. A national commission reported in 1930 that 3.5 percent of the families who had the largest medical bills paid a third of the cost of medical care in the nation.[105] The risk of uninsured charges equal to such a large portion of income naturally raised the demand for health insurance.

A fraction of American workers was covered by industrial sickness funds. Leaving aside their limited coverage, these funds were tied to employment, just as is modern American health insurance. Thus unemployment resulting from the macroeconomic disaster of the Great Depression caused workers to lose both their income and their health insurance. This double dose of bad luck was aggravated by the tendency of employers to choose to fire those employees who were in poor health. Because the unhealthy workers had been weeded out of employment and were no longer covered by the sickness funds, the remaining members of the sickness funds were healthier than normal, thus reducing the coverage costs of the funds. This led to the absurd claim that "the Great Depression improved the health of the average insured worker."[106]

There was no organized effort to achieve national health insurance during Franklin Roosevelt's New Deal, despite its achievement of compulsory unemployment compensation and Social Security. The most plausible explanations were the uncompromising opposition of the American Medical Association and the tendency of FDR to follow public opinion rather than to lead it. In fact, Roosevelt responded to the fierce lobbying opposition to universal health care by omitting it from the Social Security legislation, for fear that government-guaranteed old-age pensions would flounder in Congress unless medical care was omitted from the bill.[107]

DEATH FROM ACCIDENTS AND HOMICIDES

The title of this chapter, "nasty, brutish, and short," refers initially to the causes of death involving diseases that led to short lives and nasty deaths.[108] At least these deaths were gradual as the disease progressed, allowing young and old alike to say goodbye to their family members. But other deaths were "brutish," not allowing for a prolonged goodbye. These included deaths from accidents that occurred incidental to industrial jobs; deaths from railway accidents that killed workers, passengers, and pedestrians; deaths from automobile accidents; and deaths from homicide.

Edison's October 1879 invention of the electric light was heralded not just for the brightness and reliability of the light, but also for the ease of turning it on and off in comparison to the previous era of gas and kerosene lamps. But few accounts of the benefits of Edison's invention include the saving of lives previously lost before 1879 because of the much greater safety of electric light:

> Every year in the U.S. alone five thousand to six thousand people a year died in lamp accidents due to adulterated oil, clumsiness, and carelessness—spills and breakages, or someone leaving a lamp too near to curtains or bedclothes, failing to lower the wick before blowing out the light, or trying to extinguish a lamp by blowing down the chimney.[109]

Deaths and injuries in the workplace were at levels that seem nearly inconceivable today. President Harrison was quoted in 1892 as saying, "American workmen are subjected to peril of life and limb as great as a soldier in time of war." Indeed, deaths caused by American railroads in the three years 1898–1900 to employees, passengers, and collisions with horses and people were roughly equal to British Army losses in the three-year Boer war.[110]

The peak for railroad-related fatalities was 11,800 in 1907, and figure 7–6 shows that this amounted in that year to 138 per million members of the population. The rate declined rapidly to thirty-five in 1940 and to less than ten after

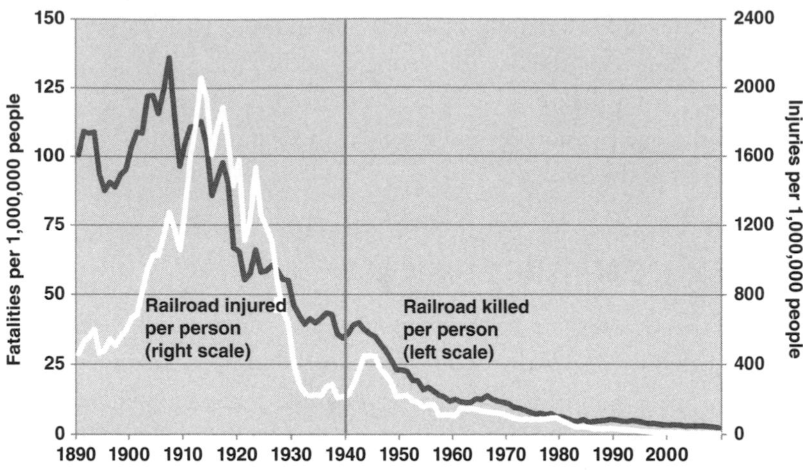

Figure 7–6. Railroad Killed and Injured per Person, 1890–2009

Sources: HSUS series Ba4768 and Ba4769, 2002 SAUS no. 1112, and 2012 SAUS table 1122.

1970. Injuries, shown on the right scale, peaked at 2,060 per million people and thereafter declined even more quickly than deaths, reaching 224 in 1940. After a temporary bulge in World War II, because of the extremely high utilization of the railway network, both railroad fatalities and injuries faded away almost to nothing after 1980. The United States was unique in its high fatality rate in the early twentieth century; the average U.S. rate in the years 1911–15 was more than six times as high as contemporary rates registered by Germany, Austria, and the United Kingdom.[111]

One reason for the higher fatality rate in the United States than in Europe was a difference in standards of construction thanks to the high cost of capital, low population density, and thin traffic on given lines. Most railroads in Europe were built from the start with grade separations, so that road traffic flowed over or under the railroad tracks. In contrast, most American railroads were built at grade level except in major cities and on some suburban railroads. British railroad bridges were built with iron, whereas many American bridges were built with wood. Furthermore, paved roads were much more developed in Europe, whereas in the United States the narrow dirt roads were dusty in summer and mud-caked in winter, offering circuitous routings between towns and cities. The straight lines followed by railroad tracks tempted many travelers to hop a freight train or just walk along the tracks, thus exposing themselves to danger. In European railway stations, fences and platforms prevented passengers or greeters from walking onto the track, but this was less true with the open design of American railway stations, which often consisted of little more than a small structure next to a track.[112]

Gradually railway safety improved, as shown by the declining fatality and injury rates displayed in figure 7–6. Better brakes, couplers, and other safety equipment, heavier and better constructed tracks and wheels, together with a gradual transition from manual to automatic signals, had virtually eliminated collisions by 1929. Deaths of railroad employees, which had reached a high of 3,400 in 1910, gradually fell as equipment was made safer and committees of employees made recommendations for changes in practices and educating workers as to the dangers of particular operations. Competition from automobiles and buses decimated short-haul railroad passenger traffic, leading to a shift from relatively dangerous rural tracks and stations to better-designed urban and suburban infrastructure.

Railroads are singled out in this section because they caused death and injuries not just among their employees, but also among passengers, pedestrians, and people, horses, and vehicles at grade crossings. Death to passengers came not just from rail travel, but also from ships. Only eight years before the massive loss of life in the *Titanic* sinking, a three-deck paddle steamer named the *General Slocum* headed up the East River carrying hundreds of German immigrants who had spent the day at a floating party. A fire broke out and oil tanks exploded, engulfing the boat in flames. As a result of bolted-down lifeboats and rotting life jackets, of the 1,300 passengers, more than 1,000 died.[113] And in 1915, on the Chicago River, the *Eastland* about to depart for a party voyage of Western Electric employees capsized, killing 844 passengers. These were only two of the most notorious of the shipping incidents in American waters that reflected poor safety precautions and ship design.

Railroad fatalities soon faded into insignificance compared to motor vehicle fatalities. The absolute number of motor vehicle fatalities first exceeded railroad deaths in 1918 and had doubled railroad deaths by 1921. The ratio of vehicle fatalities per 100 million miles traveled hit its peak of forty-five as early as 1909 and by 1922 had already fallen by half to twenty-two and again by half to eleven by 1939. The rate in 2008 was only 1.3, smaller by a factor of ten than in 1939 and by a factor of forty than in 1909. This is an example of rapid progress both before and after 1940.[114]

An apparent fan of George and Ira Gershwin noted that "the automobile is here to slay."[115] Initially in the first years after its 1900 introduction, the automobile did not travel much faster than a horse and broke down frequently, creating few accidents. But as automobile speeds increased, so did the risk of danger. Roads were narrow and rutted, and children played in the streets and became victims of automobiles. "Early cars had weak brakes, tires that blew out, headlights that glared, plate-glass windows that made them easy to flip ... no seat belts and often soft roofs or no roofs at all ... there were no drivers' education requirements, no driving exams, no vision tests, no age limits, and in most places no speed limits."[116]

During much of the past century, deaths from homicides have been roughly half as frequent as those from automobile fatalities. Figure 7–7 displays the rate per 100,000 people of homicides from 1900 to 2010, which exhibits cycles rather than a single downward or upward trend. The overall pattern is of a U, with wide tails before 1933 and after 1970 and a sharply diminished homicide rate between the early 1930s and late 1960s. There were two peaks in the homicide rate, one coinciding with the end of Prohibition in 1933 and the second at the peak of drug violence in 1980. Homicides declined by more than half from 1933 to the mid-1950s, when the rate was equal to that of 1907–10. Then they rose again to a peak in the 1980s, a bit higher than in the 1930s. By 2008, the rate had declined substantially, though not to the low levels of the 1950s.

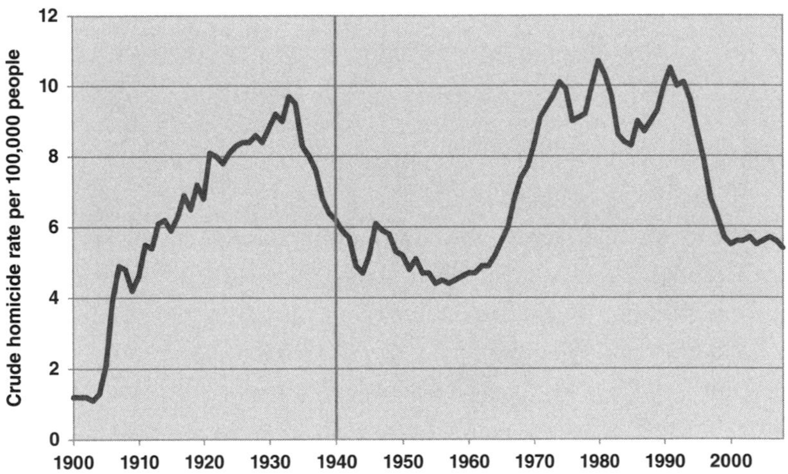

Figure 7–7. Crude Homicide Rate per Capita, 1900–2008
Sources: HSUS series Ec190 and 2012 SAUS table 312.

The absolute number of homicides in the early 1930s was about a third of motor vehicle deaths at the same time and similar to railroad-related deaths in 1917–18. What stood out was that the homicide rate in the United States was seven to ten times higher than in any European country in the early twentieth century. Homicide incidence, unlike the occurrence of railroad or motor fatalities, was not uniformly spread across the United States. In fact, in 1900, New England had a homicide rate similar to old England. Homicide rates by state show a sharp geographical distribution, with New England joined by the northern states along the Canadian border west of Wisconsin all having very low homicide rates, while the highest rates were found in the southern tier of states, led by Louisiana.[117]

In 2007, African Americans were homicide victims at almost ten times the rate of whites, and both blacks and whites in the south were more violent than their counterparts in the north. Black-on-black homicides relative to white-on-white homicides in New York City rose from three times as many to thirteen times as many between 1850 and 1950. In Steven Pinker's interpretation, democracy "came too early" to America, in contrast to Europe, where the state had long ago disarmed the people and acquired a monopoly on violence as a method of policing. The extreme was the American south, where a reliance on "self-help justice" to settle disputes and achieve retaliation was preferred to strong government-based policing. In turn, Pinker traces the southern culture back to the different origins of immigrants to the north and the south, where southerners in the mountainous frontier away from the coastal plantations mainly came from the Scotch-Irish, who arrived from the mountainous frontier of the British Isles.

But even the south was no match for homicide rates with the western frontier towns, where death rates per 100,000 could reach 100, in contrast to the rate of one in 1900 England or seven for the United States in 1925 or 2008. Pinker attributes this "anarchy" and "mayhem" to a lack of law enforcement, the ready availability of guns, a culture dominated by young men aged 15 to 30 facing a scarcity of the civilizing influence of women, and the ubiquity of alcohol. Eventually the savagery of violence in the west declined as cities grew and women arrived. But the cultural uniqueness of the American south, and the disproportionate homicide rates of black men killing black victims, remain to this day.[118] This history of black-on-black homicides unfortunately moved north with the Great Migration to industrial cities such as

Chicago and Detroit, particularly during the periods of labor shortage during World War I and World War II.[119]

THE MOST VALUABLE IMPROVEMENT OF ALL? VALUING HIGHER LIFE EXPECTANCY

A consistent theme of this book is that the major inventions and their subsequent complementary innovations increased the quality of life far more than their contributions to market-produced GDP. The national accounts dutifully record expenditures on automobiles and related services, attempting imperfectly to correct for quality changes. But in the case of the invention of motor vehicles, the GDP accounts do not include the health and aesthetic benefits of the retirement of the horse and its indiscriminate dropping of manure and urine on the urban streets, not to mention the role of the automobile in creating an entire new category of consumption known as "personal travel." Every invention has generated unmeasured benefits or consumer surplus.

But no improvement matches the welfare benefits of the decline in mortality and increase in life expectancy examined in previous sections of this chapter. Over the past three decades, economists have developed methods of placing a monetary value on gains in longevity.[120] If greater longevity raises GDP and the population in proportion, real GDP per capita does not change. But each individual is better off, because he or she has more years to enjoy that standard of living. Spouses have more years to enjoy their marriage partner instead of spending years in widowhood, while children have more years to share parental advice and affection. In a term used by Gary Becker and co-authors, "full income" refers to both market-based income produced per year and the monetary equivalent of changes in the number of years over which that income can be enjoyed.[121]

The monetary valuation of increased life expectancy should not be viewed, contrary to Nordhaus's suggestion, as a measure of the output of the health care industry.[122] As we have seen, the "health care industry" contributed little to the epochal decline in mortality between 1890 and 1950. Most of the credit is allocated above to developments outside that industry, including the arrival of clean running water and sanitary sewer pipes, reduction in food contamination and adulteration achieved by everything from refrigerated railroad cars to food and drug regulation, and the development of the Pasteur germ theory with its subsequent emphasis on controlling insects, achieving cleanliness, and changing attitudes about the breastfeeding of infants.

The estimation of the monetary value of an additional life-year made possible by decreased mortality has been developed most recently by William Nordhaus in one study and by Kevin Murphy and Robert Topel in another. Their technique shares the aim of measuring the value of an additional life-year by which to multiply the savings in life-years implied by historical mortality tables. To simplify this section, we present only the results obtained by Nordhaus.

The Nordhaus calculations of the value of improved health provide four alternative estimates that are sufficiently similar that we average their values in translating his conclusions to figure 7–8. Nordhaus expresses the value of health improvements as a share of conventional consumer expenditures, and we adjust his estimates to express them as a share of GDP. As shown, the Nordhaus calculations imply that the value of improvements in life expectancy during 1900–1950 was as large as the growth rate of real GDP per capita for all other reasons. Thus he doubles growth in potential GDP per capita from 2.05 percent per year to 4.2 percent per year. For 1950–2000, the value of increased longevity was 63 percent of the growth in the rest of GDP. Postwar growth including his health capital estimates was 3.5 percent compared to the conventional 2.1 percent.

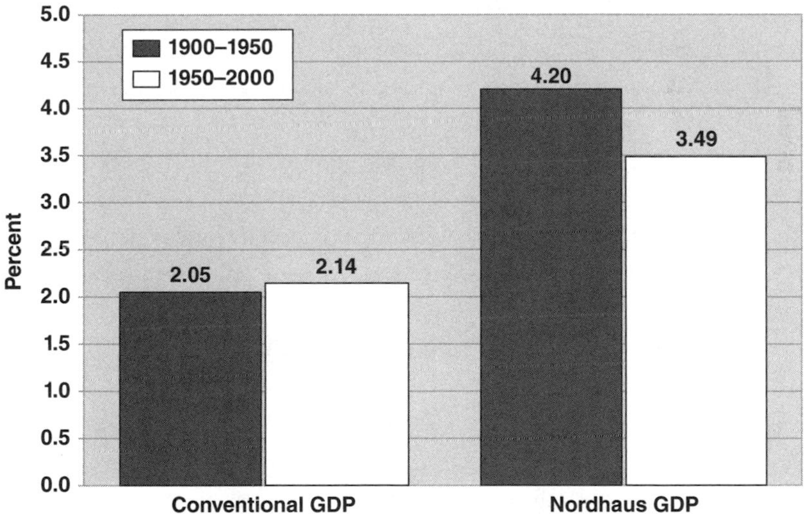

Figure 7–8. Average Annual Growth Rate in per Capita GDP with and without the Accumulation of Health Capital, 1900–1950 and 1950–2000
Sources: Nordhaus (2003) and HSUS series Ae7.

The most important conclusion to be reached from the Nordhaus study is that the health-augmented growth rate of real GDP per capita in the first half of the twentieth century was substantially higher than in the second half. Though the official measures suggest that growth was about 0.1 percent slower in the first half, the Nordhaus estimate suggests 0.7 percent faster. This result agrees with a central theme of this book that the growth rate of welfare in the first half of the twentieth century has been significantly understated relative to the second half, and this conclusion makes no allowance for the enormous amounts of consumer surplus contributed by the other inventions considered in chapters 3 through 6, including the benefits from electrification, motor vehicles, information, and entertainment.

CONCLUSION

During the 1870–1940 interval covered by this chapter, the public health and medical community came close to winning two enormous victories—against infant mortality in particular and against infectious diseases more generally. The rate of improvement in life expectancy at birth in the first half of the twentieth century was double the rate of improvement in the last half of the twentieth century. The sense of progress in 1926 was palpable in the sense that there was a great gap between what the medical community knew how to cure and actual medical outcomes. A comprehensive 1927 book on the state of American medicine provided this double-edged verdict:

> That knowledge is at hand to prevent much of the suffering and premature death caused by disease is avowed by well-known leaders in the field of medicine. The health field has a woefully ineffective distribution service, as compared with its marvelously effective production service in the laboratories of the world. We know how to do a lot of things which we don't do, or do on a wretchedly small scale.[123]

First rank among the causes of progress during 1890 to 1940 is awarded to urban sanitation infrastructure, the network of pipes bringing clean running water under pressure into the home and the different set of sanitary sewer pipes taking away the waste and effluent. The work of Cutler and Miller suggests that clean water may explain as much as three-quarters of the decline in infant mortality. Some caution is required, because deaths from nonwaterborne diseases declined as quick as or quicker than those from waterborne infections. Some credit should be given to other factors that reduced the spread of infectious diseases, including knowledge at the level of households about cleanliness and breastfeeding, the role of refrigeration and federal regulation in reducing food adulteration and contamination, the invention of window screens, and the transition during 1900–1930 from horses, with their excrement and dead carcasses, to motor vehicles.

Not just clean water, but also uncontaminated milk, contributed to the decline of infant mortality. Adulteration of milk was more common in cities, where parents bought milk from vendors, than on farms, where the milk came from the farmer's own cows or nearby sources. The reform movement calling for public health regulation that culminated in the Pure Food and Drug Act of 1906 had as its target not only adulterated and contaminated milk, but also meat slaughtered in unsanitary conditions. The purification of the milk supply is an important explanation of the timing of changes in infant mortality, which declined most rapidly in the three decades 1880–1910.[124]

Advances within the health care sector can be divided between research, hospitals, and doctors. The single most important advance in medical science was the Pasteur germ theory of disease, which by the 1880s and 1890s had led to the identification of insects and bacteria responsible for most of the infectious diseases that had caused a majority of the deaths in the late nineteenth century. Increased belief by doctors and public health officials in the validity of the germ theory spurred the advances of urban sanitation infrastructure and the regulation of food and drugs. But medical science itself contributed relatively little to the decline in mortality before 1920. Progress was made mainly in the surgical area through the development of anesthetics and antiseptics that made the process of surgery much less painful and less likely to result in death through infection. The foundations of future advances were put in place before 1920, however, with the inventions of the electrocardiogram, X-ray machine, and other basic tools of modern medicine.

In previous chapters on food, clothing, the networked house, electrification, motor vehicles, and communication as well as entertainment, the United States established the frontier of invention, innovation, and progress after 1870. But American "exceptionalism" was not entirely a virtue. We have seen in this chapter that American cities provided water and sewer pipes two or three decades later than the large cities in western Europe. The most important negative feature of American exceptionalism was the inability of the political system to adopt universal health insurance, defined as insurance that is a right of citizenship rather than being dependent on employment. Why should households suffering from the devastating loss of income through unemployment also lose their access to what should be a universal right, the ability to obtain health care services to prevent diseases and ultimately death? Bismarck figured out this greatest of all economic policy issues in the 1880s, but even now an efficient system of the provision of medical care as a right of citizenship has thus far eluded the American political system.

Chapter 8

WORKING CONDITIONS ON THE JOB AND AT HOME

> Finding work, enduring long hours, and the uncertainty of keeping a steady income dominated the lives of many and perhaps most of the working class, whether on the farm or the sea, or in the factory, the forest, or the mine. Ever present for many workers was the possibility of injury, either immediate and possibly fatal, or the gradual, insidious work-linked lung and other diseases. Those who worked most closely with the natural world—especially farmers, ranchers, fisherman, and loggers—also had to contend with the vagaries of rain, drought, sea changes, forest fires, and technological shifts that could wipe them out economically for a season or forever.
>
> —Harvey Green, 2000

INTRODUCTION

Improvements in the standard of living are usually measured by increases in consumption per person over time. This book broadens the concept of consumption using Gary Becker's theory of time use that views consumer welfare as a joint product of market-purchased goods and services and household-provided time. This framework emphasizes the parallels between home production and market production and adjusts GDP to include products produced in the home, whether a home-produced woman's dress in the 1870s or a home-baked cake in the 1950s.[1] In recent decades, analysts have attempted to go further by measuring the value of consumer surplus when new products are introduced.[2] And considerations of the value of declining mortality and increasing life expectancy, as in the previous chapter, create the biggest gains of all.

This chapter extends the concept of the standard of living to include conditions of work both outside and inside the home. In 1870, more than 80 percent of the labor force worked at jobs that were hazardous, tedious, and unpleasant. Farmers and farm laborers were subject to droughts, blizzards, floods, and insects, because their work occurred outdoors. Blue-collar craftsmen, operatives, and laborers were exposed to working conditions that were often dangerous or unsanitary, as in the heat of a steel mill, injury-prone work on the railroads, or the filth and stench of the stockyards. The transition between 1870 and 1940 and beyond gradually reduced the ratio of jobs that were arduous to those that were less taxing and in which the economist's concept of the "disutility of work" was markedly lower. The rising share of clerks, sales people, managers, and professionals made the working hours—if not delightful fun—at least less physically taxing than before. And those working hours steadily declined, from a typical sixty-hour work week in 1900 to a typical forty-hour week after 1940.

The chapter begins by describing changes in the average work experience of Americans. Labor force participation of adult males declined even as that of females increased. As more people lived beyond age 65 thanks to increasing life expectancy, the concept of retirement was invented.[3] For the few males who survived past age 65 in 1870, the male labor force participation rate in the age group 65–75 was an astonishing 88 percent. And as life expectancy was extended, the transformation of life at ages older than 65 took on new importance. The percentage of the population living past their sixty-fifth birthday was only 34 percent in 1870 but jumped to 56 percent in 1940 and then to 77 percent in 2000.[4]

Just as old age was transformed, so was youth. In 1880, time spent in full-time education dropped off rapidly after age 12, and few young people went to high school. An astonishing 50 percent of boys aged 14 and 15 were in the labor force, but child labor almost vanished by 1940 as high school education reached an ever-growing share of the population. As in other dimensions of life, female–male differences were much greater before 1940 than after. It was much less likely for 14- to 15-year-old girls than boys to participate in market work, but they were heavily engaged in home production, working as partners with their mothers in performing the many tedious tasks required to run the household. As we learned in chapter 3, most clothing for women and children was made at home from store-bought dry goods, and the daughters were fully engaged with the mother in making clothing for the family.[5]

The improvement in working conditions over time reflects both the changing mix of occupations away from those that were most unpleasant and hazardous, and, just as important, improved working conditions *within* the major occupational groups. No occupation was transformed more completely by 1940 than farming, as crude early horse-drawn plows of the 1870s were replaced by gas-powered machines after 1910, especially the ubiquitous tractor. In manufacturing, workers became more independent as electric-powered floor-mounted and hand tools replaced centralized steam power distributed inefficiently by rubber and leather belts. The iron and steel industry after 1870 gradually eliminated hot and dangerous jobs. Hideous conditions in meat-packing and other food-related industries were substantially improved during the Progressive Era of 1900–1920. Sweatshops producing apparel in appalling conditions attracted the searchlight of public opinion after the catastrophic New York Triangle Shirtwaist fire of 1911, a precursor of the deadly conditions in Bangladesh apparel factories revealed in recent years.

A consistent theme of working life before 1940 was its insecurity, including not only the risk of cyclical unemployment, but also of arbitrary dismissals when a firm fired an employee who was no longer capable of doing brute-force labor, as well as the risk of seasonal or firm-specific plant shutdowns that left the worker before 1940 without any income at all. This chapter also treats education in its multiple roles of eliminating child labor, making the life of teenagers more enjoyable, and contributing directly to economic growth. The achievement of local, state, and federal government in funding the rise of educational attainment is discussed in this chapter, and other contributions of all levels of government to growth in productivity and the standard of living are among the topics in the next chapter.

MORE LABOR FORCE PARTICIPATION FOR WOMEN, LESS FOR TEENS AND THE ELDERLY

The historical trends in labor force participation for adults are among the most familiar data in labor economics, and they reveal a great deal about the nature of the work force from year to year. As shown in figure 8–1, there was a historic transformation in the participation of adult (aged 25–64) women, changing gradually from 12 percent to 26 percent between 1870 and 1940, then surging from 32 percent in 1950 to 72 percent in 2000. Despite the widespread impression that the entry of women was a one-time process after the women's

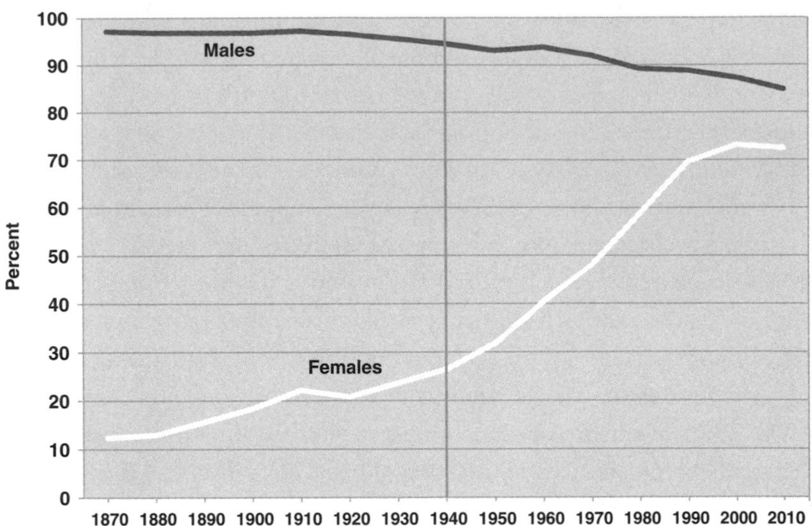

Figure 8–1. Labor Force Participation Rate by Sex, Ages 25 to 64, 1870–2010

Sources: HSUS series Ba393-Ba400, Ba406-Ba413, Aa226-Aa237, Aa260-Aa271, and 2012 SAUS tables 7 and 587.

liberation movement of the late 1960s, it actually evolved more gradually. The only decade during which female participation declined was between 1910 and 1920. The average increase in the female participation rate was 2.2 points per decade between 1880 and 1940, compared to 6.5 points per decade during 1940–2010.[6]

From 1890 to 1980, participation among women increased in all age groups, but that for young women in the 25–34 age group increased more gradually than for older women in the 45–54 age group.[7] The causes of the gradual increase in female participation before World War II, and the more rapid increase thereafter, combined higher supply caused by the time-saving made possible by modern home appliances, and higher demand as employment increased in the occupations that favored women, including clerical and sales jobs, as well as nursing and school teaching.

The participation rate of males aged 25–64 held steady at more than 95 percent during the 1870–1940 interval covered by this chapter, declining only by 0.4 percentage points per decade. In part II of the book (chapter 15), we will note the accelerated decline in prime-age male participation after 1970.

Participation rates for youth reflect expanding educational opportunities and the end of the scourge of child labor. Figure 8–2 displays participation rates by sex for the 10–15 and 14–15 age groups. In 1880, a startling 30 percent of boys aged 10–15 worked in the labor force, as did an even higher 50 percent of boys aged 14–15. Because these percentages reflect paid employment and exclude unpaid work by teenagers in farm families, the true participation rate of teenagers in the late nineteenth century must have been substantially higher. The male participation rate for ages 14–15 declined sharply, from 42 percent in 1910 to 10 percent in 1940, coinciding with the period of the greatest rate of increase in high school attendance.[8]

Figure 8–2 shows that participation rates for teenage girls were less than half that of males in each age group and at each point of time. The participation rate for girls aged 14–15 reached a maximum of 20 percent in 1910 and by 1940 had declined to 4 percent. Though participation in market work was much less important for teenage girls than for boys, the difference is nevertheless probably reversed when household work is considered. In the late nineteenth century, day-by-day household work was exceedingly onerous by modern standards, and teenage girls were called upon to be assistant mothers in every aspect of home production from hauling water to laundry to kitchen tasks to making clothes and caring for younger children.

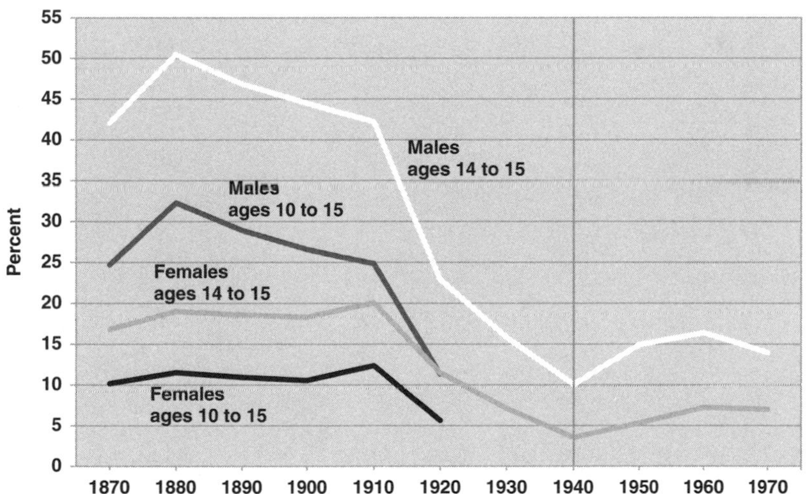

Figure 8–2. Labor Force Participation Rate by Sex, Ages 10 to 15, 1870–1970
Sources: HSUS series Ba356-Ba390.

When we examine the participation rates of older teenagers and youth as in figure 8–3, which covers the 16–24 age group, again we see a great disparity between the sexes before 1940. This narrows gradually, but most of the convergence occurred between 1960 and 1990. For young males, the participation rate declined from 87 percent in 1910 to 63 percent in 1970, followed by a brief reversal in the 1970s. Most if not all the decline in young male participation reflected the spread of high school education before World War II and the rising share of those attending college after World War II.

For males, the decline in youth participation is paralleled by an even sharper decline in participation of those aged 65–74, as shown in figure 8–4. In the early years, thanks to low life expectancy, this was a relatively small group, but it increased as a percentage of the population as life expectancy increased. From today's perspective, it seems surprising that in 1870, fully 88 percent of males in the 65–74 age group worked in the labor force. Why? They had little choice. There was no Social Security until the late 1930s, and private pension plans for farm and manual urban workers hardly existed. Because few females had jobs, the only choice for elderly men was to continue working until sickness,

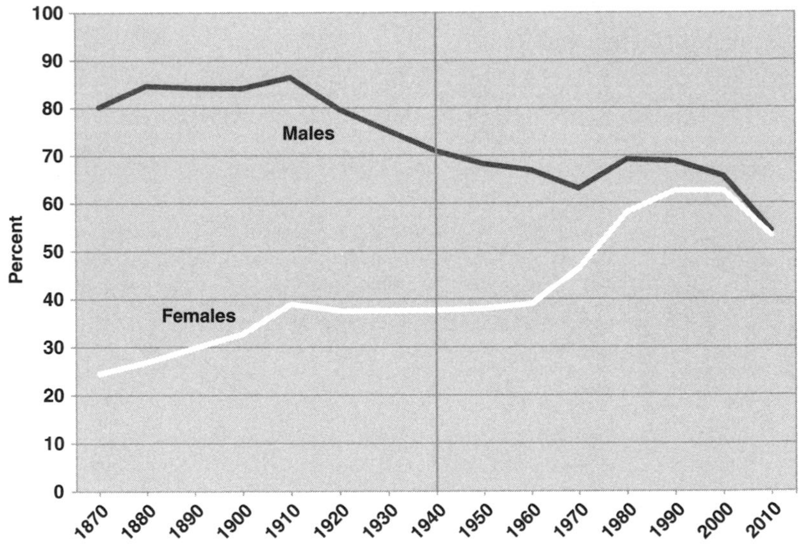

Figure 8–3. Labor Force Participation Rate by Sex, Ages 16 to 24, 1870–2010

Sources: HSUS series Ba391, Ba392, Ba404, Ba405, Aa223, Aa225, Aa257, Aa259, and 2012 SAUS tables 7 and 587.

disability, or death made that impossible. A blunt summary might say that "they worked until they dropped."

That 88 percent elderly male participation rate in 1870 raises interesting questions. We first need some perspective: In 1870, only 25 percent of Americans lived in urban areas. Such high participation of the elderly could reflect rural life in the 1870s—grandfathers helped out with family chores on the farm or in the family-owned general store. In urban settings, the elderly men may have worked not at backbreaking construction or manufacturing work but as helpers in retail and service establishments, analogous to today's elderly "greeters" at Walmarts. Male participation in the 65–74 age group declined from 88 percent in 1870 to 53 percent in 1940 to 24 percent in 1990. There was no similar decline in elderly female participation, which was at or slightly below 10 percent between 1870 and 1940 and only a bit above 10 percent from 1940 to 2010. In any case, it is clear that the phenomenon of retirement for males aged 65 or older began long before the New Deal's invention of Social Security.

The three big themes that emerge from this section are (1) a gradual movement toward equality for women in the rate of participation in the labor market, (2) the rise of education and the disappearance of child labor, and (3) the absence of the institution of retirement for elderly men in the late nineteenth

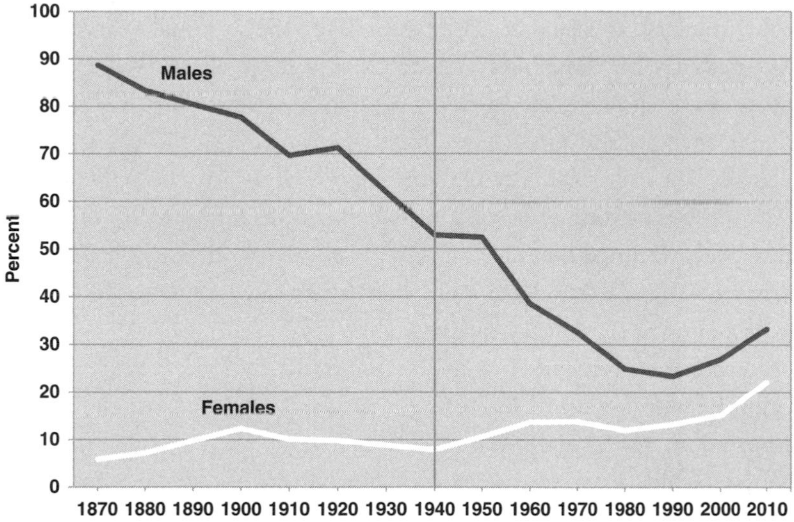

Figure 8–4. Labor Force Participation Rate by Sex, Ages 65–74, 1870–2010
Sources: HSUS series Ba401, Ba402, Ba414, Ba415, Aa238, Aa240, Aa272, Aa274, and BLS table 3.3.

century and the gradual transition to the modern world in which labor contracts and pension plans freed men (and now women) to make a transition into leisure in their sixties.

WORK: TAXING, TEDIOUS, DANGEROUS, AND UNSTABLE

The unpleasantness (economists call this the "disutility") of work declined sharply over the past fourteen decades. Though improvements in household production made possible by consumer appliances have long been an important topic in the history of economic growth, there has been less attention to the declining unpleasantness of work as economic development changed the distribution of occupations and as labor-saving electric-powered and gasoline-powered machinery reduced the difficulty of particular work tasks.

How did the relative growth and decline of industries influence the industrial structure of employment? Working conditions were more difficult and arduous in farming, mining, and manufacturing than in most other industries, so a shift in the industry mix of employment away from these industries reduced the disutility of work. For the pre-1940 period, railroad employment should also be treated as unpleasant owing to the high number of deaths and injuries of railroad employees during the years before 1930.

It is more informative to disaggregate employment by occupation rather than by industry, as displayed in table 8–1 for the terminal years 1870 and 2009 together with three intermediate dates at 1910, 1940, and 1970.[9] This decomposition allows us to develop a numerical estimate of the share of jobs that were arduous and physically difficult in contrast to those that were less unpleasant. The ordering of occupations starts with the least desirable at the top and the most rewarding of occupations at the bottom. In line (1), farmers and farm workers declined steadily from 1870 to 1970 to almost vanish by 2009. Between 1870 and 2009, fully 44.8 percent of the labor force shifted out of agriculture into some other occupation.

Blue-collar employment consists of craftsmen, operatives, and laborers, most of whom worked in mining, manufacturing, construction, utilities, transportation, and communication—for example, as telephone repair workers. These occupations increased from 33.5 percent to 39.0 percent between 1870 and 1940, then declined slowly to 1970 and sharply thereafter. Within the blue-collar category, skilled craft workers held their ground, declining only from 11.4 percent in 1870 to 8.2 percent in 2009. Operatives, many of whom

Table 8–1. Industrial Composition of the Labor Force by Type of Employment, 1870–2010

			1870	1910	1940	1970	2009
Farmers and Farm Laborers		(1)	45.9	30.7	17.4	3.1	1.1
Blue Collar	Total		33.5	38.2	39.0	35.8	19.9
	Craft Workers	(2)	11.4	11.5	11.6	13.6	8.3
	Operatives	(3)	12.7	16.0	18.2	17.8	10.2
	Laborers	(4)	9.4	10.7	9.3	4.4	1.4
White Collar	Total		12.6	19.6	28.3	37.7	41.4
	Clerical Workers	(5)	1.1	5.4	10.4	17.9	12.1
	Sales Workers	(6)	2.3	4.5	6.3	7.2	11.6
	Domestic Service Workers	(7)	7.8	5.5	4.5	1.5	0.6
	Other Service Workers	(8)	1.4	4.2	7.2	11.0	17.1
Managers, and Professionals	Total		8.0	11.6	15.2	23.4	37.6
	Proprietors	(9)	3.4	4.4	4.3	2.0	2.7
	Managers	(10)	1.6	2.5	3.7	5.9	14.4
	Professionals	(11)	3.0	4.7	7.2	15.5	20.7
Summary by Job Type	Unpleasant	(12)	87.2	74.4	60.9	40.4	21.6
	Pleasant	(13)	12.8	25.6	39.1	59.6	78.4
Alternative Classification	Disagreeable	(14)	63.1	46.9	31.2	9.0	3.1
	Repetitive	(15)	28.9	41.6	53.7	67.5	59.3
	Non-routine Cognitive	(16)	8.0	11.6	15.2	23.4	37.6

Sources for 1870–1970: HSUS series Ba1034 through Ba1046
2009: Statistical Abstract of the United States: 2011, Table 605 for self-employed plus Table 615 for employees

were assembly line workers in manufacturing, swelled as a percentage from 12.7 in 1870 to 18.2 percent in 1940 before a long decline to 10.2 percent in 2009. This shift in the structure of blue-collar employment resulted both from technological change, as robots replaced assembly line workers, and from imports and offshoring that decreased the share of employment in the manufacturing sector from its early postwar peak. Even more striking is the near disappearance of the "laborer" classification as the physical tasks of hauling and digging were replaced by motor vehicles and increasingly advanced machinery.

Although the share of blue-collar workers did not decline between 1870 and 1970, the share of farming almost vanished, offset by the increasing shares of white-collar and managerial/professional work. We note that within the category of white collar work in table 8–1, the category of domestic service workers almost vanished from 7.8 percent in 1870 to 0.6 percent in 2009. Within the managerial/professional category there was a substantial decline in the share of proprietors, particularly between 1940 and 1970, whereas there was a multifold increase in the shares of managers and professionals. The largest absolute increase in the share of managers increased after 1970, leading to accusations that American business firms had become overstaffed and bureaucratic.[10] The largest absolute increase in the share of professionals occurred earlier, between 1940 and 1970, and the increase continued at a slower pace after 1970. To some extent, the rising share of professionals mirrored the rising share of employment in the education and health sectors; also, the growth in the professional category was a natural by-product of rising college completion rates.

A crude way to summarize the transition toward lessened disutility of work is to tally the share of total employees engaged in relatively disagreeable work, whether outside, exposed to the elements; involving heavy lifting or digging; or featuring monotonous repetitive motions on the assembly line. For this purpose, we will include all those engaged in farming, blue-collar work, or domestic service as having "unpleasant" jobs and everyone else as having "pleasant" jobs. This two-way classification does not allow for nuances—for instance, that cashiers in retail stores may have jobs that are as repetitive and boring as those of assembly line workers, whereas some craft workers in manufacturing or construction create objects of which workers can be proud.

Nevertheless, the shift in the nature of work since 1870 has been striking, as the share of those in unpleasant occupations declined from an initial 87.2 percent over the years to 21.6 percent in 2009. That decline happened fairly steadily at a rate of about −5 percentage points per decade, with the slowest decline (−3.2) during 1870–1910 and the most rapid (−6.8) during 1940–70.

The story becomes slightly more complex when we shift to a three-way distinction that recognizes two dimensions of unpleasantness—work that is physically difficult and taxing versus jobs that are not physically challenging but rather repetitive and boring. This three-way distinction creates a category of truly disagreeable work, including farming, blue-collar laborers, and domestic servants. The middle category of boring and repetitious includes the jobs of blue-collar craftsmen, operatives, and all service workers other than domestic servants. The third category can be called "nonroutine cognitive" and includes the professional/managerial categories.

Taking into account the three-way distinction, the big shift over the century after 1870 was from truly disagreeable jobs mainly to repetitive occupations, leaving room for only a small shift to nonroutine cognitive employment. Only after 1970 did the change in the nature of work became unambiguously positive as nonroutine cognitive work gained at the expense of both truly disagreeable and repetitive occupations. The ratio of disagreeable to nonroutine cognitive jobs shifted from 7.9 in 1870 to 2.1 in 1940 to 0.1 in 2010, one of the great achievements of American economic growth over the past fourteen decades.

Both the two-way and three-way occupational classifications greatly understate the improvement in working conditions, for they assume that jobs in a given occupation were as taxing, arduous, boring, and/or repetitive in 2009 as they were in 1870. One only need contrast the 1870 farmer pushing a plow behind a horse or mule, exposed to heat, rain, and insects, with the 2009 farmer riding in the air conditioned cab of his giant John Deere tractor that finds its way across the field by GPS and uses a computer to optimally drop and space the seeds as the farmer reads farm reports and learns about crop prices on a fixed screen or portable tablet.

And this dimension of change extended across nearly all occupations. In our case study of iron and steel workers subsequently in this chapter, we see that some of the most uncomfortable and taxing jobs, especially those featuring exposure to extreme heat, had started to disappear as early as 1890. Just as jobs requiring heavy physical labor were phased out, working conditions changed in the repetitive jobs as well, as air conditioning reduced the discomfort of repetitive manufacturing, clerical, and sales jobs. In the postwar period, memory typewriters, mainframe computers, and personal computers eliminated repetitive retyping of documents and manual hand-entry of bank statements, telephone bills, and insurance policies.

THE WORK WEEK: FEWER HOURS AND FEWER DAYS

Regardless of whether a job was physically taxing, in the late nineteenth century, fatigue was inevitable as a result of long work hours. By 1870, when our story begins, the work week in manufacturing had declined to ten hours per day, whereas a census survey carried out in 1830 showed that eleven or more hours per day was standard at more than half the establishments surveyed. Massachusetts textile workers continued to work eleven and a half to twelve hours per day until an 1874 law mandated no more than ten.[11] In the late nineteenth century, the typical worker labored ten hours per day for six days per week. By 1920, this had declined to eight hours per day for six days and by 1940 the same number of hours for five days per week. The standard forty-hour full-time work week has remained surprisingly stable during the postwar period, seven decades of stability after such radical change in the century before 1940.[12]

The rapid decline in working hours led John Maynard Keynes in 1931 to make a famous prediction that turned out to be quite wrong—that society would be so productive that each worker would only need to work for fifteen hours per week:

> For many ages to come the old Adam will be so strong in us that everybody will need to do *some* work if he is to be contented. We shall do more things for ourselves than is usual with the rich to-day, only too glad to have small duties and tasks and routines. But beyond this, we shall endeavour to spread the bread thin on the butter—to make what work there is still to be done to be as widely shared as possible. Three-hour shifts or a fifteen-hour week may put off the problem for a great while.[13]

Figure 8–5 displays two measures of hours of work. The dark gray line exhibits hours per week for production nonsupervisory workers in the private nonagricultural sector.[14] This series declines in stages from about 58.5 hours per week in the 1890s to about 41 hours per week after 1950. The decline starts in 1900, accelerates during the decade of the teens, halts during the 1920s, and then plummets during the Depression years. If we skip over the Great Depression and

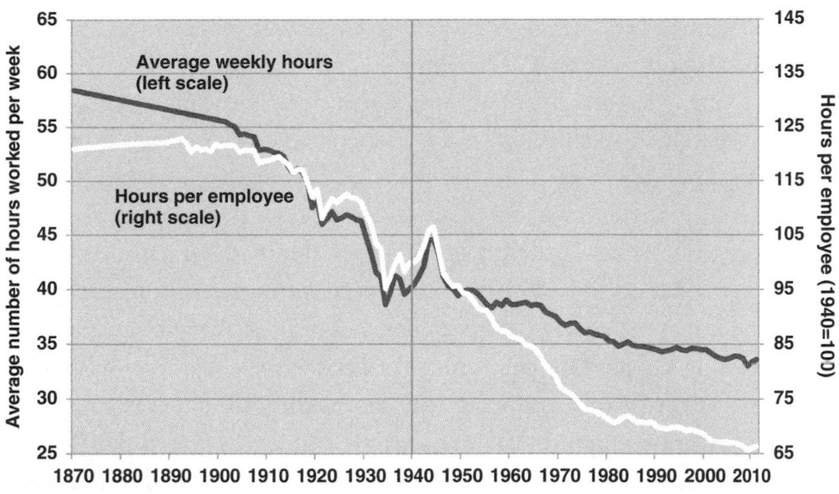

Figure 8–5. Average Weekly Hours of Production and Nonsupervisory Employees, and Hours per Employee, 1870–2013

Sources: Average weekly hours are from St. Louis FRED series AWHNONAG, 1964–2013, and are ratio linked from Jacobs (2003) Table 2-6, column 1, 1947–1963, to HSUS series Ba4575, 1900–1947, to Huberman (2004, Table 4, p. 977), pre-1900. Hours per employee are ratio linked from Kendrick (1961) Tables A-X and A-VI, 1870–1948, to BLS CES survey data, 1948–2013.

World War II, we find that hours per week declined from 48.7 to 41.1 between 1929 and 1950 after declining from 58.5 in 1900 to 49.6 in 1923.

The alternative series shown by the white line in figure 8–5 is the ratio of total hours of work to the number of total employees. This can behave quite differently. Hours per week were shorter for middle-class and upper-class employees, who are not covered by the production worker series. More important, the white line includes agricultural workers, whereas the dark gray line does not. Hence the white line declines by only about half as much as the dark gray line between 1870 and 1940, because almost half of employment in 1899 was in the farm sector, and agricultural hours were 45.5 hours per week, not the sixty or more common in manufacturing.[15]

And the postwar behavior of the two series is also quite different. The production worker series reflects the fact that full-time work hours per week have been relatively constant during the postwar years, exhibiting small fluctuations that are mainly cyclical. But the broader hours per employee series declines markedly, particularly between 1950 and 1980. This reflects primarily the entry of women into the labor force and their prevalence in part-time jobs. Also pushing down the ratio of hours worked to employment are longer vacations, more holidays, and more days of sick leave.[16]

Like so many features of American progress, from electrification to the rise of the motor vehicle to the eradication of infant mortality, progress in reducing working hours is centered on a short period of human history, 1900–1940. Claudia Goldin attributes at least part of the decline in hours during 1910–1920 to Progressive Era legislation limiting work hours of women and children. Progress in the period since 1940 not only has resulted in a minimal reduction in working hours of regular full-time jobs, but also has been counterproductive by pushing people into part-time jobs against their will as employers try to escape the expense of pension benefits and medical insurance, that in many cases they are not required to pay to part-time employees. In April 2015, fully 6.6 million people held part-time jobs who would have preferred full-time jobs but were unable to find them.

New survey data uncovered by Dora Costa reveal surprisingly little variation (except for the top income groups) in hours of work by occupation or by sex. Her large sample across numerous states in the last two decades of the nineteenth century records an average of 10.2 hours per day for men and 9.5 hours for women. Work typically went from 7:00 a.m. to 5:30 p.m., with a half-hour break for lunch. Virtually all the respondents reported working on Saturday for the same hours as on weekdays. This work effort of roughly sixty hours per week is consistent with the time series on production workers displayed in figure 8–5. The surveys used by Costa refer only to the nonfarm economy and do not include farm workers, who worked shorter hours per week over the course of the year owing to lack of activity during the winter months. Thus Costa's data provides a further verification of the dark gray line in figure 8–5 and is not in conflict with the white line based on the entire economy including farms.

Costa's survey evidence indicates that those in the bottom decile of wages in 1890 worked an average of eleven hours per day, whereas those in the top decile worked nine hours per day. The difference between working-class and middle-/upper-class hours is supported by the 1925 survey of Muncie, Indiana, by Robert and Helen Lynd, who found that typical working-class daily hours started at 7 a.m., whereas those for the business class typically started by 8:30 a.m.[17]

Interpretations of the movement for shorter hours center on the widespread belief on the part of both firms and labor leaders that a reduction in hours would improve work performance and increase production. Higher productivity and higher real wages made possible a gradual reduction of hours of work, for the onerous demands of sixty- and seventy-two-hour work weeks had created an exhausted male working class with little or no time to enjoy leisure, nor any time to help their wives with chores at home. As a result of these pressures, worker hours per week declined four times as quickly during the first two decades of the twentieth century as during the last few decades of the nineteenth century. The reasons why this occurred are complex and controversial. The few industries that were unionized led the way, and railroad employees gained the eight-hour day in 1916 as a result of the first federal government legislation limiting hours. Many states began to pass legislation limiting hours as an offshoot of the Progressive Era. Politicians also led the way, including through the 1912 Bull Moose platform plank that called for shorter hours and through Woodrow Wilson's support for an eight-hour day.[18]

THE AMERICAN FARMER: EXPOSED TO VOLATILE WEATHER, ERODING SOIL, AND UNPREDICTABLE FARM PRICES

The occupation of farming depends on the fertility of the land, the weather, and the extent to which animal and mechanical power is available to lighten the burden of the physically difficult work that men had endured for millennia. Our primary focus here is on the fertile Midwest and the Great Plains, to which millions migrated from the eastern states and from abroad. The frontier pushed westward, spurred in part by the 1862 Homestead Act, which offered 160 acres of free land to anyone who would occupy and improve it. Between 1862 and 1913, the federal government granted 2.5 million homestead claims, and 4 million settlers filed claims to 270 million acres in thirty states, 10 percent of the area of the United States at the time.[19] This encouragement by the federal government pushed the frontier westward into Oklahoma, Kansas, Nebraska, and the Dakotas. But only about 40 percent of these claims were finalized. "Drought, insect plagues, low [farm] prices, and isolation caused thousands of farm sites to be abandoned."[20]

Immigrants from Europe or from the northeast were unprepared for the variation in temperature. An early memoir from Kansas reported a temperature of 108 °F in the shade. "The winds were hot and dry and the grass, baked on the stem, had become as inflammable as hay . . . The little gardens . . . withered, and many of the women began to complain bitterly of the loneliness and lack of shade. The tiny cabins were like ovens at midday." Other hazards on the plains included the strong winds summer and winter, the deep cold in winter blizzards with little protection inside crude cabins, and plagues of insects that climaxed in the 1874 invasion of grasshoppers that ravaged crops from the Dakotas to Texas.[21]

Though the ultimate consequences of this overexpansion were not fully realized until the Dust Bowl disaster of 1934–36, the process of debasing the land began in the 1870s. As the original ground cover of the Great Plains, including buffalo grasses, was destroyed by the 1870s slaughter of the buffalo and subsequent grazing of cattle and sheep, it was further degraded by plowing for wheat crops. By the 1930s, "virtually the entire Great Plains region suffered from moderate to severe sheet erosion and slight to severe wind erosion. . . . [A] thousand tons per square mile were swept away by wind and water . . . the Mississippi River alone deposited 15 tons of sediment a second into the Gulf of Mexico."[22]

Even though the land may initially have been free, there were unavoidable expenses to setting up a farm. The Midwest was not entirely treeless, and in the forests of Ohio, Michigan, Wisconsin, and Minnesota, trees had to be cleared. It has been estimated that a month of labor plus a team of oxen were required to clear an acre. Treeless prairie offered sod that had to be broken, a difficult task owing to the "almost impenetrable tangle of roots from millennia of grasses." Estimates of the total expense of setting up a farm vary with its location and size, but one set of estimates ranges from $981 for a forty-acre farm to $3,013 for a 160-acre farm in a year when the average annual wage was about $400. As a result, many potential farmers could not save or borrow enough to own their own farms and became tenants, and in 1900, the share of farms run by tenants ranged from 60 percent at age 25 to 20 percent at age 65.[23]

No matter whether a farm was located in the dry Great Plains or the more verdant Midwest, or whether the operator was an owner or tenant, the daily routine of farm work varied little from day to day within a given season, but typical activities changed from season to season. Farm families arose at dawn, when the father and the male children headed outdoors before breakfast to feed animals, milk cows, and collect eggs. Though only a few urban dwellers were unlucky enough to have jobs cleaning up animal waste from the streets, all farm men, and particularly teenage boys, had to confront the daily or weekly tasks of cleaning animal waste from stables, pig pens, and chicken coops.[24]

The hand labor, aided by only a few farm animals, focused on planting in the spring, cultivation in the summer, and harvesting in the fall. Turning feed grasses into hay took as much work as harvesting cash crops such as corn or wheat. Cows needed attention when they gave birth, typically in the spring, and sheep were sheared in the spring. During the winter, farmers "flailed grain, shelled corn, and cured tobacco . . . they repaired fences, tools, and harness . . . pulled stumps. In the north farmers cut ice in the winter for sale or for summer use."[25]

Before mechanization had its effects in the last half of the nineteenth century, farmers were limited in the amount of land they could plant by low productivity and a limited time available to harvest. If the entire crop had to be harvested within two weeks and it required two full days of hard labor to harvest a single acre, then a farmer could not plant more than seven to ten acres per available worker. Because farm laborers were hard to find, especially at harvest time, there was a clear incentive for farm families to have many children. Other solutions were to diversify into growing crops that matured at different times, spreading the harvesting season over as many weeks as possible, and to adopt mechanical equipment soon after it was invented. The mechanization of American agriculture, though lagging behind that of manufacturing, nevertheless outpaced Europe, for the wide open spaces of the American Midwest allowed ingenious inventors to find ways of lessening the human labor needed to grow a given output of crops.[26]

For millennia farm work had been physically difficult, with long hours and constant strain on muscles. Gradually during the nineteenth century, agriculture was transformed as motive power provided mainly by humans was gradually replaced by horses working with mechanical devices and, later, by the internal combustion engines that ultimately replaced the horse. There were few horses in agriculture before the 1830s and 1840s. It was the development of mechanical implements starting with the metal plow that made horses the essential source of power on the nineteenth-century farm. Cast-iron plows were replaced several decades later by steel plows that reduced the amount of power needed to pull the plow.[27] A simple invention to reduce human drudgery was the sulky plow, which allowed the farmer to ride atop it instead of walking behind it; soon plows were developed that could cut multiple rows at the same time.[28]

Several inventors, including Obed Hussey and Cyrus McCormick, share credit for the 1833–34 invention of the mechanical reaper, which could harvest more grain than could five men working with hand scythes. McCormick's initial model was a crude device that cut the standing grain and, "with a revolving reel, swept it into a platform from which it was raked off into piles by a man walking alongside. By 1880 the bundles of grain were automatically bound with twine."[29] All these reapers, though increasingly sophisticated, had to be pulled by a team or two or more horses, and improvements were constantly made to make them lighter and less taxing for horses to pull. In addition to their role in pulling plows, reapers, and other moving machines, "horses produced stationary power for threshing, corn shelling, grinding, baling, binding, and winnowing by means of the sweeps and treadmills similar to those used to power horse ferries."[30]

The use of horses on the farm in the last two-thirds of the nineteenth century paralleled their increasing use as the prime movers of intra-urban transportation, as shown in chapter 5. Mechanization of agriculture lagged behind that of manufacturing, in part because steam engines were too expensive and bulky to be purchased by individual farmers. Thus the horse became dominant over the steam engine in farming and intra-urban transportation for the same reasons—its bulkiness and expense (additional factors inside cities were noise that disturbed citizens and vibration that destroyed the streets).[31] Unsolved until the arrival of the internal combustion engine was the problem of devising a self-propelled steam engine that could operate "on soft, uneven ground without sinking in or tipping over. In other words, a self-propelled steam engine had to be like a horse."[32]

Though drought, heat, and insects were particular problems in the Great Plains, even farmers in the most fertile areas of the Midwest within 200 miles of Chicago were suffering by the late 1880s. When they weren't protecting themselves and their animals from blizzards, they faced the consequences of growing indebtedness. Their increasing dependence on international commodity markets made the prices they received "as unpredictable as the weather." Good weather and a bountiful harvest would cause oversupply and lower crop prices, whereas higher prices caused by growing demand would induce farmers farther west, who lived on less fertile land, to plant more and send prices down again. "The situation was a severe instance of a chronic condition: Midwestern farmers lived on the edge in good times and bad."[33]

The image of the west in twentieth-century movies and television dramas has centered not on the yeoman farmer but rather on the cowboy. Until the invention of the refrigerated railway car, cattle had to be driven directly to the city where they would be consumed. The main job of cowboys was to herd the cows while they were fattening up on the range, round them up, and then to guide them in long cattle drives toward their destination. The roundup is central to the popular image of cowboy culture yet depended on the open range before the invention of barbed wire fencing that allowed individual cattlemen to protect their range land from the intrusion of cows owned by others. Cowboys did not own cattle; they were employees of the cattlemen who owned the cattle. Their working conditions have been vividly described:

> After you have mastered the cow business thoroughly—that is, learned not to dread getting in mud up to your ears, jumping your horse into a swollen stream when the water is freezing, nor running your horse at full speed, trying to stop a stampeded herd, on a dark night, when your course has to be guided by the sound of the frightened steers' hoofs—you command *good* wages, which will be from $25 to $60 per month.[34]

By 1915, many changes had occurred that mattered for the work life of farm families. Tractors began to ease the tasks of planting and cultivation for the farmers who could afford them, and combines came in small models. In 1935, 6.1 person-hours were required to harvest an acre of wheat, less than a third of the twenty that had been necessary in 1880.[35] By 1940, one California wheat farmer underlined the change by observing, "We no longer raise wheat here, we manufacture it . . . . We are not husbandmen, we are not farmers, we are producing a product to sell." Schools of agriculture and the research departments of seed companies made great strides in developing hybrid corn seeds that had greater yields and were more resistant to drought and insects. The percentage of all corn grown from hybrid seeds by 1940 had reached 24 percent nationwide and 77 percent in Iowa.[36]

This section has mainly been about farms in the Midwest and Great Plains states, and conditions there, however insecure and precarious, were orders of magnitude better than in the former Confederacy, where the sharecropping system developed, whereby ex-slaves in particular became tenant farmers. Indeed, tenant farming was much more common in the south than in the Midwest. In 1880, in the eight core Midwestern states, the share of farms that were tenant-operated was 19.2, compared to a much higher 43.1 in the six states of the Deep South. By 1920, the disparity was even greater, at 28.9 percent versus

60.9 percent, respectively.[37] These percentages include both whites and blacks; the tenancy ratio for blacks in the south was roughly 75 percent.[38]

The sharecropping system differed from standard tenancy in that the landowner retained ownership of the buildings, tools, and possibly a mule and hired the tenant and his family to do all the work needed to raise the crop, usually cotton. For his labor, the tenant would receive half of the income earned from the crop. Because the crop remained in the possession of the owner before a wage was paid, the arrangement amounted to making the tenant a wage laborer. Because the wage was not paid until after the crop was harvested, the sharecropper had to build up a debt to the owner to buy food and basic supplies. Because the debts often amounted to more than the value of the crop, the sharecroppers became, in effect, indentured servants.[39]

Life in the south in the late nineteenth and early twentieth centuries, particularly for the black sharecroppers, was striking in its isolation and its lack of connection to the modern world. Many members of farm families never traveled outside the county in which they were born. Roads were poor to nonexistent, and the only means of travel available were by foot, horseback, or wagon. Striking was the absence of medium to large-sized cities that were typical in the northeast and Midwest. Most towns were merely crossroads.

DISEASE, HEAT, AND DANGER: WORKING CONDITIONS IN NONFARM AMERICA

The 1870–1940 period covered in part I of this book encompasses the most rapid transition in American history from a largely rural to a predominantly urban nation. The percentage of the population living in urban areas (places having population greater than 2,500) grew from 25 percent in 1870 to 39 percent in 1900 to 57 percent in 1940.[40] The population of urban America grew from 9.8 million in 1870 to 74.3 million in 1940, an increase of more than sevenfold. The population of towns and cities grew not just as immigrants arrived and chose urban life in preference to rural life, but also as a result of farm-to-city migration by farmers who had been driven off their farms by failed harvests, bad weather, foreclosure, bankruptcy, and/or a belief that an urban existence would provide higher wages, better leisure time activities, and less isolation.

Next to agriculture, mining was the industry with the most taxing and dangerous working conditions. Though not subject to the vagaries of the weather or swarms of insects, mining had its own inherent perils for the large fraction of miners who worked underground rather than in open pits. Cave-ins could occur when support timbers gave way and often were caused by carelessness in response to management orders for more output. The air was always humid. Explosions were a constant threat, for dust from the mining process could be ignited by the kerosene lamps that were the only form of illumination until the 1930s. Lung disease could be caused by the mining process of any mineral, but coal was unique in its ability to permanently disable coal miners with black lung disease. In the winter, miners could go for an entire week without seeing daylight, because they started their ten-hour shift before the sun rose and ended their shift after the sun set.

> Coal dust grinds itself into the skin, never to be removed. The miner must stoop as he works in the drift. He becomes bent like a gnome. His work is utterly fatiguing. Muscles and bones ache.[41]

Close behind coal mining for abysmal working conditions were jobs in the great slaughterhouses of Chicago and elsewhere, already described in chapter 7 in connection with Upton Sinclair's novel *The Jungle* and the passage in 1906 of the Pure Food and Drug Act. From the moment workers entered the plants, they were assaulted by an unthinkable combination of odors, sights, and noises, including the squeals of animals. The Chicago establishments had developed the assembly line method of production even before Henry Ford's use of it in the auto industry. The work was not only disgusting but also boring and tedious, and each worker would stand at the same position all day doing the same "scraping, slitting, or gutting maneuver." Worse yet, the number of hours worked fluctuated unpredictably from day to day. When they left home for work in the morning, slaughterhouse workers did not know whether they would be coming home at noon or at 9 p.m.[42]

Some of the extremes of long hours and difficult working conditions darkened the lives of the hapless laborers in the iron and steel industries. Conditions worsened in the 1880s as the twelve-hour day replaced the ten-hour day, and work every other Sunday became common. As steel mills replaced ironworks, they had to operate continuously, and firms had enough control over the workers to insist on two daily twelve-hour shifts instead of three daily eight-hour shifts. Hours per week ranged from seventy-two to eighty-nine and continued so until a reform movement succeeded in having the twelve-hour day abolished in 1923.[43] An investigation conducted by the U.S. Bureau of Labor in 1910 found that nearly three-quarters of steelworkers were on a twelve-hour schedule and that on average, in that industry, laborers worked 72.6 hours per week.[44]

Competition between firms was cutthroat, and huge swings in the demand for steel made it imperative for managers to cut costs relentlessly if they were to survive. Only firms that had the lowest costs could stay in business when the price of a ton of steel dropped from $85 to $27 between the boom year of 1880 and the depressed market of 1885. The most important cost to make steel besides raw materials was labor, and firms worked ceaselessly to reduce labor requirements and, when possible, cut wages. The pace of work was intensified by foremen called "pushers." A visiting English steelmaker reported on his return from America:

> The bosses drive the men to an extent that the employers would never dream of attempting in this country, getting the maximum work out of them, and the men do not seem to have the inclination or the power to resist the pressure.[45]

Another pair of British visitors, Karl Marx's daughter Eleanor Marx Aveling and her husband, Edward, visited the United States in 1886. They found that the physical demands placed by American employers on their workers were much more severe than those prevailing in Britain. "American laborers started to work at an earlier age than their British counterparts, worked more strenuously, and died, on the average, almost a decade earlier." They found fines for the mildest violations of rules, along with blacklists and intimidation. "Many workers reported to the Avelings that they were afraid to be seen talking to them for fear of losing their jobs." Many employees were forced to sign an oath at hiring that they did not belong to and would not join any working-class organization.[46]

Not only were employees pressured to work at an unbearable pace, but their working conditions can only be described as insulting. There were no lockers for coats or packed lunches. Washrooms and toilets were few and insufficiently equipped, often lacking soap and toilet paper. Managers refused to put light bulbs in toilet rooms, hoping to discourage workers from reading instead of getting back to the job. Some factories had washing room attendants whose main job was to clock the time the workers spent: Excessive time spent in the lavatory would result in a deduction from pay. Because there were no on-premises showers, mill workers covered with filth would spill into the streets at the end of their shift, leading to complaints from other people against whom they might rub.[47]

Before machinery replaced the task, men had to hammer red-hot iron into manageable pieces. A plant superintendent described this as "[a]n exceedingly hard and laborious job. They were working constantly in a cloud of moist vapor of high temperature, which of itself was debilitating." In the words of one steel-worker, it was "working aside of hell ahead of time."[48] As machines replaced men, there was less need not only for laborers, but also for skilled craftsmen who had previously formed the metal in operations that required years of experience. The giant steel mills steadily replaced the skilled craftsmen with a homogenous work force of largely unskilled and semiskilled workers.

This trend from autonomous craftsmanship to a machine-driven homogeneous working-class labor force was noticed in the Lynds' study:

> Inventions and technology continue rapidly to supplant muscle and the cunning hand of the master craftsman by batteries of tireless iron men doing narrowly specialized things over and over and merely "operated" or "tended" in their orderly clangorous repetitive processes by the human worker.[49]

The role of mechanization in driving upward productivity in the manufacturing sector is illustrated by figure 8–6. Shown for selected intervals between 1869 and 1929 are the annual growth rate of horsepower per hour worked and output per hour worked. Though the correlation is not perfect across these time periods, we notice that in 1869–89 the two series increased together, whereas in 1889–1914 horsepower per person grew exactly twice as fast as output per worker. After a short hiatus of slow growth during 1914–19, growth in both horsepower and output per hour soared in the early 1920s and concluded the 1920s with slower but still rapid growth.

The explosion of productivity growth in manufacturing during the 1920s has long been noticed by economic historians. Paul David has argued that half of the upsurge in manufacturing productivity after 1919 can be attributed to growth in electric motor capacity. Among the reasons cited by David for the long delay in the electrification of manufacturing was the high price of electricity, as well as the time taken to develop small electric motors powerful enough to replace the previous system of shafts and belts linking individual work stations with a centralized steam or water power source. David cites as a by-product of the transition to single-unit electric machines an improvement in working conditions:

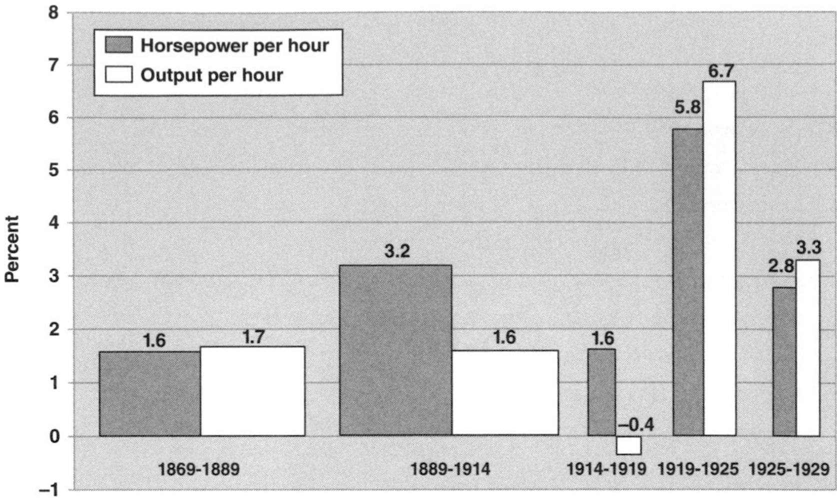

Figure 8–6. Average Annual Growth Rates of Horsepower per Hour and Output per Hour in the Manufacturing Sector, 1869–1929.
Sources: Jerome (1934) Table 15 and Kendrick (1961) Table D-II.

> Lighter, cleaner workshops were made possible by the introduction of skylights, where formerly overhead transmission apparatus had been mounted; and also by the elimination of the myriad strands of rotating belting that previously swirled dust and grease through the factory atmosphere, and where unenclosed within safety screening, threatened to maim or kill workers who became caught up in them.[50]

THE INDUSTRIAL DEAD AND WOUNDED: FATALITIES, INJURIES, AND FREQUENT UNEMPLOYMENT

Coal-mining deaths occurred at a rate of one or two per day in the late nineteenth century. "Accidents came from roof collapses, runaway coal buggies, flooding, and faulty explosives."[51] In 1930, injuries from coal mining per hour worked were almost five times higher than in manufacturing.[52] Coal miners were not alone; for all industrial blue-collar workers, life in the workplace was dangerous. During the year ending June 1907, in Allegheny County (which includes Pittsburgh), there were 526 accidental deaths of workers in the county's factories, mines, and railroad yards. In addition, 167 workers were disabled.[53] Deaths from industrial accidents in Pittsburgh per 100,000 residents almost doubled from 123 to 214 between 1870 and 1900.[54] The Lynds surveyed their working-class families in 1925 and found that one in five workers had an accident in 1923 serious enough to create an absence and hence loss of income. More than half lost fewer than eight days, but 29 percent lost three weeks or longer. The death rate came out at fifty per 100,000 workers.[55] The most dangerous industry was iron and steel production:

> Molten metal spattered the millhands. Unstable piles of iron billets stood everywhere. Hot floors burned feet through wooden-soled shoes. Molds and furnaces exploded. The machinery had no protective guards. Standing next to a hot furnace all day stirring iron, guiding it through the rolls, carrying it, dumping materials into blast furnaces, and pouring steel into molds drained workers, especially during the summer, when the mills resembled infernos.[56]

Those who chose to escape the stifling mills or stinking slaughterhouses often chose construction work, despite its unpredictable and seasonal ups and downs in labor demand. But construction workers faced their own set of dangers. They could be injured in falls or crushed to death or maimed by heavy construction materials that dropped or became dislodged. Outdoor workers in railroad yards were killed by moving trains, often at night, and immigrants who had poor language skills were particularly prone to injuries, for they did not understand warning signs or signals.

The legal protection of injured workers, or compensation of their families in the case of death, barely existed. The courts ruled in the late nineteenth century that those who accepted employment in the steel, coal, railroad, or laundry industries assumed the risk of dangers that were widely known. Carelessness on the part of fellow employees leading to injury or death was not considered the employer's responsibility. Managers often blamed industrial accidents on employee carelessness and drinking.

Though garment making might seem a safe occupation, particularly when contrasted with laboring in a steel mill or coal mine, conditions in the industry were not pleasant. The female immigrant workers who dominated work in the apparel industry, in addition to receiving low wages and working long hours, suffered from unsafe working conditions. Needles could pierce fingers and sometimes require finger amputations. Workers were typically locked in the rooms. Perhaps the best-known disaster in U.S. manufacturing history was the New York City Triangle Shirtwaist Factory fire in March 1911, in which 148 employees died, most of them young women, in conditions very similar to those of the Bangladesh clothing factory fires of 2012–13:

> As flames spread throughout the eighth floor, workers jumped to their deaths. Scores of charred bodies were found piled against closed doors. They had been kept bolted, a newspaper reported, to safeguard employers from the loss of goods by the departure of workers.[57]

There were fire escapes, but they could not handle the 700 fleeing workers. Women whose clothes and hair were on fire leaped to their deaths. This tragic event caught the nation's attention and led to reforms and regulations to improve workplace safety.[58]

As difficult as work may have been in the late nineteenth century, men had to work to provide an income for their families. But they could not always work as much as they wanted, for the economy was subject to repeated booms and busts. There was a severe depression between 1873 and 1878, and another between 1893 and 1897, with shorter downturns in the mid-1880s and after the financial crisis of 1907.[59] Between the 1907 panic and mid-1909, fully half of the 40,000 blast furnace workers in the steel industry lost their jobs.[60] In 1880, a relatively prosperous year, 30 percent of all Pittsburgh working-class men experienced unemployment lasting longer than a month.[61]

Uncertainty was widespread—not just about next year's financial situation, but also about next week's income. Workers sometimes reported for work only to find the plant or mill closed or their jobs eliminated. Firms were under no obligation to provide advance notification of termination or to provide severance pay. Layoffs could stretch from a day to a week or even several months. Instability of aggregate demand first hit the traditionally cyclical industries such as construction and steel but soon extended into the service sector. When automobile sales fell, not only were automobile production workers laid off, but so were car salespeople at automobile dealers.

At the very end of the 1870–1940 period covered in part I of this book, the blow to family income from unemployment was partially cushioned by government-managed unemployment benefits financed at the federal government level. Before the 1938 New Deal legislation, workers' compensation (WC) was handled entirely at the state level. During the decade between 1910 and 1920, all but four of the forty-eight states had passed WC legislation. Before then, unemployed heads of households had only their previous savings, if any, and private charity to provide food and shelter for their families, with help in summer, in the less congested cities, from vegetable gardens. There was little sympathy in the middle and upper classes (among whom unemployment was rare) for the effects of income variability in working-class families. In the middle and upper classes, workers were blamed for their troubles and portrayed as "dullards or as dangerous, drunken louts."[62]

WOMEN'S WORK OUTSIDE THE HOME: OCCUPATIONAL SEGREGATION, LOW WAGES, AND REPETITIVE TASKS

Paid work was much less common among married women than unmarried before World War II. Unmarried women were herded into "women's jobs," including household servants, clerks, school teachers, and medical nurses. Women worked also in manufacturing, primarily in textiles and apparel; the majority of these working women were young, childless, and/or widows.[63] Just as the mechanization of the steel industry eliminated the personal satisfaction of skilled workers and forced employees into a homogenous and highly regimented work force, so the invention of the sewing machine created the archetypal sweatshop, in which rows and rows of women sat in front of their machines producing clothing to the drumbeat of their supervisors demands for an ever faster pace of work. The harsh conditions present in 1870, before the arrival of the sewing machine, combine poor working conditions and low pay:

> I have worked from dawn to sundown, not stopping to get one mouthful of food, for twenty-five cents. I have lived on one cracker a day when I could not find work, traveling from place to place in pursuit of it . . . made shirts for eight cents apiece and by working early and late could make three in a day.[64]

Though most women did not work in the late nineteenth and early twentieth century, those who did experienced a severe disappointment if they thought that work outside the home would be easier, more pleasant, or less isolating than work inside the home. Indeed, conditions for female workers turned out to be even worse than those for men in most occupations. Women were unskilled, unorganized into any unions or other supportive groups, and crowded into a few occupations where their wages were low and their working conditions, in some cases, appalling. Firms preferred to hire women, for women were docile, cared most about their families, had little expectation of advancement, and posed no likelihood of joining a trade union or other form of protest. Most important, as machinery reduced the physical demands of work in many manufacturing industries, employers found that women could do the same work and were willing to accept a lower rate of pay. For instance, machinery changed the nature of work at shoe factories and raised the share of female employees from 5 percent in 1870 to nearly 25 percent in 1910.[65]

Many women in the work force shared the experience of blue-collar males in finding that their jobs became more routinized and less compatible with individual initiative. An example was the elimination of previously independent midwives as the male-dominated American Medical Association forced the birth process from home to hospital and virtually abolished midwifery. Female librarians, nurses, and teachers all became subject to supervision by male supervisors. But there was improvement in the situation of women as well. By the 1920s, an advance guard of females began to make their first tentative advances into management and the professions, taking jobs as

> college professors and presidents, chemists, photographers, dentists, manufacturers, and supervisors. Less affluent native-born white women entered secretarial and office work, finding places for themselves in this new and expanding sector of the work force.[66]

Part of the increase in the female participation rate from 1920 to 1940 resulted from the increased demand for clerical workers in response to the steady decline in the output share of agriculture and increased share of the service sector. Another part was a response to the great surge of secondary school attendance and graduation; high school graduation rates increased from 9 percent in 1910 to 52 percent in 1940.[67] A third cause was the gradual diffusion of electric appliances (as discussed in chapter 4), including the iron, vacuum cleaner, range, refrigerator, and washing machine. The opportunities for women to shift from household service and the apparel sweatshop to clerical and sales work steadily improved working conditions as dirty and arduous work was replaced by the cleaner and more comfortable environment of the modern office and sales floor, jobs that typically required fewer hours of work per week.

THE FEMALE FATE INSIDE THE HOME: ISOLATION AND ALL THAT LAUNDRY

The life of a working-class housewife in the late nineteenth century was little different than that of a hired domestic servant. "Marriage brings a woman a life sentence of hard labor in her home. Her work is the most monotonous in the world and she has no escape from it."[68] A child raised on a North Dakota farm in the 1890s later recalled as a grandmother details of life inside her late nineteenth-century farmhouse:

> [She] remembers the tools—doing laundry with tubs, washboards, and flatirons, cooking on a wood stove with iron pots, growing and preserving food, sewing and mending, cleaning filthy kerosene lamps—and speaks with a little nostalgia: "I'd hate to go through it again. Took us all day to do a big washing."[69]

During the interview, she guessed that electric lights arrived in her farmhouse around 1923, sooner than for most farm families, who had to wait until the 1930s and 1940s to join the modern world of electricity.

Aside from the major invention of the cast-iron stove and the minor invention of the hand eggbeater, the process of cooking was roughly the same in 1900 as a century earlier. The kitchen was the center of family life and often was the only room supplied with heat. There were bread and cakes to be baked from batter mixed by hand, vegetable chopping to be done with no Cuisinart to help, the fire to be fed. "In cooking, as in other household tasks, women still did the work of producing energy in 1900; their daughters would come to consume it."[70]

The monotonous routine of the housewife was little changed from week to week. "Only grave sickness or sudden calamity broke that proper routine: washing on Monday, ironing on Tuesday, mending on Wednesday, sewing on Thursday, extra cleaning on Friday, baking on Saturday."[71] The burden of weekly laundry was the most onerous task. In most of rural America until the 1940s, washday started with carrying in enough water to fill a large pot and heat it on a coal or wood stove, then rubbing clothes on a washboard, turning a hand wringer, and then hanging clothes on a clothes line. "When one needed to draw water, chop wood to heat it, scrub each item by hand, rinse in clear water, and then clean the ashes after, it was little wonder that those who could afford to often employed laundresses."[72] As incomes rose, some could afford to use commercial laundries, whose revenues doubled between 1919 and 1929.

A household task even more unpleasant than doing the laundry was, before the arrival of underground sewer pipes, the need to carry liquid refuse outside, including "dirty dishwater, cooking slops, and of course the contents of chamber pots." Clean water and the elimination of untreated outdoor waste not only freed women from their previous role as beasts of burden, but also was the most important of all factors that created the epochal conquest of infant mortality during the interval of 1890 and 1950.[73] Nevertheless, in 1940, 33 percent of all homes still cooked with wood or coal, 20 percent still lacked electric light, 30 percent lacked running water, 40 percent lacked an indoor toilet, 44 percent lacked a private shower or bathtub, and 58 percent lacked central heating.[74]

How much did the arrival of running water, sewers, and household appliances reduce the work effort of women at home? One estimate comes from the Lynds' survey of 120 working-class families in 1925, in which two-thirds of the responses reported that the wives worked between four and seven hours per day. The average of roughly six hours per day for seven days each week comes to about forty-two hours per week, somewhat less than the forty-eight to fifty hours per week that men were working at the same time. Three quarters of those responding reported that their mothers worked more hours, but the survey results do not indicate by how much.[75] A more significant change was found in the same survey of forty "business-class" housewives, who reported that a third had one full-time household servant, whereas the proportion for their 1890 mothers was two-thirds. The shift from full-time servants to a weekly visit was attributed to cost—"a single day's labor of this sort today costs approximately what the housewife's mother paid for a week's work."[76]

A more systematic approach to the division of the work week into types of activities has been developed by Valerie Ramey and Neville Francis. They divide the total hours per week spent by both men and women among four main activities—market work, household production, leisure time, and personal care time, the latter category including sleeping, bathing, and eating. Their definition of leisure relies on modern household surveys of how enjoyable an activity is rated. Surprisingly, on a scale of 1 to 10, work rates a level of enjoyment of 7. We note that this high ranking of the enjoyment obtained from work describes surveys taken in the 1990s, not the 1890s, and that work has become much less unpleasant, and hence more enjoyable, over that century.

Based on the survey rating of the enjoyment obtained from many activities, the types of activities classified as leisure (that is, more enjoyable than market work), include sports, playing with children, hanging out in bars, movies, reading, walking, meals out, recreational trips, hobbies, baby care, exercise, and gardening. Categories classified as household production because they are less enjoyable than market work include cooking, shopping, child and elderly care, commuting, errands, housework, home repairs, paying bills, yard work, cleaning the home and dishes, laundry, and going to the doctor, dentist or automobile repair shop.[77]

Ramey and Francis have developed estimates for the entire twentieth century of time use divided among the four basic activities of market work, home production, leisure time, and personal care. Their key result comes from a separate paper by Ramey and finds that the prime-age group of 25- to 54-year-olds experienced only a slight reduction in hours devoted to home production, from 26 hours per week in 1900 to 24.3 hours in 2005, despite the arrival of all the consumer appliances that would have seemed wondrous to behold from the perspective of 1900. The paradox is resolved when we learn that prime-age women actually did benefit from consumer appliances, reducing their weekly hours of home production from 50.4 in 1900 to a mere 31.1 in 2005, while men in the same age groups raised their weekly hours in home production from 3.7 to 17.3.[78] The Ramey–Francis estimate for age 18–64 female home production time for 1925 is 43.8 hours per week, very close to the 42-hour rough estimate obtained from the Lynds' survey already discussed.[79]

The twentieth-century transition combined two different trends—the alleviation of the burden of housework experienced by women together with the decline of market work hours of men, which allowed them to participate more actively in home production, including child care, home repairs, and yard work. The increased activity of men reflected, in part, a transition in residential location from farming, where outdoor maintenance was counted as hours of work, to suburban dads mowing their lawns and fixing up their houses. The transition from inner-city tenements to suburban settings also raised the ratio of land to family size and required more male maintenance.

The Ramey result that hours in household production hardly changed, with an increase in male hours nearly canceling the decline in female hours, looks very different when hours per person are converted to hours per household. On this basis, the data make more sense, with a decline in home production hours per household (including teenagers, women, men, and individuals aged 65 or older), from seventy-eight to forty-nine hours per week between 1900 and 2005. Though the average size of households declined by almost the same percentage during that period, from 4.7 persons to 2.6 persons, any attempt to conclude that hours per person of household production did not decline ignores the basic economies of scale of household production. Once the housewife has to produce breakfast or dinner for the family, it makes little difference whether she is cooking for two or four children.

The apparent paradox that the development of consumer appliances did not appreciably reduce time devoted to home production has an explanation provided by the Lynds' 1925 survey. Respondents reported that though the physical toil of housework had declined, this had been offset by rising standards:

> People are more particular about diet today. They care more about having things nicely served and dressing for dinner. So many things our mothers didn't know about we feel that we ought to do for our children.[80]

Joel Mokyr has labeled this conundrum—that the invention and diffusion of consumer electric appliances did not reduce hours of household production—as the "Ruth Schwartz Cowan problem."[81] His analysis is in the same spirit as the Lynds' observation but goes much further in linking it to the late nineteenth-century Pasteur germ theory of disease and the resulting increase in standards of cleanliness, requiring that more hours be spent not only in cleaning the house, but also in bathing children. Health was now viewed not as an inevitable divine retribution but as a matter of personal responsibility.

DID PROGRESS BOOST REAL WAGES?

Skilled workers such as "molders, carpenters, machinists, mule spinners, and coal miners" represented about 45 percent of blue-collar workers around 1900 and could barely afford to keep their families above a standard of living that we would associate with poverty. There would have been plenty of food on the table.[82] But their well-being was always at risk, a potential victim of unemployment, illness, or injury. Workers were paid hourly wages, and they had to show up to collect the wages. There was no sympathy in late nineteenth-century industrial America for workers who experienced bad luck. These workers were discarded, and there were plenty of eager applicants at the door, often just off the ship from Europe.

Above the level of the semiskilled were the aristocracy of the working class, the highly skilled and irreplaceable workers, "including many iron rollers, locomotive engineers, pattern makers, and glass blowers." The highest income manual workers at the turn of the century could earn incomes of $800–$1,100 yearly. At the bottom were about a quarter of the working class who lived in "total destitution. Many found their living by scavenging, begging, and hustling."[83]

Peter Shergold's careful study of twenty-two occupations in Pittsburgh (both in manufacturing and construction) in 1906 shows a 2-1 difference in the hourly wages of the most skilled workers (e.g., bricklayers) to the least skilled (common laborers). His results reinforce the view that it is simplistic to consider the American working class at the turn of the last century as a homogeneous struggling horde:

> There were two worlds among Pittsburgh's manual workers . . . . At the top of the wage pyramid were those high-skilled, high-income workers able to purchase their own homes, to wash in indoor bathrooms . . . families able to enjoy the "American standard" . . . . At the broad base of the pyramid was the city's large laboring population, crowded into hastily converted tenements and rapidly deteriorating wooden constructs, sharing outside toilet facilities and a communal faucet, living next to the noise, glare, and stench of the mills and furnaces. Here were children fighting imaginary battles along the unpaved streets and open sewers and workers to whom leisure was sleep.[84]

By 1914, the average nominal manufacturing wage had increased by 30 percent from seventeen cents per hour to twenty-two cents per hour, which translated to $2.04 per day.[85] Consider the sensation created when Henry Ford announced early in 1914 that henceforth the base wage in his Highland Park factory would be $5 per day.[86] His ulterior motive was to reduce labor turnover, combined with a bit of altruism. Labor turnover was an endemic problem at the time, due in part to the reliance of manufacturing plants on immigrant workers who were not yet married and planned to move on to another town whenever news came of better wages or working conditions. For instance, the superintendent of a mine in western Pennsylvania alleged that he had hired 5,000 workers in a single year to sustain his desired work force of 1,000.[87] The fact that unskilled work in manufacturing plants required little or no training made it easy for immigrant workers who were dissatisfied with one type of work to quit and move to another town and try something different.

Ford more than doubled the wage, but this generosity did not come without conditions, for he combined altruism with paternalism. His newly formed "Sociological Department" hired 200 agents to visit every household of the 13,000 employees and provide them with advice about a proper life style. Because Ford required employees to be married, a purpose of the agents' home visits was not just to observe standards of cleanliness but also to make sure that there was a wife. Single male employees often borrowed young unattached women to play-act the role of wives during these visits. The paternalism crept into every aspect of life. Ford provided legal staff to help workers buy houses; had a medical team of ten doctors and 100 nurses to provide health care, especially to injured workers; and arranged for language training of immigrants.

But there was no toleration for the non-American customs of immigrant workers, and 100 of them were fired for taking a day off from work to celebrate the Eastern Orthodox Christmas. The reformer Ida Tarbell visited the community, planning to expose the oppressive Ford system, yet concluded, "I don't care what you call it—philanthropy, paternalism, autocracy, the results which are being obtained are worth all you can set against them."[88]

A broader historical view of real wages is provided in figure 8–7, which plots real wages of production nonsupervisory workers against real GDP per hour, both expressed as index numbers with 1940 equal to 100. The most striking aspect of the graph is that real wages grew faster than output per hour (i.e., labor productivity) before 1940 but more slowly thereafter, particularly after 1980. The post-1980 divergence is consistent with the large literature on increasing inequality and the declining income share of labor, with a large share of productivity gains after 1980 going to the top 1 percent of the income distribution.[89]

More puzzling is the rapid growth of real wages relative to productivity before 1940, with a particular surge in real wages between 1920 and 1940 despite the decline in labor demand experienced during the decade of the Great Depression. Growth rates over intervals are plotted separately in figure 8–8. The results are quite striking. Over the seven decades between 1870 and 1940, the real wage grew almost a full percentage point faster than productivity, 2.48 versus 1.51 percent per year. But after 1940, the relationship was reversed, with productivity growth of 2.25 percent outpacing real wage growth of 1.56 percent by a difference of 0.69 percentage points.

The time interval with the fastest real wage growth was 1910–40, when the growth rate of 3.08 percent was a full percentage point faster than during 1870–1910. A plausible explanation for this shift was the role of unlimited

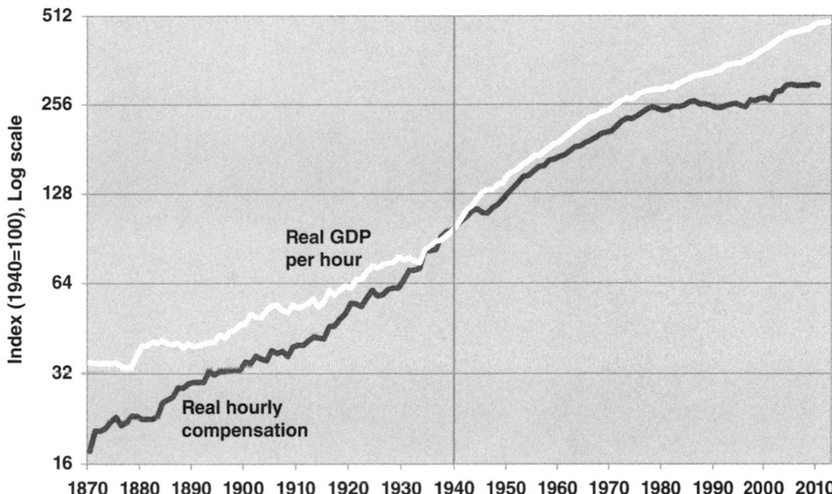

Figure 8–7. Real Hourly Compensation of Production Workers and Real GDP per Hour, Bottom 90 Percent of the Income Distribution, 1870–2012

Sources: Wages are from Production Workers Compensation from MeasuringWorth, price deflator is ratio linked from the PCE deflator 1929–2010, NIPA Table 1.1.9, to the CPI for pre-1929 from MeasuringWorth, GDP is from Balke and Gordon (1989) Table 10, 1869–1928, and NIPA Table 1.1.6, post-1928, and Total Hours are from BLS and Kendrick (1961) Appendix Table A-X.

immigration in holding down real wages in the earlier period and the end of mass immigration caused by World War I and the restrictive anti-immigration quotas passed in 1921, which saw further tightening in 1924 and 1929. The encouragement of labor unions by New Deal legislation may have been just as important, as suggested by the extremely rapid 4.64 annual growth rate of the real wage series between 1936 and 1940.

Some part of the explanation of rapid real wage increases before 1940, particularly between 1920 and 1940, may be attributable to the end of mass immigration and the encouragement of labor unions by New Deal legislation. But ultimately it was technological change that drove real wages higher. Part of this was compositional—new machines that pulled, pushed, carried, and lifted shifted the composition of employment away from the common laborer to operatives doing specialized albeit repetitive tasks and to new layers of supervisors, engineers, and repairmen to plan the layout of the machines, train new workers, and tend the machines. Firms began to raise pay to reduce turnover, for the assembly line could be slowed if an experienced worker quit and was

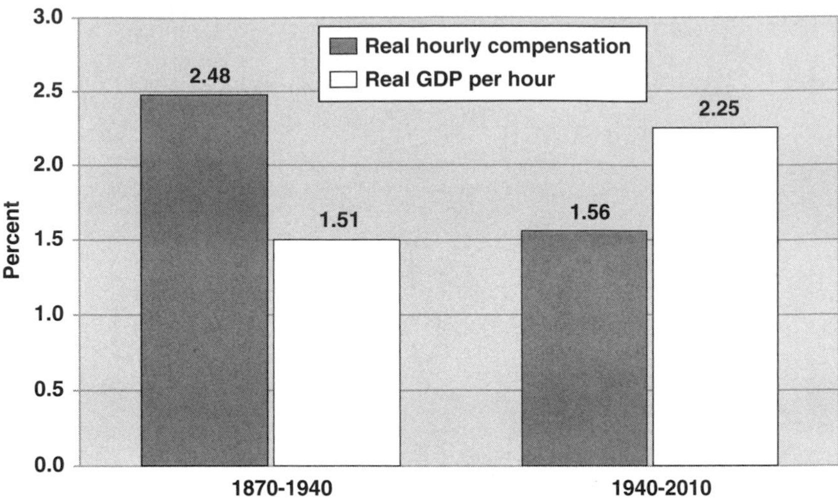

Figure 8–8. Average Annual Growth Rates of Real Hourly Compensation of Production Workers and Real GDP per Hour, 1870–2010

Sources: Wages are from Production Workers Compensation from MeasuringWorth, and price deflator is ratio linked from the PCE deflator 1929–2010, NIPA Table 1.1.9, to the CPI for pre-1929 from MeasuringWorth.

replaced by someone who could not initially keep pace. Much of this shift in the nature of employment was created by the rise of the automobile industry and its assembly line method of production and is symbolized by the contrast between the dark, satanic steel mills of the 1870s and the smoothly running Ford and General Motors assembly lines of the 1920s.

THE OPPORTUNITY COST OF EDUCATION WAS CHILD LABOR

As we learned from figure 8–2, child labor was common before 1920, especially for boys aged 14–15, whose participation rate in 1870 was 50 percent. Farmers started their children doing simple chores such as collecting eggs at ages 5 or 6. Family businesses such as restaurants also started children working very young. "I started washing dishes in the restaurant about five . . . I'd get up on a Coca-Cola box to bend over the dish though," later recalled a child laborer. Textile mills hired children deliberately because they could duck in and out of small spaces between the machines.[90] Children between the ages of 10 and 15 regularly lied about their ages in order to gain employment, often encouraged by parents who needed the extra income to fill holes in the family budget.

Full-time young workers had shifts of between eight and twelve hours. There were a well-recognized group of "boys' jobs." In coal mines, boys as young as 8 worked as "trappers," opening and closing doors so that coal cars could move through underground passages. "Breaker boys" picked through mined coal and threw out the slag. In manufacturing, boys cut cold iron into strips, opened and closed furnace doors, and opened and closed the molds for skilled glass-blowers. Boys, like adult women, were typically paid half the hourly rate of adult men, between seventy-five cents and $1.25 per day.[91]

Though most states in the north had compulsory school attendance and child labor laws by 1890, they were only erratically enforced. Southern states deliberately did not pass similar legislation in hopes of obtaining a competitive advantage over northern textile plants. But in both the north and the south, children of textile workers went immediately from school to work in textile mills. For the 14–15 age group, 76 percent of textile workers' children in the northeast and 94 percent of children in four southern states were at work.[92] Inequality was transmitted between generations by the tendency of relatively high-income parents to keep their children in school longer, as contrasted with immediate labor force entry by children from lower-income families as soon as compulsory school ended.

Farm families tended to keep their children in school longer than blue-collar workers in the cities, for there was no extra monetary compensation for the family when farm teenagers quit school to work.[93] Just as farm teenagers had more freedom than their urban counterparts, so the life of teenage boys in small towns offered more leisure and less toil, as experienced by Tom Sawyer and other young heroes of small-town novels. Sinclair Lewis wrote nostalgically of his own "fun he had had as a kid, swimming and fishing in Sauk Lake, or cruising its perilous depths on a raft . . . tramping out to the fairy lake for a picnic . . . It was a good time, a good place, and a good preparation for life."[94] For boys living in small towns, the country was necessarily always nearby. "Country roads beckoned the town boy to fish, to hunt, or simply to tramp the woods looking for excitement. The country road with barefoot boys, dogs, and fishing poles was an important part of early twentieth century small-town iconography."[95] This life could not have been more different from that of the child laborers, who were victims of their industrial environment.

The opportunity cost of extra education is a central concept that explains the differential educational attainment in different locations and social classes. The opportunity cost was highest in urban manufacturing centers, where the choice of working in manufacturing or garment sweatshops precluded further schooling entirely. The opportunity cost for rural teenagers was much lower, for they were expected to help with the planting in the spring and harvest in the early fall and were allowed (and expected) to attend school on a seasonal basis.[96] Indeed, among the highest high school graduation rates across states were in the portions of the Midwest that Claudia Goldin and Lawrence Katz called "the education belt." In 1910, the highest rates of high school graduation outside the New England states were in Iowa, Indiana, and Nebraska. All of the north central states ranked higher than any of the mid-Atlantic states. In 1910, high school completion rates in New York and New Jersey were in the same category as the states of the old Confederacy.[97]

By 1870 most children in the north and west were literate and had completed elementary school. But in 1876, the total number of high school graduates was only 20,000 per year in a population of 45 million. The ratio of high school attendance to elementary school attendance was only 6 percent. Only 1 percent of the college-age population was enrolled in institutions of higher learning in 1870.[98] The years 1910 to 1940 witnessed the most rapid phase of expansion of secondary education, as shown in figure 8–9. Though in 1910 just

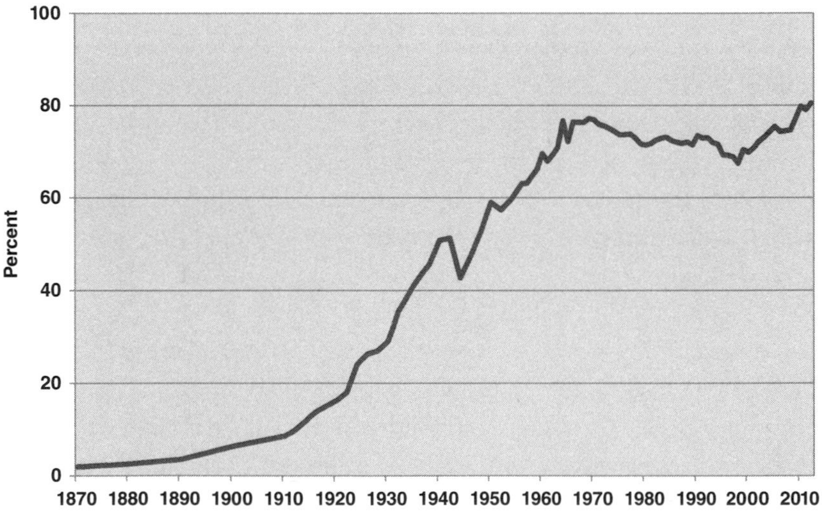

Figure 8–9. Public and Private High School Graduates as a Percentage of All 17-Year-Olds, 1870–2012

Source: HSUS series Bc264, NCES *Digest of Education Statistics* (2013), Table 219.10 after 1985.

9 percent of American teenagers obtained a high school diploma, by 1940 that percentage had reached 51 percent, and by 1970, it had reached 76.9 percent. The completion rate rose by 14 percentage points per decade during 1910–40, by 8.7 points per decade during 1940–70, and not at all after 1970. The surge in secondary school attendance and completion made possible the rapid expansion of college enrollment after World War II.

CONCLUSION

A consistent theme of this book has been that the world was revolutionized along multiple dimensions between 1870 and 1940. In every chapter, we continue to discover aspects of ordinary life that were unalterably changed between 1870 and 1940, and most of these happened over the shorter interval between 1890 and 1930. Previous chapters have shown how the world was changed by electrification, the networking of the home, motor vehicles, communication, entertainment, and the eradication of not just infant mortality, but also most infectious diseases. Life had irreversibly improved along so many dimensions; by 1930, urban America enjoyed near complete coverage with electric power, running water, sewer lines, telephone access, and town or natural gas, not to mention the nearly total replacement of the horse by the motor vehicle.

This chapter adds to the multidimensional list of improvements achieved during 1890–1930. These forty years were an era of improvement without comparison in human history, when hours of work per week were reduced, when the danger and physical difficulty of work began its long transition to more pleasant and comfortable work, when the exploitation of children in mines and factories was replaced by quiet high school classrooms, and when the taxing drudgery of household work for women was greatly lessened by running water, sewer pipes, and the first appearance of electric appliances. The Great Depression and World War II interrupted progress along these dimensions, but in the twenty-five years after the war, the benefits spread to the entire population.

The declining disutility (or "unpleasantness") of work occurred across three dimensions. Most clearly, weekly hours of work declined sharply from roughly sixty hours per week in 1890 to forty in 1940. In some extreme cases, as in the iron and steel industry, weekly hours had been seventy-two per week or more during 1890–1910. The second dimension was the shift in the occupational distribution away from backbreaking, uncomfortable, and dangerous work toward less unpleasant jobs, including as assembly line operatives and white-collar clerks. The third dimension was the most important and is the central focus of the chapter, for it describes the epochal transition from the taxing and arduous working conditions within each occupational group of 1870–1900 in contrast with the steady improvement in these working conditions after 1910.

A sharp distinction is drawn between the working conditions of the 46 percent of the 1870 work force engaged in farming as proprietors or farm laborers and the 46 percent working in blue-collar or white-collar occupations (the remaining 8 percent worked as nonfarm proprietors, managers, or professionals). The majority of those engaged in farming were proprietors who owned their own land and homes, usually subject to mortgages and debt. They had the great advantage over urban workers of being independent. There was no boss who dictated their working hours or behavior or who could dismiss them at a whim. Rather, the farmer answered to the combined "bosses" of weather, insects, and farm prices. The vagaries of the weather, the unpredictable clouds of insects, and the equally unpredictable risk of plunging farm prices made each farmer's existence not only physically taxing, but also economically risky. And whatever the hazards of being a farmer in the Midwest and Great Plains, nothing compared to the indignity and economic exploitation of the southern black sharecroppers.

This chapter replaces one's vague idea that "work was tough in the old days" with the visceral daily pain and humiliation of being a blue-collar worker in America in the late nineteenth century. The danger of coal-mining and the disgusting conditions of the stockyards were matched by the cruel conditions to which workers in the iron and steel industries were subjected by the tough policies of bosses such as Andrew Carnegie, now remembered benignly for his contributions to museums and public libraries. Shifts were twelve hours per day in conditions lacking lockers and having only primitive toilet facilities, and the heat and danger of the job itself paints a portrait of dramatic imbalance between the power of employers and weakness of workers. Managers could dismiss workers instantly for any reason, including a perception that as a worker aged, he or she was becoming physically weaker. The number of hours worked per year varied randomly, not just with the business cycle, but also when any closure for maintenance, reconstruction, or slack demand sent workers onto the streets with no compensation and no unemployment insurance.

Women faced a life of hard work, boredom, and drudgery, whether on the farm or in the city. The small percentage of women who entered the labor market found themselves cordoned off into female occupations, working to manufacture apparel or as clerks, nurses, or school teachers. They were usually paid half of male wages. Employment in the market was more common for younger women who had not yet married, and this employment was primarily in domestic service, which occupied fully 8 percent of the labor force. This world of *Upstairs, Downstairs* and *Downton Abbey* created for many women jobs that were not dangerous as male blue-collar jobs but shared with them the unforgiving discipline of fixed and long hours of work and daily rites of subservience.

The chapter traces how working conditions improved over time along multiple dimensions. The share of farm workers declined, hours of manufacturing workers declined, and workforce discipline became less tyrannical as workers protested and as the endless supply of immigrants was cut off by restrictive quotas in the early 1920s. The daily ordeal of housewives in managing their homes was made less burdensome by a series of innovations, including running water and sewer pipes, the cast-iron stove, and then the many goods available from the mail-order catalogues after 1895, especially the major electric consumer durables that became available after 1920, including the electric washing machine and refrigerator.

This chapter broadens the scope of the American standard of living. Households cared not just about how much they could buy and how easy it was to convert market-purchased goods into household-produced meals. The male bread-earners cared deeply about the difficulty of the task of earning a living—long hours and autocratic discipline gradually transitioned into shorter hours and more respect for employees. The grandchildren of the valiant and brutalized farmers, coal miners, and manufacturing workers of the 1870s and 1880s did not realize how lucky they were to be working in 1940. The conditions of work both outside of and inside of the home had finally changed for the better, after centuries and millennia of agricultural peasantry.

Changes in the occupational distribution and the arduousness of work within a given occupation continued well beyond 1940. But the decline in working hours from sixty hours weekly to the normal postwar forty-hour week was fully accomplished by 1940. In that sense, the improvements in the welfare of workers chronicled in this chapter represent yet another dimension of the unique achievement of the years 1870–1940. No other era in human history, either before or since, combined so many elements in which the standard of living increased as quickly and in which the human condition was transformed so completely.

Chapter 9

TAKING AND MITIGATING RISKS: CONSUMER CREDIT, INSURANCE, AND THE GOVERNMENT

Don't be too timid and squeamish about your actions. All life is an experiment. The more experiments you make the better.

—Ralph Waldo Emerson, 1841

INTRODUCTION

Household well-being depends not just on the level of income, but also on its volatility. This chapter is about institutions, particularly consumer credit and insurance, that allow the household to enjoy a standard of living that is less volatile over time. Consumer credit allows for the purchase of homes and consumer durables by spreading out payments over time and avoids the need to save the entire purchase price in advance. Insurance helps to reduce volatility by providing payments to compensate for losses of income during spells of unemployment, for catastrophic losses from fire, and for the loss of life of the breadwinner.

We begin with consumer credit and mortgage finance. Was consumer credit a new invention of the 1920s that allowed the consumer durables boom of the 1920s to occur? Were there fundamental changes in mortgage finance that facilitated the building boom of the 1920s that endowed America with a surfeit of office buildings, residential apartments, and houses? The oldest financial institutions are maritime insurance and life insurance, which can be dated back to the Phoenicians. How did insurance evolve during our period of 1870–1940? This chapter also covers the role of the government, mainly in mitigating both microeconomic and macroeconomic risks as it made the transition from the laissez-faire regime of the late nineteenth century to the multidimensional interventions of the New Deal.

During 1870–1940 the American economy began its long transition to a mass consumer society. In the late nineteenth century, when the majority of Americans belonged to the working class, often having arrived directly from Europe, most households lived a meager existence, spending half or more of the family income on food and drink. Yet by 1940, disposable real incomes had risen sufficiently to allow the purchase of goods that would have been considered unattainable luxuries fifty years earlier, and by 1940 almost every urban housing unit was networked, connected to electricity, gas, telephone, running water, and sanitary sewage pipes. There was enough discretionary income for families to begin buying electric appliances, and by 1929, motor vehicle registrations per household had reached 93 percent, starting from zero in 1900. How did families pay for the massive number of houses built in the roaring 1920s? Did they have access to mortgage finance and consumer credit? If so, then when did those elements of consumer finance begin, and what was the process by which they spread? Modern forms of installment buying may have expanded in the 1920s, but a pervasive reliance on consumer credit dates back to the early nineteenth century in the forms of rural general stores that offered credit to their farm customers and of pawnbrokers who similarly offered credit to their urban clientele.

Was fire and life insurance always available, and what was the nature of automobile insurance in the first few decades after the motor vehicle was invented? The first part of this chapter is devoted to consumer finance, insurance, and the mitigation of risk. Risk and uncertainty can be viewed as an externality, a byproduct of industrialization and urbanization for which the barons of industry did not have to pay.

Even in the laissez-faire environment of the late nineteenth century, the government intervened in the development of the economy in numerous ways. Government actions included a wide range of legislation, the granting of land to railroads and homesteading settlers, food and drug regulations, the establishment of land-grant universities and agricultural research stations, the patent system, deposit insurance, Social Security, and unemployment compensation, to name the main government programs that promoted economic development, mitigated risk, and increased security and well-being.

BORROWING ON THE FARM AND IN THE CITY: EARLY FORMS OF CONSUMER CREDIT

In the late nineteenth century, consumer credit was universal in rural America. Farmers purchased goods such as shoes, clothing, coffee, and alcohol from the nearby country store, which extended credit that was often not repaid until the next harvest. It was common for farmers in the north and west to buy horses, carts, harnesses, furniture, and seeds, half of the payment consisting of cash and the other half in the form of a bill to be repaid after the harvest. The administration of credit, including for dry goods and notions from the nearest general store, was informal, and customers were expected to repay when they could.

There was a very low incidence of nonpayment, as this would have resulted in a suspension of credit privileges and would have meant a loss of respect for farmers and their families in close-knit farm communities where neighbors knew their neighbors. In the beginning of the nineteenth century, "payment of debts was a virtue and inability to pay them a mortal sin."[1] Credit was developed earlier and more freely in the United States than in many European countries, in part because the typical American farmer (outside the south) owned his own land, whereas in Europe, tenant farming was more common, with large estates owned by upper-class families through inheritance over generations. Whereas in Europe the avaricious lender faced a social stigma for ideological reasons, usually religious, in the United States the borrower experienced the stigma, being considered a "penniless failure."[2]

The traveling salesman supplemented the role of the country store in providing credit to isolated farms and small towns alike. Finance for these salesmen was provided by wholesalers who were eager to sell their goods in the remote parts of rural America, and the back-up finance ultimately traced its way back to Chicago or New York.

> Such was the heavily leveraged world of frontier exchange. Everyone owed money to everyone else, and for much of the year the only way to sell anything at all was to do so "on time." It was little wonder that frontier interest rates were so high. Urban banks and wholesalers lent their credit to small-town merchants, and they in turn lent merchandise to their rural customers. … It was a risky world, with bankruptcy or foreclosure lurking around every corner.[3]

Thus a farmer could simultaneously save face and maintain his social standing within his rural community by paying his bills for the small items purchased from the local country store but face bankruptcy or foreclosure of his entire farm as the result of a catastrophic event affecting all his fellow farmers, such as a crop failure caused by drought or a nationwide decline in farm prices, as occurred in 1920–21 or in the Great Depression of the 1930s.

Farmers/owners in the north borrowed not just from the general store for everyday purchases, but also from local banks to buy their land and build their farmhouses. Because loans on farm land were not granted for longer than six to eight years, "borrowers were regularly in the market, securing new mortgages, paying new origination fees, and coping with unpredictable interest rates." The late nineteenth century was an era of deflation, which reduced farm prices and farm incomes, and the nominal value of debts was fixed and not responsive to economy-wide deflation. Farmers were further disadvantaged by the lack of a central bank and a national banking system; the farther a farmer/borrower was from New York City, the higher the interest rate he was likely to pay. Effective real interest rates in the north were at 10 percent.[4]

In between small purchases of everyday items at the general store and the purchase of land and materials to build a house, farmers also needed to finance the purchase of large pieces of newly invented farm equipment. In 1850, the farmer used equipment little changed since biblical times, but new inventions such as the McCormick reaper offered gains in productivity—if the farmer could afford to buy the machine. The contrast between a farmer's annual gross income of $600 and the $100–150 price of a McCormick reaper in 1850 was daunting. As a result, McCormick offered a $125 machine for a down payment of $35, with the balance due after harvest. This was not installment financing, however: The balance had to be paid as a lump sum.[5]

Debt was a more important issue for southern sharecroppers, for they did not own their land, buildings, or animals but rather worked for the owner/landlord. The tenants were paid a fraction of the value of the crop at the end of the harvest, and that fraction depended on the extent to which inputs used by the sharecropper had been provided by the owner. Harvest receipts were available to repay the debts that had been run up over the prior year, and often the debts could not be covered in full. The outstanding debts turned sharecropping into a form of servitude, and violence could occur if a sharecropper tried to escape to another location to void his debt obligations. Interest rates charged to sharecroppers could range from 40 percent to 60 percent. The accumulation of unpaid debts year after year was called "debt peonage," and "the high level of physical mobility in the rural South is indicative of a degree of freedom that contradicts the notion of widespread debt peonage."[6]

The use of crops to be harvested in the future as collateral for loans in the southern states allowed small farmers to obtain credit under the "crop-lien" system. The harvested crop was brought to the lienholder, who sold it and used the proceeds to pay off the farmer's debts. Because roads and railroads were rare in the south, the merchants at rural crossroads had a local monopoly and exploited it. "The [crossroads] merchant thus profited both as a lender and as a crop broker."[7] The role of the coal mine owner was similar to that of the land owners in the rural south. Debts contracted at company stores were deducted from paychecks. The tying of coal miners to debt-financed and overpriced purchases at the company store impoverished the miners and prevented them from moving away.

Urban pawnbroking dates back to medieval times and in American history to colonial times. But its role in providing consumer credit became more prominent in the early nineteenth century with the development of dense urban centers. The services of pawnbrokers were tied to the unpredictable nature of urban employment, which, as we learned in chapter 8, was unstable as a result not only of the macroeconomic business cycle, but also of the instability of employment in particular industries and at particular plants. In the Chicago stockyards, an employee returning home from work on Monday did not know whether he would be offered four, eight, or twelve hours of work on Tuesday.

The pawnbrokers' "cycle of pledging and redemption" followed weekly and seasonal patterns. Weekly events included paychecks and due dates for rent payments. Seasonal events included the pledging of winter clothing in the spring to be redeemed in the fall. In 1935, a famous New York City pawnshop recorded pledges of a silver and gold watch, a piece of cashmere, corsets, and a telescope.[8] Pawnshops became vehicles for disposing of stolen articles, and regulation of pawnshops by the late nineteenth century included limits on interest rates as well as requirements that all items and the identity of the pledger be registered with the police.[9]

Modern consumer credit originated as early as 1845 with installment sales of pianos and organs. Rising incomes allowed families, particularly in the middle and upper classes, to purchase substantial pieces of furniture, including large dining room tables, buffets, and sofas. Pawnbroking was not suited to providing loans on these large objects which could not be conveniently transported as collateral. Instead "chattel lending" developed, in which the collateral was not the object itself but the legal title to the object. This new form of lending had the additional appeal of confidentiality. In 1850, the Singer Sewing Machine Company began to sell its machines on installment to consumers through agents.[10] By the 1870s, such a machine could be purchased for as little as $1 down and fifty cents per week. This stage of installment purchases extended beyond the prosperous classes to working-class households, including recent immigrants.

The late nineteenth century also brought the development of "wage assignment" loans, similar to today's "payday" loans, in which the collateral was a legal claim on the future wages of the borrower. Administering these loans required new types of information gathering, as borrowers could lie about the amount of their wages or the security of their employment. Lenders tended to favor workers who had stable employment, such as government or clerical workers, and they sometimes resorted to bribes to gain access to the payroll records of their borrowers. In the event of failure to repay, the lender could apply to garnish a portion of the borrower's wage. Before legal measures had to be invoked, however, the lender usually was able to coerce repayment "based on the social stigma of debt."[11]

Chattel and wage assignment loans were carried out in the fringes of the legal system, surviving because of lax enforcement. More sinister were the lenders who explicitly flouted the state-enforced usury ceilings. Small lenders charging high interest rates were universally labeled "loan sharks":

> How can men be so reckless as to borrow from these agencies that are everywhere known as sharks, leeches, and remorseless extortioners? It is clear ... that the majority of borrowers have been overtaken by sudden emergencies which under their standard of living cannot be met out of income.[12]

These small lenders trapped borrowers facing a legitimate financial emergency into a state of indebtedness characterized by usurious interest rates and collection techniques that sometimes relied on violence, "often with the connivance of corrupt police, courts, municipal public servants, and payroll employees."[13] Because these forms of credit were part of the underground economy, no records exist regarding their importance or magnitude. The subterranean world of working-class credit in the late nineteenth century differed little from that of two centuries earlier, which had been described by R. H. Tawney as "spasmodic, irregular, unorganized, a series of individual, and sometimes surreptitious, transactions between neighbors."[14]

Rather than observing a straightforward shift from cash to credit in retail purchases during 1870–1940, we find that the transition was U-shaped. Initially, credit was dominant in rural America, and it played a substantial role in the form of urban pawnshops. Urbanization brought a shift from credit to cash. In 1910–12, the ever-growing A&P chain of food markets eliminated credit and converted to a cash-only policy. In the early years of the retail revolution created by large urban department stores and by mail order catalogs, most merchants required cash payment.

The department stores were able to reduce prices compared to smaller stores primarily through economies of scale, but also by refusing to discount and selling primarily for cash. The elimination of haggling and bargaining made each purchase a straightforward transaction that could be handled by a clerk without the need for a manager's involvement. However, competition among the department stores, at least in the large urban centers, slowly fostered a switch from an all-cash policy to the availability of charge accounts, initially for only the wealthiest patrons. As late as 1902, Macy's in New York maintained an all-cash policy, whereas Wanamaker's in Philadelphia had begun to offer installment payments, with no down payments, for selected large items, including pianos. Joining Macy's with an all-cash policy at the turn of the century were J.C. Penney and the catalogs of Sears, Roebuck and of Montgomery Ward.[15]

The credit policies of the great catalog merchants are recorded in the introductory pages of their thick books of offerings. Though Sears began in the late 1890s by offering C.O.D. (cash on delivery, as contrasted to cash sent with the initial order), by 1902 C.O.D. was eliminated, and all purchases had to be paid for in cash up front. In the payments technology of 1902, this meant the payment had to be submitted "by post office money order, express money order, bank draft, cash, or stamps. We do not accept revenue stamps, foreign stamps and due stamps, as they are of no value to us."[16]

The introductions to the annual catalogs are some of the most overwritten in the history of advertising. The introduction to the Sears 1902 catalog approaches 10,000 words in a tiny typeface but has a refreshing honesty. The message was clear that Sears customers constituted an egalitarian democracy. There was no discounting to any buyer, no matter how large. There was no provision of credit, because the clerical and interest expense of credit would imply a higher cost of goods for the normal cash-paying customer. The catalog cost fifty cents and was not distributed for free, so to hold down the cost of goods. These excerpts from the first two pages provide a flavor of the egalitarian approach:

> In order to maintain our incomparably low prices, prices which, quality considered, are not and cannot be met by any other house, we are compelled to ask our customers to invariably send cash in full with their orders . . . . We have discontinued making C. O. D. shipments . . . with a view to naming still lower prices, giving greater value than ever before. . . . Any house that ships goods by express C.O.D. . . . makes it impossible to furnish their customers the same values we quote on the upwards of 100,000 items in this catalogue. . . . By getting 50 cents for our big catalogue, thus doing away with nearly all advertising expense, we have effected a very great saving which has changed our selling prices accordingly.[17]

The shift toward cash payment during the 1890–1910 period and then back again to credit should not be exaggerated. During the peak years of immigrant arrival between 1900 and 1913, there were between 5,000 and 10,000 peddlers on New York's Lower East Side selling goods from house to house. The peddlers acted as middlemen between local retailers and the closely packed customers in the large tenement blocks discussed in chapter 4. Their retail suppliers provided credit to the peddlers which allowed them to sell on credit to their customers. A memoir recalled how in 1899 the author's mother bought a silk tablecloth from a peddler for nothing down and ten payments of twenty-five cents per week.[18]

When payments were made with cash rather than by credit, what did "cash" mean? The above list of payments accepted by Sears included money orders, bank drafts, "cash" (i.e., currency), and certain types of stamps. Not mentioned were personal checks, which, unlike bank drafts, carry the risk of bouncing if there are insufficient funds in the account. The distinction between payments by personal checks and by currency and coins varied across the type of transaction and the social class of the purchaser. Checks were used for all but the smallest purchases by the middle and upper classes; currency and coins were used for small transactions by the middle and upper classes and for all transactions by the working class. A 1910 report shows that in the prior year, 75 percent of retail bank deposits had been made with checks, 21 percent with currency, and 4 percent with coins. Those deposits included both payments made at the same time as the retail transaction and payments of outstanding credit incurred for previous transactions.[19]

BUY NOW, PAY LATER COMES TO DOMINATE CONSUMER DURABLE PURCHASES

Early forms of credit, such as rural loans at the general store and in southern agriculture, called for lump-sum repayment of the principal amount, usually at harvest time. Urban pawnbrokers gave loans on pledged goods and accepted a lump sum at the time of redemption. In these and other examples, the borrower repaid the loan in a single payment, a financial obligation that was daunting in the context of the low average incomes at that time. The development of the installment plan avoided the need to save up for a full repayment of the balance due. Instead, the borrower was required to repay the loan with fixed installments to be made at regular frequencies over a stated period, with the interest charge built into the periodic payments.

The installment plan is often credited with the creation of the American consumer society and particularly the durable goods and housing booms of the 1920s. But as we have seen, furniture, pianos, and sewing machines were sold to high-income families as early as 1850 on terms of one-third down and additional payments over the next two to three years. Despite the absence of credit reports in the nineteenth century, installment credit resulted in few defaults, because lenders were highly discriminatory in limiting credit to high-income families or those middle-class families who appeared to have stable lives and marriages and jobs that were likely to be free of business cycle or industry volatility.[20]

The early years of the twentieth century witnessed a rapid conversion of consumer credit. There arose a new world of consumer finance available to most of the working class that was "continuous, regular, organized, a series of increasingly impersonal, often visible bureaucratic transactions between individuals and institutions."[21] By the 1920s, phrases such as "buy now, pay later" had become commonplace. The new age of consumer credit was called by its enthusiasts "a revolution second in importance only to the great shift from handicraft to machinery."[22] Over the period between 1905 and 1915, the previous cash-only department stores began to offer installment-plan purchases of furniture and large items of household equipment that could be repossessed, as did the mail-order catalog houses.

Though most major department stores operated in 1900 on a cash-only basis, they had all converted to credit accounts by the 1920s. Marshall Field's charge business in Chicago had increased by 1929 to 180,000 accounts, double the 1920 number. Most large department stores found that sales on credit made up 50 percent to 70 percent of their business. The number of regulated small loan offices increased by a factor of six between 1913 and 1929.[23]

As compared to the loan sharks and pawnbrokers of the late nineteenth century, these large and impersonal sources of consumer finance were more aggressive in collecting payments and less tolerant of temporary personal misfortune. In the 1920s, consumer finance companies could retaliate against late or incomplete payments by garnishing wages and taking defaulting customers to court. Although the stock market collapse of late 1929 is often cited as a major cause of the Great Depression, the overreliance of households on consumer credit and their increased leverage added to the downward spiral of collapse and deflation once incomes and jobs began to be cut in 1929–30.

Few inventions have ever spread as rapidly as did the automobile between 1900, when there were no automobiles on the roads, to 1929, when the ratio of motor vehicles to American households had reached 93 percent. "The installment plan was to consumer credit what the moving assembly line was to the automobile industry."[24] The integral role of finance began with the seasonal imbalance between supply and demand. The assembly line method of production required steady production to minimize costs, but in the early days of open cars, purchases were much higher in the summer than in the winter. The large automobile companies had sufficient leverage to force the inventory overage onto the local auto dealer, who in turn needed a way to finance the large seasonal inventory of unsold autos.

The borrowing requirements of dealers led to the development of finance companies, often independent but sometimes owned by the automobile manufacturers. Martha Olney has described the development of these finance companies as a way "to preserve manufacturer power over dealers while simultaneously solving the problem of inadequate wholesale inventory financing."[25] Though automobile finance on the installment plan can be traced as far back as 1910, financing on a modern scale began in 1919 with the establishment of the General Motors Acceptance Corporation (GMAC). Although Henry Ford adamantly opposed installment buying, by 1919, two-thirds of Ford cars were sold on the installment plan, financed not by the Ford Company itself, but rather by local finance companies that cooperated with Ford dealers.[26]

By 1924, three out of every four automobiles were bought on credit. The competition among manufacturers amid the explosion of automobile sales in the 1920s led to a gradual liberalization of finance terms. Starting from a 50 percent down payment and a mere twelve months to repay, soon down payments were reduced to one-third or less, and repayment intervals extended to two years.[27] Olney has calculated that effective interest rates for car loans were typically 34 percent in the 1920s.[28]

Did the increased availability of consumer credit account for the durable goods sales boom of the 1920s? Olney's main hypothesis is that the increased availability of consumer credit created a major upward shift in the demand for durable goods, holding constant household incomes and relative prices. And, indeed, her regression analysis finds that this upward shift occurred except for three types of traditional goods largely unaffected by technological change—china, silverware, and house furnishings. But Olney's analysis is unconvincing, for she focuses entirely on demand without considering the revolutionary changes in supply.

New goods were for sale that previously had not existed, most notably electric refrigerators and washing machines. And the most important consumer durable of all, the automobile, experienced a radical decline in price and increase in quality between 1910 and 1923. The revolution made possible by the invention of electricity and the internal combustion engine, together with Olney's finding of no shift for traditional goods (china, etc.), raises the possibility that the consumer durables boom of the 1920s resulted from the availability of newly invented products at greatly reduced prices rather than the availability of consumer credit. Thus the availability of new products fueled the provision of consumer credit, and at the same time the availability of consumer credit facilitated the purchase of the new products.

Figure 9–1 compares the percentage ratio of non-structures debt as a percentage of nominal GDP with real consumer durable expenditures as a percentage of real GDP.[29] The graph raises the question of whether there actually was a durable goods boom in the 1920s. The GDP share of consumer durables had ranged from 5 percent to 6 percent between 1900 and 1910, and in the 1920s, the share rose slightly above 6 percent for five straight years, from 1925 to 1929. This hardly qualifies as something remarkable that needs to be explained; the relatively flat percentage of consumer durables spending suggests that however rapid the growth of durables spending, the sum of the other components of GDP (consumer nondurables and services, investment in structures, government spending, and net exports) was growing just as rapidly.

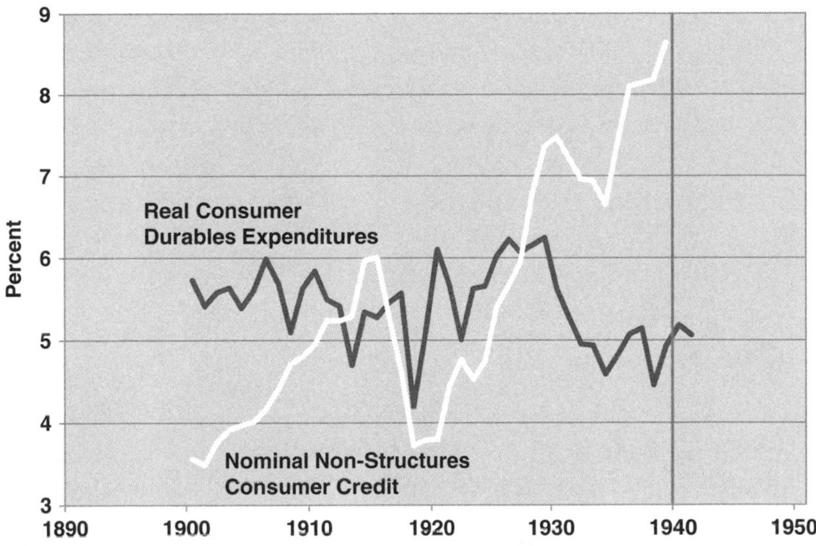

Figure 9–1. Ratios to GDP of Non-Structures Consumer Credit and Consumer Durables, 1900–1941.

Source: Olney (1991, Tables 4.1 and A.7) and Gordon (2012a, Table A-1).

Unlike the ratio of real consumer durable goods spending to real GDP, the ratio of outstanding consumer credit balances, shown by the gray line in figure 9–1, grew rapidly from 1900 to 1915–1916, then collapsed until 1919–20, then expanded rapidly through 1929–30, and then drifted down until 1934, when another burst of growth brought the ratio by 1941 far above the 1929 ratio.[30] The role of causation between consumer credit and consumer durables expenditures is dubious; the credit ratio rose from 3.6 percent to 8.6 percent between 1900 and 1939, whereas the consumer durables spending ratio actually declined from 5.7 to 5.0 percent over the same interval. The increasing availability of credit appears to be a phenomenon largely independent of the rise and fall of the share of consumer durables in total spending.[31]

During the 1920s, the market for durable goods was transformed to a credit-based system of purchase comparable in most ways to the postwar years. By 1929, installment credit financed the sales of 61 percent of new cars and 65 percent of used cars.[32] And automobiles were not alone. It has been estimated that in the late 1920s, consumer credit financed "80–90 percent of furniture, 75 percent of washing machines, 65 percent of vacuum cleaners, 18–25 percent of jewelry, 75 percent of radio sets, and 80 percent of phonographs."[33] The use of credit for luxury items, as automobiles and electric appliances were perceived to be in the 1920s, reversed the previous image of social stigma associated with borrowing. It brought to the working classes the ability to purchase newly invented products that had not even existed a generation earlier:

> Credit came to be seen as the greatest catalyst in the famous melting pot. … By creating the base for a large market it facilitates mass production, and therefore an enormous reduction in unit costs. American economic vitality in the twentieth century stems from this correspondence.[34]

THE HOUSING BOOM OF THE 1920S AND ITS ROOTS IN THE MORTGAGE FINANCE REVOLUTION

The first provider of installment loans was the U.S. government. The Harrison Act of 1800 provided for the sale of public land to farmers for a down payment of 25 percent and three additional payments stretched out over up to four years.[35] A total of 19.4 million acres of land in the Northwest Territories was sold in this way between 1800 and 1820.[36]

As early as 1890, census data show that 29 percent of homes in the United States had outstanding mortgages.[37] For instance, in the Boston area, it was typical for a family to be required to save half of the purchase price—say, $1,500 for a $3,000 house—and borrow the rest. Then a first mortgage would be obtained from a savings bank or mortgage dealer for 40 percent of the sales price ($1,200) at an interest rate of 5 to 6 percent, and a second mortgage for $300 was obtained from a real estate agent. Interest was paid semiannually over three to eight years, and the lump sum of principal was due at the end of the loan period.

The details of mortgage contracts differed between and within cities, with some loans extending for as long as twenty years. The largest holders of mortgage debt were individuals, savings banks, and building and loan associations. The latter pioneered amortized loans, in which the monthly payment included both interest and repayment of principal, so that no lump-sum payment was due when the loan matured. Though the inclusion of principal repayment raised the size of the monthly payment, this was in many cases offset by extending the length of the repayment period. Amortized loans were a valuable innovation, for they reduced risk for both lender and borrower. By the 1920s, they had become standard.

In the 1890s, most houses in Muncie, Indiana, were built for rental, but the Lynds estimated that in 1923, the rental portion had declined to only 10 percent.[38] They attribute this change to the development of "building and loan associations" after 1900, which made it possible for many members of the working class to consider homeownership. In the mid-1920s, fully 75 percent to 80 percent of new Muncie homes were built for owners, with mortgages provided by four associations, and a bank executive estimated that 85 percent of those purchases were "working men."

A parallel financial innovation was the development of the real estate mortgage bond, which greatly facilitated the enormous but unsustainable boom in building both large and small apartment buildings in the 1920s. Builders could obtain money in advance of construction to finance the entire construction project, with only minimal down payment requirements. "While only about $150 million worth had been sold before the war, total investment in real estate bonds is thought to have been approximately $10 billion by the early thirties."[39]

One reason homeownership rates soared in the 1920s as part of the massive building boom of that decade was a widespread loosening of credit conditions that allowed families to take out second and third mortgages. The value of outstanding mortgages soared from about $12 billion in 1919 to $43 billion in 1930 (i.e., from 16% to 41% of nominal GDP). Figure 9–2 plots the ratio of

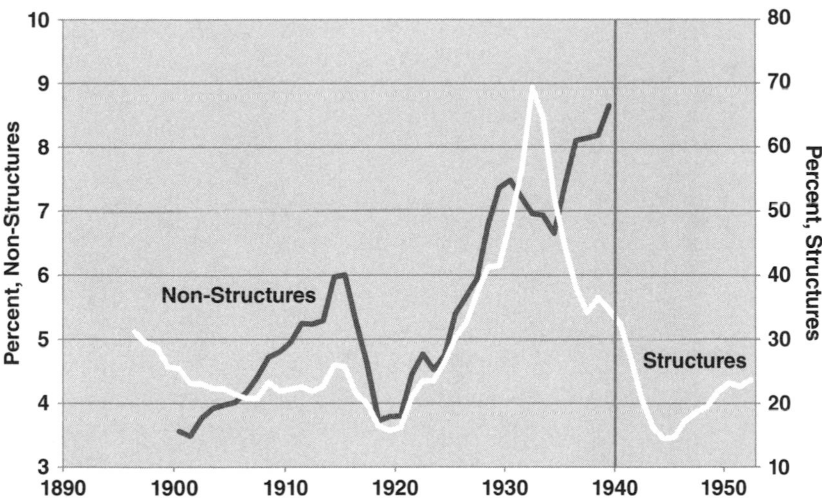

Figure 9–2. Ratios to GDP of Non-Structures Consumer Credit and Residential Structures Credit, 1896–1952.

Sources: Olney (1991, Table 4.1), Gordon (2012a, Table A-1), and HSUS series Dc903.

mortgage debt to GDP against the non-structures consumer debt ratio already examined in figure 9–1. The differing left-hand and right-hand axes indicate that mortgage debt for structures during the 1920s was consistently seven times higher than for non-structures consumer debt. The longer view in figure 9–2 shows that the value of outstanding mortgages was roughly 20 percent of GDP from 1900 to 1922.[40]

Owing to the short-term character of nonmortgage finance and the economic recovery of the late 1930s, the ratio to GDP of nonmortgage consumer credit rose by 1939 far above its 1929 value. In contrast, though the timing of the expansion of mortgage finance in the 1920s was similar, its behavior in the 1930s was entirely different. The mortgage finance ratio spiked from 41 percent to 69 percent as the economy collapsed during 1929–32 and then, because there was so little residential construction during the 1930s, declined from 69 percent in 1932 to a mere 27 percent in 1941.

Another confirmation that mortgage finance of residential structures exploded in the 1920s is provided by figure 9–3. The ratio of residential mortgage debt to residential wealth increased from 14.3 percent in 1916 to 27.2 percent in 1929. The sharp decrease evident in figure 9–3 between 1916 and 1920 is a result of wartime and postwar inflation, and the sharp increase between 1929 and 1932 is a result of deflation in the Great Contraction of

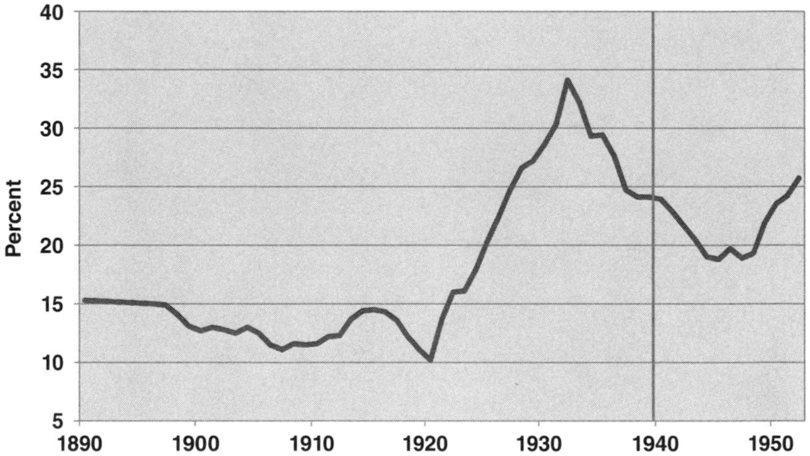

Figure 9–3. Ratio of Nonfarm Residential Mortgage Debt to Nonfarm Residential Wealth, 1890–1952.

Source: Grebler, Blank, and Winnick (1956, Table L-6, p. 451).

1929–32. The rise in prices after 1933, together with the near disappearance of residential construction during the 1930s and the years of World War II, helps account for the decline in the debt/wealth ratio between 1932 and 1948.

It was substantially easier to obtain credit for automobiles than for houses, because the collateral for the loan was moveable, and this helps to explain why automobile sales grew so rapidly in the United States compared to other countries. There are contrasting views on how difficult it was to obtain mortgage credit. The Lynds' statement that 80 percent of Muncie houses built in the 1920s were sold to owners, and that many of these new owners were working class, conflicts with Wood's unqualified remark that there was no mortgage finance available for families below the fiftieth percentile of the income distribution. "Beyond this, in a downward direction, they do not and cannot go."[41]

Overall, the most important support of the transition from rental status to homeownership was the evolution of credit institutions. Between 1890 and 1930 mortgages became easier to obtain, with lower down payments and more options for second and third mortgages. Homeownership rates crept up toward 50 percent in the nation as a whole. The positive stimulus from mortgage finance came at least temporarily to a halt as a result of bank failures in the early 1930s and revived somewhat in the late 1930s, then changed completely to a much easier financial environment after World War II.

LIFE INSURANCE: THE OLDEST FINANCIAL INSTITUTION

Insurance is the oldest form of the many financial institutions that directly affect the welfare of household members. As long ago as 900 BC on the island of Rhodes, sea law provided for contributions from the community to cover the losses of ships and cargo at sea. There started "the practice of preventing a great loss for any one individual by the acceptance of a small loss by all members of a group."[42] Life insurance developed by expanding the concept of maritime losses from the direct value of the ship and its cargo to the value of the seamen employed on the ships that were lost. During the fifteenth and sixteenth centuries, life insurance was derided as a form of gambling, particularly in France and Italy. Nevertheless, the Italians took the lead in the development of insurance, and the Italian province of Lombardy gave its name to London's "Lombard Street," the origin of modern insurance in the 1550s. The first formal life insurance policy was issued in 1583 on a William Gibbons of London, and it was "not only the oldest life insurance policy on record, but also the first known case taken to court for settlement."[43]

The first term life insurance in the United States was offered in 1759 to Presbyterian ministers in Philadelphia.[44] Until the Civil War, life insurance policies were simple documents stating the amount and conditions of coverage and the amount of the premiums. There were no cash or loan values, and life insurance was not the instrument of saving that it later became. In the last three decades of the nineteenth century life insurance was transformed into its modern form, with a large number of agents on commission aggressively selling policies with cash and loan value, and flexibility to change beneficiaries. Life insurance was based on the idea that although death is certain, the date of death is highly uncertain. But for any group of sufficient size, the percentage of that group who will die in a given year varied little except during periods of war or epidemics. By the beginning of the twentieth century, life insurance companies were regulated as to the percentage of outstanding insurance that had to be held in the form of assets available to pay benefits to policy beneficiaries.

By 1900 life insurance became known as a method of forced saving that countered the tendency of heads of working-class and middle-class households to postpone saving. Like the installment plan of consumer credit, it was based on required relatively small periodic payments that forced heads of household to set aside savings for a future rainy day, including their own death. In a journal article from 1905:

> It is not what passes through a man's hands, but what he holds on to, that gives him a competency. The holding on is difficult, and any device which helps a man to hold on to his earnings and turn them into earning capital makes for the prosperity of the country.... Nothing so far has been devised which enables so large a proportion of persons to save under such easy conditions as life insurance, hence its high rank in economic life.[45]

To the extent that the institution of life insurance raised household saving, it also raised domestic investment and fueled economic growth. Also, by providing a convenient vehicle of forced saving, it spared widows and their children from indigence or dependence on private or public charity.

By the time of this 1905 article, the assets of life insurance companies had more than doubled as a share of GDP from 4.5 percent in 1875 to 10.4 percent in 1905, as shown in figure 9–4. There was further growth to 14.5 percent in 1914 and then a decline to 8.4 percent as wartime inflation eroded the value of the nominal assets of the insurance companies, followed by a doubling to 16.9 percent in 1929 as insurance outstanding far exceeded the pace of nominal GDP growth in the 1920s. Just as the inflation of the wartime years eroded the GDP share of outstanding insurance, so the deflation and economic collapse of the Great Depression caused the ratio to soar to 37.0 percent in 1933 before beginning its decent due to economic recovery and the explosion of nominal GDP during World War II.[46] Over longer periods, the ratio grew at an annual rate of 4.0 percent between 1880 and 1905, by 2.0 percent between 1905 and 1929, and at a surprisingly rapid annual rate of 3.5 percent between 1929 and 1941. Thus the late nineteenth century and the decade of the 1930s saw the fastest pace of expansion of life insurance outstanding, as compared to nominal GDP.

Changes in the ratio of life insurance company assets to GDP does not reveal the amount of insurance in force nor the distribution of premiums and benefits. In 1915, about 25 percent to 30 percent of the population had their lives insured by policies, roughly equivalent to the share of adult males to the total population.[47] Thus life insurance was close to being universal and covered not just the middle and upper classes but nearly the entirety of the working

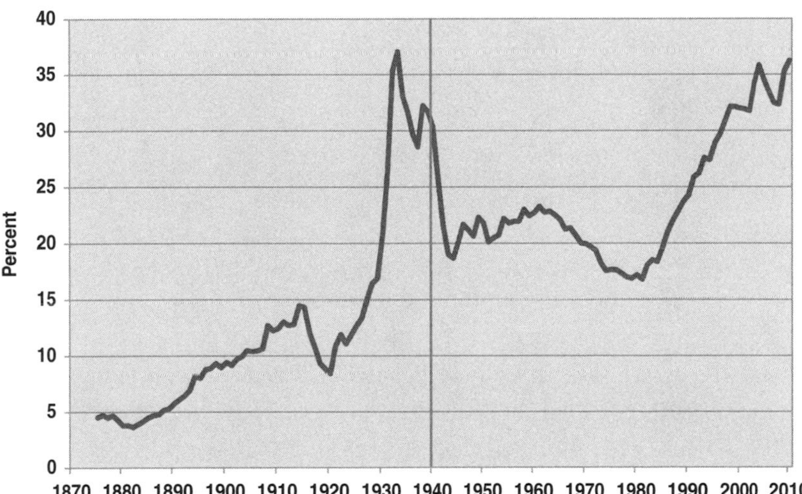

Figure 9–4. Ratio to GDP of Life Insurance Assets, 1875–2010.

Sources: Gordon (2012a, Table A-1), ACLI Life Insurers Fact Book (2013, Figure 2.1) and HSUS series Cj741.

class. The insurance covering workers' lives provided future benefits for their wives and children. Premiums in 1915 amounted to 2.8 percent of GDP, of which 2.1 percent was returned to society as death benefits and the remainder covered expenses of the life insurance companies, with any remaining surplus being added to their investments.[48] By 1926 insurance in force had reached $79 billion, or 81 percent of GDP, more than six times higher than life insurance company assets of $12.9 billion.[49]

Forced saving through life insurance made available policy loans, which in 1915 amounted to 15 percent of insurance company assets. Considering the uncertainty of employment from year to year and even from week to week, as described in chapter 8, life insurance loans provided a source of cash to tide over a family during periods of slack work for the head of household. In addition, life insurance loans were also used to make down payments on consumer credit borrowing, as well as to make lump-sum repayments at the termination date of consumer loans.

The role of life insurance agents seems remarkable from today's perspective. About 20 percent of total life insurance premiums were collected by agents who made weekly visits, which were made not just to collect premiums, but also to pay dividends and bonuses, to prepare proofs of death, and even to pay claims.

> The agent enters into the daily family life of the wage-earners. He knows all the family, their joys and griefs, their income and outgo, their pleasures, their work—their very *life;* is often their adviser, confidant and friend; and always in a representative capacity; he is what he is to those millions of people because he to them *is* the company; they know the company is back of the agent; agents may change but the company is always with them.[50]

It was in the interest of life insurance companies to minimize the death rate of their policyholders, and by the early twentieth century most large companies provided information on personal health and hygiene. Several companies distributed millions of pamphlets on topics such as avoidance of tuberculosis, care of children, purity of milk, "flies and filth," and a host of other potential hazards. Some companies even provided free medical examination and visits by nurses. This self-interested paternalism is similar to the Ford Motor Company's sociological department (discussed in chapter 8), which regularly visited the homes of workers to make sure that they were married and well-behaved.

Along with the commercial life insurance carriers discussed above, there developed side-by-side a system of life insurance offered by fraternal organizations. First offered in 1868, fraternal insurance grew until by 1915 it represented fully a third of life insurance in force, with the other two-thirds being provided by the commercial companies. This alternative system of insurance began when members of an organization were relatively young and healthy, and members were attracted by substantially cheaper rates than the insurance companies. But the fraternal plans failed to anticipate the inexorable process of aging of their members and accumulated insufficient assets to pay off their claims as members died. In New York State in 1915, fraternal orders held in assets only 2 percent of the benefit certificates that they had in force, in contrast to the 28 percent of assets held by the commercial insurance companies in the same year. As a result of inadequate asset holdings, many fraternal insurance plans failed, and others were forced to impose on their members drastic increases in rates. As a result, between 1915 and 1925, the fraternal share of insurance in force fell from 33 percent to 15 percent.[51]

FIRE AND AUTOMOBILE INSURANCE

Even today, the United States rates among the highest of all developed countries in the incidence of fires and deaths from fires. On average during 1979–92, the death rate from fires in the United States was 26.4 per million, as contrasted to 5.2 in Switzerland and 6.4 in the Netherlands.[52] Data are lacking to compare the incidence of major fires across countries over a consistent time series, but the historical record suggests that major fires that devastated large areas of central cities were periodic in the nineteenth century but, on a per-capita basis, destroyed more U.S. cities than those of Europe. Between 1849 and 1906, major fires destroyed the central areas of St. Louis, Chicago, Baltimore, and San Francisco. Since 1906, there have been plenty of fires that destroyed individual buildings or blocks, but none on the scale of the great central city fires that culminated with the 1906 San Francisco earthquake.[53] Notably, the 1989 San Francisco Bay Area Loma Prieta earthquake, which was significant enough to cause part of the Bay Bridge to tumble into the bay, did not cause a fire.

Fire insurance originated in England in the early eighteenth century as entrepreneurs created companies to insure property owners against the disastrous loss of wealth that had occurred in London's great fire of 1666, when three-quarters of the buildings in the city were destroyed. As in the case of life insurance, Philadelphia was among the first American cities to develop fire protection in the form of seven "fire extinguishing companies" by 1752, and in the same year was established the first fire insurance company in the United States, the Philadelphia Contributionship. Gradually, through the nineteenth century, fire insurance arrived at its modern form. Just as life insurance companies adopted an educational role and even medical services, so the fire insurance companies helped educate architects, builders, and fire departments about improved construction methods and other aspects of fire protection.[54]

The epochal calamities that tested the resources and organization of the fire insurance industry were the Great Chicago Fire of 1871 and the San Francisco earthquake and fire of 1906. In the case of Chicago, 49 percent of the value of the lost buildings was covered by insurance, but there was widespread concern that the insurance companies would not honor their commitments. Indeed, fifty-one of the smaller insurance companies were put out of business by their inability to pay claims. Nonetheless, most of the claims were eventually paid, and rebuilding started immediately with loans often secured by the value of land. Chicago's location at the intersection of waterways and as the nation's leading railroad hub secured its future, and funds for rebuilding were made available not just from insurance claims, but from investment funds pouring in from around the nation and the world.[55]

The San Francisco earthquake and fire can be directly compared with the Chicago event, because the price level changed little between 1871 and 1906.[56] In San Francisco, total damage was between 2.0 and 2.5 times that in Chicago, and the percentage of damage covered by insurance was the same, roughly half. Even after some insurance companies defaulted, more than 80 percent of the insurance claims were paid.[57] A fortunate aspect of the San Francisco event was that the detailed property accounts in the Hall of Public Records were not destroyed, which served as a basis for the settlement of insurance claims and other financial consequences of the disaster.[58]

Automobile insurance began with a similarity to ancient maritime insurance, to protect the vehicle (or ship) from damage to its human or material contents or to outright loss. The main difference in the development of automobile insurance is that vehicles crashed into each other, rarely the case with ships, and a determination of fault had to be made. The 1920s, as in so many other topics in this book, were the pivotal period for the development of compulsory automobile insurance. Fatalities from accidents involving the recently invented automobile were more than twenty times more frequent than today, as measured by the decline in automobile fatalities per 100 million vehicle miles from 24 in 1921 to 1.1 in 2012 (see figure 11–6).

Those early years of automobile travel resembled a free-for-all, and government agencies moved only slowly to provide stop signs and electric traffic signals. The higher rate of accidents and fatalities in the early decades of the automobile combines multiple factors—flimsy lightweight cars initially open to the elements rather than with closed bodies, the absence of driver training and driver's licenses, the dangers posed by poorly constructed two-lane roads, the absence of speed limits and police monitoring of speed, the absence of traffic control lights, and the absence of seat belts or any other safety equipment.

Although the earliest automobile insurance policy was written in 1897, liability and collision insurance sales began to soar when states, beginning with Connecticut in 1925, enacted legislation requiring the purchase of automobile insurance. Other states followed suit slowly, and some states waited until the late 1940s and early 1950s to enact compulsory insurance legislation.[59] The earliest policies resembled those of today in that they included protection for bodily injury for the occupants of both cars involved in an accident, for property damage to either car, medical payments liability, as well as liability to protect against uninsured motorists as well as collision and comprehensive coverage for minor incidents. By 1935, all these components had been integrated into a standard policy by the National Bureau of Casualty and Surety Underwriters.[60]

The two largest current providers of automobile insurance are State Farm and Allstate, the first founded in 1922 and the second in 1931. Both companies have in common that their business, then and now, has been based on an earlier life-insurance business model in which individual agents sell policies, provide information, and settle claims. The difference between the two companies is that State Farm was founded by an Illinois farmer, George Mecherle, who was offended that big insurance companies charged the same rates for city and farm customers, even though the latter were less prone to accidents. He started his company with the initial goal of providing low rates to Midwestern farmers; hence the name of the company.[61] State Farm from the beginning was a mutual company in which policyholders own shares. In contrast, Allstate was founded by the CEO of the Sears, Roebuck Company in 1931 as a way to complement Sears' existing sales of tires, batteries, and automobile accessories. Overhead was minimized by locating Allstate agents inside Sears retail stores and by offering insurance through the Sears catalog. It became a fully independent stockholder-owned company in 1995.

THE GOVERNMENT PROMOTES ECONOMIC GROWTH AND LESSENS SOME—BUT NOT ALL—SYSTEMIC RISKS

The rapid progress of the American standard of living between 1870 and 1940 was largely achieved by inventions and the innovation-driven accumulation of capital in the private sector. But despite the common description of the late nineteenth century as an era of laissez-faire, the federal government, aided by state and local governments, provided direct support of the process of growth and also intervened to limit its excesses. In this section, we include not only government measures to make life less risky—e.g., legislation to reduce contamination of meat and milk—but also those government policies that supported the overall process of economic growth.

The government intervened in the development of the economy in numerous ways. As we have seen in previous chapters, government actions included the Homestead Acts, the granting of land to railroads, the food and drug regulation introduced in 1906 and subsequent legislation, and Prohibition during 1920–33. Other government actions included the establishment of land-grant universities and agricultural research stations, the patent system, the antitrust legislation of the Progressive Era, and the array of New Deal legislation, both that directly aiming at reducing the severity of the Great Depression and that providing permanent benefits after World War II, including deposit insurance, banking regulation, Social Security, and unemployment compensation. Other aspects of government intervention had negative effects, including restrictive immigration legislation in the 1920s and high tariffs throughout the period. The remainder of this section discusses a number of these government interventions and actions to foster economic development and mitigate risk.

The Homestead Acts have always been controversial. The outright gift of western lands to anyone who might claim them has been viewed as an interference with the free market. Absent the Homestead land gifts, the unregulated role of land speculation might have induced an equivalent number of land settlers hoping to make profits by buying and then selling land at higher prices. The territories of land available through the Homestead grants were more distant from railroads and thus less desirable and valuable than the lands that the government granted to the railroads. Because no homesteading was allowed on the railroad lands, Homestead Act claimants were forced to go outside the bounds of the railroad grants to inferior land. The monopolization of the best lands granted to the railroads forced many farmers into tenancy, renting the more desirable lands owned by the railroads.[62]

During the two decades between 1850 and 1870, the federal government granted fully 7 percent of the area of the continental United States to railroads, mainly in the south and west. The resources needed to develop the vast lands and mineral resources of the west lay beyond the financial capability of any single railroad company. Without federal aid, the lands and resources would have remained inaccessible. There was a nationalistic desire to bind into the union the far-away areas of California and the Pacific northwest, and the rapid expansion of the railroads was expected to raise the value of the lands retained in the possession of the government.[63] Yet the granting of government land to the railroads was not unconditional. Instead, land was granted in proportion to the completion of a certain number of miles of new tracks, and the government did not turn over title to the granted land until the railroad had delivered on its part of the bargain.[64]

The railroad land grants created a complex set of externalities that allowed individual agricultural settlers and business operations to benefit from the increased speed of travel and degree of market access made possible by the railroad. Among these externalities were the provision of fresh vegetables from California, freshly packed meat from the Chicago stockyards sent in refrigerated cars to the east, and a variety of materials sent from Chicago to the western plains. As chronicled by James Cronon, Chicago provided the raw materials of the westward expansion as entrepreneurs floated trees down Lake Michigan from Wisconsin and Michigan to Chicago, where they were sawed into lumber and transported west to provide the wood for houses and barns on the prairie. In return, the cattle herds of the western plains were transported by rail to the Chicago stockyards, which in turn supplied the eastern United States with its supply of beef that arrived in refrigerated rail cars.

The Morrill Act of 1862 was one of the most fundamental interventions by the federal government in the process of economic growth. The so-called land-grant institutions resulted from a partnership of federal and state governments in setting aside land to launch both agricultural experimentation stations and state colleges and universities. The Morrill Act established a land-grant college in every state and territory. The resulting state universities represented a national system created by national policy. The second Morrill Act of 1890 gave rise to a separate set of all-black colleges, most of them located in the southern states. Soon full-fledged research universities, headed by world-leading institutions such as the University of Michigan and the University of California, surrounded the initial undergraduate college with a wide array of graduate schools and departments. Though most of the funding for these universities and colleges was provided by state governments, the federal government through the Department of Agriculture provided most of the funding for the agricultural research activities.[65]

The transition of American agriculture between 1870 and 1940 to much higher levels of output per person and per acre relied on more than the invention of agricultural machinery by private entrepreneurs such as Cyrus McCormick and John Deere. The government played a major role in making modern agriculture possible through the Agricultural Extension Service, which provided the research that individual farmers could not possibly perform on their own. The service did fundamental research on "the maintenance of soil fertility, the development of improved crop varieties, the control of plant diseases and insects, the breeding and feeding of animals, . . . as well as those principles which have to do with the marketing and distribution of the products of the farm." The purview of the service encompassed not just farming but also home production, providing information on food, cooking, and nutrition. A challenge was to distribute all of the research information to the local level, which consisted of 6 million individually owned farms in 1929. To achieve this goal, there were government-funded agents in every agricultural county, and demonstrations of improved farming methods were conducted in 56,000 rural communities.[66]

The land-grant colleges had to combine their original 1862 mission of providing extended education and technology transfer, particularly about agriculture, with a more general goal of providing college education for the children of farmers. By 1980, the land-grant universities accounted for 18 percent of the U.S. college student population and 66 percent of Ph.D. degrees granted annually.[67] The agricultural origin of these colleges and universities has been criticized for failing to provide opportunities for the urban working class: "There is no labor extension service, there are few short courses, no demonstration projects, no annual fairs, or any similar services for labor comparable with those for agriculture."[68]

Perhaps the most important government activity to stimulate growth was the patent office and the process of patent approval. Based on the British model as copied by individual colonies before 1776, the principle of patent protection was included in the U.S. Constitution.[69] By 1870, revisions of patent law required that inventors make public the specific details of their inventions, which helped to spread scientific and technological knowledge and encourage the next wave of inventions. The patent office was fair, respected, impartial, and not subject to bribes or corruption, and it provided strong protection to inventors and their inventions at modest cost.

The transition of the federal government from a laissez-faire regime to one of partial regulation began with the 1887 Interstate Commerce Act, which created the Interstate Commerce Commission and granted it the power to regulate railroad rates. By 1915, the ICC controlled virtually every aspect of railroad transit, just as the railroads began their decline in the face of competition from motor vehicles and, later, commercial aviation.

Some of the legislation of the Progressive Era acted to mitigate risks that arose in the conduct of business in the private economy. Diseased or spoiled beef, as well as adulteration and contamination of milk, were addressed by the initial Food and Drug Act of 1906 and subsequent legislation, as discussed in chapter 7. The 1906 act was a remarkably rapid legislative response to the appalling conditions in the Chicago stockyards described in Upton Sinclair's *The Jungle.* What Sinclair revealed about the inner workings of the stockyards was matched by Ida Tarbell's muckraking exposé of John D. Rockefeller and his Standard Oil monopoly.[70] Rockefeller was described as "the 'victim of a money-passion' that drove him to get ahead by any means possible, however dishonorable."[71] The 1890 passage of the Sherman antitrust legislation led twenty-one years later to the Supreme Court decision to break up the Standard Oil trust. Despite these steps forward to battle monopolies and to lessen the risk of illness caused by contaminated food, ordinary households continued to face an uncertain life in the early decades of the twentieth century.

States and localities provided regulation of business, enforcing weights and measures. In the 1920s, Herbert Hoover, secretary of commerce from 1921 to 1929, achieved in the business world a standardization of sizes, from nuts and bolts to automobile tires and plumbing parts.[72] Together with the assembly line, introduced in 1913 by Henry Ford, the standardization of component sizes is a little-known factor that facilitated the enormous expansion of weapons production achieved by the United States as the Arsenal of Democracy between 1940 and 1945.[73]

From today's perspective, most of the Progressive legislation was uncontroversial and overdue. However, the Prohibition legislation in effect from 1919 to 1933 exerted unprecedented government control over everyday life and was widely detested and disobeyed. The best available estimates suggest that expenditures on alcohol did not decrease as a share of GDP, as decreased consumption was offset by higher relative prices due to illegality. Productivity was not enhanced by the sobriety of employees, for they managed to obtain illegal spirits, sometimes home-brewed, to replace the beer and wine of which they were deprived. Indeed, efficiency was decreased in another dimension by the forced decentralization of alcoholic beverage production. Additional harm was done by the disappearance of federal alcohol taxes, which had to be replaced by higher income tax rates, mainly on the rich.[74]

The years covered here, 1870–1940, witnessed an extraordinary investment by the state and local governments in both education and infrastructure. This was the period when clean running water and sewer pipes reached most urban homes, an achievement that was largely financed by local governments rather than by private commerce and that could happen only once in American history. This period also witnessed the development of professional rather than volunteer police and firefighting units. State and local governments worked together to finance the expansion of education from the 1870 attainment of elementary school graduation to a transition that occurred mainly between 1910 and 1940 toward universal high school graduation.[75] Virtually all the regulation of the great inventions of the networked house (chapter 4) was carried out by state and local government, not the federal government. In the same way, licensing of automobiles and their drivers occurred at the level of state government.

Farmers were subject to droughts, deep freezes, flooding, and swarms of insects. Workers, as shown in chapter 8, were subject not just to unemployment resulting from macroeconomic business cycles, but also to day-to-day and week-to-week uncertainty about the number of hours they would be able to work at their particular employer. The income of wage earners was paid as an hourly wage, and workers were not paid for the hours that were lost when a particular plant shut down to repair the blast furnaces in the steel industry or because of a temporary hiatus in the arrival of cattle to the stockyard gate. Employment could also be lost at the whim of a foreman or supervisor if a worker appeared to be losing his physical strength or to punish any worker who complained about working conditions. A risk in rural regions was the loss of savings when the local bank failed, and the risk of insolvent banks spread to the entire nation in 1931–33 as 10,000 of the nation's 25,000 banks failed.

Over the 1870–1940 era, the most important actions to mitigate risk for the average American were achieved by the New Deal between 1933 and 1940. The first legislation with a long-run impact was the Federal Deposit Insurance Corporation, which almost completely eliminated bank failures and the consequent loss of life savings by depositors.[76] Next came Social Security in 1935, which eventually provided a stable retirement income for America's senior citizens. Unemployment benefits began as part of the 1935 Social Security Act and by 1938 had been adopted by all states. Mitigation of risk was only partial, however, as unemployment benefits never covered more than 40–50 percent of the previous wage income and were initially limited to sixteen weeks, later extended to twenty-six weeks.

New Deal programs enhanced the role of the federal government in promoting economic growth, which was already evident in the Homestead and Morrill Acts of 1862. A priority for the New Deal was the achievement of rural electrification, given the great divide between near-complete electrification of urban homes by 1929 contrasted with a lack of electricity in rural America. The Rural Electrification Administration (REA) created a substantial improvement in the standard of living for many Americans even in the dismal years when work was hard to find. While the rural electrification effort is usually associated with the southeast states and the development of the Tennessee Valley Authority (TVA), the REA was a nationwide program and brought electricity to rural communities all over the nation. One Wyoming ranch woman called the day when electricity arrived

> my Day of Days because lights shone where lights had never been, the electric stove radiated heat, the washer turned, and an electric pump freed me from hauling water. The old hand pump is buried under six feet of snow, let it stay there! Good bye Old Toilet on the Hill! With the advent of the REA, that old book that was my life is closed and Book II is begun.[77]

Other New Deal programs were developed to provide jobs and reduce unemployment. The Works Progress Administration (WPA) at its peak in 1938 created 3 million jobs, equal to about 7 percent of the labor force. The WPA specialized in infrastructure—roads and public buildings—and is credited with constructing many of today's U.S. post offices.[78] The Civilian Conservation Corps (CCC) hired mainly young men, limited in number to

330,000 at any one time, to do manual work that focused on the planting of trees, increasing the amenities of national parks, and otherwise improving the infrastructure of government-owned land. Michael Darby revealed the bizarre definition of employment in the 1930s that excluded from the employment data those working for government agencies such as the WPA and CCC, and Darby estimated that the overall unemployment rate in 1941, officially 9.9 percent, was actually a substantially lower 6.6 percent when the WPA and CCC workers are counted as having been employed rather than unemployed.[79]

CONCLUSION

The seven decades from 1870 to 1940 witnessed a revolution in the American standard of living. Previous chapters in part I chronicled advances in food, clothing, housing, transportation, information, communication, entertainment, health, and working conditions. Along all these dimensions, the quality of daily life in 1940 was entirely different from that in 1870, particularly in urban America. Likewise, this chapter has traced the arrival of the modern world of consumer credit, insurance, and government policy that created the institutions of 1940 that more closely resemble those of today than the America of 1870. Consumer credit allowed purchases to be made on the installment plan so that goods could be enjoyed before they were fully paid for, and insurance protected households from catastrophic loss in the case of a fire and provided income protection in the case of the early death from accidents or illness of the family's primary income earner.

The shift from rural to urban living brought with it a change in the provision of credit, which in 1870 rural America had been provided largely by local general stores and, for farm mortgages, by small local banks. As cities grew, a larger share of the population came to rely on urban sources of credit such as the pawn shop. The use of credit reached a nadir in the 1900–1910 decade as the cash-only mail order catalogs became an ever-growing source of clothing and implements for the rural population and as the cash-and-carry department store became a dominant source of supply in medium and large cities. Throughout the late nineteenth century, more than half of family budgets were devoted to food and clothing and most of the rest to rent (or for farmers mortgage payments), so there was not much income left over for substantial purchases of consumer durable goods.

That changed as prosperity increased discretionary income between 1910 and 1929. Consumer and mortgage credit flourished during the 1920s. The installment plan, which dated back to the 1850s for major middle-class purchases such as sewing machines and pianos, became ubiquitous for both rural and urban consumers, working-class and middle-class alike. Between 1910 and 1925, both the catalog houses and the department stores introduced installment plans as they shifted away from their earlier reliance on cash purchases. The prosperity of the 1920s was fueled by easy consumer credit as many households were able to purchase their first automobile during a decade that witnessed the increase of motor vehicles per household from 29 percent in 1919 to 93 percent in 1929. Also financed by consumer credit were the earliest major electric household appliances, mainly the refrigerator and washing machine. Mortgage credit was especially abundant and facilitated an unprecedented and unsustainable housing boom that ignored the decline in future population growth implicit in the restrictive immigration legislation of the early 1920s.

Life insurance was transformed in the late nineteenth century to an instrument of saving, with each policy having a cash and loan value. By the turn of the twentieth century, life insurance was almost universal not just among middle-class families, but also among working-class households. Life insurance loans became popular as a method of obtaining the down payment needed to buy an automobile or a dwelling. Regulations governed the financial affairs of life insurance companies, requiring that they maintain specified levels of assets sufficient to meet the regular flow of claims.

Just as private life, fire, and automobile insurance reduced the risks of everyday life, so the government provided social insurance that the private sector could not or would not supply. Before the New Deal, the primary risk-related government action was the establishment in 1906 of the Food and Drug Administration, intended to reduce the risk of adulteration or contamination of milk, meat, and other food products. More significant measures to reduce risk awaited the 1930s, when the New Deal eliminated the risk to individual depositors of bank failures through the Federal Deposit Insurance Corporation. The risk of a penniless old age was countered by the Social Security legislation, and the risk of unemployment was partly mitigated, at least for a temporary period, by government-administered unemployment insurance.

Long before the FDA and the New Deal measures, the federal government had promoted economic growth and development through free land grants to railroads, homesteaders, state colleges and universities, and state agricultural experimental stations. Incentives for innovation were provided by the well-administered U.S. Patent Office. The contribution of running water and sewer pipes to the improvement of the standard of living over the 1870–1940 period was largely financed by state and local governments, whereas the network of highways built in the 1916–40 interval was funded by a combination of state and federal resources. Although the wiring of urban America with electricity supplies had been financed by private enterprise, the extension to rural America, particularly in the south, was financed by the federal government through the Rural Electrification Administration. Finally, the federal government also intervened to moderate the excesses of monopoly with the 1887 establishment of the Interstate Commerce Commission and the 1890 passage of the Sherman Antitrust Act. Whether a specific government action mitigated risk or promoted economic growth, it supplemented the powerful forces in the private economy that propelled the epochal increase in the American standard of living between 1870 and 1940.

Entr'acte

THE MIDCENTURY SHIFT FROM REVOLUTION TO EVOLUTION

The year 1940 marks the transition from part I to part II of the book. Like any dividing point, the choice of that year is arbitrary and is made because it falls roughly halfway between 1870 and 2015. A central theme of this book, as suggested by its title *The Rise and Fall of American Growth*, is that the pace of progress sped up in one era and slowed down in a subsequent era. Figure 1–1 makes this interpretation explicit, showing that the growth of output per person increased from an initial half-century (1870–1920) to a much faster rate in the subsequent half-century (1920–70) before slowing in the final period of almost half a century (1970–2014). The best available measure of innovation, the growth of total factor productivity, is shown in figure 1–2 to have the same pattern of a speedup in 1920–70 and a slowdown in 1970–2014, to such an extent that its post-1970 growth rate was barely a third that achieved in 1920–70.

Thus the year 1940, which divides part I from part II, does not represent the borderline between fast and slow growth but rather occurs in the middle of the period of rapid growth. This interpretation can be related to the sequence of industrial revolutions. The first industrial revolution (IR #1), based on the steam engine and its offshoots—particularly the railroad, steamships, and the shift from wood to iron and steel—resulted from inventions in the period 1770 to 1820 that were sufficiently important for their exploitation to require most of the nineteenth century. The second industrial revolution (IR #2) reflected the effects of inventions of the late nineteenth century—particularly electricity and the internal combustion engine—and had its maximum effect on output per person and on productivity in the half-century 1920–70. Between 1940 and 1970, output per person and output per hour continued to increase rapidly, in part as a result of three of the most important subsidiary spinoffs of IR #2—air conditioning, the interstate highway system, and commercial air transport—while the world of personal entertainment was forever altered by television.

The third industrial revolution (IR #3), associated with information and communication technology, began in 1960 and continues to this day. Like IR #2, it achieved revolutionary change but in a relatively narrower sphere of human activity. The domain of IR #2 covered virtually the entire span of human wants and needs, including food, clothing, housing, transportation, entertainment, communication, information, health, medicine, and working conditions. In contrast, only a few of these dimensions, in particular entertainment, communications, and information, were revolutionized by IR #3. This single fact, the narrowness of the effects of IR #3, is enough to explain why growth in output per person and output per hour began to slow down after 1970. Part II of this book provides an account of progress after 1940 that combines epochal change in the dimensions of IR #3 combined with a gradual slowing in the effects of change in the numerous other dimensions of the standard of living that were radically altered by IR #2.

OUTPUT MEASURES MISS THE EXTENT OF REVOLUTIONARY CHANGE FROM 1870 TO 1940

The preceding chapters of part I have chronicled the arrival of the modern age in the years between 1870 and 1940. The quality of life in urban America changed more quickly during those seven decades than in any other era of similar length in prior human history. The inventions poured out from 1870 to 1900 and were implemented, developed further, and became pervasive in the middle decades of the twentieth century. Electricity and running water were omnipresent in urban America by 1940 but lagged behind on the farm and in the small town, whereas the revolution created by the motor vehicle benefited farmers and city dwellers alike. Change occurred in every aspect of household well-being. Most notably, the isolated dwelling unit in the urban America of 1870 had by 1940 become "networked," connected to the rest of the economy by electricity, gas, telephone, running water, and sewer lines. Although many farmers in 1940 still awaited the arrival of electricity and running water, by that date farm productivity had surged upward thanks to inventions from the reaper to the farm tractor, which became ubiquitous between 1920 and 1950.

Except in the rural south, daily life for every American changed beyond recognition between 1870 and 1940. Urbanization brought fundamental change. The percentage of the population living in urban America—that is, towns or cities having more than 2,500 population, grew from 25 percent to 57 percent. By 1940, many fewer Americans were isolated on farms, far from urban civilization, culture, and information. Moreover, many fewer were subject to the extremes of cold and heat, of drought and floods, and of periodic infestations of insects.

The extent of improvement in the standard of living is demonstrated by several humble examples. In 1870, there were no iceboxes. Between that year and 1920, the icebox became the dominant household appliance to keep food fresh, yet its effectiveness required regular deliveries of ice. The development of the electric refrigerator during 1910–1930 is a classic example of an invention that raised both consumer welfare and productivity. Consumers benefited because the refrigerator temperature was uniform, and the productivity of society increased because the chain of employees involved in cutting ice in the northern states and shipping it to the southern states became unnecessary. By 1940, roughly 40 percent of American households had electric refrigerators, a figure that reached 100 percent shortly after World War II.[1]

The standard of living tripled over these seventy years, with real GDP in 2009 prices growing from $2,770 per person in 1870 to $9,590 in 1940.[2] Yet measures of real GDP omit many of the most important gains in the standard of living over the 1870–1940 era and, to a lesser extent, since 1940. Among the many sources of advance not captured by real GDP were the brightness and safety of electric light as compared to the inconvenience, danger, and dimness of the previous kerosene and whale oil lamps.

Real GDP does not value the increased variety of food available after 1870, with the invention of processed food, from corn flakes to Coca-Cola, and the increased availability of fresh meat made possible by refrigerated railroad freight cars. Real GDP does not value the invention of the modern urban department store, which provided convenience and economies of scale in making available a wide variety of goods to the urban consumer starting in the 1870s and 1880s. Real GDP does not value the invention of the thousand-page mail-order catalog, which created a multifold increase in the selection of goods available to America's rural population in 1900, not to mention provided those goods at prices significantly lower than had previously been available.

Real GDP does not value the removal of horse droppings and urine from city streets and rural highways as motor vehicles replaced horses over the 1900–1940 interval. Real GDP does not value the increase of speed and load-carrying capacity made possible by the motor vehicle, nor the flexibility of the automobile that gave birth to a new industry called "personal travel."

Real GDP does not take account of the epochal decline in price and improvement in the quality of the motor car between 1900 and 1935, because the motor car was not included in the Consumer Price Index until 1935. In the meantime, the inflation-adjusted price of the Model T Ford fell by roughly 80 percent between 1910 and 1923.

Real GDP does not count the value of instant communication via the telegraph, of voice communication via the telephone, of reproduction of music by the phonograph, or of instant availability of news and entertainment achieved in the 1920s and 1930s by nationwide radio networks. Real GDP does not count the difference in the quality between a nickelodeon showing a few silent moving images on the screen compared to the multidimensional 1939 experience of seeing *Gone with the* Wind with color, sound, and dazzling effect for an average price of twenty-three cents.[3]

Real GDP does not value the reduction of infant mortality from 22 percent of new births in 1890 to about 1 percent in 1950. By some estimates, this change created more welfare value than the all the other sources of increased consumer welfare taken together. Real GDP does not account of the change in the body and soul when the seventy-two-hour weekly work schedule in the steel industry, accompanied by heat, sweat, and danger, was replaced by a forty-hour weekly work schedule in a clerical or professional job carried out in an air-conditioned office.

Real GDP does not value the increase in consumer surplus as clean running water arrived at the in-home tap and replaced the previous need to carry pails of water into the house from nearby wells or streams. Real GDP does not value the replacement of the outhouse and the need physically to dispose of human waste by the silent efficiency of public waste sewers that became universal in towns and cities by 1940. Real GDP does not value the comfort or privacy of taking a bath in a private enclosed bathroom in a tub or a shower as contrasted with the 1870 standard of a bath in a large bin of heated water in the communal kitchen. Real GDP does not take account of the liberation of women, who previously had to perform the Monday ritual curse of laundry done by scrubbing on a wash board, as well as the Tuesday ritual of hanging clothes out to dry. Running water, the electric washing machine and refrigerator, the motor vehicle, and all the other inventions of the late nineteenth and early twentieth centuries, are "linked in" to the GDP statistics, which means that zero value is placed on their invention.

All of this provides *prima facie* evidence that the growth rate of real GDP in the years covered by part I of this book, 1870–1940, is substantially understated in all available measures. A major research effort spanning multiple projects and investigators would be required to come close to a quantitative estimate of how much of the increase of consumer welfare during this period is understated by the standard sources of real GDP per capita. Research thus far has been confined to individual output categories. The value of railroads compared to canals has been estimated at 3 percent of real GDP per year, the invention of tractors at 6 percent of real GDP per year, and the invention of motion pictures through 1938 at 3 percent of real GDP per year. Though no studies have been carried out for the wide range of other inventions of the 1870–1940 period, including the value of the invention of electricity and internal combustion engines, it is not difficult to imagine an omitted value to economic growth amounting to 100 percent of GDP. In fact, Nordhaus's estimates of the value of increasing life expectancy in the first half of the twentieth century roughly doubles the growth rate of the standard measure of consumption expenditures (see chapter 7).

SLOWING EVOLUTIONARY GROWTH COMBINED WITH THE ICT REVOLUTION, 1940 TO 2014

The years 1940 to 1970 witnessed a continuation of rapid growth as the inventions of IR #2 altered the standard of living of every household. The chapters of part II include those that describe dimensions of life in which the pace of progress slowed after 1970 and those in which it did not. Chapter 10 shows that consumption of food and clothing, as well as the equipment of dwelling units, changed relatively little after a transition period between 1940 and 1970, when virtually every kitchen became equipped with the modern appliances, most of which were invented before 1940. Though chapter 11 recognizes that automobiles became safer and more convenient after 1940, the typical automobile of 2014 had much more in common than its 1940-model ancestor than the 1940 vehicle had with the horse and buggy of 1870, and the increased speed of travel after 1940 should be credited more to improved highways than to faster cars. Chapter 11 also chronicles the advance of commercial air transportation, which by 1970 had developed a nationwide network in which jet aircraft linked large cities with each other and with small towns; after 1970, every aspect of air travel experienced slower growth—traffic grew more slowly, prices fell less rapidly, and air travel became less comfortable as seating space tightened and as the airport experience became fraught with security inspection delays.

Health and medicine, covered in chapter 14, are another category in which progress was rapid between 1940 and 1970 but subsequently slowed. The rate of increase of life expectancy was only half as fast in the second half of the twentieth century as in the first half. A disproportionate share of medical advances took place between 1940 and 1975 and fewer occurred between 1975 and 2014. Penicillin, invented before World War II and in common use during and after the war, was joined by numerous other antibiotics and other medications such as the Salk and Sabin polio vaccines. The rate of death from cardiovascular disease reached its peak in the early 1960s, roughly at the same time when the public became aware of the dangers of smoking. The main treatments for cancer, radiation and chemotherapy, were already in wide use in the 1970s. Medicare and Medicaid were introduced in 1965 and brought medical insurance to senior citizens and to the poorest segments of the population.

Likewise, chapter 15 shows that progress in working conditions and education slowed after 1970. Child labor disappeared as the high school completion rate increased from 10 percent in 1900 to nearly 80 percent by 1970, but after that year, there was little further improvement in the percentage of youth completing high school. Thanks to the GI Bill and heavy subsidies of state colleges and universities, the rate of college completion increased more rapidly between 1945 and 1975 than afterward. The standard work week for full-time workers by 1940 had already declined from sixty to forty hours, and the unionization movement of the 1930s and 1940s achieved not only the eight-hour day, but also premium pay for overtime work. Additional progress achieved by 1970 included the civil rights legislation of 1964–65, the women's liberation movement, and the beginning of a massive shift of adult females from housework to market work.

Thus chapters 10, 11, 14, and 15 all provide evidence of a slowing of progress after 1970 in a wide variety of aspects of the standard of living, including food, clothing, housing, motor and air transportation, health, medicine, working conditions, and education. This leaves chapter 12 to convey the rapid pace of advance in the areas of entertainment and communication and chapter 13 to capture the essence of the information technology (IT) revolution. Though black-and-white television sets became universal in nearly every household during the 1950s, as did color sets in the 1960s and 1970s, by today's standards, the choice of programming was extremely limited. The enormous broadening of program choice began with cable and satellite television in the 1980s, continued with time shifting and movie rentals made possible by the video cassette and digital video recorders, and expanded further with video on demand and video streaming. The field of communications witnessed an even greater acceleration of change, particularly after the 1983 breakup of the AT&T monopoly over telephone service provision and hardware manufacturing. The fastest transition of all, as chronicled in chapter 13, was the IT revolution, as the dominance of the mainframe computer for commerce and research yielded to the personal computer in the 1980s and then in the 1990s the PC was married to communications through the development of the world wide web. After 1995, this marriage added a "C" for communication as the IT revolution became renamed the ICT revolution. The culmination of ICT development arrived in 2007 in the form of the smartphone and its own revolutionary effect on social interaction.

DIMENSIONS OF THE POST-1970 GROWTH SLOWDOWN

As we have seen, numerous dimensions of the standard of living experienced a slower pace of progress after 1970 even as others, particularly entertainment and ICT, enjoyed a continuation or even an acceleration of rapid growth. How did these conflicting trends emerge in the aggregate economic data? Despite the flaws of GDP measurement that omit many benefits from innovation and technological change both before and after 1970, in the absence of a superior alternative, we use the growth rate of real GDP per person as our basic measure of improvements in the standard of living. And we use growth in real GDP per hour as our basic measure of labor productivity.

Growth in real GDP per person by definition can be split into growth of real GDP per hour plus growth in hours of work per person. When per-person hours of work decline, as when people take longer vacations, output per person rises more slowly than labor productivity. When per-person hours of work increase, as when women shift from housework to market work, output per person rises more rapidly than labor productivity. It is important to remember that GDP is the numerator of both output per person and output per hour, so all the measurement errors in GDP already enumerated apply equally to output per person and output per hour. The denominator of the ratios, the number of persons in the population and the number of hours of work, are by comparison measured quite accurately. Thus there is no sense in which the many improvements in the standard of living that are omitted from GDP matter more for growth in output per person than for growth in labor productivity.

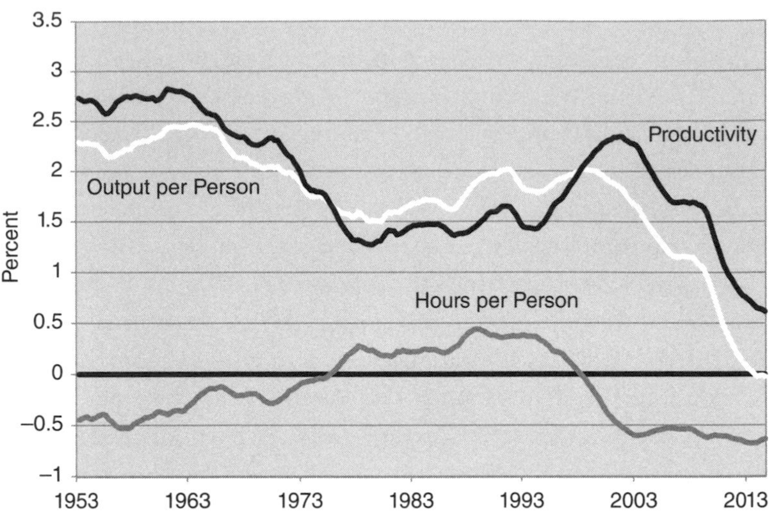

Figure E–1. Growth Trends of Output per Person, Hours per Person, and Productivity, 1953:Q1 to 2014:Q4

Figure E–1 displays for 1953–2013 the trend growth rate, adjusted to filter out the ups and downs of the business cycle, in these three basic measures of economic performance—real GDP per person, labor productivity, and hours per person. The episodic behavior of the trend in hours per person, shown by the gray line in the bottom of the graph, is critical to understanding the six decades since 1953. Hours per person registered negative growth between 1953 and 1975, then positive growth from 1975 to 1998, and then negative growth again after 1998. The general tendency for hours per person to decline over time reflects the widespread desire of workers to use some of their rising incomes to achieve shorter hours of work. This is achieved through some combination of fewer hours worked per week and fewer weeks worked per year—in other words, more vacation time. This historical tendency for hours to shorten was interrupted between 1975 and 1998 by the influx of women into the labor force. Aggregate hours of work per member of the population rose as many women made the transition from contributing zero hours of market work per person to a substantial number of hours of work. After 1998, the epoch of female entry abated to be replaced by a return to the long-run historical trend of declining hours, augmented after 2008 by the beginning of retirement of the baby-boom generation.[4]

Growth in real GDP per person by definition is equal to growth in labor productivity plus growth in hours per person. This means that by definition, the white line depicting growth in output per person is the exact sum of the black line displaying growth in labor productivity plus the gray line showing growth in hours per person. Note that the white line grew more slowly than the black productivity line during the two intervals 1953–75 and 1998–2014, when hours per person registered negative growth, and grew more rapidly than the black productivity line in the middle period of 1975–98, when hours per person recorded positive growth. Are these growth rates displayed by the white line rapid, or are they slow? We gain perspective by noting that over a longer period reaching back to 1891 and ending in 2007, output per person grew at 2.1 percent per year. When any quantity grows at 2.1 percent per year, it doubles every thirty-three years. Thus it was typical over more than a century for output per person to double every generation. For that long century, children had the expectation that on average they would be twice as well off at any given age as their parents had been at that age.

The white line in the graph representing trend growth in output per person lies above the historical trend of 2.1 percent between 1953 and 1968 and below 2.1 percent after 1968. The steady decline in the white line after 1999 reaches a value of zero in 2013 and 2014. In those years, the positive growth in labor productivity of about 0.6 percent per year was almost exactly offset by negative growth in hours per person, resulting in zero growth in the trend of output per person. More than anything else, it is this sharp decline between 1999 and 2014 in trend growth of output per person that lies behind the title of this book, *The Rise and Fall of American Growth*. During the decade 2004–2014, the negative growth rate of hours per person was relatively flat at a rate of about –0.6 percent per year, so the decline in American growth was experienced in parallel by output per person and productivity (output per hour).

The sharp decline in growth, especially in the last five-year interval 2010–14, does not appear in any government publication, for the growth rates plotted in the graph represent the hypothetical capability or "potential" of the economy to grow, abstracting from the effects of the business cycle—that is, when the unemployment rate is held constant. Actual growth can be faster than the economy's potential when the unemployment rate is falling, and the decline of the unemployment rate from 10 percent in late 2009 to 5.3 percent in mid-2015 allowed real GDP per person to grow at its actual rate of 1.6 percent per year as the recovery recovered from the trough of the 2007–9 recession. Once the unemployment rate stops declining and instead settles down at the 4.5 to 5.5 percent range that is typical after the post-recession recovery is completed, the best estimate of the economy's potential growth in output per person is shown by the value of the white line in the graph for 2014.

The disappointing performance of growth in output per person began in the mid-1960s. Clearly the white line, which must equal the sum of the black and gray lines, was dragged down by the steady decline in the black line displaying productivity growth, which averaged 2.72 percent per year during 1953–64 and then slowed steadily to an average of 1.44 percent per year for the time span 1977–94. This decline in productivity growth by almost half reflects the ebbing tide of the productivity stimulus provided by the great inventions of IR #2. Its successor, the ICT-oriented IR #3, was sufficiently potent to cause a revival in the productivity growth trend to an average of 2.05 percent during the decade 1995–2004. But the power of ICT-related innovations to boost productivity growth petered out after 2004. For the decade 2005–2014, average trend productivity growth was just 1.30 percent and by the end of 2014 had reached only 0.6 percent per year.

Thus diminishing returns from the great inventions lie behind the episodic waves of the black trend productivity growth line in the graph. The big difference between the two industrial revolutions is that IR #2 had effects that were more powerful and that lasted much longer than those of IR #3. How much did this matter? In 2014, real GDP per person was $50,600. If productivity growth between 1970 and 2014 had been as rapid as between 1920 and 1970, real GDP per person for 2014 would instead have been $97,300, almost double the actual level. That difference of $46,700 for every man, woman, and child in the U.S. stands as a dramatic symbol of the power of the second industrial revolution (IR #2) as compared to that of the third (IR #3).

Part II

1940–2015—THE GOLDEN AGE AND THE EARLY WARNINGS OF SLOWER GROWTH

Chapter 10

FAST FOOD, SYNTHETIC FIBERS, AND SPLIT-LEVEL SUBDIVISIONS: THE SLOWING TRANSFORMATION OF FOOD, CLOTHING, AND HOUSING

> The failure of the postwar subdivisions was, paradoxically, a result of their great commercial success. The making of suburbs, which had been an honorable branch of town planning, became simply a way of marketing individual houses. The developers overlooked the chief lesson of the 1920s suburbs: subdivisions should consist not only of private dwellings but also of public spaces where citizens can feel that they are part of a larger community.
>
> —Rybczynski (1995, p. 126)

INTRODUCTION

This chapter marks the transition between part I, which covers the interval 1870–1940, to part II, which treats the era since 1940. The chapters of part II treat the components of the standard of living in the same order as in part I. In contrast to part I, where during 1870–1940 each component experienced fundamental and revolutionary change, in part II the pace of change varies widely from very slow to very fast. This chapter treats food and clothing, where there was little fundamental change, together with housing and its equipment that experienced rapid improvement in quantity and quality from 1940 to 1970 but slower progress thereafter.

In chapter 3, we found that the improvement in the standard of living related to food and clothing was the least important of all the changes that occurred between 1870 and 1940. Caloric counts suggest that most people were well fed in 1870, and indeed, foreign observers marveled at the amount of meat consumed by American farmers and the urban working class. Advances from 1870 to 1940 did not include any significant increase in calories consumed but rather took the form of an increase in variety made possible by processed food and the refrigerated rail car, as well as the first regulations to control the contamination and adulteration of food.

The second necessity, clothing, experienced substantial change during 1870–1940, both in where it was made and where it was purchased. In 1870, most clothing for men and boys, as well as most shoes, were bought on the marketplace (often from rural general stores), whereas most clothing for women and girls was made at home from purchased dry goods. Progress from 1870 to 1940 involved a shift of women's apparel toward purchased rather than home-produced items, rather than any revolution in clothing quality or style. A more important change was the transformation of the experience of buying clothing. As America shifted from a rural to an urban society, the rural general store was displaced by the urban department store, and for those away from urban centers, the mail-order catalogs of Montgomery Ward and Sears, Roebuck provided a much wider variety of clothing options than could be stocked by rural or small-town merchants.

Food consumption evolved slowly after 1940. By then, food was relatively uncontaminated, and the urban retail environment featured large refrigerated cases for meat and prepared food and was well along in the transition to frozen food. The second necessity, clothing, witnessed little, if any, progress after 1940, with the single exception of synthetic fabrics that did not need to be ironed. Also, particularly after 1970, there was also a complete transition from domestic to imported clothing, together with a transition to "big-box" mass merchants such as Walmart that helped to achieve a sharp decline in the relative price of clothing.

This chapter also treats housing and its equipment, which for 1870–1940 were the subject of chapter 4. The revolution of American housing between 1870 and 1940 involved not the size or placement of houses, but rather the "networking" of the nation's housing stock. By 1940, the networking was complete, at least in urban America, with connections to electricity, gas, telephone, clean running water, and sewers. The networking that had occurred during 1870–1940 qualifies as among the most important contributions to the improvement of the standard of living achieved in all of human history.

The stock of housing and its equipment experienced major changes after 1940. Newly constructed houses in the early postwar years were small and shoddily built. The initial postwar surge of suburban housing tracts such as Levittown provided housing that was clearly inferior to the bungalows of the 1920s. Although the early postwar years reflected a decline in housing quality, gradually there was a turnaround. This chapter documents the inexorable increase in the average square feet of space in the typical single-family housing unit. Beyond size, the appliances and other equipment inside the house evolved into a form that is now taken for granted, and except for air conditioning, this transformation was largely complete by 1970.

This chapter goes beyond the size and equipment of housing units to talk about where they were located. In part thanks to deliberate government policies, suburbs were developed farther from the center city than in most other developed nations. Superhighways were built not just to connect cities, but also to facilitate commuting within cities. Unlike in Japan and western European countries, interurban passenger rail transport was not subsidized but rather was allowed to wither away. Except in the densest part of a few central cities, households were forced to use automobiles for shopping, commuting, and travel for all other reasons. Only within the past decade has there been a reversal of suburbanization as an increasingly large number of people, particularly youth who have no children, as well as empty-nesters, have shown a renewed taste for city living.

FOOD INSIDE THE HOME: THE MODERN ERA HAD ALREADY ARRIVED BY 1940

For two decades before our transition year of 1940, the concept of "normal" consumption of food and drink is elusive because of both Prohibition during 1920–33 and the Great Depression, which caused hunger and malnutrition for a substantial share of the population. By 1940, food and its marketing were, along most dimensions, quite modern—and, indeed, were much closer to the conditions of 2015 than those of 1870. Although Americans ate about the same amount of meat as they had in 1870, by 1940 they could take for granted that the meat had been transported in refrigerated rail cars and sold in refrigerated display cases. In contrast, back in 1870, there had been no refrigeration and cattle had often arrived in large cities "on the hoof," in an emaciated state.

The dominant form of meat consumption in 1940, particularly for the working class, was pork, just as it had been in 1870, but as we learned in table 3–2, overall meat consumption fell by fully a third between 1870 and 1940. One reason for the decline in meat consumption was that immigrants were used to consuming smaller quantities of meat, and their taste favored multi-ingredient meals such as stews, goulashes, and Italian dishes consisting of pasta, tomatoes, and small amounts of meat. Immigrants disdained bland American bread and cherished their ethnic bakeries, where Old World recipes were preserved.

Americans lagged European countries in the variety and quality of raw and cooked vegetables they ate. In the 1920s, only potatoes, cabbages, lettuce, tomatoes, onions, corn, sweet potatoes, and string beans were widely used. Gradually the food habits of immigrants spread to the native-born population, and American farmers began to grow asparagus, artichokes, endive, avocadoes, sweet peppers, and spinach. Sales of citrus fruit tripled between 1920 and 1940.[1]

Food retailing in the 1920s and 1930s was revolutionized by the self-service supermarket. The potential saving of labor when customers provided their own service first occurred to Clarence Saunders, the founder of the Piggly-Wiggly chain, who opened the first self-service market in 1916. The conversion to self-service and larger stores was concentrated in the 1930s but was halted by the ban on new construction during World War II. Though the first use of the term "supermarket" did not occur until 1933, by the late 1920s, self-service markets were opening with interior sizes as large as 10,000 square feet, compared with a mere 600 square feet for the typical chain store operated by A&P and others.[2] The popularity of supermarkets grew rapidly in the 1930s, aided both by the explosion of automobile ownership that had occurred in the 1920s and the acute depression, which made customers even more receptive to the low prices achieved by the self-service format. The first shopping cart was introduced in 1937, and the rise of the supermarket forced A&P to close more than half of its stores between 1936 and 1941.[3]

Despite depressed economic conditions, the 1930s witnessed not just the arrival of the self-service supermarket, but also the rapid development of the frozen food industry. The freezing technique was perfected by Clarence Birdseye in 1926, and the marketing of frozen food began in March 1930; initially, however, sales were slow, because the refrigerators of the 1930s did not have separate freezers that could maintain the necessary low temperatures. Two-temperature refrigerators were not sold until 1939, but before that, separate freezer cabinets were purchased by enough families to allow sales of frozen foods to become substantial by 1937.

The steady improvement in the American diet and the relative ease of buying food was interrupted during 1942–45 by wartime production prohibitions and rationing. Among the products rationed were sugar, fats, meats, and canned fruits and vegetables. The metal in the tin cans was diverted to war production, and coffee was rationed to conserve on ocean shipping. Out of necessity, consumption shifted to products that were not rationed, including eggs, milk products, and fresh fruit and vegetables.[4] Shortly after FDR announced his plan for "economic mobilization" in April 1942,

> every man, woman and child in America received a little cardboard-bound ration book, containing coupons that had to be presented for the purchase of specified items.... Many cheerfully gave up tinned foods and hoed their way to more healthful diets by raising fresh fruits and vegetables in Victory Gardens.... [F]or the stateside members of the greatest generation, their sacrifices amounted to sentimental gestures rather than genuine hardships.[5]

Housewives were forced to resort to "ration book gastronomy." The fact that red meat was rationed but fish and poultry were not was a harbinger of the steady shift to poultry in the postwar diet. There was a reluctant turn toward cheaper cuts of meat and organ meats such as liver, which required fewer ration points. The system worked remarkably well, although butchers were bribed and black markets for meat and coffee emerged in some places. "Home canning of vegetables flourished, with about three-fourths of the country's families putting up an average of 165 jars a year."[6]

FOOD IN POSTWAR AMERICA: A TURTLELIKE EVOLUTION

Figure 10–1 shows the share of total consumption expenditures spent on food from 1930 to 2013. Two lines are plotted, the upper line for food consumed at home and the lower line for food consumed away from home. Because food is a necessity, we should expect that the percentage of consumption devoted to food should decline over time as real income increases, and the upper line for food eaten at home is consistent with this expectation for the postwar period between 1950 and 2000. After 2000, however, the ratio stagnates, one of many

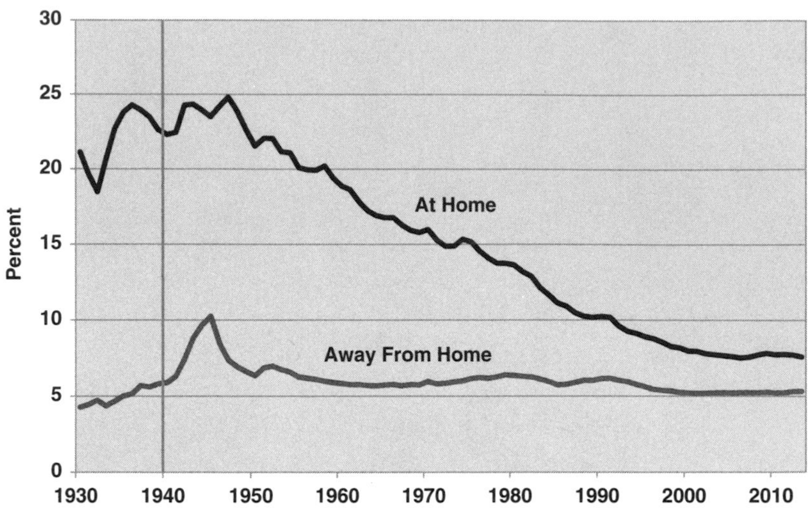

Figure 10–1. Consumption of Food at Home and away from Home, Percent Share of Total Personal Consumption Expenditures, 1930–2013

Sources: NIPA Table 2.4.5.

aspects of U.S. economic growth that indicates a decline in the rate of economic progress after 2000.

Why did the percentage of consumption expenditures spent on food fail to decline between 1929 and 1950? The answer seems obvious. During the Great Depression, the living standard receded as real income per capita plummeted, and it is not surprising that the share of expenditures on food increased temporarily as expenditures on less essential goods and services were reduced. During World War II, the production of almost all consumer durable goods was prohibited, implying that the share of perishables such as food and nondurables such as clothing had to increase as a matter of arithmetic. The share may have remained relatively high in the immediate postwar years between 1945 and 1950 due to shortages of consumer durable goods.

Though food eaten at home is a necessity, food eaten away from home is, if not a luxury, more of an option. As shown by the lower line in figure 10–1, the share in total consumption of food eaten away from home remains roughly constant (except for a temporary bulge during World War II). When we divide the bottom line in figure 10–1 by the top line, we obtain the share of food eaten away from home as a percentage of food eaten at home. The role of food eaten away from home steadily increased, from 20 percent of food eaten at home in

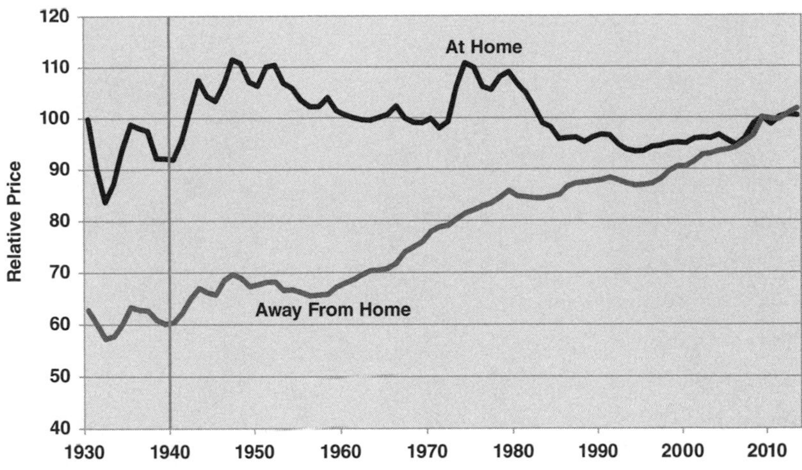

Figure 10–2. Relative Price of Food Consumed at Home and Away From Home (2009 = 100), 1930–2013

Sources: NIPA Table 2.4.4.

1929 to 29 percent in 1950, 37 percent in 1970, 60 percent in 1990, and then at a slower pace to 70 percent in 2013. The pace of transition away from food eaten at home to food eaten away from home slowed markedly after 1990.

Whereas figure 10–1 displays the share of nominal food spending in overall consumption, figure 10–2 shows us the evolution of the relative price of food. The upper line indicates that there was virtually no change in the relative price of food consumed at home, whereas in contrast, the lower line indicates a steady increase in the relative price of food eaten away from home. This rising relative price can be interpreted as a by-product of the fact that productivity growth in the service sector tends to be relatively slow, as restaurants combine food that has a constant relative price with labor that experiences a rising relative price. Even the efficiency of production methods in fast food outlets compared to traditional restaurants was not enough to stem the steady upward creep in the relative price of food eaten away from home.

How did food consumption patterns change after World War II? Table 10–1 shows the consumption of each type of food (measured in pounds per person per year) for 1940, 1970, and 2010. After declining precipitously between 1900 and 1929, meat consumption bounced back enough that annual consumption of meat per capita by 2010 had returned to the level of 1870. But its composition was much changed, especially in the long-term shift away from red meat to

Table 10–1. Apparent per Person Consumption of Foods, 1940–2010 (in pounds per person, except eggs)

	1940	1970	2010
Meat	152.2	203.4	219.4
Beef and veal	50.1	86.9	59.8
Pork	68.3	55.4	47.2
Lamb and mutton	5.9	2.9	0.9
Chicken and turkey	16.9	46.5	95.7
Fish and shellfish	11.0	11.7	15.8
Fats and oils[1]	50.1	55.7	83.9
Shortening	9.0	17.3	15.3
Butter	17.0	5.4	5.0
Margerine	2.4	10.8	3.5
Lard	14.4	4.5	1.5
Other fats and oils	7.3	17.7	58.5
Fruits[2]	202.2	237.6	255.9
Fresh	168.6	100.9	128.8
Citrus	56.7	28.8	21.4
Canned fruit	19.1	26.2	15.0
Fruit juice	7.2	96.7	97.7
Dried fruit	6.0	10.0	9.4
Frozen fruit	1.3	3.9	5.0
Vegetables[3]	291.1	321.6	389.9
Fresh	256.1	154.4	190.5
Canned	34.4	93.0	99.4
Frozen	0.6	43.7	71.5
Other		30.6	28.5
Dry beans	8.4	6.2	7.0
Total Milk Equivalent[4]	818.2	563.9	603.2
Milk and Cream	305.7	273.8	206.0
Cheese	7.9	16.4	35.2
Frozen Dairy	11.7	25.8	23.7
Eggs (numbers)	309.2	302.2	242.8
Sugar and sweeteners	108.4	132.3	140.7
Flour and Cereal Products	199	136.7	194.7

Table 10–1. *(Continued)*

	1940	1970	2010
Coffee	13.0	10.4	7.0
Total	1349.7	1420.1	1563.5

Sources: USDA ERS Food Availability Data System, HSUS (1960) G552-84, HSUS (1975) G881-915.

Notes: 1. In 2000, the number of firms reporting vegetable oil production increased, which contributed to the spike in the data.

2. Fresh includes HSUS Melon category. Data before 1970 not comparable to data afterwards, primarily for juice, dried, and frozen.

3. Includes corn for human consumption and potatoes. Subcategories before 1970 use different guidelines and are not necessarily comparable.

4. Includes butter, listed under Fats and oils.

poultry; the ratio of poultry to red meat consumption was only 14 percent in 1940 but by 2010 had reached 89 percent. This fundamental change in tastes was spurred in part by health concerns that red meat raised cholesterol levels and increased the likelihood of cardiac disease. Also the development of massive poultry farms allowed the relative price of poultry to decline relative to red meat, further encouraging the shift of consumption.

In the category of fats, the main event was the near disappearance of lard and in recent decades the sharp increase in the use of cooking and salad oils, including everything from corn and canola oil to olive oil. Sales of margarine had been boosted by the shortage of butter during World War II and remained higher than butter sales; the ratio of butter to margarine consumption shifted from 7.0 in 1940 to 0.5 in 2010.[7]

Though fruits and vegetables have become a much more important component of the American diet, a surprise in table 10–1 is that the consumption of fresh fruit declined as compared to 1940. There was a marked shift away from fresh citrus fruit toward processed fruit juice that was largely complete by 1970, in part responding to improved preservation techniques that have given more of a fresh taste to processed fruit juices. The transformation of consumption of fresh vegetables has evolved quite differently from fruits, with a decline from 1940 to 1970 followed by a partial recovery by 2010. Somewhat surprisingly, canned vegetables still remain a greater share of consumption than frozen vegetables, in part because of the widespread use of canned tomatoes to make many multiple-ingredient dishes, including homemade pasta sauces and pizza.

Consumption of dairy products and eggs peaked in the middle of the twentieth century, when it was more common than recently for cakes, pies, and other baked goods to be made at home rather than purchased in a store. Though cheese consumption has steadily increased, frozen dairy goods have been on a plateau since 1970. Flour and cereal products steadily declined from 1940 to 1970 but then turned around and made a comeback, reaching the 1940 level in 2010. This may reflect the popularity of cold breakfast cereals.

The total for all food consumption is shown in the bottom line of the table. Annual consumption of 1,563 pounds per person per year in 2010 works out to 4.3 pounds per day, up from 3.9 pounds per day in 1970 and 3.7 pounds per day in 1940. This increase had as its by-product the increase in obesity that is discussed later this chapter. At the level of individual foods, certain categories stand out as experiencing particularly large decreases and increases. For meat, the biggest percentage declines were for lamb and veal, with the greatest percentage gains occurring for shellfish, chicken, and turkey. Tastes in fruit shifted from canned fruit and fresh citrus toward apple juice, fresh grapes, and fresh noncitrus fruit. Vegetable preferences shifted away from brussels sprouts and sweet potatoes toward fresh spinach, fresh garlic, and fresh tomatoes. Dairy foods shifted from whole milk to cheese of all types.[8]

Some postwar trends extended those that had begun as long ago as 1900. The breakfast meal had changed completely from the ham and hominy heaviness of 1870 and by the 1920s had become a light meal that featured juice, coffee, cold packaged breakfast cereals, with the addition perhaps of toast or sweet rolls. The popularity of breakfast cereal was driven by incessant television advertisements of the top brands, just as it had by radio advertising in the 1930s and 1940s. With the proliferation of new refrigerators containing freezer compartments, accompanied by increasing sales of separate standalone freezers, the consumption of frozen foods expanded rapidly after World War II. By the 1950s, "TV dinners" and frozen vegetables had become everyday staples. The invention of plastics in the 1930s had made it possible for leftovers to be preserved not just in waxed paper or foil, but in plastic wrap. The replacement of fresh food cooked at home by frozen meals evoked a justified protest that the quality of the American diet had declined.

In the early postwar years, the utopian claims of the promise of frozen foods seemed farfetched, somewhat like the Jetsons' vertical takeoff car that never made the transition from dream to reality. A magazine editor in 1954 imagined a future in which frozen food had emancipated women from any need to cook, had eliminated labor strife by preventing an increase in the cost of living, and "brought abundance to American households." The euphoria about the promise of frozen foods was driven by the evolution of refrigerator and freezer technology, but fortunately the predictions of a complete takeover by frozen foods did not occur. As shown in table 10–1, frozen fruit consumption remained a small fraction of fresh fruit, and frozen vegetable consumption never equaled that of canned vegetables, much less fresh vegetables.

FOOD MARKETING FROM A&P TO WHOLE FOODS AND TRADER JOE'S

The most important change in food marketing was the gradual shift to the modern supermarket that was accomplished between the 1930s and 1960s. The share of total food sales accounted for by supermarkets soared almost overnight from 28 percent in 1946 to 48 percent in 1954 and by 1963 had reached 69 percent.[9] The stark improvement in customer satisfaction and retail productivity were accomplished by two central innovations. The first was the inclusion of all food items within a given retail structure. No longer did shoppers need to wander from butcher to baker to vegetable vendor to cheese merchant. All these items could be purchased in one visit. The second innovation was to detach the process of selection of food items from the process of paying for it. Until the early 1930s, a shopper in a multiproduct market would be asked to pay for the cheese at the cheese counter and to pay for the meat at the meat counter, with the potential for lines of customers forming at each of these unnecessary barriers. But supermarkets had shifted to a single checkout aisle for all items no matter where they were purchased in the store.[10] By 1954, the average supermarket size had grown from 10,000 square feet in the 1930s to 18,000 square feet.[11]

Before modern computer technology and barcode scanning, an invention of the 1980s, checkout clerks had to key in the price of each item that had been marked with a glued-on price tag, and the clerks had to memorize and know the price of each produce item unless there was a separate produce clerk to do the weighing and pricing. There was a rapid transition during the 1980s to the current technology, which has changed hardly at all in the past three decades: Clerks scan almost all items, including those from the deli and meat counters that have been affixed with their own barcodes.

The homogenization of food retailing represented by the large supermarket chains of the early postwar years has been replaced by a cornucopia of options. Many consumers have access to food purchases from traditional supermarkets, Whole Foods, Trader Joe's, Walmart, and Costco. We have come to take for granted blueberries in the winter; at least three grades of fresh salmon, ranging from expensive to very expensive, throughout the year; canned sardines from Spain; and a dozen varieties of balsamic vinegar from Modena and elsewhere. This increase in the variety of food that has occurred in the retail transition of 1980–2015 has taken the form of a larger variety of a given food item rather than the invention of entirely new types of food items, as occurred from 1870 to 1930 during the first wave of introduction of processed food products such as corn flakes, Jell-O, and bottled cola.

Although the small chain stores of the 1920s offered as few as 300 to 600 items, by 1950 the average supermarket stocked 2,200 items, a figure that had soared to 17,500 by 1985.[12] Despite this increase in variety, food consumption patterns did not change radically after World War II. Although several different flavors of corn flakes or shredded wheat might be available, consumer welfare was not markedly enhanced by the growth of trivial "brand extensions." Evidence began to accumulate that the growing size of supermarkets had gone too far, as sales per square foot began to decline. Much of the extra space was used to divide the store into separate departments and to group service counters for meat, fish, deli items, and even flowers and salad bars in a sequence that forced consumers and their shopping carts to find their way through all the increased variety.

Challengers to the dominance of supermarkets began to emerge in the 1970s. As supermarket chains had made the transition to fewer but larger stores, the location density of supermarkets declined and opened the way for some standard food items, tobacco, and gasoline to be sold in chain-operated convenience stores such as those of the 7-Eleven chain.[13] Because shoppers went to the nearby convenience store for just a few items, there was virtually no wait at checkout lines. Soon the large drugstore chains, now dominated by Walgreens and CVS, started building larger stores on the scale of early postwar supermarkets and combined the roles of pharmacy, over-the-counter health items, and rows of refrigerated cases little different from those in 7-Eleven containing milk and a wide variety of soft drinks.

The final evolution of postwar retailing of food involved a bifurcation between small convenience stores that challenged the supermarkets for size, quick check-out, and convenience, and the evolution of the Target, Costco, and Walmart supercenters, which combine under one roof shopping not just for food, but also for clothing, appliances, drugs, and almost everything else. Now shoppers could avoid the supermarkets altogether, using nearby convenience stores and large chain drugstores for small purchases of staples, together with the big-box stores for major shopping trips. Among the early victims of the large variety of items available at the big-box stores were the lower-priced department stores and the chains of small variety stores such as Woolworth's and Ben Franklin.

The controversy about the growth of Walmart is similar to the traditional economic classroom analysis of free trade. Imports benefit consumers with lower prices, and free trade benefits owners and workers of firms selling exports. The losers are the displaced domestic owners and workers at the firms that can no longer compete with cheaper imported goods. Walmart is similar, but with a difference. When Walmart comes to town, it lowers retail food prices by 25 percent, benefiting all consumers.[14] But it also drives local small businesses into bankruptcy, eliminating jobs of people who may be forced to shift from the freedom of individual proprietorship to the minimum-wage nonunion work environment of Walmart. And the analogy between international free trade and Walmart is incomplete, because there is no equivalence to the benefit of export jobs that are created by free trade. In fact, in its relentless pursuit of low costs and low prices, Walmart has increasingly turned to cheap imported goods and has been accused of tolerating harsh working conditions of apparel suppliers from Bangladesh and other nations.

Yet the benefit of Walmart's low prices cannot be overlooked. An arcane flaw in the official Consumer Price Index is that it does not consider the price reduction made possible by a Walmart to be a price decrease, because the CPI compares only similar items sold at the same outlets. This perennial form of CPI "outlet substitution" bias has the additional implication that the low-income part of the income distribution experiences a lower rate of inflation than the upper-income part, which spends a larger share of its purchases on scarce goods and services that rise rapidly in price, such as private college tuition and subscriptions to the Metropolitan Opera.

Supermarkets were further battered by the emergence after 1990 of upscale food chains, particularly Trader Joe's and Whole Foods, both of which shunned brand-name packaged goods and combined their own house brands with quite different approaches, from the mix of self-service prewrapped items at Trader Joe's to the multiple manned full-service counters at Whole Foods. Squeezed from below by the low prices at the big boxes and by the Spartan no-service format of Trader Joe's, and assaulted from above by the organic produce, upscale service counters, and superior selection of Whole Foods, supermarkets were condemned to a steadily declining market share, and some smaller chains went out of business.[15]

RESTAURANTS AND FAST FOOD

Our image of the postwar evolution of food consumption is of a continuing migration from cooking at home to food consumed outside the home at a combination of full-service restaurants, casual dining chains such as Applebee's, Red Lobster, and Olive Garden, and a vast variety of fast food options, including McDonald's, Burger King, Kentucky Fried Chicken, Steak and Shake, Pizza Hut, and countless others. It makes perfect sense that the share of food consumed outside the home would increase, not just because higher incomes allowed consumers to buy food prepared outside the home, but also because of the sustained increase in female labor force participation between 1965 and 1995.

Another contributor to the increase in food consumed away from home has been technology that did not exist three or four decades ago. Franchise fast food operations combine military-like training exercises with futuristic technology that allows them to deliver food to drive-through customers in two or three minutes.[16] Current workers at Taco Bell wear a three-channel headset that connects them simultaneously to the customer and the food and beverage workers. Orders are not called out to the kitchen but are entered in "point-of-sale" computer systems that have become almost universal in restaurants over the past two decades. There is perhaps no greater symbol of the attachment of American consumers to their vehicles than that 70 percent of the revenue of the fast food industry comes from the drive-through lanes, which have achieved an assembly-line efficiency worthy of Henry Ford. A primary reason why the share of food consumed away from home has increased is the manufacturing-like efficiency of the fast food outlets:

> Go into the kitchen of a Taco Bell today, and you'll find a strong counterargument to any notion that the U.S. has lost its manufacturing edge. Every Taco Bell, McDonald's, Wendy's and Burger King is a little factory, with a manager who oversees three dozen workers, devises schedules and shifts, keeps track of inventory and the supply chain, supervises an assembly line churning out a quality-controlled, high-volume product and takes in revenue of $1 million to $3 million per year, all with customers who show up at the front end of the factory at all hours of the day to buy the product.... The big brands spend hundreds of millions and devote as much time to finding ways to shave seconds in the kitchen and drive-through as they do coming up with new menu items.[17]

A major theme of this book is that the pace of technological change has been slowing, for many of the innovations made possible by computers and information technology have already occurred. This is apparent in the fast food industry, for the primary tools to provide rapid and accurate delivery of fast food to customers arriving in their own vehicles were developed in the 1990s, not within the past decade.[18]

FOOD ISSUES: INEQUALITY AND OBESITY

U.S. income inequality was high between the 1890s and 1920s and fell sharply during the Great Depression and World War II. The era between 1945 and 1975 was called by Claudia Goldin and Robert Margo "The Great Compression," after which income inequality began its multidecade increase, which still continues. The growing divide between middle- and upper-class Americans and their poorer fellow citizens has numerous causes and consequences, most of them treated in chapter 18. Here our attention turns to the relationship between income inequality, nutrition, and obesity.

There is day-and-night difference in the quality and quantity of food consumed at the top and bottom of the income distribution. At the top, the richest Americans dine in grand restaurants that charge $180 per fixed-price meal, with costs of wine not included. They buy berries from Chile and New Zealand out of season and pay Whole Foods $15 per pound for Icelandic salmon. But at the bottom, even after six decades of postwar prosperity, the bountiful average levels of American food consumption displayed in table 10–1 have not reached the poorest decile of the income distribution. In the America of 2014, many families, and especially children living in poverty, did not have enough to eat. Seventeen percent of Americans, or about 50 million people, lived in households that the U.S. Department of Agriculture calls "food insecure." This tragedy is most common in female-headed households in the southern states and in the inner areas of large cities.[19]

A new problem that influences our interpretation of advances in the American standard of living is the rising incidence of obesity. For the total population, a third of adults and a fifth of children are obese. After a century of stability between 1870 and 1970, total daily calories of food consumption after 1970 increased by more than 20 percent, enough to add fifty pounds to the average adult each year. Hardly any of this rise resulted from sugar consumption; more than half has come from fats and oils, and most of the rest from flour and cereal. Many of these extra calories are consumed away from home; this is triple the calories eaten away from home thirty years ago. Foreigners often note the large portions served at American restaurants, and drink sizes at fast food restaurants have escalated from eight to sixteen or even thirty-two ounces. As some states have required restaurants to list calorie counts on their menus, Americans have been surprised to find that a standard plate of food at a casual dining restaurant can contain 1,500 to 2,000 calories, as much as many adults should eat in a full day.[20] International comparisons support the view that the United States is an outlier in the extent of its obesity. In 2000, the U.S. percentage was 27 percent, and none of the twenty-three other countries compared had a percentage above 20 percent. Half the countries had obesity percentages below 10 percent, with Italy at 8 percent, France at 6 percent, and Japan at 2 percent.[21]

Obesity is a particular problem for the poverty population. A 2008 study by the U.S. Department of Agriculture found that children and women eligible for food stamps were more likely to be overweight than those who were not. There appears to be a systematic relationship between inequality and obesity. Analysts have concluded that the relative prices of healthy foods, including fruits and vegetables and lean meats and fish, are beyond the budget constraint of the poorest families. Much has been written about the "food deserts" without a full selection of supermarket food in poor urban ghetto areas, but studies have shown that poor people are just as likely to subsist on sugary, fat, and processed foods near well-stocked supermarkets as in food deserts.[22]

There is a substantial economic literature on the causes of increased American obesity. One study attributed 40 percent of the change to the declining relative price of food consumed at home.[23] However the data underlying figure 10–2 show that although there have been cycles in the relative price of food, there has been no long-run trend up or down in food consumed at home. On a basis of 2009 equals 100, the relative price of food was 100 in 1930, 1964, and 2009. Because the incidence of obesity has been steadily increasing in the United States, there is no support for changes in the relative price of food as a cause. Furthermore, much of the damage from fried foods, fast food, and supersized sugary drinks has occurred away from home at fast food and casual dining outlets. As shown in figure 10–2, the relative price of food away from home has steadily risen. Thus the sources of the increase of obesity must come from something other than a change in relative prices. Some authors claim that "mean weight is likely to be higher in richer countries."[24] But this is clearly wrong, considering the minor incidence of obesity in Sweden, France, and Japan.

The literature that tries to explain obesity in the United States by technical change (e.g., children playing video games instead of engaging in physical play outside) fails to confront the fact that these universal aspects of the Internet revolution do not create an obese population in the advanced nations that remain thin. Teenagers in South Korea are said to be even more obsessed with video games than American teens. This brings us back to the distinct difference of the United States compared to other advanced nations, the extent of inequality and childhood poverty. Poor children sit in idleness in front of TV screens and eat cheap fast foods high in fats and cholesterol. Upper-middle-class children eat kale salads before their trip to participate on the soccer team. Obesity is a social issue, not a technological phenomenon.

A theme of this book is that the rate of technological change has been slowing down. A new dimension of concern is that childhood obesity, especially among the poverty population, may lead to occurrence of diseases such as diabetes and heart disease that have the potential to reverse the century-long improvement in life expectancy. Although the evidence is still controversial, "these data raise the possibility that the current generation of children could suffer greater illness or experience a shorter lifespan than that of their parents—the first such reversal in lifespan in modern history."[25] We return in chapter 14 to the evidence that the poverty population is missing out on the century-long increase in life expectancy.

THE SLOW EVOLUTION OF THE SECOND NECESSITY: CLOTHING

The consumption of clothing for men, women, and children may have changed between 1940 and 2010, but the nature of this change was trivial compared to the other categories considered in this book. This section first examines the large decline in the share of consumer expenditure spent on clothing, then examines changes in how and where clothing was purchased, and finally discusses the relatively minor changes in clothing styles and quality.

Clothing declined sharply as a share of nominal consumer expenditures, in part because the relative price of clothing declined so rapidly. Figure 10–3 shows that the share of total nominal consumption consisting of clothing declined from 10.1 percent in 1940 to a much lower 3.1 percent in 2013. Already in 1940 the clothing share had declined from 13.1 percent in the year 1900.[26]

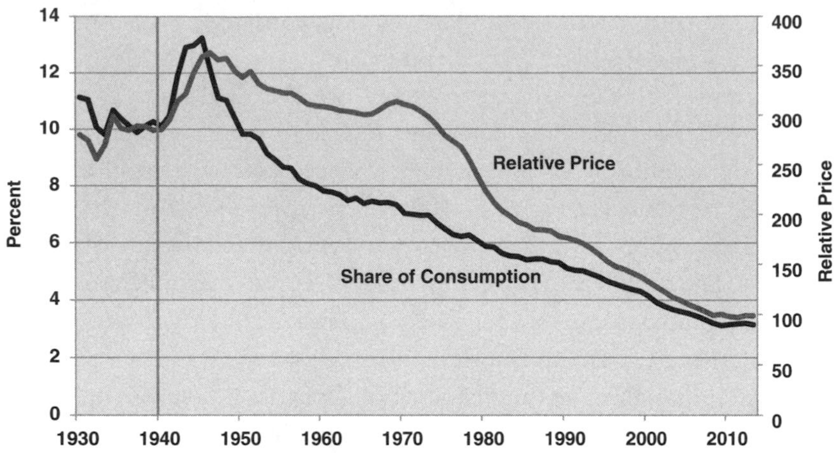

Figure 10–3. Consumption and Relative Cost of Clothing (2009 = 100), 1930–2013

Sources: NIPA Table 2.4.4., Table 2.4.5.

Expressed as an index number with the 2009 value equal to 100, the relative price of clothing was 285 in 1940, then rose to a maximum of 363 in 1946 before experiencing a steady decline to 99 in 2013. Stated another way, overall consumer inflation during 1940–2012 proceeded at an annual rate of 3.6 percent and that of apparel at a rate of 2.1 percent, for an annual reduction in the relative price of clothing of 1.5 percent per year. Thus clothing became steadily cheaper relative to other consumption goods and services over a long time period.

Was the relative price decline entirely due to the influence of imported clothing? Imports came to dominate clothing sales in the past three decades. The post-1980 years observed a near total replacement of domestic-produced clothing by imports.[27] Imports were purchased because they were much cheaper, so it is not surprising that the rate of decline of relative clothing prices more than quadrupled, from –0.6 percent per year during 1940–80 to –2.6 per year from 1980 to 2013.[28]

Thus imports drove down the relative price of clothing, which in turn stimulated a shift of inflation-adjusted real consumer spending toward clothing from other products. During the 1940–80 period before the rise of imports, real clothing purchases per person grew at an annual rate of 1.6 percent, substantially slower than the 2.4 percent annual growth of total consumption per person. In contrast between 1980 and 2012, real clothing purchases per person rose at 2.7 percent per year, substantially faster than the 2.0 percent rate for total consumption per person. This rate of increase in real purchases took the form of more items of clothing per person, not just because the relative price of clothing was falling, but because changes in tastes and styles allowed men and women to shift from formal suits costing $150–200 in today's dollars to much cheaper casual tops, shorts, and pants with prices at Walmart, Target, and elsewhere as low as $15, $25, and $35.

The transition of clothing marketing was less complex than that of food, in part because clothing sales never experienced the equivalent of the corner convenience store for food staples. The change in the marketing of clothing can be best understood if we divide clothing purchases into those done in person and those achieved remotely through a hard-copy mail-order catalog or e-commerce. Clothing sales during 1900–1945 were dominated by downtown department stores, with different selections providing higher prices and quality at some stores (e.g., Marshall Field's in Chicago) and lower prices and quality at other stores (e.g., Goldblatt's in Chicago). The same gradation of price and quality occurred everywhere, with competition between local stores rather than among national chains. After 1945, there was a rush of the dominant downtown department stores to branch out and become anchors in the early postwar shopping malls, initially located in the first ring of suburbs and later in far suburbs and exurbs.

An important source of productivity gain for food stores was the development in the 1930s of the self-service supermarket, with a single set of checkout aisles. In contrast, the department store remained departmentalized. If you bought a coffee maker, you paid for it in the small appliance section, and if you then bought a men's shirt, you paid for it in the men's shirt section. This system of decentralized payment is still used in downtown and suburban multistory department stores. The most important development of postwar apparel retailing was the shift by Walmart and its competitors to the food supermarket system of a single checkout aisle, but this required large greenfield sites where the entire retailing operation could be conducted on a single floor, with a set of checkout lanes near the single set of entry doors.

Except for the invention of manmade fabrics, quality changes in clothing were minimal between 1940 and 2013. Most changes reflected changes in taste rather than quality, such as the disappearance of fedora-type formal men's hats, the rise and fall of women's hemlines, and a shift to informal clothing styles such as "business casual" and sportswear. Changes in style and improvements in manmade fabrics led to a shift away from cotton, wool, and silk; in 2013, U.S. apparel imports consisted of 49.1 percent cotton, 48.8 percent polyester and other manmade fabrics, and only 2.1 percent wool, silk, and other fabrics.[29]

Tastes in clothing evolved gradually. Female tastes shifted from dresses to separate tops and bottoms, and women revolted from the ups and downs of hemlines by shifting from skirts to pants and pantsuits. Likewise, men wore formal suits less often and separate jackets and trousers more often. Hats for women gradually disappeared, as they had for men a decade or two earlier. The market fragmented with clothing that differed by age group and lifestyle, but the continued trend toward casual clothing created a more uniform look for men based on the universality of khaki and blue denim pants. Men began to switch from shirts with buttons to polo shirts and turtlenecks. For women, the casual trend eroded the differences between daytime and evening wear, and as more women joined the labor force, they favored clothing that they could wear to work and then out at night without changing. By the mid-1970s, jeans for women had become so common that what began as a rebellion against conformity became a unisex uniform.[30]

In the past few decades, the trends toward casual wear and sportswear has continued. Denim jeans for both women and men include overpriced, often tight-fitting designer jeans sold at upscale department and specialty stores as well as equally sturdy versions sold at big-box retailers for a fraction of the price.[31] Knit tops, tunics, skirts, pants, and sweaters have become standard women's wear. Traditional shoe styles, including dress oxfords and loafers, are being worn less often, having been partly replaced by boat shoes and all types of athletic shoes, with separate designs for jogging, tennis, and basketball. Many companies have relaxed dress codes and allowed "casual Fridays," on which suits and ties are replaced by open-neck shirts and khakis.

This section has emphasized the very slow evolution of changes in tastes and styles, together with the rapid reduction in the relative price of clothing that occurred after 1980. Most observers would consider this a prime example of the benefits of globalization and free trade, but Elizabeth Cline offers legitimate qualifications. The most obvious is the loss of manufacturing jobs, an inevitable by-product of free trade. A total of 650,000 apparel jobs disappeared in the ten-year period 1997–2007, the prime period when the supply of imports from China multiplied so rapidly. The differences of wages, and the lack of difference of productivity, made the shift to Asian imports inevitable:

> When everybody went offshore to the Orient, we opened Pandora's box. After that, you couldn't manufacture clothing without being in Asia. You can never shut that box and say we can go back to where we were. It's open. It's done. It's finished.[32]

FROM LEVITTOWN TO MCMANSIONS: THE POSTWAR EVOLUTION OF HOUSING

By 1940, the American housing stock had advanced a long way from the simple, isolated dwellings of 1870. Urban housing units by 1940 were networked with the five basics of electricity, gas, telephone, running water, and sewers. None of this existed in 1870, except for gas and water in a few upscale urban neighborhoods. The rest of this chapter chronicles the further transformation of American housing from 1940 to 2015. Our treatment starts with the characteristics of the home and its equipment, then examines quality changes in appliances and other home equipment, and concludes with issues involving the arrangement of U.S. urban areas, particularly suburban sprawl and the decay of the inner city in some urban areas.

Table 10–2 extends to 1970 and 2010 the account of "modern conveniences" in American housing beyond the 1940 data provided in chapter 4. By the time of the first U.S. Census of Housing in 1940, virtually all urban housing units had electric power, running water, and exclusive use of an indoor toilet, whereas these conveniences were much less common in rural America and particularly in the rural south. As the percentage of the population living in urban areas rose from 56.5 percent in 1940 to 73.4 percent in 1970, this alone raised the national percentage of homes equipped with modern conveniences. By then, these core attributes of modern living had spread throughout rural America.[33]

The large number of blank cells for the year 2010 in table 10–2 occurs because the share of housing units with the conveniences listed had reached 100 percent; there was no longer any need to keep track of them. Even including rural America, the coverage of electric power was complete by 1950, as was that of running water, exclusive use of flush toilets, and exclusive use of a bath or shower by 1970. Central heating reached 78 percent in 1970 and 94 percent in 2010; the failure of this percentage to reach 100 percent reflected the lesser need for heating in parts of the south and southwest regions of the country.

The most important change recorded in table 10–2 for 1970–2010 refers to the spread of air conditioning. Either central air conditioning or window units were present in 37 percent of American homes in 1970, but by 2010, they were present in 89 percent.

We can measure both the quantity and quality of newly constructed housing units. Our quantity measure, illustrated in figure 10–4, is the number of new housing units constructed ("housing starts") divided by the number of households, expressed as an index number with 1929 = 100. This series testifies to the extent of overbuilding in the 1920s and its dire consequences for the economy of the 1930s. A five-year moving average reaches a peak of 186 percent of the 1929 value in 1923–27 and then falls precipitously to 31 percent in 1931–35, a decline of 83 percent. The moving average reached its postwar peak of 146 percent in 1950–54. The housing bubble of 2002–6 raised the ratio only

Table 10–2. Percentages of Housing with Modern Conveniences, 1940–2010

		1940	1970	2010
(1) Lighting	Electric Light	79	100	100
(2) Cooking fuel	Gas or Electricity	53	98	100
	Wood or Coal	35	1	
	Other	12	1	
(3) Water Supply	Running Water	74	98	
(4) Toilet facilities	Flush - Exclusive	60	95	
	Flush - Shared	5		
	Other	35	5	
(5) Bathtub or Shower	Exclusive	56	95	
	None or shared	44	5	
(6) Central heating	All Fuels	42	78	94
	Individual Stoves, Heaters, or None	58	22	6
(7) Air Conditioning	Central		11	68
	Room Unit(s)		26	21
	None		63	11

Sources: Line (1), 1940–70. Lebergott (1976), pp. 260–88. 1970 values extrapolated to 2010. Lines (2) through (6), 1940–60. SAUS 1965, Table 1102, p. 759. Also Table 1105. Lines (2) and (6), 1970–80 and Line (7), 1960–80, SAUS 1985, Tables 1319–1320. Lines (3) through (5), 1970, SAUS 1972, Table 1159, p. 690. Lines (2) and (6)-(7) for 1980–2010 from the same sources as used for those years in Table 10–3.

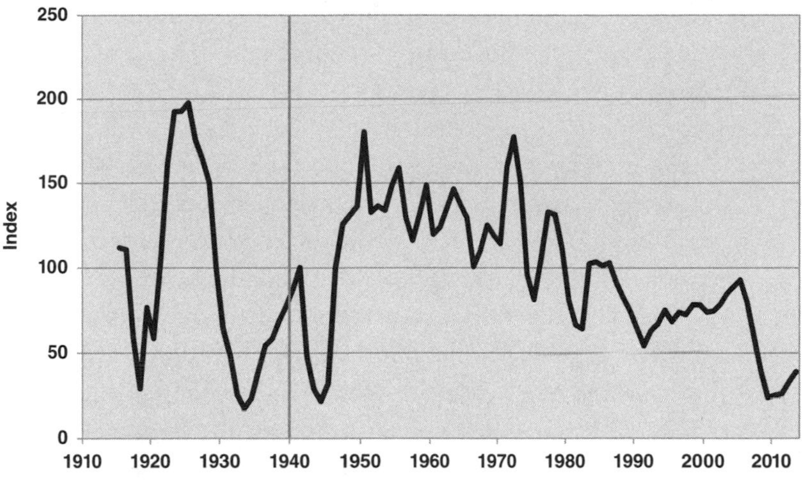

Figure 10–4. Index of Housing Starts per Household, 1915–2013 (1929 = 100)

Sources: HSUS Hc510, Hc531, and U.S. Census Bureau.

to 85 percent, and for 2009–13 the ratio was 30 percent, lower than during the worst years of the Great Depression. Overall, the construction of new housing units relative to the number of households has declined substantially in the last four decades, from an average of 135 percent of the 1929 level in 1947–72 to a much lower 78 percent during 1973–2013.

The causes of the long-term decline in the building of housing units per household include excess demand in the first decade after the war ended in 1945 that was largely satisfied by 1970, the increased relative price of construction, and the gradual slowdown in the rate of population growth. A more subtle reason is that housing units last almost forever.[34] New housing units are built on previously undeveloped lots ever farther from the city center rather than by destroying central-city housing that may be 100 or even 200 years old. The central cities and railroad suburbs of Boston, New York, Philadelphia, and Chicago were largely built up by 1929, and almost all the pre-1929 residential construction is still intact.

How does this explain the secular decline in the number of annual housing units constructed relative to the number of households? If houses last forever but people have finite lifetimes, then an ever-increasing share of the need for housing can be satisfied by houses older than average life expectancy. Those who die in 2015 at the average age of 85 were born in 1930, so the entire stock of housing built before 1930 is available as an option for the new households being formed now, requiring less new construction. The fraction of housing needs that can be satisfied by pre-existing housing rises as the rate of population growth declines.

A measure of quality is shown by the white line in figure 10–5, the average real value of housing constructed per year divided by the number of units constructed per year. This is expressed as an index number with 2005 = 100. Real spending per unit increased at a fairly steady pace between 1950 and 2006, except for an upward surge in the 1980s. We ignore the further increase after 2006 as a typical cyclical response. When housing construction collapses as in the Great Depression and in the financial crisis after 2007, larger homes continue to be constructed, and smaller "starter" houses and small apartment units bear the brunt of the collapse of construction. The upward surge in the value per unit index in 2006–9 echoed almost exactly a similar increase that occurred between the peak housing construction year of 1925 and the trough year of 1933.[35]

The tripling in the real value per unit ratio between 1955 and 2006 by definition is explained by the increase in the size of housing units—that is, the square feet of interior area times the real inflation-adjusted value of spending per square foot. Figure 10–5 helps us to understand the relative contribution

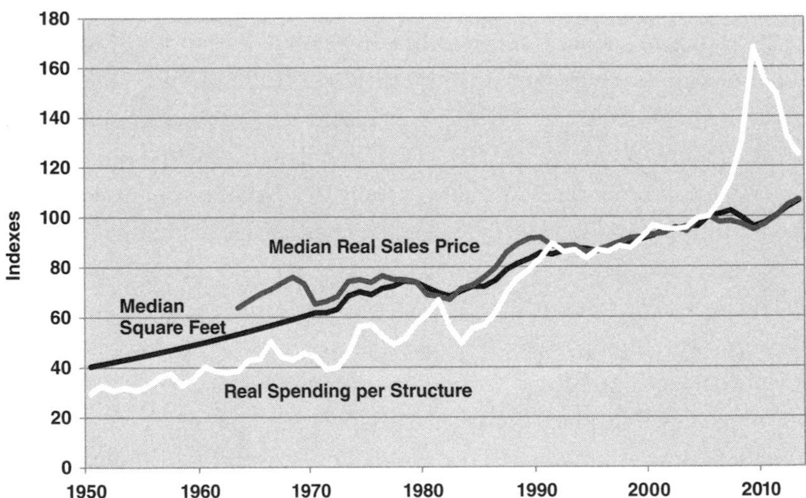

Figure 10–5. Indexes for Median Square Feet, Median Real Sales Price, and Real Spending per Residential Structure, 1950–2013 (2005 = 100)

Source: U.S. Census Bureau.

of larger units and more spending per square foot. The gray line reports the median real sales price per unit adjusted for inflation. Somewhat surprisingly, the median real sales price is tracked very closely by the black line representing the median number of square feet in a newly constructed single-family housing unit. This very close correspondence suggests that the dominant reason for the increasing real sales price was that single-family housing units have steadily become larger. The size of the median newly constructed U.S. single-family unit more than doubled over the postwar era.

More puzzling is the different path of the white line representing real value per unit compared to the gray line in figure 10–5 displaying real median sales price per unit. Here the explanation lies in the difference between the word "median" (i.e., the middle house in a ranking of houses from most to least valuable) and the word "average." The soaring real value per unit reflects a change in the mix of housing units toward relatively large houses in the top third of houses constructed, a shift toward larger size missed by the data on median square feet and median sales price. The increase in the real value compared to median sales price mainly seemed to happen in the 1980s. In the twenty-five years after 1990, the size of the median single-family house continued to creep higher, reaching 1,900 square feet in 1990 and 2,364 square feet in 2013. Half the houses by definition were larger than the median, and the largest became known as "McMansions"—both those in older suburban neighborhoods, where they replaced smaller "teardowns," and those in remote, often gated, communities on the fringes of metropolitan areas. Between 1992 and 2013, the fraction of newly constructed homes with four bedrooms or more increased from 29 percent to 44 percent, of those with three bathrooms or more from 14 percent to 33 percent, and of those with a garage holding three or more cars from 11 percent to 21 percent.[36]

The trajectory of house prices up for most of the postwar period and down after the 2006 peak of the 2001–6 housing price bubble has split the generations in their amount of wealth. Those who owned homes between 1960 and 2005 experienced enormous gains that provided a cushion of home equity against which they could borrow and that also provided income for retirement if eventually they chose to downsize. Those caught by the housing bubble of 2001–6 experienced the wrenching opposite experience of watching positive home equity rapidly sink "underwater" (i.e., turning into negative home equity). The consequences of this decline in household wealth still held back the growth rate of aggregate demand and GDP as recently as 2015.

Figure 10–5 supports the finding that there was an unambiguous increase in the quality per unit of the American housing stock over the entire postwar period. House sizes inexorably increased. More square feet allowed each newly constructed unit to have more bedrooms and bathrooms, but the postwar change in housing conditions went beyond a mere count of rooms. Starting with the earliest postwar houses, the traditional living room and formal dining room were reduced in size or eliminated in favor of the ubiquitous family room, a postwar invention, that was initially placed next to the kitchen and during most of the past three decades included within the kitchen as a "great room" in which the dinner could be cooked and eaten, children could play in an informal setting, and the family could gather after or even during dinner to watch the increasingly large TV set that was the central focus of the family room. Ironically, the family room was a throwback to the primitive 1870 kitchen, a sizeable space centered on the open hearth fireplace used for heating and cooking, and in which the family cooked, ate, played together, and even took baths in front of each other using water heated over the fire in the hearth. In 1956 *Sunset* magazine remarked on the "family room's kinship with the farm kitchen, rumpus room, and other rooms of the past."[37]

HOUSEHOLD APPLIANCES: QUANTITY AND QUALITY

Just as the size of newly constructed dwelling units continued to increase throughout the post-1940 era, so did the quantity and quality of equipment within the home. Progress focused on the kitchen, building on the transition that had already occurred between 1870 and 1940. The core labor-saving appliances of the modern era, the refrigerator and the washing machine, were first sold commercially around 1920 but, as shown in table 10–3, by 1940 had appeared in only 44 percent (for refrigerators) and 40 percent (for washing machines) of American homes.

In the early postwar years, the kitchens of many American homes achieved the standard of displays at the New York 1939–40 World's Fair that seemed so futuristic at the time. All walls were covered with matching cabinets, and the appliances included a large refrigerator–freezer, a gas or electric stove, and, in an increasing number of kitchens, the more recently developed electric dishwasher and garbage disposal. In a separate laundry room, whether next to the kitchen or in the basement, the initial wringer washing machines were soon replaced by white porcelain-finished automatic washers with a matching electric or gas dryer alongside.

Table 10–3. Percentages of Households with Selected Appliances 1940–2010

		1940	1970	2009
(1) Mechanical Refrigerator		44	100	97
(2) Separate Freezer			31	30
(3) Washing Machine	**Automatic and wringer**	40	92	82
(4) Clothes Dryer	**Gas or electric**		45	79
(5) Range (stove)	**Includes separate oven and countertop**		56	100
(6) Microwave oven				96
(7) Dishwasher			27	63
(8) Garbage disposal			26	59

Sources:
1970: SAUS 1972, Table 1162, p. 691.
2009: U. S. Department of Energy Residential Energy Consumer Survey, Tables HC3.1, HC4.1, HC5.1, HC6.1, and HC7.1.

In 1959, Richard Nixon and Nikita Khrushchev visited a model ranch house containing a well-equipped kitchen that was part of an exhibition in Moscow to show the Russians how well ordinary Americans lived. Soviet journalists scoffed that the exhibit was a fraud, since such a "Taj Mahal" could surely be afforded only by millionaires. Nixon retorted that such a house could be purchased with a $100 per month mortgage payment that was within reach of the budget of an ordinary steel worker. Foreigners in countries where apartment-dwelling is still predominate continue to marvel at the living standard of typical American middle-class families, with their two-car garages and houses large enough to store their abundance of possessions.[38]

Table 10–3 traces the postwar advance in the percentage of dwelling units equipped with specific types of appliances. These data apply to all dwelling units, whether built in 1830 or 1890 or 1955. Not surprisingly, the two most important appliances—refrigerators and washing machines—became universal first. This is clearest for the refrigerator, which had arrived in 98 percent of American homes by 1960. The washing machine never reached the same penetration, because many apartment-dwellers relied on machines that were communal to the building or went outside the apartment building to patronize Laundromats. The early data for washing machines in the 1940s and 1950s need qualification, for some of the machines in question were equipped with hand wringers to squeeze the water out of the clothes, requiring human effort no longer required by fully automatic washing machines with their mechanical spinning wash tubs.

Whereas washing machines eliminated the previous drudgery of the washboard described in chapter 8, the arrival of the clothes dryer eliminated the tedious task of hanging clothes on outside clothes lines, where the drying process could be interrupted by rain or where, in industrial cities, the clean clothes could be coated with soot and pollution. Clothes dryers took longer to reach American households than washing machines but eventually caught up. By 2010, about 80 percent of American households had automatic washers and dryers, which had been sold as matching pairs since the 1950s.

Somewhat surprisingly, the percentage of households with a stove that included an oven and cooktop was only 24 percent in 1952, rising to 99 percent by 1990. The 1952 percentage evokes skepticism, for photos of typical 1920s kitchens include stoves, and these had become universal in the kitchens of the vast number of residential units constructed in the 1920s. No appliance was more enthusiastically accepted than the microwave oven, present in only 8 percent of American homes in 1980 but in 96 percent in 2010. The combination of a built-in dishwasher and garbage disposal reached 60 percent penetration in 2010, which seems surprisingly low from today's perspective, considering the large fraction of the nation's housing stock built since 1950.[39]

First place in the modernization of the postwar kitchen is held by the electric refrigerator, which had approximated its current size and quality by 1960. Between 1930 and 1950, the average refrigerator doubled in size.[40] *Consumer Reports,* which began publication in 1936, issued its first report on refrigerators in 1938. It reported that a refrigerator could keep food cold for a third of the operating cost of an icebox. But early refrigerators were of low quality: "Food kept for any length of time in them tended to dry out. Ice accumulated relentlessly around the freezing elements, demanding frequent defrosting."[41]

There were many improvements in refrigerators after 1940, and the most important was in the basic function of being able to keep food at a specified temperature. In 1949, the criterion for the refrigerator compartment was 43 °F, gradually lowered by 1957 to the present 37 °F. In 1949, only two of the models tested could hold a freezer temperature at the required 0 °F, and the other models registered temperatures of 5 to 22 °F. It was not until 1964 that all tested models could hold a temperature of 0 to 5 °F.

Beyond its greater ability to cool or freeze food, the 1970 refrigerator was a far different appliance from its 1949 predecessor. The most important quality improvement was the addition of refrigerator defrost followed by full freezer defrost. Steady improvements included shelves in the door, a heated butter compartment, vegetable crispers, a meat compartment, and adjustable shelves. These new features were estimated to add about 10 percent to the value of a 1970 refrigerator. But this additional consumer value was swamped by the importance of improvements in energy efficiency. Between 1949 and 1983, reduced electricity use for a refrigerator of given size and quality amounted to an effective price reduction of −1.66 percent per year, which cumulates to 76 percent over that thirty-four-year interval.[42] This price reduction was overlooked by the government's Consumer Price Index (CPI), which did not measure any of the benefits to the consumer of the improvements in energy efficiency achieved by appliances. Because the same price index is used to convert dollar spending into real consumer spending, measures of real GDP understate improvements in appliance quality as a result of improving energy efficiency.

A dimension of improvement common to all appliances, including television sets, was their frequent need for repair in the early postwar years, followed by a steady improvement in reliability. *Consumer Reports* complained in 1949 that "a very high percentage of service calls on prewar refrigerators were for repair of slipping belts, poor piping and shaft seals, trouble with expansion valves, and thermostat trouble. This year's refrigerators seem to have eliminated the first three problems almost entirely."[43] By 1971, the refrigerator report purred with satisfaction, and "the overall quality differences between models were generally smaller than they had been. And a notable uptrend in quality had emerged."[44] After 1971, there were no further comments in *Consumer Reports* about refrigerator quality, indicating that a high plateau of uniform quality had been reached.

Prewar washing machines were not truly automatic and instead required users to employ a hand wringer. The sales of truly automatic washers did not surpass those of wringer models until 1952. Just as refrigerators added many new features in the early postwar years, so did washing machines, including wash-and-wear cycles and multiple temperature and water-level choices. By the early 1980s all rated machines provided three cycles, two separate automatic dispensers for bleach and softener, and continuous rather than discrete control of water level. Just as refrigerators, especially their freezer compartments, became larger, so did the capacity of washing machines, from about a ten-pound load in 1960 to about an eighteen-pound load in 1981.

Just as two decades elapsed after 1945 before refrigerators could maintain food at the desired temperature, so washing machines also gradually improved from the early models. One 1950 machine was rated "not acceptable" because "it tangled clothes so badly and so consistently." As late as 1960, most washers were unable "to get rid of large quantities of sand, or tended occasionally to redeposit some of the sand they removed onto subsequent loads."[45] Gradually, sand and lint problems were solved, and by 1982, "all the machines are designed to prevent lint from settling on clothing during the wash."[46] Overall, quality improvement in washing machines during the 1945–80 period was not as significant as for refrigerators, primarily because the big improvements of refrigerators in their ability to defrost automatically and gradually to become more energy efficient were not relevant for washing machines.

The evaluation of quality change for built-in undercounter dishwashers involves the same issues as for laundry washing machines. Dishwashers were introduced in the early 1950s, simultaneous with clothes dryers and room air conditioners. A basic dimension of quality improvement was increased interior capacity within a fixed exterior dimension. Just as washing machines increased from a capacity of a ten-pound load to an eighteen-pound load, so the dishwasher increased from six to eleven place settings between 1952 and 1980. There was a steady improvement in the basic function of getting the dishes clean. Similar to the increased flexibility of washing machine controls, dishwashers also introduced alternative cycles and water temperatures.[47]

Clothes dryers were a relative latecomer, invented in 1930 but sold only after the war. Clothes dryers did not experience any technical evolution such as that between wringer washers and automatic washing machines. They applied heat to tumble the clothes dry right from the beginning. The earliest dryers required lighting the gas flame with a match, but automatic ignition became standard by the early 1950s. As for washing machines, the main improvements were improvements in multiple heat settings and timing controls. By the 1970s, dryers had automatic sensors.

Because dryers applied heat just as refrigerators created cold temperatures, we would expect dryers to have experienced improvements in energy efficiency. These savings were relatively minor before the 1974 energy price shock but were very rapid thereafter. Energy use was cut in half during 1954–83, and because the cost of energy use for the lifetime of a clothes dryer was double its purchase price, there was a gain of consumer welfare from energy efficiency equal to 100 percent of the purchase price of a clothes dryer, even greater than for refrigerators.

The role of energy efficiency in the quality improvement of room air conditioners is even more important than for refrigerators and clothes dryers. The earliest central air conditioning appeared in Grauman's Metropolitan Theater in Los Angeles in 1923, and by the mid-1930s, air conditioning had been installed in the U.S. Capitol Building, the White House, and the U.S. Supreme Court Building, as well as in department stores, other retail markets, and a few office buildings. But the room air conditioner began its transformation of American home life only after World War II. In 1951, the room air conditioner appeared in the Sears catalog for the first time; total sales of room air conditioners leaped from 48,000 units in 1946 to 2 million in 1957.[48]

Consumer Reports was enthusiastic about air conditioning from the start and in a 1986 retrospective provided this glowing summary:

> Without air conditioning we wouldn't have Las Vegas, or Miami, or Houston, or Los Angeles. At least, not in their modern metropolitan forms that, collectively, make up the Sunbelt, the fastest growing area of the United States. Nor would we have jet air travel, manned spaceflight, submarines, or computers.[49]

We return in chapter 15 to the beneficial effects of air conditioning on productivity in two senses: First is the obvious fact that people work more efficiently when they are cool than when they are hot and sweaty. Second, air conditioning made possible a massive move of American manufacturing to the southern states and indirectly sped the process by which inefficient old multistory factories in the old northern industrial cities were replaced by new greenfield single-story structures in the south. We return in the next section to the unfortunate consequence of urban decay in the northern industrial cities hardest hit by the exodus of manufacturing jobs—and with them a substantial proportion of the early postwar population.

Room air conditioners are simple single-purpose devices designed to cool air and recirculate it. There are fewer dimensions of quality change, because there is no analogy to the multiple aspects of refrigerator quality. There were only two important improvements in quality for room air conditioners that did not involve energy efficiency. The first was the reduced weight, declining for a standard unit from 180 pounds in 1957 to seventy-five pounds in 1970. This eliminated installation expense and made possible installation by the purchaser. The second was the transition from the requirement of a heavy-duty 230-volt power source to a normal 115-volt power plug; this transition was complete by 1957. The third was that more than half of units tested in 1953 lacked thermostats and had only one fan speed. *Consumer Reports* commented in 1953 that all units are "very noisy" but in 1965 that "the top-rated models are very quiet."[50]

The energy requirements of a standard-sized window unit declined by two-thirds between 1953 and 1983. Translated into an annual growth rate, this implies that the price of the unit and the present value of its operating cost together fell by 2.6 percent per year for the thirty years between 1953 and 1983. Stated differently, the quality of a window unit with a given output increased by 2.6 percent per year for thirty straight years, implying a doubling of quality over that thirty-year period.[51]

Leaving aside audio, visual, and computer-related equipment to be discussed in chapters 12 and 13, the only new piece of household equipment introduced after 1950 was the microwave oven. First introduced in 1965 and sold in large quantities around 1980, the quality of the microwave oven evolved along the same dimensions as the washer, dryer, and dishwasher. The early models offered mechanical controls, a timer dial, and a single power setting. Later models were much improved and included a temperature probe, numerous variable power settings, and touch-panel controls.

Early microwave ovens were unnecessarily large and expensive. For most purposes, a unit with an interior capacity of half a cubic foot performed as well as the original models, which were sized at a full cubic foot. Newer models were lighter, more compact, and required less counter space. An original primitive model with no controls except an on/off switch sold in 1968 for $495. By 1986, compact models with all the electronic bells and whistles sold for an average of $191. The quality-adjusted price of the microwave oven declined at a rate of –6.7 percent per year, the quickest decline in cost for any appliance before the arrival of the personal computer. An additional dimension of improvement was product safety. There was radiation leakage in early models, but by 1985 *Consumer Reports* found that "radiation leakage was quite low in most models."[52]

Our evaluation of the quality of appliances is largely based on a detailed study that I conducted in the 1980s and that was published in 1990. There is no evidence provided here on changes in the quality of appliances after the mid-1980s, and none is needed; the basic source of my research, *Consumer Reports* product evaluations from 1938 to 1986, explicitly conclude that there was no further quality improvement in appliances after 1960 for some appliances and after 1970 for others. Though there was doubtless some additional gain in energy efficiency after the mid-1980s for the appliances that had high energy consumption—refrigerators, clothes dryers, and room air conditioners—the other dimensions of quality had reached a plateau by 1970. Though mechanical controls on washers and dryers were replaced by electronic controls in recent decades, these did not improve quality and, indeed, may have increased repair costs. The appliances examined in this section reinforce the overall theme of this book—that along many dimensions, progress was rapid until the early 1970s and then proceeded at a substantially slower pace.

SUBURBANIZATION AND SPRAWL

In 1939–40, the futuristic highways and mass-built single-family houses that had been previewed at the 1939 New York World's Fair seemed a distant dream. But in the great consumer boom that was initially fueled by forced wartime saving, that dream world swiftly became a reality. The shortage of housing at war's end was intense:

> People were doubled up with relatives, friends, and strangers. Veterans lived in converted chicken coops and camped out in cars. The need for shelter was only expected to grow as waves of demobilized veterans, wartime savings at the ready, married and formed new households.[53]

Though a few cities having well-developed commuter rail networks, such as Boston, New York, Philadelphia, and Chicago, had suburban settlements near the railroad stations from the mid-nineteenth century, in most cities the development of the suburbs awaited the spread of automobile ownership. After the depressed housing demand of the 1930s and the prohibition of residential construction during World War II, after 1945 the growing population spilled outside the city limits of the central city of each metropolitan area. Single-family housing units were built in the 1940s and 1950s in the inner suburbs, in the 1970s and 1980s in the outer suburbs, and after 1990 in what became known as the "exurbs." Spurred on by growing family sizes during the baby boom, middle-class parents fled the central city, leaving central cities in which residential segregation in some cities isolated the African American population in what became known as urban ghettoes.

The distinction between the city and the suburb can be overdone. Adjectives to describe each exaggerate the differences. Cities can be described as bad (dangerous, polluted, concrete) or good (diverse, dense, stimulating), and so can suburbs (homogeneous, sprawling, and dull vs. safe, healthy, and green).[54] In fact, many areas within the city limits closely resemble suburbs, such as Chicago's bungalow belt, built largely in the 1920s. Within New York City, most of the dwelling units of Queens and Staten Island have front and back yards. Many American cities grew by annexation of surrounding suburbs and even whole counties, and most of cities such as Minneapolis, Houston, Phoenix, and Los Angeles are largely suburban in character. The suburban-like dwellings built before 1940 were built on small lots fairly close to the street, creating compact neighborhoods where one could walk to the store or to the park. The automobile was accommodated in many areas by bisecting each block with service alleys so that the garage could be placed in the back of the lot, facing the alley rather than the street.[55]

When the war ended, the readiness of millions to pursue their suburban dream was palpable:

> It was a potent image. Soldiers returning home, after all, wanted nothing more than to get on with their lives. They wanted to start families. They wanted to purchase new homes and new cars. They wanted all of the things that had seemed impossible before the war when the country was suffering under the weight of the Great Depression. The expectation after the war was that the good life was finally here, that something better than the 1930s was ahead. Whatever they were offered by the enticing advertisements of newly available consumer goods, they were ready and willing and eager to support it, and they could afford to buy after years of high wages, high savings, and nothing to buy.[56]

Postwar suburbs were built on a vast scale with the main priority to achieve the lowest possible price. The early postwar Levittown on Long Island eventually grew to house 80,000 people, and a four-room Cape Cod cottage was marketed for $7,990 in 1949. The GI Bill meant that for many veterans, no down payment was required, and monthly mortgage payments were often lower than renting a small apartment. The interior size of the Levittown cookie-cutter houses amounted to only 750 square feet, just a third the size of the median single-family house built over the past two decades, and indeed, these houses were substantially smaller than the urban bungalows described in chapter 4.

The postwar subdivisions were oriented around the individual lot, often with much of the space wasted by a large front lawn and with any architectural charm defaced by a front-facing two-car garage integrated into the house. There was no central town square, and schools and shopping centers were scattered randomly about, each surrounded by a large parking lot, being accessible only by automobile. Nevertheless, parents valued the privacy and outdoor space available in the new suburbs and in many cases built room additions to enlarge the interior space of their tract houses.

As part of the lack of planning, most subdivision developers made no provision for commerce. Suburban residents were expected to drive to the nearest town that offered retail commerce or even to drive back into the central city to shop. Finally, starting in the mid-1950s, the suburban shopping center and shopping mall began to develop. The new regional shopping centers were the obvious solution to the swelling numbers of suburban residents who had no convenient place to shop, and the incentive to develop these centers was amplified by the relatively high incomes of the suburbanites. For instance, whereas the 30 million people that *Fortune* magazine counted as suburban residents in 1953 represented 19 percent of the total U.S. population, they accounted for 29 percent of personal income.[57] The large suburban malls became the new town centers for postwar America.

Initially, the central mall was outdoors rather than being enclosed in the mid-1950s malls such as Old Orchard near Chicago and the Garden State Plaza in Paramus, New Jersey, just over the George Washington Bridge from Manhattan. The department anchor stores could be entered either from the massive parking lots or from the interior mall, whereas most of the smaller satellite retailers faced toward the mall rather than toward the parking lot. The developer controlled signage and every other aspect of the mall, down to the type of lighting, benches, and plantings that softened the atmosphere of the mall. Central management and planning contrasted starkly with the lack of planning of the subdivisons themselves. Advantages of the malls were compared to the "inefficiencies and visual chaos" of traditional downtown shopping centers. The virtues of shopping malls were abundant:

> Parking was plentiful, safety was ensured by hired security guards, delivery tunnels and loading courts kept truck traffic away from shoppers, canopied walks and air-conditioned stores made shopping comfortable year 'round, piped-in background music replaced the cacophony of the street.[58]

Suburban sprawl and the regional shopping center did not benefit everyone. Increasingly, families in the outer neighborhoods of the central cities began to shop in the controlled shopping mall environment and shunned the previous bus or streetcar trip to the central city. As middle-class shoppers went elsewhere, downtown shopping districts were left with a clientele that lacked cars and that was dependent on public transportation. Downtown stores began to close, particularly in cities that lacked a dense public transportation network. "In promoting an idealized downtown, shopping centers ... tried to filter out not only the inefficiencies and inconveniences of the city but also the undesirable people who lived there."[59]

Artists and intellectuals were disdainful of suburbs from the start. They were repulsed by the portrayal of suburbs as "brainless utopias" in the television sitcoms of the 1950s and 1960s. Much of the negativism reflected class divisions—those leaving the cities for the new suburbs of the 1950s were the former working class who were in the process of becoming middle class, including factory workers, retail store employees, and school teachers. By the 1970s, the suburbs were stigmatized by the conformity of the subdivision cookie-cutter architecture and a perceived focus on accumulating appliances and other possessions rather than participating in the cultural events of the city.[60]

Urban density can be measured by the population per square mile of the defined land area of each metropolitan area. These range from 1,414 people per square mile in Birmingham, Alabama, to 5,319 in the massive New York metropolitan area that stretches from eastern Long Island to Princeton, New Jersey. Surprisingly, Los Angeles, despite its reputation for sprawl, is the densest U.S. metropolitan area, at 6,999 people per square mile.[61] By contrast, the population density of Manhattan is 83,286 per square mile; for the city of Paris, the figure is 63,298.[62] Research extending from 1940 to 2000 shows an unambiguous decline in the density of metropolitan areas. The causes all point in the same direction—newly incorporated urban areas tend to have lower densities than older areas, and older cities such as Houston and Jacksonville have added land through annexation faster than they have added population.[63]

The postwar development of American metropolitan areas has differed from that in other developed countries, particularly western Europe and Japan. The most obvious difference is population growth. The U.S. population more than doubled between 1950 and 2015, whereas that of the United Kingdom grew by 15 percent, that of Italy by 17 percent, and that of Germany by 18 percent. A second reason is the lack of zoning and land use regulations, such as the British green belts, that limit the extent to which large European cities can spread, and the automobile-free pedestrian zones in many large European cities that promote center-city shopping. In fact, to the extent that America has any land-use regulations, they promote sprawl by limiting suburban lot sizes to a minimum of one or two acres in many places.

A third reason is the much faster diffusion of motor vehicles in the United States than in other countries. In 1929, the United States accounted for 90 percent of the world's motor vehicle registrations. Americans were the first to choose how far from the center city to live, and to some extent their choice of a low-density solution reflected the ready availability of auto transport. But more was involved than the availability of automobiles—a fourth reason was the decision of all levels of American government to subsidize construction of urban expressways while starving public transport and passenger rail. In turn, the low density of the resulting suburban sprawl made it impossible to serve outlying areas economically with public transit. Yet another area in which public policy matters, and the fifth reason for low suburban density, is the deduction of mortgage interest payments from personal taxes in the United States but not in many other countries. This tax deduction, which grows with the size and expense of a home, has been called "the mansion subsidy" and is widely interpreted as a major cause, together with zoning laws, of the much larger house sizes in the United States than in Japan or Europe.[64]

The suburban sprawl in the United States compared to that in Europe has advantages in productivity that help to explain why the core western European countries never caught up to the U.S. productivity level and have been falling behind since 1995. Careful research studies of the sources of the European productivity advantage focus on the retail and wholesale trade sectors.[65] The ease in the United States of building highly efficient "big-box" stores near suburban interstate highway junctions raises productivity through economies of scale and the ease of segregating truck traffic from customer entrances. One only need drive through central Milan or Rome to be impressed with the small sizes of the shops and to gaze in amazement as several men carry a single mattress out of a tiny shop for delivery in a small truck to a customer who may live in a walk-up fourth-story apartment. The European land use regulations that contain suburban sprawl and protect inner-city pedestrian districts have substantial costs in reducing economy-wide productivity and real output per capita.

Another problem in the United States that barely exists in Europe is the decaying Rust Belt American industrial city, of which Detroit has become the poster child. The extent to which the population has moved away from the northern industrial cities to their suburbs and to warmer climates in the south and southwest is stunning. From 1950 to 2010, the population of the city of Chicago declined by 25.5 percent, that of Philadelphia by 26.3 percent, that of Cleveland by 56.1 percent, that of Detroit by 61.4 percent, and that of St. Louis by 62.7 percent. Though the downtowns of Chicago and Philadelphia are thriving, parts of central Cleveland, Detroit, and St. Louis resemble ghost towns. With this extent of population loss, vacant, abandoned, and demolished houses are inevitable. The British consul in Chicago told me in 2012 that his biggest surprise after three months on his new job was the "utter decay and deterioration of many Midwestern industrial cities."[66] The literature on the decline in urban density appears to have neglected the sharp loss of population in the industrial cities of the northeast and Midwest.[67]

The decay of central cities can be traced to many causes, and racial discrimination plays a major role. During the 1940s and 1950s, there was an epochal migration of southern black sharecroppers to the northern cities, particularly Chicago and Detroit, drawn initially by the employment opportunities provided in the tight labor markets of World War II. The Ford Motor Company, which had built, with government financing, the gigantic Willow Run factory that ultimately completed a heavy B-24 bomber every hour, was desperate to find workers, no matter their level of skill. Ford hired agents to circulate petitions throughout rural Mississippi and Alabama to lure African Americans to take a chance on participating in the American dream. The migration continued after the war as civilian demand flooded the factories of the industrial Midwest with orders and the need for more workers. In the late 1940s, as many as 2,000 migrants per week arrived at the Illinois Central Station in Chicago.

They found jobs, at least during the great age of U.S. manufacturing that lasted from 1941 to 1972. But they faced the problem of where to live. Crammed into tenement-like apartments designed for smaller numbers of residents, and in some cases with middle-class incomes, the black migrants wanted to buy their own houses. But contemporary America conspired to block that desire, starting with the decision of the Federal Housing Authority to "red-line" any residential area deemed "unstable." Because white residents of the areas adjacent to those where the blacks lived refused to live in racially integrated neighborhoods, they fled to the suburbs as soon as a few black families moved in, and this then caused the area to be designated as "unstable." The result was that most black families that bought houses in Chicago in the 1950s were unable to obtain conventional mortgage financing and instead relied on contract financing that sold them houses at inflated prices, with repayment contracts that carried high interest rates, and that did not allow the residents to build home equity. Hence was born the urban ghetto that spread to large areas of Chicago, Detroit, and other cities in the Midwest and northeast. It was ironic that the same federal government that a few years later in 1964 passed sweeping Civil Rights legislation was also a major factor in sustaining urban segregation and creating urban poverty.[68]

After the 1960s, central city manufacturing went into a decline that was in large part caused by globalization. Imports began to replace goods that formerly had been made in central-city manufacturing plants, and American multinational corporations moved some or all of their manufacturing operations to foreign countries. This happened at the same time as the moving of manufacturing from crowded multistory and inefficient plant structures to "greenfield" sites in the suburbs of the old northern industrial cities and increasingly to the southern states. The combined effect of all this movement has been to increase inequality, as central cities lost the unionized blue-collar jobs that had been the foundation of their prosperity in the 1950s and 1960s. Racial segregation in the suburbs was even more extreme than in the cities, enforced by government loan policies and "redlining" by local bankers.[69]

In the most distressed cities such as Detroit, Newark, and St. Louis, as jobs and residents disappeared, many owners walked away from buildings, some of which were torn down and others of which were destroyed by arson. "It became common to compare American city centers with Dresden after the war and to marvel that a country rich enough to put a man on the moon could let such a thing happen to its city centers."[70]

As American suburbs matured, problems intensified, starting with political fragmentation. Although some cities, such as Houston and Jacksonville, Florida, annexed most of their suburbs and maintained central government control, in most other cities, the central city limits were fixed, and the suburbs were governed by dozens, if not hundreds, of local, county, and single-purpose agencies. A display of a typical property tax bill for Hempstead, in Nassau County on

Long Island, shows fifteen lines for the separate agencies that benefit from the property tax on a single property.[71] In fact, there are 7,000 separate units of government in the state of Illinois.[72] This multiplicity of political entities, without the metropolitan government established in large areas such as Toronto, enables white, affluent suburban homeowners to use political dividing lines and zoning laws to evade tax burdens for welfare, schools, police, and fire protection for the poor people remaining in the central cities.

Problems built up after 1970 for reasons going beyond political fragmentation and social exclusion. On Long Island, the transition from commuting via railroad to automobile dependence severed the ties with regional institutions, devastated local merchants in cities and towns, and in the case of Hempstead "left the village a hollow shell of its former self, as its commercial and cultural functions dispersed. … [N]o centre exists as a focus of regional coordination."[73]

The increasing relative price of housing has created a new set of challenges. In 1967, the median price of a new housing unit was 2.9 times median household income, but by 2011, this had increased to 4.5 times median household income.[74] This increase reflected both the increased relative price of housing construction, the higher relative price of land in desirable areas, and the stagnation of median household income that in part emerged as a side effect of growing inequality after the late 1970s. Children of the early suburban migrants increasingly find that they cannot afford to buy housing units as convenient to centers of employment as did their parents, although the dispersion of factories, offices, and shopping centers eased what otherwise would have been an impossible time burden of commuting to the central city.

CONCLUSION: THE NARROWING SCOPE OF PROGRESS

As previewed at the beginning of this chapter, the pace of economic progress since 1940, and particularly since 1970, has not been as widespread or revolutionary as during the 1870–1940 interval treated in part I of the book. This theme is evident in the evolution of the three necessities—food, clothing, and shelter—treated here.

For food and clothing the changes that occurred during 1870–1940 were more important than anything that happened after 1940. Food consumption and marketing were transformed in the decades after 1870, as processed food was invented, as the purity and safety of milk and meat were achieved, and as the marketing of food experienced its transition from small country and city merchants to chain stores and supermarkets. The changes after 1940 have been minor by comparison. Frozen foods became an option in addition to canned and packaged products. As household income rose, the share of household income devoted to food declined precipitously, from 45 percent in 1870 to 13 percent in 2012, and a much higher share of that 2012 food consumption occurred outside the home in fast food shops and casual dining restaurants.

Developments related to food consumption were unambiguously positive before 1940 but have not been since then. After a century of food consumption of a constant number of daily calories, after 1970 calories consumed have increased by about 20 percent. And the result has been predictable—the conversion of a lean and fit America into the most obese of all developed countries. Tragically the increase in obesity has traveled hand in hand with the increase of income inequality and the failure of the United States to conquer poverty. Urban ghettoes, food deserts, and other symptoms of poverty result in the dependence of poor people on junk food. And the absence of a comprehensive nationwide health care system leaves the poor overly dependent on emergency rooms for the acute care that could have been avoided by provision of preventive medical care across all income levels.

The second necessity is clothing. The most important shift in this area, freeing of women and girls from the obligation to sew their own clothing, had been accomplished by 1940. The postwar era involved mainly a transition in styles, both at home and at work, toward a more casual and less expensive wardrobe. Retail options blossomed as Walmart and Target allowed customers to browse through large selections of clothing at rock-bottom prices, and the arrival of inexpensive imported clothing at these and other big-box stores contributed to a sharp decline in the relative price of clothing. The rise of the big-box chains had negative consequences, including the decimation of central-city department stores and the flood of imports that virtually eliminated textile and clothing manufacture as a part of the American economy.

Beyond food and clothing, this chapter has provided a multidimensional overview of changes in housing. After fifteen years in which there had been very little residential construction during the Great Depression and World War II, after 1945 the race was on to provide housing to satisfy the excess demand of the millions who as a result of the war had substantial savings and much higher wages than before the war. Additional pressure for an increase in the supply of housing came from the baby boom itself, as the population increased rapidly, by 20 percent in the decade of the 1950s alone. The cities were full, the land in the suburbs was cheap, and so America diverged from western Europe in pursuing a path of urban development that was more dispersed, with the population distributed at a much lower density, than any precedent in the urban history of developed countries. An important contributor to sprawl was arithmetic—the U.S. population more than doubled between 1950 and 2010, whereas population growth in countries such as Germany, Italy, and the United Kingdom was less than 20 percent.

Suburban development began with small houses on small lots, but all the suburban houses had yards that provided fresh air and a release from the congestion of the central city. The postwar suburbs were notable for the lack of planning of central public spaces and the lack of access to public transit. Gradually, new construction built larger houses on larger lots, and this enlargement of the typical American home continued until in 2012, the average newly constructed single-family house had triple the square feet of one built in the late 1940s. Because half of American dwellings (as of 2015) were built after 1977, these much larger houses contained all the modern appliances and were built with central air conditioning. As revolutionary as air conditioning window units seemed in the first half of the postwar era, they have become ever less necessary as the average year of construction has advanced, year by year. Newly built houses incorporated additional features that went beyond the appliances of the 1950s, including built-in microwave ovens, undercounter kitchen lighting, and ceiling fans even in air-conditioned rooms, as well as outdoor hot tubs and propane gas grills.

Though the increase in house sizes was steady, the trajectory of the adoption of the major appliances was not steady, nor was the increase in their quality. There is a sharp distinction between the first half and last half of the interval covered in this chapter. Progress was rapid in adopting appliances until by 1975, the rates of adoption had reached the same levels as prevail today, except for the microwave oven and central air conditioning. There is an uncanny similarity in the frequent evaluations of household appliances by *Consumer Reports (CR)*. Quality and capabilities were poor in the late 1940s but then improved so quickly that by 1970, the *CR* product reports agreed that quality issues and defects had all but disappeared for all major appliances, and there was no further need to report about product quality. Indeed, there is no longer any need for *CR* to publish reports on the major consumer appliances, and it rarely does so.

In addition to a sense of stasis after 1975 in the evolution of food, clothing, and household equipment, there are additional negatives to consider that partly offset the ever-growing size of houses. Among the most obvious are the inherent defects of the American urban model of low density, subsidization of public highways, and starvation of public transit. The result is routine traffic congestion, not to mention high energy consumption as distances extend from home to work. Increased income inequality has been joined by increased social inequality as the upper part of the income distribution lives in their large houses ever farther from the poor, many of whom are still trapped in central city ghettoes and food deserts.

More than for most aspects of the standard of living, the economics of housing location and the locational aspects of the quality of life are intertwined with local politics. The governance of the United States is the opposite of the model of a strong central government that collects revenue at the center and then distributes it rationally according to the merit of projects and the need of the citizens. Instead, the United States has been cordoned off into a multiplicity of local governing units that allow the most prosperous citizens to avoid transferring financial resources to poorer districts. This matters especially for local schools, which are primarily financed by local property taxes. Fiscal inequality worsens the inequality of educational inputs and consequently the educational achievement of students living in rich versus poor school districts. In this way, local school finance begets an increase of income inequality in the next generation, perhaps the most pernicious effect of postwar suburbanization in the United States.

Chapter 11

SEE THE USA IN YOUR CHEVROLET OR FROM A PLANE FLYING HIGH ABOVE

See the USA in your Chevrolet, America is asking you to call,
Drive your Chevrolet through the USA, America's the greatest land of all.

—*The Dinah Shore Chevy Show* theme song, 1952

How the curse of distance was lifted from the human race.

—T. A. Heppenheimer, 1995

INTRODUCTION

The internal combustion engine shares with the commercialization of electricity the gold medal for the two most important inventions of all time, by one of history's remarkable coincidences invented within ten weeks of each other in the fall of 1879. By 1940, the internal combustion engine had made possible automobiles, trucks, busses, and early commercial aircraft that utterly changed transportation speeds, comfort, safety, and convenience, as well as tractors that by the early 1930s had begun to revolutionize agricultural productivity. The ratio of motor vehicles to the number of American households had reached 90 percent by 1929, a year when the United States accounted for 80 percent of the world's motor vehicle production and 90 percent of its registrations.

With the post-1945 emergence of America from the Great Depression and World War II, the automobile moved the nation forward into the modern age. The pioneering efforts of Henry Ford to mass-produce the automobile and offer affordable prices for average Americans created a new product called "personal travel" and a host of new business opportunities to build supermarkets, motels, drive-in movies, drive-in restaurants, and the other new businesses made possible by the near-universal possession of personal automobiles. The increasing number of two-car families reflected in part the lack of public transportation in the suburbs that required many families to acquire a second car.

Another major contributor to postwar prosperity, the construction of the vast interstate highway system, was largely concentrated in the years 1958–72. The new multi-lane highway network greatly increased the productivity of truck drivers, shortened the duration of personal trips, and increased safety. The interstate highway system ranks along with the growing array of appliances within the home as two of the most important elements in the rapid progress of the American standard of living between 1945 and 1972, but subsequently the pace of progress was slower both inside the home and in surface travel.

Air travel increased by a factor of 300, from nine passenger miles per person in 1940 to 2,660 in 2013. Just as automobiles had gained the basic attributes of comfort and speed by 1940, the technology of air travel was already well advanced by 1940. As we shall see in this chapter, an airline trip from New York to Chicago in 1940 took little more time than in 2014, with relatively more of the journey spent in the air and less on the ground. Air travel reached its pinnacle of comfort and speed in the early 1970s, by which time both long-haul and short-haul air travel had been converted from piston engines to jets. The transition to jets was also accompanied by a substantial quality improvement in the form of reduced noise and vibration. Thus for air travel, as for so many other aspects of consumer welfare, the year 1970 is a watershed year marking the dividing line between rapid progress and slower evolutionary growth.

But the situation after 1970 was worse than a mere slowing in the rate of forward progress, because some aspects of transportation began to exhibit retardation. After dominating automobile production and sales throughout the postwar years, the big three American automobile companies (General Motors, Ford, and Chrysler) witnessed the gradual erosion of their unchallenged reign. The epochal rise and fall of General Motors, bedeviled with poor styling, safety issues, and foreign competition, ended with its 2009 bankruptcy and subsequent government bailout. Motor vehicles also raised environmental issues as they released dangerous levels of carbon monoxide, nitrous oxide, hydrocarbons, and other pollutants into the atmosphere. Though automobile travel had improved the urban environment by reducing horse pollution on city streets in the early twentieth century, air quality suffered as smog clouded cities in a blurry, brownish haze by the middle of the twentieth century. Strict government regulations requiring antipollution devices, as well as government-mandated improvements in safety equipment and fuel efficiency, have dominated changes in the quality of automobiles over the past four decades. The ability of a car or light truck to move passengers and their cargo from point A to point B has changed little since the 1950s, as travel speeds were constrained then, as now, by speed limits and congestion rather than by engine power.

Half of this chapter is devoted to the evolution of the automobile, personal travel culture, and the spread of the interstate highway network. Because there was no mention of air travel in chapter 5, the chapter on pre-1940 transportation, the second half of this chapter goes back to the beginning of U.S. commercial airline travel in 1926 and highlights the surprising extent of the progress achieved in the decade between 1926 and 1936, not to mention the further strides of air travel after World War II. No mention is made in this chapter of the decline and near disappearance of intercity passenger rail travel, whose demise was inevitable because of the low population density of the United States outside the northeast corridor and because of the heavy subsidies provided by the government to both the highway and air traffic control networks.

THE CONTOURS OF CHANGE IN POSTWAR TRAVEL

Today, travel in the United States is by motor vehicle, local urban transit, or airplane. There is no discussion here of post-1940 developments in urban transit, because they differed in each metropolitan area. Everywhere there was the early postwar replacement of the streetcar by the bus. Several areas, particularly Atlanta, Washington, and San Francisco, benefited by the development of entirely new heavy rail rapid transit systems, whereas light rail systems emerged in cities such as Dallas and Denver that previously lacked any type of fixed-rail urban transit.

Table 11–1 exhibits the history of motor vehicles per household. Trucks must be included, for consumers increasingly turned from automobiles to light trucks after 1970. One of the most surprising facts in this book, reported in chapter 5, is that, starting from zero in 1900, there were already eighty-nine motor vehicles per 100 households as early as 1929. The table traces total registrations per household for every twenty years between 1910 and 2010. After the sharp leap from two to eighty-nine in 1930, the ratio increased modestly to 113 in 1950 and then jumped to 171 in 1970. Thus the decades of the 1950s and 1960s are those when two-car households became common. Subsequent

Table 11–1. Motor Vehicle Registration per Household, Cars, Trucks, and Total, Percentages, Selected Years, 1910–2010

Year	1910	1930	1950	1970	1990	2010
Automobiles per Household	2.3	76.8	92.6	140.8	143.2	112.1
Trucks per Household	0.1	12.2	19.7	29.6	58.4	94.5
Total Motor Vehicles per Household	2.3	89.2	112.9	171.0	202.3	207.3

Sources: MV registration after 1995 from SAUS Table 1119, MV registration before 1995 from HSUS Series Df339-342

increases in the vehicles-per-household ratio were modest—to 202 in 1990 and then to 207 in 2010. Thus the great transformation of America to a motorized society was essentially over by 1970, another metric by which the early 1970s mark a dividing line between rapid and slower progress.

Figure 11–1 plots vehicle miles per person for motor vehicles and passenger miles per person for railroads and airlines on a log scale that extends from 1 at the bottom to 10,000 at the top. To the extent that most vehicle trips are taken for work or shopping involving only one occupant, the three lines in the chart are comparable. Vehicle miles per person steadily increased, but the growth rate diminished as vehicle travel became a necessity that was little changed after 1950, both in its ability to perform its basic function of transporting a passenger and cargo from one place to another and in its relative price.

By way of contrast, in the first few decades, vehicle miles per person soared from 1.3 in 1900 to 422 in 1919 to 1,623 in 1929. The annualized growth rate from 1919 to 1929 was 13.5 percent per year. Despite the Great Depression, vehicle miles per person continued to grow during the 1930s, declined sharply in World War II as a result of gasoline rationing, but then soared again after the war albeit at an ever-decreasing rate of growth. The growth rate between 1929 and 1950 was 6.2 percent, followed by an acceleration to 8.0 percent between 1950 and 1980. But then diminishing returns set in; the annual growth rate from 1980 to 2012 was a mere 1.1 percent. In fact, vehicle miles per person in 2012 were 6.4 percent *lower* than in 2004.

Airline revenue passenger miles (RPMs), also shown in figure 11–1, exhibited the same phenomenon of slowing growth. It is natural for any industry

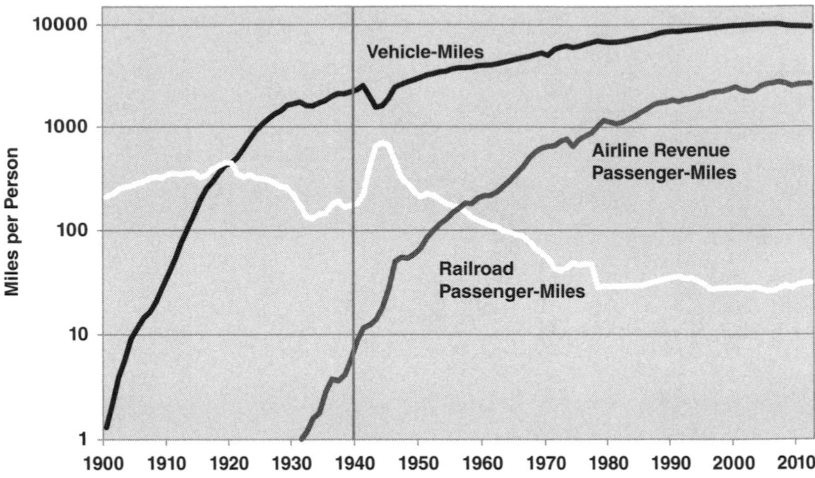

Figure 11–1. Vehicle-Miles per Person, Railroad Passenger-Miles per Person, and Airline Revenue Passenger-Miles per Person, 1900–2012

Source: Federal Highway Administration Table VM-201, HSUS series Df413-415, Df903, Df950, and Aa7, Traffic Safety Facts NHTSA Chapter 1 Table 2, SAUS 2014 Table 1120, A4A Annual Results U.S. Airlines Table, HSUS Series Df1126-1138, Airline RPM after 1948 from A4A Annual Results U.S. Airlines Table, Airline RPM before 1948 from HSUS Series Df1126-1138, National Transportation Statistics Table 1–40. Railroad Data interpolated between 1980–1990.

to experience rapid growth after a fundamental invention and then to have demand for its product level off as the product reaches maturity. Growth in RPMs per person reached 32 percent per year between 1940 and 1960, 16.5 percent between 1960 and 1980, and 7.8 percent between 1980 and 2000. Traffic tripled in the 1950s, tripled again in the 1960s, doubled in the 1970s, and almost doubled in the 1980s before slowing to a crawl. RPMs per person stopped growing after 2000, with the growth rate between 2000 and 2013 at the turtlelike pace of 0.6 percent per year.

Leaving aside the years of World War II, railroad passenger miles per person reached their peak at 448 in 1919, then began their long descent as automobile trips began to replace rail travel. Miles per person fell to 256 in 1929, and after the collapse in traffic during the Depression and peak during the war, they were back down to 225 by 1950, fell by half during 1950–59, fell by another half between 1959 and 1970, and by 2012 had declined to a mere thirty-two miles per person. In fact, air traffic surpassed rail travel as early as 1956.

THE ALREADY POWERFUL AUTOMOBILE ADDS QUALITY AND CONVENIENCE

The increase in automobile sales in the early postwar years created a two-way virtuous circle for the U.S. economy. The motor vehicle industry enjoyed sales which jumped from the business-cycle peak achievements of 5.3 million cars and trucks sold in 1929 and 4.7 million in 1941 to 7.9 million in 1950 and 9.1 million in 1955. The ability to achieve a near doubling of automobile production between 1941 and 1955 attests to postwar benefits conferred by the large additions to plant capacity made possible by federal government plant expansion expenditures during World War II (discussed in chapter 16).[1] This rapid expansion in motor vehicle production and sales fueled rapid growth in productivity and GDP, and these increases in personal income in turn enabled working families to afford not just one car but two, thus completing the virtuous circle back to increasing vehicle production and sales.

By the 1950s, the multiplicity of automobile models created a set of images defined by branding and styling. The Cadillac, Lincoln, and the Chrysler Imperial were for the ancien régime of inherited wealth and for the executive suite. The four-hole Buick Roadmaster connoted the vice president, while the three-hole Buick Century was for the rising midlevel executive, the owner of the local retail business or restaurant. Farther down the perceived chain of status were the Oldsmobile, the Pontiac, and the ubiquitous Chevrolet, America's best-selling car year after year, eagerly bought by the new unionized working class that, in its transition to solid middle-class status, could afford to equip its suburban subdivision house with at least one car, and often two.

The evolution of automobile quality in the postwar era requires a different approach than the sections in chapter 10 devoted to the improved quality of household appliances. Our study of appliance quality shows that most of the quality improvements, particularly improvements in energy efficiency, were missed by the government price indexes, so that consumer welfare benefits of improving appliance quality were omitted from GDP. The ratio of omitted benefits to those included in GDP was unity for refrigerators, double for room air conditioners, and (as we shall see in chapter 12) a ratio of ten or more times for television sets. But the official price indexes for automobiles were compiled differently, for automobiles were treated as a special case. Each year, officials of the Consumer Price Index (CPI) obtained from Detroit the estimated value of quality improvements, including each individual item, such as the cost of installing seat belts or a heavier and more crash-resistant bumper.

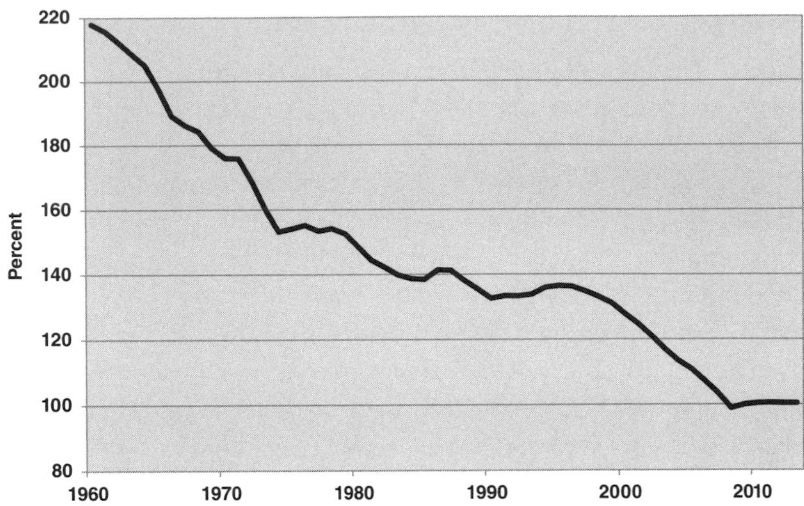

Figure 11–2. Relative Price Deflator for New Motor Vehicles, 1960–2013 (2009 = 100)

Source: Detail underlying NIPA Table 2.4.4, Series DNDCRG and DNFCRG.

It is not surprising that because of the greater attention to measuring the quality change of automobiles, the price of automobiles increased much more slowly than the overall rate of inflation. Figure 11–2 displays since 1960 the price deflator for new motor vehicles relative to that of all consumption goods and services. Over more than half a century between 1960 and 2014, the relative price fell by more than half, but its decline occurred at an irregular pace. The annual rate of change for 1960–74 was a rapid –2.4 percent per year, then a much slower –0.9 percent during 1974–90, and a near hiatus of –0.4 percent during 1990–2000, followed by a more rapid rate of –2.8 percent during 2000–2008. There was no decline at all between 2008 and 2013. The overall deflator for consumption goods and services increased between 1950 and 2013 by a factor of 7.6, but that of automobiles increased by a much smaller factor of 4.1.

The average price of a new car (including light trucks) increased from $2,300 in 1950 to $24,100 in 2012. How is this tenfold increase in price to be explained if the CPI's price index for automobiles increased only by a factor of four? By definition, the answer must be that the average quality of motor vehicles greatly improved. The white line in figure 11–3 plots the average current-dollar price of vehicles sold between 1950 and 2012, illustrating the tenfold

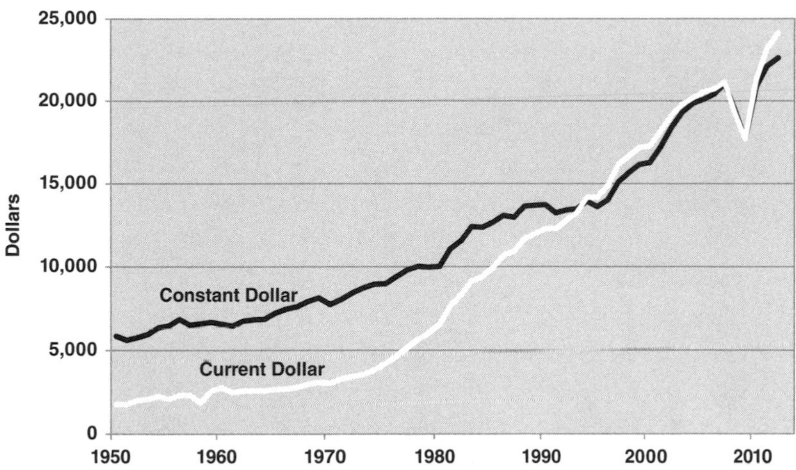

Figure 11–3. Spending per Motor Vehicle, Current and Constant 2009 Dollars, 1950–2012

Source: HSUS Table Df347-352 before 1996, SAUS 2014 edition Table 1082 after 1996. Data interpolated in even-numbered years between 1950 and 1962.

increase on a logarithmic scale. When the nominal (current-dollar) sales prices of the vehicles are converted into fixed 2009 prices, the black line records the inflation-adjusted sales price per car. Thus the black line represents the implicit quality of cars.[2] Another way of thinking about the black line is that it shows an ever-increasing amount of real quality per car. The increase in quality appears to be relatively steady, growing at 2.3 percent between 1950 and 1970, 2.5 percent between 1970 and 1990, and 3.2 percent between 1990 and 2014.

By 1940 the American automobile was already powerful, with the power of an ordinary 1940 Chevrolet rated at eighty-five horsepower and the more prestigious General Motors brands, such as Oldsmobile or Cadillac, offering engines of 110 to 125 horsepower. That is enough power to propel a large car at 100 miles per hour, far above the speed limit on any U.S. highway. By 1940, the higher-end GM cars were also offering automatic transmission, a much-appreciated improvement in automobiles that was available on half of cars sold in 1953 and more than 90 percent of cars sold by 1970.

During the early postwar years there was a steady conversion of what were initially accessories, such as automatic transmission, to standard equipment. Automatic transmission was the first and most important of the "power" additions to the standard plain-Jane automobile (such as my parents' 1950

Plymouth with its bench seats, manual transmission, and heater, but nothing else).[3] Initially, even radios were not standard on automobiles, and they were not installed on the majority of automobiles until the early 1960s. Perhaps even more important than automatic transmission was air conditioning, with 50 percent installation reached by 1970 and 84 percent by 1983. Power steering reached 50 percent installation by 1965, as did power brakes by 1970. Power windows were slower to arrive, with an installation rate of only 38 percent by 1983.[4]

The history of the affordability of motor cars is one of the most surprising facts developed in this book. Henry Ford's 1923 Model T had a total price of $265, only 11 percent of current-dollar per-household consumption expenditures in that year. My parents' 1950 Plymouth with a price of $1,520 was a much higher 33 percent. In 2012, the same calculation assesses the average $24,000 vehicle at a somewhat improved 21 percent of per-household consumption expenditures. Despite the multifold increase in the American standard of living since 1923, it may come as a surprising revelation to learn that the Model T Ford was twice as affordable relative to the incomes of that day as is today's typical motor vehicle. No wonder that the well-known automobile journalist Paul Ingrassia wrote, "Historians rightly agree that the Model T Ford is the most important car in American history."[5]

If this seems a paradox, it can be easily resolved by pointing to the very low quality of the Model T by present standards. For most of its production run, it had to be hand-cranked, was available only in one color (black), and had a flimsy body and an engine with a mere twenty horsepower. Still, though, it provided a far superior alternative to the horse, and it was supremely affordable. The mass production methods that Ford developed in the decade 1913–23 were among the essential elements that made possible the surge of productivity between 1920 and 1970 that, among other benefits, was essential in the victory of World War II as well as in achieving postwar prosperity.[6]

An important reason why the price index for automobiles increased so much more slowly than that for overall consumer expenditures was that the CPI procedures treated all government-mandated rulings as representing an increase in automobile quality. Not only were the seat belts and airbags valued as quality improvements at whatever the automakers reported they cost to add to each car, but so was the anti-pollution equipment that the government forced firms to add to vehicle engines as early as 1967. The treatment of the anti-pollution equipment was controversial, as it did not raise the quality of the automobile for the owner and in fact detracted from its value to the extent that it reduced miles per gallon of fuel efficiency. Instead, the anti-pollution equipment created a positive externality that benefited all of society, not just the owner of the automobile.

Between 1967 and 1985, the CPI methodology led to the result that automobile quality had increased by 56 percent. Of this, 12 percent was the result of safety devices, 25 percent of anti-pollution equipment, and another 12 percent of other changes, such as making automatic transmissions or power steering standard on some models.[7] By comparison, our implicit quality index over the same period increases in figure 11–3 by a similar 66 percent. We conclude that almost half of the CPI's measure of improvements in automobile quality during that period was the result of environmental regulations that did not directly benefit those who purchased the automobiles. There is no doubt that the 1970 Clean Air Act ultimately succeeded in greatly improving the nation's air and, for instance, dramatically reduced the incidence of smog in the Los Angeles basin. But the decision to treat this as an increase in the quality of a motor vehicle instead of more general government infrastructure spending remains a dubious choice by the government statisticians.

AUTOMOBILE FUEL ECONOMY, SAFETY, AND RELIABILITY

Any success in achieving a substantial increase in fuel economy is bound to be the most important contributor to automobile quality—even greater than air conditioning—because fuel consumed over the life of the vehicle costs as much as the vehicle itself. Fuel consumed just in the first four years costs 40 percent or more of the vehicle purchase price.[8] Figure 11–4 displays the average fuel economy of American passenger motor vehicles (including cars and light trucks) and records a 56 percent improvement from 15 miles per gallon in 1950 to 23.5 in 2012. Average fuel economy actually declined between 1950 and 1970 as vehicles became larger, V-8 engines became more powerful, and an increasing percentage of cars were equipped with air conditioning. The changes in fuel economy caused by the mix of different sizes and types of cars do not represent a change of the technology of achieving fuel economy.

The data underlying figure 11–4 show that average fuel economy improved by 23 percent between 1967 and 1984. But that is a significant underestimate of the improvement in fuel economy technology. The central problem is that any change in the mix of cars can raise or lower fuel economy without any change in

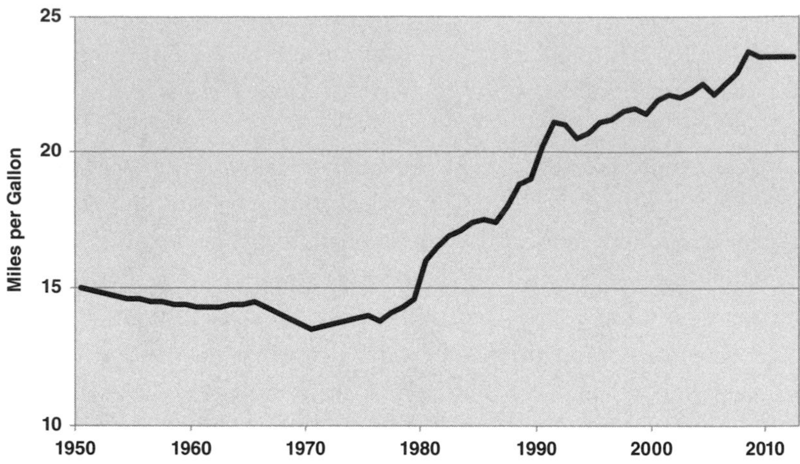

Figure 11–4. Passenger Motor Vehicles Miles per Gallon, 1950–2012
Source: U.S. Department of Energy, *2011 Annual Energy Review,* Table 2-8.

underlying fuel efficiency. For instance, a shift to smaller cars as occurred after the mid-1970s can improve fuel economy, whereas the gradual spread of automobile air conditioning takes its toll on fuel economy.[9] A rough estimate suggests that the improvement through 1984 reduced the price and raised the quality of the average car by 18 percent.[10] This leaves the period from 1984 to 2012, when fuel economy in figure 11–4 rose from 17.5 to 23.5 miles per gallon.[11] The resulting reduction in the price and increase in the quality of the average car was 12 percent, leading to a cumulative improvement in quality from 1967 to 2012 of 35 percent.[12] The increase in the implicit quality of passenger motor vehicles from 1950 to 2012 shown in figure 11–3 (which excludes the effect of fuel economy) is by a factor of 3.7. When we include the value of improved fuel efficiency, the cumulative increase in quality is by a factor of 5.6.[13]

How does this improvement in quality compare with developments before 1940, which witnessed the transition from the seven-horsepower 1906 Oldsmobile to the much more powerful and substantial cars of the late 1930s? Our crude quality index displayed in table 5–2 increases between 1906 and 1940 by a factor of 2.5. Multiply that by the postwar improvement by a factor of 5.6, and we reach the conclusion that today's average vehicle has fourteen times the quality of the 1906 car. The history of quality improvement is shown in figure 11–5 for all attributes excluding the value of improved fuel economy. In today's prices, the quality of a motor vehicle is increased further from the

$23,000 value shown in the chart for 2012 to $34,000 when we include the dollar value of improved fuel economy. Even in recent years, light vehicles have continued to add features such as anti-lock brakes, side-impact airbags, keyless entry, a backup camera, satellite radio, and others.

Another dimension of improvement in the quality of automobile travel is the rapid rate of decline in vehicle fatalities per mile traveled experienced since the birth of the automobile industry. As shown by figure 11–6, fatalities per 100 million vehicle miles have declined steadily from a peak of 45 in 1909 to a trough of 1.1 in 2012. The decline in the fatality rate between 1909 and 2012 evolved at an astounding annual rate of −3.6 percent per year or −36 percent per decade. Better-constructed and more reliable cars deserve some credit, but much of this achievement should be credited not to the makers of automobiles but to the government investments in highway infrastructure that reached their peak in 1958–72 with the construction of the interstate highway system. Until the interstates, driving on two-lane highways was inherently dangerous, as a decision to pass a slow-moving truck or tractor could potentially cause injury and often death from a collision with a car coming in the opposite direction. The interstates eliminated that source of collision. But the interstates did not create the most rapid decline in the fatality rate. That came at the beginning,

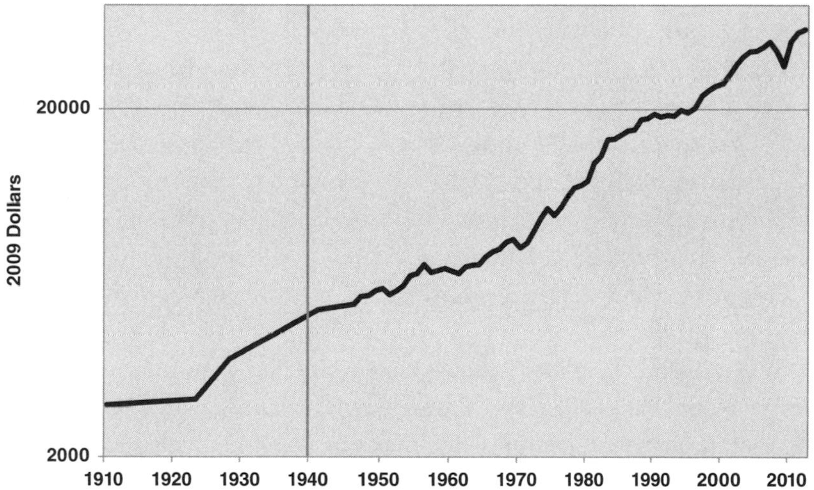

Figure 11–5. Implicit Passenger Motor Vehicle Quality, Constant 2009 Dollars, 1910–2012

Sources: Table 5-2 quality index, NIPA 2.4.3, 2.4.5, and 5.5.5.

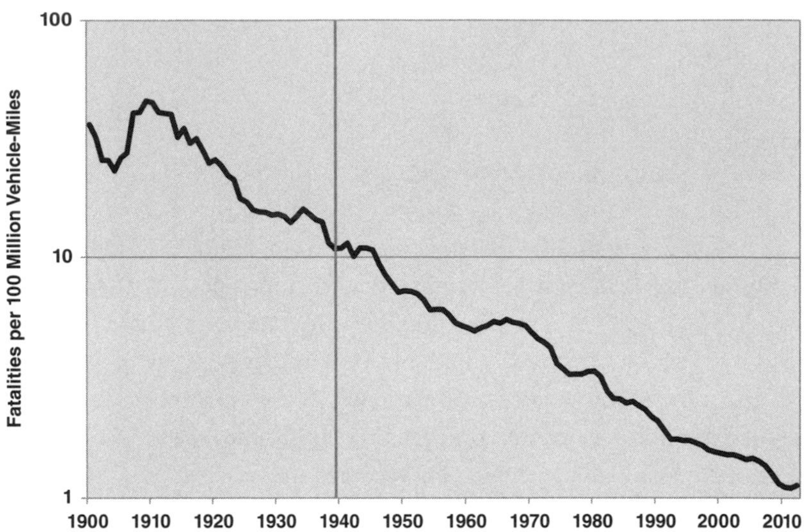

Figure 11–6. Motor Vehicle Fatalties per 100 Million Vehicle-Miles, 1900–2012

Source: HSUS Series Df415 before 1986, Traffic Safety Facts 2012 NHTSA Chapter 1 Table 2 after 1986.

when the rate fell by a factor of three between 1909 and 1926 (an annual rate of –6.2 percent) as a result of improvements in automobile quality and of the first round of improved highways.

Another aspect of automobile quality is the frequency of both routine service and repairs for operating problems. A major improvement has been in the frequency of routine servicing. In the early postwar years, an oil change was mandatory every 1,000 miles, and for an automobile that traveled 12,000 miles per year, that implied an oil change every month.[14] Today's motor vehicles need oil changes only every 7,500 miles, which is attributed to "advances in engine materials, and tighter tolerances, as well as the oil that goes into engines."[15]

The problem of automobile reliability was so significant that an economist won the Nobel Prize in large part for a journal article he wrote on "lemons," a term used at the time for automobiles that had defects in quality and reliability that were invisible to the potential buyer of used cars.[16] Frequent problems with automobiles in the 1950s and 1960s included oil leaks, exhaust smoke caused by excess oil consumption, engine overheating, and compressor failures on early automobile air conditioning units.

The frequency of repairs of American automobiles is recorded in the annual automobile issue published by *Consumer Reports* magazine *(CR)* each April.[17] Though these ratings make it easy to compare cars in a given year, they do not provide any information about what has happened to the "average"—that is, whether cars have experienced a lesser or greater need for repairs over the postwar era. *CR* in 1984 cited an average annual repair cost for a five-year-old model of $360 in current dollars, not far from the $276 per vehicle of annual nominal maintenance and repair expense per registered vehicle recorded in the national income accounts.[18] Unfortunately, similar data are not reported by *CR* in recent decades. However, the national accounts provide data on real inflation-adjusted vehicle maintenance expenditure. Figure 11–7 plots real (2009 price) maintenance and repair expenditure per 1,000 vehicle miles, and there is a slight downward tilt in the line. Comparing the first five years (1950–55) with the last five years (2009–13), the decline is 15 percent. Comparing the first two decades (1950–70) with the last two (1993–2013), the reduction is only 5 percent. These changes are substantial when cumulated over the life of a vehicle and provide further evidence that the quality of automobiles has steadily increased.

One of the most significant changes in the U.S. automobile marketplace in the postwar era was the surge of imported cars; the share of imports in new

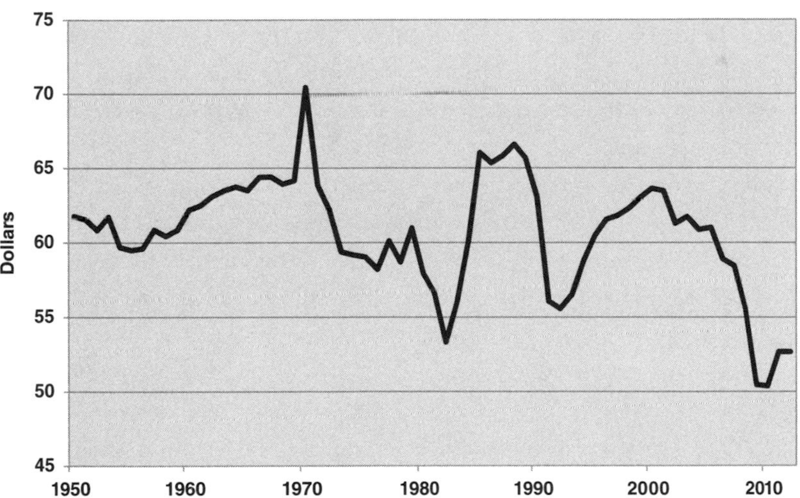

Figure 11–7. Maintenance and Repair Expenditures per 1,000 Vehicle Miles, 2009 Dollars, 1950–2013

Source: NIPA Table 2.4.3

automobile sales rose from a mere 4 percent in 1963 to an all-time peak of 42 percent in 1987. The timing of the upward surge from the mid-1970s to 1980 mainly resulted from the permanent increase in the relative price of gasoline that occurred as a result of the two "oil price shocks" of 1974–75 and 1979–81. During that brief period, the price of oil increased from $3 per barrel to more than $30 per barrel, and the price of gasoline increased from about $0.25 per gallon to $1.25 or more.[19] American companies made no mass-market small, fuel-efficient cars, having failed with the Chevrolet Corvair in the early 1960s, so the market was wide open for the invasion of imports that had already begun in the 1960s with the VW Beetle. The Japanese brands Toyota, Honda, and what was then called Datsun (now Nissan) flooded the American marketplace with small, fuel-efficient cars.

But they were not just small and fuel-efficient. They were of much higher quality than anything Detroit could produce. *CR* repair frequency records, based then as now on hundreds of thousands of questionnaires returned by readers, ranked the Japanese brands better than the American brands by an order of magnitude. The distance between the highest-rated ("much better than average") and lowest-rated cars was a giant chasm—the top category had repair incidents of 2 percent or less of questionnaire respondents, and the worst brands had incidents of 15 percent or more. The 1984 report included 198 different models, of which 147 were domestic brands and fifty-one were imported. Out of 147 domestic models, sixty-three had a black dot (much worse than average), and only one had a red dot (much better than average). Out of the fifty-one imported models, no fewer than thirty-six had red dots, and there were only two exceptions, both Volkswagens. The Japanese brands were rated by *CR* has having a frequency of repair incidence orders of magnitude better than the domestic brands.[20] In the 2014 evaluation the differences between domestic brands and foreign brands (most of them now manufactured in the United States) were narrower, but with only a few exceptions, the only red dots were for foreign brands and the only black dots for domestic brands.

The data used in this section show that there was a gradual increase in miles driven per vehicle from 9,450 in 1950 to 12,500 in 2000, followed by a decline to 12,000 in 2012. The recent decline reflects a change in lifestyles that needs to be taken into account, because a decline in miles traveled per vehicle does not necessarily indicate a decline in the standard of living. Some families may be making sacrifices because of high fuel prices, but others are making choices. The fraction of those aged 16 to 24 who have a driver's license declined from 82 percent in 1983 to 67 percent in 2010.[21] An important new development is the increased allure for young people, who are marrying and having children later in life, of living near the urban center to attach to a community of educated youth, for the restaurants and cultural life, and to be near jobs, which in some of the leading cities are increasingly concentrated downtown, including Boston, New York, Chicago, and San Francisco. Notably, motor vehicle miles per person in 2012 were no higher than in 1997.

THE INTERSTATE HIGHWAY SYSTEM BRINGS SPEED AND SAFETY

When newly elected President Dwight D. Eisenhower took office on January 20, 1953, the United States found itself at a critical historical juncture. In the decade following 1947, Americans purchased 30 million new cars.[22] These automobile owners were desperate for improved roads and highways upon which they could drive their new vehicles. Eisenhower was the ideal president for understanding the conditions of American roads. As a young soldier in 1919, he had been part of a U.S. Army expedition that traveled from Washington, D.C., to San Francisco by automobile, a trip that took sixty-two days to complete. His experiences as Supreme Commander of the Allied Forces in Europe during World War II demonstrated to him the value of having an advanced highway network. Examining the remnants of Germany's infrastructure, Eisenhower was shocked to find how quickly the Allied armies could travel along the autobahns, and he never forgot his experience with roads, both domestic and foreign.

Yet, even before the Eisenhower administration, the federal government recognized the necessity of spending money on a comprehensive national highway system to supplant the original 1916 and 1921 legislation that had created the numbered federal highway system that was largely complete by the end of the 1930s. In 1944, Congress passed the Federal Aid Highway Act, which designated 40,000 miles to be included in a new national interstate highway network. Despite the efforts of President Harry Truman, the implementation of an interstate highway network was pushed aside by the postwar financial demands of the Marshall Plan, the GI Bill, and the Korean War. Comprehensive planning to organize construction of a united network of superhighways and to manage the logistical and financial constraints would be left for the attention of President Eisenhower. By the mid-1950s, government officials had developed a detailed blueprint for the monumental system of limited-access highways spanning more than 40,000 miles.

One of the highways in particular, the Pennsylvania Turnpike, would be a shining example of what American roadways could become. Born out of New Deal public works programs, the Pennsylvania Turnpike was completed in August 1940, covering a 160-mile stretch of rough Pennsylvania terrain from Harrisburg to Pittsburgh. Initial users of the highway were amazed by the quantum leap of the achievement compared to previous highways, where two lanes encouraged passing slow vehicles and frequent deaths through collisions, and where progress was slowed by traffic signals. Travel times were slashed as the new turnpike cut through mountains. Though Americans were proud of the Pennsylvania Turnpike, they were mostly unaware that starting in late 1933 Adolph Hitler had built a network of limited-access autobahns spanning the full extent of Germany, and that these were largely complete by war's outbreak in 1939. The interstate highway system in its comprehensiveness was a belated attempt to duplicate not the Pennsylvania Turnpike but the German autobahn network over a spatial terrain roughly twenty times larger.[23]

Dwight Eisenhower signed into law the Federal Aid Highway Act of 1956, which called for 41,000 miles of interstate highways to be built at an estimated cost of $25 billion, with a planned completion date of 1969.[24] The act split the costs of the project, with the federal government assuming 90 percent of the funding and the states assumed the remaining 10 percent. The Highway Trust Fund was also established to collect revenues from gasoline sales taxes.[25] From the moment of this mandate, the interstate highways were put on firm fiscal ground. The idea to funnel federal sales taxes on gasoline into funding the highways efficiently allocated the costs of the highways to the automobile owners who were most frequent users. Figure 11–8 displays federal highway spending expressed as a ratio to potential GDP. There is a clear bulge upward in the ratio during the peak years of interstate construction during 1955–70, when the ratio was roughly double the level of spending after 1970. But even the peak years of interstate construction did not match the ratio for highway spending in the 1920s and 1930s.

Almost as soon as the first concrete slabs were laid, an immediate economic impact spread across a variety of domestic industries. Research confirms the substantial boost to business productivity created by the interstates during the 1950s through the 1970s. Of the thirty-five industries examined, all but three experienced significant cost reductions because of more versatile and cheaper transport.[26] Another study estimated that interstate highway spending

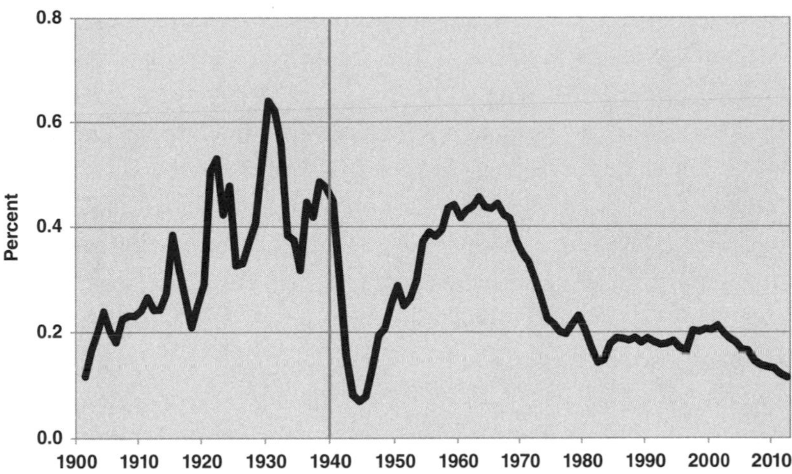

Figure 11–8. Percentage of Government Highway Spending to Potential GDP: 1900–2012

Sources: BEA FA Tables 7.5A, 7.5B, 7.6A, & 7.6B, Berry, Kendrick data (1870–1929) and BEA data (1929–2013), HSUS series Df339-342 before 1995, SAUS 2014 Table 1117 after 1995, MV Registration interpolated between 1995-2000, 2012.

contributed to a 31 percent increase in American productivity during the 1950s and then a subsequent 25 percent increase during the 1960s, but the productivity effect dwindled to a mere 7 percent in the 1980s.[27] Though these numbers are too large to be plausible, the extent of the economy-wide productivity growth slowdown in the 1970s and 1980s is consistent with the theme of this chapter—that the contributions of transportation technology and infrastructure to economic growth slowed substantially after 1970.

The interstates did not extend from coast to coast or from north to south all at once. The long stretches of four-lane road were largely completed by 1972, but small sections remained unfinished, thus delaying the full glory of the non-stop coast-to-coast and north-to south passage "without a traffic light" for another few years. In 1974, Nebraska became the first state to fully complete its single interstate route, I-80. In 1979, the first Canada to Mexico route was completed on I-5 through Seattle, Portland, the central valley of California, all the way to the San Diego border with Mexico. The completion of the first transcontinental interstate, I-80 from the George Washington Bridge in Manhattan to the western terminus of the San Francisco–Oakland Bay Bridge, did not occur until 1986, and the coast-to-coast southern interstate I-10, from

Jacksonville, Florida, to the Santa Monica coast of California, was not completed until 1990. The final link in the original interstate highway map was completed in 1992.[28]

The interstates increased mobility; research studies indicate that the early completion of interstate segments attracted higher rates of population growth. Counties previously lacking major transportation corridors underwent the highest rates of positive demographic change.[29] Even as suburbanites were adjusting to their affluent new domestic lifestyles, they also began to realize ways of spending their free time that had never before been possible, an outgrowth of the theme in chapter 5—that the automobile created as a side effect a new activity called "personal travel."

The new highway network offered the sightseeing and vacation opportunities, but after the war, travel was impeded by the absence of places to stay and to eat. In the 1950s, brand-name hotel franchises started to pop up across the country along interstates at interchanges and exits. Holiday Inn, with its ubiquitous slogan "the best surprise is no surprise," soon came to dominate the motor hotel or "motel" industry. That chain grew from twenty motels in 1956 to more than 500 in 1963.[30] Travel and tourism were direct effects of the interstate highway, and so, by connection, the highways expanded jobs not just in the construction industry, but also in motels and restaurants.

> Out of the car culture of the 1950s came a sprawling highway community similar to but larger in scope than that of the 1920s. As Americans spent more time in their cars, entrepreneurs took notice. And so the 1950s became the "drive-in" decade. Drive-in movie theaters, drive-in restaurants, drive-in banks, drive-in churches, . . . even drive-in funeral parlors. Americans, it seemed, never wanted to leave their cars.[31]

Our treatment of automobile travel has emphasized safety in the form of a reduced fatality rate, as well as substantial progress in reducing pollution as an externality produced by automobile travel. Both safety and anti-pollution devices were installed in automobiles as the result of legislative and regulatory action, and safety benefited as well by the increased percentage of vehicle travel that took place over divided limited-access interstate highways that stretched between cities and connected city and suburbs within metropolitan areas. But, as we have seen, the ratio of spending on highway construction relative to GDP fell by half after 1972, and in many metropolitan areas, traffic congestion became an increasing problem as the growth of vehicle volumes overwhelmed the capacity of the highway system, particularly during rush hours.

COMMERCIAL AIR TRAVEL FROM THE SWALLOW BIPLANE TO THE 777-300

In 1940, the dividing line between part I and part II of this book, air travel was in its infancy. The number of passenger miles per person in 1940 was equal to those for automobile travel in 1904. Nevertheless, the ten years between 1926 and 1936 witnessed by far the greatest advances in the history of commercial aircraft; nothing after 1936 comes close in its magnitude except for the introduction of jet travel in 1958. In the nearly six decades since the first jet flight, there have been no improvements at all in the speed or comfort of air travel. Changes to aircraft have been limited to the conversion of the cockpit to sophisticated electronic controls, a quantum leap in fuel economy similar to that achieved by the automobile industry, a relatively minor increase in the maximum distance an aircraft can fly without refueling, and the introduction of in-flight entertainment options on some aircraft.

Most of the improvements since the beginning of the jet age in 1958 have occurred on the ground, in the form of which routes airlines are allowed to fly, how passengers make their reservations, how many airlines are available to choose from on a given route, and how many stops are required on a typical trip. Quality improvement has not been uniformly positive. The seating space occupied by a typical passenger today is substantially more cramped than in 1958, and much more time must be spent at the airport between the time of a passenger's arrival in the terminal and the time the aircraft door closes before departure.

The story of air travel before 1940 can be told through a depiction of three events: the first U.S. commercial airline flight in 1926, the first long-haul transoceanic flight in 1935, and the first modern domestic airliner introduced in 1936. When linked together, these three events illustrate a rate of technological advance that ranks as among the most rapid in history, along with the introduction of television in the early 1950s and the Internet in the late 1990s. The distance flown in the initial 1926 flight was 411 miles, and nine years later, a plane inaugurated regular service on a route that spanned 2,398 miles.[32]

The first flight occurred on April 6, 1926, on Varney Air Lines, the corporate ancestor of United Airlines, today one of the three largest airlines in the world. Ironically, in 1934, the same Walter Varney founded Continental Airlines, which merged with United in 2010. Thus the corporate roots of both airlines can be traced to the same man. In those days, the main business of airlines was to carry airmail, and the first flight qualifies, even though it carried no passengers, because Varney had acquired the contract for the first-ever commercial airmail route granted by the U.S. Post Office. That first flight, on a plane so tiny that there was room only for one pilot and the mail, traveled on the unlikely routing between Pasco, Washington, and Elko, Nevada,[33] two important railway junctions 411 miles apart. The Swallow biplane was about the same size as a single-engine Cessna propeller aircraft used today to train aviation students at flight schools.

It was 5:30 a.m. on April 6 in Pasco, where reporters, photographers, post office officials, and a crowd of 2,500 people gathered to watch the pilot, Leon Cuddeback, prepare for the epochal flight.

> Cheers filled the air as a stagecoach pulled by a team of six horses came to a halt near the hangar and the riders handed over six sacks of mail containing 9,285 pieces weighing a total of 200 pounds. The mail was loaded aboard and mechanics began hand-pulling the Swallow's prop, but the balky engine refused to crank. Cuddeback became anxious as the 6:00 am departure time came and went. Finally, after 20 minutes of pulling, the engine caught and Cuddeback roared off for Elko.[34]

So well recorded was that day that a letter addressed to Charles J. Rose, U.S. Air Mail Field, Elko, Nevada, signed by the pilot, has pride of place today in the corporate archives of United Airlines.

Now let us flash forward five years to November 19, 1931, in an event involving Charles Lindbergh just four years after his solo transatlantic flight, the first ever, had made him the most famous man in the world. Lindbergh was sitting in an airport lounge with Igor Sikorsky, a Russian immigrant best known for inventing the first viable helicopter in 1939. Together the two men began preliminary sketches on the back of a menu, as they envisaged the plane, to be called the Sikorsky S-42, that four years later would fly the first nonstop service from San Francisco to Honolulu, 2,400 miles away.[35] And that same plane would continue onward to Manila in the Philippines, then an American colony.[36]

Through a curious victory of necessity birthing invention, aircraft designers somehow figured out how to achieve that range at a time when the newly introduced DC-3 carried only twenty-one passengers and could fly only as far as New York to Chicago. Their 1935 achievement occurred eighteen years before aircraft engineers could design a passenger plane capable of flying exactly the same distance from Los Angeles to New York. Not surprisingly, this feat inspired the imagination of a beleaguered America suffering from 20 percent unemployment during the Great Depression.

> The first flight was set for November 22, 1935. Over a hundred thousand San Franciscans were on hand, while CBS and NBC laid on coast-to-coast radio broadcasts. Short-wave facilities carried the ceremonies to Asia, Europe, and South America. The President of the Philippines spoke over the hookup. A letter from President Roosevelt stated, "Even at this distance I thrill to the wonder of it all." A band played, skyrockets flew, and Trippe (founder of Pan American) stepped to the mike. He said simply, "Pilot, you have your sailing orders. Cast off and depart for Manila in accordance therewith."[37]

Considering that it happened in only nine years, this technological leap from one pilot in 1926 carrying 200 pounds of mail a distance of 411 miles to a plane flying 2,450 miles is one of the most breathtaking of all leaps in the history of innovation. The ability of this early aircraft to fly so far was dependent on the fact that it took off from the water rather than land, being the so-called flying boat. This implied that there was no cost of airport construction on the S-42's initial 1935 route going from San Francisco to Manila by way of Honolulu, Midway, Wake, and Guam.[38]

However impressive the technology of the first transpacific flight, it had zero influence on the American standard of living, for the flights carried only twenty passengers once or twice per week. Far more important was the evolution of domestic passenger aircraft. Technological change was so rapid that the most capable plane of its time, the nine-passenger 1929 Ford Trimotor, was eclipsed in 1933 by the fourteen-passenger two-engine Boeing 247. The Boeing was the most advanced aircraft of its day, and was capable of flying from New York to Chicago, with a fifteen-minute stop for refueling in Cleveland, in 5.5 hours.[39]

But this achievement was soon eclipsed by the Douglas DC-3, the speed and range of which revolutionized the air transport industry. It was jointly conceived by Donald Douglas and C. R. Smith, the president of American Airlines, which operated its first flights, departing simultaneously from Newark to Chicago and from Chicago to Newark, on June 26, 1936. The DC-3, which could carry twenty-one passengers in seats or fourteen passengers in sleeper beds, popularized domestic air travel. With three refueling stops, eastbound transcontinental flights could cross the country in only fifteen hours. For instance, a passenger could leave Los Angeles after work and be in New York in time for lunch the next day. The round-trip fare for a sleeper seat was $285, which translates into $3,940 in today's prices. This is almost exactly the same as the current fare of $3,600 to fly from New York to Los Angeles in a business-class seat that extends into a lie-flat bed.[40]

The advance represented by the DC-3 is best captured by its description in a 1937 American Airlines timetable:

> All flights are made in 21-passenger Flagship Club Planes, the largest, most luxurious and quiet land transport planes in America. Your plane is air conditioned before departure and air cooled all the way. Your deep lounge chair brings real relaxation. The journey is short. Read a magazine, chat a while, smoke, take a nap—and then eat a delicious complimentary meal. You arrive feeling as fresh and clean as when you left home.

The timetable also provides the surprising information that the round-trip price of $1,182 (corrected for inflation 1937–2014) was less than the price of the fastest train ($1,185), and an Internet search in September 2014 reveals the remarkable fact that a comparable seat cost $1,179!

We can make further comparisons of the quality of air travel in 1936 versus 2014. The timetable mentions smoking, which was allowed on commercial aircraft for almost the entire history of the airline industry; smoking was not banned until 1998. The saving of time might appear to be a major advantage of modern aircraft, but that is deceiving. The scheduled New York–Chicago flight time in 1936 was three hours, fifty-five minutes versus two hours, thirty-five minutes today, but that includes only the time taken from gate to gate. In 1936, a passenger without checked baggage needed to be at the airport only ten minutes before departure, and the gates were immediately next to the terminal entrance. Upon arrival in Chicago, taxis would be waiting five minutes from the gate. And one could travel downtown from the airport in Chicago in a chauffeured twelve-cylinder Cadillac limousine for the equivalent of $10.50 in today's prices.[41]

In contrast, today's New York–Chicago trip is quite different. For those without bags, the fastest way to travel is to arrive by taxi. Though check-in is swift at an electronic kiosk, there is the risk of long lines at security check points. A traveler with a noon flight to Chicago on American Airlines today would typically arrive by 11:00 a.m. to allow time for the unknown length of the security line and for the walk to the gate in time to board the plane typically twenty minutes before departure. On the Chicago end, at least ten minutes are needed for passengers to get from the middle of the plane to the front door. Then the walk from the gate to the taxi line would take between five and ten minutes. Having arrived at the airport at 11:00 a.m., the traveler finally enters the taxi at 2:50 pm (Eastern Time) in Chicago. The trip in total has taken three hours and fifty minutes, exactly twenty minutes shorter than the 1936 trip.

The civilian version of the DC-3 was produced between 1936 and 1941. Its price was $1.1 million per plane in the prices of 2014, much lower than the $15 million current price of the smallest available turboprop passenger plane carrying thirty-six passengers, representing, respectively, prices of $52,000 and $416,000 per seat. Its production rate of 100 per year was the second highest in the history of the aviation industry, surpassed only by the Boeing 737 in its many versions produced from 1968 until now (157 per year). But the production rate of any aircraft in history is dwarfed by the rate of production during World War II. The miracle of the home front between 1942 and 1945 is chronicled in chapter 16, but few feats of World War II production can match that of the DC-3, which was renamed the C-47 Skytrain for military use. Total production of the C-47 during World War II was 10,000, or 2,900 per year.

The DC-3 lives on today, which is not surprising, for a total of 10,600 were produced by 1945. They were ubiquitous on U.S. airlines in the 1950s, dominating short-haul air service between smaller cities. No one knows how many are in service today around the world, but they number in the hundreds, perhaps the thousands. They are popular in Africa because they can land on dirt runways. More than ten are lined up every day at the airport in San Juan, Puerto Rico, because they are the most efficient way of flying cargo among the small Caribbean islands.

The very aircraft, the "Flagship Detroit," that operated the first American flight from Chicago to New York is owned by the Flagship Detroit Foundation and often flies around the country to visit air shows. DC-3s are used everywhere because they are cheap; one can be purchased for $100,000. Their popularity eight decades after the first flight demonstrates that the DC-3 is the best-designed aircraft in aviation history. Its ruggedness is legendary; a common saying among pilots is that "the only replacement for a DC-3 is another DC-3."

Progress in the eight decades since the first flight of the DC-3 is so gradual by comparison that it can be described briefly. Developed during the war, the four-engine DC-6 began airline operations in 1946 and was capable of flying nonstop from Honolulu to San Francisco, the same route flown eleven years earlier by the 1935 flying boat. It increased the number of passengers from twenty-one to fifty-four and cut the elapsed time from Los Angeles to Chicago from 11.5 hours to 7.8 hours. Pressurization and the associated increase in comfort was lacking on the DC-3 but was present on the DC-6 and all subsequent aircraft.

Even though nonstop service from Hawaii to the mainland had been achieved in 1935, and by 1948 Pan Am and United were each flying four daily flights on the route, there was a mysterious seven-year lag in developing an aircraft that could fly exactly the same distance from Los Angeles to New York.[42] Finally the DC-7 achieved that goal in 1953, spanning the nation in 7.8 hours, exactly half the time required by the 1936 DC-3. The Boeing 707 jet aircraft made its first flight in late 1958 and improved the quality of airline travel by eliminating the annoying vibration of piston engines. It was faster than piston planes but not twice as fast, with an elapsed Los Angeles to New York time of 4.8 hours. However, the speed improvement represented by the jet aircraft was not permanent. Today's elapsed time for every airline flying between Los Angeles and New York is 5.6 hours instead of 4.8 hours.

Technological change is normally measured by percentage change per year, and that percentage change is the greatest for the longest transcontinental routes. For the Los Angeles to New York route, the 1934–36 change from the Boeing B247 to the DC-3 reduced elapsed time at an annual rate of 8.7 percent per year, from the 1936 DC-3 to the 1946 DC-6 reduced time at a rate of 7.3 percent per year, to the 1958 Boeing 707 reduced time at an annual rate of 4.0 percent per year. Over the almost six decades since the adoption of the Boeing 707, the rate of improvement of elapsed time has become negative, at a rate of –0.2 percent per year. The decline of speed in the past six decades combines a deliberate slowdown in response to higher fuel prices and runway congestion that substantially lengthens the time between the gate and the takeoff.

Though the Boeing 707 was introduced as a long-haul aircraft in 1958 (and the competing DC-8 jetliner was introduced in 1959), it required another decade until the late 1960s for America's entire aircraft fleet to be converted to jets. By 1969, 737s, which flew at the same speed as 707s, were filling in the local routes (e.g., San Francisco to Fresno or Atlanta to Savannah). But since 1970, there has been no improvement in the passenger experience of air travel; to the contrary, it has significantly deteriorated. Today's passengers are herded like cattle through long security lines, they are crowded into airline seats that are closer together than in the 1960s, and even on a transcontinental flight they must pay extra for a cold box of food, whereas until a decade ago, they could expect a hot meal with a choice of entrees.

Our surprising depiction of air travel as experiencing remarkably little progress since 1936 neglects two overriding considerations. The first, treated in this section, is the order-of-magnitude improvement in safety measured by air crash fatalities per passenger mile. The next section focuses on the reduction in the real price of air travel that converted it from the vehicle of Hollywood celebrities in the late 1930s to the mass transportation that began in 1960 and enjoyed its fastest rate of growth between 1960 and 1972.

The improvement in aircraft safety proceeded at a lightning rate analogous to that of the TV revolution in the early 1950s or the dot-com revolution of the late 1990s. Figure 11–9 records a relatively steady rate of progress that reduced air crash fatalities per 100 billion passenger miles from 580 in 1950 to ten by 1990, an annual rate of improvement of 10.1 percent per year. As impressive as this steady progress was, it was a snail's pace compared to the revolution of complete safety that was achieved between 1994 and 2006, as the rate of improvement registered 23.2 percent per year. But then there was no more improvement to come. In the eight years between 2006 and 2014, there was only a single U.S. event, which killed forty-nine people in 2009. Otherwise, there were no airline-related fatalities at all in the United States for those eight years. The transition from a dangerous method of travel to one that was completely safe had taken barely fifty years.

If there were many airline fatalities in the past but almost none in the past eight years, what accounts for the difference? The answer comes by examining the reasons for several of the most notable events. Most famous of all was the collision over the Grand Canyon on June 30, 1956, of a TWA Super Constellation with an almost-new United DC-7, causing 128 deaths. It was caused by the failure of an air traffic controller to notify the two planes that they were headed toward each other. After an extensive investigation, the crash led to the creation in 1958 of what is now called the Federal Aviation Administration (FAA).

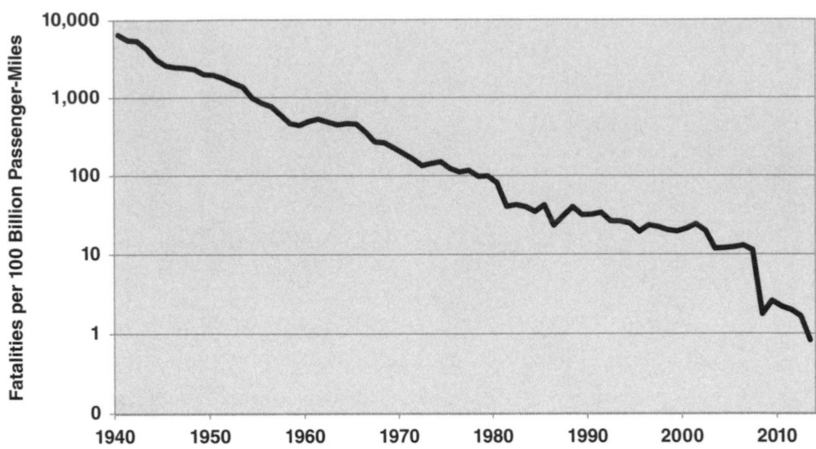

Figure 11–9. U. S. Commerical Airline Passenger Fatalities Per 100 Billion Passenger-Miles, Seven Year Moving Average, 1940–2013.
Sources: HSUS Df1120, Df1133, Df 1231, Df1236 before 1997, MIT Airline Data Project RPM and NTSB 2013 Preliminary Airline Statistics Table 3 after 1997.

Soon inadequate air traffic control faded away as a cause of airline fatalities, but still manufacturing and maintenance errors could be deadly. On May 25, 1979, an American Airlines DC-10 carrying 271 passengers and crew dived into the ground immediately after takeoff from Chicago's O'Hare airport. The cause was immediately determined to be the detachment of the left engine, which upon takeoff flipped over the top of the wing, severing hydraulic lines and damaging the left wing. The ultimate cause was determined to be faulty maintenance procedures at American Airlines. Finally, on November 12, 2001, in an eerily similar incident, an American Airlines Airbus A300 immediately after takeoff from New York's Kennedy airport dived into the Queens neighborhood of Belle Harbor, New York. The cause was determined to be pilot error, as the pilot's aggressive use of the rudder caused the tail of the plane to snap off, and before the aircraft hit the ground, both engines had fallen off the wing.

These three incidents with their very different causes—inadequate air traffic control, faulty maintenance, and pilot error—appear to have taught airlines and aircraft manufacturers many lessons. To quote the title of Ralph Nader's famous book, air travel was initially "unsafe at any speed" but now is safer than walking across the street.

AIRLINE PRICES AND THE INITIAL PROMISE OF AIRLINE DEREGULATION

In the history of the U.S. airline industry since World War II, one theme stands out. Air travel rapidly made the transition from a travel mode that was relatively dangerous and expensive to one that opened the world as an affordable destination for millions of Americans. In the words of the epigraph that opens this chapter, air travel "lifted from the human race the curse of distance." In the 1950s, travelers to Europe still mainly traveled on ships, but the jet plane within a few years caused regular transatlantic ship travel to cease. By the end of the 1960s, most ocean liners were scrapped or converted to cruise ships.

But, surprisingly, the period of most rapid decline in the real price of air travel occurred before the first flight of a jet plane. As shown in figure 11–10, the price of air travel relative to other goods and services declined rapidly from 1940 to 1960, declined at a slower rate from 1960 to 1980, and has experienced no decline at all in its relative price between 1980 and 2014. The growth rate of passenger miles traveled has mirrored the rate of change of the relative price except with the opposite sign, because lower prices stimulate the demand for any good or service.

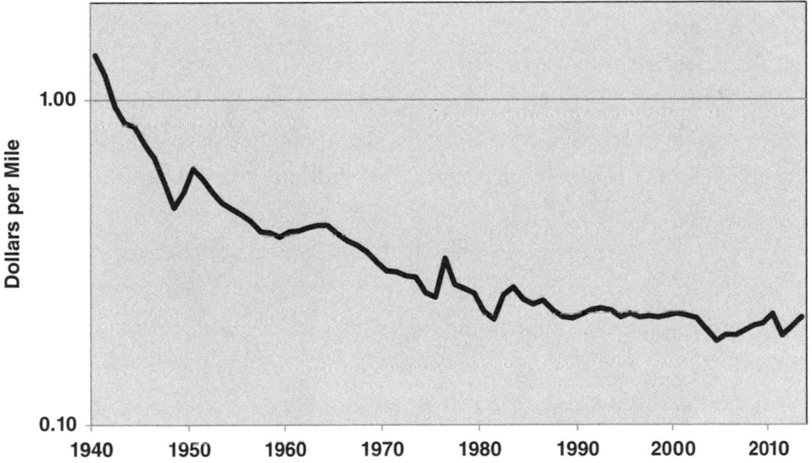

Figure 11–10. Inflation-Adjusted Passenger Price per Mile in Constant 2009 Prices, 1940–2013

Source: HSUS Tables Df1177-1228 before 1995, ratio linked forward from 1980 to 1995. After 1995 SAUS Table 1094 ratio linked forward and interpolated from 1995-2000. Airline RPM after 1948 from A4A Annual Results U.S. Airlines Table, Airline RPM before 1948 from HSUS series Df1126-1138.

Table 11–2. U.S. Domestic Air Travel, Annual Rate of Change, 1940–2013

	(1) Relative Price	(2) Passenger Miles
1940–1950	−8.1	20.5
1950–1960	−4.5	12.1
1960–1980	−2.8	9.3
1980–2013	−0.1	2.9

Sources: (1). HSUS Tables Df1177-1228 before 1995, ratio linked forward from 1980 to 1995. After 1995 SAUS Table 1094 ratio linked forward and interpolated from 1995–2000. Airline RPM after 1948 from A4A Annual Results U.S. Airlines Table, Airline RPM before 1948 from HSUS series Df1126-1138.

(2). Airline RPM after 1948 from A4A Annual Results U.S. Airlines Table, Airline RPM before 1948 from HSUS Series Df1126-1138..

Comparing the initial decade 1940–50 with the average of the period 1980–2013, we see in table 11–2 that the price and quantity measures mirror each other with opposite signs. By far the fastest annual rate of decline of the relative price (−8.1 percent per year), and most rapid rate of change of passenger miles traveled (20.5 percent per year) occurred in the initial decade of 1940–50. The rates of change are much slower in the more than three decades since 1980, with no change in relative price and annual growth of passenger miles at a rate of only 2.9 percent per year.

The 1960 to 1980 growth rate of 9.3 percent per year was sufficient for the passenger miles flown to increase by a factor of eight between 1960 and 1984; during this period, miles flown grew by 100 billion per decade. After 1960, air travel transitioned from a luxury to a standard method of travel that most families experience at least once per year and that many experience many times per year. Air travel allows college students to enjoy not only summer vacations in Europe, but also regular trips home for holidays and family events throughout the year.

For many employees air travel is a requirement for the job. At one extreme, most management consultants leave home early on Monday morning, fly to their client for the week, fly back Thursday night, and spend only each Friday in their office. College professors who are engaged in research and writing travel many times each year to annual meetings of the national association in their field, and they present and discuss papers at numerous conferences and at invited seminars at other universities.

If the speed and comfort of jet travel have not changed since the 1960s, then what has changed? The most important event of the jet age for domestic U.S. air travel was the deregulation of the airline industry, achieved in 1978 after decades of controversy. Until 1978, airlines could not fly where they wanted to fly and could not choose the price they charged to passengers. To take the case of Chicago, only United and Northwest could take passengers from Chicago to Seattle, and only American and TWA could take passengers from Chicago to Phoenix. About 30 percent of U.S. air travel required passengers to make connections, and most of these connections required passengers to change airlines. A passenger from Syracuse to Chicago could only fly on American, and onward travel to Seattle would require a lengthy walk from, say, American's gate K9 to United's gate E10.

Moreover, all airlines were required to charge the same price, which varied only in proportion to distance. The routes and prices were controlled by a government agency, the Civil Aeronautics Board (CAB). Pressure for deregulation originated in American federalism itself. The CAB was authorized to regulate interstate air travel but had no control over intrastate air travel. For decades, intrastate travel within California was deregulated, beyond the reach of the straightjacket of CAB regulation. By the early 1960s, a feisty carrier known as Pacific Southwest Airlines (PSA) had become the dominant carrier on the nation's busiest air routes, those connecting three SF Bay Area airports to four in the Los Angeles basin. In 1972, PSA operated 162 nonstop flights per day with a total of 22,000 seats between northern and southern California. PSA was the poster child for deregulation, and the primary argument by the deregulation proponents was an academic paper on PSA written by an economist, Theodore Keeler.[43]

The airline business changed radically in the first few years after deregulation. Change came immediately in the route structure. Now American could fly to Seattle, and United could fly to Phoenix. Connections that required a change of airlines all but disappeared within a few years, and the idea that an airline could fly anywhere delighted passengers but dismayed some airline employees who took for granted the route monopolies of the past. It soon dawned on airline executives that the ability to fly anywhere meant that an airline had to dominate its city, and that was achieved by large airlines merging with small carriers, a radical change accomplished between 1986 and 1990. TWA absorbed Ozark to dominate St. Louis; Northwest absorbed North Central to dominate Minneapolis and Detroit. Even PSA, the poster child of deregulation, did not survive the 1980s but rather was purchased by U.S. Airways, itself the creation of a merger between Allegheny and Piedmont Airlines.

Industrial organization economists in the decade after deregulation wrote frequently to evaluate its effects. Critics claimed that nonstop routes had been abandoned and that passengers had been forced to make plane connections through hubs dominated by a single airline. Closer study, however, revealed that many more nonstop routes were added than dropped. Although deregulation was initially expected to lower airline fares, we can see in figure 11–10 that there was no change in the real price of airline travel in the decades after the 1978 deregulation act. Instead, there was an increase in the variance of fares, as airlines could now vary the price of a given seat in order to maximize revenue, charging lower fares to personal travelers able to book weeks or months in advance and higher fares to business travelers who often booked within a day or two before the flight. Increasingly complex systems of managing airline fares (called "yield management") devised other methods of charging higher prices to business travelers, including restrictions that required those buying the lowest fares to stay over a Saturday night at the trip's destination.

However, the meaning of the price itself changed on Monday, May 1, 1981, when American Airlines stunned the industry by introducing the first frequent flyer benefit plan, dubbed "AAdvantage." Now each customer ticket purchase was linked to a frequent flyer plan number, and miles were added to a customer's mileage balance in proportion to the miles flown per flight. Competing airlines such as United were startled by the threat and scrambled to devise their own plans, which United announced on Thursday, May 4. In the early years, the rewards were exceptionally generous by today's standards. For the price of one economy ticket and 50,000 miles, my wife and I flew on TWA in first class from Chicago to London and back in 1986.[44]

The heat of competition among the big airlines became hotter in 1984 when American invented the concept of an elite level, "AAdvantage Gold." The benefit was enticing—in addition to earning miles, the "gold" member was entitled to upgrade to any seat in the first-class cabin that was available twenty-four hours in advance for a modest fee equal to about $40 for a typical flight from Chicago to New York. Today, all airlines offer four or five levels of elite status, and some members reach milestones such as 1 million or 2 million miles. Since the mid-1980s, all airlines have had alliances with particular banks to offer credit cards tied to a customer's frequent flyer account. For instance, my Chase card automatically gives me three miles for every dollar spent on United

Flights, two miles for every dollar spent on gas and groceries, and one mile for everything else.[45]

The importance of the frequent flyer plans for any discussion of price and benefits of air travel for consumer welfare is obvious: It makes the dollar price of flights an inaccurate measure of the true cost of flights. The benefits are clearest for longer flights, such as the 2,500-mile flights between the west coast and east coast. Five round trips are enough to earn a free sixth trip. That represents a price reduction of 18 percent, subject to the qualification that the free award trips are capacity controlled and are often not available for flights on the most popular days or times of travel.

THE DECLINE IN THE QUALITY OF THE CONSUMER AIR TRAVEL EXPERIENCE

But the benefits for consumers of airline marketing innovation came to an abrupt halt when American, the same airline that had invented the basic idea of the frequent flyer plan in 1981, announced in 2008 that it would begin charging customers a fee to check a bag. That fee, initially $15, is now $25, and a second bag costs $35 extra. Consider a family member going on vacation in 2014 on a $400 round-trip ticket who is now charged $25 to check the bag going to the destination and another $25 coming back. That raises the price from $400 to $450, but the rise in price is higher than that, for airlines no longer provide complimentary food in flight. Whereas hot meals were routinely served in economy class until after the World Trade center disaster of September 11, 2001, now customers must pay extra for food. If a family wants to eat anything on their vacation flight, which might be three hours or more, they would need to pay $8 each for a ham and cheese sandwich or chicken wrap.[46] Now the round-trip price, which was $400 before 2008, is $466.

Airlines now charge extra for their better seats; United charges $59 extra for a seat with thirty-four inches between rows compared to the usual economy distance of thirty-one inches. But before 1977, thirty-four-inch pitch was standard on all airlines.[47] The fact that customers today on a $200 flight are required to pay $59 extra to have the same seat space as they did in 1977 does not imply that for comparability we must add $59 to the price of a 2014 ticket. For most passengers, the extra fee is not worth it, so we shall take $15 rather than $59 as the value of the extra seat space available before 1977. This brings the round-trip ticket price up from $466 to $496. Compared to the basic ticket price of $400, the $496 represents an unmeasured price increase of 24 percent just between 2008 and 2014.

As the final dimension of decline in the quality of airline travel, consider the 200 million hours per year of valuable consumer time wasted in airline security (roughly 600 million U.S. passengers multiplied by twenty minutes per passenger). This represents an annual wasting of time worth about $8 billion. The current system of airport security all over the world represents an overreaction to the September 11, 2001, hijackings. There was only one weakness in the U.S. airline security system on September 11, and this was that the cockpit doors were flimsy. Within days, they were replaced by completely secure doors that nobody could break through. Although the security issue was completely solved within a week, fourteen years later billions of dollars per year of passenger time continues to be wasted in unnecessary additional security precautions. The pre-2001 security system, based on a quick walk through an X-ray machine to check for guns and metal weapons, would be enough.

A symbol of rising inequality, a topic treated in chapter 18, is the ever-growing chasm between domestic travel in economy class and the quality of the premium cabin on international flights, whether from San Francisco to Hong Kong or from Seattle to Amsterdam. As stated by the *Economist* in its issue of September 20, 2014:

> Nowadays those at the cheap end of the plane barely have room to open their copies of Thomas Piketty's *Capitalism,* at the top of the national best-seller lists for its lament about the new age of inequality. Airlines keep cramming more bodies into economy class while passengers, despite their moans, regard this as a fair tradeoff for cheap fares. But in the front of the cabin carriers have made seats as plush as first class seats used to be a few years earlier.[48]

One exception to the discomfort of economy-class air travel is the spread of inflight entertainment options. This has gone furthest for international travel, where on most airlines economy-class passengers can choose from a wide range of movie, audio, and game options, albeit from a small seat-back screen half or less the size of the screens showing the same entertainment options in premium classes. On domestic flights, options range from a variety of live TV options on Jet Blue and selected planes of several other airlines to no entertainment at all on Southwest. By 2014, inflight Wi-Fi had become available on most flights, although usage rates of less than 10 percent suggested that passengers did not consider Wi-Fi availability to be worth the trouble, at least for the prices charged.

CONCLUSION

This account of advances in transportation since 1940 provides a mixed assessment of the pace of progress. The number of motor vehicles per household increased rapidly through 1970 and more slowly between 1970 and 1990, then did not increase at all after 1990. Vehicle miles traveled per person also experienced an ever-decreasing rate of growth and actually registered an absolute decline between 2000 and 2014, partly reflecting a reduction in the share of the population that had a driver's license. But there was also a steady pace of improvement in automobile quality after 1970, along with an equally steady pace of decline in automobile fatalities per mile traveled.

The quality of automobiles increased by a factor of at least 2.5 between 1906 and 1940 (see table 5–2), but this was entirely missed by government data on prices and GDP, because automobiles were not introduced into the Consumer Price Index (CPI) until 1935. This chapter documents continuing quality improvements in automobiles during the postwar years. Postwar cars did not become much larger or appreciably more powerful than their 1940 ancestors, but they gradually added a host of convenience features, such as air conditioning and automatic transmissions, as well as numerous convenience, safety and anti-pollution devices. The fuel economy of automobiles increased as well. However, the price indexes used to compute GDP did a much more complete job of capturing the value of automobile quality changes in the postwar years than they did before 1940, so the omission of the value of automobile quality improvements from GDP was much more significant before 1940 than after.

Steady improvement was made in reducing motor vehicle fatality rates. Though some of this achievement was a result of government-mandated seat belts and airbags, much was the result of the greater safety inherent in the superhighways that were constructed, mainly between 1958 and 1972, as part of the Interstate Highway System. That economy-wide labor productivity grew more rapidly before 1972 than afterward is at least partly a direct effect of the interstate highway system in allowing truck drivers to cover more miles for each hour of work. More productive truck drivers translated into a reduction of transportation costs for industries across the board.

Few industries exhibited technical progress in their first decade as rapid as that experienced by commercial air transportation. The achievements of the long-haul flying boat and the medium-haul DC-3 made flying feasible, but the relative price of travel was sufficiently high to restrict demand before World War II to movie stars and other rich people on expense accounts. The democratization of air transport came in two stages, first with the large piston planes that after 1953 were able to cross the country nonstop, and then with the jet planes that followed soon after. Within barely a decade of the first Boeing 707 and Douglas DC-8 transcontinental and transatlantic flights, the entire air transport industry had converted to jet planes, including short-haul Boeing 737 and Douglas DC-9 jet aircraft suitable for serving small cities.

For air transport more than for automobiles, the early 1970s marked a transition point from rapid to slower progress. When 1970–2000 is compared to 1945–70, the more recent period has witnessed a slower decline in the relative price of air transport and slower growth in airline passenger miles flown per person. The physical experience of air travel has unambiguously deteriorated since the early 1970s as a result of tighter seating configurations and longer security lines. And the slow decline in the relative price since 1980 overstates the price decline by neglecting the shift from free meals and baggage checking to separate fees for these and other amenities, offset to some extent by the value of frequent-flyer award tickets.

Airlines were deregulated in 1978 with the promise of lower prices, but we have seen that there was no decline at all in the relative price of air travel as contrasted with rapid price declines before 1980. This suggests that the most important driver of the relative price was not the extent of regulation, but rather the development of larger and faster aircraft that, as in the case of the interstate highways and truck driver productivity, made the airline crew—especially the pilots—more productive. As successive waves of mergers have occurred in the deregulated era, the domestic air transport industry has coalesced into four major carriers with a few smaller ones nibbling around the edges, competing with each other to maximize the share of their revenue collected as ancillary fees from passengers who once were able to regard the price of an airline trip as the price of the airline ticket.

Chapter 12

ENTERTAINMENT AND COMMUNICATIONS FROM MILTON BERLE TO THE IPHONE

Mr. Public views that television set in his home as a 20th Century electronic monster that can transport him to the ball game, to Washington D.C., to the atomic blast in Nevada—and do it now. The viewer is inclined to accept it as his window to the world, as his reporter on what is happening now—simultaneously. The miracle of television is actually Man's ability to see at a distance while the event is happening.

—Gary Simpson, NBC television director, 1955[1]

INTRODUCTION

Following the so-called age of mass communication from 1870 to 1940, in which Americans benefited from an explosion of communications innovations, there occurred another dramatic shift in the way Americans consumed entertainment and information. Unlike the multiplicity of communications technologies of the previous seventy years, the post-1940 world of information and entertainment was dominated by a single behemoth: television. Though the early roots of television dated back well before 1940, commercial television did not begin until after World War II. With great rapidity, however, the advent of television would shift the American way of life to center on the home and yet, thanks to TV's grasp on popular attention and the dominance of the major networks, managed to maintain a highly public, communal character. With unprecedented speed, television entered the American living room and provided a window to the world that previously had been a distant dream.

Television did not arrive in a vacuum, for its ability to cater to audience demands in large part owed to existing broadcast structures and practices that had been pioneered by radio. Indeed, many of television's earliest stars came from the radio world, as did much of its funding. Even so, rumors of the death of radio were, as the saying goes, greatly exaggerated. Though radio quickly lost its previously dominant hold on national audiences, it survived and thrived by filling in the cracks television that could not, adapting its programming to become local and personalized. Though families no longer gathered together around the radio as a central source of entertainment, it had become a reliable personal companion, particularly on commuting and shopping trips in the car.

Motion pictures were more greatly affected by TV. After World War II, weekly cinema attendance plummeted as people chose instead to watch TV from the comfort and convenience of their own homes. Beyond the initial investment in the television set, a family did not need to pay for transportation or tickets when they could make use of their television set for free. The popularity of motion picture stars was eclipsed by that of television characters such as Lucille Ball, who seemed to become another member of the family, or Milton Berle of Texaco Star Theater, soon dubbed "Uncle Miltie."

Yet, like radio, the "old" medium of the motion picture proved to be adaptable. Though weekly movie admissions fell from 60 percent to 20 percent of the population (see figure 6–5), they did not fall to zero. After the arrival of cable television in the 1980s, the new medium increasingly relied on the film industry for programming. Just as the VCR and DVD would later become unexpected boons for the movie business, television proved to be a cash cow for Hollywood and did little to reduce the importance of the feature film in popular culture. Far from disappearing, the cultural currency of the motion picture changed from a single receiving location, the movie theater, to multiple access points, including television and, later, personal computers and smartphones.

In the meantime, the audience experience of television continued to improve. As screens increased in size and gained higher definition, prices fell. By the mid-1970s, the majority of Americans were watching their favorite programs in color. The invention and expansion of cable television provided far greater consumer choice, as well as facilitating a more reliable, high-quality color picture. Later on, the invention of the VCR, followed by the DVR, allowed people to watch their favorite programs on their own schedule, bringing new levels of "time-shifting" control to the viewer.

The evolution of music listening proceeded, albeit at a slower rate than television. For much of the period after 1940, the phonograph record continued to dominate, although innovations in recording technology produced a higher-quality listening experience. The shellac record and record changer were replaced by vinyl long-playing records providing stereophonic sound. More significant changes in recording quality, accessibility, and convenience arrived with the cassette tape and, later, the compact disc. Soon, the CD would eliminate many of the imperfections of sound recording while further extending playing time. By the end of the twentieth century, despite the apparent similarity of its disc shape, the phonograph of the 1940s and 1950s had been almost completely supplanted by CD technology.

Interpersonal communication also experienced significant change, first in the sharp reduction in the price of long-distance calls. The arrival of the mobile phone in the 1980s brought a new element of immediacy, in recent years becoming cost-effective enough to surpass the home landline telephone as the central nexus of personal communication. During this time, the cell phone has become a new form of multimedia, with the smartphone allowing users to search the web, send texts and e-mails, listen to music, and watch movies, in addition to the primary function of making calls, all while on the go.

Just as interpersonal communications have become more instantaneous, so too has the transmission of news. Starting with radio during World War II, and later adapted to TV, on-site live reporting was a fairly novel practice in 1940. Instant transmission contributed to the long, slow decline of the print newspaper, further hastened by cable news channels such as CNN and by news obtained directly from the Internet. At the same time, television news greatly improved on the primitive week-old newsreels of 1930s and 1940s movie houses.

The continuing rapid evolution of entertainment and communication throughout the era since 1940 provides a contrast to the previous two chapters. Quality and quantity improvements in food and clothing consumption (as discussed in chapter 10) were negligible, and there was a distinct slowing of progress in equipment of housing units and in the quality of household appliances after 1970. Likewise, in chapter 11 we learned that 1970 marked a dividing line in the development of the nation's highway system and in the quality of the commercial air travel experience. No such slowing after 1970 occurs in this chapter; if anything, the arrival of smartphones and social media in the past decade constitutes an acceleration rather than a slowing of progress.

THE EARLY YEARS OF TELEVISION

Although television's golden age did not occur until the 1950s, the origins of TV's technological breakthrough took place long before that. In the 1870s, Sir William Crooks, among others, helped develop the cathode ray tube, which would become the foundation for transmitting television images, although television experimenters did not recognize this until the end of the nineteenth century. Previously, experimenters had tried to transmit images with mechanical devices, but in 1897 Karl Ferdinand Braun created the cathode-ray oscilloscope, which exposed electronic signals to visual observation. Boris Rosing, in St. Petersburg, expanded on this technology ten years later, achieving weak images on a photoelectric cell connected to an altered Braun tube.

In the following decades, other scientists continued to modify Braun and Rosing's innovations, but the biggest contributions would come from two men in the 1920s and 1930s. One was Vladimir Zworykin, an immigrant from Russia, now working for American corporate giants to develop a camera tube that would solve the missing link in transmitting a television image.[2] The other was Philo T. Farnsworth, a young man from Rigby, Idaho, who worked independently of the large companies, establishing his own laboratory in San Francisco.

Zworykin first worked for Westinghouse, where he developed the iconoscope, which could increase the light sensitivity of the electronic camera, thus improving the image detail. In 1928, the demonstration of this device that could transmit a photoelectric television image immediately drew attention, not least from David Sarnoff, the vice president and general manager of RCA, who offered Zworykin additional research funding. Sarnoff extended support for television research even farther when RCA took control of the radio research operations of GE and Westinghouse in 1930.

Meanwhile, Farnsworth, without the copious financial backing of a corporation such as Westinghouse or RCA, was busy developing his own version of the tube. Though he may not have had an extensive technical education equal to Zworykin's, Farnsworth had been interested in the idea of television since he was 15 years old, studying photoelectricity and the cathode-ray tube from his Idaho home. Farnsworth's accomplishments between 1926 and 1938, at a cost of $1 million compared to the $9 million spent by RCA, were integral contributions to television's move toward commercialization.[3]

Farnsworth's independent innovations did not go unnoticed by the big corporations. RCA, caught off guard when Farnsworth applied for an electronic television patent in 1930, quickly filed a patent interference suit against him. The courts, however, sided with Farnsworth, and by August the 24-year-old had his television patent. This would not be the last conflict between Farnsworth and RCA, and the independent inventor won a majority of the numerous patent proceedings.[4] With the innovations of Zworykin and Farnsworth having brought television standards to a level where it could start being marketed commercially, Sarnoff took decisive action forever to link his name and his nascent National Broadcasting Company with the arrival of the new medium. In April 1939, at the New York World's Fair in Flushing Meadows, in front of reporters and the cameras of NBC, Sarnoff declared:

> It is with a feeling of humbleness that I come to this moment of announcing the birth in this country of a new art so important in its implications that it is bound to affect all society. It is an art which shines like a torch of hope in a troubled world. It is a creative force which we must learn to utilize for the benefit of all mankind.[5]

At this point, broadcasting was still only experimental. On July 1, 1941, however, the FCC finally approved commercial standards, and the CBS and NBC New York stations became WCBW and WNBT, the first two commercial television channels. Although televisions were still a rarity and were mainly limited to local broadcasting in New York and a few other metropolitan areas, prime airtime costing about a tenth the radio rate, modern television had nonetheless begun. Only five months later, though, the bombing of Pearl Harbor and the United States' subsequent entrance into World War II would delay television's rise to prominence and give radio five more years in the sun.[6]

WORLD WAR II AND THE LAST HURRAH OF THE OLD MEDIA

In May 1942, in order to direct all available resources to the war effort, the War Production Board prohibited further building of television stations. NBC and CBS quickly cut TV broadcasting, a hiatus that would last until the summer of 1944. Meanwhile, radio entered the peak of its influence as the essential conveyor of war news to a population hungry for every shred of news about the evolution of combat. Radio had such universal reach that 62 million Americans—nearly half of the population—were listening on December 8, 1941, when FDR delivered his "date which will live in infamy" speech. In addition to its continuing position of dominance, radio played a significant practical role in the war effort, in a variety of ways. On the battle lines, the walkie-talkie was a useful new tool for military communication.

Outside of the frontlines, radio proved fundamental to the promotion of patriotism and citizen responsibility for the war effort, including appeals to Americans to purchase War Bonds. The most notable of these appeals occurred on February 1, 1944. Other approaches to promoting wartime patriotism involved integrating themes of war into existing programs or creating new programs that focused primarily on the war effort. In so doing, radio helped raise consciousness about rationing. It also contributed to the sense of a shared national cause. In many of these programs, such as *This Is War!*, "the producer's aim was to inspire, frighten, and inform all at the same time."[7] Radio news also underwent important qualitative transformations that would have a lasting influence on the way radio and later television informed the population about current events. One such shift was the appearance of live, on-site reports. Whereas news coverage had previously consisted of delayed reports read from a broadcasting studio, suddenly Americans could receive information directly from the battle zones.

Radio broadcasters gave the details of the unfolding war as it was happening *now.* It was more urgent and real than any newspaper could provide. Indeed, "Murrow's historic coverage of the Nazi bombing raids over London and of the resilience of the British people signaled a change in how Americans learned about world events. Radio obliterated time and distance in its coverage of World War II, in a way that the printed word could not match."[8] This wartime heyday of radio news, however, was not to last. Even though television could build no stations during the war, the young upstart was not standing still. Technical research and innovation continued, as Zworykin developed the image-orthicon to improve light sensitivity and RCA and CBS experimented with color images.[9]

The motion picture industry, like radio, boomed throughout the war. During these years, 23 percent of Americans' recreational spending went to the movie industry. In the summer of 1946, an article in *Variety* magazine talked about the "Film Industry's Fattest Six Months in History," during which the box office receipts were $1.7 billion as 90 million people a week, more than 60 percent of the population, attended movies.[10] Generally, they went to see double features, with a newsreel, sandwiched between features, showing moving images of what Americans were being told through radio. They conveyed the goosestep march of the Nazis and the heroic roll of American tanks, accompanied by uplifting music and narration.

The Japanese unconditional surrender, signed on the deck of the battleship *Missouri* on September 2, 1945, let loose the energy of the American economy to achieve as rapid a reconversion as possible to peacetime production. Although radio initially benefited from this as well, nothing about peacetime, besides the end of rationing, was more anticipated than the emergence of television. Though it took a few years for the television industry to achieve widespread production and distribution, by 1950, its surge through the nation had begun. The end of World War II signaled the dawn of the golden age of television.

TELEVISION'S GOLDEN AGE

When the war ended, privately owned television sets still numbered in the tens of thousands and were located primarily in the New York City area. By 1950, 9 percent of American households owned a television set, a proportion that had increased to 64.5 percent only five years later. This increase in percentage ownership by 13 points per year is the fastest diffusion of any appliance or device in history, faster than the smartphone after 2003 or the tablet after 2010. By 1955, no less than 97 percent of households were within reception range of a television signal. Television entered more than 90 percent of homes by the early 1960s.

While set ownership became universal almost overnight, as shown in figure 12–1, the availability of programming, particularly in smaller cities, was delayed by the decision in 1948 by the Federal Communications Commission (FCC) temporarily to "freeze" the granting of television stations. The number of television stations was capped until 1952 at a mere 108, and sixteen of these were in the three metropolitan areas of New York, Chicago, and Los Angeles.[11]

In the early years of television, when it was still a rarity in American households, TV-watching had a highly social character. For a while, televisions could mainly be found in public places, and the tavern often became the locus where people of the neighborhood would congregate to watch TV. If one's neighbors owned a TV, those neighbors usually became suddenly far more popular, often hosting "TV parties." Children would spend hours away from home to take advantage of the neighbors' television set, and maybe even to convince their parents to get one of their own, if only to keep an eye on them.[12]

In fact, this was one of the major drivers of television purchases. According to one early study conducted in 1949 of television owners in the New York

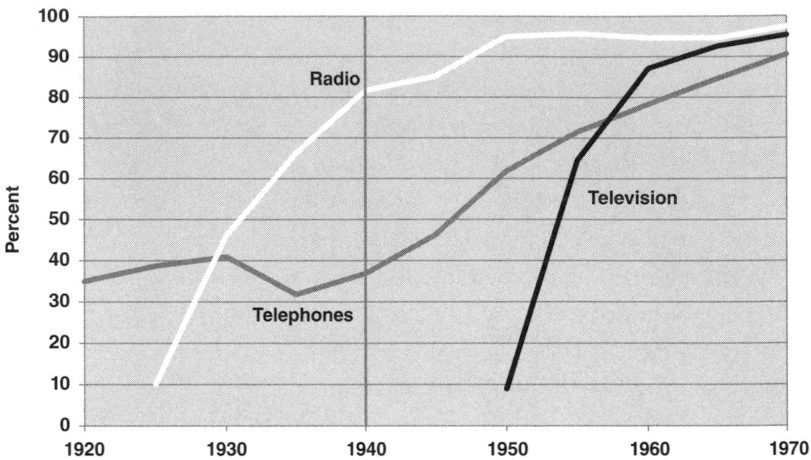

Figure 12–1. Telephone, Radio and Television Ownership as Percentage of Households, 1920–1970

Source: SAUS (1999), Series 1440, US Census Bureau.

area, 18 percent said they had bought a TV set because their children wanted one, whereas 15 percent said they had been watching at friends' houses and now wanted to get one for their own. The most popular reason for buying a set, with about a third of respondents in the study citing it, was to watch sports.[13] During the formative years of commercial television, programming was almost exclusively local. Distinct from the network-dominated nature of the radio age, early television fostered a local presence. Everyone who could access the TV knew the local newscaster and weatherman.

Network television arrived as early as 1946, when the first coaxial television cable, connecting New York, Philadelphia, and Washington, D.C., allowed viewers in all three cities to watch the Joe Louis–Billy Conn heavyweight boxing match. Five years later, AT&T had built a coaxial cable system from coast to coast that could connect to around 95 percent of American television sets. Thus the national television network was born. Over the next three decades, the networks would wield unparalleled influence in the television business, with 1982 being the first year in which the proportion of network affiliate stations dropped below 80 percent of the total number of stations.[14]

The division of the United States into four time zones immediately created a problem for network executives. Broadcasting an 8 p.m. show in New York simultaneously to Californians at 5 p.m. was impracticable. As a solution, the coaxial cable would bring each network programs instantly to a control center in Los Angeles, where movie cameras were set up to film the programs for rebroadcast three hours later. Those who grew up in the Pacific time zone will remember the fuzziness of the network programs as compared to the much higher quality of the live local TV shows. Only the introduction of the videotape recorder in 1957 allowed westerners to rejoin the country and enjoy live television programming with the same degree of picture quality as their east coast brethren.[15]

The national networks united the population with the new "window on the world." Ironically, the medium that made the private home the center for recreation also generated a sense of shared, public experience. "The normal way to enjoy a community experience was at home in your living room at your TV set."[16] On a given day at the office, the most animated topic of conversation at the watercooler likely revolved around the shenanigans that Lucy had gotten into on last night's episode of *I Love Lucy*. Radio, too, had enjoyed a substantial national presence in its glory days. However, the appeal of television and its characters was stronger. On January 19, 1953, when CBS broadcast the episode of *I Love Lucy* in which Lucy has a baby to coincide with Lucille Ball *actually* giving birth, 68.8 percent of the country's television sets were tuned in.[17] Two years later, half of the entire population watched as Mary Martin played "Peter Pan" on television.[18]

Also at the top of the ratings was Milton Berle from *Texaco Star Theater*. Berle's outrageous costumes and slapstick comedy became such a centerpiece of Americans' Tuesday nights that, at least according to one account, sudden drastic drops in Detroit's reservoirs were the result of viewers all waiting until his show was over, then going to the bathroom all at once. In any case, during one show, when Berle ad-libbed, saying, "Listen to your Uncle Miltie," he became the nation's uncle.[19]

Television was built, in part, on the back of radio's successes, co-opting funds, broadcasting structures, and stars from the older medium. The instant shift of preferences is measured by surveys of listening and viewing hours. Between 1948 and 1955, average daily radio listening per home fell from 4.4 hours to 2.4. In TV homes, this number was even lower, at 1.9 hours, even as TV-viewing in such households averaged 4.9 hours a day.[20] The importance of television to leisure time would continue to grow, and by 2005 the average household spent more than eight hours a day watching television, as is shown in figure 12–2.[21] Television also affected how people devoted time to social activities. In 1965, television owners spent less time on social activities outside the household, as well as less time sleeping, grooming, gardening, and doing

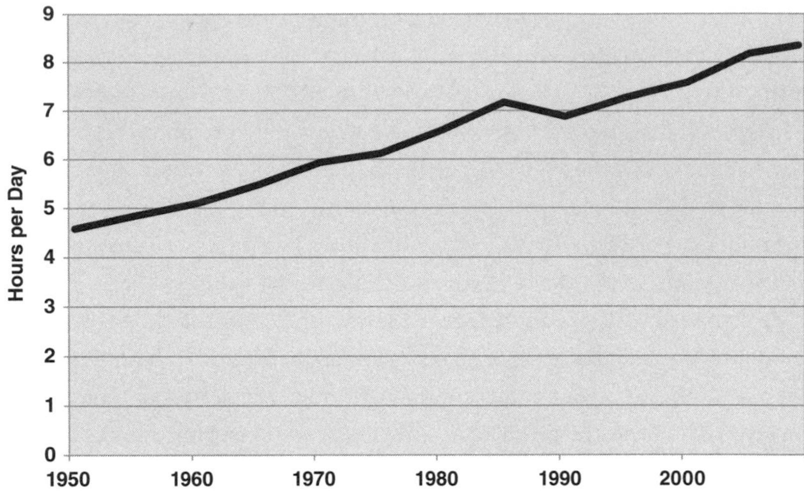

Figure 12–2. Household Television Viewing Time, 1950–2009
Source: "TV Basics" (2012), p. 6.

laundry than people without television. By 2005, television, as a primary activity, consumed nearly half of all free time—more than half if television viewing was a secondary or tertiary activity, that is, done at the same time as one or two other, more central activities.

The impact of television was not limited to shifts in time usage. As a private window to the public world, from the start television, like radio before it, became a social equalizer. Despite the small picture size and high price of early television sets, by 1960 virtually every household had one. One could enjoy the same programs as anyone else from the comfort of one's own home, free from possible stigma. As one southern African American stated:

> It permits us to see things in an uncompromising manner. Ordinarily to see these things would require that we be segregated and occupy the least desirable seats or vantage point. With television we're on the level with everyone else. Before television, radio provided the little bit of equality we were able to get. We never wanted to see any show or athletic event bad enough to be segregated in attending it.[22]

This is to say nothing of TV's ability to influence public opinion. Perhaps the most famous example of such influence was the first debate in the 1960 presidential campaign between Richard Nixon and John F. Kennedy.[23] During the debate, Nixon, who refused to use makeup, looked haggard and irritated, whereas Kennedy, taking full advantage of the transmitted image, looked sharp, handsome, and engaged in the debate. According to CBS's president at the time, "Kennedy was bronzed beautifully...Nixon looked like death." While radio listeners were relatively split on who won, those who watched the debate on television overwhelmingly thought Kennedy was the winner. Kennedy's eventual victory in the election is often attributed to TV's effect on the audience in that first debate.[24] Just as significant was television's role in the Civil Rights movement. On March 7, 1965, a group of peaceful protestors, marching against segregation from Selma, Alabama, to Montgomery, was attacked by the sheriff of Selma and a band of state troopers. Images of the vicious aggression of the police, captured and broadcast to the nation by the television networks, inspired a push against such violent bigotry, which soon culminated in Lyndon B. Johnson's signing into law the Voting Rights Act of 1965.[25]

The power of the television age wielded political, social, and cultural influence that few other innovations in any sphere could match, and it "was hailed as the ultimate communication experience, delivering a dream of spatial transportation that had, since the nineteenth century, fascinated the modern imagination."[26] It is little wonder, then, that so many predicated that the rise of television would cause the death of print media, radio, and the motion picture. In truth, however, these old media evolved rather than perished, as when Mark Twain cabled from London in 1897, "The reports of my death are greatly exaggerated."[27]

OLD MEDIA IN THE TELEVISION AGE

In the postwar years, movie attendance experienced a precipitous drop. Whereas more than 60 percent of Americans on average had attended the cinema each week in 1946, by the mid-1950s attendance was hovering under 25 percent, a level that has remained fairly stable to this day (see figure 6–5). It is not hard to see how television contributed to this decline.

Movie theaters were emptier than they had ever been. Throughout the years, cinemas sought new ways to attract audiences. Technology was one of the main approaches, including 3D films and large formats, including Cinerama. Color, still absent from standard televisions, became far more prevalent in motion pictures, rising from 12 percent of films in 1947 to 58 percent in 1954.

None of these approaches proved successful.[28] Around the same time, the drive-in movie theater arrived, less a response to television than a result of the booming car culture. Though the drive-in theater developed considerable cultural and nostalgic value, it did little to stem the flow of audiences out of theaters, nor did the refurbished megaplexes of the mid-1990s.

Yet the motion picture survives. The construction boom of the 1990s demonstrates a stubborn staying power of the movie theater. Although it may not represent a serious rival to TV, the cinema continues to provide a unique large-screen experience that cannot be matched in the living room.[29] This staying power is not always readily apparent in the numbers. After an average of around 500 films released per year in the United States during the 1930s, only 369 were released in 1950, and 232 in 1954.[30] By 1960 and 1970, film releases stabilized at around 200 per year.[31] However, most of the films that disappeared were of B- and C-grade quality, and they were replaced by big-budget blockbusters.[32] There was still room for a critical masterpiece such as *The Godfather* to spur millions of Marlon Brando impersonations and for *Star Wars* to burst onto the scene and become a cultural icon and box office success, to this day trailing only *Gone with the Wind* in inflation-adjusted domestic gross revenue.[33]

In 1956, CBS telecast *The Wizard of Oz,* the first major Hollywood film broadcast on a top television network. A few years later, the film became an annual event on network television, doing more to cement it as a classic than had its time in theaters.[34] By 1975, movies made up more than half of all network primetime programming, as well as 80 percent of programming on nonaffiliated stations. As one writer put it: "More people than ever before are seeing Hollywood films, but most of them are not paying Hollywood for the privilege." However, the networks did pay the Hollywood studios rental fees to show the movies. For instance, NBC paid $10 million in 1974 to broadcast a two-night special of *The Godfather.* The investment paid off, for NBC won the ratings war on those nights. Through TV, the motion picture still wielded considerable cultural and economic influence.[35]

Though television virtually eliminated network radio, local radio stepped in, with advertising for local stations continuing to grow slowly but steadily over the years. Many of these stations made use of a Top 40 format, in which a disc jockey played the best-selling records over and over again. In the 1960s, stations became increasingly specialized, some adopting all-news formats and others a blend of news, talk, and sports, whereas others settled into musical specialties, becoming stations for "golden oldies" or "underground rock," among others.[36]

Radio's adaptation to fill the entertainment niches left vacant by television was not limited to programming decisions. The very character of radio listening also was transformed. Because the TV had supplanted the radio as the piece of furniture that brought the family together, radio use took on a more personal dimension. As a teenager and college student, I had a small AM radio and sometimes dialed around at night to find the clear-channel radio station that was the farthest away.[37] The transistor reduced the cost of radio and enabled people to use pocket-sized radios wherever they went, and there were soon more radios than households.[38] Between 1940 and 1970, the car radio grew from being a feature in 30 percent of cars to being in 95 percent of them.[39] In short:

> Radio didn't die. It wasn't even sick. It just had to be psychoanalyzed.... The public didn't stop loving radio despite TV. It just [started] liking it in a different way—and radio went to the beach, to the park, the patio and the automobile.... Radio has become a companion to the individual instead of remaining a focal point of all family entertainment. An intimacy has developed between radio and the individual. It has become as personal as a pack of [cigarettes].[40]

IN LIVING COLOR: CHANGES IN TELEVISION QUALITY

Though the 1950s were television's golden age, TV still lacked a high-quality picture and real consumer choice. In the next forty years, four major changes took place that transformed how viewers experienced television. First was the steady improvement of television sets with rates of quality increase that were unprecedented for any consumer product before the arrival of the personal computer. Second was the arrival of color television, coupled with increasing technical mastery over picture definition, which brought more realistic and vibrant images. Third was cable television, which provided innumerable viewing options. And fourth was the VCR, or videocassette recorder, which revolutionized television-watching by putting scheduling choices in the hands of the audience, eventually to be replaced by the technically superior digital video recorder (DVR). Figure 12–3 shows the rise in percentage of households reflecting these changes.

In chapter 10 we discovered that refrigerators, washers, clothes dryers, and room air conditioners experienced major quality improvements in the first three decades after the war that share three characteristics. First, the quality changes occurred early in the postwar era and were largely completed by 1970.

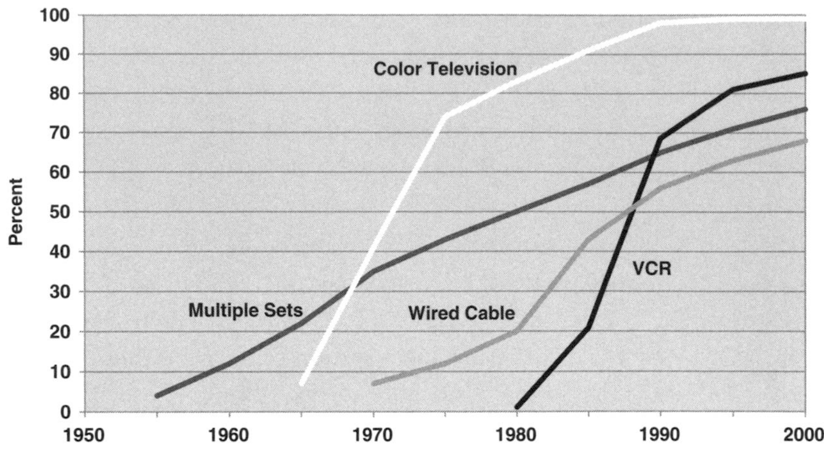

Figure 12–3. Multiple Sets and Color TV, VCR, and Wired Cable Ownership as Percentage of Households, 1955–2000

Sources: Data for households with multiple sets and VCR from "TV Basics" (2012), p. 2. Data for households with color TV and wired cable from "Television Facts and Statistics–1939 to 2000" (2001).

Second, by far the largest quantitative effect of the improvements came through improved energy efficiency. Third, the cumulative effect of these improvements from 1947 through 1983 was massive. Improvements in quality—that is, previously unmeasured components of consumer surplus that were not included in the GDP data—amounted to 100 percent of the cost of refrigerators and clothes dryers and 200 percent of the cost of room air conditioners.

The value of quality changes in these appliances pales next to the previously unmeasured quality improvements in TV sets. Over the course of TV's history, sets have become larger, picture quality has improved, and prices have come down. For $350 my parents in 1950 bought a black-and-white RCA table model with a nine-inch screen the shape of a pumpkin; purchase of the set required the additional purchase of a $50 annual service contract. For $418 in current dollars, a customer in August 2014, could purchase a forty-inch high-definition LED color set with theater surround sound and equipped with Internet hookups enabling video streaming.[41]

The dimensions of improved quality include not just larger and clearer TV pictures. Other types of improvements included a radical reduction in weight that made TV sets portable, light enough to carry from room to room. Repair costs, which were estimated at $50 per year in the late 1940s, virtually disappeared after the transition from vacuum tubes to solid-state electronics had been completed by the early 1960s. The arrival of solid-state electronics also created a large gain of energy efficiency. Long forgotten and now taken for granted are early improvements such as "remote control, quartz tuning, stereo speakers, multiple audio and video jacks, and tuners able to handle more than the original 82 VHF–UHF channels."[42]

My study of the quality of TV sets covered the years 1952–83 and was based on product evaluations from *Consumer Reports* and outside evaluations from reliable sources like MIT. In the early years, repair costs were a much larger component of the cost of owning a television set than electricity costs. Between 1950 and 1986, the incidence of repairs for black-and-white sets was reduced by a factor of thirty and for color sets between 1964 and 1986 by a factor of ten. The *Consumer Reports* data on the incidence of repairs is among the best of any source of changes in quality, as it is based on the responses of hundreds of thousands of readers who fill in the annual *Consumer Reports* questionnaire. In contrast to the $50 per year service contracts of 1950, by the 1960s, repair costs had virtually disappeared and manufacturers were able to offer free-repair warranties for a year or longer. Similarly, energy consumption for black-and-white TV sets fell from 250 watts to 60 watts between 1948 and 1981, whereas consumption for color TV sets fell from 350 watts in 1964 to 110 watts in 1981.

When all these dimensions of quality improvement are put together, the "true" annual rate of price decline for 1952–83 was –4.3 percent per year, compared to the price decline of—1.0 percent registered by the CPI. Because CPI data are used to create real GDP, the understatement of the true price decline in the CPI automatically created an equally large understatement of the increase in the growth of the TV component of real GDP.[43] The difference of –3.3 percent per year cumulates over the thirty-one-year time span to 278 percent, implying that the unmeasured consumer surplus provided by development of the television set in 1983 is almost triple the amount spent on the TV sets themselves.

This adjustment is doubtless an understatement, making no allowance for the improvement in picture quality. In a 1950 *Consumer Reports* evaluation, five of fourteen rated sets were labeled "poor" or "unacceptable" for their picture quality. By 1967, the evaluation was the opposite: "the top-ranked sets showed clearer, crisper pictures than any we have seen."[44] By 1984 an author wrote of the latest models that "the first thing you notice is that the picture is sharper, brighter, and more contrasty in broad daylight. . . . The main reason the picture is sharper than in the past is that many of the better sets use a so-called comb filter, which separates the color signal from the black and white signal."[45]

Unlike home appliances ("white goods"), in which there were only minimal quality improvements after 1972, TV sets have continued until the present day rapidly to increase in quality. The transition was particularly significant between 2000 and 2014, with the twin innovations of flat screens and high definition. A basic TV had a ten-inch screen in 1950, a nineteen-inch screen in 1983, and a forty-inch HD screen in 2014. Thus screen sizes doubled and doubled again, but in 2014, screen sizes had expanded far beyond forty inches. For $1,000 one could buy a sixty-inch HD set that had 2.2 times the viewing area of a forty-inch set, ten times the typical viewing area of a 1984 set, and thirty-six times the viewing area of the typical 1950 set.[46]

The quality and picture size of TV sets increased between 1983 and 2014, while their price plummeted. The starting point for a comparison of prices is the average price of $700 for fifteen different 1983 nineteen-inch models rated by *Consumer Reports.*[47] The average price of nineteen-inch TV sets dropped to $327 in 1992 and $161 in 1999, for an average rate of price change of –9.0 percent per year. The price dropped almost as rapidly for twenty-seven-inch models, which had an average price in *Consumer Reports* of $657 in 1992, $423 in 1999, and $321 in 2004, for an average rate of price change of –6.0 percent per year. As time went on the size of TV set models rated by *Consumer Reports* continued to increase. The average price of thirty-two inch models declined from $773 in 1997 to $559 in 2004, a rate of price change of –4.6 percent per year. The rate of price decline increased radically with the introduction of HD plasma and LCD sets, first rated by *Consumer Reports* in 2003 and 2004. As one example, the average price of thirty-two inch LCD models decreased from $2,916 in 2005 to $382 in 2014, for an average rate of price change of –22.5 percent per year. Larger plasma and LCD HD sets declined at an even faster rate in the decade ending in 2014.[48]

Previously we have noted the substantial understatement in the rate of price decline by the CPI for television sets in the period 1952–83, when the CPI decreased at an annual rate of 3.3 percent slower than the alternative price index discussed above. This understatement continued between 1983 and 1999, when the CPI declined at a rate 4.0 percent slower than the average price of nineteen-inch and twenty-seven-inch sets (–3.8 percent per year for the CPI as compared to –7.8 percent for the average prices listed in *Consumer Reports).* The 4.0 percent annual rate of price decline cumulates over the sixteen years 1983–99 to an additional 89 percent of unmeasured consumer benefit from television sets, and combined with the 278 percent understatement from 1952 to 1983 amounts to a total understatement for 1952–99 of 525 percent (2.78 × 1.89 = 5.25).

However, starting in 1998 the methodology of the CPI was changed to introduce a hedonic price index for TV sets, a method that controls for quality change along numerous dimensions, including not only picture size and high-definition resolution, but additional features as well, such as connectivity to the Internet. As a result of this change in methodology, there was virtually no difference between the CPI and the average prices of HD sets obtained from *Consumer Reports* in the decade ending in 2014, during which the CPI for TV sets registered a rate of price change of −20.4 percent per year. This is an important example of a theme that runs throughout this book, that the understatement of the consumer surplus provided by new products, the HD television set in this case, has been smaller in recent years than earlier in the postwar era, not to mention during 1870–1940.

None of these estimates include the value of the transition from black-and-white to color television, yet that transition was one of the most important events in the history of entertainment. Since the mid-1970s, color television has become a staple in almost every American household. At the same time, picture definition has continuously improved, with ever higher gradations of resolution until, as of May 2012, more than 70 percent of households had an HD-capable television set, compared to less than 15 percent in November 2007.[49] Today Americans watch the Rose Bowl Parade on a large, flat screen with a colorful brilliance and crisp clarity that could have only been dreamed of when color TV first arrived sixty years ago.

Another major change to the TV audience's experience was the advent of cable television, which began as a device to improve TV reception in distant locations. A few men, independently seeking ways to bring a clear picture to their own homes located in small isolated towns, found a simple but effective solution. They erected antenna towers where landmarks would not obscure the signal and then ran connecting wires to their television sets. Soon, they were providing cable services to their own and neighboring towns for a subscription cost of around $2 or $3 a month.[50] Cable television maintained its small-scale, local character until the 1960s, when viewer demand for sports programming brought it into conversations about national entertainment. Even then, however, cable faced obstacles. At first, the FCC, concerned about questions of broadcasting piracy on the part of cable providers, heavily regulated the expansion of CATV.

In the 1980s, however, cable television would finally have its day, as the consolidation of cable providers enabled them to overcome initial investment and installation costs.[51] From 1980 to 1990, the percentage of TV households with wired cable almost tripled, from 20 to 56.[52] Unlike early CATV, the main benefits of a cable subscription lay in variety. Viewers' options extended far beyond the three networks and a smattering of local channels. People could now watch a station devoted entirely to music videos or, if they were willing to pay extra for premium cable, could see movies on HBO, free from advertising interruption, twenty-four hours a day.

This expansion of viewing options spelled the end of the networks' dominance. The percentage of stations that were network affiliates dropped below eighty in 1982 for the first time since 1947. Only five years later, this proportion was down to 60.7 percent.[53] Moreover, between 1986 and 1999, the networks' audience share was cut in half, to less than thirty percent.[54] While networks still received, on the whole, more viewers than the smaller, newer stations, the days when a single show such as *I Love Lucy* or *Texaco Star Theater* represented a universally shared experience were gone. Cable, too, however, lost its edge for satisfying the consumer. Despite increasing competition from satellite TV, cable providers raised prices at three times the rate of inflation between 1998 and 2003 after an FCC decision to deregulate prices. Moreover, the cable services industry has consistently received some of the lowest marks in customer satisfaction.[55] As satellite continued to establish its place in the television market, and as digital entertainment has started to establish a foothold, cable subscriptions dropped from nearly two-thirds of American households in 2000 to just under 52 percent of homes by 2010.[56]

Another major development in television was the video cassette recorder (VCR). Entering American markets in the late seventies, the videotape recorder allowed its owners to record their favorite programs to watch whenever it best suited them. In what has been called "time-shifting," for the first time the viewer, not the broadcasting station, now had control over when TV was watched. With little delay, the VCR was purchased by most American families. Whereas just over 1 percent of homes were equipped with VCR in 1980, it had reached 68.6 percent of households by 1990 and 81 percent by 1995.[57] In fact, the popularity of VCRs was so great that the value of VCR shipments exceeded that of washing machines by 1983.

A partial cause of this growth was the VCR's rapid price reduction from $1,200 in 1978 to less than $250 by 1987. This rate of price decline of 17 percent per year exceeded that of any other appliance, albeit for only nine years. And this rate greatly understates the true rate of price decline, because quality change was very rapid in the first few years. The earliest models had electromechanical switches rather than electronic controls, and these were a constant cause of repair incidents as the controls were prone to jamming. The earliest models also lacked any programming capability and even lacked a remote control.[58] By 1982 "super deluxe" VCRs arrived that were initially very expensive but quickly declined in price; these included infrared remote control, fourteen-day programming capability, and multiple recording heads.[59] Because the VCR was not introduced into the CPI until 1987, all of this gain in consumer surplus resulting from the falling price and greatly improved quality was entirely missed in the GDP statistics.

Another reason for the popularity of the VCR, beyond its time-shifting capabilities, was the prerecorded video business. Not only could viewers decide when they watched TV programming, but also they could choose to watch Hollywood films in their homes that were not scheduled for TV. Because purchasing such prerecorded tapes could cost up to $80, rentals became the typical means for watching these videos, a convention that persisted up until the videotape was overtaken by the DVD player and DVR recorder, as discussed hereafter.[60]

TRANSITIONS IN MUSIC

During the first three decades of the postwar era, the phonograph was still king. During the war and in the immediate years that followed, the 78 rpm record remained the best way, outside of a live radio performance, to listen to music. The 78 had plenty of problems, though, with poor sound quality and short playing time that necessitated the constant use of record changers, even to hear just one classical song. The war, however, spurred a "revolution in sound" that solved these problems. In 1948, Columbia introduced the 33⅓-rpm disc, a record that brought long-playing capabilities to its listeners. The idea of the LP was not new. Thomas Edison had, in fact, produced a record in 1926 with around forty minutes of reproduction, although it had been highly unreliable and low-quality. The new 33⅓ differed from records of the past in its use of vinyl. As opposed to the 78's blend of shellac and various filler substances, vinyl was a highly durable and unbreakable material. The change lengthened the record's average life and enabled producers to cut much finer grooves into the record, which both improved sound quality and increased the possible number of revolutions and, thus, the playing time of the disc.

This was the birth of the album, as Americans could now sit and listen to a disc that played up to a half-hour per side, with very high quality. RCA, just months after Columbia's release of the LP, released the 45-rpm record. Despite using vinyl microgroove technology, the 45 brought higher-quality sound than the 78 but not long-playing capabilities.[61] While the 33⅓ introduced the concept of the album, the 45, as a single, was less expensive and gained its own following with youth audiences, as it became the vehicle for rock 'n' roll:

> For a time, the 45 R.P.M. record was the ultimate adolescent artifact. It was cheap as an allowance and easily transportable; it set just the right tempo for Saturday night. For a couple of American generations, a stack of 45's on a chubby spindle evokes a time of sweaty hands and quickened heartbeats, blue lights in the basement rec room.... Of course, the 45 itself bore witness to the idea that nothing is forever. It distilled transitory teenage romance into three-minute segments.[62]

In the past, music recordings of an artist followed fame. In these years, the 45 was the maker of fame. It made the stars of the day and influenced the stars of the future.[63]

The magnetic tape recorder, another recording innovation to come out of World War II, took some time before it made its full impact. Though the sound was not of the highest quality, it offered longer recording time and could be edited easily, unlike the phonograph disc, which relied on recording a song once through. Thus artists could double-track the vocals to harmonize and strengthen the sound of their singing voice or delete and tape over mistakes.[64] Though the tape recorder received limited use during the 1950s, mainly by independent artists such as Chuck Berry or to archive bebop from jazz clubs, the introduction of the tape cassette in the sixties signaled its true entrance into the spotlight. The tape cassette was user-friendly, compact and portable, and it was capable of playing forty-five minutes of music per side of tape. Sound quality and playing time continued to improve over the following decades.

The tape cassette democratized music. People who lacked the resources to record in the studio now had an avenue to make music and sell it commercially, as happened with the emergence of rap music in the late 1980s. The consumer could become the producer, and the varieties of music expanded as independent recording became more practicable. In addition to providing more diverse and participatory music options, the cassette tape made it easier to access one's favorite music. One could listen to a full album of one's choice while driving a car to work, an option not available with even the new and improved phonograph-based record discs.[65] The emergence of the portable Walkman, a precursor to today's iPod, allowed people to take music with them wherever they went. As one Walkman user noted, "It's totally liberating.... At the push of a button, you can be somewhere else with your music."[66]

It would be the compact disc, however, that received the most accolades, for it was able to respond to the problems of both the record disc and the tape cassette. Using a laser instead of microgrooves, the CD could play longer than either, up to seventy-five minutes on a single disc. The user also had the option of randomizing the order of songs. Perhaps most important, the CD recreated and even improved on the sound quality of vinyl records, as cassette tapes could not, while still being an accessible, portable option.

From 1978 to 1988, the sale of vinyl records fell 80 percent, a result more of the cassette tape than the CD, which was not introduced until 1982. By 1988, CD sales outpaced those of vinyl records,[67] and by 1991, they overtook cassette tapes as well. The CD reached its peak in 2002, when it accounted for more than 95 percent of sales, a number that would decrease quickly thanks to the iPod and digital music downloading, to be discussed later.[68]

From World War II until the end of the twentieth century, the way Americans listened to music changed in significant ways. Though the phonograph was the main source of recorded music for the first thirty years, thanks to the vinyl microgroove record, the cassette tape and then the CD ruled the final portion of the century, largely because of their mobility. Music was not, however, the only sphere of life in which mobility had become a paramount characteristic.

CAN YOU HEAR ME NOW? THE EXPANSION AND MOBILIZATION OF TELECOMMUNICATIONS

In 1940, the telephone had still reached only about 40 percent of American homes.[69] Prices remained high, especially for long distance calls. Such calls had to be patched through by an operator, or several operators, using a manual switchboard. As subscribers increased in number, so too did the number of possible connections at the square of the number of subscribers. This exponential growth meant that the number of operators and size of the switchboards themselves had to keep expanding, unless the process could be streamlined. The first automatic toll switch, located in Philadelphia in 1943, allowed a single operator, rather than a team of operators, to connect users to a long-distance phone number, though the operator still had to dial up to nineteen digits. The real breakthrough came in 1951 when AT&T introduced Direct Distance Dialing. In the new system, a caller could forgo the operator by dialing ten digits, the first three of which represented a unique area code for a particular part of the country. The initial area codes all required that the middle digit be "0" or "1," and the largest metropolitan areas were recognized by the low digits of their area codes (New York 212, Washington 202, Los Angeles 213, and Chicago 312).

The first call of this system, between Mayor Leslie Downing in Englewood, New Jersey, and Mayor Frank Osborne in Alameda, California, on November 10, 1951, took only eighteen seconds to connect from coast to coast. Just thirty-six years earlier, the first transcontinental phone call between New York and California had taken more than twenty-three minutes for five different operators to connect. Barriers of time and distance on the telephone were beginning to fade away.[70] Before the end of the decade, around 80 percent of the country's telephones could be reached by 60 percent of subscribers through direct dialing. However, there were still issues of switching capacity that made long-distance phone calls unreliable and inaccessible to many. In large cities, switchboards were overloaded, whereas in rural areas, they were costly and inefficient. The solution was to convert to automatic dialing of all telephone calls.[71]

The breakthrough toward such automation had come in 1948 with the invention of the transistor, which would also prove integral to the development of the computer. The transistor, invented by Walter Brattain, John Bardeen, and a team of Bell Labs scientists, facilitated electronic design and circuitry. This development quickly directed many experts to work on applying electronics to telecommunications switching, and in 1960 the stored-program control system, one of the earliest electronic switching systems, was applied commercially in Morris, Illinois.[72] By the 1970s, AT&T's Traffic Service Position System essentially brought a national standard of automation to telephony. Compatible with nearly all Bell System local and toll switching systems, TSPS eliminated the need for an operator in many tedious tasks, such as collecting tolls. Meanwhile, nearly all subscribers could reach one another through direct distance dialing.[73]

The efficiency gains from automation improved simultaneity, convenience, and cost of telephone calls by reducing the need for intermediate operators. These developments helped reduce the price of a three-minute phone call from New York to San Francisco from more than $75 in 1939 to about $3 in 1981. In the same time, rates from New York to London fell from more than $240 to just under $6.[74] As a result of rate reductions and accompanying growth in subscriptions over this period, the average number of daily toll calls per capita rose more than eleven times.[75] Moreover, by 1990, 93 percent of American families had a telephone, compared to 40 percent fifty years earlier.[76]

Just as the residential landline telephone was establishing a firm foothold in nearly every American household, the cellular phone was introduced. Mobile phones had been around for some time, but they had to remain within close range of a transmitting station. In the 1970s, a cellular system consisting of a network of receiving and transmitting towers, or "cells" began to be established. As a cellular phone moved, its signal switched to the nearest cell.[77] In the early days car phones dominated the cellular industry, largely because portable hand-held phones were too bulky and heavy to carry around. The Motorola 8000, introduced in 1984, was often compared to a brick. By 1988, only 5 percent of cellular phone sales in the United States were of hand-portables. Moreover, the cell phone was still mainly a tool for business, and calls were generally short and to the point. Films such as *Wall Street* (1987) presented cell phones as a symbol of status and financial success.[78]

Only toward the end of the 1990s did the cell phone begin to affect the life of the average American, with the number of subscribers growing from just over 5 million in 1990—or about 2 percent of the population—to nearly 110 million, or 39 percent of Americans, by the year 2000. During that time, the number of cell sites increased proportionally, and the average monthly bill decreased by nearly half. After 2000, the cell phone overtook the residential telephone as the standard means of telecommunication. Whereas the residential telephone accounted for 75 percent of American phone service expenditures in 2001, this percentage was down to 37.3 by 2009. In 2010, there were almost 2.6 cell phones for every household,[79] and, by 2013, 91 percent of American adults had one, as can be seen in figure 12–4.[80] As shown in that figure, Americans increasingly canceled their land-line service as they came to rely entirely on mobile phone communication.

The explosion of the cellular phone into American life changed many social and cultural practices. For the first time, "Where are you?" could be used outside of a game of hide-and-seek, as a telephone number was no longer limited to one location. Parents were always just a few button dials away from hearing their child's voice, which probably came as a comfort to them, though the ever-present proximity of parental voices was considered a *decrease* in the standard of

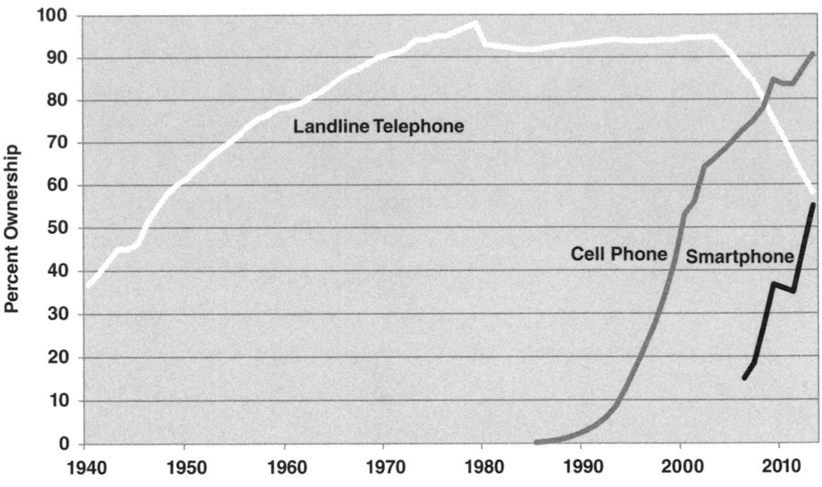

Figure 12–4. Shifts in Telephone Ownership, 1940–2013

Sources: Landline telephones after 2002 from Blumberg and Luke (2013). Landline telephones 1940–2001 from SAUS (2012), "No. HS-42: Selected Communications Media: 1920 to 2001," US Census Bureau. Cell phones from 1985–2000 from US Department of Transportation.

living by many a college student. One of its biggest effects was on the planning of social gatherings:

> By the time I got my first phone, its purchase was not so much a fashion statement or the result of any love of shiny new technology as it was a necessity: if I wanted a social life then I had better get my hands on one. My friends had long dispensed with the traditional method of arranging nights out well in advance, establishing firm details such as where and precisely when we would meet. Instead, a vague indication of plans would be finalized at the last minute, coordinated in real time through texts and quick calls. I got a phone because I did not want to be left out.[81]

The cell phone has its drawbacks, such as the intrusion of someone else's phone conversation into one's personal space. With the advent of the smartphone, to be discussed in the next section, one often sees a table full of people at a restaurant, each with their eyes glued to their own small screen as they send text messages. People instinctively check their phones every ten minutes, never free from their self-imposed obligation constantly to scan the latest updates on their social networks. Yet the cell phone has provided freedom for spontaneity, an increased sense of security, and an end to being out of touch.

THE NEWS

Immediacy also came to characterize Americans' consumption of news. The early years of television news were experimental works in progress. When TV news programs showed footage, they did so often days or weeks after the fact and taken from newsreel clips, because television cameras still had trouble producing a good picture outside of studios. As time went on, television news became more substantive and produced more of its own film footage.[82] The improvement in television quality was accompanied by a corresponding decline in the cinema newsreel, which was all but dead by the mid-1960s.

Television news, on the other hand, increasingly gained a quality and credibility that the newsreel lacked. The information came first from a familiar anchor, with footage used for the most part as a substantive complement rather than purely as an eye-catching distraction. Indeed, the familiarity of the network anchors helped television news surpass not only the newsreel, but also the newspaper, as the main source of news. For example, Walter Cronkite, "[with] his wholesome manner and appearance, his studied fairness, his twinkle in the midst of seriousness . . . was deeply trusted by millions when he was the anchor of the 'CBS Evening News.' He was even mentioned as a suitable candidate for vice-president."[83]

The effect of TV news went beyond the ability to present a familiar, trusted face to deliver the top stories. Like radio, television news was immediate, but it also wielded the power of the image to evoke strong feelings in the viewer. In addition to coverage of the day's top stories, television news also developed more in-depth journalistic programs. The news documentary reached new heights in 1968 with the introduction of CBS's *60 Minutes,* still, after forty-seven years, one of the top ten highest-rated network TV programs, week after week.[84] Cable television delivered CNN as the first twenty-four-hour news station in 1980.[85] By the 1990s, so many channels were available that one could choose to listen to political talk from the left (MSNBC), center (CNN), or right (Fox News) of the political spectrum. In the largest metropolitan areas, there was even a twenty-four-hour local cable channel (e.g., NY-1 in the New York area and CLTV in Chicago).[86]

Unsurprisingly, after reaching all-time highs in the postwar years, newspaper circulation per household soon began a gradual but continuous decline, dropping from 1.4 per household in 1949 to 0.8 in 1980 and to less than 0.4 in 2010 (see figure 12–5).[87] The newspaper's quantitative decline was accompanied by qualitative changes. Before radio and TV delivered an immediacy of reporting that the papers could not match, newspapers were essentially bulletins for the most recent developments off the wire. They provided bare facts of what was happening in the world, with little analysis or interpretation, although those facts were often determined by a "certain fast-and-loose, devil-may-care attitude," because the incentive was to be the first to print the newest scoop.[88]

With television, newspapers had no chance of reporting the biggest stories first. To compete, papers endeavored to provide more comprehensive coverage or to uncover special-interest stories that had not reached the TV broadcasts. Rather than printing the news and leaving it for the reader to decipher the meaning, newspapers began integrating analysis into their stories. The success of the weekly news magazines, such as *Time* and *Newsweek*, which distilled often complicated events of the week into orderly, easily understood synopses for the reader, spurred imitation from the newspapers. Moreover, TV made sports so popular that by the 1980s, many newspapers devoted around 20 percent of

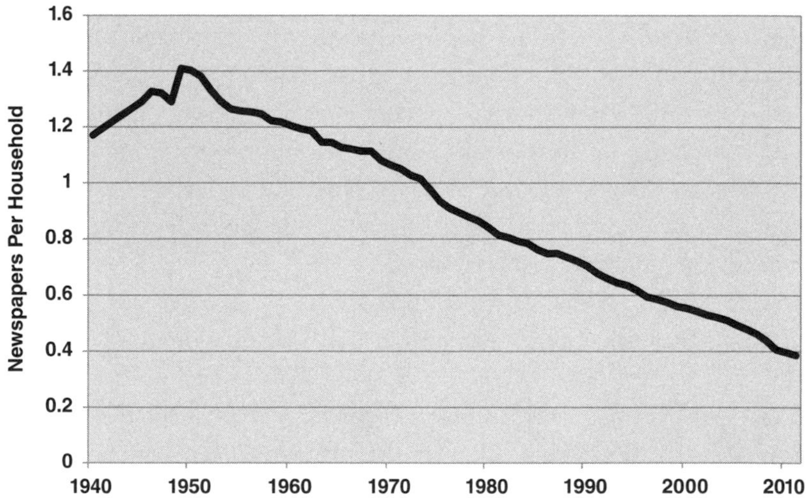

Figure 12–5. Newspaper Circulation Per Household, 1940–2011
Source: Newspaper Association of America (2012).

their news space to a separate sports section.[89] Thus, though newspapers were unable to halt their steady decline, they did carve out a niche in spaces that television could not fill.

By the late 1990s, both television and the newspapers faced a new competitor, news delivered over the Internet. Google searches allowed any specific piece of news, such as a stock price quotation or a sports score, to be located immediately. A brief bulletin heard on the radio could be fleshed out by reading a longer story obtained through Google. Between 2003 and 2012, even as ad revenues for online newspaper editions nearly tripled, overall revenues were cut in half, for the print editions were losing advertisers more quickly than online editions could make up for lost revenue.[90]

Though television remains Americans' primary source for news, with more than 87 percent of respondents in a 2014 poll saying they had used it for news in the past week, 69 percent were now using laptops and computers as well. The large majority of smartphone and tablet owners use such devices for news. Meanwhile, radio provided 65 percent of Americans with news, while newspapers reached 61 percent of the adult population.[91] As TV news is able to relate current events so that viewers feel a part of current events, Internet news provides the benefits of up-to-the-minute, convenient, personalized content. Blogs and chat groups have further diverted attention from traditional media. However, neither venue for news is without its flaws. Because of the power of the image, events of visual impact often supersede issues of more substantive importance, such as the economy's weak labor market or political gridlock in Washington.[92] With Internet news, studies have found that reading speed and retention are lower when people use a digital screen, raising questions of how beneficial is the current transition toward digital news.[93]

DIGITAL MEDIA: THE PERSONALIZATION AND FRAGMENTATION OF ENTERTAINMENT

A theme throughout this chapter is that unlike for some other aspects of the standard of living discussed in other chapters, there has been no slowing in the rate of progress of entertainment and communication. The move toward digital media began in the 1990s, and the transformation accelerated through the past fifteen years. From music to movies to television, entertainment has increasingly shifted to digital devices and in many ways transformed its own social meaning. In music, the first step toward digitalization was the MP3 in the late nineties, a high-compression file that could be downloaded onto computers and play music. File-sharing, whereby people would "rip" music from a CD into MP3 form and then distribute music files to others for free, made music more accessible than before because of the large quantity of music that could be stored on a small, portable device.

When it was introduced in 2001, the iPod separated itself from the pack of MP3 players with its intuitive click wheel interface and its compatibility with iTunes. In turn, iTunes integrated the market for digital music and one's own personal music library into a single user-friendly computer application. One could choose one of thousands of songs from the pocket-sized device, and, for the first time, the user had almost total control over the listening experience. The iPod replaced the portable CD player, for a user's library of CD albums could be uploaded into the iTunes program at zero cost. Suddenly a choice among hundreds of albums, limited only by the size of one's existing CD collection, could be heard and sorted by song or artist, or MP3 songs and albums could be purchased for reasonable prices from the iTunes store.

Though the iPod was the most influential driver of the shift to digital music and has maintained its favored position, it has been joined by several other innovative sources of music. The websites Pandora and Spotify have taken the radio format to the Internet and personalized it, streaming music according to the listener's stated preferences. For instance, Spotify allows users unlimited access to its entire library of 30 million songs for a monthly subscription of around $10—or for free, if one is willing to listen to advertisements.[94] These changes in music delivery not only increased the portable capacity and convenience of acquiring and listening to music, but also made music listening highly personal. Wherever one has access to the Internet, one can listen to favorite songs or to any of millions never heard before.

The shift toward digital audiovisual entertainment evolved in stages. The prominence of the VCR met its demise on two fronts in the late 1990s and early 2000s. The DVD, or digital video disc, was introduced to the United States in 1995, and by 2006, more American households had a DVD player (81.2 percent) than a VCR player (79.2 percent).[95] A lighter and more compact device than the videocassette, DVDs also provided higher definition and expanded capabilities, such as menu selections and skipping scenes. By 2011, nearly 87 percent of households owned DVD players. This transition is summarized in table 12–1.

On the other front, the DVR, or digital video recorder, emerged at the turn of the century to challenge the VCR as the principal time-shifting device. While

Table 12–1. Home Access to Media in 2011

	Percentage of Households	
	1970	**2011**
Cell Phone	0	87.3
DVD Player	0	86.7
Internet at Home	0	77.1
Peronsal Computer	0	80.9
Satellite Dish	0	26.3
Video Game System	0	35
VCR	0	69.6
MP3 Player	0	45.3
HDTV Capable	0	69.8
DVR	0	41.3
Television	95.3	98.9

Source: "TV Basics" (2012).

the VCR created a revolution in how people watched TV, the DVR's main contribution was to improve the convenience of time-shifting, as recording became as simple as clicking a button on the remote. All recordings were located in one place without taking up the space of tens or hundreds of videotapes. Though less than half of American households had a DVR in October 2013,[96] on average about thirty minutes per day was spent watching time-shifted TV.[97]

Another important development has been the emergence of online video streaming. From video sharing on YouTube to the copious movie and television offerings on Netflix, the number of viewing options has exploded, with people in full control of when, where, and what they watch. With more than 30 million subscribers in 2014 to a streaming service that had only begun in 2007, Netflix has led the way as audiovisual entertainment has found its new home on the Internet.[98] Before its success in video streaming, Netflix pioneered the business of renting DVD movies by mail and within a few years drove the retail rental giant Blockbuster into bankruptcy and liquidation.

Like the coming of television, the move toward digital entertainment dominance has not pushed aside the old audiovisual media. Rather, just as the motion picture shifted and adapted to changing circumstances in the second half of the twentieth century, TV and movies have done the same in the digital age. At first seen as a threat by the movie industry, DVDs became a cash cow and even caused Hollywood to increase movie production and variety to fill store shelves with DVDs.[99] Sites such as Netflix have the potential to do the same.

Digitalization has also affected the written word. Though around 70 percent of adults read a book in print in 2013, the proportion of those who read an e-book was up to 28 percent from just 17 percent two years earlier. Though e-readers such as the Kindle started the shift toward digital books, the tablet has become popular as a device well-suited for reading.[100] The advent of the smartphone, beginning with the BlackBerry and continuing with the iPhone, made entertainment mobile in the same way the earlier cell phones had made communications mobile. In January 2014, 58 percent of American adults owned a smartphone,[101] an impressive number considering that the first smartphone, the BlackBerry, entered U.S. markets in 2003. With a smartphone, one could listen to music, send text messages and e-mails, watch sports highlights, or read a magazine article on one device, all while waiting in line at the supermarket.

> We carried a first- or second-generation mobile phone because communication was desirable, even essential, on the move. But we are now carrying around a new object, one that might trick us into thinking that it is merely an extended phone, but is in fact, I think, a radically new personal device. The smartphone... is not just a phone. It's a computer. And computers are unique—they are, in a crucial respect, unlike any other technology—and uniquely important in the history of the modern world.[102]

Indeed, for some people, the smartphone's auxiliary functions have superseded typical phone uses. Of the 63 percent of adult cell owners who used their phones to go online as of May 2013, 34 percent used the phone as their primary means of accessing the Internet, and 81 percent sent or received text messages. Around half of cell phone owners—and presumably the large majority of smartphone owners—accessed email, listened to music, downloaded applications, and used GPS capabilities.[103] One of the main developments, unique to the smartphone, was the application, or "app." Introduced in 2008, the Apple iPhone App Store has rapidly expanded its offerings from 500 initial apps to more than 700,000. Ranging from games to portals for social networks or news publications, apps have seen more than 30 billion downloads.[104] The smartphone and its Twitter app have been largely responsible for the success of that social networking company, as 78 percent of the approximately 60 million monthly active users in the United States access it using mobile phones.[105]

CONCLUSION

Of all the components of the American standard of living, the quality of entertainment and communications advanced fastest and farthest throughout the 1940–2014 era. There has been no post-1970 slowdown in the pace of progress such as occurred for food, clothing, household appliances, and air travel. Technologies that have become integral parts of the American household were unknown, or at most distant dreams, in 1940. Today, however, the TV, introduced by David Sarnoff at the 1939 World Fair, can be found in nearly every home and is used by more than 88 percent of adults each day. In fact, the majority of homes have more than one TV, through which they can be transported to any part of the world, to a highly anticipated sporting event, or through which they can view a recent movie, without commercials, through mail movie rental or video streaming.

The initial benefits of television were followed by a sequence of further innovations, large and small. The quality of television sets steadily improved so much that for the same price of roughly $400, the repair-prone nine-inch black and white set of 1950 has been replaced in 2014 by a dazzling forty-inch LED high-definition color set with surround stereo sound. For most of the postwar period the enormous improvement in the quality of TV sets relative to their price was understated by the CPI, the official government price index. Between 1952 and 1999 we estimate that for every dollar of spending on TV sets recorded in real GDP, quality improvements have delivered $5 of unmeasured benefits. Since 1999 improved CPI methodology has eliminated this source of price-index understatement of consumer benefits. The radical declines in the prices of HD television sets by a factor of ten between 2004 and 2014 have been accurately tracked by the CPI, which declined by a rate of more than 20 percent per year during that decade. This provides an example of a theme of this book, that the extent of understatement of the benefits of new and improved products has been less significant than in the earlier postwar years and particularly before World War II.

The transition to color by 1970 brought new life and reality to the television screen, and cable expanded viewers' options, providing a plethora of narrow-interest alternatives to the broad-based appeal of the networks. Starting in the late 1970s, the VCR and, later, the DVR put full time-shifting control into the hands of audience members, allowing them to watch at times that fit their schedule. Such choice and control were unprecedented; at no time in history had one been able to decide at a moment's notice to watch an opera, a baseball game, or a myriad of other program types.

Platforms for listening to music went through several phases of transformation. Although the phonograph continued to dominate the music scene for three decades after the 1940s, from the 1970s on new technologies made music mobile. The portability of music listening devices, from transistor radios to the Walkman and the iPod, was matched by an ever-expanding storage capacity and playing time. In communications, the price of long-distance calls declined steadily until today phone users take for granted that all long-distance domestic calls, even across 3,000 miles of distance, are covered by a fixed-price phone plan. Mobile phones continue this trend by erasing constraints not only of distance, but also of location. A spontaneous phone call from wherever one happens to be is taken for granted today, whereas seventy years ago, a connection between two locations could take several minutes and cost as much or more than the hourly wage. In the past two decades digitalization has brought convenience and personalization throughout the world of entertainment and communication.

Chapter 13

COMPUTERS AND THE INTERNET FROM THE MAINFRAME TO FACEBOOK

> If the automobile had followed the same development as the computer, a Rolls Royce would today cost $100 and get a million miles per gallon, and explode once a year killing everyone inside.
>
> —Robert X. Cringely, *InfoWorld* magazine

INTRODUCTION

The improvement in the performance of computers relative to their price has been continuous and exponential since 1960, and the rate of improvement dwarfs any precedent in the history of technology. The wonders achieved by computers and, since the mid-1990s, by the Internet have misled many analysts into believing that the current rate of economy-wide progress is the fastest in human history and will become even more rapid in the future. The basic flaw in this faith in an acceleration of technological change is that even if the contribution of computers to economic growth were increasing, the share of total GDP represented by computers is too small to overcome the great majority of economic activity where the pace of innovation is not accelerating and, indeed, in many aspects is slowing down.

ICT is the standard acronym for information and communication technology, and the share of total spending by business firms and households on ICT hardware and software, including Internet and phone connection charges, amounted to only 7 percent of the economy in 2014. Even if the performance-to-price ratio of ICT equipment were to rise by 20 percent per year, a hypothetical zero rate of progress in the other 93 percent of the economy would yield a growth rate of overall economic performance of only 1.4 percent per year.

The magical advance of computer technology over the past half century discussed in this chapter is even more impressive than the advances in entertainment and communication discussed in chapter 12. This contrasts with the slowing pace of innovation discussed in chapter 10 on food, clothing, housing, and appliances, and in chapter 11 regarding surface and air transportation.

The chapter begins with the mainframe computer, which allowed the computerization of many routine and tedious business operations as long ago as 1960. The first bank statements, telephone bills, and insurance policies were produced by mainframes in the 1960s, and airline reservations systems were gradually automated in the 1960s and 1970s. The tedious typing and retyping of legal briefs and book manuscripts was eliminated in the 1960s and 1970s by the memory typewriter. Electronics made possible the modern copying machine, and the Xerox Company became one of the hot corporations of the 1960s. At the same time as the personal computer arrived in the early 1980s, two other fundamental innovations were made in the form of the ATM cash machine and the retail barcode scanner.

In the beginning of the 1980s, the personal computer became accessible with software choices that enhanced personal productivity, including word-wrapped word processing, spreadsheet calculations, and gaming. Academics, authors, and others whose jobs involved writing and manuscript preparation flocked to the personal computer. Long before the arrival of the Internet, computers within business firms were connected with "T-1 lines" that operated at broadband speeds, and so within the firm, the New York office could send messages and trade files with the San Francisco or London office as early as the 1980s.

The rise of the Internet utterly transformed the role of the PC for individuals by allowing it to communicate with the outside world, just as communication inside business firms had been possible for most of the previous decade. Academics began sending e-mails in the early 1980s, and e-commerce and web searches began with the Netscape web browser in 1994. With the quick reach that the Internet provided to the general public for information, communication, and entertainment, a new era began for professionals and ordinary citizens alike. Just as electricity and indoor plumbing networked American homes (chapter 4), the Internet networked the American people. Search engines enabled people to find the cheapest airline tickets and the weather in Savannah next Saturday. Just as cheaper telephone calls had made letter writing obsolete by the early 1970s, so e-mail began to encroach on the previous centrality of telephone calls as a means of communication. Increasingly, news did not come from newspapers tossed onto our porches or from the nightly TV news, but from online versions of traditional news media and from new forms of information called "blogs."

The rise of the Internet and the computer also opened the market for e-commerce. Large superstores such as Walmart became gigantic consumers of data, which allowed them to predict sales from historical trends, as well as to undercut the prices of their competitors. Amazon was founded in 1994 and gradually over the past two decades has developed into an e-commerce juggernaut that put many small independent book stores out of business and then ultimately crushed the bricks-and-mortars giant Borders. Consumers have benefited from e-commerce in many ways, for instance by being able to find menus on the websites of all but the smallest restaurants and to make airline, hotel, and restaurant reservations electronically without having their phone calls placed on hold.

The chapter concludes by comparing the familiar benefits of the Internet with its costs, some of which are subtle. There still remains a gap in Internet access and, more important, Internet literacy that can add to the shortfall of educational achievement of the minority and poverty population. The Internet has brought with it a set of concerns that did not exist twenty years ago, including hacking, identity theft, privacy, Internet bullying, and (in the views of some observers) a decline of attention spans and literacy, especially among American teenage boys. Another set of problems has to do with the payoff of investments in modern technology. Elementary and secondary schools have made large investments in ICT without any evident improvement in test scores. Colleges spend vast sums on smart classrooms that require ubiquitous handholding by support staff, without any apparent benefit to educational outcomes. Beyond the classroom, families have increasingly turned from personal to electronic communication, and young children are obtaining access to electronic devices. For adults, the constant connection to their smartphones, email, and social media means increased levels of multitasking and hyperconnectivity, both of which may hinder productivity and even create danger in the form of texting while driving.

THE TECHNOLOGICAL REVOLUTION AND THE DEATH OF MOORE'S LAW

In the early 1970s, Seymour Cray, known as "the father of the supercomputer," was turning heads in the computer industry. The Cray-1 system was a supercomputer that held a world-record speed of 160 million floating-point operations per second and had an eight megabyte main memory. The computer had no wires that were longer than four feet, and it could fit in a small room. In 1976, the Los Alamos National Laboratory bought the Cray-1 system for $8.8 million, or $36.9 million in today's inflation-adjusted dollars.[1]

The sharp contrast between the Cray-1 and today's most ordinary laptops represents progress so rapid that it is hard to grasp. In mid-August 2014, the Walmart website offered for $449 a Lenovo laptop with six gigabytes of memory, or 750 times the memory of the Cray-1, and the ability to do 1,000 times as many calculations per second as the Cray-1. Beyond speed and memory, other benefits of the everyday laptop over the fastest computer in the world in 1976 include being able to watch video, access the Internet, and communicate with people halfway across the world on a system that can fit on the lap without the burden of an industrial-grade cooling system.

Leaving aside the increased connectivity, the sheer increase in computing power represented an increase in the performance-to-price ratio of the Lenovo compared to the Cray at an astounding annual rate of 44 percent per year. And yet this increase has been vastly understated in the U.S. national income accounts, despite its use of a hedonic price index for computers, because—with one exception hereafter discussed—research on computer prices has overlooked the necessity of directly comparing mainframe and PC prices. And yet it is trivial to calculate that the price of the computing power contained in the Cray of $8.8 million fell to $0.60 between 1976 and 2014.

The technology industry is unique in the rapid growth that it has achieved since 1960 in the performance-to-price ratio of the products it has produced. The classic description of the uniqueness of technical advance in the computer industry is provided by Moore's Law, set out a half century ago by Gordon Moore, a cofounder of Intel. His long-term projection was a doubling of chip density every two years. "The number of transistors incorporated in a chip will approximately double every 24 months."[2] This converts to an annual growth rate of 34.7 percent, almost as fast as our calculation of the transition from the Cray supercomputer to the Lenovo laptop.[3] Moore's Law is a misnomer, it being rather a conjecture that semiconductor producers subsequently adopted as an industry standard.

Figure 13–1 summarizes the evolution of Moore's Law starting with the 1971 Intel 4004 with 3,500 transistors and ending with the 2014 Intel 15-Core Xeon Ivy Bridge with 4.31 billion transistors.[4] The chart shows how remarkably close the transistor count stays to the Moore's Law trend line. However, estimates of the rate of improvement of computer quality based on memory and speed inherently underestimate the improved performance relative to price by failing to place any value on more advanced ways of accessing memory (flash drives versus floppy disks), more advanced input–output connectors (USB ports instead of serial and parallel ports), shorter boot times, better audio/video capability, and the enormous increase in portability and reduction in weight that have occurred since 1982. The earliest PC screens in 1982 were monochrome green and black, not full-color, and the DOS interface required typing multiple commands instead of scrolling with a mouse or, more recently, using a touchscreen.

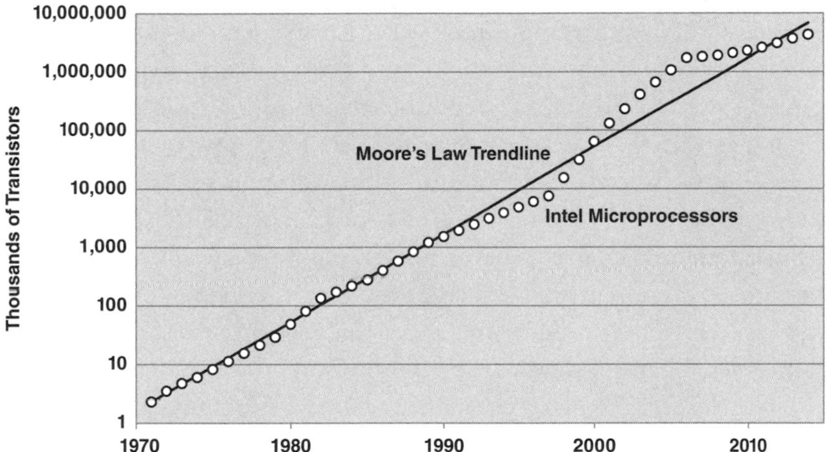

Figure 13–1. Moore's Law and Thousands of Transistors in Intel Microprocessors, 1971–2014

Sources: Intel "Microprocessors Quick Reference Guide" 1971–2008 (http://www.intel.com/pressroom/kits/quickreffam.htm), "Intel Previews Intel Xeon® 'Nehalem-EX' Processor" 2010 (http://www.intel.com/pressroom/archive/releases/2009/20090526comp.htm), "Westmere-EX: Intel's Flagship Benchmarked" 2011 (http://www.anandtech.com/show/4285/westmereex-intels-flagship-benchmarked), "Product Brief: Intel® Itanium® Processor 9500 Series" 2012 (http://download.intel.com/newsroom/archive/Intel-Itanium-processor-9500_ProductBrief.pdf), "Intel shares details of 15-core Xeon chip, Ivytown" 2014 (http://www.pcworld.com/article/2096320/intels-15core-xeon-server-chip-has-431-billion-transistors.html).

William Nordhaus's research on the history of computer power over the past two centuries makes two important comments about the comparison of Moore's Law to growth in computational speed and cost:

> First, it is clear that rapid improvements in computational speed and cost predated Moore's forecast [in 1965]. For the period 1945–1980, cost per computation declined at 37 percent per year, as compared to 64 percent per year after 1980. Second, computational power actually grows more rapidly than Moore's Law would predict because computer performance is not identical to chip density. From 1982 to 2001, the rate of performance as measured by computer power grew 30 percent per year faster than Moore's Law would indicate.[5]

Nordhaus's estimate of a 64 percent per year decline in the performance-adjusted price of computers after 1980 conflicts with the price declines of roughly 20 percent per year for mainframes between 1957 and 1984 and in the range of 20 percent to 30 percent for personal computers after 1984. Part of the discrepancy is that Nordhaus has quantified the sharp step downward in the price–performance ratio embedded in the transition from mainframes to PCs, just as we have done in our comparison of the Cray mainframe with the Lenovo laptop. Whatever the reasons for the differences between our Cray/Lenovo annual rate of price reduction of 41 percent and Nordhaus's estimate of 64 percent, there is no doubt that computer prices have declined more quickly than those for any other product in the history of invention.

However figure 13–1 also contains startling evidence that Moore's Law has finally suffered a major slowdown below its historic 34.7 percent growth rate. If we look closely at the relationship between the dots and the straight line, we notice that the dots are above the line in the late 1990s and the beginning of the 2000s but then decline to below the Moore's law line thereafter. We can calculate that the Moore's Law line rises on average since 1970 at 34.7 percent per year. This speeded up to 60.1 percent per year during the period 1997–2006 and then fell by a factor of almost six, to 11.5 percent, for 2006–2014.

The sharp speedup and then collapse of the Moore's Law growth line is shown clearly in figure 13–2. The growth rate of the dots in figure 13–1 can be calculated and plotted as a centered five-year moving average. The Moore's Law line is horizontal at the traditional Moore's Law growth rate of 34.7 percent per year. The actual outcome has differed sharply on both the up side and the down

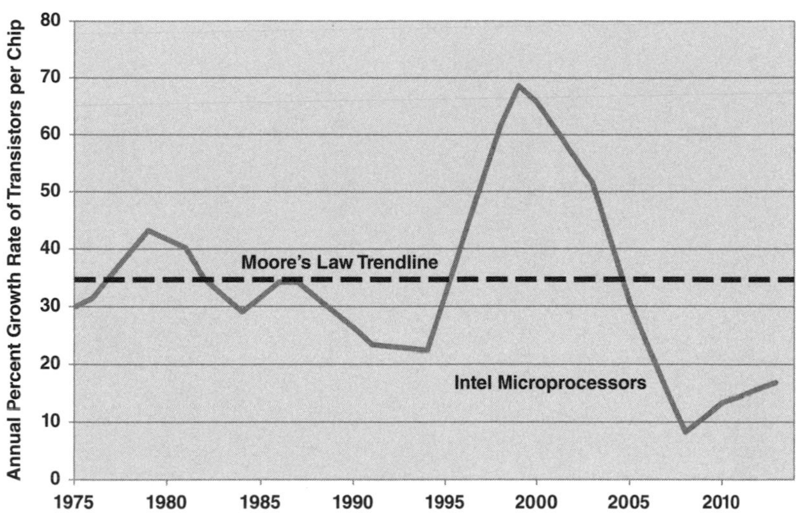

Figure 13–2. Moore's Law Is Violated by the Irregular Rate of Increase of the Number of Transistors on a Chip, 1975–2014
Source: See figure 13–1.

side. Instead of doubling every two years, during the go-go period of 1997 to 2006, the doubling interval dropped to fourteen months. But since 2006, the doubling time tripled from the traditional two years to six years.

Why did the growth rate in figure 13–2 jump in the late 1990s and collapse after 2006? In e-mail correspondence, the distinguished economist Hal Varian, now the chief economist at Google, explained that technological change in desktop and laptop computers has come to a halt "because no one needs a superfast chip on their desktop," so research has shifted into trying to improve larger computers in data centers as well as battery life of portable devices. He concludes, "The most important issue is whether the slowdown is a demand-side or supply-side phenomenon. My view is that it is demand-side." He goes on to cite a prophetic 2002 article titled "The Lives and Death of Moore's Law."[6]

The rest of this chapter asks how well this gusher of computer performance, at least the part that happened before 2006, was translated into what matters—the growth of real GDP per hour and per capita, and the creation of consumer surplus not captured by real GDP. We postpone until chapter 17 the implications of the remarkable slowdown of the past decade and its implications for future productivity growth, with the slowdown in the operation of Moore's Law joining a list of other evidence that diminishing returns have set in.

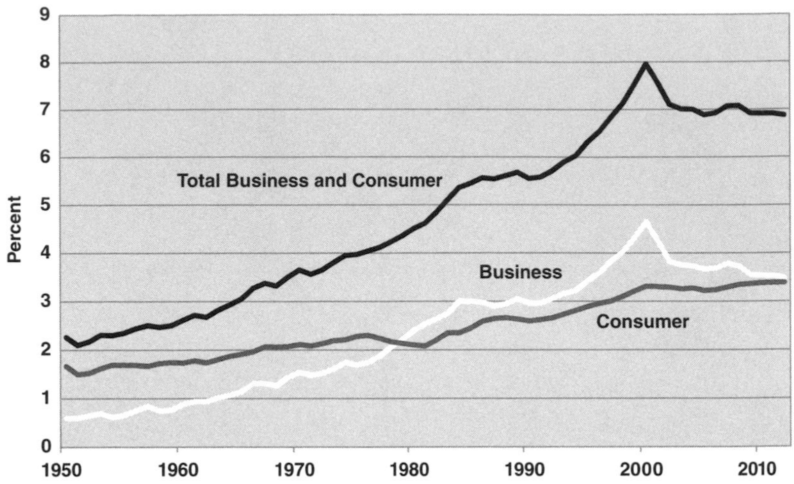

Figure 13–3. Share in Nominal GDP of Business Computer Hardware and Software and of Consumer Video, Audio, and Computer Equipment and Telecommunication Services, 1950–2013
Source: Bureau of Economic Analysis (NIPA Tables 1.1.5, 2.4.5, 5.5.5., 5.6.5.)

Figure 13–3 plots the share of three different forms of ICT spending in GDP. The largest share is ICT investment by business firms. The smaller categories are two types of consumer spending, that on audio, visual, photo and information processing equipment, and the consumer service components of Internet and telecommunications services. This is where the monthly land-line and smartphone bills are tabulated. Business investment in ICT exhibits two periods of rapid growth—from 1975 to 1984 and, after a short hiatus, from 1991 to 2000. These two periods of quick growth are followed by slow growth during 1985–95 and negative growth during 2000–2005. The top line in figure 13–3 is the total of business and consumer spending and has the same pattern of peak in 2000 and then decline as the business component.

BIGGER IS BETTER: MAINFRAMES AND EARLY NETWORKS

On February 15, 1946, the *New York Times* published an article titled "Electronic Computer Flashes Answers, May Speed Engineering." The War Department scientists at the University of Pennsylvania revealed one of World War II's top secrets, "an amazing machine which applies electronic speeds…to mathematical tasks hitherto too difficult and cumbersome for solution."[7] The

ENIAC, or Electronic Numerical Integrator and Computer, computed mathematical problems 1,000 times faster than ever before and had not a single moving mechanical part, but weighed thirty short tons, took up 1,800 square feet, consumed 175 kilowatts of power, and had several miles of wires. Impressed with the size of this colossus, some joked that when the ENIAC was turned on, the lights in Philadelphia dimmed.[8]

Airline passenger traffic exploded with double-digit growth after the end of World War II, but flight booking was done entirely by hand. As early as 1946, American Airlines started working with Teleregister to develop the "Reservisor" that could handle an additional 200 passengers daily with twenty fewer agents. By 1956 a larger and faster version could process 2,000 reservations a day and cut response times to half a second, but the process was not fully electronic, requiring punch cards for each reservation. American Airlines leaped ahead of the other airlines and developed a fully electronic system that became fully operational in 1964. SABRE supported more than 1,000 terminals from two IBM 7090 computers and could process 83,000 daily phone calls.[9] Unlike the Reservisor, the system took over all booking functions and did not require any use of punch cards.

The life insurance industry needed to handle large volumes of data, and electromechanical punched-card tabulating equipment was already a staple in the industry dating back to the 1930s. An IBM assessment noted, "Insurance companies were among the largest and most sophisticated users of punched-card machines in the late 1940s and 1950s."[10] During the Second World War, many insurance actuaries and other employees worked for the military in projects involving statistics, code-breaking, bombsights, and operations research.[11] This is one of many examples emphasized in chapter 16 of the spillover of technologies developed under wartime conditions to raise productivity in the postwar economy. The large life insurance companies in 1954–55 rushed to buy the first commercially available computer, the UNIVAC 1. Progress was slow, because the initial computers did little more than juggle data read from punch cards and printed by punch-card printers.

The banking industry went through three phases of electronic evolution involving the use of the mainframe computer, the development of credit cards, and the early ATM cash machines. As early as 1934, IBM had introduced the IBM 801 Bank Proof Machine, which listed and separated checks, endorsed them, and then recorded the totals. It represented a milestone in the history of check clearing. By the 1960s, the typical bank system consisted of an IBM 1401 computer, which could receive data from either punched cards or a magnetic character reader. Tellers could now locate customer information, process it, and print the results within seconds at each teller window. One of the first 1401-based banking systems was installed at the Pacific National Bank in Seattle in August 1961, and the bank increased its checking account update speed from three checks per minute to seventy-five.[12]

Credit cards created an entirely new form of payment. The legend goes that the financer Frank McNamara was entertaining clients at Major's Cabin Grill in 1949. The stereotypical New York power lunch was embarrassingly brought to halt when the bill arrived and McNamara realized that he had left his wallet in a different suit. He had to call his wife to bring over money to pay the tab. Suitably embarrassed, McNamara began working with his lawyer Ralph Schneider and friend and retail-store magnate Alfred Bloomingdale to create a multipurpose charge card. A year later, they started Diners Club, the first charge card company, with a network of twenty-seven restaurants.[13] However, the BankAmericard, established in 1958, quickly became the most popular credit card and in 1976 was renamed Visa. The modern-day VISANet system, as of 2012, is connected to 200 countries or territories, 15,000 financial institutions, 2 million ATMs, millions of merchant outlets, 2 billion cards, and 68 billion transactions per year.[14]

Despite the benefits that IBM processing systems brought to banks and the ease that credit cards made to payments, customers could make deposits and withdraw cash only during specified bank hours. The idea of the modern networked automated teller machine (ATM) was conceived by a former IBM engineer, Donald Wetzel. There were two main barriers that Wetzel had to overcome to convince banks to adopt the ATM—costs and acceptance. Wetzel recounts:

> The mentality of people at that time was, remember, "we want to deal face-to-face with people. People are not going to walk up to a machine and use it. In fact we don't want them to do that, we want them coming to the bank and talking to us, because then we can sell them on some other things."[15]

The inherent benefits of an ATM were customer-based: It decreased the time required for a transaction and offered the convenience of being available for use 24/7. In time, the ATM evolved from a novelty that banks advertised to a service that consumers took for granted.

The mainframe, which often occupied an entire air-conditioned room or even a separate building, contrasted in size with the miniature barcode. After several decades of trial and error in development, on June 26, 1974, Sharon Buchan scanned the sixty-seven-cent price of a ten-pack of Wrigley's Juicy Fruit gum using a laser scanner, the first time an item was scanned and sold using the Universal Product Code (UPC). Despite the technology being available by the mid-1970s, barcode adoption was slow. In 1977, around 200 stores in the United States had scanning facilities. Acceptance involved the usual chicken/egg dilemma that new products experience. Few items were UPC registered, and another barrier was the $133,000 price of a scanning system for a retail store with ten checkout lanes. In 1976, a *Business Week* headline grimly described "The Supermarket Scanner That Failed." However, by 1980 scanners had improved in quality, the price had decreased exponentially, and an estimated 90 percent of grocery products had UPC registration.

THE COMPUTER REVOLUTION GOES TO WORK AND THEN COMES HOME

The popularization of photocopying occurred at the same time as the mainframe computer became viable, as the Xerox 914 photocopier was unveiled to the public in 1959. This 650-pound behemoth could print an astounding 100,000 copies a month but needed a carpenter just to uncrate it, a specific employee to operate it, its own twenty-amp electric circuit, and a wary eye to make sure that it did not overheat—the machine had an unfortunate tendency to catch on fire if it got too hot. The machine launched Xerox as one of the hottest companies of the 1960s and 1970s, and the model 914, which had a seventeen-year production run, was labeled by *Fortune* as "the most successful product ever marketed in America measured by its return on investment."

Other than by using a mainframe, in the 1960s the basic tasks of multiplication and division could be performed only two ways, either crudely by a slide rule or precisely on a Marchant calculator that would take several seconds as it went "clunk clunk" to obtain the precise value. We wonder today at the mechanical calculations necessary to produce the great classics of economic research (e.g., John Kendrick's 1961 magisterial volume of output and productivity data, which remains the primary source for what happened on the supply side of the economy before 1929). The world changed instantly in 1970 when for a pittance one could buy an electronic calculator. Instantly not just the Marchant machine but the slide rule were rendered obsolete.

The typewriter is a device that may be found today in a museum or in the home of a nostalgic writer, but it was still the universal tool of commerce in the 1970s. The addition of memory to the electric typewriter starting in the 1960s dramatically changed the process of writing and eliminated tedious retyping of manuscripts. Though the term "word processor" is commonly associated with modern software such as Microsoft Word, the rudimentary concept is a device that can record, edit, and play back keystrokes. In 1964, the first word processor, the IBM Magnetic Tape/Selectric Typewriter (IBM MT/ST), was introduced. This meant that it could record text typed on a roll of magnetic tape and allowed individuals automatically to reproduce previous documents.

For a brief period, the transition from the mainframe and memory typewriter to the personal computer was bridged by word-processing minicomputers. Wang Laboratories became famous for its production of word processing machines. The 1200 Word Processor connected a Wang minicomputer to an IBM Selectric typewriter and allowed storage of text and offered many features to edit text, including inserting text, deleting text, and skipping characters and lines. The individualized Wang Office Information System, introduced in 1976, had a screen and was an affordable office machine that was quickly adopted by law firms, educational services, and other businesses.

The catalyst that sparked the personal computer revolution was the Altair computer released in 1975 by Micro Instrumentation and Telemetry Systems (MITS). The system was not very exciting for anyone except for hobbyists and collectors, for it featured neither keyboard nor screen, and its only output was flashing lights. The most significant part of the Altair was that MITS hired two students to adapt the BASIC programming language for the Altair. These were Paul Allen, a recent Washington State University dropout, and Bill Gates, who would use his Altair money to drop out of Harvard. In April 1975, they together founded Microsoft. A month earlier, another computer legend, Steve Wozniak, had attended the Homebrew Computer Club in California and was immediately inspired by what he saw. He began work on his own personal computer, the Apple Computer or the Apple I, and got his friend, Steve Jobs, to help with sales. The computer had more memory and a cheaper microprocessor than the Altair and could be plugged into any television to use as a screen. Soon Jobs and Wozniak began work on the Apple II, which included a keyboard and a color screen as well as an external cassette tape (soon replaced with floppy disks).

It was IBM's first personal computer (PC), introduced in 1981, that revolutionized the market and soon made the Wang minicomputer and the memory typewriter obsolete. It broke two longstanding IBM traditions by using other companies' products in the computer hardware (the Intel 8088 chip) and incorporating an operating system made by Microsoft rather than by IBM. Another break from IBM tradition was that rather than keeping the design secret, IBM released its specifications to the public so that independent software developers could design programs to run on it. Sales were initially expected to be 250,000 units in five years. In less than four years, 1 million had been sold.[16]

The earliest PCs let loose a torrent of feverish development of software, with each new version making the previous version obsolete. Lotus 1-2-3 was the leading spreadsheet software of the 1980s, and WordPerfect was the leading word processing software. So rapidly were new versions of WordPerfect released that by 1992, only a decade into the PC era, it reached version 6.0. PCs quickly appeared on the desks of virtually everyone in the business world and in an increasing number of homes, particularly those of authors, academics, designers, and a host of other professionals.[17] As the decade of the 1990s began, the world had the hardware and software to become connected through the Internet. Instant communication through e-mail came first, and the world had only a few years to wait before the first widely used web browser brought the world to every desktop and laptop PC.

FROM THE INTERNET REVOLUTION TO THE SOCIAL REVOLUTION

The beginnings of the Internet mirrored the creation of the computer. Much like the ENIAC computer system, the Internet's origins began with the U.S. military. Though ideas and concepts of a globally connected network emerged throughout the 1950s, the ARPANET team, composed of two dozen engineers and scientists, emerged from the Pentagon's Advanced Research Projects Agency in 1969. ARPANET was built to link distant computers so that multiple individuals could share time on a single mainframe computer. Later that same year, ARPANET facilitated the first successful computer link between UCLA and Stanford Research Institute. By 1971, there were more than twenty connected sites or nodes.[18] While on-line services such as Prodigy, CompuServe, and American Online arose in the 1980s, where users used telephones to connect to a central system that dispensed electronic information, these systems were rudimentary precursors to the modern World Wide Web owing to the small amount of information shared, the limited number of simultaneous users, and the inability to handle large amounts of traffic.

Long before the arrival of web browsers, e-mail was used not just in offices but by individuals accessing the Internet using telephone dial-up lines to services such as aol.com. Employees of companies could often access the Internet through an e-mail account hosted by their employer, as many of my academic colleagues and I did beginning in the late 1980s. From its inception, e-mail had extraordinary power, because it combined instant communication with the the ability to include documents and other information as attachments.

In December 1991, the first server in the United States was installed at the Stanford Linear Accelerator System, and the World Wide Web became accessible. The first browser was released at the same time. In September 1993, the National Center for Supercomputing Applications released Mosaic, which quickly came to dominate other web browsers and was soon dubbed the "killer app" of the Internet.[19] However, if any year can be anointed as the beginning of the Internet revolution, it is 1995. The introduction of Windows 95 was a sensation, creating long lines of eager buyers waiting for hours in front of stores that would sell it before the doors opened on August 24, 1995.[20] This version of Windows represented the transitional moment in the history of the Internet in that Microsoft's Internet Explorer, a web browser derived from Mosaic, was available as an add-on to Windows 95. An excited observer wrote, "The Internet is slow, superficial, chaotic, nerdy, hostile, and largely a waste of time. You just gotta try it."[21]

Figure 13–4 uses U.S. Census data to display the adoption of the PC and Internet in American households. The initial PC adoption rate is noticeably slower than that of the Internet, taking thirteen years to reach 30 percent in contrast to the mere seven years after the release of Mosaic for Internet use to reach 30 percent. By historical standards adoption of the PC and the Internet was somewhat slower than of television, which had required only the five years between 1950 and 1955 to go from 5 percent to 65 percent ownership.

From today's perspective, the Internet of 1995 was extremely limited and indeed almost useless except for e-mail. On the early web browsers, you could see pictures of Paris or London, but you couldn't make a hotel reservation or plan a trip. You could hear only snippets of a song or movie, not the entire thing. Access from offices was through relatively fast T-1 lines, but access to the Internet from home or from hotel rooms could be made only via dial-up services, which were slow and quirky. Figure 13–5 displays the percentage of households with dial-up and broadband access and shows that broadband access by 2005 had surpassed dial-up, which has by now almost disappeared.

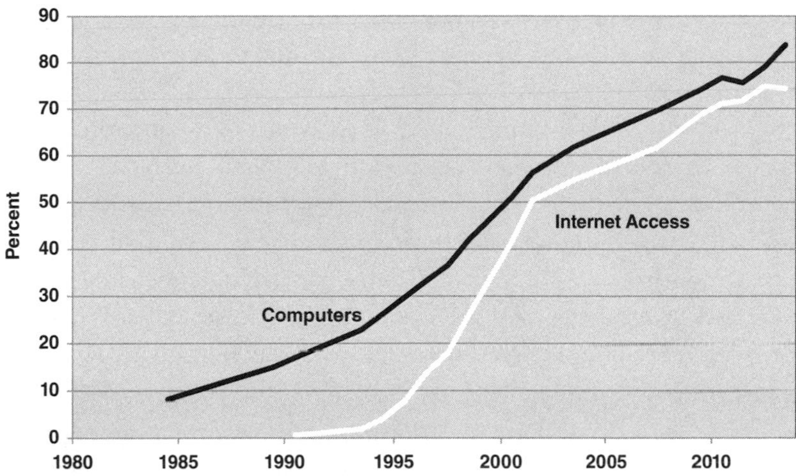

Figure 13–4. Percentage of Households with Computers and Households with Internet Access, 1984–2013

Source: US Census Bureau, "Computer and Internet Access in the United States" (2012 and 2013).

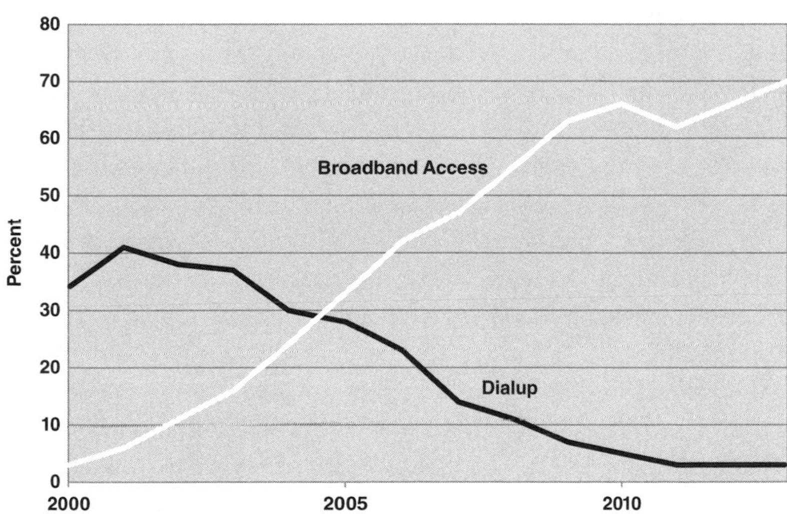

Figure 13–5. Percentage of Households With Internet Access by Broadband and Dialup, 2000–2013

Source: Pew Research Center, "Home Internet Access" (2013).

Today we routinely book airline and hotel reservations on the web and choose restaurants by reading reviews on Trip Advisor and other travel sites. The website Trivago offers to "compare hotel prices on 217 booking sites at once." Pandora and Spotify create services on which we can not only listen to music but also find songs of similar genre and style. Netflix offers suggestions for streamed movies, and Amazon examines our past purchases and tries to get us to purchase ten books in addition to the one we are planning to purchase. Wikipedia is our modern-day gigantic encyclopedia, which if published in print would require 2,052 volumes to house the 4.6 million articles in the English language and double that to include articles in all of the 270 available languages.[22] No longer is a desktop or laptop PC required to access the world, for a pocket-sized smartphone can do the same with the extra convenience of a touchscreen and innumerable apps. College students can keep up via Facebook with their friends from high school. A hashtag on Twitter can spark a revolution. No longer can governments censor the ideas obtained by their citizens, although some (as in China) are still trying.

Though e-mail continues to be indispensable for the many people whose jobs depend on exchanging files and web links, gradually e-mail has been replaced for communication by social media and social networking. The former creates social interaction among people in which they share or exchange information and ideas in virtual communities and networks. Social networking is narrower, a platform to build relations among people who share interests, activities, or background. For instance, YouTube is largely a social media website on which the primary purpose is to view videos. LinkedIn is largely a social networking service or online social network, for its primary purpose is to help people connect with others in related businesses or fields of study. LinkedIn has become a worldwide network of business cards and has become a primary way for people, particularly young adults beginning their careers, to find and change jobs. Facebook, Google +, and Twitter combine aspects of both to create multiplatform websites.

Almost by definition, the attraction of any social media site depends on how many users there are. If 90 percent of the people with whom you interact speak English and only 10 percent speak French, then it is quite likely that you will work harder to perfect your English than your French. Thus the power of social media is determined by the popularity of the platform. In 2005, only 8 percent of adults said they used social media. A service called Myspace was then the leading social media network, and Facebook, created by Mark

Zuckerberg in his Harvard dorm room, was still only a year old. Eight years later, in 2013, social media use in adults had reached 72 percent. Teenagers and young adults had an adoption rate of close to 90 percent. Many business interactions still remain focused on e-mail, but social networks dominate personal interactions.

E-COMMERCE: THE AMAZON REVOLUTION

The e-commerce revolution in retailing has created both incalculable benefits for consumers and unmitigated pain and bankruptcy for some types of traditional retailers in categories in which the essence of a purchase is to be able to choose easily among a wide range of possible options. Amazon, founded in 1994, initially sold books. Although a half decade elapsed before it became the dominant merchant of books, the appeal of its concept was immediate.

Traditional book retailing in 1994 consisted of two types of book sellers. The large nationwide chain stores—for instance, Barnes and Noble, Borders, and Waldenbooks—had hundreds of branches. Supplementing the large chains were small, specialized book shops. Small bookstores allowed customers to visit an entire store devoted to, say, cookbooks, or mystery novels, or even comic books. Because only the largest cities could support these specialists, it was often necessary for customers to travel long distances to reach them. But for most of the population they were unnecessary, because one of the large chains was around the corner. Amazon stepped into this environment in 1994, and immediately the benefits of its revolution became clear. Soon it became possible to search for any book by author, title, or subject category. Soon the software became more sophisticated, as each user would have an account that provided Amazon with the history of previous purchases. If a customer had previously shown a preference for a particular type of mystery novel, then on the Amazon search stream would appear eight or ten illustrated book covers of that type of mystery novel under the heading "You Might Also Like…" Soon the availability of any type of book became so appealing that many, and eventually most, book customers stopped going to bookstores. By 2003, my neighborhood highbrow specialized shop, Great Expectations, closed for good. And in 2011, the large nationwide chain Borders declared bankruptcy and closed all its stores, as had Waldenbooks several years earlier. If all it sold was books, Amazon would have changed retailing forever, but the imagination of its founder Jeff Bezos went far beyond that. He soon realized that he could sell *anything.* Today, Amazon sells

232 million products to a user base just in the United States of 244 million customers, defined as those who have purchased anything within the past twelve months.

The basic concept of customer loyalty was not lost on Amazon, and it figured out how to build customer loyalty by providing a unique benefit. Founded in 2005, Amazon Prime costs $99 per year, and it provides an irresistible lure by eliminating the only disadvantage of mail-order services—the cost of shipping. Amazon Prime customers are entitled to unlimited free shipping, guaranteed to arrive two days after an order is placed. There are now 20 million Prime members, and they spend twice as much per year as other Amazon customers.

The Amazon revolution has brought selection, convenience, and free shipping to millions of customers, but it has created problems in its wake beyond the bankruptcy of Borders and specialized bookstores. Through most of Amazon's history, it charged no sales tax, implying that states and localities have been deprived of billions of dollars of sales tax revenues. As a longer-term effect, by reducing the demand for all types of merchandise in brick-and-mortar retail stores, it has weakened the economy by creating an excess supply of space in retail shopping malls. In the future, there will be fewer jobs for construction workers building new shopping malls and fewer jobs for clerks, stocking staff, and managers at retail stores. We return to this theme in chapter 17 as we explore the central theme of this book, the ever-growing set of forces that are slowing American economic growth to a crawl.

CONCLUSION

Achievements of the computer revolution thus far extend from the first commercial mainframe, the Univac I introduced in 1954, to the iPhone 6, introduced in September 2014. The rapid development of computing technology has brought together not just new ideas but ultimately a complete change in how people communicate and obtain information. Gordon Moore, the cofounder of Intel, provided one of the most accurate predictions in the history of science when he guessed in 1965 that the power of computer chips would double every two years. The pace accelerated to doubling every16 months during the late 1990s but since 2006 has slowed to doubling every four to six years. Moore's Law died because there was no demand for the engineering expense necessary for it to continue: Existing chips are powerful enough to perform all required functions on desktop and laptop computers.

The computer revolution began in the 1960s and 1970s with mainframe computers, which were so large that they often filled an entire room and required a separate custom-built source of air conditioning. The early computers allowed telephone bills to be created automatically, eliminated telephone operators as phone calls began to be switched electronically, made possible ATM cash machines that replaced many bank teller jobs, and allowed airlines to handle an upsurge in traffic while eliminating the tedious manual task of making and keeping track of reservations.

Computers did not have to be large to make a difference. In 1970, the handheld electronic calculator was invented, eliminating overnight both the mechanical calculator and the slide rule. In 1981, the mainframe computer went on a diet, shrinking in size from units that filled a room to a small box with a screen that would fit on any desk in the office or at home. Soon the typewriter became obsolete, for documents could be changed again and again without retyping. Any calculation could be done with a single formula applied to hundreds or thousands of numbers, thanks to the magic of electronic spreadsheets. Although the personal computer was initially perceived as a specialized tool mainly useful for computer hobbyists, statisticians, writers, and researchers, its appeal broadened to the entire population when web browsing was invented in the early 1990s.

The World Wide Web gave individuals entirely new options to obtain information, communicate with one another, and make purchases without any need to travel to a store. Information became free, print encyclopedias became obsolete, and a few keystrokes in a search window could obtain any information in a second. For instance, the previous section of this chapter contains the impressive statistic that Amazon sells 232 million products. How did I know? I typed into the Google search box "how many products does Amazon sell?" and the answer appeared on my computer screen in a fraction of a second. Communication has also been revolutionized. Long ago, telephone calls eliminated personal letters, and then e-mail eliminated many types of telephone calls. Now communication is possible by many new options, including Facebook, Twitter, and Skype, which allows a soldier in Afghanistan to have daily video chats with his parents in Nevada.

The benefits of the computer and the Internet, though overwhelmingly positive, have begun to raise concerns about some side effects of the revolution. The first problem is the exacerbation of inequality. Lack of access to computers and the Internet inside the home greatly handicap the efforts to succeed in school of students whose families live in poverty, for they are competing with the majority of students, who have computers at home and who have parents who show how to use them. Internet illiteracy, the inability to navigate through this new source of learning and information, creates a handicap that can last a lifetime.

Another less familiar problem is that we may be creating too much data. Ronald Coase, a University of Chicago economist who won the Nobel Prize, long ago warned that "if you torture the data long enough, it will confess to anything." Information on the Internet is bountiful and varied, but for all the valuable resources, there are flawed resources as well. At the level of students from elementary school to college, the Internet makes possible Internet bullying. The Internet allows both good and bad ideas to travel around the world instantly, and the Internet can not only create revolutions like the Arab Spring, but also spread disillusionment and misleading information.

There are other problems with the new world of constant connectivity. Teenagers, especially boys, have so much distraction available online that increasingly they have difficulty concentrating in school. Like anyone, instead of doing their homework, they can watch a YouTube video, check up on a friend's Facebook page, or play video games with friends. Psychologists worry that this early exposure to the Internet can change human interaction, and school officials grow concerned about adopting technology without a strong positive effect on test scores and class engagement.

The computing revolution has brought a new level of convenience, connectivity, and collaboration to at least 80 percent of the population. A farmer who has a smartphone today has better and faster access to a wide variety of information than a university professor did only two decades ago. As important as the computer and Internet revolutions have been, the comparison of their benefits with those achieved between 1870 and 1970 creates an illuminating contrast to be developed subsequently, in chapter 17.

Chapter 14

ANTIBIOTICS, CT SCANS, AND THE EVOLUTION OF HEALTH AND MEDICINE

> Gleaming palaces of modern science, replete with the most advanced specialty services, now stood next to neighborhoods that had been medically abandoned, that had no doctors for everyday needs, and where the most elementary public health and preventive care was frequently unavailable. In the 1960s many began to observe that abundance and scarcity in medicine were side by side. After World War II, medicine had been a metaphor for progress, but to many it was now becoming a symbol of the continuing inequities and irrationalities of American life.
>
> —Paul Starr, 1982

INTRODUCTION

Chapter 7 examined the rapid progress made in the sphere of public health and medicine from 1870 to 1940, when a confluence of environmental, social, and medical advances both extended and improved American lives. The greatest beneficiaries of these health improvements were children, as most of the life expectancy gains were owed to significant reductions in infant mortality. After 1940 the nature of the achievements and approaches to public health underwent considerable change. Most important, the rate of growth in American life expectancy slowed to about half the pace of the previous seventy years. What growth in life expectancy did occur was different in character than before, for it consisted mainly of reductions in death rates for older Americans rather than infants.

This change in character draws attention to one of the major themes of this chapter, the shift in medicine from curing acute infectious diseases to managing chronic illnesses. By the 1950s, the acute infectious killers had, by and large, been eliminated. This left chronic diseases, such as heart disease and cancer, as the main threats to American health. These prominent ailments now required long-term management and care and resulted in more gradual, piecemeal improvements, compared to the swift advances of the earlier period.

At the same time, the realm of public health was becoming increasingly centered around professional medicine. Though it had been recognized in the seventy years before 1940 that environmental factors and social behavior were the most powerful bulwarks of public health, the seventy years that followed concentrated on medical care and centered on pristine, technology-laden hospitals, staffed by increasingly specialized personnel. The result of this emphasis combined slowly improved health outcomes with perpetually rising costs for the consumers of medical care. Meanwhile, patterns of inequality in the health system have persisted. Gradually, the United States has become the least efficient major developed nation in terms of the delivery of healthcare, as indicated by cross-country comparisons of medical expenditures per person versus life expectancy.[1] This shift toward slower progress reinforces the overall theme of part II of the book, as suggested already in chapters 10 and 11, that the pace of progress slowed down, particularly after 1970, from its rapid pace in 1870–1940 as recorded in part I.

This chapter interweaves these major themes with examinations of specific developments in American public health and medical care. We start with an overview of the evolution of life expectancy and mortality rates since 1940. Then follows a more detailed chronicle of progress in the first decades of the post-1940 era, when the pace of innovation was rapid as one important invention followed another, from antibiotics to the polio vaccine. The discussion then turns to the rise in the importance of chronic diseases, particularly heart disease and cancer, and determines that today's most effective treatments were already being applied by the late 1970s. There follows an account of how public knowledge and social behavior have continued to play a part in the improvement of public health.

We then examine the increasing professionalization of America's healthcare system, exploring how the roles of doctors have changed and how expensive medical technologies have permeated the procedures of modern hospitals. The chapter concludes with an examination of America's uniquely flawed health financing system, which matters because the lack of medical care coverage as a right of citizenship in the United States, in contrast to other nations, deprives millions of access to medical care, leaving diseases to go untreated and the death rate to be higher than necessary. Though progress in health and medicine continues, it is at a slower pace than in the first few decades of the post-1940 era, and issues ranging from the speed and cost of development of new drugs to the prospects for curing cancer and dementia constitute major obstacles to continued progress.

CHANGES IN LIFE EXPECTANCY AND DEATH RATES

After the rapid growth in life expectancy before 1950, American life expectancy continued to grow, albeit at a more moderate pace. The average American in 1950 enjoyed twenty-five years' longer a life expectancy at birth than in 1880. By 2008, average life expectancy at birth had gained about nine additional years from the 1950 figure. Even within the postwar period, life expectancy manifested apparent diminishing returns. A newborn in 1975 could be expected to live nearly eight years longer than one thirty-five years earlier; thirty-three years later, however, additional life expectancy was only five years more than in 1975.[2] In short, lives were extended more before World War II than after. This trend, unsurprisingly, was reflected in death rates. In the first forty years of the twentieth century, the death rate per 100,000 people dropped 37.2 percent. In the sixty years that followed, it fell 19.4 percent.[3]

The growth in life expectancy not only slowed, but also fundamentally changed. Much of the life expectancy gains of the seventy years before 1950 came from drastic reductions in infant mortality. Whereas overall life expectancy at birth increased only 13 percent between 1950 and 2008, life expectancy for Americans aged 60 years rose more than 33 percent.[4] This shift toward improving life expectancy in the older age groups is not surprising, for once infant mortality was all but eliminated and more people were living longer, chronic diseases came to dominate as the major sources of mortality in the second half of the twentieth century. Indeed, "By 1945 more than two-thirds of all deaths were attributed to chronic diseases, including heart disease, cancer, and stroke; only twenty-five years earlier two-thirds had been from infectious diseases."[5] Thus it was attention to these chronic diseases that drove life expectancy gains during the second half of the century.

The biggest killer of the twentieth century was heart disease. Unlike most diseases, the mortality rate due to major cardiovascular diseases increased between 1900 and 1940 and did not begin to recede until the mid-1960s (see figure 14–1). Of the approximately 1,720 deaths per 100,000 people in 1900, heart disease claimed 345.2, or 20 percent. By 1940, it was the cause of 485.7 of the 1,080 deaths per 100,000 people, or almost 45 percent of all deaths. At its peak in 1963, heart disease was the cause of more than 55 percent of all deaths,[6] but by then a movement toward reducing its incidence was well under way, with many aspects of prevention and treatment already established, including control of blood pressure, better-equipped emergency rooms, and separate coronary care units in hospitals. Heart disease remains the leading cause of death in the United States today, accounting for 24.2 percent of deaths in 2010.[7]

The decline from 1963 to 2010 in the share of heart disease as a cause of death was the indirect result of the steady increase in cancer mortality, for those who did not die from heart disease lived longer and were more vulnerable to contracting other diseases, chiefly cancer. Killing only sixty-four people per 100,000 in 1900, the mortality rate from cancer grew to 120.3 in 1940 and 200.5 in 2000.[8] By 2010, cancer was responsible for 23.3 percent of all deaths, close to the share for heart disease.[9] Moreover, the fight against cancer has proven to be more difficult than against other leading killers. "Even as research and treatment efforts have intensified over the past three decades and funding has soared dramatically, the annual death toll has risen 73 percent—over one and a half times as fast as the growth of the US population."[10]

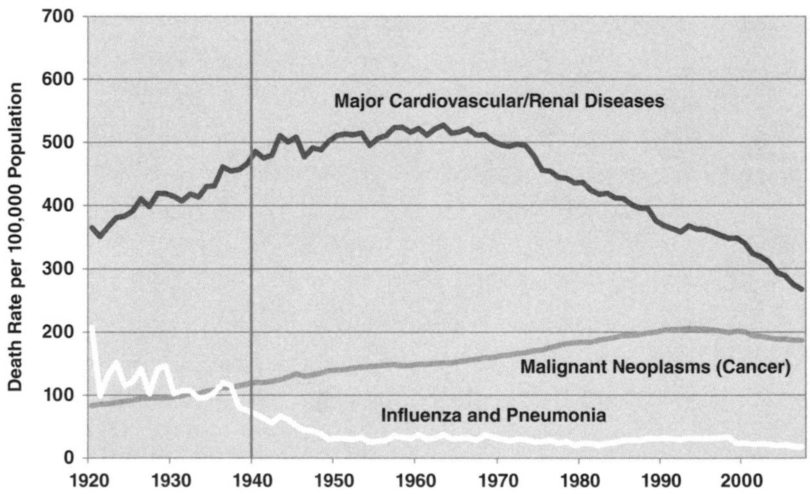

Figure 14–1. Death Rates by Selected Major Causes, 1920–2007

Sources: SAUS (2006, 2012), "Historical Statistics," No. HS—13.

Taken together, heart disease and cancer accounted for 47.5 percent of all deaths in 2010. In third place were chronic lower respiratory diseases (e.g., emphysema and chronic bronchitis), with a mortality rate of 45 per 100,000, followed by cerebrovascular diseases and (after accidents) Alzheimer's disease, with mortality rates of 41.9 and 27 per 100,000, respectively.[11] A study by the American Academy of Neurology claims that Alzheimer's may be far more deadly than is recognized and "may contribute close to as many deaths in the United States as heart disease or cancer."[12] Even the more cautious estimates of the CDC indicate that the mortality rate from Alzheimer's increased more than 70 percent between 1999 and 2011.[13]

HEALING FROM WAR: EARLY POSTWAR INNOVATIONS

By the time World War II ended, one of the most important medical innovations in human history was already primed for widespread production and had earned itself a reputation as a wonder drug: penicillin. The first antibiotic, penicillin was versatile enough to cure "almost instantly such diseases as pneumonia, rheumatic fever, and syphilis, which had been greatly feared and often fatal."[14] Indeed, cases of syphilis, which occurred at a rate of 372 per 100,000 people in 1938, had fallen to 154.2 by 1950 and to sixty-eight in 1960, a testament to the antibiotic's ability to kill the infection before it spread.[15] Pneumonia, previously called the "Captain of the Men of Death," was now easily curable, and by 1954 it caused only a quarter as many deaths of children ages 1–4 as in 1939. The effect on rheumatic fever and rheumatic heart disease was even greater, with the death rate falling 90 percent between 1940 and 1960.[16]

The discovery and subsequent development of penicillin came about largely by accident when, one night in 1928, the Englishman Alexander Fleming discovered a large patch of mold surrounded by a sterile ring on a dirty dish that had been left out for weeks. After finding that the mold had killed the growth of some types of bacteria, Fleming began experimenting to uncover the antibacterial feature of the mold. What started as an investigation in a small laboratory would by World War II become a large, coordinated, interdisciplinary team effort subsidized by the U.S. government.[17] This effort marked the birth of large-scale drug research and development that would grow in size and complexity in the following decades.

As the war came to its end, penicillin became available in U.S. pharmacies in the summer of 1945 and soon afterward in pharmacies around the world. By this time, the drug had already become very affordable, with a price per dose of just 6.5 cents. Given its efficacy and low cost, it immediately became widely used. "Between 1948 and 1956, the US market for penicillin increased sevenfold to more than 450,000 kg, or 3 grams for every person in the country." Even as other antibiotics followed penicillin's lead and entered the market in the postwar years, the trailblazing drug maintained its cure-all aura to the point that "patients were demanding that 'no one person should be allowed to die without having been given penicillin.'"[18] A more sober assessment of penicillin's impact concluded:

> Penicillin's public-health effect was to sustain and continue pre-war improvements in mortality and morbidity, but its dramatic effects on the course of many particularly feared conditions also transformed the ways people thought about their lives in the post-war years. Compared to the pre-war atmosphere of self-reliance, self-discipline, and, of course, guilt in the event of failure to maintain health, infection now came to be seen as a technical problem susceptible to a pharmaceutical solution.[19]

Following penicillin an array of other antibiotics quickly arrived. In fact, 50 percent more new drugs were approved by the FDA between 1940 and 1960 than in the fifty-one years that followed, as is shown in figure 14–2.[20] Like penicillin, most other new antibiotic drugs became affordable in the immediate postwar years, as they were largely competing with each other and declined in price together.[21] The antibiotic streptomycin, when supplemented with a regimen of several other antibiotics, has been credited with the elimination of tuberculosis as a major disease, at least within the United States.[22] The incidence rate of the disease—which had already declined fivefold from 1900 to 1940, decreased by another two-thirds between 1944 and 1960. By 2001, fewer than six in 100,000 Americans reported a case of tuberculosis.[23]

Other postwar benefits emerged from wartime research, including improved resuscitation therapy to prevent and treat shock, as well as safer, more effective blood replacement techniques.[24] In 1947, Dr. Stephen S. Hudack performed the first joint replacement surgery, after about eight years of experimenting with artificial joints. In 2010, there were more than 1 million joint replacement surgeries in the United States, the effect of which can be measured by analyzing the influence on quality-adjusted life-years (hereafter QALYs), a metric calculated by multiplying the additional years of life achieved by a medical procedure by the assessed quality of that extra year (which falls between 0 and 1, 1 being

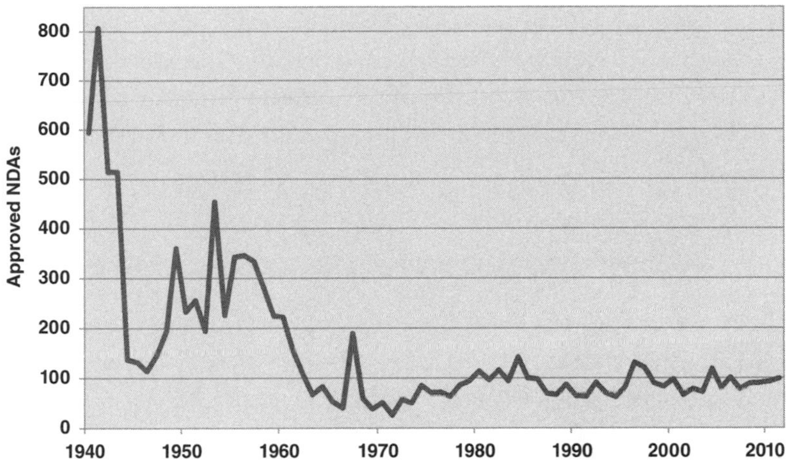

Figure 14–2. Approved New Drug Applications, 1940–2011

Source: US FDA (2013). "Summary of NDA Approvals & Receipts, 1938 to the Present," last updated January 18. Retrieved from http://www.fda.gov/AboutFDA/WhatWeDo/History/ProductRegulation/SummaryofNDAApprovalsReceipts19.

perfect health).[25] One study found that on average, hip replacement surgery provides an additional 0.8 QALYs over five years.[26]

Another important advance of the early postwar years was the development of a polio vaccine. Polio was not a particularly important killer, and mortality rates from polio were quite small. Nonetheless, the disease had become very visible thanks to Franklin Delano Roosevelt, and, more important, "it was deeply feared as the leading crippler of children." It is a testament to how effectively so many deadly diseases, especially childhood ailments, had already been virtually eliminated in the first half of the century that the risk of polio was such a prominent source of worry in the 1940s and early 1950s.

The annual March of Dimes, a campaign to raise money for research to fight polio, drew more public support and money than any other health campaign.[27] This public support was rewarded with the development of the Salk vaccine in 1955, which proved extremely effective after the largest clinical trial in history, in which more than 400,000 American children took the immunization. Five years later, the Sabin vaccine, also for polio, earned the surgeon general's recommendation and would soon become the more prevalent of the two immunizations.[28] By the late 1960s, the polio virus had been entirely eliminated in the United States.[29] These developments can be seen as the culmination of a long history of eliminating childhood diseases since

1890, just as antibiotics had nearly eliminated many of the most prevalent infectious diseases. As Robert Bud writes: "One can think of the middle of the twentieth century as the end of one of the most important social revolutions in history—the virtual elimination of infectious disease as a significant factor in social life."[30]

A SHIFT IN FOCUS: THE CAMPAIGNS AGAINST CHRONIC DISEASES

With infectious illnesses dwindling to insignificance, the focus shifted to chronic ailments, particularly cardiovascular disease (CVD) and cancer. Cardiovascular epidemiology, the branch of medicine specifically concerned with heart disease, was established in the late 1940s. For the first time, members of the medical profession began in-depth investigations into the risk factors contributing to heart disease, assessing factors such as geography, cholesterol levels, high blood pressure, smoking, and dietary habits. Heightened attention to the cardiovascular epidemic led to a rapid improvement in understanding and a multidimensional campaign to fight the disease.[31]

By the mid-1960s, just as CVD mortality rates peaked, many of the methods of treatment and prevention prevalent today had already been developed. In the middle of the decade, a series of reports from the De Bakey Commission "noted with pride that research in high blood pressure had resulted in the development of drugs to lower blood pressure levels. Atherosclerosis of major arteries was being attacked 'surgically with gratifying results' and artificial arteries had been invented. Cardiac pacemakers were now available, implanted in more than 5,000 living adults. Anticoagulant drugs were in use."[32]

Even the first heart transplantations had been conducted by the late 1960s, although for the first several decades they remained rare owing to relatively low survival rates. Only in the 1980s did heart transplantation become effective, with one-year and five-year survival rates of 85 percent and 75 percent, respectively.[33] Nonetheless, transplants remain relatively rare and have played a minor role compared to the CVD treatments already available in the early 1960s. Pacemaker implantations, of which there were 188,700 in 2009, are far more common than heart transplants.[34] Other treatments that taken together are even more important in contributing to the continuing decline in CVD incidence since the 1970s have included the widespread use of statins to reduce cholesterol, and the increased use of coronary interventions such as cardiac catheterization and coronary artery bypass graft surgery.

In addition to drugs and new technologies, important progress in the fight against CVD was achieved by better public knowledge of risk factors and preventive measures, facilitated by informational campaigns. According to one 1994 study, about 40 percent of the decrease in CVD deaths since 1975 were attributable to treatment and a larger 51 percent to prevention.[35] The decline in smoking prevalence was just one of the many ways in which increased general knowledge contributed to better health outcomes. Stroke, one of the main cerebrovascular diseases, followed an almost identical path as that of heart disease, with a mortality rate that declined by half after its peak in the early 1960s.[36]

In recent years, however, the great successes in the fight against heart disease have experienced a slower rate of progress. Since the late 1970s, the rate of decline in coronary heart disease (CHD) mortality rates has slowed from about 4 percent per year in the late 1970s to 2.5 percent more recently. Among men aged 35 to 54, the dropoff was even more pronounced, as the annual rate of decline in the 2000s was only 0.5 percent, whereas that of the 1980s had been 6.2 percent. These recent trends are a cause for concern that progress might have stopped or even have reversed: "Health officials in the United States, which rarely leads the world in any health indicator, have long celebrated the status of the United States as the country that has led the decline in CHD. Early signals of reversal threaten this status: the United States might become the poster child not of the conquest of CHD but of its resurgence."[37]

One cause of the slowdown in the rate of progress has been the increase in the incidence of obesity, already covered in chapter 10. International comparisons support the view that the United States is an outlier in the extent of its obesity. In 2000, the U.S. percentage was 27 percent, and none of the other twenty-three countries had a percentage above 20 percent. Half the countries had obesity percentages below 10 percent, with Italy at 8 percent, France at 6 percent, and Japan at 2 percent.[38]

Unlike cardiovascular disease, cancer steadily grew during the twentieth century, with a mortality rate three times higher in 2000 than in 1900, as shown by figure 14–1. Most of the major approaches to treating cancer had been developed by the 1970s. Before World War II, the primary methods of treating cancer were surgery and radiation therapy. Surgery could cure cancer only if the tumor was localized enough to be entirely removed. Radiation therapy, which dated back to the 1896 invention of the X-ray, was meant to control small tumor growths that had not or could not be surgically removed.[39] The practical application of cancer chemotherapy emerged from World War II. Mustard gas was shown to cause atrophying in victims' bone marrow and lymph nodes, suggesting that it could possibly suppress cell division in cases of leukemia and lymphoma. From this knowledge, American doctors in the early 1940s experimented with nitrogen mustards on cancer cells, with some success.[40] In 1948, Sidney Farber, the so-called "father of chemotherapy," was able to induce the first complete remission in a child with acute leukemia by using chemical agents.[41] By the 1960s, chemotherapy was successfully inducing long-term remissions and, in some cases, fully curing patients with Hodgkin disease or acute leukemia, and by the 1970s, it was being applied to most types of cancer, just as it is today.

More sophisticated techniques for cancer detection were also developed in the 1970s. Computed tomographic (CT) imaging, which provided more precise 3D imaging than an X-ray, started to make its presence felt in the 1970s and became widespread by the 1980s, in most cases eliminating the need for intrusive exploratory surgery.[42] The mammogram procedure to detect breast cancer was introduced in 1973.[43] Though these innovations provided very important functions for detection and prevention, they have also been plagued by criticism of waste. CT exams cost thousands of dollars, and anywhere from 5 percent to 30 percent of the 75 million performed in 2009 are said to have been unnecessary. Moreover, concerns about CT scans' *causing* cancer have become a large topic of debate, with one estimate claiming that the CT scans performed in 2007 alone could produce nearly 29,000 future cases of cancer.[44]

Even within existing methods of treatment for cancer, innovations since the 1970s have been relatively sparse. For example, in chemotherapy, "in recent years, there has been a plateau in the evolution of the clinical results obtained with this modality treatment. In some cases, the limitations of chemotherapy observed during the early days still apply."[45] Even though the United States declared an unofficial war on cancer in 1971 with the National Cancer Act, the percentage of Americans dying from cancer, even when adjusted for the fact that Americans are living longer, was no better in 2004 than it was in 1970. Part of the increased prevalence of cancer as a cause of death is the result of success in treating CVD, so that millions who previously would have died of coronary disease are now dying of cancer instead. Writing in 2004, Clifton Leaf and Doris Burke characterized the slow progress in treating cancer: "Thirty-three years ago, fully half of cancer patients survived five years or more after diagnosis. The figure has crept up to about 63 percent today." Progress has been sluggish in spite of the nearly $200 billion, adjusted for inflation, that was spent in America, between 1971 and

2004, to combat cancer. According to Clifton Leaf and Doris Burke, this failure to make more rapid progress arises from a damaged system of research and development, in which publishing papers on very specific issues earns funding while the big picture falls by the wayside. A survivor of prostate cancer was quoted saying, "It's like a Greek tragedy. Everybody plays his individual part to perfection, everybody does what's right by his own life, and the total just doesn't work."[46]

A summary of post-1970s medical developments would not be complete without mention of the HIV/AIDS pandemic. While scientists still debate the disease's origins, it is certain that HIV, or the human immunodeficiency virus, made its way to North America in the late twentieth century. HIV is a retrovirus spread primarily through sexual intercourse or sharing hypodermic needles. Left untreated, HIV will eventually lead to AIDS, or acquired immune deficiency syndrome, a condition where the body's immune system is seriously compromised. People with AIDS are extremely vulnerable to a wide range of diseases. Left untreated, people who have AIDS have a three-year life expectancy, which falls to twelve months once an AIDS patient becomes ill.[47]

When it first came to the attention of the U.S. medical community in 1981, AIDS was a terrifying mystery. No one knew how it was transmitted, why it was occurring primarily in certain subsets of the population, or how it could be treated. Even after HIV was discovered as the mechanism, an infection was a slow but certain death sentence. AZT, approved by the FDA in 1987 as the first anti-HIV drug, was a promising treatment but proved to be only somewhat effective at slowing the progress of AIDS and was accompanied by many negative side effects. By 1995, more than a half-million cases of AIDS had been reported in the United States, and more than 300,000 Americans had died of AIDS, making it the leading cause of death among Americans aged 25–44.[48]

One of the revolutions of modern medicine was the development of ART, or antiretroviral therapy. ART is essentially a group of drugs that act collectively to prevent the virus from replicating. Though ART is not a cure for AIDS, it causes HIV to remain dormant in the body and thus prevents AIDS from developing. Improvements in ART over the last twenty years have turned a diagnosis of HIV from a death sentence to a chronic, treatable disease while softening the negative side effects of the drugs. These developments have improved the quality of life for the 1.2 million Americans currently living with HIV.[49] In fact, thanks to ART, people with HIV can have "an almost normal lifespan without experiencing serious illness related to their HIV infection," something unheard of a mere twenty years ago.[50]

TRANSFORMATIONS IN PUBLIC AWARENESS OF HEALTH ISSUES

Changing perceptions of cigarettes represent the most important postwar development in public awareness of health-related issues. At the beginning of the twentieth century, cigarette consumption was modest, but over the next sixty years it spread very rapidly, becoming almost ubiquitous in the 1950s. Like cardiovascular mortality rates, cigarette consumption peaked in 1963, when more than 4,300 cigarettes were consumed per person, as shown in figure 14–3. After remaining at a plateau above 4,000 per person through 1977, consumption declined steadily to 1,230 by 2011, largely as the result of a comprehensive campaign to raise awareness of the deleterious health effects of smoking.

Nonetheless, tobacco use is still estimated to contribute an estimated $200 billion per year in added healthcare and lost productivity costs,[51] and the pace of reductions in smoking rates appears to be slowing. Though smoker prevalence fell 17 percentage points (from 42.4 to 25.5) in the twenty-five years after 1965, in the nineteen years that followed, it fell only another 5 points, to 20.6 percent, as shown in figure 14–3. This is in large part because smoking has remained hard to eliminate among the poorest segments of American society. According to a

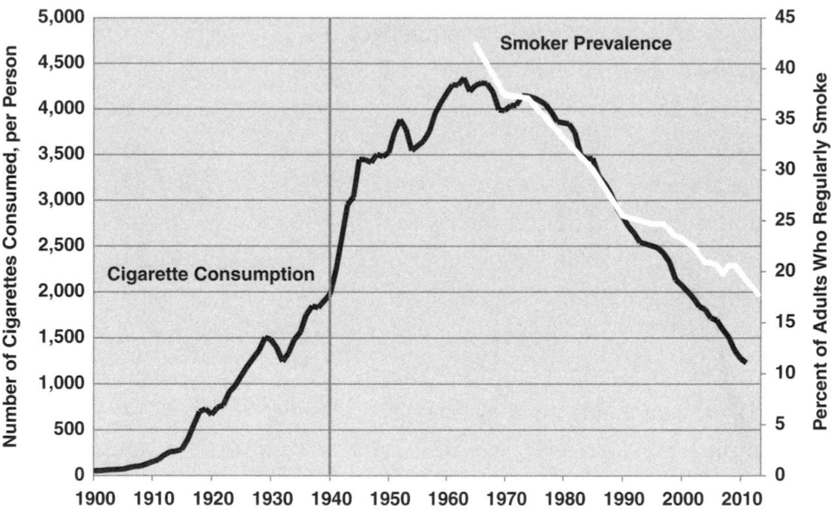

Figure 14–3. Annual Cigarette Consumption per Person and Adult Smoker Prevalence, 1900–2013

Sources: American Lung Association (2011). "Trends in Tobacco Use," Tables 2, 4. CDC (2014). "Current Cigarette Smoking Among Adults—United States, 2005–2013." CDC (2012). "Consumption of Cigarettes and Combustible Tobacco—United States, 2000–2011."

recent study, though the adult smoking rate has fallen 27 percent since 1997, for the poor it has fallen only 15 percent, an important reason why life expectancy is increasing more slowly at the bottom of the income distribution.[52]

World War II and succeeding decades also witnessed a newfound commitment to improving mental health. During the war, more than 850,000 American soldiers saw treatment for "psychoneurotic" issues, and the presence of psychiatric medical officers in the military multiplied by nearly 100. Afterwards, the field of mental health became more important and gained increased acceptance. As described by Paul Starr: "Psychiatry, previously concerned primarily with the care of the insane, had been institutionally marginal in America before World War II. Now it moved into the 'mainstream' of American medicine and American society and enormously expanded its claims and its clientele. Whereas formerly its province was mental illness, now it became mental health."[53] Though the effects of psychiatry can be hard to quantify, the reduction of a social stigma surrounding questions of mental health allowed many Americans to find help. Even today, cases of serious mental illness are estimated to cost more than $190 billion in lost earnings per year.[54]

Another dimension of increased public awareness concerns the connection between public health and air pollution. In the 1960s, air pollution was a very visible problem, with many major American cities, particularly Los Angeles, enveloped in thick, hazy smog, described by one resident as a "blanket of orange." Though the relationship between air pollution and health was not fully understood, it seemed obvious that breathing toxic air would degrade lung health. Recognizing air pollution as a national problem, in 1963 Congress passed the Clean Air Act, the first law intended to control air pollution rather than merely study it. Seven years later, the act was substantially amended to set specific minimum standards of air quality. Since then, many other legislative acts on both the local and national level have established further quality standards and limits on emissions and, as a result, Los Angeles, the poster child of oppressive smog, has ozone levels today that are 60 percent lower than they were in the mid-1970s.[55]

According to one recent study, this reduction in smog levels had substantial effects on life expectancy throughout much of the nation between 1980 and 2000, accounting for about 15 percent of the 2.7-year increase in life expectancy over that two-decade interval.[56] Studies in other countries have demonstrated substantial connections between reduced air pollution and additional QALYs.[57] The diminution in air pollution not only lengthened many American lives but also raised the quality of life, reducing the "hacking" or "crackling cough" of people living in dense smog.[58] Though the health benefits of this environmental change are not as significant as those brought about by the spread of sewer pipes and elimination of open sewage waste early in the twentieth century, it is another example of how changes outside of the purely medical sphere can significantly affect public health.

ACCIDENTS AND VIOLENCE

Health problems go beyond those related to disease. Today, accidents are the fifth most prevalent cause of death in the United States, claiming more than 126,000 lives in 2011, or 40.6 per 100,000 people. As shown by the top line in figure 14–4, the accident mortality rate was relatively stable at between seventy and ninety between 1900 and 1940, then fell rapidly to thirty-five in 1990 before retreating back up to forty-one in 2011. The failure of the accident rate to decline before 1940 was entirely due to the prevalence of automobile accidents. The lower line in figure 14–4 shows that the non-automobile mortality rate declined by half from ninety-four in 1906 to forty-six in 1940 and then further to a minimum of eighteen, reached in 1980, before rising back up

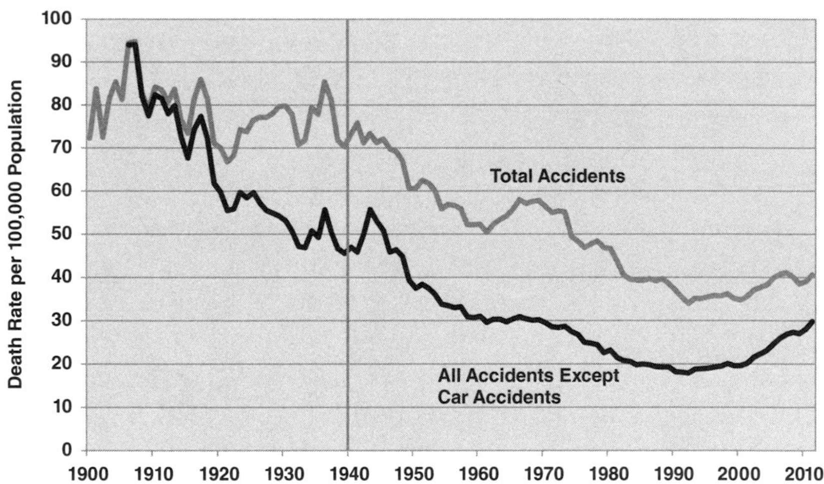

Figure 14–4. Death Rate per 100,000 Population from Accidents, 1900–2011

Sources: HSUS Table Ab945 for death rates by total accidents until 1998. CDC (2011), "Deaths: Final Data for 2011" for 1999–2011. SAUS (2012), "Historical Statistics," No. HS--13 for death rates by motor vehicle accident.

to thirty in 2011. We return to the sources of the increase in nonautomotive accidents in chapter 15; we have already seen in chapter 11 that the continuous decline in the automobile accident death rate was the joint achievement of better highways and the inclusion of safety equipment on new automobiles, including seat belts, air bags, and better bumper protection.

The contribution of violence to mortality rates is today about an eighth that of accidents but still provides an integral perspective on Americans' changing standards of living. The homicide rate exhibited cycles through the twentieth century, with peak rates between eight and ten per 100,000 population, both between 1921 and 1936 and again between 1970 and 1996 (see figure 7–8). The increase in murders in the 1970s and 1980s was accompanied by an increase in other less serious crimes, changing citizens' perceptions of the world around them. Steven Pinker describes this change:

> The flood of violence from the 1960s through the 1980s reshaped American culture, the political scene, and everyday life. Mugger jokes became a staple of comedians, with mentions of Central Park getting an instant laugh as a well-known death trap. New Yorkers imprisoned themselves in their apartments with batteries of latches and deadbolts, including the popular "police lock," a steel bar with one end anchored in the floor and the other propped against the door. [One] section of downtown Boston...was called the Combat Zone because of its endemic muggings and stabbings.[59]

Though homicide rates and other important measures of crime would not decline until the 1990s, the 1970s saw the beginnings of progress in another sphere of violence—abuses against women. In a shift in cultural norms that can be partly attributed to the feminist movement of the 1970s, especially Susan Brownmiller's 1975 bestseller *Against Our Will,* the incidence of rape began to decline in the late 1970s. This trend accelerated in the 1990s, and by 2009, the rate of rape was just a fifth of its 1973 level. Around the same time, other manifestations of violence against women, such as domestic violence, began trending downward.[60]

In the 1990s, improvements in gender-related violence were joined by more widespread gains. From muggings to murders, almost all types of violent crime sharply dropped in the last decade of the millennium. The homicide rate, which stood at 10.5 victims per 100,000 people in 1991, was reduced to only 5.5 by 2000 and has seen hardly any variation since then.[61] Explanations for the sharp decline in violence abound, from better and smarter law enforcement to a simple "civilizing" of American cultural norms, as Pinker puts it. One controversial theory has held that *Roe v. Wade* (1973), by legalizing abortions and consequently reducing the number of unwanted births and uncared for children, was largely responsible.[62]

CHANGES IN THE MEDICAL PROFESSION

As public knowledge of health issues was shifting, so, too, was the medical profession experiencing rapid change. The struggle for the professional autonomy of doctors had been achieved by the 1920s. The widespread construction of hospitals and formal training institutions, as was documented in chapter 7, had been spearheaded by medical professionals. The influence of the medical profession included its successful efforts to resist the nationalization of health insurance, as had been achieved in so many other countries, an effort that has had a lasting effect on America's healthcare system. Such efforts helped ensure "a health care system whose organization, laws, and financing reflect the priorities of the medical profession to provide the best clinical medicine to every sick patient, to enhance the prestige and income of the profession, and to protect the autonomy of physicians."[63]

Despite physicians' achievement of autonomy in most areas of medicine in the 1920s, pharmaceuticals remained an area over which doctors held little sway in a "wild West" environment of unregulated pharmacies. This changed in 1938, when Food and Drug Administration (FDA) legislation promulgated drug regulations, including the classification of some drugs as needing a physician's prescription. The effects of such regulation began to be felt most strongly after World War II, when many of the new drugs introduced required a prescription. Between 1940 and 1965, sales of prescription drugs rose from accounting for only 12 percent of pharmacy sales to 40 percent. The control of prescriptions gave the medical profession additional control over most realms of healthcare. The big drug corporations that had been established after World War II were able to turn their attention from the consumer and focus their advertising attention on medical professionals. By 1961, around 60 percent of the advertising budgets of the twenty-two biggest drug firms was directed toward physicians.[64]

Around the same time, the profession was beginning a transformation toward specialization. In 1940, less than a quarter of doctors in active practice were specialists. Salaries for specialists were far higher than those for general practitioners. As a result, the rising generation of physicians shifted their career goals toward becoming full-time specialists. The percentage of doctors classified as specialists rose from 24 percent in 1940 to 69 percent in 1966.[65] High incomes for specialists, supplemented by a third-party-payer insurance system that was highly lucrative for hospitals and their staffs—especially after the implementation of Medicare and Medicaid—helped attract more Americans to the medical profession throughout the second half of the century. Indeed, starting in 1960, the ratio of doctors to 10,000 population started a steady climb from thirteen in the 1950s to thirty-one by 2009 (see figure 7–5).[66]

The unrivaled autonomy of the medical profession began to erode after the 1950s. As hospitals became larger and more complex, administrative control fell increasingly into the hands of professional administrators.[67] Patients also began to challenge the authority of the medical profession. While "for the most part, the authority of the doctor was unquestioned" in 1960, with the surgical profession even earning such high praise as being called a "religion of competence,"[68] by the early 1970s patients were demanding greater say in how they were treated. What had always been a tradition of "doctors know best" changed in 1972 when a federal appeals court in Washington, D.C., for the first time established a legal requirement for informed consent. "According to the new standard, the physician had to tell the patient whatever 'a reasonable person' would want to know in order to decide whether to accept the treatment." In 1973, responding to increasing pressure from healthcare consumers, the American Hospital Association came out with a Patients' Bill of Rights.[69] By Paul Starr's account, "nowhere was the distrust of professional domination more apparent than in the women's movement. Feminists claimed that as patients, as nurses, and in other roles in health care, women were denied the right to participate in medical decisions by paternalistic doctors who refused to share information or take their intelligence seriously."[70]

Part of the reason for the loss of trust in the medical profession was related to the movement toward specialization. Whereas in the past Americans' main connection to the medical community was through a primary-care physician (i.e., a general practitioner who formed long-term relationships and recommended a specialist as something of a last resort), in the second half of the twentieth century, many patients were increasingly bounced from specialist to specialist, with little coordination to avoid overlap and excessive costs.

Today, fewer than 30 percent of American doctors are generalists, compared to at least 50 percent in most other advanced countries, prompting some to classify the decline in primary care as "the silent crisis undermining US health care."[71]

ELECTRONICS, TECHNOLOGY, AND THE MOST RECENT MEDICAL INNOVATIONS

The role of electronic technology centers on new methods of scanning. The CT scan from the 1970s provided a more accurate method of internal imaging and detection. Its disadvantages include a cost of several thousand dollars per scan and concerns about its potential to cause cancer through excess radiation.[72] The CT scan was soon supplemented by a radiation-free imaging technology, magnetic resonance imaging (MRI). First introduced in 1977, the MRI provided an alternative to the CT scan that had both comparative advantages and weaknesses in imaging different parts of the body.[73] Use of both MRI and CT scans has increased by an annual rate of more than 8 percent per year since the mid-1990s, demonstrating both their diagnostic potential and continuing high costs, with more than $100 billion spent annually on medical imaging, including positron emission tomography (PET) scans, ultrasound, and nuclear medicine tests.[74]

Beyond improved imaging processes, the most important technological medical innovations of the past forty years are yet to be realized. One is the human genome project, which, by analyzing complex DNA sequences, is attempting to determine connections between certain ailments and specific gene sequences. The promise of genomic medicine lies in the possibility of diagnosing diseases or risk factors very early on, even perhaps from birth, as well as developing drugs that are directed more precisely at particular gene sequences, so that ultimately medications may be developed that are personalized to the particular genetic structure of each patient.

Despite its potential, "for most areas of medicine, the uptake of genomics has been slow." Though the project was started in 1995, the proper "evidentiary framework needed to convince the FDA to approve genomic tests, insurance companies to cover them, and physicians to use them" has yet to be developed. Moreover, even a proponent of the technology acknowledges that "it remains to be seen whether genomic medicine will actually improve health, when efforts to implement simpler clinical and preventive strategies have failed."[75] Nevertheless, molecular diagnostics have been growing rapidly and, it has been estimated, will soon account for a third of all diagnostic test costs.

Another area that holds promise but that has had little mainstream effect to date is stem cell therapy. As a regenerative therapy, the field of stem cell transplantation provides a ray of hope in today's age of chronic, degenerative diseases. However, though stem cell therapy has been practiced since the late 1980s for bone marrow transplants,[76] its practical application has thus far failed to extend far beyond that. The very prevalence of the phrase "stem cell research," compared to the relative absence of the phrase "stem cell therapy," attests to the therapy's limited practical implementation: In 2008, according to Google's Ngram Viewer, the first phrase was used eleven times more often than the second in a sample of more than 5 million books.[77] Skeptical investors have been hesitant to throw their support behind further research and development. Jeffrey O'Brien writes, "Long time horizons, regulatory hurdles, huge R&D costs, public sentiment, and political headwinds have all scared financiers. Wall Street isn't interested in financing this particular dream."[78] In short, the realization of the stem cell therapy dream appears to lie relatively far in the future.

Today, though bright ideas and human ingenuity abound—as exemplified by the concepts of genomic medicine and stem cell therapy—translation into practical, clinical applications are relatively rare. Part of this discrepancy stems from the ever-increasing costs of developing new medical innovations. As we noted in figure 14–2, new drug approvals have stagnated since the 1960s. A more basic measurement of drug industry innovation is to use new molecular entities (NMEs), which contain previously unused chemical functional groups and form the fundamental, chemical base for families of related drugs. Since the 1950s, according to Bernard Munos, companies have produced NMEs at a steady pace, even though they have made ever-increasing investments into research and development, with the costs of NMEs rising 13.4 percent per year over those six decades.[79] Even the world's biggest pharmaceutical company, Pfizer, which invested around $7 billion in research and development in new drugs in 2007 alone, came out with relatively few drugs in the first decade of the 2000s, and some of them were little more than combinations of old drugs. Other companies have developed spinoffs of old drugs that can cost more than twenty times more than their predecessors without producing any measurable improvements in outcome.[80] As Victor Fuchs and Alan Garber succinctly sum up the situation: "marginal improvements from the last dollar we now spend are small."[81]

Two reasons for the rising costs and diminishing returns on investment, according to Jan Vijg, are stringent regulatory standards and the skewed nature of modern linkages between research and clinical practice. Today, a handful of adverse outcomes out of tens of thousands of trials can derail a promising prospective treatment in the current risk-averse regulatory environment. "Intolerance for even a minimum of casualties, unavoidable in testing powerful new therapeutic approaches, has now reached a level that effectively constrains any further attempts to seriously innovate in this area." Had the regulatory norms of today existed in the 1940s, Vijg argues, innovations such as kidney dialysis and antibiotics might never have come to fruition.

At the same time, the connection between the clinical and research branches of medicine has become increasingly detached. Whereas clinicians often used to be the ones to experiment with unknown methods and techniques to cure patients—as was the case in the development of kidney dialysis—the research sphere, like the rest of the medical profession, has undergone a movement toward specialization. As we have seen previously, incentives in cancer research have turned toward favoring the expansion of specialized knowledge for knowledge's sake: "Unfortunately, the unraveling of molecular pathways, not their use in clinical interventions, is the way to get scientific recognition, publications and promotion. Ironically, to publish a paper in a top journal describing merely a new cure for cancer has much less priority than hard core science providing an interesting mechanism." Meanwhile, even when research does reach the clinical, pragmatic stage, patients hesitate to take part in experimental treatments. "In contrast to the old days today there are therapies for about everything.... Hence, they prefer to stick with the old, proven therapies and are highly reluctant to participate in something new. Only terminally ill people see some benefit."[82]

In spite of these formidable barriers and the generally stagnant trends of the past several decades—from unchanging cancer treatments to static new drug approvals—medical optimists continue to extol inventions such as diagnostic robots[83] or 3D printing of internal organs. Even if robots and 3D printing can improve the efficacy of surgery, however, the gains will likely be minor compared to the achievements of the decades between 1940 and 1970, including antibiotics and the development of the basic tools to fight CVD and cancer. Furthermore, as we will see in the following section, the problems of the U.S. medical system lie not in the scarcity of advanced modern technology, but rather, at least to some extent, in its overuse.

HOSPITALS: GLEAMING PALACES OF SCIENCE AND WASTE

Like so much else, hospitals, which had by 1940 attained their essential character as places of healing rather than places to die, experienced rapid growth in the aftermath of World War II. A catalyst to extensive hospital construction was the 1946 Hill–Burton Act, which over the following twenty years would help fund 4,678 hospital projects. Setting minimum standards for hospital provision, such as the guideline of having 4.5 hospital beds per 1,000 population, the legislation made particular progress in providing access to hospitals for low-population, rural areas, especially in the previously underserved south. This expansion of facilities and services was reflected by general hospital admissions, which rose by 26 percent in the six years after 1946; hospital inpatient services, which were "perceived as an unambiguous social good," would continue to expand until major changes in hospital administration in the 1980s reversed the trend.[84]

Hospitals of all kinds, bolstered by increased funding and freed in large part from considering cost constraints thanks to third-party hospital insurance, greatly expanded staff and equipment, including high-tech machinery. As early as 1960, almost every short-stay hospital, no matter how small, had diagnostic X-rays, clinical laboratories, and postoperative recovery rooms. This proliferation of hospital services and equipment only grew after the implementation of Medicare and Medicaid, with more than half of all not-for-profit hospitals having intensive care units in 1969, compared to only a seventh in 1961. At the same time, the rate of surgical operations was steadily growing from the 1960s through 1980. The American hospital by the early 1980s had become, in the words of the Blue Cross and Blue Shield Association president, a "technological emporium."[85]

Hospitals had become gleaming palaces, furnished with an abundance of highly trained personnel and sophisticated medical technologies that had the potential to cure diseases and extend life expectancy. But these opulent facilities came at a cost. One of the main drivers of medical inflation, the price of hospital care, doubled in the 1950s.[86] In the 1960s, the rate of medical inflation was twice that of general price inflation.[87] Such high expense might have been acceptable if hospital spending had been efficient and effective. But it was neither. Because hospitals focused on creating subspecialty departments and integrating expensive technologies for which they would be generously reimbursed, relatively little effort was devoted to community education and preventive measures that would have significantly reduced costs and improved patient outcomes.

The "medical arms race" is a frequently used term by those describing the evolution of American hospitals. No overall supervisory body prevents a hospital corporation from building a satellite state-of-the-art hospital embodying the latest high-tech imaging equipment in close proximity to the existing hospital of a competing hospital chain. This duplication of hospital resources tends to happen most often in affluent suburbs, where the population is well insured against the costs of all kinds of treatment.[88] Costs are pushed higher by the excessive purchasing of high-tech medical imaging equipment. For example, in Indiana in 1978, there was one CT scanner for every 100,000 people, compared to one per 1 million in Canada and one per 2 million in Britain, with no apparent advantage in outcomes. Another example of failed coordination and oversupply of medical equipment and personnel makes the case even more strongly:

> Two new hospitals, both half empty, within a few blocks of each other in one city neighborhood; half a dozen hospitals in another city equipped and staffed for open heart surgery, where the number of cases would barely keep one of the centers busy; empty beds the rule rather than the exception in obstetric and pediatric services across the nation; aged chronically ill patients lying idle in $60 a day hospital beds because no nursing home beds are provided; overloaded emergency rooms, and under-used facilities and services that have been created for reasons of prestige rather than need.[89]

In short, hospitals were providing a myriad of services, but not those of the highest medical priority, and were doing so at great expense. The lack of coordination combined with an unequal provision of services. As Paul Starr writes in the epigraph to this chapter, these supposed cathedrals of medical progress "stood next to neighborhoods that had been medically abandoned, that had no doctors for everyday needs, and where the most elementary public health and preventive care was frequently unavailable."[90] Indeed, as wealthier and middle-class Americans had moved to the suburbs in postwar years, many hospitals had followed the money, creating ethnic and social redlining, a tendency that has, to this day, not been corrected.

One of the most glaring examples of such inequity is the University of Chicago's Medical Center. Located on the south side of Chicago, where so much of the city's gun violence takes place, the hospital closed down its trauma center in 1988, ostensibly to cut costs, making the closest trauma ward to many parts of the south side more than ten miles away. In spite of community protests and studies finding that transportation time can affect chances of survival, no trauma center has been reopened in the area. In 2010, an 18-year-old named Damian Turner was shot in a drive-by shooting only blocks from the University of Chicago Medical Center but had to be taken by ambulance to a hospital more than eight miles away, where he soon died of his injuries.[91]

In the late 1970s and 1980s, the character of hospitals shifted toward more profit-oriented behavior. Despite the expectation that proprietary for-profit hospitals would be more efficient than their counterparts, a 1981 study found that their daily costs were 23 percent higher. "They would continue to duplicate expensive equipment available elsewhere in the community because the costs can be recovered through the insurance system. Though they may be exceedingly efficient in maximizing reimbursement rates, this sort of efficiency does not necessarily benefit their patients or the rest of society."[92]

In most recent years, the proliferation of HMOs and other managed care organizations has seen some success in cutting costs. Primary care doctors are more common, with less emphasis on specialization and expensive technology. This shift in emphasis comes with the tradeoff that patients are sometimes undertreated in these systems. Nonetheless, many modern hospitals remain, in large part, "less a health center . . . and more a mechanical treatment station."[93]

ASSESSING THE VALUE OF EXTENDED LIVES

Because most of the gains in life expectancy over the past six decades came not from reducing childhood mortality rates, but rather from extending the lives of older people, chronic, degenerative ailments that were once relatively rare problems have plagued the growing elderly segment of the population. The relatively slow gains in life expectancy have also been characterized by a lower quality of life in the years that were gained. Whereas a child who was cured of influenza or diphtheria in the first half of the twentieth century likely could look forward to a relatively normal, healthy life, today a 70-year-old who has been treated for heart disease has constant monitoring and management to look forward to, with a real chance of developing a degenerative illness such as Alzheimer's disease. Just in the twelve years after 1999, deaths from Alzheimer's per 100,000 people rose from sixteen to twenty-seven,[94] and at least one estimate says those figures drastically understate the role of the degenerative disease, placing Alzheimers' true death toll at more than 160 per 100,000, which would make it the third largest killer in the country. Its overall presence in the population would be even larger.[95]

The risk of degenerative disease must be weighed against the many sources of an improved quality of life. From hip replacements to air quality improvements, there have been an array of contributions to higher QALYs for modern Americans. Even many seniors who do not face problems as serious as Alzheimer's disease or other degenerative illnesses such as Parkinson's disease will spend their additional years in and out of hospitals where they will receive "high-tech, high-cost interventions" while they "suffer from a lack of low-tech, 'high-touch' services" such as visiting nurses and nurses' aides and will experience hardships with respect to housing, transportation, shopping, and social services. "If the elderly, at age sixty-five, could choose the pattern of spending that they prefer, many might opt for a mix very different from the one they will actually receive. They might prefer more focus on the quality of life, even at the expense of a small decrease in average life expectancy."[96]

There is no doubt that medical technology continues to move forward and has achieved numerous improvements that have yielded benefits far in excess of their costs. David Cutler and Mark McClennan examine five types of medical procedures in which substantial benefits have been achieved at modest, or zero, increase in cost. For instance, improvements in heart attack survival rates over the period 1984–98 yielded a one-year increase in life expectancy worth $70,000 at a mere $10,000 cost of improved medical technology. Improvements over 1950–90 in the care of low-birthweight infants yielded a similar 6-1 benefit-cost ratio. Better treatment of depression and more effective techniques of cataract surgery achieved benefit increases with no increase in costs. Only for breast cancer, the fifth type of medical intervention that they studied, did benefits fail to exceed costs.[97]

In the basic data on life expectancy great progress has been made in reducing inequality, but along other dimensions that quest has been more elusive. Today the average life expectancy at birth for African Americans is 3.5 years shorter than that of whites, compared to a 7.6-year differential in 1970 and nearly double that in 1900.[98] Nonetheless, health imbalances still exist for the most socioeconomically disadvantaged groups. In 2011, the rate of infant mortality within the black population was double that in the white population.[99]

With cardiovascular disease, America's leading killer, "the social class gap in heart disease deaths may be increasing as the rates of heart disease decline faster among higher social classes."[100] Part of this, no doubt, is related to the fact that the poor have been slower to eliminate risk factors such as smoking and obesity. For cancer, the five-year survival rate between 2001 and 2007 was 68.6 percent for whites and 59.4 percent for blacks.[101] And some of the presence of inequality in health outcomes relates to education, not just to race. As Sabrina Tavernise reported in 2013:

> A study last year found that white women without a high school diploma lost five years of life expectancy between 1990 and 2008, a measure of decline last seen among Russians in the economic chaos that came after the fall of the Soviet Union. This year, researchers at the University of Wisconsin found that mortality for women had gone up in more than 40 percent of the counties in the United States since the early 1990s.[102]

A less-known cause of increasing life expectancy, also with a differential effect across income groups, is the effect of air conditioning on heat-related mortality. A study of the temperature-mortality relationship emerged with two primary findings. First, the mortality impact of days with a mean temperature exceeding 80 °F has declined since 1960 by almost 70 percent. Second, this entire decline in heat-related fatalities can be attributed to the diffusion of residential air conditioning. To the extent that the low-income population has been the last to be able to equip their residences with air-conditioning units or central air conditioning, this cause of reduced mortality would provide a further explanation, albeit probably small, for the differential increase of life expectancy between rich and poor Americans.[103]

RAISING THE STANDARD OF LIVING GOES BEYOND INCREASING LIFE EXPECTANCY

Most of this chapter has focused on the achievements of the medical care system in achieving an increase in life expectancy and a reduction in mortality rates. In addition numerous innovations have improved the quality of life without having any impact on longevity. We have already examined the development in the early postwar years of hip and knee replacement surgery, which have produced significant increase in QALYs, the quality of a life year made possible by the surgery. There has been a steady improvement in replacement surgery through better techniques and materials. In 2014, there were 719,000 total knee replacement surgeries and 332,000 total hip replacement operations.[104]

The birth control pill has been called "after penicillin the most important pharmaceutical development of the 20th century." For millennia couples had attempted to control the number of births, but methods were clumsy, reducing spontaneity, and were often unreliable. During the 1950s, research on a birth control pill proceeded rapidly, starting from a pill synthesized in Mexico City from a type of Mexican yam that had a long been used by Mexican women. The efforts to develop the pill combined the activism of Margaret Sanger, the head of the organization that would later become known as Planned Parenthood, and the scientist Gregory Pincus. After large-scale clinical trials were held in Puerto Rico in the mid-1950s, the pill gained FDA approval in 1960. It was an instant success, and by 1965 6.5 million women were using it. Over the years, the pill has remained controversial because of side effects, and lower doses with fewer side effects have been developed.[105]

In 1965, the Supreme Court ruled that married couples had the right to use birth control on the grounds that privacy was protected by the Constitution, although millions of unmarried women were still denied use in twenty-six states. Finally, in 1972, the Supreme Court legalized birth control for all citizens regardless of marital status. The pill was an important factor that brought the baby boom of 1947–64 to an end and encouraged women, who could now control the number and timing of children, to enter the labor force. The years of the most rapid increase in the labor-force participation rate of women were 1965–85—that is, starting soon after the pill became widely available in the early 1960s.

Birth control pills did more than allow the spacing and number of children; they also increased the spontaneity of sex, which could take place without the previous need to insert a diaphragm in women or put on a condom for men. Another important innovation that came later was a medical cure for erectile dysfunction. Sildenafil, developed by two Pfizer research lab employees, was synthesized in 1989 and, starting in the late 1990s, sold by Pfizer under the brand name Viagra. Soon Viagra was joined by competing drugs, including Cialis. To the extent that these drugs make sex possible, as people age, for people who would otherwise have stopped having sex, it can be said to contribute to the quality of life measured by QALYs.

Dentistry has not been discussed in this chapter, for it has little effect on the length of life, but note should be made of progress that has raised the quality of life. Research on adding fluoride to water was carried out in the 1930s to determine the optimal ratio of fluoride to water that would protect against tooth decay without staining teeth. Grand Rapids, Michigan, in January 1945, became the first city to have its water fluoridated, and a year later, my own city of Evanston, Illinois, became the site of a test to determine whether fluoridation resulted in a reduction of tooth decay compared to nearby towns. Fluoridation became the official policy of the U.S. Public Health Service in 1951, and by 1960, water fluoridation was widespread. Fluoridation now reaches 64 percent of the U.S. population, one of the highest percentages in the world, and the development of fluoridated toothpaste has further caused a decline in the prevalence of tooth decay. In one controlled experiment comparing the Irish Republic, which had fluoridated water, and Northern Ireland, which did not, fluoridation was shown to reduce tooth decay by 56 percent.[106]

PAYING FOR HEALTHCARE

Although around 16 percent of the American population lacked health insurance in 2010[107]—compared to the universal coverage enjoyed by citizens in the great majority of other developed nations—the United States still spent significantly more per person than any other country, with no corresponding advantage in health outcomes. Figure 14–5 plots the Group of Seven nations' life expectancies against health expenditures per person. The countries are arranged

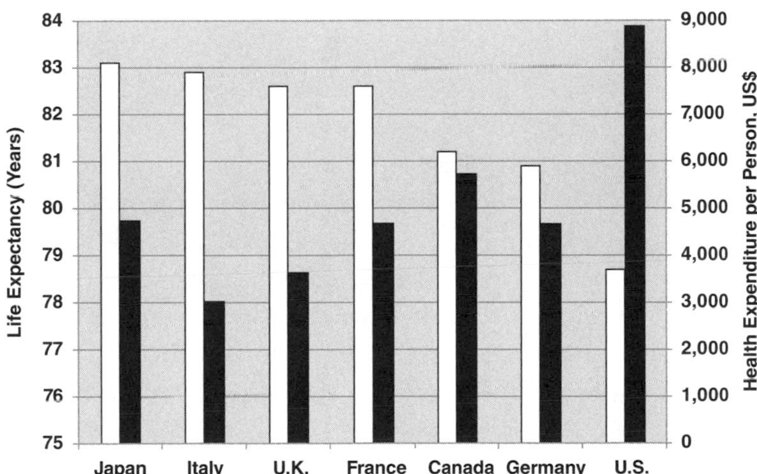

Figure 14–5. Life Expectancy versus Health Expenditure per Person, Group of Seven Countries, 2012

Source: The World Bank (2014). "World Development Indicators," Tables 2.15 and 2.21.

from left to right in order of decreasing life expectancy. Although American per person health expenditure was more than twice that of Italy and the United Kingdom, life expectancy in the United States was about four years shorter. Perhaps the most telling comparison, because of their considerable similarities, is between the United States and Canada. U.S. per person health care spending was nearly 55 percent higher than Canada's, and its life expectancy was 2.5 years shorter. What elements of the U.S. medical care system make it so relatively expensive and ineffective?

This question as it applies to the United States versus Canada has been studied directly by Alexis Pozen and David Cutler. They focus on the two-thirds of total cost difference attributable to physicians and hospitals and are able to allocate the high level of U.S. spending to three categories. They conclude that 39 percent of the U.S. excess is due to administrative expenses, 31 percent to higher incomes of medical practitioners, and 14 percent to additional procedures (e.g., extra tests); they are unable to allocate the remaining 16 percent of spending differences to a specific cause. They are careful to qualify their results. Higher physician incomes in the United States, for instance, may reflect higher incomes of all skilled occupations and may be necessary to induce young people to enter the medical profession. The additional procedures in the United States may be excessive or effective viewed individually, but they have not been sufficient to offset the 2.5 year shortfall of life expectancy in the United States. The likeliest indicator of waste is the high amount of administrative expense in the United States, due in large part to the complexity of the insurance system and the need for extra nonclinical workers in doctors' offices and in hospitals to deal with insurance-related administrative paperwork.

The high costs and inefficiency built into the structure of the U.S. medical care system has its roots in the early 1930s with the creation of Blue Cross, for hospital care, and Blue Shield, for physician payments. Previously payment had come from patients in a direct exchange to their physicians on a fee-for-service basis. Blue Cross introduced the modern idea of insurance, in which individuals pay premiums into a collective pool that a third party can then pay out for necessary medical expenditures. In 1940, only 12 million people had private health insurance, but during World War II, with wages frozen, many businesses sought to attract employees by offering health benefits tied to employment. After that, not only did third-party insurance plans begin to establish themselves as a primary method of making medical payments, but employment became the most important criterion in obtaining coverage.[108]

The link to employment made the system regressive, for those lacking a steady income, or those who worked part-time or small businesses that were unable to afford insurance, were forced to pay out of their own pockets for medical services. In the case of major illnesses the medical bills faced by the uninsured could lead to personal bankruptcy.

Some remedy for this problem came in the mid-1960s with the enactment of Medicare and Medicaid, federal government programs aimed to protect the most vulnerable in society, the elderly and the poor. These programs were quite successful at extending care to the previously underserved. Whereas in 1964 the poor saw doctors around 20 percent less frequently than the nonpoor, by 1975, this relationship had been entirely reversed.[109] Similarly, from 1965 to 1985, the proportion of hospital inpatients who were 65 years or older rose from 16 percent to 30 percent.[110] However, though these programs expanded coverage, they also enlarged the growing third-party insurance system that contained incentives for excessive spending. Indeed, between 1950 and 1980, healthcare expenditures as a share of GNP more than doubled, from 4.5 to 9.4 percent, largely as a result of a set of skewed incentives created by a predominantly third-party-payer system.[111]

> Just as hospital insurance removed individual anxieties about paying large hospital bills, it removed considerations of cost constraints from hospital billings. Hospitals could pass increased costs on to insurers, who could pass them on again to millions of subscribers, sick and well, in small increases in hospital insurance premiums. The potential of a third-party payment system unleashed an unprecedented demand for hospital services. It was a demand that could be stimulated by the suppliers, that is, by the doctors and hospitals themselves. Hospital expenditures and reimbursement mechanisms drove each other, in an expansionary spiral.[112]

During the 1960s and 1970s it could at least be said that hospital efforts, if excessive and misdirected, were relatively attentive to the needs of the patient. This began to change in the 1980s, when the "overtly profit-making ethos" came to the fore. Until then, hospitals were directly reimbursed for their costs. But then Medicare, in an attempt to standardize cost reimbursements, specified standardized reimbursement rates for 467 diagnosis-related groups (DRGs). Hospitals quickly took advantage of this opportunity to take the fixed per-treatment reimbursement and raise profits by cutting the costs of treatments, often by reducing the quality of patient care:

> Not surprisingly complaints soon came from patients and their advocates charging that seriously ill Medicare patients were being inappropriately discharged from hospitals, that many patients were given incomplete information on their rights of discharge appeal and on options for posthospital care, and that some hospitals were denying admission to patients with multiple serious conditions.... Since hospitals could keep any differences between the actual cost of services for a given case and the amount received per DRG, the system gave administrators an incentive to press doctors to give minimal service, justified on grounds of fiscal efficiency.[113]

This shift was not simply a case of a few anomalous abuses. As shown in figure 14–6, the amount of care patients received fell rapidly on average after 1980 as hospitals cut both the number of patients admitted and, more significant, their length of stay. The average length of stay for all patients fell from 7.3 days in 1980 to 4.9 days in 2000. The decline was even more marked among the

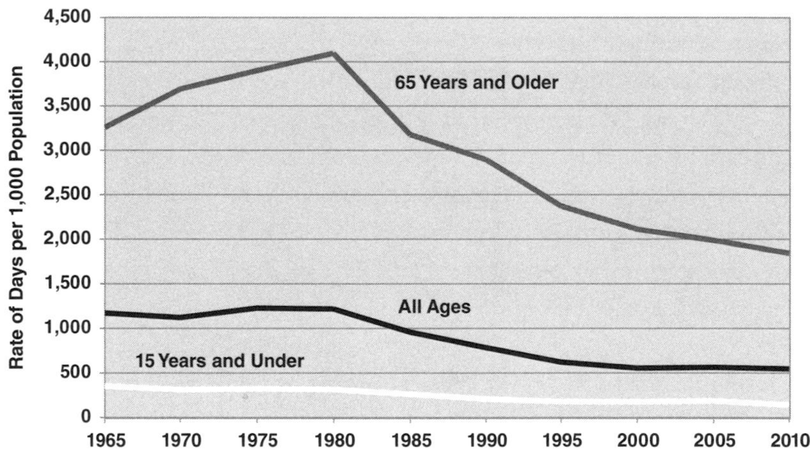

Figure 14–6. Rate of Days of Care for Patients Discharged from Short-Stay Hospitals

Sources: US Department of Health and Human Services (1989), "Trends in Hospital Utilization: United States, 1965–1986," *CDC*, Table 2. CDC (2006, 2010), "National Hospital Discharge Survey." HSUS Table Aa204-217.

elderly, as their 1970 length of stay of 12.6 days fell by more than half to just 6 days by 2000.[114] According to one study, patients admitted to the hospital for a broken hip were discharged after just seven days in 1998, compared to the twenty they would have stayed in 1981. "Although better surgical techniques and the expanding availability of rehabilitation hospitals provide a partial explanation, the authors of the study . . . concluded that the patients were also in relatively worse health as they were discharged."[115]

The development of managed care organizations began in the early 1970s. Paul Elwood, a pediatric neurologist and hospital administrator, had come to admire the Kaiser Permanente and Mayo clinic group practices, with fixed fees replacing fee-per-service and salaries for doctors removing the incentive for medical practitioners to provide excessive testing and services. Ellwood, feeling that the first priority of these entities should be to keep people healthy, proposed calling them "health maintenance organizations" (HMOs).[116] Ellwood's persuasive powers contributed to the development of the HMO Act of 1973, but with a twist. The Nixon administration's legislation sanctioned the idea of HMOs but broadened the concept beyond Ellwood's ideal model of group practices in the mold of Kaiser and Mayo. Throughout the 1980s and 1990s, HMOs became steadily more popular as employers welcomed the idea of a new principle of financing medical care that promised to reduce costs. But most of this growth was provided by the major for-profit commercial insurance companies, which by 1997 accounted for fully two-thirds of the HMO business.[117]

The shift away from the group practice model made a crucial difference. Whereas at Kaiser, Mayo, and similar organizations, treatment choices were made by staff physicians, the new for-profit managed plans "set their own criteria and imposed it on their physicians from afar, frequently requiring the physicians to obtain prior approval for referrals, tests, and procedures."[118] Further affecting the quality of care were financial incentives that based a physician's income not on health outcomes but on how effectively the doctor had succeeded in reducing expenses. The health care literature provides numerous examples of disability and death caused by HMO coverage limitations.

In a reaction against the restrictions, insurers developed preferred provider organizations (PPOs), which have been described as "half-hearted" HMOs in that they impose only some of the access limitations. For instance, PPOs usually provide some insurance coverage even if a patient does not visit a preferred provider, and patients have responded to this greater freedom of choice enthusiastically by choosing PPO in preference to HMO coverage when employers offer that choice. By 2010 PPOs were the dominant form of health plan, covering 56 percent of employees with insurance coverage, as compared to 19 percent for HMOs, 21 percent for various hybrid-type health plans, and a mere 1 percent for traditional fee-for-service plans. This represented a nearly complete rejection of fee-for-service plans, which had accounted for 73 percent of covered employees as recently as 1988.[119]

The overriding questions about managed care, including HMOs, PPOs, and other variants, concern its effects on costs and quality of medical care. In the mid-1990s there was considerable optimism that a turning point had been reached, as was justified by the time path of the share of health care spending in GDP, as displayed in figure 14–7. Notice that the spending share began to creep up in the 1960s and 1970s and then rose rapidly, at four times the overall rate of inflation, in the late 1980s and early 1990s. But then the share stabilized and rose only from 13.5 percent to 13.8 percent between 1993 and 2000, and spending in 2000 was about $300 billion lower than had been projected in 1993.[120] Unfortunately, this progress in cost-containment was short lived, as between 2000 and 2009 the medical spending share rose until in 2010 it accounted for 17.7 percent of GDP.

Jonathan Cohn has ascribed this cost resurgence to the fact that managed care organizations had already reduced all the costs they could without

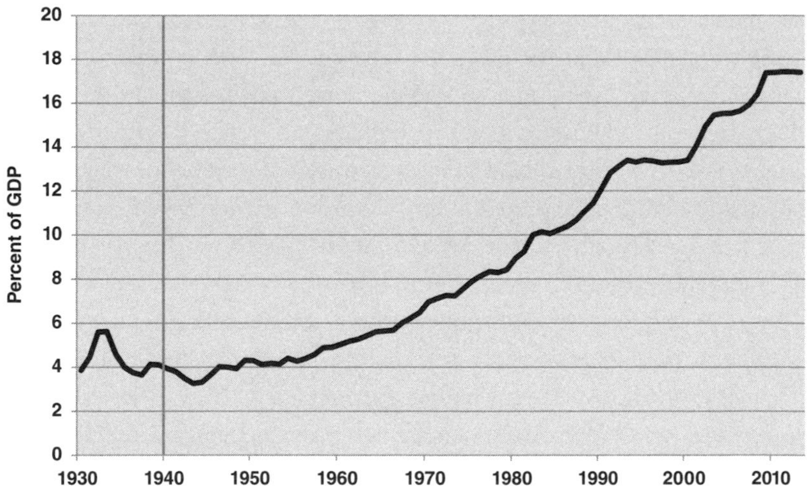

Figure 14–7. Health Spending as a Percentage of GDP, 1930–2013
Source: HSUS Ab952 before 1960, CMS "National Health Expenditure Accounts" after 1960. Data extrapolated for gaps before 1948.

having a severe negative effect on health outcomes. William Schwartz claimed that their initial cost-cutting success was unsustainable for a different reason, for many proprietary organizations had artificially reduced their premiums to drive out competition, a practice that could not last.[121] A more obvious cause of the renewed rise in the spending share was the rapid shift from more restrictive HMOs to less restrictive PPOs as the PPO share among covered employees rose from 38 percent in 1999 to 56 percent in 2010. Whatever the case, the continuing upward creep of the medical spending share of GDP indicated that the initial promise of cost containment through managed care could not be sustained.

The restrictions imposed by HMOs and, to a lesser extent, PPOs, as well as the anecdotal evidence of harm done by those restrictions, would seem to support the conclusion that HMOs reduce the quality of medical care. Yet, surprisingly, there is no firm evidence of a quality reduction. In his 2000 review of research studies, David Dranove concluded:

> Overall, the evidence suggests that HMOs score higher on some dimensions of quality and lower on others, and on many other dimensions quality is about even. . . . The mixed empirical evidence belies the many complaints about HMOs. Physicians complain the loudest, apparently unwilling to accept even the possibility of reduced quality in exchange for $300 billion of savings. Perhaps conditioned by the complaints of their physicians, patients are complaining as well.[122]

Cutler and Wise (2006) concur that "summary reviews of the literature suggest no outcome differences between managed care and traditional insurance coverage." And they agree with Dranove that despite cost savings and no adverse impact on health, "managed care is not very popular."[123]

The long evolution of managed care with all its complexity did not change the basic facts that the U.S. medical care system remained by far the most expensive in the world while providing only partial coverage. On the eve of the passage of the Patient Protection and Affordable Care Act of 2010, better known as Obamacare, 16 percent of U.S. citizens lacked health coverage, higher than the 12 percent who had lacked insurance in 1987.[124] The burden of lack of coverage has mostly, contrary to the popular narrative, fallen not on the unemployed or extremely poor, but instead on the working poor. Thanks to a steady decline in employment-based health insurance, by the early 2000s about 80 percent of the uninsured were working Americans who were neither poor enough to qualify for Medicaid nor in a position to bargain for a job with health benefits.[125] Among those were citizens who needed and were willing to pay for insurance to cover a pre-existing condition but who were denied coverage because of that very condition.

It is too early to determine the overall effect of Obamacare on the share of health care spending in GDP or the efficacy of medical care. The program has three beneficial features. First, it deals directly with the coverage gap for those who lack employer-paid coverage but have income too high to qualify for Medicaid. Second, the law explicitly prohibits insurers from denying coverage to those who have pre-existing conditions. And third, the law provides substantial subsidies to help pay for coverage.

The average cost of the most popular "silver" plan in 2014 before subsidies was $4,100, with annual deductibles ranging from $6,000 for individuals to more than $12,000 for a family of four. Two factors mitigate these high costs. First, the average subsidy on a silver plan was $3,300 per year, reducing the annual premium cost to $828 per year, or only $69 per month. In fact, 85 percent of those who signed up for health coverage under Obamacare in 2015 were eligible for subsidies. Second, despite the high deductibles, an extensive set of preventive screening tests is offered free of any copays, including blood-pressure and cholesterol tests, immunizations, mammograms, and colonoscopies, as well as one annual health checkup. Any further medical procedures found to be necessary as a result of preventive screening would be paid for by the patient up to the limit of the deductible.[126]

The problems with Obamacare begin with its complexity. An inquiry in February 2015 to the Obamacare website healthcare.gov for my state of Illinois lists 142 different plans, each offering a different menu of premiums, deductibles, and copays. A more serious problem than complexity is the restricted nature of provider networks and their apparent instability. Many people who were previously insured received notice that their longtime insurance policies did not meet the requirements of the Affordable Care Act and were forced to shop for a new policy, often finding it difficult to locate a plan that included their previous family doctor. Stories abound of patients being required to travel long distances to be treated by in-network specialists to avoid paying large sums to see out-of-network specialists who may be nearby. Doctors shift in and out of networks frequently, resulting in bills for uncovered services from physicians who have exited a particular network. Instability in the composition of the networks creates obsolescence for lists of included doctors, and up-to-date information is hard to obtain. Asked whether a doctor was part of a plan, an insurer's representative "said he didn't know because doctors came in and out of the network all the time, likening the situation to players switching teams in the National Basketball Association." Other complaints include ever-changing lists of drugs that are covered, that require high copays, or that are not covered at all.[127]

The complexity and restrictions of Obamacare contrast notably with the simplicity of Medicare and its single-payer system, from which most doctors and hospitals accept payments. In its effort to obtain passage of the Affordable Care Act in 2010, the Obama administration did not attempt to base the plan on the single-payer model or even to provide a public payer option, apparently fearing an onslaught of opposition from lobbyists for the private insurance industry. Although it is much too soon to gauge the effects of Obamacare on health wellness indicators such as life expectancy, it is encouraging that, as shown in figure 14–7, the long-term increase in the share of medical care spending in GDP appears to have stopped, at least temporarily, during 2010–13, even before Obamacare enrollments began in 2014.

CONCLUSION

The U.S. health care system changed dramatically after 1940 in its methods of treating illness, in its organization of care delivery, and in its methods of payment. The most important post-1940 innovations occurred early on, between 1940 and the late 1970s. Indeed, the 1940s and early 1950s represented the culmination of a social revolution that by and large eradicated the influence of infectious diseases on everyday American life.[128] After the quantum leaps of progress made possible by Pasteur's germ theory and improved water treatment and waste removal, the invention of penicillin and other antibiotics during and after World War II delivered the finishing blows to the potency of many infectious illnesses. The main treatments for cardiovascular disease and cancer were mostly developed by the 1970s. In the case of heart disease, a variety of preventive and palliative approaches was available by the early 1960s, at which time the incidence of heart disease began its slow but steady decline. The war on cancer has not been as successful, and there have been few breakthroughs since the development of modern imaging technologies and of treatments such as chemotherapy and immunotherapy that were in widespread use by the 1970s.

Progress was achieved in part through the expansion of public knowledge and awareness of health issues. The reduction of smoking and other risk factors was integral to the decline of heart disease, and greater public emphasis on cleaning up air and water pollution had a positive impact on life expectancy and quality-adjusted life years. Meanwhile, mortality from accidents maintained a steady decline, and violence in America has continued to experience up and down cycles, with a cyclical peak as recently as the early 1990s followed by marked improvement since then.

After 1970, an increasingly specialized medical profession shifted emphasis toward high-tech, expensive machinery, turning hospitals into both "technological emporiums" and cold "mechanical treatment centers." The share of medical care spending in GDP began its inexorable upward creep after the early 1960s, and simple preventive measures that could have limited cost increases while also improving public health were underemphasized by hospitals and their doctors. At the same time, practical medical innovations were occurring less often and the rate of development of new drugs slowed to a crawl as it faced the obstacles of burdensome regulations and skyrocketing costs.

The rising medical care share of GDP was largely driven by a health insurance system based on incentives to supply a higher volume of high-tech services without regard to cost. This fee-for-service system reflected the wishes of a medical profession that embraced a free-market ideology and independence from government intervention, resisting the movement in the rest of the developed world toward universal health care provided as a right of citizenship rather than conditional on covered employment. The gradual shift toward managed care organizations after 1980 had by 2010 largely replaced the fee-per-service system but had not ended the dependence of insurance coverage on employment. By 2013, the share of medical care spending in GDP, which was only 4 percent between 1930 and 1960, had reached 18 percent, yet a sixth of the population still lacked insurance and life expectancy at birth in the United States was between two and four years shorter than in other developed countries providing universal care.

Research assessments of managed care did not uncover any systematic decline in quality compared to the traditional fee-for-service system, although the distinction between in-network and out-of-network providers made managed care quite unpopular. The problem of limited networks was exacerbated by Obamacare, which suffered from the complexity of hundreds of different plans, each offering narrow provider networks that were plagued with relatively high provider turnover. At least Obamacare helped to bridge the coverage gap with medical insurance that was subsidized along a sliding scale depending on income, that was available without denial for pre-existing conditions, and that required all providers to offer preventive screening tests free of charge to patients.

Meanwhile, the payoff from technological change has been disappointing relative to the rapid progress achieved between 1940 and the late 1970s. Innovations in medical research based on the genome and stem cells, while initially promising, have thus far been slow to produce effective new drugs and therapies. The breakthroughs that have been achieved recently have been largely in the realm of disease management rather than cure, and many of them have been made available only at relatively high cost.[129] Further extensions of life expectancy based on improved treatment of physical illness are bringing ever more Americans into the age range of vulnerability to Alzheimer's and other forms of dementia. Although large expenditures on medical research and treatment will doubtless continue to result in a slow continuing advance in life expectancy, they are unlikely to change the rank of the United States as having by far the most expensive medical care system among the developed countries along with one of the lowest levels of life expectancy.

Chapter 15

WORK, YOUTH, AND RETIREMENT AT HOME AND ON THE JOB

> The $20 hourly wage, introduced on a huge scale in the middle of the last century, allowed masses of Americans with no more than high school education to rise to the middle class. It was a maker, of sorts. And it is on its way to extinction.
>
> —Louis Uchitelle, 2008

INTRODUCTION

By 1940 working conditions on the job and in the home had already improved significantly from the toil, danger, and drudgery of the late nineteenth century. Most of the exodus from the farm to the city had already occurred. Large and small machines, most of them powered by electricity, had replaced the most dangerous factory work, such as that of the 1890 steelworker. An increasing fraction of jobs was in clerical and sales occupations that, however boring and routine, were safer and more comfortable than life on the farm or in the factory. The reduction in work hours from sixty to forty hours per week had already been achieved by 1940, and the forty-hour week was still standard in 2015.

Similarly, working conditions inside the home for women had improved by orders of magnitude. By 1940 most urban homes had central heating fueled by oil or natural gas, so wood and coal did not have to be hauled in. Clean running water had replaced the need for the housewife to carry pails of water into the home for laundry, cooking, and bathing. By 1940, about 40 percent of the households owned an electric refrigerator, and 44 percent owned some type of electric washing machine. Along these and other dimensions, working conditions improved more dramatically from 1870 to 1940 than they have in the decades since 1940.

During the years of the baby boom between 1947 and 1964, women were busy raising children and therefore few considered market work a viable option. But starting in the late 1960s the female labor force participation rate began its gradual upward climb until a peak was reached in 1999. There is a debate in the economics literature over whether the universal adoption of electric household appliances between 1945 and 1965 had any effect on fertility or labor force participation. The temporary rise in the fertility rate during the baby boom period is best viewed as a change in taste for raising children caused more than anything by the hardships imposed by the Great Depression and World War II. Women flooded into the marketplace not in the 1950s, when most kitchens became equipped with the basic set of home appliances, but rather a decade or two after the appliances arrived.

The postwar period brought both progress and new problems. The share of the labor force engaged in manufacturing peaked in 1953 at about 30 percent and then declined, slowly at first, but then more rapidly after 1980 as the substitution of machines for labor, together with a surge of imported manufactured goods, eliminated jobs in one American manufacturing industry after another. By 2015 the share of manufacturing jobs in the labor force had fallen to 10 percent, and the disappearance of steady, well-paying union jobs brought with it a gradual erosion of the mid-1950s assumption that a blue-collar worker with no more than a high school education could own a suburban house and at least one car, if not two.

Beneficiaries from improvements in working conditions included not only adult males and females, but also youth, particularly teenagers, as child labor was replaced by universal high school education. The high-school completion rate steadily climbed from 10 percent in 1900 to 75 percent in 1970, with little further advance since then. Many students, particularly from the minority and poverty populations, fail to complete high school and are thus condemned to spend their lifetimes working in a succession of manual, routine jobs paying little more than the minimum wage.

During the early postwar period, the United States led the world in the percentage of young people completing college, thanks in large part to the GI Bill, which paid all college expenses for millions of veterans returning home from the war. But in the past two decades, the U.S. college completion rate has dropped from first place in the international league tables to no better than fifteenth. Although the percentage earning four-year degrees has continued to creep up over the past decade to about a third, in recent years as many as 40 percent of these college graduates have been unable to find jobs requiring a college education. Even when adjusted for inflation, the price of college has increased by a factor of ten since the 1950s.[1] Rampant cost inflation has caused the price of a college education to spiral ever upward, and although fellowships and scholarships lighten the burden, particularly at the most selective schools, students have been forced to accumulate a burden of student debt that has now reached $1.2 trillion.

Just as the quality of life for youth was transformed as child labor disappeared and high school completion became nearly universal, so there was a revolution in the life of the elderly after 1940. In the pre-1920 era, there was no concept of "retirement." Workers "worked until they dropped"—that is, they kept working until they were physically unable to do their jobs, after which they became dependent on their children, or on church charity and other kinds of private welfare programs. The first step in the old-age revolution was the passage of the Social Security legislation of 1935 that provided for a nationwide old-age pension system. All workers would make contributions during their lifetime and then reap the rewards in the form of a guaranteed and secure Social Security pension.

While Social Security payments were relatively small, they were often supplemented by defined-benefit pension plans for employees of large corporations in the private sector and in most unionized public-sector jobs. Workers could now afford to retire when their pension payments began. The concept of retirement soon evolved as a time of leisure and generated a boom in the construction of golf courses, retirement homes, and retirement cities such as Sun City, Arizona, and there was a massive exodus from the northeast and north central states to states in the Sun Belt from California to Florida. As life expectancy has increased while the retirement age for Social Security remained fixed until recently, the portion of life spent in retirement has steadily grown, and the question of future funding for the Social Security system remains a hot potato that is regularly kicked down the road.

FROM FARM AND FACTORY TO THE OFFICE CUBICLE: BETTER PAY AND SAFER WORKING CONDITIONS

The backbreaking toil associated with farming and blue-collar labor gave way to the physical ease of jobs in accounting, administration, engineering, management, and sales. Technological innovations that made workers much more productive from 1900 to 1940 allowed them to make a seamless transition into white-collar employment, especially because the unemployment rate with the exception of two recession years remained at 5.5 percent or below throughout the two decades between 1950 and 1970.[2]

The decline of the percentage of employment in agriculture was inexorable but did not occur at a steady pace. It required the forty years between 1900 and 1940 for the agriculture employment percentage to decline from 40 percent to 20 percent. Progress since 1940 is displayed in figure 15–1, which shows that the percentage declined by half from 20 percent to 10 percent by 1953, by another half from 10 percent to 5 percent by 1967, and eventually to a low plateau of 2 percent during 2000–2013. The introduction of advanced machinery replaced farm tasks requiring physical labor, making that labor redundant on the farm but eagerly solicited in urban blue-collar and white-collar jobs, at least during the first half of the postwar era.

The transition from farming and blue-collar jobs to white-collar employment produced a significant increase in annual salaries and socioeconomic status. This rise in income levels was a major factor in the historic expansion of the middle class and its standard of living through the latter half of the twentieth century. With the decline of the American manufacturing sector and the rise of the service sector, jobs for many Americans became safer as workers left

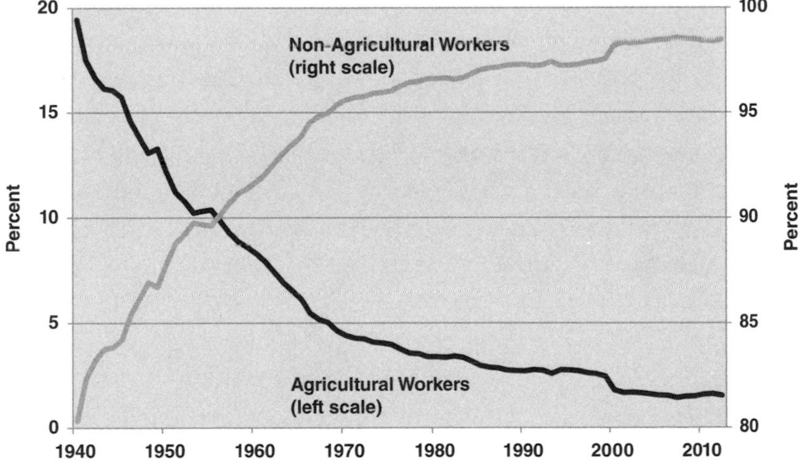

Figure 15–1. Percentage of Employed Civilian Labor Force in Agricultural and Non-Agricultural Work, 1940–2012

Source: Table B-35, Department of Labor (Bureau of Labor Statistics), ratio linked back from 1940 to 1947.

dangerous industrial work for the minimal physical demands of the office cubicle. The growth of white-collar jobs improved safety around the workplace, and safety also greatly improved within manufacturing and mining. In the coal mining industry, the annual fatality rate per 100,000 miners dropped from 329 during 1911–1915 to twenty-five during 1996–1997.[3] The reduction in injuries and fatalities across mining and manufacturing lifted the scourge of income loss and disability for thousands of households.

Just as the invention of air conditioning facilitated the flight of retirees to sunny southern destinations, so it also benefited the productivity, not to mention the comfort, of clerical and other white-collar workers. Productivity was estimated to have been raised by 25 percent among government typists during the 1950s as a result of air-conditioning, and it was rated as the chief boost to worker productivity by 90 percent of American firms in a 1957 survey. And while air-conditioning ended sweltering conditions in the workplace, overall health saw a boost from lowered mortality rates. Rates of illness and death during heat waves were reduced as the percentage of households with central or room air conditioning increased from near zero in 1950 to 68 percent in 1993 to nearly 90 percent in 2013.[4] Once the home was air-conditioned, housework became more productive and leisure-time activities more enjoyable.

> Seasonal cycles were determined by weather. Workers' productivity declined in direct proportion to the heat and humidity outside—and on the hottest days employees left work early and businesses shut their doors. Stores and theaters also closed down, unable to comfortably accommodate larger groups of people in stifling interiors. Cities emptied in summers.... Houses and office buildings were designed to enhance natural cooling, and people spent summer days and evenings on porches or fire escapes.[5]

Along with indoor plumbing, electricity, household telephones, and a host of other late nineteenth- and early twentieth-century inventions, the air conditioner is an iconic example of the impact of technology on the American standard of living. Because most indoor jobs benefited from air conditioning by 1970, that single invention may help to explain why the growth rates of labor productivity and total factor productivity were so much higher before 1970 than after that date.

Unprecedented growth in real wages in the 1950s and 1960s enabled families that had a high school graduate as the head of household to move into the rapidly spreading suburbs.

> The expanding middle class had in it two distinct kinds of workers: white-collar and blue-collar. Back then, thanks to the wages won for him by his union, the blue-collar man (the gender specification is unavoidable) could live next door to the white-collar man—not to the doctor, perhaps, but to the accountant, the teacher, the middle manager. This rough economic equality was a political fact of the first importance. It meant that, in a break with the drift of things in pre-war America, postwar America had no working class and no working-class politics. It instead had a middle-class politics for an expanding middle class bigger in aspiration and self-identification than it was in fact—more people wanted to be seen as middle-class than had yet arrived at that state of felicity. Socialism in America, the German political economist Werner Sombart wrote in 1906, foundered upon "roast beef and apple pie," a metaphor for American plenty. The expanding middle class of the postwar era—property owning, bourgeois in outlook, centrist in politics—hardly proved him wrong.[6]

The clear overlap between blue-collar and white-collar ambitions and success from the 1940s until the 1970s symbolized the egalitarian experience of a diverse and stable middle class. Claudia Goldin and Robert Margo chronicle the "Great Compression" of the American socioeconomic classes between 1945 and 1975. They assert that "if the decade of the 1980s created the rust belt, then surely the 1940s created the steel belt."[7] This, combined with a gradual increase in the supply of educated workers, maintained the small variation in the wage structure for that thirty-year time period. A fortunate set of circumstances thus allowed the wage disparities of the late nineteenth and early twentieth centuries to narrow.

Just as the Great Compression coincided with the golden age of economic expansion, so the post-1975 rise of income inequality has taken place in an environment of slower overall economic growth. By some measures the median real wage has barely increased in the past three or four decades. During the years of the Great Compression, job diversity, steady incomes, and quality education were self-reinforcing. But more recently, the bottom half of the income distribution has begun to drop out of the middle class.

> If the average income of one's neighbors (and/or its correlates) indirectly affects one's own social, economic, or physical outcomes, then income segregation will lead to more unequal outcomes between low- and high-income households than their differences in income alone would predict. In a highly segregated region, then, higher-income households may be advantaged relative to lower-income households not only by the difference in their own incomes but by the differences in their respective neighbors' incomes.[8]

The correlation between average neighborhood income levels and individual socioeconomic status is exacerbated when the top groups take home an ever-increasing share of income and wealth. Between 1970 and 1998, the average income in the top 0.01 percent of the income distribution jumped from fifty to 250 times the economy-wide average income level.[9] The sharp division between the very top incomes and the average has replaced the Great Compression by the "Great Divergence." We return to the causes and consequences of rising income inequality in chapter 18.

THE FEMININE REVOLUTION: ROSIE THE RIVETER BECOMES A BABY-BOOM HOMEMAKER AND THEN A WHITE-COLLAR PROFESSIONAL

The most important change in postwar labor markets was the rise of female labor force participation. Millions of women had obtained their first experience with work in the marketplace during World War II, when 5.2 million women entered the labor force. "Rosie the Riveter" became an overarching symbol for American female patriotism and service during the war, as the economy struggled to overcome an acute shortage of adult males. Thanks in part to the earnings of women, the war made possible a massive stockpile of savings, for workers were paid unprecedented wages yet had little to buy thanks to rationing and production prohibitions. The ratio of personal saving to household disposable income peaked in 1943 and again in 1944 at 27 percent, far above the normal peacetime ratio of 5 percent to 10 percent.

The end of the war in 1945 brought millions of returning veterans eager to return to civilian employment and to resume a normal civilian life, in which raising a large number of children was regarded as an essential component. American households were ready to spend on whatever the rapidly reconverted factories could produce. All those labor-saving devices that had been invented in the 1920s and refined in the 1930s were soon on sale, and by 1960, the prewar American kitchen had been modernized, and new kitchens had been built in 20 million newly constructed housing units. With less time needed for chores, there was more time to care for children, and the fertility rate soared from 2.4 in 1945 to 3.3 in 1947, then slowly rose to 3.8 in 1956, but dropped back down to 2.4 by 1970.[10]

The high fertility rate kept women busy with the work of raising children and taking care of the house. By one estimate, "The average of sixty housewives of time spent on home production was 56 hours per week. This estimate included time spent in meal preparation and cleanup, care of clothing, house cleaning and repairing, shopping, physical care of children, oversight of children, and management of the household."[11] These homemakers worked longer hours and more days than their husbands, who typically worked between thirty-eight and forty hours per week. The larger the number of children, the greater the burden of work. Valerie Ramey's time use study specified that "if the youngest child was under one year of age, the housewife spent 17 hours more per week on home production. Each child age six or above added almost two extra hours. If the youngest child was between one and five years old, the housewife spent almost seven extra hours per week."[12]

Cultural expectations drove down the age of marriage from the male and female ages of 24.3 and 21.5 in 1940 to 22.6 and 20.4 in 1970.[13] "In 1960, 60 percent of women who entered college quit before graduation, often to earn their Ph.T., as the practice of dropping out to Put Hubby Through school was jocularly called."[14] This common practice was reflected in popular culture, which portrayed American women as accepting domestic responsibilities for the sake of stability. For example, an article from *Seventeen* magazine stated, "being a woman is your career, and you can't escape it. There is no office, lab, or stage that offers so many creative avenues or executive opportunities as that everyday place, the home."[15]

Children kept women at home, but those without children or with grown children faced a daunting degree of antifemale discrimination, not just in obtaining jobs, but also in climbing the educational ladder necessary to start a career in a profession like medicine or the law. There is no better example than Sandra Day O'Conner, who later became a Supreme Court Justice but upon graduation from Stanford Law School was turned down for interviews by forty law firms and initially managed to obtain work only as a legal secretary.[16]

> Women were vigorously discouraged from seeking jobs that men might have wanted. "Hell yes, we have a quota," said a medical school dean in 1961. "Yes, it's a small one. We do keep women out when we can. We don't want them here—and they don't want them elsewhere, either, whether or not they'll admit it." . . . In 1960 women accounted for 6 percent of American doctors, 3 percent of lawyers, and less than 1 percent of engineers. Although more than half of federal government employees were women, they made up 1.4 percent of civil-service workers in the top four pay grades.[17]

Starting in the mid-1960s, the end of the baby boom resulted in a prolonged period of growth in female labor force participation, as shown in figure 15–2. Despite the baby boom the labor force participation rate (LFPR) for "prime-age" females (aged 25–54) had already inched up from 34.9 percent in 1948 to 44.5 percent in 1964. Then began the period of most rapid growth to 69.6 percent in 1985 and then to a peak of 76.8 percent in 1999, followed by a slow decline to 73.9 percent in 2014.

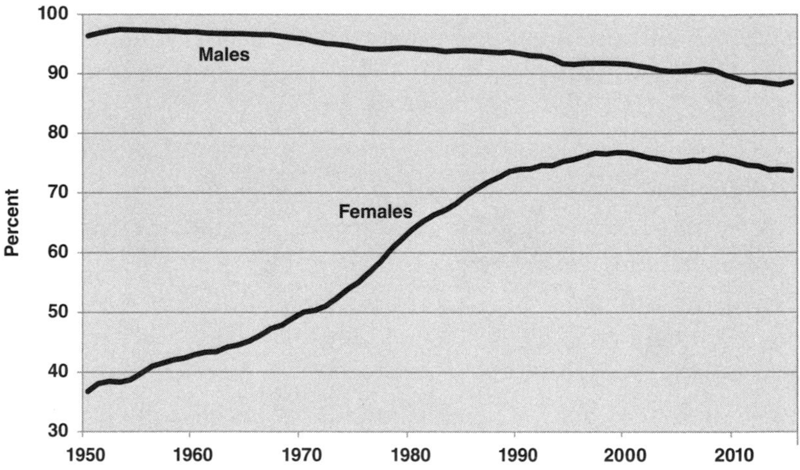

Figure 15–2. Labor Force Participation Rate by Gender, Ages 25 to 54, 1950–2015

Source: Bureau of Labor Statistics, LNS11300061 and LNS 11300062.

Also shown in figure 15–2 is the contrast between the male and female LFPR. After a period of stability between 1948 and 1964, the prime-age male LFPR began to decline very slowly, from 96.8 percent in 1964 to 93.9 percent in 1984, 91.7 percent in 1999, and 88.2 percent in 2014. The difference in the male and female rates narrowed rapidly until 1999 and then remained stable; the male LFPR minus the female LFPR was 14.9 percentage points in 1999 and an almost identical 14.3 percentage points in 2014. We return in chapter 18 to the post-1999 decline in the LFPR for prime-age males and females, one of the "headwinds" that reduces hours of work per member of the population and thus contributes to slower growth in real GDP per person than in real GDP per hour.

As female participation rose through the 1970s and 1980s, so did female educational attainment. As a result of this together with a decline in gender discrimination, women found themselves climbing the employment ladder toward white-collar professional careers with advancement opportunities. Claudia Goldin, who calls it the "Quiet Revolution," describes this period after 1970: "With more accurate expectations, they could better prepare by investing in formal education and they could assume positions that involved advancement. That is, they could plan for careers rather than jobs."[18] Women began to become accepted as career-track professionals whose progress went far beyond the traditional pink-collar occupations. In 1960, 94 percent of doctors were white men, as were 96 percent of lawyers and 86 percent of managers. By 2008 these numbers had fallen to 63 percent, 61 percent, and 57 percent respectively.[19] The new environment was described in the early 1990s by Shirley Bigley, then a vice president of Citibank:

> It was right in my vintage when the numbers of women dramatically started to change. My law school class was about 40 percent female, and it never occurred to me when I was younger that I wasn't going to go to college and professional school. For the first time, the 1990 census shows women outnumbered men in Maryland in "professional specialty" occupations—a U.S. Census Bureau category that includes everything from doctors, lawyers, and scientists to teachers, nurses, and librarians.[20]

By 1970, cultural norms had changed enough to make labor market participation for women acceptable even if they had children still living at home. The labor force participation rate of mothers whose youngest child was between ages 6 and 17 rose from 54.9 percent in 1975 to 69.9 percent in 1985 and to 76.4 percent by 1995. Similar increases were observed even for women with the youngest child younger than age 6. In some cases, very successful mothers pursued their careers while their husbands stayed at home with the children.

> Seven of the 18 women who are currently CEOs of Fortune 500 companies—including Xerox's Ursula Burns, PepsiCo's Indra Nooyi, and WellPoint's Angela Braly—have, or at some point have had, a stay-at-home husband. So do scores of female CEOs of smaller companies and women in other senior executive jobs. Others, like IBM's new CEO, Ginni Rometty, have spouses who dialed back their careers to become their powerful wives' chief domestic officer.[21]

Although the gender gap has not disappeared, since 1970 there has been substantial progress toward wage equality. As shown in figure 15–3, the percentage of annual median female wages to male wages jumped from 58.8 percent in 1975 to 71.6 percent in 1990 and 77.4 percent in 2010. The ratio for weekly

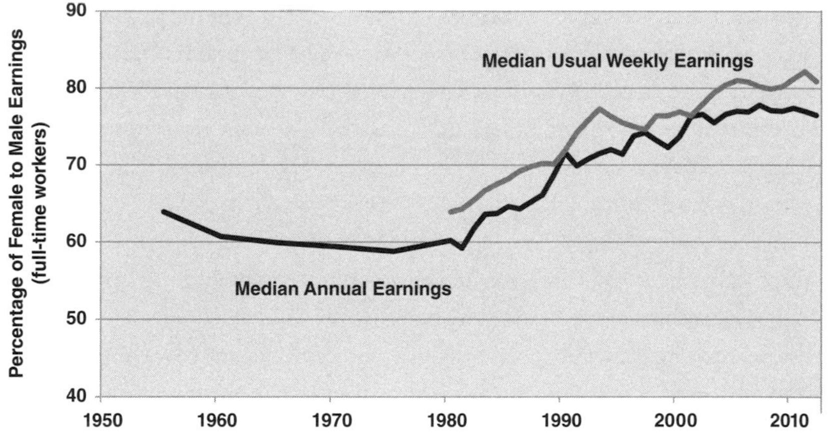

Figure 15–3. Gender Wage Ratio and Real Earnings: Median Annual Earnings and Median Usual Weekly Earnings, 1955–2012

Source: Annual data: 1955: Francine D. Blau and Marianne A. Ferber, *The Economics of Women, Men, and Work*, 2nd ed. (Englewood Cliffs, NJ: Prentice-Hall, 1992); U.S. Census Bureau, *Income, Poverty, and Health Insurance Coverage in the United States: 2010,* Table A-5, Weekly data: 1970 and 1975: Blau and Ferber (1992); 1980–2011: Weekly and Hourly Earnings Data from the Current Population Survey. 2013: Weekly Data from U.S. Bureau of Labor Statistics, *Median Usual Weekly Earnings of Full-Time Wage and Salary Workers by Selected Characteristics, Annual Averages.*

earnings was an even higher 81 percent; the less favorable ratio for annual earnings reflects the smaller number of weeks per year worked by women compared to men.

In recent years faster progress for women has been accompanied by slower progress for men. Women aged 30 or younger make more money, on average, than their male counterparts, with the exception of in the three largest U.S. cities.[22] What's more, three men lost their jobs for every woman during the recent recession.[23] Much of this is a result of male domination of blue-collar industries versus female dominance in white-collar work; males constitute 87 percent of workers in manufacturing and 71 percent in construction.[24] The combination of the rising share of women working in the professions, together with the dominance of male employment in declining industries, implies that many women have been able to surpass men in terms of job stability and advancement.

However there remains the fact that as of 2010, the median female-male ratio of annual earnings was still only 77 percent, even though the percentage of women completing college has exceeded that of men for more than three decades. As pointed out by Goldin (2014), the fraction of the gender wage gap that can be explained by identifiable characteristics "decreased over time as human capital investments between men and women converged. Differences in years of education... narrowed. In consequence, the residual portion of the gap rose relative to the explained portion."[25] Goldin's analysis of the residual gap distinguishes two different sources of gender-related wage differences, those between occupations and those within occupations. Despite the increased professionalization of female occupational choices, the occupational composition of women is still quite different than men, particularly when skilled pink-collar occupations are compared with skilled blue-collar occupations. For instance, virtually all midwives are female, and virtually all cement contractors are male. Goldin concludes that these occupational choices explain only about a third of the residual gender wage gap, leaving the remaining two-thirds to be explained within occupations.

Goldin's analysis of within-occupation wage differences centers on the age profile, which shows that "something happens that decreases women's earnings relative to those of men as they age." Stated another way, the positively sloped age profile of male wages is steeper than female wages. For women born around 1963, the earnings gap is 10 percent for the age group 25–30 and widens to 35 percent for the age group 45–50. This age-related gender gap differs greatly across occupations. Among business executives and lawyers in particular, long hours are rewarded with a disproportionate increase in pay, and there is a large penalty for the time flexibility that women need around periods of childbirth. The key ingredient in these occupations is that there is low substitutability between one employee and another in a task to be done—a particular person must be available all the time to take responsibility. In Goldin's characterization:

> Not all positions can be changed. There will always be 24/7 positions with on-call, all-the-time employees and managers, including many CEOs, trial lawyers, merger-and-acquisition bankers, surgeons, and the US Secretary of State.[26]

At the other extreme are occupations in which one employee can easily substitute for another. For instance, pharmacists have pay that is more linear in working hours and suffer virtually no penalty for part-time employment. Other occupations that offer time flexibility without a penalty or with only a small penalty include physicians, dentists, optometrists, and veterinarians. Long-term trends have shifted pharmacy employment from small proprietor-owned drugstores and single-doctor medical practices to large chain drugstores and medical group practices, and these larger groups make individuals less indispensable and more substitutable with their peers.

UNIVERSITY BOUND: THE GROWTH, BENEFITS, AND RISING COSTS OF COLLEGE EDUCATION

The occupational shift of Americans away from farm and blue-collar manual work to white-collar, managerial, and professional jobs both caused an increased demand for higher education and was made possible by the growing supply of college-educated people. Figure 15–4 shows two different series for college completion, one for people aged 25–29 and the other for all those older than 25; the latter series is higher, reflecting college completion by those age 30 or older, many of them veterans of World War II, the Korean War, or the Vietnam War. The percentage for those aged 25–29 is a better yardstick of college completion for the general population and exhibits an increase from 5 percent in 1940 to 10 percent by 1966 to 20 percent in 1990 and then to 32 percent in 2013.

Along with the overall increase in college attainment has come the rise of the female percentage of total enrollment and the decline in the male percentage. As shown in figure 15–5 the male–female percentage was noticeably skewed by the

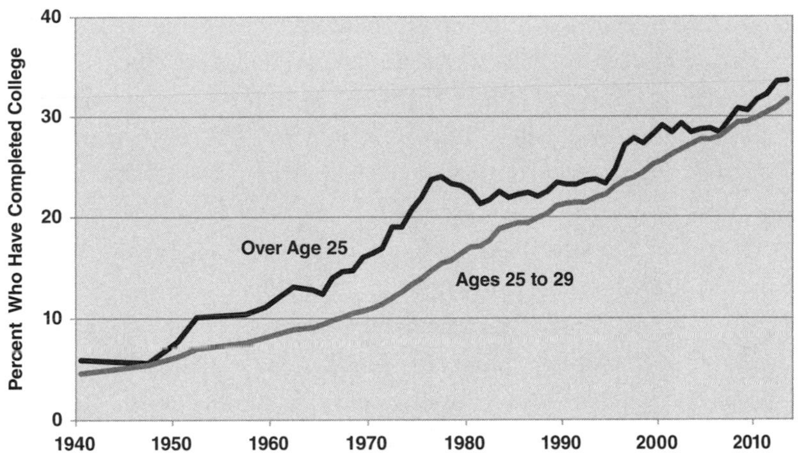

Figure 15–4. Percent of People Who Have Completed College: Over Age of 25 and Between Ages of 25 to 29, 1940–2012

Source: 1947 and 1952 to 2002 March Current Population Survey, 2003 to 2013 Annual Social and Economic Supplement to the Current Population Survey (noninstitutionalized population, excluding members of the Armed Forces living in barracks); 1950 Census of Population and 1940 Census of Population (resident population).

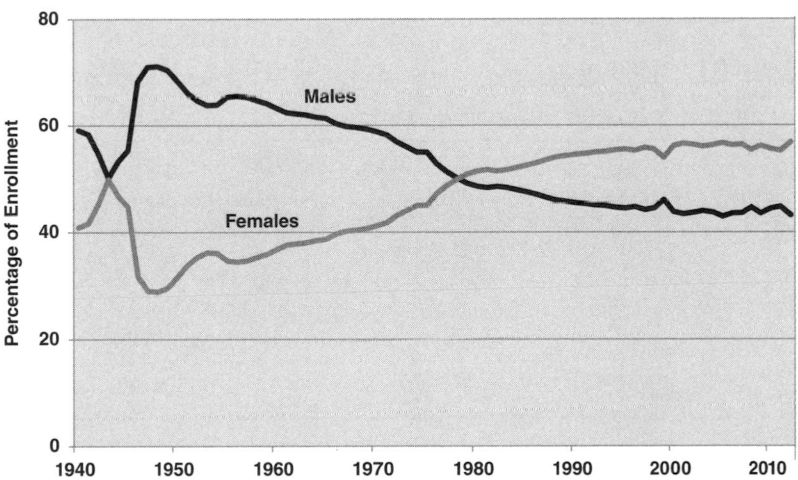

Figure 15–5. Percentage of Enrollment in Institutions of Higher Education by Gender, 1940–2012

Source: HSUS Table Bc523-526 before 1995, SAUS Table 240 after 1995, interpolated 1940, 1942, 1944, 1958, 1960, & 1962.

absence of males during World War II, followed by the bulge in the male percentage to 72 percent in 1949–50, the peak years of impact of the GI Bill. There was a smaller post-Korea bulge in the mid-1950s, then a steady decline until the male percentage fell below 50 percent in 1978. In 2013, the most recent year plotted in figure 15–5, the female–male split was 58–42. Table 15–1 documents the steady progress of women aged 25–64 as they have transitioned from 78 percent having earned no more than a high school diploma in 1970 to 67 percent having earned more than a high school diploma in 2010. The percentage of women in this age group who have a four-year college degree has advanced at a steady pace of 6 percentage points per decade from 1970 to 2010.

Problems with American postsecondary education extend beyond the decline in the male percentage of college graduates. The first of these is the rising real cost of college education and the limited job opportunities available to four-year college graduates since the financial crisis of 2008–9. Student loan debt reached more than $1 trillion in 2014, an amount greater than either outstanding credit card or automobile loan debt.[27] And student debt must be repaid regardless of whether the graduate obtains a job in an occupation requiring a college degree or not. A nontrivial number of college graduates emerged from college burdened with debt yet able only to find menial jobs driving taxis or working as baristas at Starbucks. Many graduates were forced to move back

Table 15–1. Educational attainment of women in the labor force, 1970–2010 (Percent distribution of women in the civilian labor force, aged 25 to 64)

Year	Less than a high school diploma	High school graduates, no college	Some college, no degree, or associate's degree	College graduates
1970	33.5	44.3	10.9	11.2
1980	18.4	45.4	17.4	18.7
1990	11.3	42.4	21.9	24.5
2000	8.5	31.6	29.8	30.1
2010	6.8	26.4	30.3	36.4

Note: Due to rounding, the sum of percent distributions may not equal 100. Data for 1970, 1980, and 1990 are for March of each year and the educational attainment categories are based on the number of years of school completed (i.e. less than 4 years of high school, 4 years of high school and no college, 1 to 3 years of college, and 4 years or more of college). Data for 2000 and 2010 are annual averages and refer to the highest diploma or degree received.

Source: "Educational attainment of women in the labor force, 1970–2010," *Bureau of Labor Statistics* (December, 2011).

in with their parents, thus delaying the normal timing of household creation, marriage, and children.

The stagnation of American educational attainment is best measured by the diminishing pace of improvement for those cohorts twenty-five years apart. The real advance came between those born in 1925 (now aged 90), who received on average 10.9 years of schooling, and those baby-boomers born in 1950 (now aged 65), who received 13.2 years. Jump ahead another twenty-five years to those born in 1975 (now aged 40), and attainment crept up only from 13.2 to 13.9 years.[28] The slowing advance of educational attainment is one of the underlying causes of the slowing rate of productivity growth since 1970.

Despite the inability of somc college graduates to find jobs requiring a college education, nevertheless college graduates experience a more favorable labor market outcome than their peers who fail to graduate from a four-year college. Figure 15–6 shows that since 1992, the unemployment rate of four-ycar college graduates has consistently been roughly half that of high school graduates. Those who have attended college but have failed to obtain a four-year college degree have unemployment rates closer to those of high school graduates than to those of four-year college graduates. Although this might make college appear to be a good investment for everyone, the average outcome for all four-year college graduates disguises a high variance across occupations and college

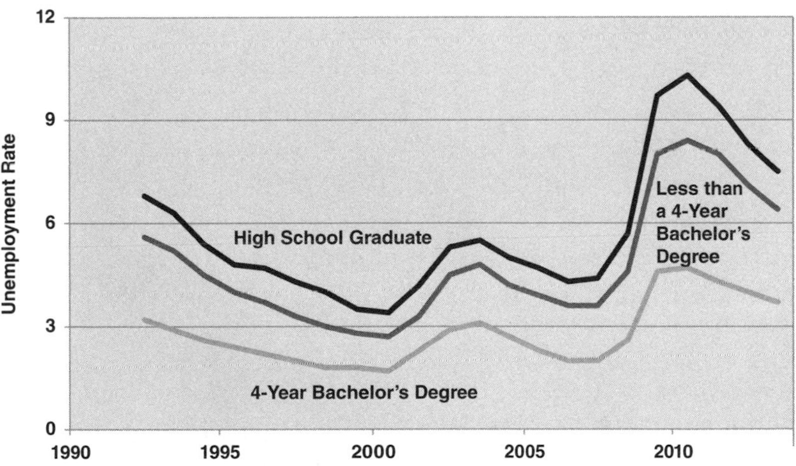

Figure 15–6. Unemployment Rates by Educational Attainment, 1992–2013
Source: Bureau of Labor Statistics, Labor Force Statistics from the Current Population Survey, Series IDs LNU040227662, LNU04027689, and LNU04027660.

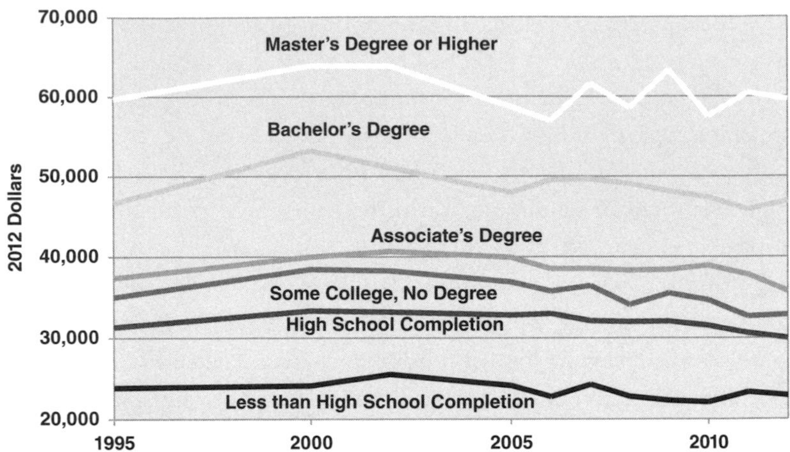

Figure 15–7. Median Annual Earnings: Full-Time Workers Aged 25 to 34 by Educational Attainment, 1995–2012

Source: 502.30, U.S. Department of Commerce, Census Bureau, Current Population Survey, March 1996 through March 2013, interpolated between 1995, 2000, 2002, and 2005–2012.

majors. An engineering graduate is almost sure to have a low unemployment rate, whereas a graduate in English, art history, or music does not have the same probability of employment in a job requiring a college education.

Just as college students have superior outcomes, at least on average, in unemployment rate, so do they for median annual real earnings, as shown in figure 15–7. Each successive step up the educational ladder provides a boost in average earnings. In 2002, high school dropouts earned $23,000 per year, high school graduates $30,000, those with a four-year bachelor's degree $47,000, and those with a master's degree or higher $60,000. All salaries plotted in figure 15–7 are adjusted for inflation, so it is striking that there was no growth at all in real earnings for any group over these seventeen years of data, and in fact there were slight declines for those with less than a bachelor's degree.

PENSION PARADISE: RETIREMENT AND LIFESTYLES IN OLD AGE

The percentage of retirement-age people in the total population, as shown in figure 15–8, displays a steady increase from 7.1 percent in 1940 to 11.3 percent in 1980 and then to 13.1 percent in 2010. The percentage reflects not just

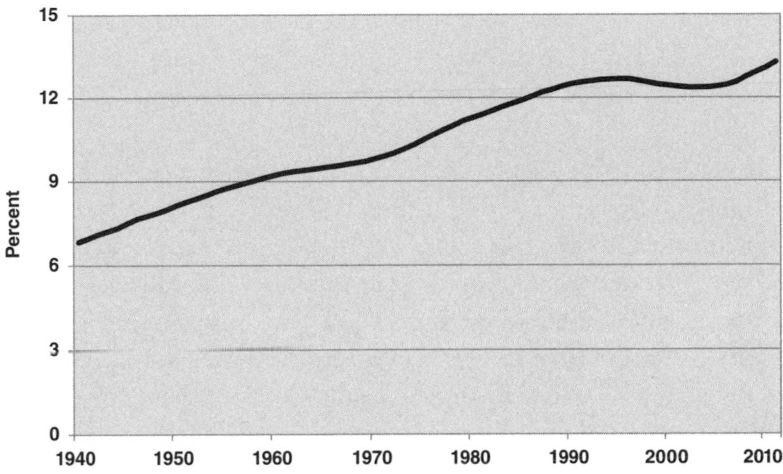

Figure 15–8. Percentage of Retirement Age People to Total Population, 1940–2011

Source: Table B-34, Department of Commerce (Bureau of the Census).

increased life expectancy but also the differing number of births in each decade, as well as changes over time in the extent of immigration. The temporary plateau of the percentage between 1995 and 2005 echoes the dearth of births in the Great Depression and World War II years, and the retirement of the baby boomers begins to become visible starting in 2008.

In the 1920s, before passage of the 1935 Social Security Act, private pension programs offered comfortable benefits to a relatively small proportion of the population. Tax reform in 1921 had provided an incentive for many private companies to provide tax-exempt pensions and compensation plans.[29] By 1930, a tenth of the workforce benefited from private pension coverage.[30] But the Great Depression largely eliminated this safety net, leaving elderly workers unemployed and without an income:

> With the onset of the Great Depression in 1929, businesses began having great difficulty acquiring cash to meet operating expenses, including rising pension payments. Profits plummeted and, as a result, employers were forced to cut costs drastically, including pension benefits. As a result, more firms began to require employees to contribute toward their plans. Some companies actually abolished their pension plans, while others reduced the amount of benefit payments. In cases

where plans were terminated, some retirees could expect to receive no further payments. And few new fully employer-financed plans were created in the 1930s.[31]

Along with its introduction of the Social Security system in 1935, New Deal legislation forced reforms in private pension plans. The new system ensured that "no longer would workers face destitution when superannuated, and thus stand in need of capitalist welfare. Nor did the lack of suitable old age pensions, at least for the rank-and-file workers, impede a systematic corporate retirement policy."[32] A new threefold savings plan ensued, with government securing the bare minimum while company pensions and private savings added to the funds available for retirees. Social Security played an influential role in regenerating private pension programs in individual firms. Coverage under private pensions grew from 7 percent of the labor force in 1940 to about 28 percent by 1960.[33]

Social Security was revolutionary in its ability to provide funds on a national scale for the elderly to sustain an adequate lifestyle after retirement from work. Though company defined-benefit pensions and defined-contribution 401(k) retirement investments have played a role over the years, Social Security has been central to the reduction of the poverty rate among the elderly, from 35 percent in 1959 to 10 percent by 2003.[34] Workers who were aged 65 or older in the late 1940s and 1950s had spent their prime years experiencing the Great Depression and World War II and were thus accustomed to dealing with harsh economic realities. After World War II, this generation could look forward to a stable old age financed by Social Security and, in an increasing share of cases, by private pension plans as well. A growing convergence and declining inequality characterized the lifestyles of the retired generation of the 1950s just as the next generation of workers was enjoying steady increases in wages and benefits.

The golden age of pensions occurred in the 1970s. Worries about the insolvency of Social Security and private pension plans lay far in the future. Pension participation in the private sector jumped to 45 percent in 1970, whereas private plans held 7 percent of U.S. financial assets by 1970, a multifold increase as compared to the 2 percent holding in 1950.[35] A breakthrough came when the Employee Retirement Income Security Act, also known as ERISA, was passed by Congress in 1974. This legislation forced companies to provide adequate pension plans and mandated that pension benefits be "vested"—that is, guaranteed, after a minimum number of years of employment. In addition ERISA founded the Pension Benefit Guaranty Corporation, which guaranteed the payment of basic pension benefits and in 2010 paid benefits to 1.3 million workers from 4,140 terminated pension plans.[36]

The combination of increased life expectancy and the increased income of retirees led to a new industry that catered to senior citizens. In 1960, Del Webb Development launched its first master-planned, age-restricted community for "active adults," the 26,000-unit Sun City, located in Maricopa County, Arizona. By 2013, the number of these age-restricted communities had risen to 771. Many offer facilities ranging from tennis and racquetball courts to golf courses, indoor and outdoor swimming pools, and fitness centers.[37] Comfortable living in retirement-oriented communities and expectations of maintaining pre-retirement standards of living have become commonplace, and for many retirees, the standard of living in these leisure-oriented communities in the Sun Belt exceeded what had been available before retirement in older and more crowded Snow Belt locations.[38]

Retirement since 1950 has been described as "a period of enjoyment and creative experience, and as a reward for a lifetime of labor, increasingly shorter. Mass tourism, low-impact sports such as golf, and mass entertainment such as films, television, and spectator sports provide activities for the elderly at a low price."[39] Typical time schedules in retirement involve more time spent in each individual everyday activity, with the obvious exception of work. For example, the total population watches an average of 2.75 hours of TV per day, whereas retirees watch TV an average of 4.2 hours per day. Retirees also spend more time relaxing, thinking, and reading than average Americans, by a margin of 1.3 to 0.3 hours per day.[40]

There is a stark contrast between those who retired between the 1940s and the 1960s, known as the GI generation, and the modern-day baby boomer generation that is currently entering into retirement. A large portion of the GI generation retirees removed themselves from all types of work after an arduous lifetime of hard labor in factories, mines, and farms. With the white-collar revolution of American jobs and the extension of life expectancy, many baby boomers are choosing to work full-time beyond age 65.

Progressive growth of the elderly population has led to increased concerns over the financial sustainability of retirement. Americans find themselves living longer lives and adjusting to more affluent lifestyles, which translates into a costly extended retirement period. The need for more financial resources has come into conflict with the gradual replacement by firms of defined-benefit pension plans with defined-contribution plans. The latter impose on the retiree the risks of financial market fluctuations. Though Medicare provides protection against catastrophic illness and hospital costs, most Medicare supplement plans involve high copayments that will increase as a burden on elderly budgets if the relative price of medical care continues to increase.

When it was enacted in 1965 as part of the Great Society social welfare programs, Medicare contributed to the golden age of retirement in the 1970s by supporting the medical costs of the retired population. The problem for Medicare, which showed early signs of weakness in the 1980s and has since been further exposed, is that it relies on public taxpayer funding to foot most (but not all) medical bills. The aging of the population will drive up the costs of Medicare for the foreseeable future. Between 2012 and 2037, it is estimated, the number of Medicare beneficiaries who will enroll in the program will grow by 36 percent or 18 million people, and Medicare spending as a percentage of GDP is projected to increase from 3 percent to 5 percent of GDP.[41]

> Each day, 10,000 baby boomers retire and begin receiving Medicare and Social Security benefits. And while five workers supported the benefits of each retiree in 1960, there will be only two workers funding each retiree by 2030. Those who dismiss long-term budget projections should re-read the last paragraph. The retirement of 77 million baby boomers into Social Security and Medicare is not theoretical projection. Demography is destiny.[42]

As fiscal strains are being placed on Social Security, Medicare, and other traditional pension programs, the Great Recession of 2007–9 and the slow subsequent economic recovery have dramatically reduced private savings. As a result of a shift by employers from defined-benefit to defined-contribution 401(k) pension plans, employees now have the latitude to withdraw funds from their own pension plans to tide themselves over periods of low income or unemployment. By September 2008, 60 percent of U.S. workers held about $3 trillion in 401(k) plan-related assets.[43] The percentage of workers on a defined-benefit pension plan has decreased from 30 percent in 1983 to 15 percent in 2013, and about 33 percent of retirees 65 and older live only on Social Security.[44] As the S&P 500 stock market average collapsed from its peak of 1568 in October 2007 to its trough of 680 in March 2009, many holders of 401(k) assets did exactly the opposite of standard advice for stock market investments—they converted their stock holdings into cash and thus "bought high and sold low."

By modern retirement standards, as established since the 1970s, "if a household of any income level finds that inadequate resources force upon it a dramatic reduction in its standard of living after retirement, that is evidence of inadequate retirement planning."[45] This expectation is under serious threat based on recent data that 49 percent of middle-class workers will be poor or near poor during retirement.[46] For many workers, having limited funds in savings accounts is forcing them to remain in the labor force after their desired age of retirement.[47] Age discrimination laws that prohibit the refusal to hire the elderly facilitate the process of remaining in the workforce, although many workers who are 50 or older find it difficult to find new jobs in their own occupation if they are unlucky enough to be laid off or if their employer goes out of business.

Age discrimination laws, moreover, are difficult to enforce. In one study of 4,000 résumés sent to firms, otherwise identical resumes identified the age as varying between 35 and 62. The younger workers were 40 percent more likely to be called back for an interview than were workers older than 50.[48] Employer claims that older employees are incapable of performing given tasks run up against the realities of the lessening physical difficulty of work and the improved average physical condition of the elderly.

> But don't older people bring lots of problems, too? Literature is full of examples of difficult-to-manage older people, from Shakespeare's King Lear to Charles Dickens' Jeremiah Flintwinch. However, today's oldies are in far better shape than those of earlier generations. If Mick Jagger and Keith Richards can go on touring into their late 60s, their contemporaries can at least be trusted with a desk and a computer. People's muscles do weaken with age. But few jobs require brawn these days: in America 46 percent of jobs make almost no physical demands on workers.[49]

CONCLUSION

On the job and at home, working conditions have improved significantly but at a slower pace in the seven decades since 1940 than in the seven decades leading up to 1940. Changes between 1940 and 1970 continued the trends of safer, less physically demanding work that began at the turn of the twentieth century. Workers no longer found themselves stuck in the toil of backbreaking work on the farm, in the mine, or in the factory that often pushed them to their physical limits. Already by 1940, the average workweek had leveled off at around forty hours, down from sixty hours per week in 1900. The period between 1940 and 1970 witnessed the white-collar transition toward stable, upwardly mobile careers. The improvements in workplace safety, in part brought by the shift away from blue-collar jobs, assisted toward this end by lengthening the span of the working life and the long-term earning power of most workers. The period between 1940 and 1970 also witnessed the most rapid improvement in working conditions of housewives at home, for the transition from household drudgery, manual laundry work, and the hauling of fuel and water was largely complete as the major household appliances became nearly universal by 1970.

Though the change in working conditions on the job and at home improved more rapidly during 1940–70 than thereafter, the chronology was different for the marked change in the role of females in the workplace and in society. Only after the mid-1960s did the fertility rate decline from the baby-boom years, allowing women to shift from home to market work as the chosen use of their time. In the early postwar years, college classrooms were dominated by men, but by the late 1970s, females had become half of those completing college, and by 2013, they constituted 58 percent of college graduates. As women increasingly earned college degrees, they began to gain a fair share of advanced professional degrees, particularly in medicine but also in law and business.

The chronology for educational attainment, like that for working conditions on the job and at home, exhibits a more rapid pace of improvement before 1970 than afterward. Child labor disappeared before World War II as the percentage of the population finishing high school exceeded half and finally by 1970 settled down at its apparent long-term value of three-quarters. College educational attainment expanded rapidly in the postwar years, spurred on by the free access to college made possible by the GI Bill. The increasing share of the population with high school diplomas and then college degrees helped pave the way for a transformation from a working-class society before World War II to a middle-class society afterward. The gradual increase in human capital as educational attainment advanced allowed more workers to shift into the more desirable occupations of professional, proprietor, and manager.

The income security of the elderly improved rapidly after the adoption of the Social Security legislation of the 1930s and the spread in the postwar years of defined-benefit pension plans, many negotiated as part of union collective bargaining agreements. Workers responded by retiring as early as age 62 and turning to a life of leisure, often moving to country club and golfing communities in the Sun Belt. As life expectancy increased, the length of the retirement years stretched to twenty years and beyond, raising concerns about the financial viability of the system. Indeed after the 1980s firms increasingly closed defined-benefit pension plans and replaced them with 401(k) defined-contribution plans that were vulnerable to the naïveté of retired workers about investments and also to early withdrawals by workers suffering from temporary unemployment or loss of a job by a spouse.

Two of the topics treated in this chapter identify potent sources of economic growth that are in the process of becoming weaker. The great transition of women from home to market work, together with the lessening of discrimination against the black population, has created a better allocation of talent and investment in human capital. One research study has estimated that this shift may have accounted for as much as 15 percent or 20 percent of U.S. economic growth during the period 1960–1990 but is clearly becoming less important as the female labor force participation rate has declined since 2000 and as wage gaps between white men and black men have reached a steady plateau since 1990.[50] The other source of slowing growth is the diminishing rate of increase of educational attainment. The percentage of the population completing high school reached a plateau long ago in 1970, and although the percentage obtaining a four-year college degree has continued to increase slowly, a relatively large share of recent college graduates has been unable to obtain a job requiring a college education. The rapidly rising cost of college education and heavy indebtedness of recent college graduates create the possibility that the increase of college degree attainment may soon cease or even begin to reverse.

Entr'acte

TOWARD AN UNDERSTANDING OF SLOWER GROWTH

The conclusion of chapter 15 marks the transition from part II to part III of the book. We have now taken a close look at the mixed record of progress, depicted in chapters 10–15, from 1940 to 2014. Throughout the different dimensions of the growth experience, the decades since 1940 do not exhibit the same uniformity of revolutionary change as occurred between 1870 and 1940. Instead, the year 1970 marks a distinct break point between faster and slower growth. The ten decades between 1870 and 1970 deserve their accolade, awarded in chapter 1, as the "special century." The inventions of the second industrial revolution (IR #2) gathered momentum between 1870 and 1920 and then between 1920 and 1970 created the most rapid period of growth in labor productivity experienced in American history, bringing an utter change from 1870 in most dimensions of human life. The inventions of the third industrial revolution (IR #3), though revolutionary within their sphere of influence—entertainment, communication, and information technology—did not have the same effects on living standards as had electricity, the internal combustion engine, running water, improving life expectancy, and the other Great Inventions of the special century, not to mention the improvement in the human condition as work hours declined from 60 to 40 per week.

By definition, growth in output per person equals growth in labor productivity plus growth in hours worked per person in the population. Starting in the late 1960s, there was a distinct slowdown in labor productivity growth. However, growth in output per person avoided suffering a similar slowdown until after 2000, because its growth rate exceeded that in labor productivity by the contribution of rising hours of work per person. This occurred as women shifted from house work to work in the market, meaning that each woman who made this shift raised average hours of market work for the population as a whole. Since 2000, we have seen a sharp decline in growth in output per person and its two components—growth in productivity and in hours of work per person—after corrections for the ups and downs of the business cycle. Because the basic data are unambiguous in registering a significant and deepening growth slowdown, the book's title, *The Rise and Fall of American Growth*, has become a statement of fact. We are now ready in part III to explore some of the reasons why growth was so rapid during 1920–70 and why it has been slowing down since 1970.

THE MIXED RECORD OF GROWTH SINCE 1970

The aggregate record across all sectors of the economy shows that productivity growth slowed down markedly after 1970 and experienced a brief revival during 1996–2004 that most analysts attribute to the influence of the invention of the web, search engines, and e-commerce, as well as to the sharp spike of investment in information and communication technology (ICT) equipment. In the past decade, productivity growth has been even slower than it was between 1970 and 1996. This story of slowdown, revival, and further slowdown, as told by the economy-wide data, conceals substantial differences in performance across sectors of economic activity.

Among the sectors examined in the chapters of part II, entertainment and communication (chapter 12) and digital equipment (chapter 13), led the pack by exhibiting faster growth after 1970 than before. Between 1950 and 1970, broadcast TV was limited in choice to the three big commercial networks and public television, and there was little change beyond the arrival of color and of larger screens. Innovation accelerated after 1970 with the explosion of choice made possible by cable and satellite TV, with time-shifting made possible by the video-cassette recorder and digital video recorder, and with rental followed subsequently by streaming of movie videos. Communication changed little until the break-up of the Bell telephone monopoly in 1983, after which accelerating change created ever smaller and more capable mobile phones, followed by the merger of the computer and the mobile phone in the form of the smartphone, introduced with the BlackBerry in 2003 and the iPhone in 2007. Compared to entertainment and communication, which continued enjoying rapid and steady progress to the present day, the progress of the digital revolution was more episodic. The third industrial revolution (IR #3) based on personal computers, the web, and search engines exhibited a pronounced peak in its effects on labor productivity during 1996–2004, and its driving force—Moore's Law, governing the increased density of computer chips—showed signs after 2005 of slowing down.

At the other extreme from the fast growth exhibited by entertainment and ICT, innovations in the effects of food and clothing on the standard of living were minor. In the seventy years before 1940, food had experienced major change in the invention of processed food, the avoidance of contamination and adulteration, the benefits of refrigeration, and the rapid change in food marketing from the country store through stages to the modern supermarket which began to spread in the 1930s. As described in chapter 10, progress in food availability and marketing continued after 1940 but was relatively minor. More capable refrigerators allowed the 1916 invention of frozen food to become widely used, and there was a further increase in food variety, including out-of-season and organic produce. Rising prosperity allowed a major shift from the consumption of food at home to food away from home, creating food options from fast food outlets to pizza delivery to a wide range of upscale and downscale sit-down restaurants. Similarly, there was nothing after 1940 to compare with the pre-1940 shift as women became able to buy their own clothes instead of having to make them at home. Postwar changes in clothing involved mainly a shift in styles to more casual clothing and a shift from domestically produced to imported clothing that was substantially cheaper and that allowed the accumulation of wardrobes featuring more items.

The theme of incremental progress following revolutionary change applies with force to the housing of the American family, which by 1940 in urban America had witnessed the nearly complete transition from the isolation of 1870 to the fully networked house, connected to the outside with electricity, gas, and telephone lines, as well as running water and waste disposal pipes. The end to hauling—of pails of water, wood, and coal—was among the most important advances in the human condition that had ever occurred, and it was almost complete in urban America by 1940. No change after 1940 compared with the networking revolution, except for the gradual arrival of each of the network components to small towns and farms in the decades between 1940 and 1970, a transition aided by a mass movement of households from farm to city. The big change in farm and city alike between 1940 and 1970 was the arrival of modern gas and electric appliances that ended housewife drudgery and created the modern kitchen that by 1970 looked much like today's kitchens except for cosmetic touches and the ubiquitous microwave oven, a post-1970 arrival. Two changes were continuous throughout the postwar period, with no evident slowdown after 1970, and provided clear evidence of an ongoing rise in the standard of living. These were the steady increase in the size of newly constructed houses and the gradual conversion to air conditioning, first to room air conditioners initially sold in the early 1950s and then to central air conditioning, which by 2010 had been installed in two-thirds of housing units.

Chapter 11, on transportation, finds little improvement in travel by motor vehicle after 1970, a year by which most of the interstate highway system had been completed, replacing antiquated and dangerous roadways. Reduced motor vehicle fatality rates since 1970 have resulted mainly from government-mandated safety devices and improved roads. Though after 1970 automobiles did not change in their ability to move passengers and their cargo from points A to point B at a given speed, there was a steady increase in the quality of the automobiles making those journeys, thanks not only to safety devices but also to convenience and comfort items such as automatic transmission and air conditioning, as well as improved fuel economy.

Our treatment of airline travel finds little improvement after 1970, a year when the conversion from piston to jet planes was complete. Along most dimensions, particularly seating comfort, meal service, and airport security, the quality of the air travel experience declined after 1970. Despite the promise of deregulation in 1978, the reduction in the relative price of air travel per mile flown was substantially slower during 1980–2000 than in 1950–80 and has been even slower than that since 2000. Just as automobile fatality rates have experienced a steady decline with no hiatus after 1970, so too have airline fatality rates, which since 2006 have fallen close to zero thanks to better aircraft and engine design, improved air traffic control, and shifts in maintenance procedures.

The evolution of medicine and physical health can be divided into three stages. The great achievement of the conquest of infant mortality had been largely completed by 1950, and the plague of infectious diseases had been conquered. As a result, the rate of improvement of life expectancy was twice as fast in the first half of the twentieth century as in the second half. Progress, as chronicled in chapter 14, shifted to a second stage after 1940 with the invention of antibiotics, particularly penicillin, and with the advance of knowledge in how to treat heart disease and cancer. Most of today's treatments for heart disease had been developed by the 1960s, and the incidence of cardiovascular diseases declined after reaching a peak in 1963. Radiation and chemotherapy treatments for cancer had also largely arrived in their present form by 1970. In the third stage since 1970, life expectancy has continued to improve at a steady pace, albeit slower than before 1950, with a substantial contribution being made by the reduction in smoking together with incremental improvements that increase survival rates from surgery. Senior citizens have benefited by the greater mobility in old age made possible by widespread access to hip and knee replacement surgery.

Conditions of work improved more slowly after 1940 than before. Nothing that happened after 1940 for the adult male worker compared to the reduction in the discomfort of physical labor made possible by shorter hours, more capable machinery, and the shift from farm to city. Nothing that happened after 1940 for the adult female housewife compared to the replacement of hauling of water, wood, and coal by the networked house with its electricity, gas, telephone, water, and sewer connections. Nothing that happened after 1940 for male teenagers compared to the elimination of child labor and its replacement by universal high school education. And nothing that happened after 1940 was as important to the life of the older generation as the establishment in 1935 of Social Security, although the 1965 introduction of Medicare came close. The other dominant sources of progress of the postwar era shared by citizens of all ages have been the civil rights and voter legislation of 1964–65, the end of the Jim Crow regime of overt subjugation and segregation in the south, and, most important of all, the liberation of women who flooded into the labor force after the mid-1960s. By 1980, women had become the majority of college students and had begun to enter the professions, most notably in medicine but also significantly in law and business.

THE EXTENT OF OUTPUT MISMEASUREMENT DECLINED AFTER 1970

A central theme of this book, previewed in chapter 1 and summarized in the entr'acte between parts I and II, is that official measures of real GDP fail to capture many aspects of the revolutionary changes that have occurred since 1870. Because real GDP is the numerator both of output per person and output per hour, this tendency of real GDP measures to understate progress implies that the growth rate of these key ratios has been systematically understated. The previous entr'acte provided many examples of revolutionary changes between 1870 and 1940 in the standard of living that were missed by the real GDP data, because no allowance is made for the value ("consumer surplus") that consumers receive from newly invented products and services.

Among the most important examples of improvements not valued in real GDP are the brightness, convenience, and safety of electric light; the improved variety and reduced risk of food contamination made possible by refrigeration; the removal of horse droppings and urine from city streets and rural highways as motor vehicles replaced horses; the dimensions of change in human activity made possible by the speed and carrying capacity of the motor vehicle and commercial aviation; the value of instant communication made possible by the telegraph and telephone; and the value of entertainment delivered by the invention of the phonograph, radio, and motion pictures. Some would place even more value on the arrival of clean running water that eliminated the previous drudgery of carrying water into and out of the home; the transition from the outhouse to the indoor toilet and bathroom; the transition from child labor to high school education as the typical experience of teenage males; and, perhaps above all, the value of the reduction of infant mortality from 22 percent in 1890 to 1 percent in 1950.

These changes, which provided immense value to all households, rich and poor alike, had arrived in urban America by 1940 and in farms and small towns by 1970. How did the understatement of real GDP growth compare in the 1940–2015 era covered by part II of the book? First on many lists of improvements excluded from real GDP growth would come the changes in comfort, productivity, and geographical location made possible by the spread of air conditioning. Price indexes utterly failed to capture the value of the quantum leap in the quality of TV sets and the variety of entertainment available on them. Improvements in medical practice and scientific knowledge, particularly about the dangers of smoking, made possible continuing incremental improvements in life expectancy that were not valued by real GDP. Reductions in accident, motor vehicle, and air travel fatality rates continued unabated throughout the post-1940 period. Social changes, including civil rights legislation and the entry of women into the labor force and then into the professions, created unmeasured value of a different kind than that produced running water and household appliances' creation of a transition away from female household tedium and drudgery.

But in other respects, the extent of undervaluation of real GDP changes was less after 1970. Two aspects of the advance in the standard of living, the increased real quality of automobiles and the larger size of newly constructed housing units, were incorporated into real GDP with relative accuracy. After 1986, the price indexes used to create real GDP captured most, if not all, of the rapid improvement in the ratio of performance to price of mainframe and personal computers. Most of all, the extent by which growth in real GDP was understated became less important for a more basic reason—that the nature of change itself became less revolutionary after 1970 than in the special century that ended in 1970. Those who complain that real GDP and productivity statistics do not give credit to the multiple functions of the smartphone are correct as far as they go, but they often fail to realize that real GDP changes have understated progress since the beginning of recorded economic history and for innovative changes far more important than the multifunction smartphone.

THE SOURCES OF FASTER AND SLOWER GROWTH

Why was growth in labor productivity and in total factor productivity (TFP) so quick during 1920–70? Why did the pace of growth slow after 1970? Will future growth accelerate from the slow pace of the past decade, as is forecast by enthusiasts whom we will collectively label the "techno-optimists"? Or is future growth more likely to resemble the disappointments of the recent past? There is no shortage of big questions, each of enormous importance. The chapters of part III provide a set of suggestions and speculations intended to inform the debate and advance the discussion.

Chapter 16 looks into the past rather than the future. It probes into the underlying data on labor and capital input and on TFP to provide a striking portrayal of economic progress. Not only was TFP growth much more rapid during the half-century 1920–70 than it had been before or has been since, but within those fifty years, the growth of TFP by decade steadily sped up from the 1920s to 1930s to a peak in the 1940s, followed by a symmetric downward series of steps into the decades of the 1950s, 1960s, and 1970s and beyond. There was a leap in TFP between 1929 and 1950 as real GDP more than doubled even as labor and especially capital input grew far less rapidly. Our search for an explanation centers on the timing and magnitude of the Great Depression and World War II, both of which caused the inventions of the second industrial revolution, particularly electric motors and assembly-line methods, to have their full effect on productivity years earlier than might have otherwise occurred.

In chapter 17, the question shifts from why growth was so rapid before 1970 to why it has slowed since 1970. The basic answer is provided by the underlying distinction between the industrial revolutions. The utter change in everyday life made possible by the inventions of IR #2 occurred in the special century between 1870 and 1970, but by that year, their main effects had already taken place. Unlike IR #2, the digital revolution IR #3 had a less powerful overall effect on productivity growth, and the main effect of its inventions occurred in the relatively short interval of 1996 to 2004, when the invention of the Internet, web browsers, search engines, and e-commerce created a fundamental change in business practices and procedures that was reflected in a temporary revival of productivity growth. The core of chapter 17 demonstrates that the late 1990s represented a temporary, rather than a permanent, upswing in the pace of progress The most recent decade, 2004–14, has been characterized by the slowest growth in productivity of any decade in American history, and this verdict of the productivity data is echoed by continuity rather than change in business practices in the worlds of offices, retail stores, hospitals, schools, universities, and the financial sector.[1] In short, the changes created by the Internet revolution were sweeping but were largely completed by 2005. The major exception, the invention and dissemination of the smartphone, has thus far not had a visible effect on the productivity data as did the Internet revolution of the late 1990s.

Chapter 17 concludes that the effect on productivity growth of innovation over the next twenty-five years will resemble that achieved within the last decade—that is, slower than during the 1995–2004 revival decade, but by no means negligible. In contrast, chapter 18 strikes a more pessimistic note about the prognosis for the future of the standard of living based on the power of gale-force headwinds that are currently operating to slow the growth of the standard of living for the majority of Americans. First among the headwinds is increased inequality. Fundamental changes in the American economy began in the late 1970s to create a steady multi-decade increase in the share of total income earned by the top 1 percent of the income distribution. Causes of faster income growth at the top include the superstar effect for compensation of sports and entertainment stars; a winner-take-all syndrome enriching those perceived as being the best in the professions, and a sharp increase in the ratio of the pay of top business executives relative to average employee pay. Forces pushing down incomes in the middle and the bottom include the shrinking role of labor unions, the declining real value of the minimum wage, and the combined roles of automation and globalization in shrinking the availability of well-paying middle-income blue-collar and white-collar jobs. Growing inequality implies that whatever may be the growth rate of real income per person for the economy as a whole, the growth rate for the bottom 99 percent of the income distribution will be substantially slower.

Other headwinds are also explored in chapter 18. The historic role of rising educational attainment as a creator of productivity growth began to fade after 1970, when completion of high school reached a plateau of 75 percent to 80 percent. Though the four-year college completion rate continues to rise slowly, increasing numbers of college graduates face a dearth of available jobs that require a college education. Though on average college completion still pays off in higher lifetime incomes and a lower incidence of unemployment despite the rising incidence of college debt, not everyone is average. Those who major in subjects not having a ready job market or who take substantially longer than four years to complete the degree can encounter a problematic future in which the rewards of a college degree do not balance the debt incurred to obtain it. Taken together, these forces combine in the educational headwind, the failure of rising educational attainment to make its historic contribution to productivity growth.

Any force that holds back future productivity growth also has a similar effect on growth in output per person, for the two grow at identical rates if hours of work per person remain constant. But after rising thanks to female labor force entry between the mid-1960s and late-1990s, the trend in hours per person shifted sign from growth to shrinkage after the year 2000. As a result of this decline in hours per person, which we label the "demographic headwind," the growth of output per person has been slower than that of productivity. The labor force participation of prime-aged (25–54) men and women has declined since 2000, and since 2008, the overall labor force participation rate has begun to decline further as a result of retirement of the baby-boom generation. This headwind will continue to hold down the growth of output per person over the next two decades. A final "fiscal headwind" is ahead thanks to the inevitable future increase in the ratio of federal government debt relative to GDP over the next two decades if current entitlement and tax policies continue. Some combination of benefit reductions and tax increases must be enacted by then, which will reduce the future growth of disposable personal income. Adding to the force of the headwinds are adverse sociological trends, particularly the decline of marriage as an institution, leading to the prediction that the increasing fraction of children growing up in single-parent households will be more likely to drop out of high school and engage in criminal activity.

Chapter 18 concludes that this combination of four headwinds—inequality, education, demographic, and fiscal—will combine to imply future growth in the disposable income of the bottom 99 percent of the income distribution that is likely to be barely positive and substantially slower than growth in the labor productivity of the total economy. Because these sources of slower growth are deep-seated and have sources that extend back for decades, solutions to achieve faster growth are difficult to devise and are inevitably controversial. The book concludes with a "postscript" minichapter that outlines some of the policy directions that seem most likely to be fruitful.

Part III

THE SOURCES OF FASTER AND SLOWER GROWTH

Chapter 16

THE GREAT LEAP FORWARD FROM THE 1920s TO THE 1950s: WHAT SET OF MIRACLES CREATED IT?

> I refuse to recognize that there are impossibilities. I cannot discover that anyone knows enough about anything on this earth definitely to say what is and what is not possible.
>
> —Henry Ford

INTRODUCTION

The Great Leap Forward of the American level of labor productivity that occurred in the middle decades of the twentieth century is one of the greatest achievements in all of economic history.[1] Had the economy continued to grow at the average annual growth rate that prevailed during 1870–1928, by 1950 output per hour would have been 52 percent higher than it had been in 1928. Instead the reality was a 1928–50 increase of 99 percent, a marked acceleration of the pace of economic growth compared to everything that had created growth in the six decades before 1928, including the Roaring Twenties themselves.

At first glance it may seem a surprise that so much of the progress of the twentieth century occurred between 1928 and 1950. The Great Inventions of the late nineteenth century had by 1928 already reached most urban households. Light was produced by electricity in cities and towns alike, and almost all urban housing units were connected by then not just to electricity, but also to gas, telephone, running water, and sewer lines. The motor vehicle had a more widespread effect than electricity, transforming not just urban but also rural

America. By 1926, fully 93 percent of Iowa farmers owned a motor vehicle, starting from 0 percent in 1900, and the ratio of motor vehicle registrations to the number of households in the entire country had by 1929 reached 90 percent.[2]

Part of the puzzle of the Great Leap Forward is that the data and history do not provide us with a steady unbroken record of progress between 1928 and 1950. Rather, the operation of the normal economy was obscured as the decade of the Great Depression was followed by the production miracle of World War II. The macroeconomic "lights out" is like a blackout curtain that prevents us from determining any aspect of normal macroeconomic behavior during the depression and war years. From 1929 to 1933, output, hours of work, and employment collapsed. With so many machines idle and so many buildings empty, we can learn little about the pace of technical progress or innovation during those years. And the distortions continued through the partial recovery of 1933–37, the severe recession of 1938, and then the continuous explosion of economic output from 1938 to 1945 as the economy was revived by wartime spending so enormous that in 1944, military spending amounted to 80 percent of the size of the entire economy in 1939, and real GDP in 1944 was almost double that of 1939.[3] And then, to the surprise of many economists, after the stimulus of wartime spending was removed swiftly in 1945–47, the economy did not collapse. Some mysterious elixir had converted the production achievements of the Arsenal of Democracy into a postwar cornucopia of houses, automobiles, and appliances.

Our task in this chapter is to shed light on this fundamental puzzle in American economic history: What allowed the economy of the 1950s and the 1960s so unambiguously to exceed what would have been expected on the basis of trends estimated from the six decades before 1928?[4] Our analysis in this chapter takes the word "leap" seriously. It combines substance and speculation, and asks not just about the pace of innovation, but also about what could have happened with the lights out that permanently changed the economy's capacity to produce.[5] Though this book is about long-run trends in the standard of living rather than about business cycle fluctuations, tantalizing questions are suggested by the interaction of cycles and trends. Did the Great Depression permanently retard U.S. growth? Would postwar prosperity have occurred without World War II? How were labor input, capital input, and productivity transformed between 1928 and 1950?

The chapter begins by quantifying the leap. The first step is to ask: "The leap in what?" By definition output per person is equal to labor productivity (output per hour) times hours per person. We define the "leap" for each of these three components relative to a trend line that grows after 1928 at the same rate recorded by each concept between 1870 and 1928. We discover that by 1950, productivity growth was far above the earlier trend, whereas real GDP per person was modestly above the previous trend—and that by definition implies that hours per person were below their historic trend.

The search for explanations begins with elementary economics. An increase in real wages tends to boost productivity as firms substitute capital for labor. The New Deal passed legislation that made it much easier for labor unions to organize. In addition to pushing up real wages, labor unions also largely achieved their century-old goal of the eight-hour day. As a result, hours per person were markedly lower in the early postwar years than they had been in the 1920s.

The traditional measure of the pace of innovation and technological change is total factor productivity (TFP)—output divided by a weighted average of labor and capital input.[6] The measure of labor input allows for changes not only in the number of labor hours that are worked in a given year, but also in the average educational attainment of the labor force. Our measure of capital input is newly developed for this book and adjusts for unusual aspects of investment behavior during the 1930s and 1940s; details of these adjustments are provided in the data appendix.

The most novel aspect of this chapter is its assertion that World War II itself was perhaps the most important contributor to the Great Leap. We will examine the beneficial aspect of the war both through the demand and supply side of the economy. The war created household saving that after 1945 was spent on consumer goods that had been unavailable during the war, the classic case of "pent-up demand." A strong case can be made that World War II, however devastating in terms of deaths and casualties among the American military (albeit much less than the greater toll of deaths and wounded among other combatants), nevertheless represented an economic miracle that rescued the American economy from the secular stagnation of the late 1930s. In fact, this chapter will argue that the case is overwhelming for the "economic rescue" interpretation of World War II along every conceivable dimension, from education and the GI Bill to the deficit-financed mountain of household saving that gave a new middle class the ability to purchase the consumer durables made possible by the Second Industrial Revolution.

The supply effects are more subtle and interesting and include a vast expansion of the nation's capital stock as the government paid for new factories and equipment that were then operated by private firms to create aircraft, ships, and weapons. The expansion of government capital began during the 1930s and included not just factories to produce military goods during the war itself, but a surge of investment in infrastructure in both the 1930s and 1940s, as the nation's highway network was extended and major projects such as the Golden Gate Bridge, the Bay Bridge, the Tennessee Valley Authority (TVA), and the Boulder (later, Hoover) Dam were completed. Another supply channel boosted productivity through "learning by doing." The supply constraints of the 1942–45 war forced each firm to devise new techniques to boost output while constrained by limited capital and labor resources.

The explanation of the Great Leap then turns to the innovations of the 1920s that had not been fully exploited by 1929, as well as to the additional inventions of the 1930s and 1940s. By some measures, the 1930s were the most productive decade in terms of the numbers of inventions and patents granted relative to the size of the economy. Previous chapters of this book have pointed to technological progress during the 1930s, including in the quality and diffusion of electric appliances, improvements in the quality of automobiles, the arrival of commercial air transport, the arrival of network radio programs available in every farm and hamlet, the culmination of growth in motion picture quality and attendance, and continuing improvements in health with the invention of the first sulfa drugs. Inventions in the 1930s and 1940s also occurred in other areas not explicitly treated in previous chapters of the book, especially chemicals, plastics, and oil exploration and production.

HOW BIG WAS THE LEAP? OUTPUT, PRODUCTIVITY, AND HOURS

Throughout this book, we have equated the concept of the "standard of living" to real GDP per person while recognizing that increases in real GDP per person greatly understate the rise in the true standard of living—that is, household welfare. This understatement arises because of the inherent difficulty of measuring the value of new inventions, all of which are excluded from historical measures of real GDP. The use of official real GDP data in this section recognizes that there is an unknown degree of understatement of growth rates as a result of the unmeasured benefits of new inventions.[7]

The magnitude of the Great Leap Forward is illustrated first in figure 16–1. The straight upward-sloping line on the log scale represents the trend of growth between 1870 and 1928 in output per hour and output per person, each

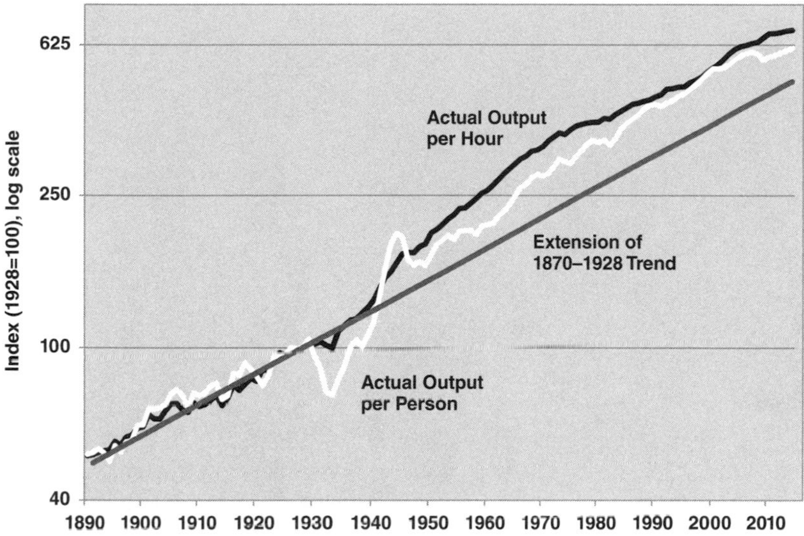

Figure 16–1. Actual Values of Output per Hour and Output per Person Compared to Extension of Their 1870–1928 Trends, 1928=100, 1890–2014

Sources: See Data Appendix for all figures in chapter 16.

growing at an annual rate of 1.9 percent per year. But actual output per hour and output per person did not behave alike after 1928. The main features of figure 16–1 pop off the page. First, deviations of actual values from the trend lines were minor before 1928. But starting with the Great Depression, the two lines diverge radically, both from trend and from each other. Output per person, as shown by the white line, collapsed during 1929–33 and soared during World War II. Then, during the postwar years, output per person was between 10 percent and 20 percent above trend (from 1947 to 1964) and then between 20 percent and 35 percent above trend (from 1965 to 2014). Output per hour (labor productivity) hardly declined at all in the Great Contraction of 1929–33 and was back to its trend by 1935. By 1941, productivity was 11 percent above trend, then reached 32 percent above trend by 1957 and 44 percent above trend in 1972. The post-1928 productivity growth miracle is perhaps the central puzzle in the American economic history of the twentieth century.

Figure 16–2 helps us better understand why the time path of output per person and of labor productivity diverged so much after 1928. It displays the percent deviation from trend of output per hour and per person and also adds an additional third line, the deviation from the historical 1870–1928 growth

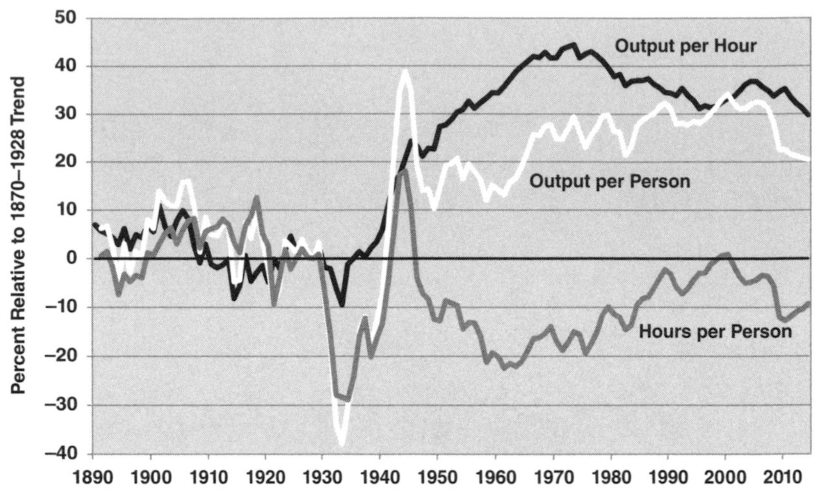

Figure 16–2. Log Ratio of Actual Values to Extension of 1870–1928 Trends of Output per Hour, Output per Person, and Hours per Person, 1890–2014

path of hours per person. Several distinctive time intervals stand out. The Great Depression of 1929–41 exhibits a parallel collapse and recovery in output per person and hours per person, implying by definition that output per hour showed little cyclical variation in the 1930s. The giant peak of all series, as achieved during World War II in 1944, reveals that the great upsurge of output per person from 1933 to 1944 was almost evenly divided between output per hour and hours per person.

The core of the puzzle addressed in this chapter occurs immediately after the war. Output per person dropped from 39 percent to 14 percent above trend between 1944 and 1950. Hours per person declined even more, from +18 to −13 percent, over the same time span. The big surprise was that labor productivity appears to have permanently increased as a result of the war. Table 16–1 shows the percent log ratios to the 1870–1928 trend for the three series for selected years. These are the base year of 1928, 1941 (the last year before World War II), 1944 (the peak year of war production), 1950, 1957, and finally the pivotal year 1972, when the ratio of labor productivity to trend reached its postwar peak.

The story told in table 16–1 identifies a set of questions to be addressed in this chapter. First, note that output per hour moved steadily higher relative to

Table 16–1. Percent Log Deviation from Extension of 1870–1928 Trend, Selected Years

	1928	1941	1944	1950	1957	1972
Output per Hour	0	11.0	20.7	27.3	32.3	44.0
Output per Person	0	6.4	38.8	14.6	16.3	26.8
Hours per Person	0	−4.6	18.1	−12.8	−15.9	−17.2
Real Wage[a]	0	13.7	19.5	26.2	38.5	56.2

Sources: Data underlying Figures 16–2 and 16–3.
Note: Trend for real wage refers to 1891–1928.

the 1870–1928 trend in each of the years shown. Why did this productivity growth surge occur? The deviations from trend of hours per person are somewhat easier to understand and include the role of labor unions in achieving the eight-hour day in the 1935–50 interval, as well as the baby boom itself in raising the population of children and thus reducing hours of work for the total population as mothers stayed home to take care of their families during the 1950s. Because the decline in hours per person relative to trend was not as large in magnitude as the rise in productivity, the postwar economy enjoyed a level of output per person substantially above the extension of the 1870–1928 trend.

WHAT CAUSED HIGHER REAL WAGES? THE ROLE OF THE NEW DEAL AND LABOR UNIONS

To explain the upsurge in labor productivity, the best place to start is with basic economic theory. In a competitive market, the marginal product of labor equals the real wage, and economists have shown that labor's marginal product under specified conditions is the share of labor in total income times output per hour.[8] If the income share of labor remains constant, then the growth rate of the real wage should be equal to that of labor's average product, the same thing as labor productivity. Could an increase in real wages have caused, directly or indirectly, the upsurge in labor productivity that occurred between the 1920s and 1950s?

Figure 16–3 copies from figure 16–2 the black line that shows the percent deviation of output per hour from its 1870–1928 trend line. Compared to this is shown the deviation from trend of the best available measure of the real inflation-adjusted wage.[9,10] In the late 1930s, the real wage began to rise more quickly than its pre-1928 trend, as did labor productivity. As shown in

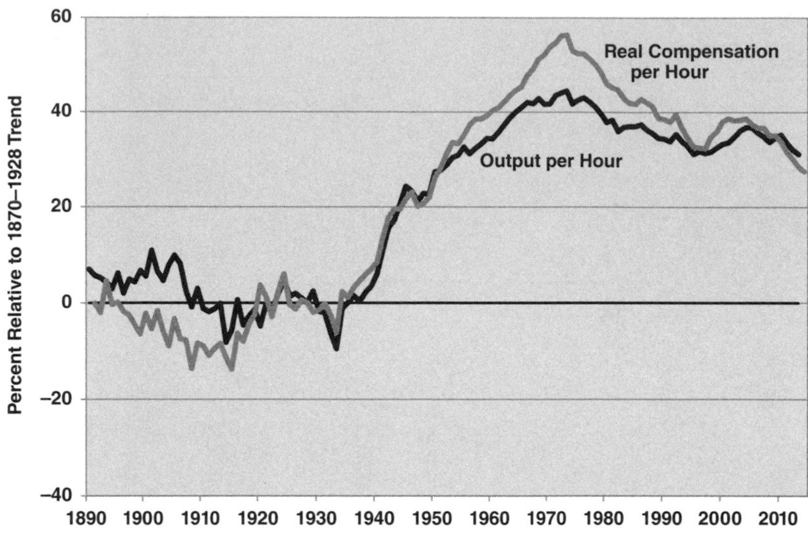

Figure 16–3. Log Ratio of Actual Values to Extension of pre-1928 Trends of Output per Hour and Real Compensation per Hour, 1890–2014

figure 16–3 and in the fourth line of table 16–1, by 1941 the real wage was already almost 14 percent above trend, somewhat higher than the 11 percent ratio to trend of labor productivity. The rise of the real wage may reflect in part the effects of New Deal Legislation, particularly the National Industrial Recovery Act of 1933–35 and the National Labor Relations Act of 1935. Because only a few industries were unionized in the late 1930s, primarily those dealing in automobiles and other durable goods, the effect of unions in boosting real wages may have spilled over to other less unionized industries. The index of the real wage relative to trend remained roughly the same as for productivity through 1950 and then between 1950 and 2007 was higher than the same ratio for productivity.[11]

The fact that both the real wage rose above its trend by more than productivity between 1950 and 1973 implies that labor's share in total income increased over this interval. The reverse occurred during 1973–2014. The growth of labor's share in the 1950s and 1960s is part of the phenomenon that Claudia Goldin and Robert Margo have called with reference to the distribution of income "The Great Compression," and the gradual shrinkage of labor's income share after the mid-1970s is consistent with rising inequality over the past three decades. We return to the inequality phenomenon in chapter 18.

The increase relative to the pre-1928 trend of both the real wage and labor productivity was in part a result of a long history of labor union agitation for higher wages and shorter hours that culminated in the 1930s. The eight-hour day was a provision of the National Labor Relations ("Wagner") Act of 1935, which set out new rules that governed the formation of unions and the conduct of free elections for labor union recruitment. Three years, later the modern system of the forty-hour week with mandatory time-and-a-half overtime for hours beyond forty was put into effect by the New Deal's Fair Labor Standards Act, passed in 1938.

The shift to the eight-hour day must have had a direct effect in boosting productivity. Edward Denison has called attention to the effect of shorter hours in reducing worker fatigue and thus improving worker efficiency. In addition, many establishments reorganized themselves to reduce business hours and conduct the same amount of business in eight hours as they formerly did in ten hours per day. However, the main upward stimulus to productivity must have come from the impetus of higher hourly wages, particularly in the late 1930s, that led firms to economize on the use of labor. This helps us to understand the explosion of productivity during World War II.

THE ROLE OF LABOR QUALITY: THE SURGE IN EDUCATIONAL ATTAINMENT

The study of the sources of productivity growth is called "growth accounting" and was pioneered by Robert Solow in the 1950s, with seminal additional contribution in the 1960s from Edward Denison, Zvi Griliches, and Dale Jorgenson.[12] This approach subdivides the growth in labor productivity into four categories:

Increases in labor quality, usually represented by changes in educational attainment
Increases in the quantity of capital relative to the quantity of labor
Increases in the quality of capital

The leftovers, alternately called "total factor productivity" or "the residual" or even "the measure of our ignorance." While often treated as a measure of innovation and technical progress, the residual incorporates every aspect not just of major innovation but

> of incremental tinkering and anything else that improves efficiency, including the movement from low-productivity jobs in agriculture to higher-productivity jobs in the cities.

"Labor quality" is often measured by educational attainment, and there were significant increases in the educational attainment of American youth both before and after World War II. Between 1900 and 1970, the high school graduation rates of U.S. teenagers rose from 6 percent to 80 percent, a truly monumental change that contributed to productivity growth. By 1940, half of American youth had completed high school, and a substantial fraction of the rest had experienced high school classes before dropping out. This created a more capable work force to confront the production challenges of the Arsenal of Democracy during 1941–45. Workers who had a high school education were better able to operate new and more complex machinery, both on the assembly line and in the office.

The period of most rapid increase in four-year college graduation rates was in the decade 1940–50. This was thanks in large part to the GI Bill, passed in 1944, which provided financing for every World War II veteran to attend college at the expense of the federal government. Because 16.1 million people, or 12 percent of the 1940 population, had served during the war, the effect was substantial and swamped the nation's colleges with new enrollees during 1946–49. The GI Bill also provided for support if a veteran wanted to complete a high school degree, as well as low-interest loans for home purchase and unemployment compensation for a veteran's first year out of the military.

There are other ways of expressing the improvement in educational attainment. The fraction of the U.S. workforce who had only an elementary school education declined from 75 percent in 1915 to 30 percent in 1960 to a mere 3 percent in 2005.[13] Over the same 1915–2005 interval, the fraction who had four-year college degrees, post-graduate degrees, and enrollment in college courses (without graduation) increased from 4 percent to 48 percent.

Because the rise in educational attainment proceeded at a steady pace before and after 1928, it does not contribute anything to the explanation of the main puzzle explored in this chapter: Why did labor productivity grow so much more quickly between 1928 and 1972 than it had before 1928? The increase of educational attainment, an undeniably positive creator of economic growth, cannot be counted among the factors that generated the Great Leap Forward between the 1920s and 1950s. For the missing causes, we must look elsewhere.

CAPITAL AND TFP: THE MIDCENTURY EXPLOSION OF PRODUCTIVITY

Standard production theory relates output to the quantity and quality of labor and capital. The preceding section examined the role of changes in the quality of labor made possible by higher educational attainment. Changes in the quantity and quality of capital are another possible source of the jump in labor productivity between the 1920s and 1950s. As economists in the early 1960s marveled over the richness of John Kendrick's seminal 1961 contribution to the data of growth accounting, one startling change leaped off the page. The ratio of output to capital input (the average productivity of capital) almost doubled between the 1920s and the 1950s.

The doubling is reproduced in figure 16–4, which displays the ratio of GDP to capital input from 1920 to 1972. The upper line shows the ratio of real GDP to the same concept of capital that Kendrick used, as updated from current data sources.[14] After hovering very close to 100 percent of the 1928 value during 1923–29, the ratio dropped to 78 percent during the worst years of the Great Depression, returned to 95 percent in 1935 and 144 percent in 1941, and then reached a peak of 220 percent during 1944. The big surprise came after the war, when many economists predicted that the economy would sink back into the dire conditions of the 1930s. The output-capital ratio dropped only to

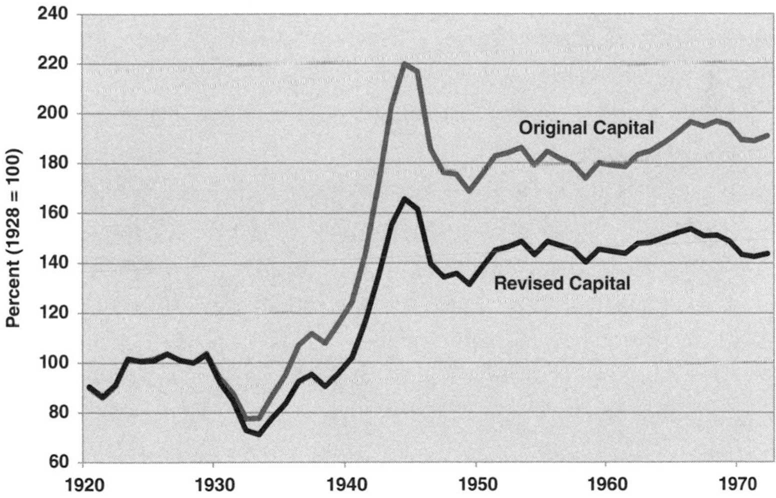

Figure 16–4. Ratio of GDP to Two Alternative Concepts of Capital Input, Original and Revised, 1920–1972

176 percent in 1950, an enormous change compared to 1928, and the average ratio between 1950 and 1972 was 185 percent.

Subsequent research summarized in the data appendix has identified three sets of measurement issues that contribute to the jump of the output-capital ratio between the 1920s and 1950s. Because mismeasurement causes capital to be understated in the 1950s relative to the 1920s, substitution of a new adjusted series on capital input raises capital in the 1950s and in tandem reduces the output-capital ratio, as shown by the lower line in figure 16–4. In contrast to the 1950 ratio of 176 percent based on the official data, that ratio in 1950 is a much lower 141 percent in the revised data. Thus roughly half of the post-1935 jump in the output-capital ratio can be attributed to the measurement issues examined in the data appendix.

Though the adjusted output-capital ratio shown as the lower line in figure 16–4 was in 1972 still 147 percent of its 1928 value, gradually the ratio fell to 108 percent by 2013. Put simply, the nation's output grew much more quickly than its capital input between 1928 and 1972 and then much more slowly from 1972 to 2013. The annualized growth rate of the output-capital ratio between 1928 and 1972 was 0.9 percent per year and then fell at –0.8 percent per year from 1972 to 2013. This history raises deep questions that we will ponder for the rest of this chapter. What factors caused the adjusted ratio to increase from 100 in 1928 to an average of 150 percent during 1950–72? Many issues await our attention, including the effect of the depression and war on production practices and industrial efficiency, as well as the underlying pace of innovation from the 1920s to the 1950s and beyond.

We now have all the ingredients needed to determine the growth history of total factor productivity (TFP), the best available measure of innovation and technological change.[15] The calculation of TFP is mechanical and equals output divided by a weighted average of labor and capital input, with standard weights of 0.7 for labor and 0.3 for capital.[16] Labor input equals aggregate hours of work multiplied by an index of educational attainment.[17] Capital input equals the adjusted concept developed in the data appendix. The resulting growth rates of TFP are displayed in figure 16–5, which displays the annual growth rate of TFP for each decade between the initial decade 1890–1900 and the extended decade 2000–2014. The horizontal labels identify the final year of each decade, and so the highest bar in the graph labeled "1950" refers to the average annual growth rate of TFP during the decade 1940–50.

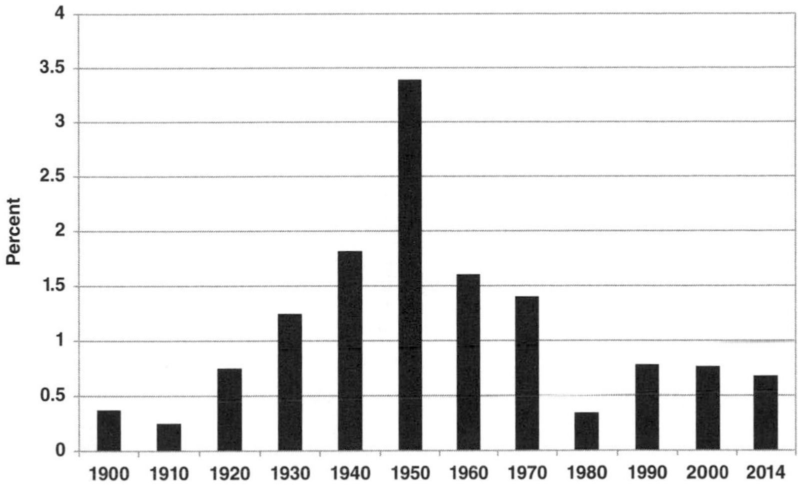

Figure 16–5. 10-Year Average Annual Growth in Total Factor Productivity, 1900–2014

Note: The average annual growth rate is over the ten years prior to year shown. The bar labelled 2014 shows the average annual growth rate for 2001–14.

This history of TFP growth has the appearance of an up-and-down "staircase" with steps of unequal height. The singularity of the 1940–50 decade leaps off the page. This graph confirms Alex Field's emphasis on the 1930s as a more productive decade than the 1920s, as well as the pickup in TFP growth in the 1920s compared to the 1890–1920 interval. Called into question is the verdict of Moses Abramowitz and Paul David (regarding World War II) that "the war . . . imposed restrictions on civilian investment, caused a serious reduction in private capital accumulation and retarded normal productivity growth."[18] Labor productivity and TFP soared during World War II, and the cessation of defense production did not prevent the wartime productivity gains from becoming permanent.

The TFP growth history laid out in figure 16–5 poses a daunting set of questions for the rest of the chapter. What was it about the innovation process that allowed TFP growth steadily to accelerate from the 1920s to 1930s to 1940s and then slow down thereafter? What was it about the growth process that allowed the *level* of TFP to remain high even after wartime production ceased in 1945–46? To what extent did the productivity explosion of the late 1930s and the 1940s benefit from inventions and innovations in the 1920s and

1930s that had a delayed impact? In the next section, the analysis begins with the effects of economic disruption in the 1930s and 1940s, and subsequently turns to the timing and effect of inventions during the first half of the twentieth century.

EXPLANATIONS ROOTED IN THE DISRUPTIONS OF THE GREAT DEPRESSION AND WORLD WAR II

What were the causes of the epochal jump in the output-capital ratio and of TFP between 1928 and 1950? To what extent could the causes be connected to the disruptions associated with the Great Depression and World War II? The first topic is the interplay between rapidly rising real wages and declining hours per week, both of which made labor more expensive to employ. The second issue is complementary, the effect of cost-cutting during the desperate decade of the 1930s that forced firms to make do with fewer employees and the high-pressure priority for maximum production during World War II that had the same effect of raising labor productivity through some combination of higher machine speeds and greater work effort. The third effect is the role of government infrastructure that was built in the 1930s and whcther this would have occurred had the Great Depression not occurred.

Rising Real Wages. Earlier this chapter, we have traced the upward surge of the real wage of production workers during the 1930s and attributed it in large part to New Deal pro-labor legislation. Did the rising real wage cause a substitution away from labor toward capital? Though capital spending was depressed during the 1930s and during World War II, this was mainly true for structures (which accounted for 77 percent of the value of the capital stock in 1928). Equipment investment rebounded strongly in the 1930s. The ratio of equipment investment to the value of equipment capital was 13.6 percent in 1928 but rose above that to 14.4 percent in 1936, 16.1 percent in 1937, 15.8 percent in 1940, and 17.1 percent in 1941. At least some part of this buoyant performance of equipment investment may have represented a substitution from labor to capital that raised labor productivity. Moreover, the new capital investment of the late 1930s reflected continuing innovation. Railroad locomotives, trucks, tractors, and industrial equipment manufactured in the late 1930s were all of substantially higher quality than their counterparts of the 1920s.

The High-Pressure Economy of World War II. All the indexes of output, hours of work, and productivity soared during 1942–45. This is not surprising, for the entire economy converted to a maximum production regime in which every machine and structure was used twenty-four hours per day if enough workers could be found to staff three shifts. As shown in figure 16–2, previously, labor productivity did not exhibit even a hiccup of decline after 1945. Though hours per capita collapsed as Rosie the Riveter switched roles from factory worker to mother in the baby boom, labor productivity continued to rise farther above its 1870–1928 trend.[19]

As early as 1941 the economy was straining against a shortage of capacity in manufacturing. The capacity use rate for the steel industry reached 97 percent in 1941, as high as in any other year during World War II. Machine tools were in short supply as early as the spring of 1940, and by the spring of 1941, the owner of a leading machine tool supplier shook his head at the backlogs, stating that "the demand is infinite."[20] Though the most famous example of "learning by doing" was the drastic reduction in the number of days needed to produce a standard Liberty freighter ship built by Henry Kaiser in his Richmond, California, and Portland, Oregon, shipyards, the pressure for maximum production must have yielded permanent improvements in production techniques under conditions of war that would not have occurred in peacetime. The Kaiser shipyards began in 1942 with a schedule of fully eight months to complete a Liberty ship, but by the next year, the completion time had been reduced to a few weeks. In a unique contest between the two shipyards, an entire ship was actually put together at each yard from prefabricated parts in four days. This supreme production achievement was made possible in part by letters from more than 250 employees suggesting ways to make production more efficient.[21]

The shipyard example can be generalized to the entire manufacturing sector. Recent accounts of the Arsenal of Democracy focus not just on the Kaiser shipyards, but also on Henry Ford's mammoth factory that built B-24 bombers. The Ford plant was built in less than a year, starting in March 1941, and turned out its first plane in May 1942. The plant had originally been designed to produce bombers at the unbelievable rate of one per hour, but it was a long struggle to achieve that rate. In a classic example of learning by doing, the production rate gradually increased, reaching seventy-five per month in February 1943, 150 per month in November 1943, and a peak of 432 per month in August 1944.[22]

And the Kaiser and Ford examples were only the best known of continuous learning by doing throughout the war in the form of continuous cost reduction and efficiency improvement.

> Pontiac had reduced the cost of its complex Oerlikon anti-aircraft gun by 23 percent. Chrysler's Dodge division . . . engineers figured out how to make [shortwave radar systems] at 57 percent less cost than eight months earlier. The company's gyrocompasses . . . were costing 55 percent of the original fee.

Throughout the war, patriotism and the sense of purpose bonded workers and management together, and workers were more eager to raise efficiency (often in ways that made their lives easier) than before. The most obvious reason why productivity remained high after World War II, despite the end of the military emergency, is that *technological change does not regress.* People do not forget. Once progress is made, no matter under what circumstances, it is permanent.

The impressive performance of productivity in the late 1930s suggests that had aggregate demand collapsed after World War II as defense spending dried up, the toll would have been taken on employment rather than on productivity. But demand did not dry up; rather, it shifted almost immediately from military to civilian purchases. In 1946–47, the floodgates of demand were let loose, and after swift reconversion, manufacturers strained to meet the demand for refrigerators, stoves, washing machines, dryers, and dishwashers, not to mention automobiles and television sets. As they struggled to fill orders that seemed almost infinite, they adopted all that they had learned about efficient production in the high-pressure economy of World War II.[23]

Virtually every firm making consumer goods (except for basic food and clothing products) had been forced to make something else during World War II, and every one of these producers learned to be more efficient from the process. During the war, jewelry makers made artillery fuses, producers of lawn mowers made shrapnel shells, manufacturers of postal meters made bomb mechanisms, makers of mens' shoes made helmet liners, manufacturers of vacuum cleaners made gas mask parts, and makers of wheelbarrows shifted to production of ammunition carts for machine guns.[24] Every part of the postwar manufacturing sector had been deeply involved in making military equipment or its components, and the lessons learned from the war translated into permanent efficiency gains after the war.

Though wartime production demands may have had a permanent effect in raising the use of capital and the level of efficiency, earlier attempts to smooth the production flow and raise efficiency date back to the 1920s. Then began a deliberate managerial effort to improve use of facilities and to save on inventories of in-process of finished products. This might help to explain the paradox of rising labor productivity and TFP growth in the 1930s despite the decline in the overall utilization of capital and labor. New methods were making it possible to raise the output-capital ratio and TFP despite low aggregate demand, helping explain why the Great Depression reduced input of labor hours more than it reduced labor productivity. This has been attributed in part to the shift in the structure of retailing to large corporations such as Marshall Field, Macy's, and Sears Roebuck, which demanded a constant flow of goods from their suppliers.[25]

There is a debate in the literature about whether World War II improved consumer welfare. Despite the prohibition of production of most durable goods, real consumption per capita (2009 dollars) remained roughly the same in 1944 as in 1941.[26] Robert Higgs has argued that the official data on real personal consumption expenditures are overstated, because the growth of true consumer prices in the wartime regime of price controls is substantially understated.[27] If the data on current-dollar consumption are correct, then any unmeasured increase in true consumer prices becomes an unmeasured decrease of the same percentage magnitude in real consumption spending. Sources of unmeasured price increases include bribes, black markets, and unmeasured declines in the quality of goods and services, including the need to wait in lines and distort consumption choices due to rationing, crowding due to migration, and a shortage of housing exacerbated by declines in rental housing maintenance due to rent controls.

Three responses to this critique range from narrow to broad. At the narrow level, the shift of 12 million people, or 9 percent of the 1940 population, into the armed forces implies that there were 9 percent fewer civilians to share the available personal consumption expenditures. Because measured real consumption was roughly the same in 1944 as in 1941, this implies that real consumption per civilian increased by 9 percent. There may well have been measurement errors, but these would have had to be greater than 9 percent for us to conclude that there was any decline in real personal consumption expenditures per member of the civilian population. All the food, clothing, and housing for the 12 million in the military (whether it be in barracks, camps, or on ships) was provided by the government and counted in wartime government spending rather than personal consumption expenditures.

A broader and more important point is that the wartime prosperity, despite its inconveniences, marked a sea change in the outlook and expectations of the entire nation after a decade of grinding depression and unemployment that appeared without end, a world of "secular stagnation" in the famous phrase of

Harvard's Alvin Hansen. The Great Depression had a searingly negative effect on the nation's sense of well-being. Through most of the 1930s, a sizable portion of the population was badly fed, clothed, and housed. This extreme poverty was eliminated by the war economy. The reduction in the economic distance between the least well-off and the rest of the population significantly lifted everyone's sense of well-being. Thus the stagnant material consumption levels of World War II may not have been thought very important for much of the population. Even if 1944 total consumption was no higher than 1941, the year 1941 seemed like paradise as it achieved a level of total real consumption fully 28 percent higher than the average annual consumption expenditures of 1930–39. Indeed, despite his negative assessment of consumer welfare in World War II, Higgs agrees with this broader point:

> The war economy . . . broke the back of the pessimistic expectations almost everybody had come to hold during the seemingly endless Depression. In the long decade of the 1930s, especially its latter half, many people had come to believe that the economic machine was irreparably broken. The frenetic activity of war production . . . dispelled the hopelessness. People began to think: if we can produce all these planes, ships, and bombs, we can also turn out prodigious quantities of cars and refrigerators.[28]

The third and even more important point is that this chapter is not about how much was produced or consumed during World War II, but rather how and why the economy was able to achieve such a "great leap" in labor productivity and total factor productivity when the 1950s are compared to the pre-1928 growth trend. The war itself may have contributed to postwar achievement directly, as explored in this section, or may, by distorting the timing of economic advance, have masked the influence of innovations and other forms of progress that were already well under way in the years leading up to 1941.

Wartime Facilities. Though private capital input stagnated during 1930–45, the amount of capital input financed by the government surged ahead throughout that fifteen-year interval. Of particular interest was the creation of new plant facilities paid for by the government but operated by private firms to produce military equipment and supplies. The wages, salaries, and profits earned in these government-owned plants were counted as part of national income originating in the private sector. Studies of productivity and TFP growth have traditionally compared real value added in the private sector with capital input financed by the private sector, neglecting the World War II government-financed increases in the nation's stock of structures and productive equipment.[29] The starkest omission from the data on capital used in World War II product comes from a single startling fact: The number of machine tools in the U.S. *doubled* from 1940 to 1945, and almost all of these new machine tools were paid for by the government rather than by private firms.[30] Not all the government-financed facilities were in manufacturing. In 1942–44, as an emergency measure, the government financed the construction of the "Big Inch" and "Little Big Inch" petroleum pipelines over the 1,300 miles from Texas to New Jersey to provide for the safe shipment of oil in wartime conditions when the previous method of transport by sea was threatened by German submarine attacks. Both pipelines became part of the nation's postwar infrastructure and are in use to this day.

Some of the government-owned factories were on a massive and unprecedented scale. Previously we have cited learning by doing at Henry Ford's government-financed plant in Willow Run, Michigan, which at its 1944 peak was producing one bomber per hour in what was called "The World's Greatest Room." Fully 50,000 workers were employed there.[31] The feat of bringing together millions of parts and fasteners at stations extending linearly for more than half a mile was unprecedented in the history of mass production. Necessity was the mother of invention, and the Ford Willow Run plant, together with the Kaiser shipyards, stands as perhaps the most persuasive example that World War II created a permanent increase in what firms, equipment, and workers could achieve together under the pressure of a government-financed regime that guaranteed fixed markups—i.e., consistent profits—and real wages higher than any work force had known from the beginning of time. Henry Ford perhaps said it best in the epigraph that begins this chapter—in 1942–45, the production genius of the United States, led by the automobile industry, stretched its imagination to perform feats never before imagined, but after imagination took over and the wartime goals were achieved, the economy did not forget.

LONG-TERM EXPLANATIONS: URBANIZATION, THE CLOSED ECONOMY, AND THE IMPROVEMENT OF CAPITAL QUALITY

Urbanization and the Decline of Farming. Now we turn to the complementary set of explanations of the great leap forward that do not rely on specific events related to the Great Depression or World War II. In searching for explanations of the rapid growth of TFP after 1929, we start with urbanization, which by moving workers from less productive agricultural jobs to more productive urban occupations contributes to the economy-wide advance of TFP growth. Did urbanization advance at a quicker pace between 1920 and 1960 than it had before or has since? The urban share during the slow productivity growth period of 1890–1920 grew from 35.1 percent to 50.8 percent. From 1920 to 1960, it rose from 50.8 percent to 69.7 percent, about the same rate per decade. Thus urbanization by itself does not explain the post-1928 acceleration in productivity and TFP growth.

Immigration and Imports. Between 1870 and 1913, roughly 30 million immigrants arrived on American shores; they crowded into central cities but also populated the Midwest and the plains states. They made possible the rapid population growth rate of 2.1 percent per year over the same interval, and the new immigrants created as much demand as supply in the sense that there was no mass unemployment caused by their arrival—and in fact the unemployment rate in 1913 was only 4.3 percent.[32] All those new people required structures to house them, factories to work in, and equipment inside the factories, so the new immigrants contributed to the rapid rise of capital input.

Contrast this with the shriveling up of immigration after the restrictive immigration laws of 1921 and 1924.[33] The ratio of annual immigration to the U.S. population dropped from an average 1.0 percent per year during 1909–13 to 0.25 percent per year during 1925–29, and the growth rate of the population fell from 2.1 percent during 1870–1913 to 0.9 percent between 1926 and 1945.[34] The anti-immigration legislation has long been cited as a cause of the Great Depression, in the sense that the overbuilding of residential and nonresidential structures in the 1920s was based on an expectation of continued rapid population growth that did not occur.[35]

Both the immigration legislation and the draconian regime of high tariffs (the Ford–McCumber tariff of 1922 and the Smoot–Hawley tariff of 1930) converted the U.S. into a relatively closed economy during the three decades between 1930 and 1960. The lack of competition for jobs from recent immigrants made it easier for unions to organize and push up wages in the 1930s. The high tariff wall allowed American manufacturing to introduce all available innovations into U.S.-based factories without the outsourcing that has become common in the last several decades. The lack of competition from immigrants and imports boosted the wages of workers at the bottom and contributed to the remarkable "great compression" of the income distribution during the 1940s, 1950s, and 1960s.[36]

Thus the closing of the American economy through restrictive immigration legislation and high tariffs may indirectly have contributed to the rise of real wages in the 1930s, the focus of innovative investment in the domestic economy, and the general reduction of inequality from the 1920s to the 1950s.

CAN THE INNOVATIONS OF THE 1920s AND 1930s EXPLAIN THE GREAT LEAP?

Our account in part I of this book of the great inventions distinguishes between the original invention and the subsidiary subinventions made possible by the initial invention. The two most important inventions of the late nineteenth century were electric light and power and the internal combustion engine, and these are often described as a "General Purpose Technology" (GPT) that can lead to the creation of many subinventions.[37]

Subinventions made possible by electricity as a GPT are such fundamental drivers of productivity as elevators; electric hand and machine tools; electric streetcars, elevated trains, and underground subways; the whole host of consumer appliances starting with the electric iron and vacuum cleaner and followed by the refrigerator, washing machine, clothes dryer, dishwasher, and many others; and, finally, air conditioning, which arrived in movie theaters in the 1920s, in some office buildings in the 1930s, and in the American home in the 1950s and 1960s. A similar list of subinventions made possible by the internal combustion engine as a GPT includes the car, truck, bus, and taxi; supermarkets; suburbs; and all the aspects of personal travel, including motels and roadside restaurants, as well as air travel.

Though we have no need to choose between electricity and the internal combustion engine as the most important GPT of all time, an author in 1932 provided a persuasive case that the most important invention of all time was the discovery of how to transform mechanical power into electricity, which then could be transported by wires for long distances and then retransformed into whatever form of energy might be desired. This passage is interesting also for its perspective on how much of the modern world had already been invented at the time of its writing in 1932.

> Without it not only would the street car again be horse-drawn, but the automobile and the airplane would stop. For without electromagnetic sparking devices, how could gasoline engines function? The electric

> light would, of course, disappear, and with it the greatest guarantee of safety after twilight in the great cities. The telephone and telegraph would be idle, and the daily newspaper would therefore become of merely local interest... Radiotelegraphy, telephony, and broadcasting would all disappear. Power plants would have to be associated with every separate factory, because long-distance transmission of power would cease. The rivers could furnish power only to factories situated on their banks.... Hospital practice would again be without X-ray appliances, and households would be without electric work-lightening devices. Ships in distress at sea, no longer able to signal their S O S calls and no longer provided with gyrocompass, radio direction finding, or fire-signaling apparatus, would often sink, as formerly, with none to rescue or help.[38]

Those attempting to explain the great leap forward in terms of inventions often cite Alfred Kleinknecht (1987), who counted up inventions by decade and declared that the decade with the greatest number of important inventions was the 1930s. In fact, if we include the 1920s, 1930s, and 1940s, these three decades contributed twenty-six out of the thirty-nine most important inventions in Kleinknecht's list of the twelve decades between 1850 and 1970. My reading of the history of invention suggests the reverse—that the 1930s were distinguished by subsidiary subinventions rather than the discovery of fundamental GPTs. For instance, the 1930s were a defining decade in the perfection of the piston-powered military and commercial aircraft, but this was not a new GPT. It represented the marriage of the 1879 invention of the internal combustion engine with the 1903 aerodynamic design of the Wright Brothers that made possible the first flight. Similarly, the invention of television in the 1920s and 1930s combined the 1879 invention of wireless transmission with the 1907 Lee De Forest invention of the vacuum tube which had previously made commercial radio possible.

Alexopoulos and Cohen (2010) have made an important contribution to the history of innovation, although their study is limited to 1909–49. They criticize the use of patent data as a measure of the pace of innovation for two basic reasons—because the date of the basic invention may be decades earlier than the introduction of a commercially viable version and because a patent provides no information about the future commercial viability of the idea.[39] Instead, they conduct an exhaustive search of the Library of Congress catalogue for handbooks and other books about technology and compare the date of the first book(s) on an innovation with its date of initial commercialization. Their count supports Field's emphasis on the 1930s, especially after 1934, as a period having a larger count of technical books published than any other interval in their forty-year period. The average number was between 500 and 600 between 1911 and 1934, then soared monotonically to 930 in 1941 and averaged about 750 between 1942 and 1949.[40]

Worthy of consideration as a GPT is Henry Ford's introduction of the assembly line to automobile manufacture, dating from December 1, 1913.[41] Developed from the ideas of many predecessors, dating back to Richard Garrett's 1853 English steam engine factory, the assembly line revolutionized manufacturing and deserves equal credit with electric motors for achieving the acceleration of TFP growth which began in the 1920s (as is evident in figure 16–5). Moses Abramowitz and Paul David attribute the rapid spread of the techniques of mass production to Ford's "deliberate policy of openness" about his detailed methods of operation that "contributed to the rapid diffusion of these new techniques throughout American manufacturing."[42] It is interesting to contrast the very slow arrival of electric motors in manufacturing as emphasized by the same David as contrasted to the rapid diffusion of the assembly line technique.

The assembly line, together with electric-powered tools, utterly transformed manufacturing. Before 1913, goods were manufactured by craftsmen at individual stations that depended for power on steam engines and leather or rubber belts. The entire product would be crafted by one or two employees. Compare that with a decade later, when each worker had control of electric-powered machine tools and hand tools, with production organized along the Ford assembly-line principle. An additional aspect of the assembly line was that it saved capital, particularly "floor space, inventories in storage rooms, and shortening of time in process."[43]

It is likely that electric power and the assembly line explain not just the TFP growth upsurge of the 1920s, but also that of the 1930s and 1940s. There are two types of evidence that this equipment capital was becoming more powerful and more electrified. First is the horsepower of prime movers, a data series available for selected years for different types of productive capital, and the second is kilowatt hours of electricity production. Analysts have long emphasized the role of both horsepower and electricity use as explanations of high productivity in American manufacturing relative to other nations.[44] Table 16–2 displays on the

Table 16–2. Horsepower of Prime Movers and Kilowatt Hours of Net Production of Electric Energy, 1929=100, Selected Years 1899–1950

	1899	**1909**	**1919**	**1929**	**1940**	**1950**
(1) Variable Depreciation Private Equipment Capital in 1950 Dollars	34	57	82	100	120	164
Horsepower						
(2) Automotive	0	1	16	100	176	309
(3) Factories	49	84	101	100	110	170
(4) Farms	13	34	76	100	156	231
(5) Electric Central Stations	5	13	33	100	134	220
(6) Average of Auto, Factories, Farms	20	40	64	100	147	237
(7) Ratio of Horsepower to Equipment Capital	61	70	79	100	123	145
	1902	**1912**	**1920**	**1929**	**1941**	**1950**
(8) Variable Depreciation Private Equipment	39	63	84	100	123	164
Kilowatt Hours						
(9) Industrial Establishments	14	54	70	100	177	242
(10) Electric Utilities	3	13	43	100	178	357
(11) Total	5	21	48	100	178	333
(12) Ratio to Equipment Capital	13	34	58	100	145	203

Sources: HSUS Colonial Times to 1957, Series S2, S6, S11, S13, S19, and S33.
Variable Depreciation Private Equipment Capital from the data underlying Figure 16–4.

top line for selected years the constant-dollar value of private equipment capital developed in the data appendix.[45]

Total horsepower is shown as an index number (1929=100) for four categories of equipment: automotive, factories, farms, and electric central stations. In absolute magnitude, the horsepower installed in the nation's fleet of vehicles swamped every other type of equipment capital, but unfortunately, the horsepower data do not distinguish automobiles used for personal travel from those used for business travel, nor from trucks and buses. Milestones for automotive horsepower include the surpassing of the horsepower of work animals by 1910 and of railroads by 1915. Horsepower in factories increased much more slowly, and the index numbers for 1940 and 1950 are very similar to those for the private equipment series. A puzzling aspect of the factory horsepower data is the absence of any growth in the 1920s. Horsepower on farms and in electric generating stations increased more rapidly than private equipment after 1929.

Because any index of total horsepower is swamped by the automotive category, we take a simple arithmetic average of the index numbers for automotive, factories, and farms, omitting electric utility generation on the ground that it is an intermediate good rather than private investment. The ratio of horsepower to equipment capital, shown on line 7 of table 16–2, rose modestly by 13 percent per decade during 1899–1919, then accelerated to 24 percent per decade in the 1920s, 21 percent in the 1930s, and 17 percent in the 1940s.

Unlike the horsepower series, which starts out with a substantial base of installed steam power in 1899, the kilowatt-hour series starts from zero in 1882 and thus would be expected to exhibit the fastest growth rates in its early years. Nevertheless, impressive growth is registered in the 1930s and 1940s. Particularly noteworthy is the series on electricity generated by industrial establishments, which grew by 57 percent between 1929 and 1941, more quickly than the 36 percent of the 1920s or 31 percent of the 1940s. When expressed as a ratio to private equipment capital, the growth rate of industry-generated electricity grew at 18 percent in the 1920s, 36 percent in the 1930s, and only 3 percent in the 1940s. The ratio of total kilowatt hours, most of which was generated by electric utilities, to private equipment capital grew at 54 percent in the 1920s, 37 percent in the 1930s, and 34 percent in the 1940s.

Overall, the increase in the horsepower of motor vehicles and the use of electricity rose much more quickly than did equipment capital in the 1930s and 1940s. While the stock of private equipment rose by 50 percent (in logs) between 1929 and 1950, motor vehicle horsepower tripled and total electricity production rose by 3.3 times. Total registrations increased between 1929 and 1941 by 45 percent for trucks and more than tripled for buses. All these additional trucks and buses were much more powerful in 1941 than they had been in 1929. Though we do not have separate horsepower data for trucks and buses, we learned above in table 5–2 that automobile horsepower in a typical popular low-priced car increased from twenty horsepower in Ford's Model T, which dominated the 1913–25 interval, to forty horsepower in Ford's Model A, introduced in 1928, to eighty-five horsepower in the 1940 Chevrolet. The horsepower of trucks and buses must have increased at comparable rates.[46]

Field finds that the most important industries contributing to the productivity upsurge of the 1930s were manufacturing and transportation/distribution. This chapter thus far has pointed to two separate sources of productivity growth in transportation/distribution, the heavy government investment in highways, and the much higher horsepower of the nation's trucking fleet in 1941 compared to 1929. The rapid rise of electricity production after 1929 by industrial enterprises provides solid evidence that the use of electricity by industrial machinery grew rapidly during the 1930s and contradicts Field's judgment that the 1930s represented the "tail end" of the "electrification transition."[47] Higher electricity use in the 1930s reflected the continuing adaptation to electric equipment not just in manufacturing, but also in the form of refrigerated cases in wholesaling and retailing and the widespread use of electric production methods in the rest of the economy, including the earliest examples of air-conditioned movie theaters and office buildings.[48]

The great expansion of electricity production in the 1930s and 1940s was made possible by economies of scale, for larger electric-generating boilers produced electricity at a lower unit cost. Throughout the 1930s and 1940s, increasing size was combined with higher temperatures and pressures as technology made tightly sealed boilers more reliable.[49] The evolution of higher thermal efficiency and productivity in the electric utility example is an example not of a breakthrough invention but of "incremental tinkering," a constant striving to improve existing technology. Totally new inventions as well as incremental tinkering are the fundamental sources of growth in TFP, and the data do not allow us to distinguish between them.

Beyond the productivity-enhancing role of electricity and the internal combustion engine, which innovations drove productivity growth in the 1930s and 1940s? The distribution system was revolutionized by the movement to chain stores and self-service stores that started around 1910 and continued during the 1920s and 1930s. The number of chain food stores quadrupled during the 1920s, achieving a major boost to productivity. But chain stores initially operated by the old-fashioned "counter and shelf" system in which the customer stood in line at each separate department and the clerk both selected the item from the shelf and received payment. It was when chain stores developed self-service, much of which happened after 1930, that the real productivity gains occurred as the customers did the walking and selecting, and the number of employees needed to run a store fell by half or more.

As important as was progress in the transportation and distribution industries, innovation and discoveries exploded after 1929 in the petroleum and related chemical industries. An epochal moment in the history of the American petroleum industry occurred with the discovery, in October 1930, of the east

Texas oil field, which has been called "the largest and most prolific oil reservoir in the contiguous United States."[50] The chemicals industry, dominated by German firms in the late nineteenth century, took off in the U.S. in the 1930–50 period. Many types of plastics had been invented before 1930. Among these were celluloid (1863), polyvinyl chloride (1872), cellophane (1908), bakelite (1909), and vinyl (1927). But the timeline of plastics inventions highlights the 1930s as perhaps the most fruitful innovative period in the history of the industry, with polyvinylidene chloride (1933), low-density polyethylene (1935), acrylic methacrylate (1936), polyurethanes (1937), polystyrene (1938), Teflon (1938), nylon (1939), and neoprene (1939). Of all the inventions on the plastics timeline, five were invented between 1839 and 1894, four more between 1894 and 1927, and seven in the brief period 1933–39.[51] Field lists numerous practical byproducts of developments in the chemical industries in the 1930s, including coatings that doubled the lives of railroad ties, quick-drying lacquers that reduced the time required to paint a car from a few weeks to a few hours, and the introduction of stainless steel and chrome. Plastics often saved fuel, fabrication, and capital costs.[52]

The productivity of motor vehicles depended not only on the power of their engines, which increased rapidly from 1920 to 1940, but also on the quality of their tires. Advances in rubber technology made it possible to equip trucks and tractors with larger and more durable tires. In fact, the early 1930s were the period when tractors became powerful enough, and their tires became large enough, to allow the revolution in agricultural productivity which they made possible. Field conjectures about the role of larger engines and better tires, along with the first (pre-interstate) national highway system, in allowing trucks to begin in the 1930s to compete with rail as a carrier of the nation's freight.[53]

A much more prosaic but very important improvement happened in the 1920s that represents a potential source of productivity gains. The "American manufacturing system" had always been known for standardization and its ability to turn out identical components of a product. In chapter 2, we recorded the marvel of European observers at the 1851 Crystal Palace expedition of the American achievement: "Almost all of the American machines did things that the world earnestly wished machines to do."[54] But standardization of parts was not achieved in 1851. There was a proliferation of multiple products for which the purpose was identical; in 1917 it was disclosed that the number of different varieties of single-bit ax offered for sale in the United States to chop down a tree was 994,840. "In this wide range were thirty-four models, four grades, thirty-five brands, eleven finishes, and nineteen sizes."

One of the most important improvements in American industrial efficiency was the establishment by Herbert Hoover of the National Bureau of Standards. Its aim was to create a system of uniformly sized parts, down to screws and bolts, aimed at "simplification of practice, elimination of waste, conservation of materials, minimum training of workers, reduction and savings in supply purchasing and unwieldy inventories, defeat of confusion, and speed in production."[55] One of the triumphs of standardization was the production of millions of universal joints during World War II, required to transform uniform velocity from the driving to the driven shaft of high-speed vehicles. Standardization of parts allowed the Bendix design for these joints to be manufactured by twenty-three additional companies that had no previous experience. An enormous improvement of industrial efficiency was made possible by standardization of such mundane components as nuts, bolts, and screws and the drive to standardization that had begun in the 1920s.[56]

CONCLUSION: WHAT CAUSED THE GREAT LEAP FORWARD?

The most fundamental question of modern economic history is why after two millennia of no growth at all in per capita real output from Roman times to 1750, economic growth moved out of its hibernation and began to wake up.[57] More relevant for our times is the second most important question, why growth has slowed since the 1960s and early 1970s not only in the United States and Japan, but also in much of western Europe. Though the timing of economic growth in Japan and Europe was different as a result of wartime destruction and interwar economic disruption, the slowdown is real; indeed, during the past two decades, labor productivity in the European Union has grown at half the pace of the United States. The third question is the focus of this chapter, why U.S. economic growth was so rapid during the middle of the twentieth century, particularly between 1928 and 1950.

The topic of this chapter focuses on the timing of U.S. economic growth and is as simple as it is perplexing. Why does a decadal plot of growth in U.S. labor productivity and TFP since 1890 look like a trek over a mountain, gradually ascending to the decade of the 1940s and gradually descending since then? The second and third questions are intertwined, for the post-1972 growth slowdown is considered a disappointment precisely because the pace of growth during 1928–72 was so rapid and so unprecedented.

The answers to both the second and third questions are fundamental to this book. This chapter has sought to quantify and then determine the causes of the great leap of labor productivity and TFP growth between the late 1920s and early 1950s, thus accounting for how TFP growth in the decades of 1930–40 and 1940–50 outpaced any others in American history. What was so special about that two-decade interval in which normal economic activity was disrupted by the Great Depression and World War II?

There are many possible explanations, and it is impossible to rank the quantitative importance of most. However, throughout this chapter, we have been able to rule out several potential causes. Education is ruled out, for the secular advance in educational attainment was just as important between 1910–28 and 1950–72 as between 1928–50. Similarly, the shift of Americans from rural farms and small towns to urban life in places having more than 2,500 population proceeded, if anything, slightly slower during 1928–50 than it had between 1870 and 1928.

The most novel aspect of this chapter is its suggestion that the Great Depression and World War II directly contributed to the great leap. Had there been no Great Depression, there probably would have been no New Deal, with its NIRA and Wagner Act that promoted unionization and that directly and indirectly contributed to a sharp rise in real wages and a shrinkage in average weekly hours. In turn, both higher real wages and shorter hours helped to boost productivity growth rapidly in the late 1930s, before the United States entered World War II. Substitution from labor to capital as a result of the jump in the real wage is evident in the data on private equipment investment, which soared in 1937–41 substantially above the equipment investment:capital ratio of the late 1920s.

Another more subtle effect of the Great Depression may have been the reorganization of business after the sharp drop in output and profits generated severe cost-cutting, most notably in the dismissal of employees. Yet output did not fall to zero in the 1930s, and the output that was produced with a lower number of employees reflected new ideas and techniques of efficiency, many of them carried over from the 1920s. Our evidence on the horsepower of motor vehicles, which greatly increased over the 1930s, suggests that the power and efficiency of electric machine tools and hand tools may have similarly experienced a substantial improvement in the 1930s.[58] Indeed, our evidence in table 16–2 implies that there was a sustained increase during 1929–50 in horsepower per unit of constant-cost capital equipment, as well as a vast increase in the amount of electricity consumed per unit of capital.

Less speculative is the productivity-enhancing learning by doing that occurred during the high-pressure economy of World War II. Economists have long studied the steady improvement over time in the speed and efficiency with which Liberty freighter ships were built. The most remarkable aspect of the surge in labor productivity during World War II is that it appears to have been permanent; despite the swift reduction in wartime defense spending during 1945–47, labor productivity did not decline at all during the immediate post-war years. The necessity of war became the mother of invention of improved production techniques, and these innovations, large and small, were not forgotten after the war.

In addition to the increased efficiency of existing plant and equipment, the federal government financed an entirely new part of the manufacturing sector, with newly built plants and newly purchased productive equipment. The high level of postwar productivity was made possible in part because the number of machine tools in the U.S. *doubled* between 1940 and 1945.[59] The amount of additional productive equipment that the federal government purchased to produce private sector output was staggering. Between 1940 and 1945, the federal government purchased productive equipment that amounted to roughly 50 percent of the stock of privately owned equipment that existed before the war in 1941.[60] And because it was all purchased between 1941 and 1945, this capital was more modern and productive than the stock of privately owned capital that existed in 1941.

Going beyond explanations that emerge from the sequence of the Great Depression followed by World War II, we need to consider the pace of innovation itself. Perhaps the most important source of the Great Leap Forward was the increased quality of machinery, as represented by the large increases in horsepower and kilowatt-hour of electricity usage per dollar of equipment capital. For every 100 units of electricity that were added to the productive process during 1902–29, another 230 units were added between 1929 and 1950. Paul David has rightly emphasized the long delay between the first electric power station in 1882 and the revolution in manufacturing productivity in the early 1920s. But this focus on the 1920s as the breakthrough decade misses that the full force of electricity expansion in manufacturing and the rest of the economy took place between 1929 and 1950.

The trauma of the Great Depression did not slow down the American invention machine. If anything, the pace of innovation picked up in the last half of the 1930s. This is clear in the data assembled by Alexopoulos and Cohen on technical books published. The dominance of the 1930s, or more generally the period 1920–1950, is supported by Kleinknecht's count of inventions by decade. Previous chapters have provided evidence of rapid progress in radio, the quality of motion pictures, and a sharp jump in the quality of motor cars. By 1940, automobile manufacturers had achieved the dream of producing automobiles that could go as quickly as the highways would allow them to travel; the development of highways worthy of this technical marvel would wait until the construction of the interstate highway system, largely achieved during 1958–72.

Little attention has been paid in this book to oil and plastics, for these are intermediate goods. However, from the discovery of the east Texas oil field to the development of many types of plastics now considered commonplace, the 1930s added to its luster as a decade of technological advance. The use of plastics in every kind of producer and consumer durable was on the cusp of reality in 1941 before production was diverted to wartime uses. A favorite photograph of the hardships of the World War II home front shows women painting stripes on their legs to replace the rayon and nylon stockings that were no longer available.

Two overriding conclusions emerge from this study of one of the great puzzles of economic growth. First, World War II saved the U.S. economy from secular stagnation, and a hypothetical scenario of economic growth after 1939 that does not include the war looks dismal at best. Second, much more than in traditional economic history, the Great Inventions of the late nineteenth century, especially electricity and the internal combustion engine, continued to alter production methods beyond recognition not just in the 1920s but in the 1930s and 1940s as well. Alex Field revitalized U.S. economic history by his startling claim that the 1930s were the "most progressive decade." For us to determine that labor productivity and TFP growth were even quicker during 1941–50 does not diminish the boldness of Field's imagination with his claim or the depth of evidence that he has marshaled to support it.[61]

Chapter 17

INNOVATION: CAN THE FUTURE MATCH THE GREAT INVENTIONS OF THE PAST?

We wanted flying cars, instead we got 140 characters.

—Peter Thiel

INTRODUCTION

The epochal rise in the U.S. standard of living that occurred from 1870 to 1940, with continuing benefits to 1970, represent the fruits of the Second Industrial Revolution (IR #2). Many of the benefits of this unprecedented tidal wave of inventions show up in measured GDP and hence in output per person, output per hour, and total factor productivity (TFP), which as we have seen grew more rapidly during the half-century 1920–70 than before or since. Beyond their contribution to the record of measured growth, these inventions also benefited households in many ways that escaped measurement by GDP along countless dimensions, including the convenience, safety, and brightness of electric light compared to oil lamps; the freedom from the drudgery of carrying water made possible by clean piped water; the value of human life itself made possible by the conquest of infant mortality; and many others.

The slower growth rate of measured productivity since 1970 constitutes an important piece of evidence that the Third Industrial Revolution (IR #3) associated with computers and digitalization has been less important than IR #2. Not only has the measured record of growth been slower since 1970 than before, but, as we have previously suggested, the unmeasured improvements in the quality of everyday life created by IR #3 are less significant than the more profound set of unmeasured benefits of the earlier industrial revolution. Though there has been continuous innovation since 1970, it has been less broad in its scope than before, focused on entertainment and information and communication technology (ICT), and advances in several dimensions of the standard of living related to food, clothing, appliances, housing, transportation, health, and working conditions have advanced at a slower pace than before 1970.

This chapter addresses the unknown future by examining closely the nature of recent innovations and by comparing them with future aspects of technological change that are frequently cited as most likely to boost the American standard of living over the next few decades. Innovation is proceeding apace, and almost weekly the stock market rewards newly created firms with initial public offering (IPO) valuations of a billion dollars or more. There is no debate about the frenetic pace of innovative activity, particularly in the spheres of digital technology, including robots and artificial intelligence. Instead, this chapter distinguishes between the *pace* of innovation and the *impact* of innovation on the growth rates of labor productivity and TFP.

The chapter begins with a historical overview of the source of inventions since 1870 and emphasizes a U-shaped history in which the role of the individual inventor dominated the late nineteenth century, followed by most of the twentieth century, when major inventions occurred within the research laboratories of giant corporations. After 1975, the individual entrepreneur returned as the modern electronic age was created by individuals such as Bill Gates, Steve Jobs, and Mark Zuckerberg.

Equipped with this historical background, we then examine the quantitative record of progress. The post-1970 years have not witnessed a uniformly slow advance of TFP. Instead the impact on TFP of the inventions of IR #3 were centered on the decade 1994–2004. We describe changes in business practices in the office, in the retail sector, and in the banking and financial sector and find in all cases that current methods of production had been largely achieved by 2004. Along numerous quantitative measures that compare the 1994–2004 decade with the recent past, we find a marked slowing down, leading to the suggestion that the wave of innovation in the late 1990s may have been unique, unlikely to be repeated over our forecasting horizon of the next quarter-century.

The chapter then looks into the future, providing numerous historical examples in which forecasts of the future development of technology turned out to be relatively accurate. We focus on the development of robots and artificial intelligence and assess the forecasts made by "techno-optimists" that the U.S. economy is on the verge of a new surge of productivity growth at the cost of massive future job destruction, as robots replace large numbers of jobs, and as highly sophisticated computer algorithms eliminate analytical jobs from legal searches to personal financial analysis. The chapter concludes with an alternative version of the future in which the job destruction by robots and artificial intelligence proceeds slowly, just as it has over the past several decades. The economy will be able to maintain relatively full employment as the fruits of computerization cause the composition of job types and categories to evolve only slowly rather than in a great rush. The rate of advance of labor productivity and TFP over the next quarter century will resemble the slow pace of 2004–15, not the faster growth rate of 1994–2004, much less the even faster growth rate achieved long ago during 1920–70.

INNOVATION THROUGH HISTORY: THE ULTIMATE RISK-TAKERS

The entrepreneurs who created the great inventions of the late nineteenth century—not just Americans, including Thomas Edison and the Wright Brothers, but also foreigners such as Karl Benz—deserve credit for most of the achievements of IR #2, which created unprecedented advances in the American standard of living in the century after 1870. Individual inventors were the developers not just of new goods, from electric light to the automobile to processed corn flakes to radio, but also of new services such as the department store, mail-order catalog retailing, and the motel by the side of the highway. Although this book's coverage begins in 1870, we should not neglect the role of individuals before that year. Among the Americans notable for pre-1870 inventions are Samuel F. B. Morse for his 1844 invention of the telegraph and Cyrus McCormick for his 1834 invention of the reaper. They were preceded by many British inventors going back to Thomas Newcomen and James Watt (the inventors of the steam engine) and George Stephenson (who shares in the invention of the railroad).

Most studies of long-term economic growth attempt to subdivide the sources of growth among the inputs, particularly the number of worker-hours and the amount of physical capital per worker-hour, and the "residual" that remains after the contributions of labor and capital are subtracted out. That residual, defined initially in Robert Solow's pioneering work of the 1950s, often goes by its nickname "Solow's residual" or by its more formal rubric "total factor productivity" (TFP). Though primarily reflecting the role of innovation and technological change, increases in TFP also respond to other types of economic change going beyond innovation, for instance the movement over time of a large percentage of the working population from low-productivity jobs on the farm to higher-productivity jobs in the city. Solow found, to his own surprise and to others', that only 13 percent of the increase in U.S. output per worker between 1910 and 1950 resulted from an increase in capital per worker; this famous result seemed to "take the capital out of capitalism."

The usual association of TFP growth with innovation misses the point that innovation is the ultimate source of all growth in output per worker-hour, not just the residual after capital investment is subtracted out. Capital investment itself waxes and wanes depending not just on the business cycle but also on the potential profit made possible by investing to produce newly invented or improved products. Without innovation, there would be no accumulation of capital per worker. As Evsey Domar famously wrote in 1961, without technical change, capital accumulation would amount to "piling wooden plows on top of existing wooden plows."[1]

Technological change raises output directly and induces capital accumulation to create the machines and structures needed to implement new inventions. In addition, innovations are the source of improvements in the quality of capital—for example, the transition from the rotary-dial telephone to the iPhone, or from the Marchant calculator to the personal computer running Excel. The standard technique of aggregating capital input by placing a higher weight on short-lived capital such as computers than on long-lived capital like structures has the effect of hiding inside the capital input measure the contribution of innovation in shifting investment from structures to computers.[2]

This leaves education and reallocation as the remaining sources of growth beyond innovation itself. However, both of these also depend on innovation to provide the rewards necessary to make the investment to stay in school or to move from farm to city. This is why there was so little economic growth between the Roman era and 1750, as peasant life remained largely unchanged. Peasants did not have an incentive to become educated, because before the wave of innovations that began around 1750, there was no reward to the acquisition of knowledge beyond how to move a plow and harvest a field. Similarly, without innovation before 1750, the reallocation of labor from farm to city did not happen. It required the innovations that began in the late eighteenth century and that created the great urban industries to provide the incentive of higher wages to induce millions of farm workers to lay down their plows and move to the cities.[3]

Thus every source of growth can be reduced back to the role of innovation and technological change. Pioneers in the development of particular products and industries have been described by Schumpeter as "innovators," those "individuals who are daring, speculative, restless, imaginative and, more pertinently, eager to exploit new inventions."[4] Thus innovators, particularly when acting by themselves or in small partnerships, are the ultimate risk-takers. Their inventions may lead them to create large firms, or their inventions may be supplanted by alternatives that are more efficient and perform better. Or they may have a promising idea and fail to find a source of funding for development of that idea. Invention at the level of the individual "is anything but mechanical, automatic, and predictable. Chance plays a tremendous role."[5]

Few descriptions of the role of risk and chance in the process of invention are as evocative as that of D. H. Killeffer, writing in 1948:

> Inventions do not spring up perfect and ready for use. Their conception is never virginal and must be many times repeated. One seldom knows who the real father is. The period of gestation is long with many false pains and strange forebirths.... Few of the children of the mind ever survive and those only after many operations and much plastic surgery.[6]

William Baumol offers a related caution. Entrepreneurs contribute to economic growth far more than the narrow word "innovation" can convey.

The explosion of U.S. entrepreneurial innovation after the Civil War is documented in figure 17–1, which displays the ratio of patents relative to the total population from 1790 to 2012. The large jump in patents during the 1860–1880 period coincides with the dates of the great inventions of the second industrial revolution, including electric light and power (1879, 1882), the telephone (1876), and the internal combustion engine (1879). Patents per capita remained at a plateau over the interval between 1870 and 1940. There was then a dip through 1985 followed by an explosion, particularly after 1995. Average ratios in figure 17–1 over successive intervals are 18 for 1790–1830, 89 for 1830–1870, 344 from 1870 to 1940, 275 from 1940 to 1985, and then 485 from 1985 to 2012.

The last three decades of the nineteenth century were the glory years of the self-employed American entrepreneur/inventor. Horatio Alger–like fantasies were conjured up by the concrete achievements of inventors like Bell and Edison, whose names were widely known and whose latest inventions were publicized and discussed. The goal of becoming an individual entrepreneur, a

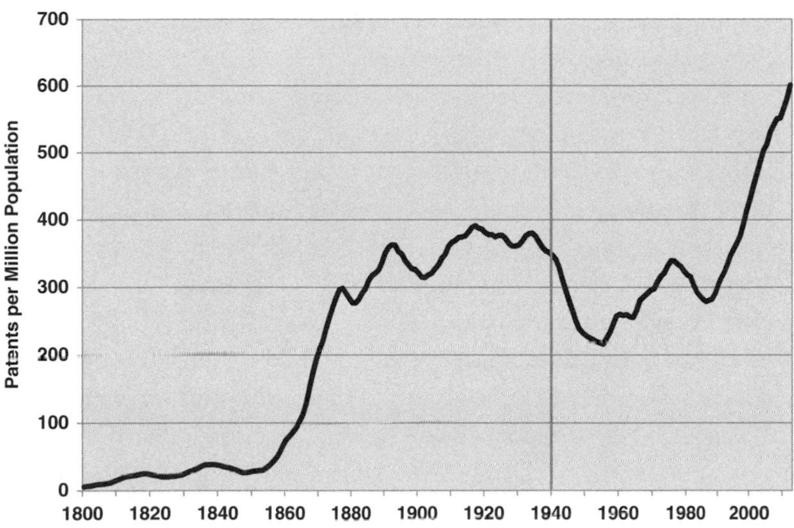

Figure 17–1. U.S. Patents Issued Per Million Population, 10 year Moving Average, 1800–2012

Source: www.uspto.gov/web/offices/ac/ido/oeip/taf/h_couints.pdf, column labeled "Utility Patents (Inventions)."

"self-made man," excited dreams of young men, even if few would be able to follow the steps of social mobility pioneered by Edison. Nevertheless, many of the manufacturing firms of this era were founded by owners who had begun as ordinary workers. To start one's own business—that is, to be an entrepreneur—was a badge of success; to remain a mere employee "was to forsake a life of striving for a condition of dependency—itself a sign of moral failing."[7]

The U-shaped interpretation of entrepreneurial history starts with a primary role for individual entrepreneurs, working by themselves or in small research labs like Edison's.[8] By the 1920s, the role of the individual entrepreneur reached the bottom part of the U, as innovation came to be dominated by employees working for large corporate research laboratories. Much of the early development of the automobile culminating in the powerful Chevrolets and Buicks of 1940–41 was achieved at the GM corporate research labs. Similarly, much of the development of the electronic computer was carried out in the corporate laboratories of IBM, Bell Labs, and other large firms. The transistor, the fundamental building block of modern electronics and digital innovation, was invented by a team led by William Shockley at Bell Labs in late 1947.[9] The corporate R&D division of IBM pioneered most of the advances of the mainframe computer era from 1950 to 1980. Improvements in consumer electric appliances occurred at large firms such as General Electric, General Motors, and Whirlpool, while RCA led the early development of television.

But then the process began to climb the right side of the U as the seminal developments of the transition from mainframes to personal computers and the Internet were pioneered by individual entrepreneurs. A pivotal point in this transition was the decision of IBM, the developer in 1981 of the first widely purchased personal computer, to farm out not just the conception of the operating system software, but also the ownership of that software, to two young entrepreneurs, Paul Allen and the Harvard dropout Bill Gates, who had founded Microsoft in 1975. The Third Industrial Revolution, which consists of the computer, digitalization, and communication inventions of the past fifty years, has been dominated by small companies founded by individual entrepreneurs, each of whom created organizations that soon became very large corporations. Allen and Gates were followed by Steve Jobs at Apple, Jeff Bezos at Amazon, Sergei Brin and Larry Page at Google, Mark Zuckerberg at Facebook, and many others.

The left side of the entrepreneurial U is well documented. The percentage of all U.S. patents granted to individuals (as contrasted with business firms) fell from 95 percent in 1880 to 73 percent in 1920, to 42 percent in 1940, and then gradually to 21 percent in 1970 and 15 percent in 2000. Of the remainder, until 1950, almost all were granted to U.S. firms, but after 1950, the share going to foreign firms soared until in 2000 the 85 percent not granted to individuals were divided almost evenly, with 44 percent going to U.S. firms and 41 percent to foreign firms. Nicholas attributes the decline in the share of independent invention to the growth of "complex capital-intensive areas such as chemicals and electricity."[10]

The declining role of individuals occurred not just because of the increased capital requirements of ever more complex products, but also because the individuals who developed the most successful products formed large business enterprises, including Bell, Edison, and Ford, among many others. Edison's early light bulb patents ran out in the mid-1890s, leading to the establishment of General Electric laboratories to develop better filaments. By the same time Bell's initial telephone invention had become the giant AT&T, which established its own laboratory (which eventually became known as Bell Labs); by 1915, it had developed amplifiers that made feasible nationwide long-distance telephone calls.[11] Successive inventions were then credited to the firm rather than to the individual. Furthermore, a natural process of diminishing returns occurred in each industry. The number of patents issued in three industries that were new in the early twentieth century—the automobile, airplane, and radio—exhibit an initial explosion of patent activity followed by a plateau—or, in the case of automobiles after 1925, an absolute decline.[12] Richard Nelson describes this pattern as widespread:

> Following the breakthrough of a basic invention, there is at first a rising, then a falling, rate of increase in practical adoptions of the new invention. In time the new invention is made obsolete by still newer inventions, and its use declines or falls off entirely.[13]

Individual inventors flourished in the United States in part because of the democratic nature of the patenting system. From the beginning, the U.S. patent system was self-consciously designed to be different from European systems, "and nearly all of [the] alterations can be viewed as extending effective property rights in technological discoveries to classes of the population that would not have enjoyed them under traditional intellectual property institutions."[14] Detailed specifications of any patented invention were required to be made public immediately, and the patent fee was set at only 5 percent of the amount charged in Britain.[15] Patents solved the problem of theft of intellectual property in an environment in which inventors needed to learn about the latest inventions that might be complementary or perhaps a key ingredient in their own newest developments. In the United States, trade in patented technologies through licensing was much more extensive than in Europe, and as a result, "technologically creative people without the capital to go into business and directly exploit the fruits of their ingenuity were major beneficiaries."[16]

The low cost of patents fostered a unique aspect of American invention—that many of the inventors had only an elementary or secondary education. The patent system allowed them to develop their ideas without a large investment in obtaining a patent; once the patent was granted, even inventors who had a low personal income were able to attract capital funding and also to sell licenses. The U.S. patent system was revolutionary "in its extension of effective property rights in to an extremely wide spectrum of the population. Moreover, it was exceptional in recognizing that it was in the public interest that patent rights, like other property rights, should be clearly defined and well enforced, with low transaction costs."[17]

The democratic nature of the U.S. patent system may help to explain why so many of the Great Inventions of the late nineteenth century happened in the United States rather than in Europe. In a famous example discussed in chapter 6, on February 14, 1876, both Elisha Gray and Alexander Graham Bell arrived at the patent office to register their competing telephone technologies. Bell arrived a few hours earlier and became rich and famous, and Gray was forgotten. Years earlier, Antonio Meucci had developed his own version of the telephone but could not afford the patent application process in Italy.

Appearing to contradict the U-shaped evolution of innovation by individuals is the failure of the patent share of individuals to turn around after 1980. Instead, that share remains flat at 15 percent, down from 95 percent in 1880. This may be explained by the more rapid formation of corporations by individuals in the past three decades than in the late nineteenth century. Though the Harvard dropout Bill Gates may be said to have invented personal computer operating systems for the IBM personal computer, almost all Gates's patents were obtained after he formed the Microsoft corporation in 1975 (six years before IBM granted Microsoft the right to design and sell software for the earliest IBM PC). The same goes for the other individuals who developed Google's search software and Facebook's social network. Even though this wave of innovation is credited by the Patent Office to firms rather than individuals, it was made possible by individual inventors and entrepreneurs more directly than the earlier twentieth-century inventions of Bell Labs and the other large corporate research organizations.

THE HISTORICAL RECORD: THE GROWTH OF TOTAL FACTOR PRODUCTIVITY

We previously learned in figures 1–2 and 16–5 that growth in total factor productivity (TFP) was much faster between 1920 and 1970 than either before 1920 or since 1970. Now we take a closer look at the behavior of TFP growth for the years since 1970. Shown by vertical bars in figure 17–2 are the growth rates of TFP for 1890–1920, 1920–1970, and three subperiods since 1970. The first of these intervals, 1970–94, exhibits TFP growth of only 0.57 percent per year, less than a third of the 1.89 percent growth rate achieved in the fifty years before 1970. Then the two most recent decades between 1994 and 2014 are shown separately, with TFP growth notably faster in 1994–2004 than in the other two post-1970 intervals. Black is used to fill in the bars for the two

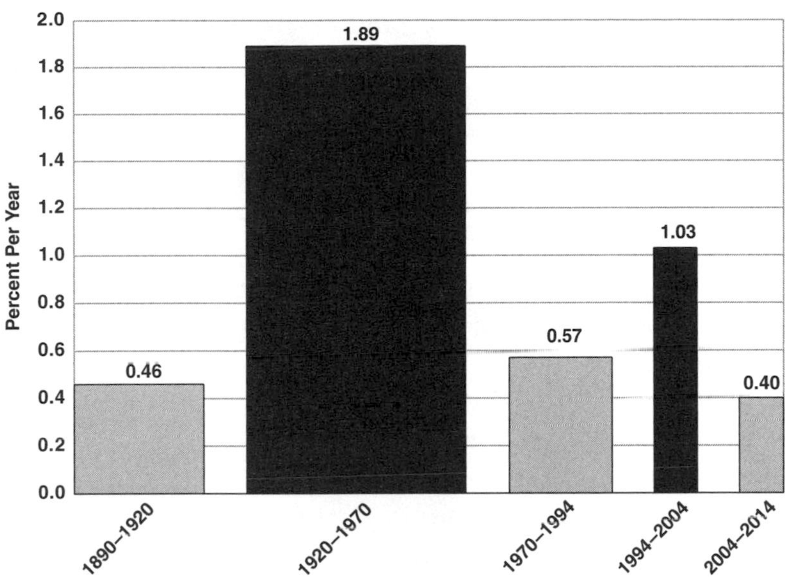

Figure 17–2. Annualized Growth Rates of Total Factor Productivity, 1890–2014

Source: Data underlying Figure 16–5.

periods with relatively rapid TFP growth—1920–70 and 1994–2004. Light gray is used to show the contrast with all the other intervals in which TFP growth is below 0.6 percent per year.

The contrast between the black and gray bars in figure 17–2 supports our interpretation that the great surge in the level of TFP was achieved primarily between 1920 and 1970 and was the result of the implementation and extension of many of the great inventions associated with the Second Industrial Revolution (IR #2) of the late nineteenth century. The brief revival of TFP growth in 1994–2004 reflects the contribution of the Third Industrial Revolution (IR #3) associated with computers and digitalization. Judged by their contributions to TFP growth, the two industrial revolutions were quite different—IR #2 created a great surge of TFP growth that lasted for a half century, while IR #3 caused a revival in TFP growth during 1994–2004 that was much shorter lived and smaller in magnitude.

The overwhelming dominance of the 1920–70 interval in making possible the modern world is clearly demonstrated. Though the great inventions of IR #2 mainly took place between 1870 and 1900, at first their effect was small. Paul David has provided a convincing case that almost four decades were required after Edison's first 1882 power station for the development of the machines and methods that finally allowed the electrified factory to emerge in the 1920s. Similarly, Karl Benz's invention of the first reliable internal combustion engine in 1879 was followed by two decades in which inventors experimented with brakes, transmissions, and other ancillary equipment needed to transfer the engine's power to axles and wheels. Even though the first automobiles appeared in 1897, they did not gain widespread acceptance until the price reductions made possible by Henry Ford's moving assembly line, introduced in 1913.

Why did the growth of TFP accelerate so rapidly after 1920, and why was the influence of IR#2 so profound? The saga of the roaring 1920s, followed by the dislocations of the Great Depression and World War II, disguises a rapid pace of innovation and implementation that started in the 1920s and took flight (both figuratively and literally) in the 1930s and 1940s, a story told in chapter 16. The digital revolution, IR #3, also had its main effect on TFP after a long delay. Even though the mainframe computer transformed many business practices starting in the 1960s, and the personal computer largely replaced the typewriter and calculator by the 1980s, the main effect of IR #3 on TFP was delayed until the 1994–2004 decade, when the invention of the Internet, web browsing, search engines, and e-commerce produced a pervasive change in every aspect of business practice.

Growth in output per person, our best measure of the rate of improvement in the standard of living, can proceed no faster than growth in output per hour unless hours worked per person exhibit an increase. Yet the ongoing retirement of the baby-boom generation, as we shall see in chapter 18, is already causing a decline in hours worked per person that is likely to continue for most of the next twenty-five years. Thus future growth in output per person will fall short of growth in output per hour, bringing labor productivity growth and its ultimate source, the pace of innovation as measured by TFP, to center stage in any discussion of the future of growth in American well-being. Accordingly, the chronology of figure 17–2 raises three important questions that will concern us throughout the rest of this chapter. First, why was the main effect of IR #3 on TFP so short-lived that its duration was limited to the 1994–2004 decade? Second, why was TFP growth so slow in the most recent 2004–14 decade? Third, what are the implications of slow recent TFP growth for the future evolution of TFP and labor productivity over the next quarter century?

ACHIEVEMENTS TO DATE OF THE THIRD INDUSTRIAL REVOLUTION

The third industrial revolution (IR #3) encompasses the digital age of information and communication technology (ICT), beginning with the first mainframe computers in the late 1950s and continuing until today and beyond. As we have seen, its main impact on TFP growth was limited to the 1994–2004 decade. It was driven by an unprecedented and never-repeated rate of decline in the price of computer speed and memory and a never-since-matched surge in the share of GDP devoted to investment in information and communication technology (ICT) investment.

The mediocre performance of TFP growth after 2004 underlines the temporary nature of the late 1990s revival. More puzzling is the absence of any apparent stimulus to TFP growth in the quarter-century between 1970 and 1994. Mainframe computers created bank statements and phone bills in the 1960s and powered airline reservation systems in the 1970s. Personal computers, ATMs, and barcode scanning were among the innovations that created productivity growth in the 1980s. Reacting to the failure of these innovations to boost productivity growth, Robert Solow quipped, "You can see the computer age everywhere but in the productivity statistics."[18] Slow TFP growth in this period indicates that the benefits of the first round of computer applications partially masked an even more severe slowdown in productivity growth than would have occurred otherwise in the rest of the economy.

The achievements of IR #3 can be divided into two major categories: communications and information technology. Within communications, progress started with the 1983 breakup of the Bell Telephone monopoly into nonoverlapping regional monopolies. After a series of mergers, landline service was provided primarily by a new version of AT&T and by Verizon, soon to be joined by major cable television companies, such as Comcast and Time-Warner, that offered landline phone service as part of their cable TV and Internet packages.

The major advance in the communications sphere was the mobile phone, which made a quick transition from heavyweight bricklike models in the 1980s to the sleek small instruments capable by the late 1990s of phoning, messaging, e-mailing, and photography. The final communications revolution occurred in 2007 with the introduction by Apple of the iPhone, soon to be imitated by Google's Android operating system installed on phones manufactured mainly by foreign-owned companies such as Korea's Samsung. By 2015, there were 183 million smartphone users in the United States, or roughly sixty per

100 members of the population.[19] Though landline phone service was dominated by one or two providers in most metropolitan areas, landline phones were becoming increasingly irrelevant in the presence of smartphones; six companies competed vigorously to attract smartphone subscribers.

The "I" and the "T" of ICT began in the 1960s with the mainframe computer, which eliminated boring and routine clerical labor previously needed to prepare telephone bills, bank statements, and insurance policies. Credit cards would not have been possible without mainframe computers to keep track of the billions of transactions. Gradually electric memory typewriters and later personal computers eliminated repetitive retyping of everything from legal briefs to academic manuscripts. In the 1980s, three additional standalone electronic inventions introduced a new level of convenience into everyday life. The first of these was the ATM, which made personal contact with bank tellers unnecessary. In retailing, two devices greatly raised the productivity and speed of the checkout process: the barcode scanner and the authorization devices that read credit cards and within seconds denied or approved a transaction.

The late 1990s, when TFP growth finally revived, witnessed the marriage of computers and communication. Suddenly within the brief half-decade interval between 1993 and 1998, the standalone computer was linked to the outside world through the Internet, and by the end of the 1990s, web browsers, web surfing, and e-mail had become universal. The market for Internet services exploded, and by 2004, most of today's Internet giants had been founded. Throughout every sector, paper and typewriters were replaced by flat screens running powerful software. Professors no longer need to subscribe to or store academic journals. Instead they can access JSTOR, which has 8,000 subscribing institutions and provides full-text access to more than 2,000 journals.[20]

Although IR #3 was revolutionary, its effect was felt in a limited sphere of human activity, in contrast to IR #2, which changed everything. Categories of personal consumption expenditures that felt little effect from the ICT revolution were the purchase of food for consumption at home and away from home, clothing and footwear, motor vehicles and fuel to make them move, furniture, household supplies, and appliances. In 2014, fully two-thirds of consumption expenditures went for services, including rent, health care, education, and personal care. Barber and beauty shops were joined by tanning and nail salons, but the ICT revolution had virtually no effect. A pedicure is a pedicure regardless of whether the customer is reading a magazine (as would occur a decade ago) or reading a book on a Kindle or surfing the web on a smartphone.

This brings us back to Solow's quip—that we can see the computer age everywhere but in the productivity statistics. The final answer to Solow's computer paradox is that computers are not everywhere. We don't eat computers or wear them or drive to work in them or let them cut our hair. We live in dwelling units that have appliances much like those of the 1950s, and we drive in motor vehicles that perform the same functions as in the 1950s, albeit with more convenience and safety.

What are the implications of the uneven progress of TFP as shown in figure 17–2? Should the 0.40 percent growth rate of the most recent 2004–14 decade be considered the most relevant basis for future growth? Or should our projection for the future be partly or largely based on the 1.03 percent average TFP growth achieved by the decade 1994–2004? There are several reasons, beyond the temporary nature of the TFP growth recovery in 1994–2004, to regard those years as unique and not relevant for the next several decades.

COULD THE THIRD INDUSTRIAL REVOLUTION BE ALMOST OVER?

What factors caused the TFP growth revival of the late 1990s to be so temporary and to die out so quickly? Most of the economy has already benefited from the Internet and web revolution, and in this sphere of economic activity, methods of production have been little changed over the past decade. Across the economy, paper-dependent business procedures had by 2004 been replaced by digitalization, and flat screens were everywhere. The revolutions in everyday life made possible by e-commerce and search engines were already well established—Amazon dates back to 1994, Google to 1998, and Wikipedia as well as iTunes to 2001. Facebook, founded in 2004, is now more than a decade old. Will future innovations be sufficiently powerful and widespread to duplicate the relatively brief revival in productivity growth that occurred between 1994 and 2004?[21] Supporting the data showing that TFP growth was less than half as quick during 2004–14 as during 1994–2004 is the appearance that changes in business practices have been substantially slower within the most recent decade than during the prior decade.

A Slowing Transformation of Business Practices. The digital revolution centered on 1970–2000 utterly changed the way offices function. In 1970, the electronic calculator had just been introduced, but the computer terminal was still in the future. Office work required innumerable clerks to operate the keyboards of electric typewriters that had no ability to download content from the rest of the world and that, lacking a memory, required repetitive retyping of everything from legal briefs to academic research papers. Starting from this world of 1970, by 2000 every office was equipped with web-linked personal computers that not only could perform any word-processing task, but also could perform any type of calculation at blinding speed as well as download multiple varieties of content. By 2005, flat screens had completed the transition to the modern office, and broadband service had replaced dial-up service at home. But then progress slowed. Throughout the world, the equipment used in office work and the productivity of office employees closely resembles that of a decade ago.[22] And business productivity continues to enjoy the permanent increase in personal comfort on the job that was achieved between 1930 and 1970 by the introduction of air conditioning into every office setting.

A part of the great transition that was achieved in the 1980s and 1990s was the catalog revolution. Even before the web became pervasive in the late 1990s, libraries had already converted from wooden boxes of paper card catalogs to electronic catalogs that doubled not only as search tools but as inventory managers, indicating for every search result whether the book or periodical was on the shelf. The parts departments at automobile dealers made a transition at the same time to electronic catalogs from enormous binders into which multiple replacement pages had to be inserted every day. Hardware stores, book stores, garden nurseries, and, indeed, any retail store selling a large number of varieties of products shifted to electronic catalogs over proprietary computer networks even before the web allowed direct consumer contact with each merchant's catalog. The important point is that this transition from paper to electronic catalogs happened fifteen to twenty-five years ago and represented a one-time-only source of a jump in the *level* of productivity—hence a temporary rather than permanent increase in the *growth rate* of productivity.

In the past decade business practices, while relatively unchanged in the office, have steadily improved outside of the office as smartphones and tablets have become standard business equipment. A television service repair person arrives not with a paper work order and clipboard, but rather with a multipurpose smartphone. Product specifications and communication codes are available on the phone, and the customer completes the transaction by scrawling a signature on the phone screen. Paper has been replaced almost everywhere outside of the office. Airlines are well along in equipping pilots with smart tablets that contain all the information previously provided by large paper manuals. Maintenance crews at Exelon's six nuclear power stations in Illinois are the latest to be trading in their three-ring binders for iPads. The switch to tablets boosts productivity by eliminating not just the expense of the paper but also of photocopying and filing. "Interactivity, from email to downloads, means that maintenance workers can use tablets to get answers more quickly."[23]

A leading puzzle of the current age is why the near-ubiquity of smartphones and tablets has been accompanied by such slow economy-wide productivity growth, particularly since 2009. One answer is that smartphones are used in the office for personal activities. Some 90 percent of office workers, whether using their office personal computers or their smartphones, visit recreational web sites during the work day. Almost the same percentage admit that they send personal e-mails and more than half report shopping for personal purposes during work time. "Tracking software suggests that 70 percent of employees visit retail sites."[24]

Stasis in Retailing. Since the development of "big-box" retailers in the 1980s and 1990s, and the conversion of checkout aisles to barcode scanners, little has changed in the retail sector. Payment methods have gradually changed from cash and checks to credit and debit cards. In the early years of credit cards in the 1970s and 1980s, checkout clerks had to make voice phone calls for authorization, then there was a transition to terminals that would dial the authorization phone number, and now the authorization arrives within a few seconds. The big-box retailers brought with them many other aspects of the productivity revolution. Walmart and others transformed supply chains, wholesale distribution, inventory management, pricing, and product selection, but that productivity-enhancing shift away from traditional small-scale retailing is largely over. The retail productivity revolution is high on the list of the many accomplishments of IR #3 that are largely completed and will be difficult to surpass in the next several decades.

What is often forgotten is that we are well into the computer age, and many Home Depots and local supermarkets have self-checkout lines that allow customers to scan their groceries or paint cans through a standalone terminal. But except for small orders, doing so takes longer, and customers still voluntarily wait in line for a human instead of taking the option of the no-wait self-checkout lane. The same theme—that the most obvious uses of electronic devices have already happened—pervades commerce. Airport baggage sorting belts are mechanized, as is most of the process of checking in for a flight. But at least one human agent is still needed at each airline departure gate to deal with seating issues and stand-by passengers.

While the main impact on retail productivity growth of big-box stores and warehouse clubs had largely occurred by a decade ago, the past decade has witnessed the continued rapid growth of e-commerce that inherently operates at a higher level of labor productivity than brick-and-mortar retail stores. While nominal annual e-commerce sales grew 11-fold from 2000 to 2014, the share of e-commerce in all retail sales in 2014 was still only 6.4 percent, a fraction too small for e-commerce to have a major impact on productivity growth in the overall retail sector, much less in the economy as a whole (see Hortaçsu and Syverson, 2015, p. 7).

A Plateau of Activity in Finance and Banking. The ICT revolution changed finance and banking along many dimensions from the humble street-corner ATM to the development of fast trading on the stock exchanges. Both the ATM and billion-share trading days are creations of the 1980s and 1990s. Average daily shares transacted on the New York Stock Exchange increased from only 3.5 million in 1960 to 1.7 billion in 2005 and then declined to around 1.2 billion per day in early 2015. Figure 17–3 shows the average annual growth rate of shares transacted over five-year intervals, with the first bar referring to 1960–65 and the final (negative) bar displaying the growth rate for 2010–15.[25] Nothing much has changed in more than a decade, except for the ups and downs of stock prices, and despite all those ATMs—and a transition by many customers to managing their bank accounts online rather than by visiting bank

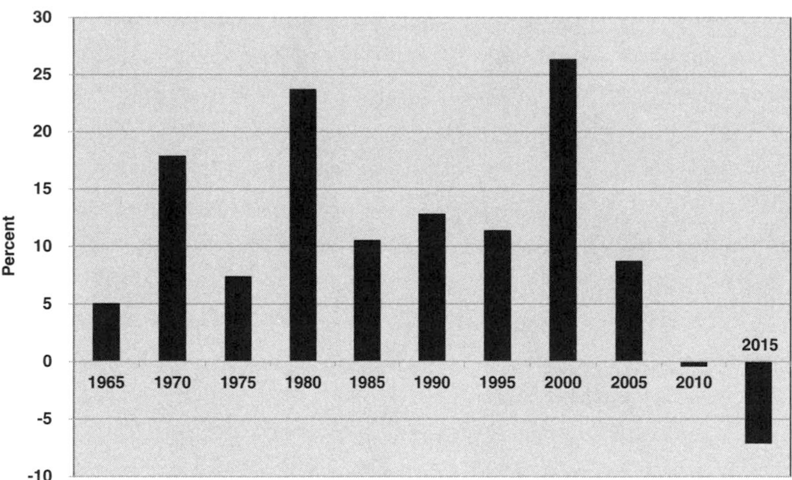

Figure 17–3. Average Annual Growth Rate of Daily Shares Traded on New York Stock Exchange, 1960–2015

Source: https://www.nyse.com/data/transactions-statistics-data-library. Each column reflects the annualized growth of the average volume traded in the first full week of each year.

branches—the nation still maintains a system of 97,000 bank branches, many of which are empty much of the time, and employment of bank tellers has declined only from 484,000 in 1985 to 361,000 recently.[26] James Bessen explains the longevity of bank branches in part by the effect of ATMs in reducing the number of employees needed per branch from about twenty in 1988 to a little more than thirteen in 2004. That meant it was less expensive for a bank to open a branch, leading banks to increase the number of bank branches by 43 percent over the same period between 1988 and 2004. This provides an example that the effect of robots, in this case ATMs, in causing a destruction of jobs is often greatly exaggerated. Bessen shows also that the invention of bookkeeping software did not prevent the number of accounting clerks from growing substantially between 1999 and 2009, although other evidence suggests that corporate financial software is continuing to reduce employment in corporate finance departments.[27]

The Home and Consumer Electronics. Each of the sectors discussed above (office work, retailing, finance, banking) went through fundamental and transformative changes in the 1980s and 1990s. Only within the past decade have computer hardware, software, and business methods ossified into a slowly changing set of routines. In contrast to the decade or so of stability in procedures at work, life inside the home has been stable not for a single decade, but for nearly a half century. By the 1950s, all the major household appliances (washer, dryer, refrigerator, range, dishwasher, and garbage disposer) had been invented, and by the early 1970s, they had reached most American households. Besides the microwave oven, the most important change has been the comfort provided by air conditioning; by 2010, almost 70 percent of American dwelling units were equipped with central air conditioning.

Aside from air conditioning, the major changes in the home in the half century since 1965 were all in the categories of entertainment, communication, and information devices. Television made its transition to color between 1965 and 1972, then variety increased with cable television in the 1970s and 1980s, and finally picture quality was improved with high-definition signals and receiving sets. Variety increased even further when Blockbuster and then Netflix made it possible to rent an almost infinite variety of motion picture DVDs, and now movie streaming has become common. For the past decade, homes have had access to entertainment and information through fast broadband connections to the web, and smartphones have made the web portable. But now that smartphones and tablets have saturated their potential market, further advances in consumer electronics have become harder to achieve. The sense that technical change is slowing down in consumer electronic goods was palpable at the 2014 Consumer Electronics Show (CES):

> But in some ways, this show was a far cry from the shows of old.... [O]ver the years it has been the place to spot some real innovations. In 1970, the videocassette recorder was introduced at CES. In 1981 the compact disc player had its debut there. High definition TV was unveiled in 1998, the Microsoft Xbox in 2001. This year's crop of products seemed a bit underwhelming by comparison. The editor of...a gadget website [said] "this industry that employs all of these engineers, and has all of these factories and salespeople, needs you to throw out your old stuff and buy new stuff—even if that new stuff is only slightly upgraded."[28]

Decline in Business Dynamism. Recent research has used the word "dynamism" to describe the process of creative destruction by which new startups and young firms are the source of productivity gains that occur when they introduce best-practice technologies and methods as they shift resources away from old low-productivity firms. As shown in figure 17–4, the share of all business firms

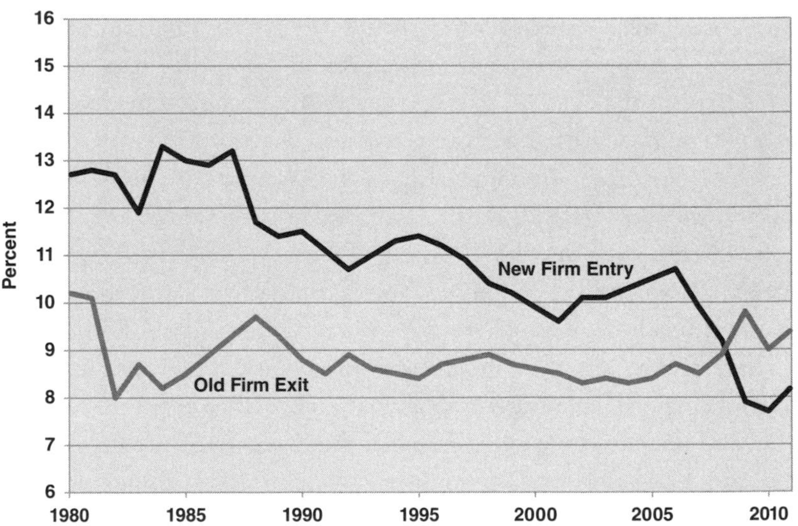

Figure 17–4. Rate of New Firm Entry and Old Firm Exit, 1980–2011
Source: Hathaway and Litan (2014).

consisting of young firms (aged five years or younger) declined from 14.6 percent in 1978 to only 8.3 percent in 2011 even as the share of firms exiting (going out of business) remained roughly constant in the range of 8–10 percent. It is notable that the share of young entering firms had already declined substantially before the 2008–9 financial crisis.[29] Measured another way, the share of total employment accounted for by firms no older than five years declined by almost half from 19.2 percent in 1982 to 10.7 percent in 2011. This decline was pervasive across retailing and services, and after 2000 the high-tech sector experienced a large decline in startups and fast-growing young firms.[30] In another measure of the decline in dynamism, the percentage of people younger than 30 who owned stakes in private companies declined from 10.6 percent in 1989 to 3.6 percent in 2014.[31]

Related research on labor market dynamics points to a decline in "fluidity" as job reallocation rates fell more than a quarter after 1990, and worker reallocation rates fell more than a quarter after 2000. Slower job and worker reallocation means that new job opportunities are less plentiful and it is harder to gain employment after long jobless spells. "For the employed it hampers their ability to switch employers so as to move up a job ladder, change careers, and satisfy locational constraints.... [J]ob mobility facilitates wage growth and career advancement."[32] This line of active current research has uncovered multiple dimensions of the declining "dynamism of American society" as indicated by the declining pace of startups, job creation, job destruction, and internal migration.[33]

OBJECTIVE MEASURES OF SLOWING ECONOMIC GROWTH

Thus far this section has provided two measures of a slowing pace of economic progress—the end of growth in stock market shares transacted and a sharp decline in business dynamism measured by the rate of entry of newly created business firms. These indicators coincide with the sharp decline in the growth of TFP that occurs when the most recent decade, 2004–14, is compared with the prior decade, 1994–2004. We now turn to additional objective measures that uniformly depict an economy that experienced a spurt of productivity and innovation in the 1994–2004 decade but that has slowed since then, in some cases to a crawl.

Manufacturing Capacity. The Federal Reserve reports monthly its Index of Industrial Production and Industrial Capacity, as well as the ratio of the two, the rate of capacity utilization. Shown in figure 17–5 is the annual growth rate of manufacturing capacity since 1980. The uniqueness of the 1994–2004 decade is evident, as the five-year growth rate of manufacturing capacity proceeded at

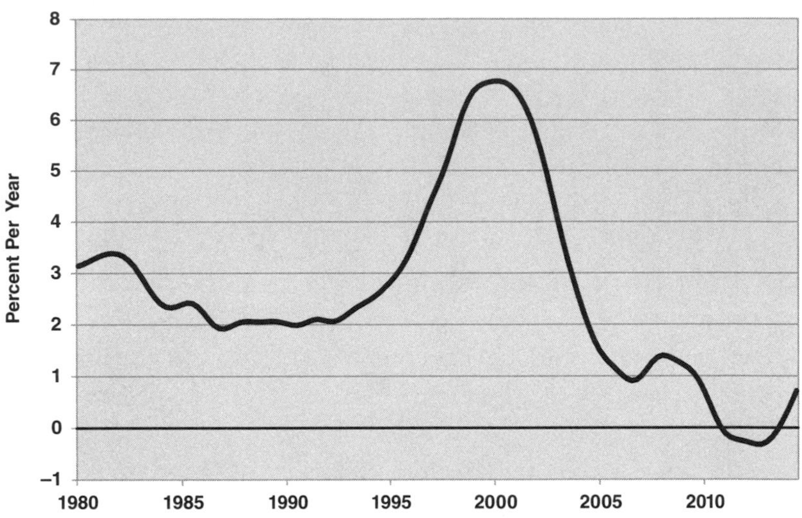

Figure 17–5. Quarterly Annualized Five-Year Change in Manufacturing Capacity, 1980–2014

Source: www.federalreserve.gov/datadownload/default.htm, G.17.

an annual rate between 2 percent and 3 percent from 1972 to 1994, surged to almost 7 percent in the late 1990s, and then came back down, reaching a negative growth rate in 2012. The role of ICT investment in temporarily driving up the growth rate of manufacturing capacity in the late 1990s is well known. Martin Baily and Barry Bosworth have emphasized that if ICT production is stripped out of the manufacturing data, TFP growth in manufacturing has been an unimpressive 0.3 percent per year between 1987 and 2011.[34] Daron Acemoglu and coauthors have also found that the impact of ICT on productivity disappears once the ICT-producing industries are excluded; their finding is that for the remaining industries there is no tendency for labor productivity to grow faster in industries that are "ICT-intensive"—that is, that have a relatively high ratio of expenditures on computer equipment to their expenditures on total capital equipment.[35]

Net Investment. The second reason that the productivity revival of the late 1990s is unlikely to be repeated anytime soon is the behavior of net investment. As shown in figure 17–6, the ratio of net investment to the capital stock (shown as a five-year moving average) has been trending down since the 1960s relative to its 1950–2007 average value of 3.2 percent. In fact, during the entire period 1986–2013, the ratio exceeded that 3.2 percent average value for

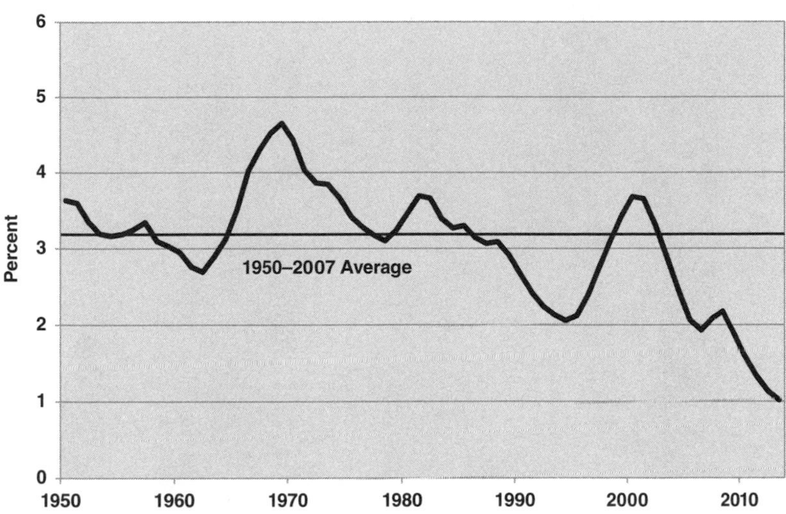

Figure 17–6. Five-Year Moving Average of Ratio of Net Private Business Investment to Private Business Capital Stock, 1950–2013

Sources: BEA Fixed Assets Accounts, Tables 4.1, 4.4, and 4.7.

only four years, 1999–2002, that was within the interval of the productivity growth revival. The 1.0 percent value of the moving average in 2013 was less than half of the previous value in 1994 and less than a third of the 3.2 percent 1950–2007 average. Thus the investment needed to support a repeat of the late 1990s productivity revival has been missing during the past decade.

Computer Performance. Another piece of evidence that the late 1990s were unique refers to the rate of improvement in computer performance. The 1996–2000 interval witnessed the most rapid rate of decline in performance-adjusted prices of ICT equipment recorded to date. The quicker the rate of decline in the ICT equipment deflator, the more quickly the price of computers is declining relative to their performance, or the more quickly computer performance is increasing relative to its price. As shown in the top frame of figure 17–7, the rate of decline of the ICT equipment deflator peaked at −14 percent in 1999 but then steadily diminished to barely minus 1 percent in 2010–14. The slowing rate of improvement of ICT equipment has been reflected in a sharp slowdown in the contribution of ICT as a factor of production to growth in labor productivity. The latest estimates of the ICT contribution by Gilbert Cette and coauthors declines from 0.52 percentage points per year during 1995–2004 to 0.19 points per year during 2004–2013.[36]

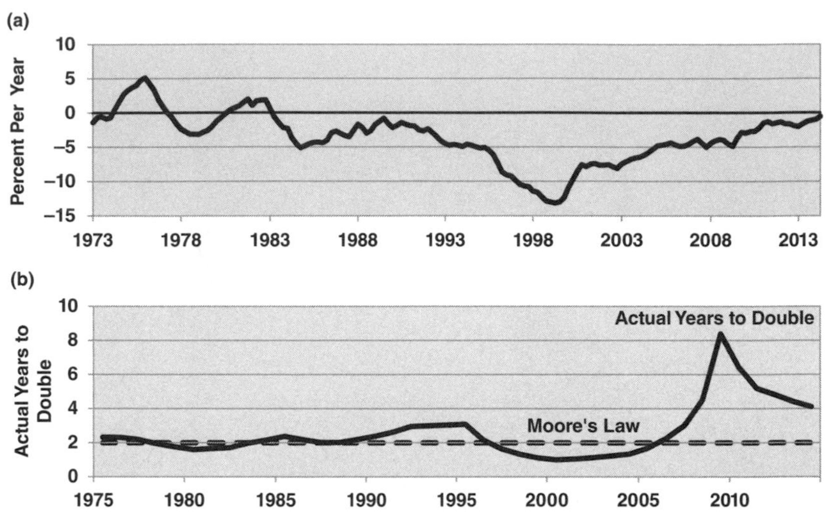

Figure 17–7. a. Annual Change of Price Index for Information and Communication Technology, 1973–2014. b. Years Taken for Number of Transistors on a Chip to Double, 1975–2014

Source: (a) NIPA Table 5.3.4. (b) Data underlying Figure 13–1.

Moore's Law. We learned in chapter 13 that the late 1990s were not only a period of rapid decline in the prices of computer power, but also simultaneously a period of rapid change in the progress of computer chip technology. Moore's Law was originally formulated in 1965 as a forecast that the number of transistors on a computer chip would double every two years. The horizontal dashed line in the bottom frame of figure 17–7 at a vertical distance of two years represents the prediction of Moore's Law. The black line plots the actual doubling time, which followed the predicted value of almost exactly two years with uncanny accuracy between 1975 and 1990. Then the doubling time crept up to three years during 1992–96, followed by a plunge to less than eighteen months between 1999 and 2003. Indeed, the acceleration of technical progress in chip technology in the bottom frame of figure 17–7 was the underlying cause of the rapid decline in the ratio of price-to-performance for computer equipment shown in the top frame. The doubling time reached a trough of fourteen months in 2000, roughly the same time as the peak rate of decline in the computer deflator. But since 2006, Moore's Law has gone off the rails: The doubling time soared to eight years in 2009 and then declined gradually to four years in 2014.

Kenneth Flamm examines the transition over the past decade toward a substantially slower rate of improvement in computer chips and in the quality-corrected performance of computers themselves. His data show that the "clock speed," a measure of computer performance, has been on a plateau of no change at all since 2003, despite a continuing increase in the number of transistors squeezed onto computer chips. He concludes:

> The weight of empirical evidence developed and reviewed in this paper suggests that since 2003, there have been notable reductions in both the rate of price decline, and in the pace of technical innovation, in the semiconductor manufacturing industry generally, and the microprocessor manufacturing industry in particular.... [T]here will be a significant and widely felt economic downside to a reduction in the rate of innovation in semiconductor manufacturing. A slackening of declines in IT hardware prices will, through the same causal links, reduce productivity growth across the broad economy relative to what it would have been had the faster pace of innovation continued.[37]

These four factors unique to the late 1990s—the surge in manufacturing capacity, the rise in the net investment ratio, the trough in the rate of decline in computer prices with the associated decline in the contribution of ICT capital to labor productivity growth, and the shift in the timing of Moore's Law—all create a strong case that the dot-com era of the late 1990s was unique in its conjunction of factors that boosted growth in labor productivity and of TFP well above both the rate achieved during 1970–94 and during 2004–14. There are no signs in recent data that anything like the dot-com era is about to recur—manufacturing capacity growth turned negative during 2011–12 and the net investment ratio fell during 2009–13 to barely a third of its postwar average.

CAN FUTURE INNOVATION BE PREDICTED?

What is in store for the next twenty-five years? Will technological change accelerate and push TFP well above its rate of the past forty years? Or does the slow TFP growth achieved in the most recent 2004–14 decade indicate that the dot-com revolution of the prior 1994–2004 decade was sui generis, an accomplishment unlikely to be repeated? Before speculating about the future, we need to ask whether any such attempt at forecasting is feasible.

The usual stance of economic historians, including my colleague Joel Mokyr, is that the human brain is incapable of forecasting future innovations. He states without qualification that "History is always a bad guide to the future and economic historians should avoid making predictions."[38] He assumes that an instrument is necessary for an outcome. As an example, it would have been impossible for Pasteur to discover his germ theory of disease if Joseph A. Lister had not invented the achromatic-lens microscope in the 1820s. Mokyr's optimism about future technological progress rests partly on the dazzling array of new tools that have arrived recently to create further research advances—"DNA sequencing machines and cell analysis," "high-powered computers," and "astronomy, nanochemistry, and genetic engineering." One of Mokyr's central tools in facilitating scientific advance is "blindingly fast search tools" so that all of human knowledge is instantly available.

Mokyr's examples of future progress do not center on digitalization but rather involve fighting infectious diseases, the need of technology to help reduce the environmental pollution caused by excess fertilizer use, and the evocative query, "Can new technology stop [global warming]?" It is notable that innovations to fight pollution and global warming involve fighting "bads" rather than creating "goods." Instead of raising the standard of living in the same manner as the past two centuries of innovations that have brought a wonder of new goods and services for consumers, innovations to stem the consequences of pollution and global warming seek to prevent the standard of living from declining.

Mokyr and other historians scoff at any attempt to forecast the future; any pessimist gazing into the future is condemned for a lack of imagination and doomed to repeat the mistakes of past pessimists. But the common assumption that future innovation is non-forecastable is wrong. There are historical precedents of correct predictions made as long as fifty or 100 years in advance. After we review some of these, we will return to today's forecasts for the next quarter-century.

An early forecast of the future of technology is contained in Jules Verne's 1863 manuscript *Paris in the Twentieth Century,* in which Verne made bold predictions about the Paris a century later in 1960.[39] In that early year, before Edison or Benz, Verne had already conceived of the basics of the twentieth century. He predicted rapid transit cars running on overhead viaducts, motor cars with gas combustion engines, and street lights connected by underground wires. In fact, much of IR #2 was not a surprise. Looking ahead in the year 1875, inventors were feverishly working on turning the telegraph into the telephone, trying to find a way to transform electricity coming from batteries into electric light, trying to find a way of harnessing the power of petroleum to create a lightweight and powerful internal combustion engine. The atmosphere of 1875 was suffused with "we're almost there" speculation. After the relatively lightweight internal combustion engine was achieved, flight, humankind's dream since Icarus, became a matter of time and experimentation.[40] Some of the most important sources of human progress over the 1870–1940 period were not new inventions at all. Running water had been achieved by the Romans, but it took political will and financial investment to bring it to every urban dwelling place. A separate system of sewer pipes was not an invention, but implementing it over the interval 1870–1930 required resources, dedication, and a commitment to using public funds for infrastructure investment.

A set of remarkable forecasts appeared in December 1900 in an unlikely publication medium—the *Ladies Home Journal.* Some of the predictions were laughably wrong and unimportant, such as strawberries the size of baseballs. But there were enough accurate predictions in this page-long three-column article to suggest that much of the future can be known.[41] Some of the more interesting forecasts follow:

- "Hot and cold air will be turned on from spigots to regulate the temperature of the air just as we now turn on hot and cold water from spigots to regulate the temperature of the bath."
- "Ready-cooked meals will be purchased from establishments much like our bakeries of today."
- "Liquid-air refrigerators will keep large quantities of food fresh for long intervals."
- "Photographs will be telegraphed from any distance. If there is a battle in China a century hence, photographs of the events will be published in newspapers an hour later."
- "Automobiles will be cheaper than horses are today. Farmers will own automobile hay-wagons, automobile truck-wagons... automobiles will have been substituted for every horse-vehicle now known."
- "Persons and things of all types will be brought within focus of cameras connected with screens at opposite ends of circuits, thousands of miles at a span.... [T]he lips of a remote actor or singer will be heard to offer words or music when seen to move."

The Jules Verne 1863 and the *Ladies Home Journal* 1900 visions of future technological progress were true leaps of imagination. Somewhat less challenging were predictions of the future made at the 1939–40 New York World's Fair. By then, IR #2 was almost complete in urban America, so it is no surprise that the exhibits at the fair could predict quite accurately the further complements to IR #2 inventions, such as superhighways. A future of air-conditioned homes and businesses was no intellectual stretch at the fair, for air conditioning in movie theaters began in 1922 and was nearly ubiquitous in theaters and new office buildings by the late 1930s. Television was introduced at the fair, and it was easy to predict then that television over the next two decades would follow the American model of commercially supported radio, with entertainment provided over several large networks spanning the continent. Although commercial aviation was primitive in 1939, still it was easy to forecast from the rapid progress in the size and speed of aircraft over the 1920–40 period that much larger aircraft could fly much longer distances, and indeed within only a few years the DC-6 and DC-7 were spanning the continent and the globe before the epochal introduction of the Boeing 707 jet in 1958.

What was missing at the 1939–40 World's Fair was any vision of the computer revolution that created IR #3. But Norbert Wiener, a visionary, in a 1949 essay that was ultimately rejected by the *New York Times*, got a lot of the future of IR #3 right. Among his 1949 predictions were these:

> These new machines have a great capacity for upsetting the present basis of industry, and of reducing the economic value of the routine factory employee to a point at which he is not worth hiring at any price.... [I]f we move in the direction of making machines which learn and whose behavior is modified by experience, we must face the fact that every degree of independence we give the machine is a degree of possible defiance of our wishes. The genie in the bottle will not willingly go back in the bottle, nor have we any reason to expect them to be well-disposed to us.[42]

Just as some inventions have come as a surprise, including the entire electronics and digital revolutions, other anticipated inventions never came to pass. Dick Tracy's wrist radio in cartoon comic strips of the late 1940s finally is coming to fruition seventy years later with the Apple Watch. The Jetsons' vertical commuting car/plane never happened, and in fact high fuel costs caused many local helicopter short-haul aviation companies to shut down.[43] As Peter Theil quipped, "We wanted flying cars, instead we got 140 characters."

THE INVENTIONS THAT ARE NOW FORECASTABLE

Despite the slow growth of TFP recorded by the data of the decade since 2004, commentators view the future of technology with great excitement. Nouriel Roubini writes, "[T]here is a new perception of the role of technology. Innovators and tech CEOs both seem positively giddy with optimism."[44] The well-known pair of techno-optimists Erik Brynjolfsson and Andrew McAfee assert that "we're at an inflection point" between a past of slow technological change and a future of rapid change.[45] They appear to believe that Big Blue's chess victory and Watson's victory on the TV game show *Jeopardy* presage an age in which computers outsmart humans in every aspect of human work effort. They remind us that Moore's Law predicts endless exponential growth of the performance capability of computer chips—but they ignore that chips have fallen behind the predicted pace of Moore's Law after 2005. The decline in the price of ICT equipment relative to performance was most rapid in the late 1990s, and there has been hardly any decline at all in the past few years. Exponential increases in computer performance will continue, but at a slower rate than in the past, not at a faster rate (see figure 17–7).

The theme of this chapter is that the main benefits for productivity growth provided by the digital Third Industrial Revolution were centered on the decade between 1994 and 2004. Since 2004, the pace of innovation has been slower, but certainly it has not been zero. The new portability of the web made possible by smartphones and tablets has continued to change business practices and consumer well-being. When we examine the likely innovations of the next several decades, we are not doubting that many innovations will continue to occur but rather are assessing them in the context of the past two decades of fast (1994–2004) and then slow (2004–14) growth in TFP. Will the next wave of innovations change business practices in a revolutionary way, as did the dot-com revolution of the late 1990s, or will innovation cause productivity to increase at an evolutionary pace, like that of the most recent decade?

The future advances that are widely forecast by Brynjolfsson, McAfee, and others can be divided into four main categories—medical, small robots and 3D printing, big data, and driverless vehicles. Enthusiasts of "big data" sometimes label this category of advance as "artificial intelligence." It is worth examining the potential of each of these categories of future innovation in turn to create a boost in TFP growth back to the level achieved in the late 1990s.

Medical and Pharmaceutical Advances. The most important sources of longer life expectancy in the twentieth century were achieved in the first half of that century, when life expectancy rose at twice the rate it did in the last half. This was the interval when infant mortality was conquered and life expectancy was extended by the discovery of the germ theory of disease, the development of an antitoxin for diphtheria, and the near elimination of contamination of milk and meat as well as the conquest of air- and water-distributed diseases through the construction of urban sanitation infrastructure.[46] Many of the current basic tools of modern medicine were developed between 1940 and 1980, including antibiotics, the polio vaccine, procedures to treat coronary heart disease, and the basic tools of chemotherapy and radiation to treat cancer, all advances that contribute to productivity growth.

Medical technology has not ceased to advance since 1980 but rather has continued at a slow and measured pace, and life expectancy has continued to improve at a steady rate (as shown in figure 7–2), while the mortality rate for cardiac-related diseases has steadily declined. It is likely that life expectancy will continue to improve at a rate not unlike that of the past few decades. There are new issues, however. As described by Jan Vijg, an eminent geneticist, progress on physical disease and ailments is advancing faster than on mental disease, which has led to widespread concern that in the future there will be a steady rise in the burden of taking care of elderly Americans who are alive but in a state of dementia.

Pharmaceutical research has reached a brick wall of rapidly increasing costs and declining benefits, with a decline in major drugs approved each pair of years over the past decade, as documented by Vijg. At enormous cost, drugs are being developed that will treat esoteric types of cancer at costs that no medical insurance system can afford. Vijg is highly critical of the current regime of drug testing in the United States as inhibiting risk taking, an example of the overregulation of the U.S. economy.[47] The upshot is that over the next few decades, medical and pharmaceutical advances will doubtless continue, while the increasing burden of Alzheimer's care will be a significant contributor to increased cost of the medical care system.

Small Robots and 3D Printing. Industrial robots were introduced by General Motors in 1961. By the mid-1990s, robots were welding automobile parts and replacing workers in the lung-killing environment of the automotive paint shop.[48] Until recently, however, robots were large and expensive and needed to be "caged off to keep them from smashing into humans." The ongoing reduction in the cost of computer components has made feasible ever smaller and increasingly capable robots. Gill Pratt enumerates eight "technical drivers" that are advancing at steady exponential rates. Among those relevant to the development of more capable robots are exponential growth in computer performance, improvements in electromechanical design tools, and improvements in electrical energy storage. Others on his list involve more general capabilities of all digital devices, including exponential expansion of local wireless communications, in the scale and performance of the Internet, and in data storage.[49]

As an example of the effects of these increasing technical capabilities, inexpensive robots suitable for use by small businesses have been developed and brought to public attention by a 2012 segment on the TV program *60 Minutes* featuring Baxter, a $25,000 robot. The appeal of Baxter is that the cost is so cheap and that it can be reprogrammed to do a different task every day. Other small robots are mobile and can move around the factory floor. Often the robots work with humans rather than replacing them.[50] These small robots are no different in principle from the introduction of machinery dating back to the textile looms and spindles of the early British industrial revolution. Most workplace technologies are introduced with the intention of substituting machines for workers. Because this has been going on for two centuries, why are there then still so many jobs? Why in mid-2015 was the U.S. unemployment rate close to 5 percent instead of 20 or 50 percent?

David Autor has posed this question as well as answered it: Machines, including futuristic robots, not only substitute for labor, but also complement labor:

> Most work processes draw upon a multifaceted set of inputs: labor and capital; brains and brawn; creativity and rote repetition; technical mastery and intuitive judgment; perspiration and inspiration; adherence to rules and judicious application of discretion. Typically, these inputs *each* play essential roles; that is, improvements in one do not obviate the need for the other.[51]

Just as Baxter cooperates with human workers, other robots do not just displace workers but also make the remaining workers more valuable and create new jobs, including those who are building and programming the robots.

The complementarity between robots and human workers is illustrated by the cooperative work ritual taking place daily in Amazon warehouses, often cited as a frontier example of robotic technology. Far from replacing all human workers, in these warehouses the Kiva robots do not actually touch any of the merchandise but rather are limited to lifting shelves containing the objects and moving the shelves to the packer, who lifts the object off the shelf and performs the packing operation by hand.[52] The tactile skills needed for the robots to distinguish the different shapes, sizes, and textures of the objects on the shelves are beyond the capability of current robot technology. Other examples of complementarities include ATMs, which, as already noted, have been accompanied by an increase, rather than a decrease, in the number of bank branches, and the barcode retail scanner, which works along with the checkout clerk without replacing these employees, with little traction thus far for self-checkout lanes.

The exponential increase in computer speed and memory has apparently raced far ahead of the capability of robots to duplicate human movements. Though Google is experimenting with robots shaped like wild animals that can run at great speeds, so far robots are having great difficulty simply standing up. The recent finals of a three-year competition in which research teams developed the latest robots, "saw robots fall every which way. They fell on their faces. They fell on their backs. They toppled like toddlers, they folded like cheap suits, they went down like tonnes of bricks."[53]

Daniela Rus, Director of MIT's Computer Science and Artificial Intelligence Laboratory, provides a summary of some of the limitations of the robots developed to date. Robotic reasoning is limited, and "the scope of the robot's reasoning is entirely contained in the program.... Tasks that humans take for granted—for example, answering the question, 'Have I been here before?'—are extremely difficult for robots." Further, if a robot encounters a situation that it has not been specifically programmed to handle, "it enters an error state and stops operating."[54] Surely multiple-function robots will be developed, but it will be a long and gradual process before robots outside of the manufacturing and wholesaling sectors become a significant factor in replacing human jobs in the service, transportation, or construction sectors. And it is in those sectors that the slowness of productivity growth is a problem. For instance, consider the task of folding laundry, which is simple and routine for humans no matter their level of education:

> No machine can yet match a human's dexterity and problem-solving abilities when attacking a pile of irregular shaped clothes of different

fabric types and weight. The difference between picking up a lace nightgown versus unraveling a pair of crumpled jeans knotted with other clothes is a calculation that requires massive computing power and a soft touch.[55]

3D printing is another revolution described by the techno-optimists. Its most important advantage is the potential to speed up the design process of new products. New prototypes can be designed in days or even hours rather than months and can be created at relatively low cost, lowering one major barrier to entry for entrepreneurs trying to attract financing for their startups. New design models can be simultaneously produced at multiple locations around the world. 3D printing also excels at one-off customized operations, such as the ability to create a crown in a dentist office instead of having to send out a mold, reducing the process of creating and installing a dental crown from two office visits to one. Thus it may contribute to productivity growth by reducing certain inefficiencies and lowering barriers to entrepreneurship, but these are unlikely to be huge effects felt throughout the economy. 3D printing is not expected to have much effect on mass production and thus on how most U.S. consumer goods are produced.

Big Data and Artificial Intelligence. The core of the optimists' case lies not with physical robots or 3D printing but with the growing sophistication and humanlike abilities of computers that are often described as "artificial intelligence." Brynjolfsson and McAfee provide many examples to demonstrate that computers are becoming sufficiently intelligent to supplant a growing share of human jobs. "They wonder if automation technology is near a tipping point, when machines finally master traits that have kept human workers irreplaceable."[56]

Thus far, it appears that the vast majority of big data is being analyzed within large corporations for marketing purposes. The *Economist* reported recently that corporate IT expenditures for marketing purposes were increasing at three times the rate of other corporate IT expenditures. The marketing wizards use big data to figure out what their customers buy, why they change their purchases from one category to another, and why they move from merchant to merchant. With enough big data, Corporation A may be able to devise a strategy to steal market share from Corporation B, but B will surely fight back with an onslaught of more big data. An excellent current example involves the large legacy airlines with their data-rich frequent flyer programs. The analysts at these airlines are constantly trolling through their big data trying to understand why they have lost market share in a particular city or with a particular demographic group of travelers.

Every airline has a "revenue management" department that decides how many seats on a given flight on a given day should be sold at cheap, intermediate, and expensive prices. Vast amounts of data are analyzed, and computers examine historical records, monitor day-by-day booking patterns, factor in holidays and weekends, and come out with an allocation. But at a medium-sized airline, JetBlue, twenty-five employees are required to monitor computers, and the humans must constantly override the computers' decisions. The director of revenue management at JetBlue describes his biggest surprise since taking over his job as "how often the staff has to override the computers."[57] Another example of the use of artificial intelligence is in apparel retailing. "At Macy's, for instance, algorithmic technology is helping fuse the online and the in-store experience, enabling a shopper to compare clothes online, try something on at the store, order it online, and return it in person. Algorithms...let companies target offers to specific consumers while they are shopping in stores."[58]

Marketing is just one form of artificial intelligence that has been made possible by big data. Computers are working in fields such as medical diagnosis, crime prevention, and loan approvals. In some cases, human analysts are replaced, but often the computers speed up a process and make it more accurate, working alongside human workers. New software allows consumer lending officers to "know borrowers as never before, and more accurately predict whether they will repay."[59] Vanguard and Charles Schwab have begun to compete with high-priced human financial advisers by offering "robo-advisers," online services that offer automated investment management via software. They use computer algorithms to choose assets consistent with the client's desired allocation at a cost that is a mere fraction of the fees of traditional human advisers. Thus far, robo-advisers mainly appeal to young people who have not yet built up much wealth; this application of artificial intelligence has not yet made much of a dent in advising high-net-worth individuals. It has been estimated recently that the combined assets under management by robo-advisers still amounts to less than $20 billion, against $17 trillion for traditional human advisers.[60]

Another use of artificial intelligence is now almost two decades old: the ability to use modern search tools to find with blinding speed valuable nuggets of existing information. The demand for legal associates has declined in part because of the ability of computerized search tools to carry out the process of discovery and search for precedents. "Computers are reading millions of documents and sorting them for relevance without getting tired or distracted.... As such analytical power expands in scope, computers will move nearer to the heart of what lawyers do by advising better than lawyers can on whether to sue or settle or go to trial."[61]

These examples of advanced search technology and artificial intelligence indeed are happening now, but they are nothing new. The quantity of electronic data has been rising exponentially for decades without pushing TFP growth out of its post-1970 lethargy, except for the temporary productivity revival period of 1994–2004. The sharp slowdown in productivity growth in recent years has overlapped with the introduction of smartphones and iPads, which consume huge amounts of data. These sources of innovation have disappointed in what counts in the statistics on productivity growth, their ability to boost output per hour in the American economy. As shown in figure 17–2, there has been no response at all of TFP growth to the 2007 introduction of the smartphone or the 2010 introduction of the smart tablet.[62]

Driverless Cars. This category of future progress is demoted to last place because it offers benefits that are minor compared to the invention of the car itself or the improvements in safety that have created a tenfold improvement in fatalities per vehicle mile since 1950. The most important distinction is between cars and trucks. People are in cars to go from A to B, much of it for essential aspects of life such as commuting or shopping. Thus the people must be inside the driverless car to achieve their objective of getting from point A to point B. The additions to consumer surplus of being able to commute without driving are relatively minor. Instead of listening to the current panoply of options, including Bluetooth phone calls, radio news, or Internet-provided music, drivers will be able to look at a computer screen or their smartphones, read a book, or keep up with their e-mail. The use of driverless cars is predicted to reduce the incidence of automobile accidents, continuing the steady decline in automobile accidents and fatalities that has already occurred. Driverless car technology may also help to foster a shift from nearly universal car ownership to widespread car sharing in cities and perhaps suburbs, leading to reductions in gasoline consumption, air pollution, and the amount of land devoted to parking, all of which should have positive effects on quality of life if not on productivity growth.

That leaves the potential future productivity advantage offered by driverless trucks. This is a potentially productivity-enhancing innovation, albeit within the small slice of U.S. employment consisting of truck drivers. However, driving from place to place is only half of what many truck drivers do. Those driving Coca-Cola and bread delivery trucks do not just stop at the back loading dock and wait for a store employee to unload the truck. Instead, the drivers are responsible for loading the cases of Coca-Cola or the stacks of bread loaves onto dollies and placing them manually on the store shelves. In fact, it is remarkable in this late phase of the computer revolution that almost all placement of individual product cans, bottles, and tubes on retail shelves is achieved today by humans rather than robots. Driverless delivery trucks will not save labor unless work is reorganized so that unloading and placement of goods from the driverless trucks is taken over by workers at the destination location.

The enthusiasm of techno-optimists for driverless cars leaves numerous issues unanswered. As pointed out by Autor, the experimental Google car "does not drive on roads" but rather proceeds by comparing data from its sensors with "painstakingly hand-curated maps." Any deviation of the actual environment from the pre-processed maps, such as a road detour or a crossing guard in place of the expected traffic signal, causes the driving software to blank out and requires instant resumption of control by the human driver.[63] At present, tests of driverless cars are being carried out on multilane highways, but test models so far are unable to judge when it is safe to pass on a two-lane road or to navigate winding rural roads in the dark. In the words of computer expert Rus:

> So far, that level of autonomous driving performance has been possible only in low-speed, low-complexity environments. Robotic vehicles cannot yet handle all the complexities of driving "in the wild," such as inclement weather and complex traffic situations. These issues are the focus of ongoing research.[64]

A future of driverless cars and trucks raises issues of legal liability that are now just beginning to be considered. Nonetheless, both Google and Tesla have announced plans to introduce certain aspects of driverless car technology in the near future, first as a type of highway autopilot not too far removed from the older technology of cruise control. Perfection in electronic devices is still years away, as has been demonstrated by defects in voice-activated computer controls:

> Voice-activated command systems and their software often are badly outdated or unreliable, leading to a tide of customer complaints and

research questioning how safe they really are.... Voice control can be extremely buggy and the struggle to get them to work can cause a driver to miss traffic hazards.... *Consumer Reports* magazine found that problems with infotainment systems—music players, navigation and hands-free systems linking smartphones—are now the No. 1 reason for complaints.[65]

CONCLUSION

The title of this chapter asks, "Can the future match the great inventions of the past?" The criterion for "match" refers to the standard economic measure of the impact of innovation and technological change, that is, the growth rate of total factor productivity (TFP). Innovation is judged to have a high impact when TFP growth is relatively fast and to have a low impact when TFP growth is relatively slow. This standard of comparison across eras creates a distinction between the *pace* of innovation and the *impact* of innovation on TFP. We contrast the hyperactive pace of innovation at the current time (with multi-billion-dollar initial public offerings of tech-related new companies almost every week) with its apparently weak impact, judging by the slow pace of TFP growth exhibited in the data for the past decade.

This book has interpreted the ups and downs of TFP growth since the late nineteenth century as the result of successive industrial revolutions. The most remarkable fact about TFP performance is that rapid growth was not spread out evenly over the twelve-plus decades since 1890 but rather was concentrated in the middle of the twentieth century, with an average annual rate of TFP growth of 1.89 percent per year between 1920 and 1970. In 1970–2014, by contrast, the growth rate was only 0.64 percent per year, just a third the pace of 1920–70.

This chapter argues that the 1920–70 upsurge in TFP growth reflected the importance of the great inventions of the Second Industrial Revolution (IR #2). Our interpretation is that the digital Third Industrial Revolution (IR #3), though utterly changing the way Americans obtain information and communicate, did not extend across the full span of human life as did IR #2, with the epochal changes it created in the dimensions of food, clothing, housing and its equipment, transportation, information, communication, entertainment, the curing of diseases and conquest of infant mortality, and the improvement of working conditions on the job and at home. The surge of TFP growth during 1920–70 culminated with three offshoots of IR #2 that reached their current form forty years or more ago, with only minor changes since: highway travel via the interstate highway system, jet commercial air travel, and ubiquitous air conditioning.

The focal point of impact for IR #3 came in the decade 1994–2004, when TFP grew at a rate of 1.03 percent per year, little better than half that of 1920–70 but substantially faster than the rates of 0.57 percent per year for 1970–1994 and 0.40 for 2004–14. In our interpretation, there was a one-time-only revolution in business practices that coincided with the marriage between personal computers and communication that occurred when Internet browsers were introduced in the mid-1990s. Offices made the transition from piles of paper and filing cabinets to flat screens and cloud storage. Paper library card catalogs and parts lists made their transition to searchable video screens. TFP growth responded, but when by 2004, the main elements of the web-enabled transition had taken place, the *level* of TFP had achieved a higher plateau, and the *growth rate* of TFP then slowed appreciably.

No one can foresee the future, but we can ask whether the future is more likely to resemble the dot-com decade of 1994–2004 or the most recent decade, 2004–14. This chapter has assembled two types of evidence that the more rapid growth of TFP during 1994–2004 represented a temporary upsurge that is unlikely to be repeated. Descriptive assessments judge the pace of change in business practices, whether in the office, the retail store, or financial markets, to have slowed markedly after the rapid transition to modern methods achieved during the 1994–2004 decade. Six types of objective measures all show a peak of activity during the late 1990s and a sharp slowdown, stasis, or even decline in the most recent decade. These include the number of daily transactions on the New York Stock Exchange, the rate of creation of new business firms, the growth of manufacturing capacity, the rate of net investment, the rate of improvement in the performance of computer equipment relative to its price, and the rate of improvement of the density of computer chips.

The chapter calls attention to an apparent conflict between the excitement of techno-optimists regarding the newly enhanced capacity of artificial intelligence to mimic and surpass human activity, versus the slow ongoing growth of TFP over the past decade. One resolution is that the replacement of human jobs by computers has been going on for more than five decades, and the replacement of human jobs by machines in general has been going on for more than two centuries. Occupations such as financial advisers, credit analysts, insurance agents, and others are in the process of being replaced, and these displaced workers follow in the footsteps of victims of the web who lost their jobs within the past two decades, including travel agents, encyclopedia salesmen, and employees of Borders and Blockbuster. Yet these previous job losses did not prevent the U.S. unemployment rate from declining to a rate near 5 percent in 2015, because new jobs were created to replace the jobs that were lost.

Most of us in our daily life encounter many different types of employees, and we can play a game I call "find the robot." Besides the ATM, the other robot I occasionally encounter is the automated e-kiosk check-in machine at airports; this innovation was rolled out between 2001 and 2005 and has thinned the ranks of airport ticket counter personnel, just as earlier airline web sites largely displaced travel agents and airline telephone agents; yet the rest of the employees needed to run an airline are still there, including skycaps, baggage handlers, flight attendants, pilots, air traffic controllers, and gate agents. Goods are still placed on supermarket shelves by store employees and by the drivers of delivery trucks for beer, bread, and soft drinks. Checkout lanes at retail markets are still manned by clerks rather than robots, and self-checkout lanes are few and far between. Haircuts, massages, and manicures are still exclusively the province of human workers, as are restaurants with their cooks and wait staff. Hotels still have front desk personnel, and if they offer room service, it is delivered by humans rather than robots. Far from occurring overnight, the shift to robots and job-destroying artificial intelligence is occurring at glacial speed.

Innovation alarmists write articles with titles such as "How Robots and Algorithms Are Taking Over" and predict that output will increasingly be produced by robots and computer algorithms.[66] Two visions compete in their forecasts for the next several decades: The techno-optimists predict much more rapid productivity growth as jobs are destroyed, and that the counterpart of exploding productivity growth is to be an age of persistent mass unemployment. The opposite vision extrapolates from the most recent decade and predicts "more of the same," consisting of growth rather than shrinkage of employment combined with the same historically low rate of growth of labor productivity observed during 2004–14. The symmetry of these opposing views belies the usefulness of the traditional adjectives "optimistic" and "pessimistic." The techno-optimists focus on machines replacing humans and are thus optimistic about future productivity growth while pessimistically forecasting a future of job destruction and mass unemployment. The techno-pessimist view favored here recognizes the many dimensions of advance of robots and artificial intelligence while stressing the slowness of their macroeconomic effects and the many sectors of the economy in which the interaction of workers and machines has changed slowly, if at all, in the past decade. Just as the techno-optimists are pessimistic about job growth, the techno-pessimists are optimistic that job growth will continue and that new jobs will be created as rapidly as technology destroys old jobs.

How can we choose between these sharply opposite visions? Numbers do not lie. Far from soaring toward the techno-optimists' vision of mass unemployment, the U.S. unemployment rate has declined rapidly, from 10.0 in October 2009 to 5.3 percent in June 2015, and seems likely to decline below 5.0 percent by 2016. And far from exploding as people are replaced by machines and software, labor productivity has been in the doldrums, rising only 0.5 percent per year in the five years ending in the second quarter of 2015, in contrast to the 2.3 percent per year achieved in the dot-com era of 1994–2004.[67] Now that the American economy has arrived back at a state of relatively full employment, it is hard to maintain the case that robots and artificial intelligence are creating a new class of the permanently unemployed.

The problem created by the computer age is not mass unemployment but the gradual disappearance of good, steady, middle-level jobs that have been lost not just to robots and algorithms but to globalization and outsourcing to other countries, together with the concentration of job growth in routine manual jobs that offer relatively low wages. The gradual slowing of economic growth examined in this book combines disappointing productivity growth over the past decade with a steady rise of inequality over the past three decades. In the next chapter, we turn from the technological origins of the rise and fall of productivity growth to the headwinds that have intervened to prevent most Americans from enjoying real income gains equal to the growth of economy-wide output per hour. These headwinds constitute barriers to the equal distribution of productivity gains, including the effects of rising inequality, educational stagnation, declining labor force participation, and the fiscal demands of an aging population.

Chapter 18

INEQUALITY AND THE OTHER HEADWINDS: LONG-RUN AMERICAN ECONOMIC GROWTH SLOWS TO A CRAWL

> The American family is changing—and the changes guarantee that inequality will be greater in the next generation. For the first time, America's children will almost certainly not be as well educated, healthy, or wealthy as their parents.
>
> —June Carbone and Naomi Cahn, 2014

INTRODUCTION

The impact of innovations and technological change in chapter 17 was measured by their effect on total factor productivity (TFP), which is an average for the total economy of real GDP divided by a weighted average of capital and labor inputs. There is no guarantee that every member of society will share equally in the bounty of economic progress. This chapter looks more closely at the very different outcomes that have occurred in the top of the income distribution as contrasted with the middle and bottom of the distribution. When the income gains at the top are stripped away, the growth in total income available to be divided up among the bottom 99 percent grows more slowly than income for the nation as a whole.

Just as 1970 was a watershed in chapter 17, the dividing point between rapid and slow growth in TFP, so there was a parallel and independent transition between equal growth for all before 1970 and unequal growth after 1970. By several measures, including median real wages and real taxable income in the bottom 90 percent of the income distribution, there has been no progress at all.

Other measures of income growth below the top 1 percent yield positive, rather than zero, growth—but at a rate substantially slower than averages that include the top 1 percent.

Steadily rising inequality over the past four decades is just one of the headwinds blowing at gale force to slow the growth rate of the American standard of living. The others that receive attention in this chapter are education, demographics, and government debt. Additional headwinds such as globalization, global warming, and environmental pollution are touched on more briefly. The overall conclusion of this chapter is that the combined influence of the headwinds constitutes an important additional drag on future growth going well beyond the post-1970 slowdown in the impact of innovation evident in chapter 17.

This chapter begins with a multifaceted treatment of the history of the American income distribution since the first income tax records became available 100 years ago. The rapid pace of advance in incomes at the top, particularly within the top 1 percent, can be explained by a set of factors that have boosted top incomes, including the economics of superstars, changing incentives for executive compensation, and capital gains on real estate and the stock market. Income stagnation for the bottom 90 percent of the distribution has a different set of causes, including the effect of automation in destroying middle-income jobs, an erosion of the strength of labor unions, the decline in the purchasing power of the minimum wage, the effect of imports in the shrinkage of the manufacturing sector, and the role of both high-skilled and low-skilled immigration.

The education headwind is important both by itself and as a source of growing inequality. Throughout the postwar years, starting with the GI Bill, which allowed World War II veterans to obtain a college education at the government's expense, the United States was the leader among nations in the college completion rate of its youth. But in the past two decades, the United States has stumbled, with its college completion rate now down in the league tables to tenth or below. And the American youth who enter college, regardless of whether they complete it, now face a combined burden of outstanding debt of more than $1 trillion. Educational problems are even deeper in U.S. secondary schools, which rank in the bottom half in international reading, math, and science tests administered to 15-year-olds. Most serious is the high degree of inequality in reading and vocabulary skills of the nation's children at age 5, the normal age of entrance to kindergarten; middle-class children have a spoken vocabulary as much as triple that of children brought up in poverty conditions by a single parent.

The third "demographic" headwind refers to the population viewed not as a single entity but as groups and subgroups within the total. The most important aspect of U.S. demography is the bulge in the birth rate between 1946 and 1964, the so-called "baby boom." Because the Social Security system allows retirement at three alternative ages—currently 62, 66, or 70—the effects of baby-boom retirement are spread out, beginning in 2008 and extending to 2034.[1] Other demographic issues include the shift in work patterns, as the percentage of those 55 and older who choose to remain in the work force has increased, even as labor force participation rates for all age and gender groups younger than 55 have declined. Taken together, the effect of baby-boom retirement and declining labor force participation at younger ages reduces the number of hours worked per person and implies that the standard of living defined as output per person must grow more slowly than labor productivity, which is defined as output per hour.

Government debt is the fourth headwind, because the ratio of government debt to GDP is predicted to increase steadily in the future. The growing ratio of retirees to working taxpayers will soon require remedies that change the current set of rates for Social Security taxes and/or change the calculation of benefits; the Social Security trust fund is currently projected to decline by 2034 to a level below which it cannot pay for its current schedule of obligations, whereas the Medicare trust fund will reach exhaustion level in 2030. At some point, measures must be taken to rein in persistent fiscal deficits by structural reforms that combine raising tax revenue and reducing expenditures. By definition, any increase in tax rates and/or decreases in transfer payments must reduce the growth of personal disposable income below that of pre-tax income.

The combined effects of growing inequality, a faltering education system, demographic headwinds, and the strong likelihood of a fiscal correction imply that the real median disposable income will grow much more slowly in the future than in the past. When combined with the implications of a smaller effect of innovation on productivity since 1970, there is little room for growth at all. When all the headwinds are taken into account, the future growth of real median disposable income per person will be barely positive and far below the rate enjoyed by generations of Americans dating back to the nineteenth century.

The combined effect of the four headwinds—inequality, education, demographics, and government debt—can be roughly quantified. But more difficult to assess are numerous signs of social breakdown in American society. Whether measured by the percentage of children growing up in a household headed by one parent instead of two, or by the vocabulary disadvantage of low-income preschool children, or by the percentage of both white and black young men serving time in prison, signs of social decay are everywhere in the America of the early twenty-first century. These problems are examined in this chapter, and a set of directions for policy changes is presented in the subsequent postscript.

THE FIRST HEADWIND: DIMENSIONS OF RISING INEQUALITY

Throughout this book, progress has been measured by the rate of advance of *average* real GDP per person or per hour. Such averages, or mean values, may be misleading if the pace of improvement benefits those who have high incomes more than those who have middle or low incomes. When the distribution of income, of wealth, or of any other quantity becomes skewed toward those at the top, then the median value of the series grows more slowly than the mean value. And this is just what has happened in the United States over the past four decades. In this section, we examine three separate data sources, the first based on tax records, the second on U.S. Census Bureau data, and the third on a combination of tax and census data that take into account the effect of taxes and transfers in redistributing after-tax income toward lower-income households.

Thomas Piketty and Emmanuel Saez pioneered the use of income tax data to study the evolution of top incomes compared with the incomes of those below the top. Their data for the United States go back to 1917, just a few years after the introduction of the U.S. income tax in 1914. They address the problem that the proportion of those with low and medium incomes who pay taxes varies from year to year and era to era. Their now widely accepted solution is to use standard macroeconomic data derived from the national income accounts to estimate total income and then to subtract the top incomes, based on tax records, to obtain the value of incomes below the top.[2]

Figure 18–1 summarizes the central Piketty–Saez results for most of the past century, 1917–2013. Growth rates are shown for three time intervals divided at 1948 and 1972 and for three groups, the bottom 90 percent, the top 10 percent, and the average covering all income earners. White bars display the growth rate of pre-tax income (including capital gains) for the bottom 90 percent, black bars for the top 10 percent, and gray bars for the growth in average income. Each of the three eras displays a distinctly different outcome..

During 1917–48, incomes became substantially more equal. Real incomes in the bottom 90 percent grew at 1.43 percent per year, more than double the

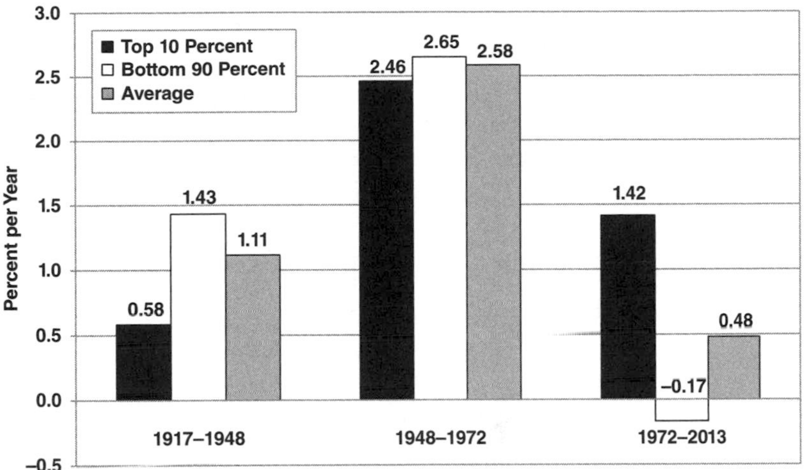

Figure 18–1. Growth Rate of Real Income, Top 10 Percent, Bottom 90 Percent, and Average, Selected Intervals, 1917–2013

Source: Calculated from Alvaredo, Facundo, Anthony B. Atkinson, Thomas Piketty and Emmanuel Saez, The World Top Incomes Database, http://topincomes.g-mond.parisschoolofeconomics.eu/, 6/25/2015. Average income for each percentile, including capital gains.

0.58 percent growth rate for the top 10 percent, with the average at 1.11 percent. This was the result of the equalizing influence of the Great Depression, World War II, and the many income-leveling programs instituted in the 1930s and 1940s, including the minimum wage, legislation encouraging the formation of labor unions, and the GI Bill, which sent millions to college and lifted them from their working class origins to middle-class status.

The remarkable fact about the middle 1948–72 period is not just that incomes grew at roughly the same rate for the bottom 90 percent, the top 10 percent, and the average, but that real incomes for each group grew so rapidly. The average growth rate of real incomes of 2.58 percent in 1948–72 was more than double the 1.11 percent growth rate of 1917–48 and more than five times the 0.48 percent growth rate of 1972–2013. The two-and-a-half decades after 1948 were a golden age for millions of high school graduates, who without a college education could work steadily at a unionized job and make an income high enough to afford a suburban house with a back yard, one or two cars, and a life style of which median-income earners in most other countries could only dream.

But all that changed after the early 1970s. A giant gap emerged between the growth rate of real income for the bottom 90 percent and the top 10 percent of the income distribution. Average real income in the bottom 90 percent was actually lower in 2013 than it was in 1972. In fact, peak real income for the bottom 90 percent of $37,053 in 2000 was barely higher than the $35,411 achieved in 1972, and by 2013, that average had declined from 2000 by 15 percent to $31,652. Meanwhile, the average real income for the top 10 percent doubled from $161,000 in 1972 to $324,000 in 2007, followed by a modest retreat to $273,000 in 2013.

A second source of data related to income inequality comes from the Census Bureau, which provides data on mean and median real household income going back to 1975. Table 18–1 compares the census growth rates for 1975–2013 and two subperiods divided at 1995, and these are compared in the same table to the Piketty–Saez data for the period since 1975. As shown in the top frame of table 18–1, mean real census income growth exceeded median growth by a substantial amount—by 0.61 percentage points during 1975–95, by 0.33 points during 1995–2012, and by 0.47 points for the two periods taken together, 1975–2012.

Growth rates of the Piketty–Saez data are reported for the post-1975 period in the bottom frame of table 18–1. The rows display respectively the growth rate of real income per taxable unit for the top 10 percent, bottom 90 percent, average of all 100 percent, and the difference between growth of the average and the bottom 90 percent. The difference is 0.70 percentage points for all three periods shown. It is interesting to compare the growth of mean census income with the growth of average Piketty–Saez income; we should expect the latter to be somewhat more rapid, for the concept includes capital gains, which

Table 18–1. Growth Rates of Real Income, Alternative Measures, 1975–2013

	1975–2013	**1975–1995**	**1995–2013**
Mean Household Income	0.77	1.15	0.35
Median Household Income	0.29	0.54	0.02
Mean minus Median	0.47	0.61	0.33
	1975–2013	**1975–1995**	**1995–2013**
Top 10 Percent	1.60	1.84	1.34
Bottom 90 Percent	−0.09	−0.01	−0.18
Average	0.60	0.68	0.52
Average minus Bottom 90	0.70	0.70	0.69

Sources: Median and mean household income from US Census Bureau, *Income and Poverty in the United States: 2013,* Table A–1. Percentile income from data underlying Figure 18–1.

are excluded in the census income data. Despite this conceptual difference, for the full 1975–2013 interval, mean census income growth of 0.77 percent per year is slightly higher than Piketty–Saez average growth of 0.60 percent.

Recently criticism of the Piketty–Saez and Census Bureau data has complained that they reflect only market income and ignore the effect of taxes and transfers.[3] Not surprisingly, an adjustment for taxes and transfers reduces the difference of income growth between the average including the top income group and the average excluding that top group. Tax rates paid by high-income individuals are substantially higher than those paid by most taxpayers, and indeed most households in the bottom half of the income distribution pay little or no federal income tax. Social Security, Medicare, and employer-paid health care premiums are transfer payments that benefit those in the middle of the income distribution, whereas food stamps, the earned-income tax credit, and Medicaid transfer payments are primarily directed to households in the bottom of the income distribution.

The most comprehensive analysis that adjusts for taxes and transfers is published regularly by the Congressional Budget Office (CBO). The concept of market pre-tax income is more comprehensive than for Piketty–Saez and the census data and rises more rapidly than the alternatives.[4] As shown in column (1) of table 18–2, CBO average pre-tax market income grows during 1979–2011

Table 18–2. Annual Growth Rate of Two Concepts of Income by Distributional Group, 1979 to 2011

Income Group	Market Income	Post-Tax Post-Transfer Income
	(1)	(2)
Top One Percent	3.82	4.05
81–99 Percentile	1.39	1.60
20–80 Percentile	0.46	1.05
1–20 Percentile	0.46	1.23
Average All Percentiles	1.16	1.48
Average 1–99 Percentile	0.87	1.28
Difference, All vs. 1–99	0.29	0.20
Difference, All vs. Median	0.70	0.43

Source: CBO, *The Distribution of Household Income and Federal Taxes, 2011*

at 1.16 percent per year, substantially more quickly than the 0.70 and 0.77 percent average growth rates of Piketty–Saez and the census over a slightly longer time period. After taxes and transfers are taken into account, average income grows at 1.48 per year. As would be expected, the statement of income growth after taxes and including transfer payments has the greatest effect on the lowest income group in the 1–20 percentile, raising income growth for that group from 0.46 percent per year before taxes and transfers to 1.23 percent per year after taxes and transfers. The top 1 percent also gains from the adjustment for taxes and transfers, although not by nearly so much, and has an annual growth rate of 4.05 percent per year post-tax and transfers as compared to 3.82 percent without those adjustments.[5]

When we consider the future of American growth, we care not just about growth of average income per capita, but also about growth of income per capita for the median American household. Figure 18–2 exhibits the differences between the annual growth rate of the average and bottom 90 percent for Piketty–Saez, as well as the differences between average and median growth for the census data and for the CBO data without and with the adjustments for taxes and transfers. Because the CBO data are superior to the other data sources, and because well-being depends on income after taxes and transfers, we take the right-hand bar in figure 18–2 as most relevant.[6] It shows that the difference

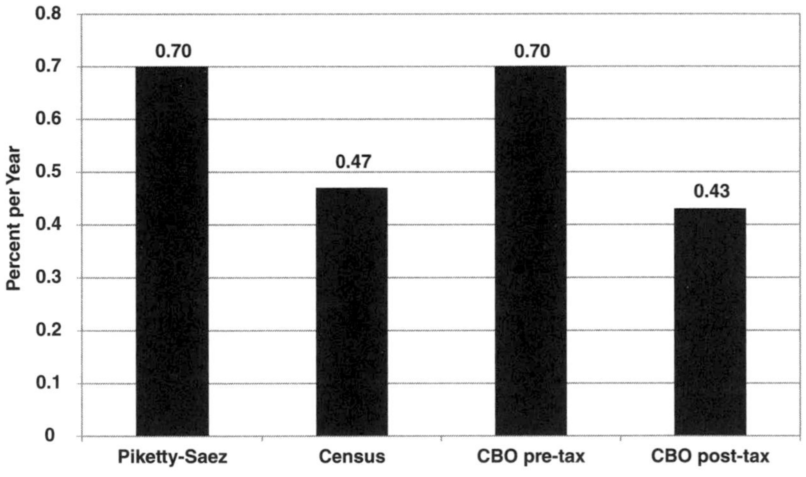

Figure 18–2. Shortfall Below Average Income Growth of Growth for the Bottom 90 percent (Piketty-Saez) and for the Median (Census and CBO)
Sources: Tables 18–1 and 18–2. CBO from 1979 to 2011, others from 1975 to 2013.

between average and median growth in the adjusted CBO data is 0.43 percent per year for 1979–2011.

If income inequality continues to grow over the next several decades as it has in the past three decades, how much slower will be the growth of median income relative to average income? The best indicator of what has happened in the past comes from the CBO data adjusted for taxes and transfers. If the future shortfall of median income growth relative to average growth were to continue at a rate of 0.4 percent, this implies that a projection of average future growth in per-person income of, say, 1.0 percent per year, would translate into a projection for median growth of 0.6 percent per year.

DOWNWARD PRESSURE ON WAGES OF THE BOTTOM 90 PERCENT

Which factors have influenced the evolution of the income distribution below the ninetieth percentile? The mid-1970s mark the turning point between an era of steadily rising wages in the middle and bottom of the income distribution to a new era during the past four decades when wages have grown little at the bottom and have increased much more rapidly at the top. The great stagnation of American wages over the last three decades has led many observers to believe that the economy is broken in a fundamental way. What caused the turnaround forty years ago?

Between 1929 and 1945 incomes at the top grew more slowly than at the middle and the bottom, creating the shift toward greater equality that Claudia Goldin and Robert Margo have called "the Great Compression." Between World War II and 1975, incomes at the top and bottom grew at roughly the same rate, and as a result, the compression lasted for about three decades. Three factors stressed by Goldin and Margo as supports for the compression were the rise of unionization and decline of both trade and immigration.[7] These three factors, which date back to the 1930s, convincingly explain the low level of inequality in the period 1945–75, and their reversal provides an important part of the explanation of increased inequality after 1975. In this section, we examine this reversal, consisting of the decline in unionization, and the rise of imports and immigration, along with two other factors generally credited as sources of increased inequality—namely, automation and the decline in the real value of the minimum wage. Subsequently, we turn to the role of education as a source of higher inequality as wage gains for college-educated workers have contrasted with wage stagnation for high school graduates and high school dropouts.

The percentage of U.S. employees in unions declined rapidly from 27 percent in 1973 to 19 percent in 1986, and then more slowly to 13 percent in 2011.[8] The falling rate of unionization has reduced wages, and particularly the median wage.[9] The decline in the rate of unionization combines market forces, particularly the shrinkage of manufacturing jobs and shift in consumer demand from goods to services, together with the aggressive anti-union stance adopted by many employers. The stagnation or outright decline in wages has been exacerbated by an increased tendency of firms, particularly in manufacturing and construction, to hire workers from temporary staffing agencies that pay relatively low wages and offer few if any fringe benefits. Firms benefit not only from lower labor costs but from increased flexibility in adjusting the supply of worker-hours to meet demand.

The share of imports in U.S. GDP increased from 5.4 percent in 1970 to 16.5 percent in 2014. Labor embodied in imports is a substitute for domestic labor. For this reason, the increase in the import share of GDP has contributed to the decline in the relative wages of unskilled and middle-skilled workers. In one particularly striking analysis, David Autor and co-authors calculated that imports from China between 1990 and 2007 accounted for about a quarter of the decline in manufacturing employment during that period and that they also lowered wages, reduced the labor force participation rate, and raised publicly financed transfer payments.[10] The inroads of imports go beyond final goods, because both firms and countries increasingly specialize in different stages of production. For instance, increases of automobile parts more than doubled between 2001 and 2014, from $63 billion to $138 billion, and caused many U.S. parts manufacturers to close their domestic factories and in some cases to "offshore" parts production to foreign countries, particularly Mexico.[11] Taken together, increased import penetration and outsourcing represent the combined effects of globalization on the levels of both employment and wages in the domestic economy. In the case of the automotive parts industry, the effects of globalization included a decline in median wages from $18.35 in 2003 to $15.83 per hour in 2013.[12]

Immigration accounted for more than half of total labor force growth in the United States over the decade between 1995 and 2005.[13] A complementary measure is that the share of foreign-born workers in the labor force steadily grew from 5.3 percent in 1970 to 14.7 percent in 2005.[14] Economic research supports the view that immigrants reduce the wages of domestic workers by a small amount and that the effect is greatest on domestic workers lacking a high school degree. Many low-skilled immigrants disproportionately take jobs and enter occupations already staffed by foreign-born workers—for example, restaurant workers and landscape services—and thus their main effect is to drive down wages of foreign-born workers, not domestic workers. The previous literature has noted the fact that among high school dropouts, wages of domestic and foreign-born workers were almost identical up to 1980, but by 2004, foreign-born workers earned 15–20 percent less.[15]

Downward pressure on wages in the bottom 90 percent would have occurred even if there had been no erosion of unionization nor a growth of imports or immigration. The steady pace of automation—the replacement of jobs by machines—would have contributed to a decline of the relative incomes of those in the bottom 90 percent. Relatively high-paying manufacturing jobs have eroded, as the share of manufacturing employment in the United States declined from 30 percent in 1953 to less than 10 percent currently. The automation effect overlaps with "skill-biased technical change" that results in the destruction of routine jobs that are close substitutes to software-driven computers, and these job losses have occurred not just in the assembly lines of manufacturing plants, but also in such routine office occupations as typist, bookkeeper, clerk, receptionist, and others. Automation did not create a permanent state of mass unemployment, as once was feared by pessimists, and the economy was able to attain an unemployment rate below 5.0 percent in the business cycle expansion that ended in 2007, and the unemployment rate in 2015 has again declined close to 5.0 percent.

Instead of massive job loss, the *composition* of jobs has changed, with more jobs created at the top and bottom of the occupational distribution and a hollowing out of the middle. This transformation has been dubbed the "polarization hypothesis" and has been extensively documented in recent years by labor economists.[16] Upper-level jobs such as those held by managers and professionals are often called "non-routine abstract" occupations. Middle-level jobs such as those held by assembly-line manufacturing workers, bookkeepers, receptionists, and clerks have been called "routine" occupations, whereas those at the bottom have been called "manual" jobs. One result of the loss of middle-skilled routine jobs is that middle-skilled workers are forced to compete for low-skilled manual jobs, thus raising the supply relative to the demand for manual workers. The result has been a decline in wages for those with relatively low skills, high school graduates and high school dropouts, as shown below in figure 18–3. The overall level of wages is reduced as the composition of employment shifts from

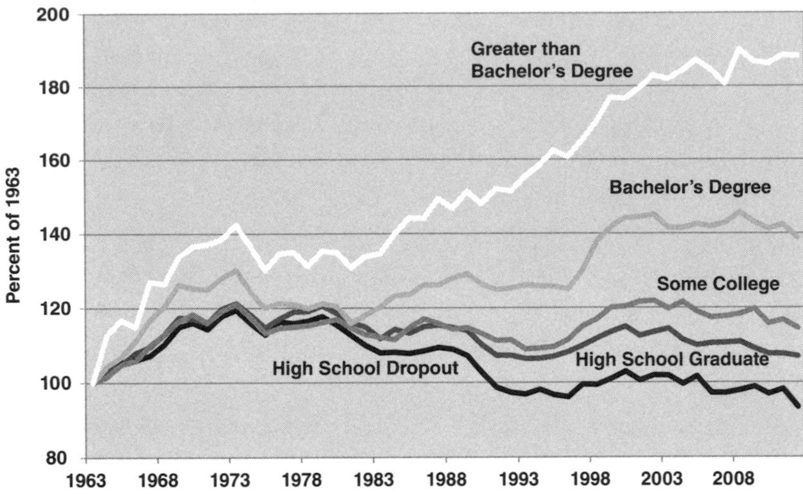

Figure 18–3. Real Weekly Earnings by Educational Attainment, 1963 = 100, 1963–2012

Source: Autor (2014b), Figure 6.

relatively well-paid manufacturing jobs to the wide range of typically low-paid jobs in retail, food services, cleaning, and groundskeeping.

Beyond the effects of deunionization, rising imports, the flow of immigrants, and automation, a fifth fact that has tended to increase inequality within the bottom 90 percent of the income distribution is the erosion of the minimum wage. Stated in constant 2011 dollars, the minimum wage decreased between 1979 and 1989 from $8.38 to $5.87. It reached a low point of $4.68 in 2006 before being raised to $7.25 in 2009. Several authors contend that the erosion of the real minimum wage accounts for much of the increase of inequality as represented by the ratio of incomes in the tenth percentile to those in the ninetieth percentile.[17]

It seems plausible that the decline of relative incomes below the ninetieth percentile since the late 1970s has been caused, at least in part, by the declining bargaining power and density of unions, by the increased importance of imports and immigration, by the inroads of automation, and by the decrease in the real minimum wage. Frank Levy and Peter Temin provide a complementary interpretation that places more emphasis on a change in political philosophy from what they call the "Detroit Consensus" of the late 1940s to the Reagan-initiated "Washington Consensus" of the early 1980s. The main point that Levy and Temin add to our preceding summary is that highly progressive taxes, with 90 percent marginal tax rates for top-bracket earners in the 1940s and 1950s, sent a signal that high incomes were unacceptable.[18] Beginning with the Reagan tax cuts, that element of the policy support of the great compression began to erode, and CEO compensation surged ahead from twenty times average worker pay in 1973 to 257 times higher in 2013, when the average CEO pay of publicly traded companies reached $10.5 million.[19] The pay gap is even greater for retirement saving, in which it is typical for departing CEOs to receive multi-million-dollar retirement plans. A particularly blatant example was the CEO of Target, who was replaced in May 2014 after a massive credit card hacking data breach and received a retirement package of $47 million, about 1,000 times the average balance that workers at Target have saved in that company's 401(k) plan.[20]

Recently, there has been substantial publicity for the plight of fast food workers, most of whom are paid little more than the minimum wage. The bottom 20 percent of American workers classified by income earn less than $9.89 per hour, and their inflation-adjusted wage fell by 5 percent between 2006 and 2012, while average pay for the median worker fell 3.4 percent. Holding down wages is an explicit corporate strategy at many retail firms.[21] The *Wall Street Journal* writes,

> Economic changes over the past decade have led to a decline across the country in well-paying jobs, such as those in manufacturing, and an increase in jobs that pay less, such as those in hotels and food services.... Positions are increasingly being filled not with the young and inexperienced, but by older and more skilled workers who can't find other jobs.[22]

The Caterpillar Corporation has become a poster child for rising inequality. It has broken strikes in order to enforce a two-tier wage system in which new hires are paid half of existing workers, even though both groups are members of the same labor union. In contrast, there was an 80 percent increase during 2011–13 in the compensation of Caterpillar's CEO, whose quoted mantra is "we can never make enough money...we can never make enough profit."[23] Foreign companies such as Volkswagen continue to open plants in the nonunion right-to-work states. By lowering wages compared to wages in union-dominated northern states, these foreign transplant factories help keep overall U.S. manufacturing employment from declining further. But any progress in arresting the decades-long decline in manufacturing employment appears to be contingent on maintaining worker wages at about half the level that the automobile union had achieved for its workers before the bankruptcy of General Motors and Chrysler. In the 2009–2013 recovery, manufacturing regained only 600,000 of the 6 million jobs that had been lost since 2001, and most of those were contingent on hiring workers at wage rates that were substantially lower than were common in manufacturing as recently as 2001.[24]

INCREASED INEQUALITY AT THE TOP

Table 18–2 focused on the gap between the growth rate of average real income since 1975 as contrasted either with income growth at the median (i.e., fiftieth percentile) of that distribution. Much of the increase of inequality has resulted from increased skewness within the top decile. Even within the top 1 percent, income gains are much faster the higher one rises into the stratosphere of the top 0.1 percent and the top 0.01 percent. It is useful in identifying the sources of rising incomes at the top to use a three-way distinction between superstars in the sports and entertainment industries, other highly paid and highly skilled workers, and the controversial additional category of CEOs and other top corporate managers.

The economics of superstars is a concept originally invented by Sherwin Rosen, who explained the extreme skewness in occupational categories dominated by superstars as the results of particular characteristics of demand and supply.[25] On the demand side, audiences want to see the very best talent, not the second-best, so income is highly skewed because the ability of top superstars to fill large entertainment venues and to sell recordings is an order of magnitude greater than that of the second-best stars. On the supply side, the performer exerts the same effort whether ten or 10,000 witness the performance. Superstar premia reflect a particular type of skill-biased technical change. Rosen suggested that a succession of innovations going back to the phonograph boosted the size of audiences who can hear a given performance and thus increased the incomes of superstars by many multiples. The sharp rise of superstar incomes since the time of Rosen's 1981 article reflects the further development of technology, including cable TV, rentable videotapes and DVDs, Internet-based movie streaming, YouTube videos, and downloaded music.

A second group of high-income individuals also reflects the operation of the market—that is, of supply and demand. Important professions, especially top-ranked lawyers and investment bankers, earn incomes that are determined by market demand for the services provided by their firms, whether an enormous law firm such as Chicago's Sidley Austin or an investment bank such as Goldman Sachs. These market-driven professionals differ from superstars in that their product is not amplified by electronic media. They are still tied down by the need to meet in person with clients and to attend legal proceedings with adversaries in person. This second group goes beyond lawyers and investment bankers to include anyone whose individual services are in high demand, including those in publishing, design, fashion, medicine, and even in the top ranks of academics.

CEOs and other top corporate officers represent a distinct third group. An ample literature suggests that CEO pay is not set purely on the market, but rather is set by peer CEOs who sit on compensation committees. Lucian Bebchuk and Yaniv Grinstein provide a managerial power hypothesis that drives top executive pay well above the market solution.[26] The pay of the top five corporate officers in 1,500 firms increased by almost twice as much between 1993 and 2003 as their regression model could explain. These authors report the striking fact that the ratio of top-five compensation to total corporate profits for their 1,500 firms rose from 5.0 percent in 1993–95 to 12.8 percent in 2000–2002.

It is clear from the literature that the rise of executive pay is dominated by the growth in the role of stock options. Brian Hall and Jeffrey Liebman propose two alternative explanations; they juxtapose a market-driven explanation against a managerial power explanation. Their first proposed explanation is that the use of stock options has increased so dramatically because corporate boards want to tighten the relationship between pay and performance. Their second proposed explanation, complementary to their first, is that boards want to increase CEO pay and choose option grants as a "less visible" method that is less likely to incite stockholder anger.[27]

There are doubtless overlaps and interactions among the superstar, top talent, and CEO explanations of rising inequality. After becoming rich for whatever reason, those at the pinnacle of the income distribution multiply their earnings by investing in the stock market and more esoteric investments such as private equity and hedge funds. Wealth gains were particularly extreme between 1983, when the S&P 500 stock market average was at 120, and 2000, when the S&P 500 average for the year reached 1477. This represents a real rate of return including dividends of 14.3 percent per year.[28] Not only do households below the ninetieth percentile of the income distribution own few stocks (except indirectly through retirement plans), but they are also prone to perverse market timing. A Federal Reserve study showed that more than 5 million households sold out of the stock market when it was low in 2009–10 and that only those in the top 10 percent of the income distribution have increased their holdings of stock since then.[29] Some of this tendency of lower-income households to "bail out" of the market when it is low may come from a necessity to liquidate assets in the face of unemployment caused by a business cycle slump.

A recent study by the Pew Research Center quantified the trajectory of real wealth increases by dividing American households into an upper group comprising 21 percent of households, a middle group comprising 46 percent, and a lower group accounting for the remaining 33 percent.[30] For the large middle group, the real inflation-adjusted value of wealth stagnated over three decades, growing only from \$94,300 in 1983 to \$96,500 in 2013. Over that thirty-year period, real wealth in the bottom group actually fell, from \$11,400 to \$9,300. In contrast, the top group enjoyed an exact doubling of real wealth, from \$318,100 in 1983 to \$639,400 in 2013. Though the emphasis of this book on the standard of living primarily refers to real income per person, the evolution of real wealth cannot be ignored, for the "safety net" aspect of wealth accumulation has a profound effect on welfare by providing self-insurance against the loss of a job or an accident or illness that reduces the ability to earn income. Real wealth stagnation for the bottom 80 percent of the U.S. income distribution is a powerful indicator supporting the view that the growth in well-being has slowed in the past three decades.

EDUCATION AS A SOURCE OF GROWING INEQUALITY

The preceding two sections examined sources of downward pressure on wages and incomes in the bottom 90 percent and the sources of rising relative incomes in the top 1 percent of the income distribution. In addition, a bifurcation has occurred within the bottom 90 percent, with wage stagnation and decline in the bottom percentiles combined with faster income growth in the eightieth and ninetieth percentiles, although not nearly so rapid as in the top 1 percent. Education is the chief source of this spreading out of the income distribution, for growth in the compensation of those who complete a four-year college degree has far outpaced those who drop out of high school. Earnings outcomes of those who have two-year college degrees, who have achieved partial completion of four-year college degrees, and those who have high school diplomas have experienced intermediate outcomes between the extremes represented by four-year college completion at the top and high school dropouts at the bottom.

The analysis of the rewards earned by workers who have different amounts of educational attainment starts with the basic proposition that the earnings of workers is determined by their productivity—that is, how much they produce from an hour of work. The value of that hour depends on demand and supply—that is, the value to the employer of what an employee can produce and the number of workers who are capable of completing the required tasks. As the percentage of Americans who complete college has increased, the supply of college graduates has risen relative to those with less educational attainment. That increase in relative supply was particularly rapid between 1964 and 1982 and was sufficiently fast relative to the increase in the relative demand for college graduates to cause the college wage premium to shrink slightly in the 1970s. After 1982, the growth in the relative supply slowed and that in relative demand increased, so the college wage premium increased between 1982 and 2000. This rise in the college wage premium has been sufficient to explain essentially all of the rise in earnings of those at the ninetieth percentile relative to those at the tenth percentile between 1984 and 2004.

Figure 18–3 shows the evolution of the real wage of full-time male workers in five education groups expressed as a ratio to the real wage of that group in 1963.[31] The lines are arrayed from top to bottom by the amount of education, with the top line plotting the real wage of those with education beyond the four-year bachelor's degree and the bottom line depicting wage changes of high school dropouts. Each point plotted represents the wage relative to 1963, so the final point of 97 percent plotted for 2012 for high school dropouts represents a 3 percent wage decline from 1963 to 2012, whereas the final point of 188 percent for those having earned beyond a bachelor's degree indicates a 88 percent increase in the real wage since 1963. The spreading apart of the five lines, showing greater wage gains with a higher educational attainment, indicates that the relative demand for highly educated graduates grew more quickly than their relative supply. It is important to note that the increasing earnings of those who have a college degree or greater increased relative to wages of high school graduates and dropouts not just because the college graduates were doing so well, but also because the groups at the bottom were doing so poorly.

The growth of earnings in the five groups did not proceed at a uniform pace. The upsurge in college graduate real wages occurred in two relatively short periods, first between 1964 and 1972 and then between 1996 and 2000. Between 1972 and 1996, and then again after 2000, the real wage of college graduates stagnated. For high school graduates, there were several phases in the evolution of the real wage: an increase during 1964–72, then a long slow decline from 1972 to 1990, stagnation to 1996, a partial recovery during 1996–2000, and then stagnation again between 2000 and 2012. The outcomes for those who have some college lie in between those for college graduates and high school graduates but are closer to the latter, whereas high school dropouts had a real wage trajectory that fell gradually, between 1974 and 2000, to about 10 percent below that for high school graduates. The erosion in wages for high school graduates and dropouts is a result of all the factors already cited—the decline in unionization and the minimum wage combined with the increase in imports and immigration, together with the ongoing role of automation.[32]

We can divide the real wage for bachelor's degree recipients by that for high school graduates to plot the evolution of the college wage premium relative to its 1963 value, as in figure 18–4. The college wage premium increased over the past half-century, but not at a uniform pace. After an initial upsurge between 1964 and 1967, the premium stagnated until 1973, when by 1982 it declined back to the 1963 level. It then increased steadily from 100 percent

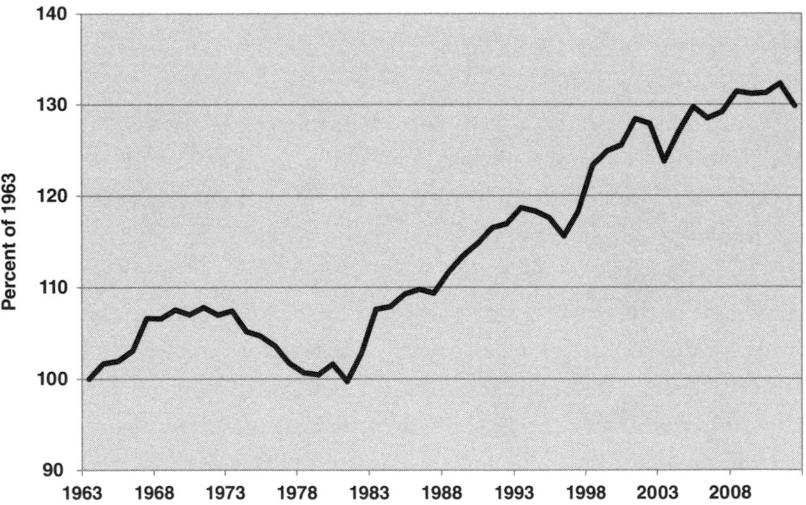

Figure 18–4. Real Weekly Earnings, Percent Ratio of College Graduates to High School Graduates, 1963=100, 1963–2012

Source: Calculated from data underlying Autor (2014b), Figure 6.

to 128 percent of the 1963 level between 1982 and 2001, followed by little further growth. The decline in the premium in the 1970s can be attributed to the rise in the relative supply of college graduates that took place in the 1960s and 1970s. The increase in the premium from 1982 to 2001 coincides with a period of relatively slow growth in the relative supply of college graduates, and the sharp increase between 1996 and 2001 may also reflect the rapid increase in the demand for skills during the dot-com boom of the late 1990s. The flattening of the premium after 2005 appears to be the result of a renewed increase in the relative supply of college graduates, but it also reflects the decline in the demand for non-routine abstract jobs that set in after 2000.[33]

As the supply of college-educated workers has increased, a growing fraction of college graduates have been forced to accept jobs that do not require a college education. As shown by Paul Beaudry and co-authors, after 2000, there was a decline in the share of college graduates working in non-routine abstract occupations and an increase in those working in manual jobs.[34] This represents a sharp turnaround from the 1990s and placed further downward pressure on the wages paid for routine manual work. Beaudry explains the decline in the demand for non-routine abstract workers as the complement of the post-2000 decline of investment in high-tech information and communication technology equipment in the investment bust that followed the late 1990s dot-com boom.

So far we have expressed real wages and the college wage premium relative to their values in 1963. What is the dollar equivalent of these values? The monetary value of the college wage premium is substantial. The 2012 annual full-time earnings gap between college graduates and high school graduates was $35,000 for men and $23,000 for women. A two-earner household with both husband and wife having college degrees would have an annual earning $58,000 higher than a two-earner household consisting of two high school graduates. The present discounted value of obtaining a college degree relative to a high school degree by 2008 had reached $590,000 for men and $370,000 for women.[35] These substantial rewards to college graduation include the additional income earned by those who gain postgraduate professional degrees, for which college graduation is a necessary prerequisite.

The effect of education on inequality extends beyond the direct effect of schooling on earnings in the current generation, because well-educated parents tend to bestow numerous advantages on the next generation. Typically, college-educated men and women marry each other, earn two incomes enhanced by the college degree, and have their children after marriage rather than out of wedlock. They nurture their children and read to them, enhancing their vocabulary advantage over children from less educated parents. Highly educated parents also have the money to enrich their children's lives through exposure to museums, sports, music lessons, and a variety of books. They tend to live in suburbs where local schools provide a richer diet of educational choices, including more counseling to pass Advanced Placement tests and to gain admission to top-ranked universities, where the admissions process tends to discriminate in favor of alumni. Scores on the SAT college admission tests tend to be highly correlated with parental income. All these advantages reduce social mobility and establish a self-perpetuating educational elite, for almost all high income families send their children to four-year college, whereas virtually none of the poorest Americans do so. College completion for households in the top quarter of the income distribution rose between 1970 and 2013 from 40 percent to 77 percent, whereas for those in the bottom quarter, it increased only from 6 percent to 9 percent.[36]

EDUCATION AS THE SECOND HEADWIND

The higher earnings of those with a college and postgraduate degrees reflects their higher productivity on the job. For the economy as a whole, this implies that aggregate productivity growth depends positively on the growth of educational attainment. Every high school dropout becomes a worker who is unlikely ever to earn much more than the minimum wage for the rest of his or her life.

The surge in high school graduation rates was a central driver of twentieth-century economic growth. But gains in overall educational attainment have become slower since 1980, implying that education has become a headwind in the sense that its smaller contribution to economic growth has reduced the growth rate of productivity and per-person income. This section examines the slowdown in the advance of educational attainment, the evidence that the U.S. education system is turning out students who have poor achievement levels compared to their international peers, and the role of tuition inflation and college student debt as an impediment to college completion, particularly for those from low- and middle-income family backgrounds.

Since Edward Denison's first 1962 attempt at measurement, growth accounting has recognized the role of increasing educational attainment as a source of economic growth.[37] Claudia Goldin and Lawrence Katz estimate that educational attainment increased by 0.8 years per decade over the eight decades between 1890 and 1970. Over this period, they also estimate that the improvement in educational attainment contributed 0.35 percentage points per year to the growth of productivity and output per person.[38] In separate research, I have adjusted Denison's estimates for 1913–79 to current BLS methodology and find an average contribution of education of 0.38 percent per year, almost identical to that of Goldin and Katz.

The increase of educational attainment has two parts, that referring to secondary education and the other relevant for higher education. High school graduation rates increased from less than 10 percent of youth in 1900 to 80 percent by 1970, and the percentage of 18-year-olds receiving bona fide high school diplomas has since fallen, to 74 percent in 2000, according to James Heckman. He found that the economic outcomes of those who earned not a high school diploma but rather a General Education Development (GED) certificate performed no better economically than high school dropouts and that the drop in graduation rates could be explained, in part, by the rising share of youth who are in prison rather than in school.[39] The United States currently ranks eleventh among the developed nations in high school graduation rates and is the only country in which the graduation rates of those aged 25–34 is no higher than those aged 55–64.[40]

The role of education in holding back future economic growth is evident in the poor quality of educational outcomes at the secondary level. A UNICEF report lists the United States eighteenth of twenty-four countries in the percentage of secondary students that rank below a fixed international standard in reading and math. The international PISA tests in 2013, again referring to secondary education, rated the United States seventeenth in reading, twentieth in science, and twenty-seventh in math.[41] A recent evaluation by the ACT college entrance test organization showed that only 25 percent of high school students were prepared to attend college as evidenced by adequate scores on reading, math, and science.

At the college level, the problems combine an interaction between a decline in the international league tables of college graduation rates with the issues of affordability and student debt. During most of the postwar period, a low-cost college education was within reach of a larger fraction of the population than in any other nation, thanks both to free college education made possible by the GI Bill and to minimal tuition for in-state students at state public universities and junior colleges. The United States led the world during most of the last century in the percentage of youth completing college. The percentage of the 25–34 age group who have earned a BA degree from a four-year college has inched up in the past fifteen years from 25 percent to 32 percent, but the United States is now ranked twelfth among developed nations, after having been ranked second as recently as 2000.[42]

And the future does not look promising. The cost of a university education has risen since 1972 at more than triple the overall rate of inflation.[43] Between 2001 and 2012, funding by states and localities for higher education declined by fully a third when adjusted for inflation. In 1985, the state of Colorado provided 37 percent of the budget of the University of Colorado, but in 2013, it provided only 9 percent. Even when account is taken of the discounts from full tuition made possible by scholarships and fellowships, the current level of American college completion has been made possible only by a dramatic rise in student borrowing. Americans now owe $1.2 trillion in college debt. Though a four-year college degree still pays off in a much higher income and lower risk of unemployment than for high school graduates, still more than half of recent college graduates were unable to find a job requiring a college education. This "underemployment rate" was 56 percent for 22-year-olds, declining to about 40 percent for 27-year-olds, and the inability of so many college graduates to find appropriate jobs is consistent with the evidence, already cited, from Beaudry, Green, and Sand, arguing that there has been a reversal in the demand for non-routine abstract cognitive skills since 2000.[44]

Students taking on large amounts of student debt face two kinds of risks. One is that they fall short of the average income achieved by the typical college graduate through some combination of unemployment after college and an inability to find a job in their chosen field of study. Research has shown that on average, a college student taking on $100,000 in student debt will still come out ahead by age 34, with the higher income made possible by college completion high enough to offset the debt repayment. But that break-even age becomes older if future income falls short of the average graduate. There is also completion risk. A student who drops out after two years never breaks even, because wages of college dropouts are little better than those of high school graduates. These risks are particularly relevant for high-achieving students from low-income families—Caroline Hoxby has shown that they seldom apply to elite colleges, which are prepared to fund them completely without debt, so they wind up at subpar colleges, loaded with debt.[45]

The poor achievement of American high school graduates spills over to their performance in college education. Many of the less capable enter two-year community colleges, which currently enroll 39 percent of American undergraduates, whereas the remaining 61 percent enroll in four-year colleges. The Center on International Education Benchmarking reports that only 13 percent of students in two-year colleges graduate in two years, although the percentage rises to 28 percent after four years. The low graduation rates reflect the need for most students to work part-time or full-time in addition to their college classes, as well as the poor preparation of the secondary graduates who enter community colleges. Most community college students take one or more remedial courses.[46]

Just as the defects of American secondary education make successful college careers less likely, so does the great inequality of financing of American elementary education feed through to poor high school performance and an excessively large rate of high school dropouts. The American elementary school system is financed by property tax revenue that allows wealthy suburbs to provide lavish facilities to their students who already have a head start thanks to their parents' income and home tutoring, whereas the students from poverty families often face acute budget cutbacks and school closings as a result of shrinking inner city enrollments and inadequate local property tax revenue. The United States is also failing to follow the lead of other nations in providing free preschool education. Across the rich nations, an average of 70 percent of 3-year-olds are enrolled in some kind of education program, whereas in the United States, that percentage is 38 percent.[47]

THE THIRD HEADWIND: DEMOGRAPHY

The demographic headwind refers to a set of forces that have changed hours per person (*H*/*N*), thus driving a wedge between the growth of productivity and the growth of output per person. The organizing principle to understand its significance is a definitional identity that relates total output (Real Gross Domestic Product or *Y*) to aggregate hours of work in the total economy (*H*) and the total population (*N*):

$$\frac{Y}{N} \equiv \frac{Y}{H} \cdot \frac{H}{N}. \tag{1}$$

Equation (1) states the truism that the standard of living measured by output per person (*Y*/*N*) by definition equals labor productivity or output per hour (*Y*/*H*) times hours per person (*H*/*N*). By decomposing output per person into productivity and hours per person, equation (1) helps clarify the relationship between chapters 17 and 18 of this book. In chapter 17, the past, present, and future of productivity (Y/H) growth was related to innovation, the fundamental driver of higher output per worker-hour. Chapter 18 identifies economic headwinds that change productivity, those that change hours per person, and those that influence neither aggregate variable but rather, in the case of inequality, reduce median real income growth relative to the economy-wide average.

The crucial H/N term can be further decomposed into hours per employee (H/E), the employment rate as a percentage of the labor force (E/L), and the labor force participation rate (L/N):

$$\text{(2)} \qquad \frac{H}{N} \equiv \frac{H}{E} \cdot \frac{E}{L} \cdot \frac{L}{N}$$

The most important demographic events in the postwar United States were the baby boom of 1946 to 1964, the influx of women into the labor force between 1965 and 1995, and the retirement of the baby boom generation starting around 2008. The entry of the baby boom generation into the work force in the 1970s boosted hours per person, while the influx of women permanently raised the *level* of hours per person and raised its *growth rate* during the transition period, roughly 1965–95. Positive growth in hours per person allowed output per person to grow faster than labor productivity, as in equation (1).

The retirement of the baby boomers will reduce hours per person independently of any other cause over a long transition period extending from 2008 to 2034. There is more to the demographic headwind, however, than the retirement of the baby boomers. The labor force participation rate (L/N) fell from 66.0 percent in 2007 to 62.9 percent for the full year 2014 and further to 62.6 percent in June 2015. Because the working-age population is 250 million, the decline in L/N by 3.4 percentage points (66.0 minus 62.6) implies a loss of 8.5 million jobs, most of them permanently.

Economic research has concluded that about half the decline in the participation rate was caused by the retirement of the baby boomers and the rest by a decline in the participation of those younger than 55. Those who have stopped looking for jobs and have thus dropped out of the labor force consist of workers who have lost their jobs in an economic setting in which they do not expect to be employed again, and a sizeable fraction of them have been able to obtain Social Security disability benefits.[48] To call attention to the plight of these victims of deindustrialization, in late July 2013, President Obama toured several

Rust Belt cities that have lost most of their manufacturing jobs base. Cities such as Galesburg, Illinois; Scranton, Pennsylvania; and Syracuse, New York now mainly rely on government, health care, and retail jobs. In Scranton, 41.3 percent of those older than 18 have withdrawn from the workforce, and in Syracuse, that percentage is an even higher 42.4 percent.[49] The devastating effect of manufacturing plant closures throughout the Midwest is captured by remarks of the newly appointed British consul-general in Chicago, who toured the Midwest during the autumn of 2013, in the first three months of his four-year term. Asked for impressions of his travels, he said, "What surprised me most was the deterioration and decay of the former one-factory small and middle-sized manufacturing towns."[50]

What does the 2007–14 experience imply for the future? We will optimistically assume that the dropping out of those younger than 55 has run its course, and that the only source of the further decline in the participation rate will be baby boomer retirement. Several scholars have estimated that the retirement of the baby-boom generation will cause hours per person (H/N) to decline by −0.4 percent per year, and this implies that future growth in average output per person (Y/N) will be 0.4 points slower than that of labor productivity (Y/H). At the end of this chapter, the effects of declining labor force participation will be combined with those of the other headwinds to provide a projection for future growth in median real disposable income per person.[51]

THE FOURTH HEADWIND: REPAYING DEBT

The future reckoning for government finance will arrive over the next several decades. The official projections of the Congressional Budget Office (CBO) currently estimate that the federal ratio of debt to GDP will stabilize between 2014 and 2020 and then rise steadily to 100 percent by 2038. But the CBO estimates paint too rosy a scenario, because its forecast of future growth in output, and hence in federal tax revenue, is too optimistic. The CBO, as a result, has understated the future rise in the debt: GDP ratio. For 2024, the official CBO forecast is a ratio of 78 percent; mine is 87 percent. For 2038, the CBO is at 100 percent; my forecast is roughly 125 percent.[52]

But even the CBO projects that trouble lies ahead beyond 2020. The Medicare trust fund is predicted to reach a zero balance in 2030, and the zero-balance date for Social Security is projected to occur in 2034. By definition, any stabilization of the federal debt-GDP ratio, compared to its likely steady increase with current policies, will require more rapid growth in future taxes and/or slower growth in future transfer payments. This is the fourth headwind, the near inevitability that over the next several decades, disposable income will decline relative to real income before taxes and transfers, reversing the trends of the past quarter-century. This is the inevitable consequence of an aging population and slowing population growth.

A sole focus on the federal debt ignores the unfunded pension liabilities of many of America's states and localities. The bankruptcy of Detroit has led municipal bond experts to ask whether Illinois and Chicago could be far behind, not to mention other large states that have massive unfunded pension liabilities. A reasonable, albeit arbitrary, forecast is that the future growth in tax rates and/or slower growth of government transfers will reduce the growth rate of disposable income in the future by 0.1 percent per year relative to income before taxes and transfers.

SOCIAL CHANGE AT THE BOTTOM OF THE INCOME DISTRIBUTION

The first part of this chapter addressed the issue of steadily rising inequality in the United States by presenting a set of alternative measures of mean vs. median income. However, the status of those at the middle and bottom of the income distribution goes beyond a lack of growth in money income. Social conditions are decaying, and clearly there is a chicken and egg two-way causality between stagnant incomes and social dysfunction. A lack of job opportunities may be responsible for declining marriage rates and for the sharp increase in the percentage of children living with only one parent. But also social problems may disqualify some for employment, especially if a prison term is involved.

The decline of marriage as an institution among Americans who lack a college education is relevant to the future rate of productivity growth, because children—particularly boys—who grow up in households lacking a father are more likely to drop out of high school and become engaged in criminal activity. An important source of this sociological change is the evaporation of steady, high-paying blue-collar jobs. Partly because men without a college education have lacked the incomes and steady employment to be attractive marriage partners, and partly because women have become more independent as opportunities in the labor market have opened up for them, fewer couples are getting married. Much of this reflects the importance that females place on having an employed spouse, as well as that there are only sixty-five employed men for every

100 women of a given age. Among young African Americans, there are only fifty-one employed men for every 100 women, reflecting in large part the high incarceration rates of young black males. Many young people view financial stability as a prerequisite for marriage, so the reluctance to marry interacts with the wage stagnation of the past three decades.[53]

For white high school graduates, the percentage of children born out of wedlock increased from 4 percent in 1982 to 34 percent in 2008 and from 21 percent to 42 percent for white high school dropouts. For blacks, the equivalent percentages are a rise from 48 percent to 74 percent for high school graduates and from 76 percent to 96 percent for high school dropouts.[54] Not only is the rate of marriage declining, but almost half of all marriages fail. The number of children born outside of marriage is drawing equal with the number of children born within marriage. June Carbone and Naomi Cahn summarize the implications for the future:

> The American family is changing—and the changes guarantee that inequality will be greater in the next generation. For the first time, America's children will almost certainly not be as well educated, healthy, or wealthy as their parents, and the result stems from the growing disconnect between the resources available to adults and those invested in children.[55]

Charles Murray has documented the decline of every relevant social indicator for the bottom third of the white population, which he calls "Fishtown" after a poor area of Philadelphia. He admirably presents his data in a series of charts that uniformly extend from 1960 to 2010. For the white population of Fishtown, the percentage of married couples in which at least one spouse worked forty or more hours in the previous week declined from 84 percent in 1960 to 58 percent in 2010. The breakup of the family is documented by three complementary indicators all referring to the 30–49 age group: percent married down from 85 percent to 48 percent, percent never married up from 8 percent to 25 percent, and percent divorced up from 5 percent to 33 percent.[56]

Murray's most devastating statistic of all is that for mothers aged 40, the percentage of children living with both biological parents declined from 95 percent in 1960 to 34 percent in 2010. The educational and inequality headwinds interact, leading to the prediction of a continuing slippage of the United States in the international league tables of high school and college completion rates.

Separately, the growth of college student debt leads to a prediction of delays in marriage and child birth and a decline in the rate of population growth, which aggravates the other sources of the future growth slowdown, particularly the fiscal headwind.

Other sources support Murray's emphasis on social decline in the bottom third of the white population. A recent study showed that between 1979 and 2009, the cumulative percentage of white male high school dropouts who had been in prison rose from 3.8 percent to 28.0 percent. For blacks over the same time interval, the percentage who had been in prison rose from 14.7 percent to 68.0 percent. That is, fully two-thirds of black male high school dropouts experience at least one spell in prison by the time they reach 40 years old. For black graduates from high school (including those with GED certificates), the percentage in prison rose from 11.0 percent to 21.4 percent.[57]

Any kind of criminal record, and especially time in prison, severely limits the employment opportunities available to those whose prison sentences are ending. According to the FBI, no less than a third of all adult Americans have a criminal record of some sort, including arrests that did not lead to convictions; this stands as a major barrier to employment.[58] The increased sophistication of electronic records make it easier for prospective employers to learn about stains in the past of a prospective job applicant. The diminished probability of employment in turn feeds back to the likelihood of marriage, for women are not attracted to men who have no capability of earning an income from legal activity.

> State laws prohibit the employment of convicted felons in occupations ranging from child- and dependent-care providers to barbers and hairdressers. Some states also cut off their access to public employment, which has been an important source of work for inner-city minorities. . . . Many employers are wary of employing convicted felons because of mounting case law delineating their liability risks for "negligent hiring."[59]

OTHER HEADWINDS

Discussions of headwinds often turn to two additional barriers to growth that are difficult to quantify, "globalization" and "energy/environment." This section places these additional headwinds in perspective without attempting to quantify their importance.

Globalization is difficult to disentangle from other sources of rising inequality. Plant closings caused by offshoring are responsible for part of the demographic headwind by causing prime-age workers to leave the labor force when their one-factory town experiences a plant closure. There has been a major loss of high-paying manufacturing jobs that long antedates the 2008 financial crisis and 2007–9 recession. Roughly half of the 7 million person loss of manufacturing jobs between 2000 and 2011 occurred before 2008.[60] The period 2000–2007 witnessed the maximum impact of the increase in Chinese manufacturing capacity that flooded the United States with imports, boosted the trade deficit, and caused plant closings and ended the chance of millions of workers to enjoy middle-income wages with no better than a high school diploma. The main reason why the economy experienced an economic expansion rather than contraction in the years leading up to 2007 was the housing bubble, which allowed many of the displaced manufacturing workers to obtain temporary jobs in the construction industry.

Globalization is also responsible for rising inequality through another channel. The United States has benefited from foreign investment, particularly in the automotive industry, but this has been directed almost exclusively at the right-to-work states, largely in the south, where foreign firms are free to pay workers whatever they want. Wages of $15 to $20 per hour, compared to the old standard of $30 to $40 per hour achieved before 2007 in union states such as Michigan and Ohio, are welcomed by residents of the southern states as manna from heaven, and new plant openings are greeted by long lines of hopeful workers at the hiring gates. Globalization is working as in the classic economic theory of factor price equalization, raising wages in developing countries and slowing their growth in the advanced nations.

Another potential headwind concerns the possible effects of global warming and other environmental issues, and a possible tailwind has emerged in the form of greatly increased U.S. domestic oil and natural gas production as a result of horizontal fracking. Though the extent and likely effects of global warming are subject to debate, there is little doubt that they are occurring and will create weather events—whether coastal flooding or more frequent and violent tornadoes—that will reduce future economic growth and raise insurance premia. Future carbon taxes and direct regulatory interventions such as the CAFÉ fuel economy standards will divert investment into research whose sole purpose is improving energy efficiency and fuel economy. Regulations that require the replacement of machinery or consumer appliances with new versions that are more energy-efficient but operationally equivalent impose a capital cost burden. Such investments do not contribute to economic growth in the same sense as such early twentieth-century innovations as the replacement of the icebox by the electric refrigerator or the replacement of the horse by the automobile.

One of the world's experts on global warming, William Nordhaus, has quantified its effects on economic growth. A surprising aspect of his research is that the impact of a 3 °C warming in the global temperature in the next seventy years would reduce global real GDP per person by only around 2.5 percent.[61] That translates as an annual subtraction of growth of –2.5/70, or 0.036 of a percentage point per year, trivial compared to the estimates in this paper of a negative effect of –0.4 percent for demography as a result of baby-boom retirement. Nordhaus's estimates are based on a hypothetical failure of worldwide policy to take explicit new measures to fight global warming.

Vast new fields of gas and oil made possible by fracking have created a cheap source of energy. In assessing the importance of fracking, a distinction must be made between oil and gas fracking. The price of oil is set in world markets, so additional oil discoveries may ultimately make the United States oil-independent but will not make oil prices lower in the United States than in the rest of the world. Because natural gas cannot be easily transported between continents, the gas fracking revolution in the United States is more of a boon. The cheaper price of gas that is unique to the North American continent will lead to a welcome substitution of gas for oil and coal, helping to reduce the growth of carbon emissions as well as reducing costs in energy-intensive industries.

CONCLUSION: FORECASTING FUTURE GROWTH IN THE STANDARD OF LIVING

This chapter on the headwinds and the preceding chapter 17 on the slowing pace of innovation have identified a set of forces that will retard future U.S. economic growth compared to the past. In this concluding section, we consider the implications for the future growth of labor productivity (output per hour) and the standard of living (output per person) over the next two to three decades, roughly the period 2015–40. It is not enough to project future growth in average output per person if inequality continues to increase, because rising inequality implies that median growth in output per person will be less than average growth. Similarly, in the event that future taxes are raised and/or transfer payments are cut to limit the rise in the ratio of public debt to GDP, then real median disposable income will grow more slowly than real median income before taxes and transfers are taken into account.

By definition, our forecast of growth in output per person must equal the forecast growth in output per hour plus projected growth in hours per person. Thus our forecasting task begins by translating the analysis from chapter 17 on the past behavior of output per hour—that is, labor productivity—into a projection of future productivity growth. As shown in the first four lines of table 18–3, the record of actual productivity growth since 1948 can be divided into four distinctly different eras. Rapid growth of 2.71 percent per year prior to 1970 contrasts with relatively slow growth of 1.54 percent per year between 1970 and 1994. Then came the dot-com–related revival to a rate of 2.26 percent between 1994 and 2004, followed by the end of the revival with growth in 2004–15 of 1.00 percent, even slower than during 1970–94.

A substantial portion of chapter 17 was devoted to the contrast between the 1994–2004 productivity revival decade and the 2004–14 slowdown decade. Our conclusion was that the revival was a one-time event that is unlikely to be repeated. Most of the benefits of the conversion of business methods and practices from the age of paper and filing cabinets to the new age of web-connected computers, digital storage, and digital search, came together in the upsurge of productivity growth during 1994–2004. The transition to slower growth after 2004 was pervasive and included a decline in business dynamism in the form of the reduced

Table 18–3. Actual and Forecast Growth Rate of Output per Hour, 1948–2040

	Actual Growth	Education Adjustment	Growth Net of Education Adjustment
1. 1948–1970	2.71		
2. 1970–1994	1.54		
3. 1994–2004	2.26		
4. 2004–2015	1.00		
5. Weighted Average of 1970–94 and 2004–15	1.38	−0.30	1.08
6. Forecast Growth 2015–40			1.20

Source: Output is GDP from NIPA Table 1.1.6. Hours are an unpublished series for total-economy hours obtained from the BLS.

Note: Growth rates in lines 1–4 refer to the second quarter of each year shown.

entry of new firms, the decline to near zero in the growth of manufacturing capacity after a temporary upsurge in the late 1990s, a decline in net investment to far below the postwar average, a greatly reduced rate of decline in the ratio of computer prices to performance, and the apparent demise of Moore's Law governing the rate of improvement in the density of transistors on computer chips.

The implication of these dimensions of temporary upsurge followed by slowdown is that the productivity revival decade of 1994–2004 is not relevant to our task of forecasting future productivity growth. Instead, we treat that decade as the climactic bringing together of the fruits of digital invention that could only happen once, that was not repeated in the 2004–14 decade, and that is unlikely to be repeated in our twenty-five-year forecast interval. Leaving this decade aside, we instead consider the implications of the other years of the post-1970 era—namely, 1970–94 and 2004–15—which exhibit 1.54 and 1.00 percent per year productivity growth, respectively. As a precedent for future growth, these two intervals (weighted by the number of years in each interval) average out at 1.38 percent per year, as shown in line 5 of table 18–3.

However, to base our forecast for the future on this 1.38 percent average rate would ignore the implications for productivity of the slowdown in the growth of educational attainment emphasized by Goldin and Katz and others, as well as recent evidence, already reviewed, of an upward shift in the percentage of college degree holders who upon graduation are unable to obtain a job requiring a college degree. Dale Jorgenson and associates have estimated that future productivity growth will be reduced by 0.3 percent per year by the diminished contribution of education, and in table 18–3, we apply their –0.3 percent adjustment factor in line 4 to mark down the 1.38 actual growth rate to a 1.08 percent adjusted rate that is relevant in its implications for future productivity growth.[62] Rounding up slightly to veer in the direction of optimism, the forecast growth rate of productivity for 2015–40 is taken to be 1.20 percent per year. Though this rate may appear to be pessimistic compared to the short-lived revival years of 1994–2004, it represents a goal that seems ambitious from the perspective of mid-2015. In quarterly data, the annual growth rate of productivity in the five years ending in the second quarter of 2015 was only 0.50 percent.

We now turn in table 18–4 to the implications of a 1.20 percent future growth rate of productivity to the likely growth in output per person, which depends on the behavior of total hours per person. To arrive at a forecast of the future rate of decline of hours per person, we choose not to speculate on any further decline in the participation rate of the sub-55 age group and rather to

Table 18–4. Actual and Forecast Annual Growth Rates of Productivity and the Standard of Living

	Actual 1920–1970	Actual 1970–2014	Forecast 2015–2040
1. Labor Productivity *(Y/H)*	2.82	1.62	1.20
2. Hours per Person *(H/N)*	−0.41	0.15	−0.40
3. Real GDP per Person *(Y/N)*	2.41	1.77	0.80
4. Median vs. Average	0.20	−0.43	−0.40
5. Median Real GDP per Person	2.61	1.34	0.40
6. Real Disposable Income vs. GDP	−0.36	0.12	−0.10
7. Real Median Disposable Income per Person	2.25	1.46	0.30

Notes for actual 1920–2014 values. Forecasts for 2015–2040 are discussed in the text.

Lines 1–3. From data underlying Figure 16–1 and 16–2. See Data Appendix.

Line 4. 1920–1970 from data underlying Figure 18–1. 1970–2013 from Table 18–2, bottom row, column 2.

Line 5. Sum of Line 3 and Line 4.

Line 6. 1920–2014 from NIPA Table 2.1, deflated by the GDP deflator. 1920–70 refers to 1929–70.

Line 7. Sum of Line 5 and Line 6.

extrapolate hours per person based only on the fact that the baby-boom generation will retire on a roughly predicable schedule during 2015–34. This will cause hours per person to decline at a rate of −0.4 percent per year, as shown in table 18–4, line 2. The implication, as shown on line 3, is that real GDP per person will grow at 0.8 percent per year during 2015–40, much slower than the growth rates of 2.41 percent achieved during 1920–70 and of 1.77 percent per year since 1970.

Income became more equal during 1920–70, as shown in table 18–4, line 4, when the "great compression" boosted median income growth per person at a rate almost 0.2 percent faster than average income growth per person. Then, during 1970–2014, income became less equal. When adjusted for taxes and transfers, median income growth per person proceeded at a rate 0.43 percent per annum slower than average growth. To project future growth in median real income per person, we need to conjecture whether income inequality will continue to widen or whether the trend toward more unequal incomes slows down or stops entirely. The factors that have driven rising inequality are powerful and look likely to continue. Globalization will continue to cause imports and offshoring to erode the base of middle-income jobs, as will the gradual but steady advance of robots, big data, and artificial intelligence, as discussed in chapter 17.

Beyond a continuation of past trends, the outlook for inequality confronts the elements of social change discussed in this chapter. Just as we have taken the past performance of actual productivity growth to provide our guidepost to the future, we do so for inequality and assume that median real income per person will grow at 0.4 percent per year slower than average real income per person, roughly the same rate as calculated from recent research for the growth of median versus average income during 1979–2011. The result of this 0.4 point subtraction is median growth of 0.4 percent per year compared to 0.8 percent for average growth, as shown on line 5 of table 18–4. The final adjustment is to recognize the inexorable rise in the federal government debt to GDP ratio. There is no way of knowing now how these fiscal problems will be resolved, let alone when or how quickly. In line 6 of table 18–4, we assume that a future fiscal adjustment by raising taxes and lowering transfer payments will result in disposable income that grows 0.1 percent slower than pre-tax income, roughly reversing the 1970–2014 period when disposable income grew at 0.12 percent faster than pre-tax income.

The bottom line of table 18–4 represents the combined effect of the projections made for future growth in productivity, hours per person, inequality, and fiscal policy over the next twenty-five years. Our choices in the right column of table 18–4 represent an attempt to weigh the precedents set by past actual performance together with likely future trends such as baby-boom retirement, low social mobility, the implications of single-parent households for the future achievement levels of the next generation of adults, and the fiscal adjustments made necessary by an aging population.

Figure 18–5 summarizes the differences between the actual outcome, now displayed for the near-century between 1920 and 2014, and the projected values. The left two bars are for the past and the future and refer to the annual growth rate of output per hour. The next two bars show the past and future for output per person, and so on for growth in median real income per person and real disposable income per person. The shortfall of projected future growth as compared to actual past growth reflects the decline in the impact of innovation on productivity as examined in chapter 17 and the headwinds discussed in this chapter. In short, the innovation slowdown and four headwinds—inequality, education, demography, and debt—convert the historical record that achieved 2.1 percent growth of income per person for nearly a century to a bleak future in which median real disposable income will barely grow at all.

As with any forecast, the projected growth of labor productivity and the subtractions for the effects of the headwinds could be too high or too low. The

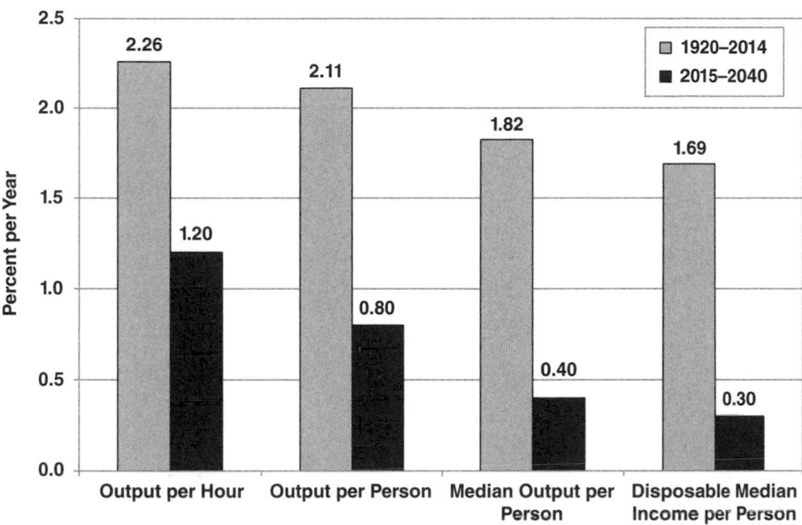

Figure 18–5. Annual Growth Rate of Alternative Real Income Concepts, Actual Outcomes 1920–2014 and Projected Values 2015–2040

Source: Data underlying Table 18–4.

choice for future productivity growth of 1.20 percent per year, though slow by the standards of 1920–70 or 1994–2004, exceeds the actual 1.00 percent growth rate registered over the past eleven years and far exceeds the 0.50 percent per year growth rate achieved over the past five years. The subtraction for declining hours per person reflects only baby-boom retirement and optimistically assumes that the fifteen-year decline in the labor force participation rate of those younger than 55 has come to an end. The subtraction for inequality assumes that the forces driving the divergence in top incomes from median incomes will continue and will not be exacerbated by the increasing share of children growing up in single-parent households. The final subtraction for future fiscal retrenchment is modest and does not fully reflect the feedback from slowing real GDP growth in restricting the future growth in federal tax revenues, nor the need for fiscal retrenchment at the state and local government level. Overall, though the bottom-line forecast of a mere 0.3 percent growth rate in real disposable median income may seem startling, each step in this "exercise in subtraction" is well supported by our analysis of chapters 17 and 18 and is also consistent with the history of American economic growth over the past decade.[63] Are there policies that could mitigate the sources of slowing growth? We turn to a set of feasible policy options in the postscript.

Postscript

AMERICA'S GROWTH ACHIEVEMENT AND THE PATH AHEAD

DECLINING GROWTH: INNOVATION AND THE HEADWINDS

This book's title, *The Rise and Fall of American Growth,* might seem to imply a sense of success followed by failure, but that is not the message to be conveyed. What is remarkable about the American experience is not that growth is slowing down but that it was so rapid for so long, and that the United States has maintained its productivity leadership over the leading nations of western Europe since the late 19th century. Instead, the rise and fall of growth are inevitable when we recognize that progress occurs more rapidly in some time intervals than in others. There was virtually no economic growth for millennia—until 1770—slow growth in the transition century before 1870, and for the United States, remarkably rapid growth in the revolutionary century ending in 1970, followed by slower growth since then. American growth slowed down after 1970 not because inventors had lost their spark or were devoid of new ideas, but because the basic elements of a modern standard of living had by then already been achieved along so many dimensions, including food, clothing, housing, transportation, entertainment, communication, health, and working conditions.

The 1870–1970 century was unique: Many of these inventions could only happen once, and others reached natural limits. The transition from carrying water in and out to piped running water and waste removal could only happen once, as could the transition for women from the scrub board and clothes line to the automatic washing machine and dryer. After 1970, innovation excelled in the categories of entertainment, information and communication technology: Television made its multiple transitions to color, cable, high-definition, flat screens, and streaming, and the mainframe computer was joined by the personal computer, the Internet and the World Wide Web, search engines, e-commerce, and smartphones and tablets.

The timing of the stream of innovations before and after 1970 is the fundamental cause of the rise and fall of American growth. In recent years, further downward pressure on the growth rate has emerged from the four headwinds that are slowly strangling the American growth engine. Rising inequality has diverted a substantial share of income growth to the top 1 percent, leaving a smaller share for the bottom 99 percent. Educational attainment is no longer increasing as rapidly as it did during most of the 20th century, which reduces productivity growth. Hours worked per person are decreasing with the retirement of the baby-boom generation. A rising share of the population in retirement, a shrinking share of working age, and longer life expectancy are coming together to place the federal debt/GDP ratio after the year 2020 on an unsustainable upward trajectory. These four headwinds are sufficiently strong to leave virtually no room for growth over the next 25 years in median disposable real income per person.

PERSPECTIVES ON AMERICAN ECONOMIC PERFORMANCE

The United States emerged from World War II with an unprecedented economic and political dominance. From 1948 to 1973, the Great Compression in the income distribution brought rapid increases in real wages from the top to the bottom, and the world's first mass consumer society was created: Ordinary citizens could finally afford the cars, televisions, appliances, and suburban houses that industry stood ready to produce. Enlightened government made a free college education and low-cost mortgages available for returning veterans and in a whirlwind of legislation passed the Civil Rights Act of 1964 and the Voting Rights Act of 1965 and, also in 1965, introduced Medicare for senior citizens and Medicaid for those in poverty. Women moved into the labor market and into higher education and the professions with such success that by 2010, 58 percent of those receiving bachelor's degrees were female.

The industrial leadership of the United States during the 1870–1970 century has given way to a mixture of advance and decline. Though manufacturing employment has declined steadily as a share of the economy, American inventions have established a new phase of dominance. Though few computers and smart devices are being manufactured in the United States, almost all the software and organizational creativity of the modern digital age has originated within U.S. borders. Of the ten most valuable companies in the world, eight are located in the United States. The continuing stream of innovations spawned by America's inventors is fueled by funding from America's sophisticated and aggressive venture capital industry, and due credit should be given to government-funded science and to the role of the U.S. Department of Defense in the early development of the Internet.

Contemporary America exhibits many other signs of health besides frenetically active markets for inventors and entrepreneurs. Research and development is at an all-time high as a percent of GDP, and the development of new drugs by the pharmaceutical industry is also dominated by American firms. Innovations in the exploration and production of shale oil and gas have reduced America's import dependence faster than was predicted only a few years ago. America's top private and public research universities have a near monopoly in the league table of the world's top thirty institutions of higher education. Finally, America's population is not aging as rapidly as are populations in western Europe or Japan, both because of a higher fertility rate and thanks to continued immigration from around the world.

All these advantages are sources of solid strength for the U.S. economic system that are likely to persist over our forecast horizon of the next quarter-century. In the shorter run, the U.S. unemployment rate has declined from 10 percent in late 2009 to almost 5 percent—compared to more than 11 percent in the Eurozone. Jobs are being created at the rate of 2.5 million per year. Assuming the continuation of slow inflation, there is still room for unemployment to decline further and for employment to grow before running into the constraints set by slowing population growth and declining hours of work per person.

THE POTENTIAL FOR POLICY CHANGES TO BOOST PRODUCTIVITY AND COMBAT THE HEADWINDS

The potential effects of pro-growth policies are inherently limited by the nature of the underlying problems. The fostering of innovation is not a promising avenue for government policy intervention, as the American innovation machine operates healthily on its own. There is little room for policy to boost investment, since years of easy monetary policy and high profits have provided more investment funds than firms have chosen to use. Instead, educational issues represent the most fruitful direction for policies to enhance productivity growth. Moreover, overcoming aspects of the education headwind matters not only for productivity growth. A better educational system, particularly for children at the youngest ages, can counter increasing inequality and alleviate the handicaps faced by children growing up in poverty.

The inexorable rise of inequality can be countered at the top by higher taxes on the highest earners who have captured so much more of the income pie than was true forty years ago. At the bottom, an increase in the minimum wage and an expansion of the earned-income tax credit can divert more of the economic pie to those in the bottom half. The decline in marriage, which stems in part from the absence of men, many of whom languish in prison, can be countered to some extent by a reform of incarceration policy and a further movement toward drug legalization. Creative policies to reform education are available from preschool to middle school to higher education. Inequality can be alleviated and productivity growth promoted by combating overly zealous and regressive regulations. The demographic headwind that is shifting the share of the population from working to retirement status can be offset by new immigration policies that substantially raise legal limits while emphasizing the education and work experience of would-be immigrants. The post-2020 fiscal reckoning does not require higher payroll taxes or lower retirement benefits, as new sources of fiscal revenue are available from drug legalization, increased tax progressivity, tax reform that eliminates most tax deductions, and a carbon tax that provides incentives to reduce emissions.

TOWARD GREATER EQUALITY OF OUTCOMES

Increasing inequality combines rapidly rising incomes at the top with stagnant incomes at the middle and bottom. Policies to influence inequality face a fundamental asymmetry, because we want to make those in the bottom 99 percent more productive and find ways for them to earn higher incomes, but we have no parallel desire to make those in the top 1 percent less productive, nor to find ways for them to contribute less to the economy and to society. Policies to increase the equality of outcomes narrow the disparity between top and bottom by reducing disposable income at the top and raising it at the bottom.

Progressivity of the Tax System

The share of income earned by the top 1 percent almost tripled, from 8 percent in 1974 to 22 percent in 2014, and the share of the top 0.01 percent quintupled over the same period, from 1 percent to 5 percent.[1] Many high-income earners, particularly sports and entertainment stars, earn pure rents (the excess of their pay over the next best job they could obtain). CEO pay as a ratio to average worker pay increased from 22 times in 1973 to 352 times in 2007, and further evidence of rent is seen in that the ratio increased by a factor of 16 when CEOs were performing the same functions as before.[2] One policy solution is to tax these rents by introducing "super-bracket" tax rates applicable to those making more than, say, $1 million and another higher rate for those making more than $10 million. Another pro-equality policy change would be to make tax rates on dividends and capital gains equal to those on regular income, as was in effect between 1993 and 1997, thus ending the current anomaly whereby Warren Buffett pays a lower tax rate than his secretary. Still another step toward equity would be to eliminate the provision in tax law that exempts from taxation the increase in the value of financial assets passed on through inheritance.[3]

The Minimum Wage

The most frequently proposed policy measure to boost the growth rate of real wages at the bottom is to increase the federal minimum wage, which is currently set at $7.25. This is 12 percent less than the average value of the minimum wage in the 1960s, expressed in 2014 prices.[4] Over the same 50 years, real compensation per hour rose by 115 percent, an indicator of how inadequate was the legislated real value of the minimum wage in keeping up with overall compensation.[5] Standard economic theory implies that an increase in the minimum wage would raise the unemployment rate of the low-wage workers. However, a substantial body of economic research indicates little or no employment effect. The current economic situation of 2015–16 is a particularly appropriate time to raise the minimum wage, as the U.S. labor market currently has a record number of job openings and is creating low-skill jobs at a relatively rapid rate.

Earned Income Tax Credit

The EITC rewards low-income parents for working and has had a large positive effect on net income for its beneficiaries. It has also achieved dramatic improvements in the well-being of children in those families, including a reduction in the incidence of low birth weight, an increase in math and reading scores, and a boost in college enrollment rates for the children who benefited. Making the EITC more comprehensive and generous is widely supported, and recent research indicates that expanding the EITC is a complement to raising the minimum wage, not a substitute for it.[6]

Incarceration

The imprisonment rate, expressed as a share of the population, in the United States is eight to ten times higher than in the largest European countries. Incarceration is an issue that relates to inequality, for those sent to prison are primarily ill-educated and poor. Their imprisonment prevents them from completing their education and deprives them of contact with their children, and when they are released, their criminal record becomes a major handicap to finding employment. Even what jobs are available are usually of the most menial type, for years of incarceration cause job skills to erode. A research study found that 60 percent of those released from prison were unemployed one year after release.[7] Individual lives are ruined by sentences that are too long and by parole and probation policies that are too inflexible. Cash bail policies condemn many poor people accused of crimes to spend time in prison while awaiting sentencing. Several million children grow up while a parent is in prison, hampering their childhood development.

The U.S. prison system is estimated to cost taxpayers $74 billion per year, using up government revenue that could otherwise be used to address a host of measures directed at inequality.[8] The policy solutions to this aspect of inequality are unique in that they would reduce government spending rather than require new expenditures. Some of the saving could be devoted to programs to deal with drug addiction and mental health issues experienced by those released from prison. It is not enough for the needed reforms to impose shorter sentences, for decades of imposing long sentences have left many older men in prison who are now of little threat to society. Only a widespread movement toward pardoning can make an appreciable dent in the prison population.

Drug Legalization

The case for drug legalization rests on the high costs and limited effectiveness of drug prohibition. Jeffrey Miron and Katherine Waldock have tallied up the costs of drug prohibition as of 2010 at $88 billion per year.[9] Legalization would allow half of this to be avoided through saving in police enforcement, court costs, and the capital and personnel costs of the portion of the prison system required to house drug offenders. The other half of the potential savings represents currently foregone tax revenue, assuming that legal drugs would be taxed at rates comparable to tobacco. These cost estimates do not count the less tangible effects of incarceration for drug offenses, such as the loss of civil liberties and the negative consequences of a criminal record for future income and employment.

TOWARD GREATER EQUALITY OF OPPORTUNITY

Preschool Education

Though preschool is universal for 4-year-olds in countries such as Britain and Japan, in the United States, only 69 percent of that age group is enrolled in preschool programs, ranking U.S. participation as number 26 among OECD countries, with the poorest children least likely to be enrolled. The United States is ranked 24th for the fraction of 3-year-olds participating in preschool programs, with a 50 percent enrollment percentage as compared to at least 90 percent in such countries as France and Italy. The United States ranks poorly not just in the age at which children enter preschool, but also in class sizes and per-pupil expenditures.[10]

The benefits of preschool education apply to all students, but particularly to those growing up in low-income families. Children of poor parents, who themselves have a limited educational attainment, enter kindergarten at age 5 suffering from a large vocabulary gap that limits their performance in elementary and secondary education and that leads to high dropout rates—and often to criminal activity. Age 5 is too late for the educational system to intervene in the learning process, for by then, the brain has already developed rapidly to build the cognitive and character skills that are critical for future success. Poor children lack the in-home reading, daily conversation, and frequent question/answer sessions so common in middle-class families, particularly those in which both parents have completed college.

James Heckman and others have studied follow-up data on outcomes of children who have completed experimental preschool programs.[11] They estimate that one program yielded a per-year return of 7 percent to 10 percent, consisting of increased school and career achievement together with reduced costs of remedial education as well as lower health and criminal justice system expenditures. They argue that preschool education for at-risk children from poor families pays for itself in the long run, and that each dollar yields a higher return than if that dollar were added to spending on elementary and secondary education. Effective preschool education is devoted not only to vocabulary and other learning skills, but also to "character skills such as attentiveness, impulse control, persistence and teamwork." [12]

Secondary and Higher Education

Preschool comes first, because each level of disappointing performance in the American educational system, from poor outcomes on international PISA tests administered to 15-year-olds to remedial classes in community colleges, reflects the cascade of underachievement that children carry with them from one grade to the next. No panacea has emerged in the form of school choice and charter schools, although there has been much experimentation—with some notable successes in which children from low-income backgrounds have earned high school diplomas and gone on to college.[13] An important component of the inequality and education headwinds is the U.S. system of financing elementary and secondary education by local property taxes, leading to the contrast between lavish facilities in rich suburbs which coexist with run-down, often outmoded schools in the poor areas of central cities. A shift of school finance from local to statewide revenue sources would reduce inequality and improve educational outcomes. Ideally, schools serving poor children should have the resources to spend more than those serving well-off children, rather than less as at present.

High costs and rapidly escalating student debt have emerged as the leading problems in American higher education. Despite substantial scholarship aid, particularly at wealthy private universities, by 2015 student debt had reached $1.2 trillion, and young people faced with hundreds of dollars per month in student loan repayments are delaying household formation, marriage, childbirth, and home ownership. The most promising policy initiative would be to shift student loans to a system of income-contingent repayment administered through the income tax system. Though federal student loans have recently introduced income-contingent repayment options, those originating in the private sector offer no such options, and so far relatively few students have chosen the income-contingent option. Australia serves as a model: College education is free for students while in college, after which a fraction of the cost is repaid through the income tax system, based on a percentage of taxable income. During a spell of unemployment or if income is below a particular threshold, no payment is due until an adequate job is found. The system is subsidized in that 20 percent of the outstanding debt is never repaid.[14]

Regressive Regulation

Throughout American economic life, regulatory barriers to entry and competition limit innovation by providing excessive monopoly privileges through copyright and patent laws, restrict occupational choice by protecting incumbent service providers through occupational licensing restrictions, and create artificial scarcity through land-use regulation. They contribute to increased inequality while reducing productivity growth. There is broad agreement among policy experts that copyright laws are overreaching by criminalizing copyright infringement and prohibiting noncommercial copying—an anomaly in the Internet Age. Patent laws have expanded too far by protecting software and business methods.[15]

Morris Kleiner has calculated that the percentage of jobs subject to occupational licensing has expanded from 10 percent in 1970 to 30 percent in 2008.[16] Licensing reduces opportunities for employment, limits the ability of new entrants to create small businesses, and restricts upward mobility for lower-income individuals. By contributing to a reduction in the rate of entry of new firms, licensing is one of the sources of the decline in "business dynamism" noted in the literature cited in chapter 17. Edward Glaeser has called restrictive zoning and land use regulations a "regulatory tax" that transfers wealth from the less affluent to more affluent and promotes housing segregation by keeping poor people away from rich people and that, by inflating housing prices, encourages potential residents to move away from the most productive metropolitan areas to less productive areas, where housing is cheaper.[17] All these instances of excessive regulation are relevant to inequality, for they redistribute income and wealth to those who are protected by their copyrights, patents, licenses, and land-use restrictions. Rolling back these and other excessive regulations is one available policy lever to alleviate inequality and boost productivity growth, with the qualification that many of the regulations are imposed at the state and local level and are outside the direct reach of federal government policy.

THE DEMOGRAPHIC AND FISCAL HEADWINDS

The demographic headwind reduces hours per person with the retirement of the baby-boom generation and, over the past decade, a decline in the labor force participation of those younger than 55. The fiscal headwind is caused by an increase in the ratio of people in retirement who do not earn incomes or do not pay income taxes to working people who do earn incomes and do pay taxes. Policy solutions include immigration, to raise the number of tax-paying workers, together with tax reforms that would raise revenue and improve tax equity. A carbon tax, desirable on environmental grounds to reduce carbon emissions, has the side benefit of generating substantial revenue to help alleviate the fiscal headwind.

Immigration

Reform of immigration can be accomplished in a way that raises the average skill level of the working-age population and that thus contributes to the growth of labor productivity. One avenue for reform would be to end the practice of denying residency to foreign-born graduates of U.S. universities, a "self-imposed brain drain." A promising tool to promote high-skilled immigration and raise the average quality of the U.S. labor force would be one such as the Canadian point-based immigration system, in which a point calculator is used to rate each immigrant applicant based on his or her level of education, language skills, and previous employment experience, among other criteria.[18] The definition of skills could be broad and could include blue-collar skills, many of which are currently in short supply in the U.S. The potential to increase the number of immigrants is revealed by the contrast between Canada's annual immigration quota, equal to 0.8 percent of its population, and the U.S. annual legal limit, equal to 0.3 percent of its population.

Tax Reform

A substantial gain in equity and in tax revenue could be achieved by adopting Martin Feldstein's longstanding recommendation to limit "tax expenditures"—his term for the many deductions built into the income tax system. All deductions, in contrast to tax credits, make tax savings rise with income, so eliminating the deductions will improve the equity of the tax system. Feldstein provides details of one plan that would raise federal tax revenues by $144 billion annually without ending charitable deductions.[19]

A carbon tax, widely supported as the most direct method of controlling carbon emissions, can address the fiscal headwind. Revenue from a carbon tax can be used to avoid raising payroll taxes or to avoid reducing retirement benefits. The CBO has estimated that a tax of $20 per ton of carbon dioxide emissions would raise $115 billion per year.[20]

The Fiscal Reckoning

The fiscal headwind originates in increased life expectancy and in the rising ratio of retired people to working people. A fiscal fix can come from three sources of extra tax revenue—the specified increases proposed above in taxes on income at the top, tax reform that eliminates or sharply limits tax deductions, and a carbon tax. Revenue from all three sources is available to stabilize the federal debt-GDP ratio and to fund the most important policy reform—the provision of universal preschool with special tutoring and enrichment programs for very young children in the poverty population. To the extent that new tax revenues are obtained by raising taxes on top incomes and by tax reforms that mainly affect the top half of the income distribution, they provide revenue to stop the growth of the debt-GDP ratio without reducing the disposable income of the median income earner.

Final Thoughts

Table P–1 summarizes 10 categories of proposed policy intervention, linking each to the related headwinds. In addition, for 7 out of 10 of the policy categories, the words "productivity growth" appear in the table, indicating that the policy category has the potential to boost the growth rate of labor productivity by increasing labor skills and human capital. These categories include a more generous EITC that improves the learning environment of poor children, policies to keep people out of prison and shorten their sentences, reforms at all levels of education, combating regressive regulations, and a shift in immigration

Table P–1. Policy Directions to Address the Headwinds and Slow Productivity Growth

Tax System Progressivity	Inequality and Fiscal
Minimum Wage	Inequality
Earned-Income Tax Credit	Inequality and Productivity
Incarceration and Drug Legalization	Inequality, Demographic, Fiscal, and Productivity
Pre-School Education	Inequality, Education, and Productivity
Public School Financing	Inequality, Education, and Productivity
Income-Contingent College Loans	Inequality, Education, and Productivity
Regressive Regulations	Inequality and Productivity
Immigration	Demographic, Fiscal, and Productivity
Tax Reform	Inequality and Fiscal

policy toward nearly automatic admission of those who have high levels of education and skills.

The sources of slow productivity growth, rising inequality, and declining hours of work per person rest on fundamental causes that will be difficult to offset. There is no claim here that even were all proposed policy initiatives implemented, median disposable real income per person would be boosted by more than a few tenths of a percent above the rate that would occur without these policy changes. Yet, whatever their effect on economic growth, these measures, taken together, would create a more equal, better-educated society, together with new sources of tax revenue to resolve the fiscal headwind and pay for new high-priority government programs—particularly preschool education.

ACKNOWLEDGMENTS

My lifelong interest in the measurement and sources of economic growth can be traced back to my graduate school job at MIT in the summer of 1965, and my first note of gratitude is to Frank Fisher and Edwin Kuh for hiring me as an assistant on their growth project. These acknowledgments are written almost exactly fifty years ago to the month after I first noticed the doubling of the U.S. output-capital ratio between the 1920s and the 1950s and the accompanying sharp discontinuous jump in total factor productivity, puzzles that pose the questions addressed in this book and in particular in Chapter 16 on the "Great Leap Forward." My intellectual debts begin with John Kendrick for his epochal 1961 book that compiled the core data on U.S. output and inputs back to 1869 upon which we still rely today for the years prior to the late 1920s. Edward Denison inspired my interest in the sources of growth, and the controversial issues that Denison debated in 1967 with Zvi Griliches and Dale Jorgenson formed the basis for a line of research that has continued throughout my career. From his role in hiring me for my first academic job to his untimely death in 1999, Griliches was my intellectual mentor and inspiration.

The book's central theme that the great inventions of the late nineteenth century lifted everyday life out of tedium and drudgery has an unusual origin. Sometime in the 1980s my wife and I stayed at a bed and breakfast in southwest Michigan, where there was a rotating bookshelf of books for guests to leave and pick up. It was there that I discovered Otto Bettmann's little known but classic book *The Bad Old Days: They Were Really Terrible,* full of illustrations of the perils of nineteenth century life, from locomotive boilers blowing up to milk being diluted with water and chalk. Bettmann's book more than any other source was the inspiration for my 2000 article, "Does the New Economy Measure Up to the Great Inventions of the Past?"

In turn, the idea of extending the theme of the great inventions into a book-length project was first suggested to me by David Warsh, a distinguished journalist who specializes in keeping track of the economics profession and its evolving ideas, and by Seth Ditchk, economics editor of the Princeton University Press (hereafter PUP). Within a week of my conversations with them at the AEA meetings in Chicago in early 2007, I described the book as a "figment" in an e-mail on January 10, 2007, to my colleague Joel Mokyr, who is the editor of the PUP series on economic history, and he immediately invited me to do the book for his series. It took forever for me to come up with a formal prospectus and chapter outline, and this was circulated for comment early in 2009, followed by the PUP contract in October, 2009.

Meanwhile Joachim Voth suggested that we jointly organize a conference in May 2010 at his home university in Barcelona around the theme of how to quantify the value of new inventions, and he cleverly titled the conference "Cornucopia Quantified." A session at the conference was devoted to two trial chapters of my book, written from a very different outline than has emerged in the present volume. I am grateful for all the ideas that I picked up at the conference, especially the comments at the session on my book chapters by David Edgerton, Mokyr, and Voth.

While the process of writing the chapters that appear here did not begin until the summer of 2011, as long ago as 2008 I began hiring one or more research assistants each year to find, compile, and highlight the book and article sources. My deep gratitude extends to all of those who worked as RAs on the book, including Ryan Ayres, Andrea Dobkin, Burke Evans, Tyler Felous, Robert Krenn, Marius Malkevicius, William Russell, Andrew Sabene, Neil Sarkar, Spencer Schmider, Conner Steines, John Wang, Scott Williams, Edwin Wu, and Lucas Zalduendo.

The book might never have been completed but for the released time and RA financial support provided by the Kauffman Foundation. I am grateful to Robert Litan, who encouraged me to apply for an initial grant and to Dane Stangler for supplemental support of the last stages of writing and editing the manuscript.

As chapters emerged numerous distinguished economists agreed to read them, and I have worked hard to incorporate the suggestions of all those who read chapters, including David Autor, Steven Davis, Ian Dew-Becker, David Dranove, Benjamin Friedman, Robert Gallamore, Joshua Hausman, Richard Hornbeck, Megan McCarville, Valerie Ramey, Hugh Rockoff, Ian Savage, Joseph Swanson, Burt Weisbrod, and Mark Witte.

Singled out for special thanks is Robert M. Solow, who supervised my MIT PhD thesis that was devoted to the puzzle of the 1920–50 doubling of the output-capital ratio, the same "great leap forward" phenomenon studied in this book's Chapter 16. During the summer of 2014 Solow not only read five chapters of the book manuscript but also celebrated his 90th birthday.

When I sent him the first draft of Chapter 16, it struck me that in a way I was submitting a much improved version of my PhD thesis forty-seven years late!

My colleague and PUP series editor Joel Mokyr was consistent in his encouragement and provided many constructive comments. The two referees for the PUP, Alex Field and Lou Cain, made many contributions to the final manuscript. I am especially grateful to Field not just for his trenchant comments but for his own discoveries of the rich trove of inventions and other dimensions of progress that occurred during the 1930s. Cain's suggestions were uniformly helpful, and he deserves credit for the final chapter organization of the book.

Seth Ditchik as Princeton University Press editor provided not just the inevitable nagging as chapters were slow to appear during 2011–13, but he maintained a healthy skepticism at my initial attempts to find an appropriate title for the book. The final title is his idea, and he deserves full credit for it and for many other aspects of the book, large and small, too many to recount. Thanks also go to Madeleine Adams, the developmental editor; Karen Fortgang, production editor; Samantha Nader, editorial assistant; and to Pete Feely and his staff who facilitated the conversion of the book manuscript into print.

My ultimate thanks go to my wife of 52 years, Julie, who did much more than tolerate the piles of books that littered my home office for four years. She has been a sounding board for many of the ideas in the book and a sharp and constructive critic right up to the last stages. The dedication to her at the beginning of the book, with its reference to a Gershwin song, is a symbol of our mutual fondness for the Great American Songbook, yet another achievement of America's great leap forward from the 1920s to the 1950s.

Robert J. Gordon
Evanston, Illinois
August 2015

DATA APPENDIX

ABBREVIATIONS IN SOURCE NOTES TO FIGURES AND TABLES

In the source notes to the figures and tables throughout the book, HSUS refers to the *Historical Statistics of the United States, Millennial Edition*, Cambridge University Press, accessed online through the Northwestern University Library. SAUS refers to the Statistical Abstract of the United States, Government Printing Office, of the designated year. NIPA refers to the National Income and Product Accounts, accessible at bea.gov.

SOURCES FOR SPECIFIED FIGURES

This data appendix provides sources for the data series involving the combination of several different data sources into new time series and index numbers. Sources for figures and tables that display data sources copied from primary sources are listed underneath each figure and table.

FIGURE 1–1

Growth rates over the listed intervals of time are taken from the data developed for figure 16–1 as described hereafter.

FIGURE 1–2

Growth rates over the listed intervals of time are taken from the data developed for figure 16–5 as described hereafter.

FIGURE FOR ENTR'ACTE BETWEEN PARTS I AND II

Output refers to real GDP, population refers to the working-age population (ages 16+) from the monthly BLS Current Population Survey, and hours of work refer to total economy hours, a quarterly unpublished series obtained each quarter from the BLS. Shown are Kalman trends for these series, developed by extracting from each series its correlation over time with the gap between that actual and natural rates of unemployment. Development of the series for the natural rate of unemployment is described in Gordon (2013).

FIGURE 16–1

Real GDP 1889–1929, Kendrick, Table A-XXII. 1929–2014, NIPA Table 1.1.6. Trend 1870–1928 calculated by linking to Berry (1988) for 1870–1889.

Population 1870–1998 HSUS series Aa7, linked to U.S. Census Bureau for 1998–2014.

Hours of work 1889–1948, Kendrick, Table A-XXII. 1948–2014 unpublished BLS series for total economy hours. Trend 1870–1928 calculated by assuming that hours per member of the population were unchanged 1870–1889.

FIGURE 16–2

All series are ratios of actual values to 1870–1928 trends, using the same data as figure 16–1.

FIGURE 16–3

Actual output per hour and its trend are taken from figure 16–1.

The real wage for 1891–1929 is from measuringworth.com and refers to the average nominal wage of production workers in manufacturing divided by the Consumer Price Index.

The nominal wage per hour for 1929–2014 is obtained by taking total employee compensation from NIPA Table 1.10, line 2, and dividing it by the index of hours as described above in the sources for figure 16–1. This is converted into a real wage series by use of the Personal Consumption Deflator from NIPA Table 1.1.4.

FIGURE 16–4

Actual GDP is taken from the sources of figure 16–1. "Original Capital" is the same as the "Official Capital" line as plotted in figure A–1. Sources are described in the next section of this Data Appendix. "Revised Capital" in figure 16–4 corresponds to the line in figure A–1 labelled "Add Government Capital," with methods described in the remainder of this Data Appendix.

FIGURE 16–5

Total factor productivity is the geometrically weighted average of the ratio of real GDP to labor input and the ratio of real GDP to capital input, with respective weights of 0.7 and 0.3.

Labor input consists of hours from the sources of Figure 16–1 multiplied by an index of labor quality, taken from the "educational productivity index" of Goldin-Katz (2008, Table 1.3, column 2, p. 39). The Goldin-Katz index is available for 1915–2005. Our educational index is extrapolated backward from 1915 to 1890 using the Goldin-Katz 1915–1940 growth rate, and it is extrapolated forward from 2005 to 2014 using the Goldin-Katz 1980–2005 growth rate.

Capital input consists of the new capital series described in the rest of this Data Appendix, shown for 1920–1970 in figure A–1 by the line labelled "Add Government Capital."

ADJUSTMENTS TO CAPITAL INPUT

The official data on the U.S. capital stock are provided by the Bureau of Economic Analysis Fixed Asset accounts (BEAFAA) back to 1925 and show that the quantity of capital input in the private economy actually *declined* between 1929 and 1945. These data greatly underestimate the increase in capital input between 1929 and 1945, and hence they overestimate the jump between the 1920s and 1950s in the average productivity of capital and of total factor productivity (hereafter TFP). In this section, we develop four alternative series for capital input that extend from 1889 to 2013, extending the data back from 1925 to 1889 through use of the estimates provided by Kendrick (1961). Figure A–1 shows each of these four series as an index number with 1928=100 to highlight differences among the four concepts between the 1920s and the 1950s. Because the differences among the series that matter for TFP are limited to the interval 1920–72, figure A-1 covers only those fifty-two years rather than the full 125 years for which each concept is calculated. In the subsequent sections, we indicate the sources for the data and the nature of the adjustments made to improve the measurement of capital input.

PRIVATE EQUIPMENT AND STRUCTURES

All data involving capital in this appendix and in chapter 16 have been recalculated to state real quantities in the fixed prices of 1950 rather than in the fixed

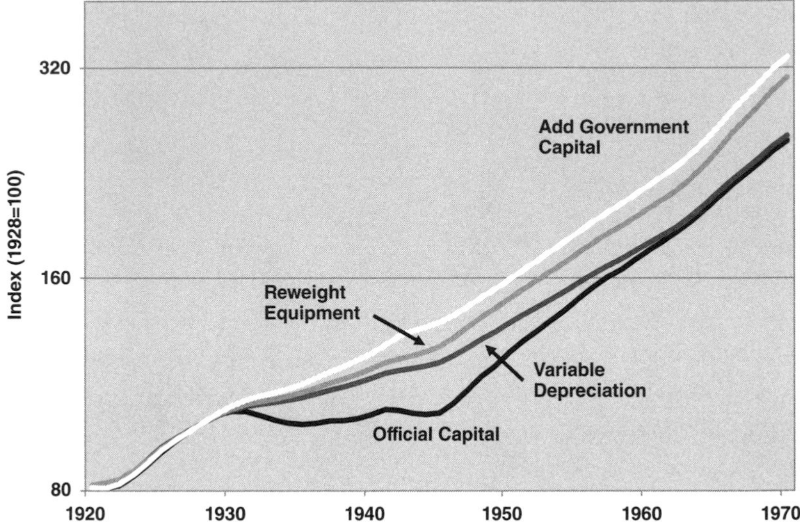

Figure A–1. Four Alternative Concepts of Fixed Residential and Nonresidential Capital Input, 1928=100, 1920–1970

prices of 2009 used in the published BEAFAA data. This eliminates changes in relative prices between 1950 and 2009 as a source of changes in such ratios as output to capital or government capital to private capital. This is appropriate, because the main focus of chapter 16 is on the change in the relationship between output and inputs between the 1920s and the 1950s, not between the 1950s and the recent decade.

Current cost estimates are taken from BEAFAA Table 2.1, lines 2 and 35. Quantity indexes are taken from the same lines of Table 2.2. Quantity indexes are multiplied by the 1950 current dollar value from Table 2.1 to create a constant dollar series in 1950 dollars, hereafter denoted $1950. The corresponding series for equipment and structures for 1889–1925 are taken from Kendrick (1961), Table A-XVI, columns 7 and 9, and are ratio-linked to the $1950 series at 1925.

The black line in figure A–1 exhibits the total of private equipment and structures as recorded in the BEAFAA. After a history of steady growth before 1929, this series stops growing between 1929 and 1944. The official series for private capital then turns sharply in 1945 from no growth to a rapid growth rate that continues throughout the postwar era. A fifteen-year hiatus in the growth of something as basic as the nation's capital stock raises red flags that something may be wrong, and it is. This leads us to make a transition to a new measure of capital input.[1] The differences between the various concepts help us understand the great leap of TFP between the 1920s and 1950s.

VARIABLE RETIREMENT

The BEA computes the capital stock by the standard "perpetual inventory" method. It starts with a value in the first year and then obtains the capital stock in the second year by adding gross investment in the second year and subtracting depreciation in that year. The key problem involves depreciation, which is based on a fixed numerical schedule that does not respond to current economic conditions. This assumption breaks down when there is a collapse of gross private investment, as occurred for most years between 1930 and 1945.

Buildings are normally torn down when profitability calculations suggest that there is a better use of the same plot of land. The official data assume that buildings constructed between 1880 and 1930 were torn down on a fixed schedule during the 1930s and early 1940s even though nothing was being built to replace them. Yet the streets of Manhattan in 1939 were not full of empty lots where pre-1930 buildings had been torn down. Instead, pre-1930 buildings remained in place throughout the 1930–45 period and helped produce output during those years.[2] The extent of the cessation of structures investment is summarized in the contrast of the ratio of gross investment in private structures to the capital stock of those structures—that ratio declined from an average of 4.8 percent during the years 1925–1929 to 1.1 percent in 1933 and did not exceed 4.0 percent until 1946. In fact, the average ratio of structures investment to structures capital in 1931–45 was only 39 percent of its average during 1925–29.[3]

A symbol of the hiatus in building construction, and with it building demolition, is provided by New York and Chicago. In New York, the tallest building was the Empire State Building, completed in 1931 and not surpassed until the World Trade Center was completed in 1974. In Chicago, the tallest building was the Board of Trade, completed in 1930, not surpassed until the construction of the Prudential Tower in 1957. In this long interval of minimal construction, buildings were not torn down, and hence the official BEA data overstate depreciation and understate the capital stock during the period 1930–45.

The same problem plagues the BEA data on producers' durable equipment. Though the productive lives of such assets are shorter, the phenomenon is the same.

When the Great Depression sharply reduced the ratio of gross equipment investment to equipment capital from 14.5 percent in 1929 to 6.5 percent in 1932, the pace of retirement of old equipment did not remain steady. The epochal achievement of the 1941–45 Arsenal of Democracy relied heavily on machinery that had been built in the 1920s and not retired "on schedule" during 1930–41. World War II has been called "the war of motors." The capacity of the American industrial establishment to build motors for trucks, tanks, and airplanes was vastly superior to that of any other country. In 1929, the United States produced 80 percent of the world's motor vehicles. Support for the view that retirement ages for equipment are extended during periods of weak investment comes from the machine tool industry. The percentage of American machine tools more than ten years old jumped from 46 percent in 1930 to 71 percent in 1940 and then declined to 42 percent as the stock of machine tools doubled during World War II (see below).[4]

The variable depreciation adjustment alters the BEA assumption of a fixed depreciation pattern to a variable depreciation pattern that equals BEA depreciation times the ratio of gross investment to the capital stock relative to its mean value. Thus, in 1933, when gross investment was low relative to the capital stock, depreciation was also low; similarly, in 1955, when gross investment was high, depreciation was also high.

The calculation begins with the series on current cost depreciation and a quantity index of depreciation from BEAFAA Tables 2.4 and 2.5, lines 2 and 35, which are combined to create depreciation of equipment and structures in constant 1950 dollars for 1925–2013. A series on gross investment of equipment and structures in constant 1950 dollars for 1901–2013 is created from BEAFAA Tables 2.7 and 2.8, lines 2 and 35. The ratio of gross investment to the capital stock (I/K) is then calculated, as is the mean of this ratio from 1925 to 1972. BEA depreciation is multiplied by an adjustment factor, which is the I/K ratio divided by its 1925–72 mean. Then the adjusted capital stock is calculated as a perpetual inventory using the new depreciation series in place of the official BEA depreciation series, using the standard formula $K_t = K_{t-1} + I_t - D^*_t$, where K is the capital stock, I is gross investment, and D* is the adjusted depreciation series. The adjustment is discontinued in 1964 when the adjusted capital series converges to the official BEA capital series.

Here is an example for the adjustment to equipment deprecation for the year 1933. The average investment-capital ratio for 1925–72 is 15.4 percent, but the actual ratio for 1933 is only 6.9 percent, or 0.45 of the average. This factor of 0.45 is multiplied by BEA depreciation of $12.7 billion (in 1950 dollars) for an adjusted depreciation amount of $5.7 billion. Because depreciation is much lower than the BEA assumption that depreciation is unaffected by the slump of investment, the adjusted capital stock grows more rapidly than the BEA capital stock. Adjusted depreciation is less than BEA depreciation during 1930–44 except for the years 1937, 1940, and 1941 and greater than BEA depreciation in 1937, 1940–41, and 1945–63. For structures adjusted depreciation is less than BEA depreciation in 1930–45 and greater than BEA depreciation in 1945–63.

The result of the variable retirement calculation is shown by the dark gray line in figure A–1. Adjusted capital input grows faster than the official capital series during the years of low investment (1930–45) and more slowly thereafter. The variable retirement series converges to the official capital measure in 1964. The variable depreciation adjustment makes no difference for capital growth between 1929 and 1964 but plausibly rearranges the level and growth rates of capital input to correct for the BEA error in assuming fixed depreciation rates.[5] The new capital measure is identical to BEA capital for 1964–2013.

USER COST WEIGHTS FOR EQUIPMENT

The next adjustment recognizes the contribution of Jorgenson and Griliches (1967) and much subsequent research. Equipment investment is different than structures investment. The lifetime of equipment in service is much shorter than that of a structure. At one extreme, a laptop computer is replaced every three to five years. In the middle would be a tractor, truck, or car used for business that might be sent to the scrapyard after twelve to fifteen years. At the long end of longevity would be structures, many of which last for multiple decades and some for more than a century.

Many commercial buildings within the central parts of the nation's cities were built during the building boom of the 1920s and are now ninety years old. The core buildings in New York's Rockefeller Center are now eighty-five years old. Most residential structures last almost forever, and the topography of urban and suburban America allows the tracing of the transition from the Georgian townhouses of the early *nineteenth century* to the Queen Anne Victorians of 1880–1900 to tiny and forbidding Levittown structures of the early postwar years to the McMansions of today. Most residential construction has been on new sites, and relatively little has been torn down.[6] Structures last for a long time, but the life of equipment is shorter—and the implication of this leads inexorably to the conclusion that the "user cost" of equipment capital is much higher than for structures simply because equipment does not last as long and thus has a higher depreciation rate. Postwar data on capital input as compiled by the Bureau of Labor Statistics (BLS) weight equipment and structures by user cost, but these BLS data are not available for years before 1948. Because our major interest is in what happened between 1928 and 1948, we must develop our own user cost weights for the BEAFAA measures of equipment and structures.

The light gray series in figure A–1 shows that capital grows more rapidly when equipment and structures are weighted by user cost. The method allows for the shift within equipment capital from longer lived trucks and industrial machinery to short-lived computers and other electronic equipment. The multiplier on equipment relative to structures is calibrated to rise gradually from 3.0 in 1925 to 5.9 in 2013. The rate of change of this multiplier is adjusted so that the growth rate of the resulting capital input series is similar to the BLS series on fixed capital in the private sector. This adjustment matters more after 1972 than during the 1920–72 span of figure A–1.

GOVERNMENT CAPITAL

The final adjustment is for government capital, much of which consists of roads, highways, and other infrastructure that adds to productivity in the private sector, as well as government buildings and military facilities that contribute to the output of the government sector. The available data on government capital, however, must be treated carefully. Though all government structures provide a factor input to the total economy, the same is not true for the recorded totals of government equipment. Most government equipment in the BEA Fixed Assets accounts consists of military weapons, such as bombers, fighters, and naval combat vessels. These weapons do not produce output in the same sense as do nondefense government equipment and structures.[7]

The current-cost net stock of government assets comes from BEAFAA Tables 7.1A and 7.1B and includes line 3 for total structures, line 37 for federal nondefense equipment, and line 51 for state and local equipment. The real quantity indexes come from the same lines of Tables 7.2A and 7.2B and are converted into a real series in 1950 dollars. The white line in figure A–1 shows the effect of adding these components of government capital to the reweighted private capital stock. Government capital rises relative to private capital throughout the 1930s thanks to New Deal projects and highway construction and reaches its peak relative to private capital toward the end of World War II in 1944.

The role of government capital is shown in more detail in table A–1. Shown in the table are four categories of government structures—buildings, highways, military facilities, and other infrastructure (mainly dams and water/sewer projects). It is important to note that buildings include not just office buildings housing government workers, or schools for teachers and pupils, but also the substantial amount of "government-owned, privately operated" (GOPO) capital built as part of the effort to win World War II. When Henry Ford built a factory to assemble B-24 bombers, the cost of construction was not paid for by the Ford Motor Company, but rather by the U.S. federal government.[8] It was counted not as part of the capital stock in the private sector, but rather as part of the stock of government structures.

Table A–1 expresses each type of government structure assets as a percentage of private nonresidential structures assets, adjusted to incorporate variable depreciation.[9] This contrast shows how much government structures grew relative to private structures. By 1941, the ratio had already increased from 35.4 percent in 1928 to 58.0 percent and by 1944 had reached 68.6 percent, almost double the 1928 percentage. Somewhat surprisingly, the relative important of government to private structures did not decline after World War II. The total ratio shown on line (5) of table A–1 declines slightly between 1944 and 1950 from 68.6 percent to 66.1 percent and then increases further to 74.9 percent in 1957 and 93.4 percent in 1972.

The sources of these increases in the relative importance of government structures are subdivided among four categories shown in the first four lines of table A–1. Government buildings include all those buildings that house government employees, including state capitols, city halls, schools, state-owned colleges,

Table A–1. Government Structures as Percent of Private Nonresidential Structures, 1950 Dollars

	1928	1941	1944	1950	1957	1972	Change 1928-72
(1) Buildings	9.8	16.1	21.6	20.9	25.2	32.4	22.6
(2) Highways	12.7	20.1	19.2	19.1	22.2	31.6	18.8
(3) Military Facilities	4.1	5.6	11.9	10.9	11.2	8.9	4.8
(4) Other Infrastructure	8.2	14.8	16.5	15.1	16.2	21.2	12.9
(5) Total Government Structures	35.4	58.0	68.6	66.1	74.9	93.4	58.0

Table A–2. Percent Log Change from 1928 in Alternative Concepts of Capital Input

	1928	1941	1944	1950	1957	1972
(1) Official BEA Capital	0	4.2	2.6	22.2	47.1	99.7
(2) Variable Retirement	0	16.0	18.3	32.2	50.7	101.4
(3) Reweight Equipment	0	19.4	22.9	40.1	61.3	121.7
(4) Add Government Capital	0	25.1	30.9	46.3	68.3	128.0
(5) Full Adjustment, line (4)-(1)	0	20.9	28.9	24.0	21.2	28.3

facilities for police and fire protection, and prisons. Government highways are a large separate category. Military facilities include army bases, navy port facilities, naval bases, and training facilities. "Other infrastructure" includes "conservation and development" such as the building of levees or the maintenance of national and state parks, water supply facilities, sewage treatment facilities, and an "other" category. The Hoover Dam and the Tennessee Valley Authority (TVA) facilities, built in the 1930s, are examples of "other infrastructure."[10]

Table A-2 shows the percent log change from 1928 to five specified years of the four capital input series plotted in figure A–1, and several surprising results stand out. Of the total change between official and revised capital shown on line (5), most of the revision occurred between 1928 and 1941. The revised capital stock relative to 1928 is 25.1 percent higher in 1941 compared to only 4.2 percent for the official series, for a revision of 20.9 percent (25.1–4.2). Of this revision, more than half consists of introducing variable depreciation, which makes sense because gross investment was below normal more in the 1930s than in any other decade. The reweighting of equipment boosts the 1928–41 increase in capital by 3.4 percent and the addition of government capital by 5.7 percent.

The revision of 28.3 percent is identical in 1944 and 1972, but the composition of the revisions is very different. In 1944, the official capital measure is 2.6 percent above 1928, whereas the revised measure is 30.9 percent higher. Of that 28.3 percent difference, 15.7 percent is contributed by variable retirement, 4.6 percent by reweighting equipment, and the remaining 8.0 percent by adding government capital. Continuing past 1944, the contribution of variable depreciation gradually disappears through the mid-1960s, whereas the contribution of reweighting equipment becomes steadily more important as equipment investment grows relative to structures investment in the postwar years. Finally, the contribution of government capital, not surprisingly, peaks in 1944 but is still substantial in the other years shown.

NOTES

PREFACE

1. This record of when the idea hatched is due to three unusual aspects of my youth. I wrote regular letters to my parents before the long-distance telephone became sufficiently affordable to make letters obsolete. The second unusual aspect was that both my parents were PhDs in economics and welcomed my reflections about economics and my economist teachers. And third, my parents saved every letter.

1 INTRODUCTION

1. Maddison (1999).
2. Landsberg (2007).
3. Bryson (2010, p. 22).
4. These percentages for urban and rural America in 1940 are presented in table 4–4.
5. Haines (2000, Table 4.2, p. 156).
6. See Becker (1965).
7. Denison (1962).
8. This nontechnical description of price index bias omits certain details: the GDP data are compiled by the Bureau of Economic Analysis (BEA), whereas the price index for consumer goods and services, the Consumer Price Index (CPI), is compiled from direct price comparisons by field agents of the Bureau of Labor Statistics (BLS). A full discussion of price index bias is contained in the 1996 report of the Boskin Commission. See www.ssa.gov/history/reports/boskinrpt.html.
9. See Hausman and Leibtag (2007).
10. Goldin and Katz (2008, Table 1.3).
11. The capital input data are original series developed for this book from detailed sources discussed in the appendix.
12. Gordon (2000).
13. The average TFP growth rate in the three intervals is 0.46, 1.89, and 0.65, respectively. Thus growth in the post-1970 interval is barely a third of that in the 1920–70 interval.
14. David (1990).
15. Solow (1987).
16. See Field (2003, 2011).
17. Between 2006 and 2014, there was only one fatal commercial aircraft crash of a U.S.-based commercial airliner: Colgan Air Flight 3407, outside Buffalo, New York. During this period, U.S. airlines carried about 5 billion passengers.
18. McCloskey (2014).

2 THE STARTING POINT

1. Based on per-capita income, in 2010 dollars, of $3,714 for the United States versus $5,038 for the UK. This calculation is based in turn on Maddison (1995) for the UK and Germany, and for the United States a ratio link from current U.S. NIPA data back to 1929 with Maddison's data before 1929.

2. Bryson (2010, pp. 22–23). The 1851 origins of the term "American System of Manufactures" is traced to commentary about the 1851 Exhibition (Hounshell, 1984, p. 331).
3. The U.S. population was 23.2 million in 1850, 31.5 million in 1860, 39.9 million in 1870, and 50.3 million in 1880. The population of the entire British isles (including southern Ireland) was 27.4 million in 1851. The population of united Germany was 41.1 million in 1871 and 45.2 million in 1880.
4. Bryce later served as the British ambassador to the United States between 1907 and 1913.
5. Bryce (1888/1959, vol. II, pp. 557–58).
6. Mokyr (2009).
7. Europeans had previously put together elements of the telegraph, including electromagnets. However, Samuel Morse was the first to develop a commercially viable and successful telegraph system.
8. Details from Ambrose (2000, pp. 365–67).
9. Ambrose (2000, p. 366).
10. See Mokyr (2009).
11. Evidence on train speeds in 1870, 1900, and 1940 is provided in chapter 5.
12. Population data from Historical Statistics of the United States (HSUS), series Aa7.
13. Malthus (1798), as quoted by Haines (2000, p. 143).
14. Haines (2000, table 4.3, p. 158).
15. Haines (2000, p. 155).
16. Haines (2000, table 4.2, p. 156).
17. Severson (1960, pp. 361–62).
18. Haines (2000, p. 193).
19. Alexander (2009, p. 57).
20. Another exclusion was households for whom the cost of fuel was included in the rent rather than as a separate item of expenditure.
21. Gallman (2000, Table 1.10, p. 30).
22. The division into disaggregated types of consumption in this paragraph is calculated from HSUS series Cd378 to Cd410.
23. McIntosh (1995, pp. 91–92).
24. McIntosh (1995, pp. 82–83).
25. Hooker (1981, p. 275).
26. Caloric intake data are provided for the UK by Floud et al. (2011, figure 4–7, p. 163). Data for the United States are available in the same source (table 6–6, p. 314).
27. Alexander (2009, p. 78).
28. Hooker (1981, p. 220).
29. Details from Alexander (2009, pp. 78–79).
30. Munn (1915, p. 27).
31. McIntosh (1995, p. 91).
32. Quotations from Bettmann (1974, pp. 110–13).
33. Details from Carroll (2010).
34. Fite (1987, p. 47).
35. Details from Schlereth (1991, pp. 142–43).
36. Danbom (2006, p. 97).
37. Clark (1964, p. 131).
38. Schlereth (1991, p. 91).
39. The radiator was invented in 1855–57 by Franz San Galli in St. Petersburg, according to http://en.wikipedia.org/wiki/Radiator.
40. Strasser (1982, p. 57).
41. Among other sources, the history of the toilet is available at www.victoriaplumb.com/bathroom_DIY/history_of_toilets.html.
42. http://plumbing.1800anytyme.com/history-of-plumbing.php.
43. Strasser (1982, p. 97).

44. Danbom (2006, p. 96). Further discussion of consumer finance and mortgage debt is provided in chapter 9.
45. Shergold (1962, p. 153).
46. Kleinberg (1989, p. 72).
47. Streightoff (1911, pp. 84–85).
48. Strasser (1982, p. 28).
49. A Google search of "House styles of 1870" in July 2011 called forth a listing on *oldhouses.com* of 131 current real estate listings of houses built between 1870 and 1880.
50. www.localhistories.org/middleclass.html.
51. Carr (1909, pp. 18–22).
52. Quoted by Greene (2008, pp. 1–2).
53. Greene (2008, p. 167).
54. Rosenzweig (1983, p. 48).
55. Facts on Coney Island from http://en.wikipedia.org/wiki/Coney_Island.
56. Kleinberg (1989, p. 109).
57. Schlereth (1991, p. 288).
58. Starr (1982, p. 113).
59. Danbom (2006, p. 98).
60. Melosi (2000, p. 90).
61. Melosi (2000, p. 75).
62. My colleague Louis Cain tells me that a current flowing at about 3.33 cubit feet per second would purify waste from a human population equivalent of 3 million in about 100 miles.
63. Greene (2008, p. 175).
64. Brinkley (1997, pp. 120–21).
65. Larsen (1990, pp. 65–66).
66. The occupational categories are as listed in the *HSUS*, which provides data by decade from 1860 to 1990. In updating the table to 2009, numerous small categories had to be rearranged. No category of domestic servants is listed for 2009, so we counted in that category "personal and home care workers." Construction helpers and vehicle cleaners were added to those listed in the source as "laborers." Farmers are those listed as self-employed and engaged in agriculture, whereas farm laborers are all employees in the farming, fishing, and forestry industries.
67. Fite (1987, pp. 38–39).
68. Fite (1987, p. 55).
69. All data in this and the previous paragraph were calculated from the HSUS, series Da16, Da24, Da159, Da530–553, Da644, and Da1277–1283.
70. Details in this paragraph come from Greene (2008, pp. 193–95) and Pursell (2007).
71. Clark (1964, p. 39).
72. Lears (2009, pp. 133–34).
73. Brinkley (1997, pp. 117–18).
74. Larsen (1990, pp. 72–73).
75. Bedford (1995, pp. 18–19).
76. Thernstrom (1964, p. 145).
77. Thernstrom (1964, p. 98).
78. Katz, Doucet, and Stern (1982, p. 128).
79. The details are taken from a fire insurance map of Philadelphia dated 1872, as recounted by Greene (2008, p. 173).
80. www.digitalhistory.uh.edu/historyonline/housework.cfm.
81. McIntosh (1995, p. 79).
82. www.digitalhistory.uh.edu/historyonline/housework.cfm.
83. Alexander (2009, p. 68).
84. Fishlow (1966, pp. 418–419).

85. Schlereth (1991, p. 245).
86. Soltow and Stevens (1981, p. 121).
87. Span (2009, p. 5).
88. Katz, Doucet, and Stern (1982, p. 85).
89. Kleinberg (1989, p. 239).

3 WHAT THEY ATE AND WORE AND WHERE THEY BOUGHT IT

1. The 1888–91 BLS surveys limit responses to "normal" families that have a husband and wife, no more than five children younger than 14, and no boarders. This contrasts with both the MBLS and the Chapin (1909) results, which include boarders, a relatively large source of family income in Chapin's data. The BLS sample is limited to wage earners in heavy industries such as iron and steel, coal, cotton, wool, and glass. One might expect that workers in these industries would have earned above-average wages owing to the unpleasantness of the work involved. The data for the 1901 surveys are different again, having a cutoff of $1,200 per year but including both wage and salary incomes. Thus we should expect the mean level of income and consumption to be higher in the 1901 survey. Otherwise, the exclusion restrictions for the 1901 survey were the same as in 1888–91—namely, the definition of a "normal" family. The 1917–19 BLS survey was intended to determine the share of food in household expenditures during World War I, when expenditures on food rose much more than the prices of other commodities. The survey was collected from white urban families.
2. We use the CPI that combines Rees's (1961) price index for 1890–1914 with the official CPI after 1914. See Officer (2011) at www.measuringworth.com/uscpi/.
3. See Chapin (1909, pp. 198–228).
4. The USDA apparent consumption series equals production, usually measured in pounds, adjusted for animal feed, seed, industrial purchases, exports, and ending stocks While the USDA series extends only back to 1909, it can be linked together with other series that extend back to 1800.
5. Dr. John Wilson, as quoted by *Southern Cultivator*, Vol. 18, p. 295, 1860.
6. Quote from Hooker (1981, p. 217).
7. See Lynd and Lynd (1929, p. 157). *Middletown: A Study in Contemporary American Culture*, the Lynds' study, is discussed in depth in chapter 4.
8. Strasser (1982, p. 21).
9. Levenstein (1988, p. 25).
10. Quote from Chapin (1909, p. 136).
11. Craig, Goodwin, and Grennes (2004, p. 327).
12. See Lebergott (1996, p. 76). Lebergott acknowledges Warburton's work but chose not to use his estimates of illegal alcohol consumption during Prohibition. Likewise, the current NIPA table 2.4.5, measuring personal consumption expenditures, assumes that alcohol consumption was nonexistent from 1929 (when the table starts) to 1933, the end of Prohibition.
13. See Warburton (1932, pp. 260–61).
14. The $5 billion estimate appears in Warburton (1932, p. 260).
15. Lebergott's total of nominal expenditure on alcohol for 1914 is $1.4 billion; see Lebergott (1996, Table A1, p. 148). Nominal GDP is from Gordon (2012a, Appendix Table A-1).
16. This list is created from Shaw's (1947, pp. 108–10) Table II-1, which lists the value of finished manufactured commodities by major and minor category.
17. Schlereth (1991, p. 132).
18. Panschar and Slater (1956, p. 95).
19. Strasser (1982, p. 24).
20. Root and de Rochemont (1981, pp. 158–59).
21. Coppin and High (1999, p. 19).

22. Van Camp and Underwood examples are from www.foodtimeline.org/foodpioneer.html. The 1855 origin date of Worcestershire sauce comes from the bottle in my kitchen cabinet. Details about Borden come from Root and de Rochemont (1981, pp. 159–60).
23. Hooker (1981, p. 214).
24. See Cowan (1983, p. 73).
25. Quote from Hooker (1981, p. 215).
26. www.thecoca-colacompany.com/heritage/ourheritage.html. None of the six detailed lists of food consumption for individual families in Chapin (1909, pp. 154–61) includes any bottled nonalcoholic drinks, although several list consumption of beer and wine and one lists hard liquor. Only in 1928 did Coca-Cola bottle sales exceed soda fountain sales, and many of those bottles were consumed outside the home.
27. See Schlereth (1991, p. 164).
28. www.kelloggcompany.com/company.aspx?id=39. See also Hooker (1981, p. 213).
29. McIntosh (1995, p. 99).
30. Examples from Fernandez (2010, p. 3).
31. Details about Clarence Birdseye from Gallagher (2012).
32. Chapin (1909, pp. 158–59).
33. This family was remarkably well fed, despite what appears to us to be a low income, thanks to the extremely low nominal food prices of 1907. We can also use this list to identify those manufactured food products that may have existed in much smaller quantities, or not at all, in 1869. Food that would be classified as manufactured accounted for between 53 percent and 83 percent of expenditures, depending on how the meat was processed. When we put the 1907 data together with growth rates for manufactured foods, we surmise that much of the difference in the 1869 and 1907 diet consisted of those items classified as manufactured.
34. See Levenstein (1988).
35. See McIntosh (1995, p. 105).
36. See http://news.bbc.co.uk/cbbcnews/hi/find_out/guides/tech/ice-cream/newsid_3634000/3634978.stm.
37. See Hooker (1981, pp. 327–28).
38. Clark (1964, p. 9).
39. Quote from Strasser (1982, p. 18).
40. See Schlereth (1991, p. 142).
41. An excellent source on life in turn-of-century American small towns is Jakle (1982).
42. Cooper (1922, p. 38).
43. Lebhar (1952, pp. 23–25).
44. Lebhar (1952, pp. 88–89).
45. Shergold (1962, p. 121).
46. Jakle (1982, p. 123).
47. Shergold (1962, p. 127).
48. Strasser (1982, p. 256).
49. Quote from Weaver (2010, p. 261).
50. The political battles between A&P and its opponents are chronicled by Levinson (2011).
51. Shergold (1962, pp. 118–19). The original source is listed by Shergold (1962) as John T. Holdsworth, *Economic Survey of Pittsburgh* (Pittsburgh, 1914).
52. Hausman and Leibtag (2007) have estimated that the arrival of a new Walmart store in a town reduces the price of food by 25 percent, of which 20 percent is the direct effect of lower Walmart prices and the remaining 5 percent price reductions by the pre-existing food retailers.
53. Hooker (1981, p. 209).
54. Kleinberg (1989, pp. 106–8).
55. See Kleinberg (1989, pp. 109–10).

56. Henderson (1956, p. 812).
57. Details are from Bettmann (1974, pp. 114–18).
58. Batchelor (2002, p. 106).
59. See Klein (2007, p. 211).
60. See McIntosh (1995, p. 101).
61. Steckel (2008, pp. 134–36).
62. The data come from HSUS series Bd653.
63. Steckel (2008, p. 144).
64. The Warren–Pearson food price index (HSUS Cc115, 1910–14 = 100) was as follows every ten years over the period of declining stature between 1830 and 1890: 1830: 94, 1840: 102, 1850: 84, 1860: 96, 1870: 139, 1880: 96, 1890: 86. Thus these numbers remain in the relatively narrow range between 84 and 102 over this entire sixty-year period except in 1870, which saw higher figures as a result of temporary inflation caused by the Civil War.
65. Floud et al. (2011, p. 306).
66. Details on rural clothing come from Danbom (2006, p. 97).
67. Kidwell (1979, p. 80).
68. Dry goods, as mentioned earlier, are fabrics bought from retailers and subsequently cut and sewn at home into clothing. Notions are items such as buttons or thread that were used to make clothing.
69. Cohn (1940, p. 290).
70. These years are chosen because I have hard copies of these catalogs at hand. Moreover, the years are convenient, spanning half of our 1870–1930 period when ready-made clothes became dominant and the Sears catalog became a major force in marketing them.
71. See Sears (1902, pp. 1100–1115).
72. See Kidwell (1979).
73. Cohn (1940, pp. 292–94).
74. Sears (1902, pp. 1103–4).
75. Cohn (1940, p. 325).
76. Cohn (1940, p. 315).
77. This quote from P. T. Barnum comes from Barron (1997, p. 159).
78. Tension between rural customers and country merchants is a theme developed by Barron (1997, p. 158).
79. Quote from Schlereth (1991, p. 144).
80. See Hendrickson (1979, pp. 28–29).
81. See Hendrickson (1979, pp. 43–44).
82. See Benson (1979, p. 205).
83. Clark (1986, p. 127).
84. See Laermans (1993, p. 87).
85. See Lebhar (1952, p. 11).
86. Emmet-Jeuck (1950, pp. 35–37).
87. Strasser (1982, p. 257).
88. Schlereth (1991, p. 156).
89. Emmet-Jeuck (1950, pp. 93, 163). Circulation was less than 1 million in 1902 and grew by 1928 to 7.2 million. Considering that each catalog in 1928 contained 1,200 pages, fully 8.5 *billion* illustrated pages were distributed in the spring of 1928 and almost as many again in the fall of 1928. Data on households from HSUS series Ae1.
90. Boorstin (1973, p. 133).

4 THE AMERICAN HOME: FROM DARK AND ISOLATED TO BRIGHT AND NETWORKED

1. Before 1870 the only network was town gas, which provided a connection with dwellings, mainly of the upper classes and mainly in large northeastern cities.

2. Haines (2000, table 4.2, p. 156).
3. A typical 160-acre farm translates to 7 million square feet, a square 2,640 feet by 2,640 feet. That would place a house in the center of a farm 2,640 feet, or half a mile, from the nearest farmhouse.
4. "The single-family detached house is found almost universally in the country and villages. Double houses and row houses are common in many of our cities" (Gries 1925, p. 25).
5. Riis (1890/1970).
6. Lubove (1962).
7. Barrows (1983, p. 418).
8. The U.S. census has maintained a consistent borderline between urban areas and rural nonfarm areas with a dividing point at a population of 2,500.
9. Doan (1997, p. 12).
10. Brown (1994, table 3.6A, p. 62). The year 1918 represents the first of six comprehensive Consumer Expenditure Surveys from 1918 to 1988 analyzed in Brown's book. Other facts about housing in 1918 are reported in subsequent sections of this chapter. A defect of Brown's approach is that she does not report averages across all those surveyed but rather presents her data separately for laborers, wage earners, and salaried families. Data from her book reported in this chapter refer to wage earners, the middle group.
11. The dates chosen for this paragraph correspond to the 1882 birth year of my maternal grandfather, followed by 1910 for my mother, and 1940 for me.
12. Muncie data as quoted by Jackson (1985, p. 50). Quote also from Jackson (1985, p. 50).
13. The source is Winnick (1957, p. 71) and the span of coverage is 1900–1950.
14. The 35 percent decline may be exaggerated because of a shift between partial surveys for the 1910 ratio to the comprehensive 1940 census of housing for the 1940 ratio.
15. Winnick (1957, p. 72).
16. Details of the organizations and commissions carrying out these surveys are provided by Wood (1919, pp. 7–8).
17. Wood (1919, p. 8).
18. Chapin (1909, pp. 75–84).
19. Wood (1931, p. 4).
20. Bettmann (1974, p. 43).
21. Jackson (1985, p. 90).
22. Details in this paragraph come from Alexander (2009, p. 157) and Fairbanks (2000, p. 24).
23. Fairbanks (2000, p. 26).
24. Nye (1998, p. 94).
25. Alexander (2009, p. 158).
26. Fairbanks (2000, p. 29).
27. Bryce (1888/1959, p. 558).
28. Jackson (1985, p. 59).
29. Mumford (1961, p. 497).
30. Sidney Fisher, quoted by Jackson (1985, p. 43).
31. Wood (1931, p. 34). Sam Bass Warner Jr., in his preface to *The Zone of Emergence*, describes the formation of the titular community as "emergence from the slum into the main stream of American life" through the growth of new forms of transportation; Wood (1931 p. 1).
32. Hayden (2003, p. 73) refers to the Chicago developer Samuel Eberly Gross who "operated on a much larger scale, subdividing lots and building thousands of brick and wood houses, which could be purchased on long-term plans." Hayden's book provides a detailed case study of Gross, complete with numerous advertisements for his developments spanning the 1885–91 period and his collusive relationship with developers of streetcar lines.
33. Bigott (2001, p. 34).
34. This and other details in this paragraph are taken from Keating (2004, p. 76).
35. Schlereth (1991, p. 93).

36. Doucet and Weaver (1991, table 1, p. 562). "Expensive housing" in this period cost between $1.30 and $1.70 per square foot. The author has a building permit for his former house in Evanston, Illinois, built in 1894 for $10,000. This had about 5,500 internal square feet, for a construction cost of $1.80 per square foot.
37. Chapin (1909, pp. 58–59).
38. Alexander (2009, p. 166).
39. The author's parents took in a boarder from the nearby University of California at Berkeley in the late 1940s. The author let out two rooms on the third floor of his house for Northwestern graduate students in the late 1970s.
40. Clark (1986, p. 93).
41. Detailed plans in Clark (1986, pp. 75, 79) contain room dimensions that total about 1,000 square feet for eight-room houses, one of which quotes the building cost in 1860 at $800 to $1,000. A more elaborate 1880s house containing about 3,000 square feet is quoted as having a construction cost between $6,500 and $7,000 (p. 81).
42. Clark (1986, p. 82).
43. Jackson (1985, p. 99).
44. Keating (2004, figure 5.13, p. 164) displays an 1874 map of Hinsdale, Illinois, sixteen miles west of central Chicago, showing some districts with lots sizes twelve times larger than in other districts. My city of Evanston, Illinois, twelve miles north of central Chicago, was largely built between 1865 and 1900 and has lot frontages ranging from thirty feet to 200 feet.
45. In our subsequent treatment of housing after World War II in chapters 11 and 17, we examine exceptions to this generalization in the form of "McMansion" teardowns in some rich suburbs where larger homes were built on the same plot to replace a smaller pre-1929 house. Also, in central cities, postwar high-rise apartment rental and condominium structures always replaced something smaller built in a previous era, whether residential or commercial.
46. This is the theme of chapter 6 of Clark (1986), "The Bungalow Craze."
47. "The California bungalow moved . . . eastward into Chicago during the early 1900s. Chicago served as the great international clearing center for ideas in materials and housing design. The mid-American metropolis had figured prominently in the introduction of the balloon frame in the 1830s and it grew into a vital marketplace for lumber, millwork, hardware, and machine tools" (Doucet and Weaver 1991, p. 564).
48. Bigott (2001, p. 32).
49. Sonoc (2003, p. 8) displays a map showing the crescent shaped bungalow belt that extended between inner city industrial areas and the suburbs outside of the city limits. Bungalows also dominated the landscape of inner suburbs, including Berwyn and Cicero.
50. Bigott (2001, p. 52).
51. Clark (1986, p. 171).
52. Sonoc (2003, p. 14) displays a typical bungalow floor plan with dimensions. The ground floor is twenty-five feet wide and fifty feet deep, for a ground floor area of 1,250 square feet. Another plan provided by Bigott (2001, p. 50) has exterior dimensions of twenty-eight feet wide and fifty feet deep, for a ground floor area of 1,400 square feet. Shanabruch (2003, p. 64) displays an advertisement for Chicago bungalows on lot sizes of forty by 172 feet, which amounts to a sixth of an acre.
53. Sonoc (2003, p. 16).
54. Details from Sonoc (2003, p. 16).
55. The estimate of $1 per square foot comes from my inspection of several floor plans provided by Clark (1986, pp. 171–78). Clark (p. 182) also quotes the *Ladies' Home Journal* for 1908 describing a variety of bungalow models costing $1,000, $2,000, or $3,000. The cost of land ranged from $150 to $450 in Chicago during the boom years of 1915–29 (Shanabruch 2003, p. 55).
56. Details of Sears bungalows at $2,129 and $2,076 are provided in Bigott (2003, p. 44).
57. Schlereth (1991, p. 92).
58. Sichel (2011, figure 3b).

59. Bigott (2003, p. 41).
60. Bigott (2001, p. 33). Bigott (2001, p. 45) contrasts the seventy house designs in the Sears catalog for 1926 (ranging in price from $986 to $4,365) to only two bathroom designs: "All consumers wanted was a toilet with a quick and rapid flush that made its contents disappear before refilling with water."
61. Lot sizes in the 1880s are given as 62.5 feet of frontage times 125 feet of depth, or 7,813 square feet. Typical lot sizes in the 1920s were forty feet of frontage and depth of perhaps 100 feet owing to the "common practice of sawing off the back of a lot [to] insert an additional house fronting on the side street" (Lynd and Lynd 1929, p. 94). Thus lot sizes fell by almost half, and blocks that previously contained eight lots now had "ten, twelve, or even fourteen."
62. Lynd and Lynd (1929, p. 29).
63. Lynd and Lynd (1929, p. 100).
64. Jakle (1982, p. 64).
65. Lane (1935, p. 15).
66. Details are from Wood (1931, pp. 33–34). Her source is Newman (1928).
67. Bryce (1888/1959).
68. Bryce (1888/1959, p. 558).
69. HSUS series Da19.
70. Alexander (2009, p. 59).
71. Lynd and Lynd (1929).
72. The song, written by Walter Donaldson, was published and first recorded in 1918 and was extremely popular in the years after World War I, being recorded by many contemporary singers.
73. Both quotes from Lindop (2009, p. 57).
74. Lebergott (1996, pp. 260–88).
75. This statement is subject to the qualification, suggested by the data reviewed later, that coal and fuel oil were still used for urban residential heating well after 1930, as was wood, for heating of farm dwellings.
76. Basic scientific data on lumens and comparisons between fuel lamps and electric lamps are contained in Nordhaus (1997, table 1.2, p. 35).
77. Nordhaus (1997, table 1.2, p. 35).
78. Stotz (1938, p. 6).
79. Brox (2010, p. 69).
80. Details about kerosene come from Brox (2010, chapter 5), and those about town gas come from the same source (chapter 4) and also from Jonnes (2003, p. 58).
81. Previous filament lamps had been made back to the 1840s; see the brief historical review in Nordhaus (1997, p. 37). Many more details about the early experiments to achieve electric light in several countries are contained in Brox (2010, chapters 6 and 7).
82. Jonnes (2003, p. 63).
83. Jonnes (2003, p. 65).
84. Brox (2010, p. 117).
85. See Nordhaus (1997, table 1.3, p. 36).
86. Nordhaus (1997, table 1.5, p. 49).
87. Nordhaus (1997).
88. Brox (2010, p. 164).
89. Electric power production from HSUS series Dh219, population from Aa7. The log annual growth rates are 10.0 percent per year from 1902 to 1915 and 11.4 percent from 1915 to 1929.
90. Nominal price per residential kilowatt-hour from HSUS series Db235. Annual GDP deflator from Gordon (2012a, Appendix Table A-1).
91. Quoted by Strasser (1982, p. 78).
92. Brox (2010, pp. 163–64) and Strasser (1982, p. 74).
93. The 1928 Sears catalog devoted an entire page (p. 910) to the attributes of its top-line "Water Witch" wringer machine. Because these products were new and unfamiliar, even the most mundane details were explained, including the "splashproof motor" and "self-lubricating ball bearings."

94. A careful search has revealed that Sears did not sell an electric refrigerator until 1931. Even then, the cabinet and refrigeration unit were shipped separately, and the customer was expected to install the refrigeration unit in the cabinet (Sears catalog, 1931, pp. 650–51).
95. Prices for 1919 and 1926 and production rates are from www.fundinguniverse.com/company-histories/Frigidair-Home-Products-company-History.html.
96. 1928 Sears catalog (pp. 662–63).
97. The 1928 Sears catalog (pp. 660–61) lists twelve models of electric vacuum cleaners ranging in price between $19.95 and $37.50.
98. Electricity consumption data from HSUS series Db241.
99. Platt (1991, table 30, p. 251).
100. Lynd and Lynd (1929, p. 98).
101. Alexander (2009, p. 160).
102. Galishoff (1980, p. 35).
103. HSUS, series Dh236.
104. Ogle (1996, p. 9).
105. Among other sources, the history of the toilet is available at www.victoriaplumb.com/bathroom_DIY/history_of_toilets.html.
106. http://plumbing.1800anytyme.com/history-of-plumbing.php.
107. The details of cisterns, pumps, piping, and cesspools are provided by Ogle (1996, chapter 2). Her chapter 3 provides details on indoor plumbing fixtures in the middle of the nineteenth century.
108. Burian et al. (2000, pp. 39–41).
109. The percentage of running water during 1890 to 1920 is taken from Bailey and Collins (2011, p. 192).
110. Lynd and Lynd (1929).
111. Facts and quotes taken from various pages in Lynd and Lynd (1929, chapter 9).
112. Bigott (2001, p. 52).
113. Details from Sears catalog of 1908, p. 604. Average working-class income in 1908 taken from Chapin (1909) to be roughly $750 per year, or about $15 per week.
114. Holohan (1992, pp. 3, 15).
115. Carpenter (1898, p. 175).
116. Holohan (1992, p. 5) reports visiting a house in upstate New York in 1989 and observing the intact "mattress radiator" steam system installed in a house when it was constructed in 1857.
117. The author has a copy of the announcement of the construction of his 1889 house in Evanston, Illinois, as containing "hot water heat" from the *Inland Architect*, April 1889, p. 61. A similar listing for his house in the *Chicago Tribune*, March 31, 1889, mentions "hardwood floors with hot-water warming apparatus."
118. Lynd and Lynd (1929, p. 96).
119. Lynd and Lynd (1929, p. 96).
120. Gordon and van Goethem (2007, pp. 181–83) have surveyed the empirical evidence on the value of the modern conveniences. Here their central values are converted from logs to percentage increases. For instance, the regressions they examine suggest that a unit having one complete bathroom rents for a log value of 0.6 more than a unit with no bathroom. A log value of 0.6 translates to a percentage increase of 82 percent.

5 MOTORS OVERTAKE HORSES AND RAIL: INVENTIONS AND INCREMENTAL IMPROVEMENTS

1. In fact, the last horse omnibus on Fifth Avenue in New York City was retired one year *after* the opening of the IRT subway system.
2. Canals were used for freight travel, particularly of bulk commodities, long after they became obsolete for passenger travel.
3. The grain output estimate comes from Steckel and White (2012, table 5), which develops a counterfactual for 1954 in which tractors were absent and all the actual production would be produced by horses.

This would require farm acreage to increase from the actual 1954 total of 329 million to 429 million, of which the 100 million difference represents the acres required to grow the feed for the horses.

4. Smil (2005, p. 103).
5. This framework, in which the subsidiary follow-on inventions raise the utility of the initial invention, is developed by Bresnahan and Gordon (1997, pp. 8–11).
6. The transatlantic steamships also served millions of immigrants who arrived in steerage, but they had no effect on the lives of immigrants after the immigrants arrived. However, the immigration of Europeans in these cramped steerage confines provided much of the economic dynamism of the late nineteenth century.
7. Air travel accounted for only 2.4 percent of intercity passenger miles in 1939.
8. The 1861 railroad map appears on the endpapers of Cronon (1991).
9. Many books and articles have been written about this speech, which it is frequently argued, propelled Lincoln from a regional leader into a national phenomenon, indirectly securing his election to the presidency and resulting in the survival of the Union.
10. Details from White (2011, pp. 1–2).
11. See Greene (2008, pp. 43–44).
12. Maps contrasting western railroads in 1879, 1885, and 1893 are provided by White (2011, pp. xxxvi–xxxix and 494). From north to south, the seven lines were the Canadian Pacific north of the U.S.–Canadian border, the closely parallel Great Northern and Northern Pacific, the closely parallel Union/Central Pacific, Kansas Pacific, and Santa Fe, and near the Mexican border the Southern Pacific from New Orleans to Los Angeles.
13. The best recent source is White (2011). Classic earlier references include Chandler (1977).
14. Stilgoe (2007, p. 115).
15. System revenue passenger miles from the Bureau of Transportation Statistics.
16. As shown in table 5–1, in 1870 elapsed railroad times between major cities were between twenty and twenty-five miles per hour.
17. Cronon (1991, p. 77) displays iso-travel time graphs for 1830 and 1857.
18. This and other details in the previous two paragraphs come from Cronon (1991, pp. 76–78).
19. Cronon's account is based on a memoir written in 1888 by the merchant William McDowell Burroughs.
20. White (2011, pp. 48–49).
21. Before 1913, the catalogs and orders were sent by the U.S. Postal Service, but the packages themselves were delivered by private companies such as Wells Fargo, which had their own fleet of wagons and, later, trucks. See Stilgoe (2007, pp. 136–37).
22. Hughes (1983, p. 201).
23. Young (1998, p. 32).
24. Jakle (1982, p. 16).
25. The guide changed its title over the years. The 1900 title is listed as the source for table 5–1.
26. There was no train service between Chicago and either Denver or Los Angeles in 1870.
27. For short routes like Portland to Bangor, the tables show both express and local trains side by side. For long-distance routes such as Chicago to Los Angeles, elapsed end-to-end times are shown in summary tables, and local all-stop trains are shown in separate tables on subsequent pages—e.g., Chicago–Kansas City and Kansas City–Albuquerque on the Santa Fe.
28. Supporting the conclusion that times were slow is an anecdote that the Santa Fe ran a "Deluxe Limited" just once per week from Chicago to Los Angeles with an elapsed time of sixty-three hours, implying an average speed of thirty-five miles per hour (Stilgoe 2007, p. 109). One reason for the slow speed was the requirement for layovers for fueling, water, crew changes, and inspections.
29. The short-lived 1860–61 Pony Express averaged nine miles per hour between Sacramento, California, and St. Joseph, Missouri. See Chapman (1932, p. 112).
30. Moline (1971, table 2, pp. 32–33) provides a table of elapsed times and transfer times for rail travelers from Oregon, Illinois, the county seat of a county directly west of Chicago located on five mainline train lines, to about seventy-five separate destinations. He provides numerous examples of train travel

between Oregon and towns forty miles away taking between four and eight hours because of long layovers at connecting points. In contrast to these speeds of five to ten miles per hour, the ninety-one miles to Chicago could be covered at a speed of twenty-nine miles per hour.

31. Stevenson (1892, pp. 27–28).
32. Quoted without a source by Bettmann (1974, p. 176).
33. Bettmann (1974, p. 176).
34. Reed (1968).
35. Source: www.greatachievements.org/?id=3854.
36. Pullman data from HSUS (1960), series Q 139 and Q 140.
37. Details about Pullman porters from Holbrook (1947, pp. 329–39).
38. Source: www.uprr.com/aboutup/history/passengr.shtml.
39. Holbrook (1947, p. 451).
40. The "star" image of the city's shape in the railroad age is provided in Monkkonen (1988, p. 178).
41. Monkkonen (1988, p. 162).
42. Facts about the early omnibus come from McShane and Tarr (2007, pp. 60–61).
43. Miller (1941/1960, p. 13).
44. Quoted by Jackson (1985, p. 35).
45. Miller (1941/1960, p. 70).
46. Kipling (2003, pp. 210–11).
47. Quoted by Sandler (2003, p. 8).
48. Jackson (1985, p. 39).
49. Young (1998, p. 16) reports that one horse could pull twenty passengers, or two horses could pull thirty passengers, on Chicago horse-drawn streetcars.
50. Greene (2008, p. 179).
51. Jones (1985, p. 29).
52. Miller (1941/1960, p. 32).
53. Young (1998, p. 16).
54. Miller (1941/1960, pp. 30–31).
55. McShane and Tarr (2007, p. 121).
56. The early history of the San Francisco cable car is provided in Miller (1941/1960, pp. 35–41).
57. Details about Chicago cable cars come from Young (1998, pp. 22–23).
58. Sandler (2003, p. 13).
59. Miller (1941/1960, p. 45).
60. Hilton (1982, pp. 235–36).
61. Miller (1941/1960, p. 45).
62. Miller (1941/1960, pp. 61–69). A recognition of Sprague's achievement also appears in Greene (2008, p. 188).
63. Jones (1985, table 3–1, p. 31). See also Miller (1941/1960, p. 101).
64. The photo is dated 1909 and depicts gridlock at the corner of Dearborn and Randolph Streets in central Chicago. It is displayed in Young (1998, p. 53).
65. Nye (1998, p. 173).
66. Miller (1941/1960, pp. 74–75); Hood (1993, p. 51).
67. Young (1998, p. 55).
68. Details from Miller (1941/1960, pp. 78–81). I am grateful to Ian Savage for providing additional details.
69. Miller (1941/1960, p. 91).
70. Quoted by Sandler (2003, p. 47).
71. Speeds from Hood (1993), p. 53 for elevated, p. 98 for express subway, which could operate at forty miles per hour between stations.
72. Though in New York 60 percent of public transit rides were on rapid transit (subways and elevated), in London, the percentage was only 12 percent. Miller (1941/1960, p. 185).

73. Facts in this paragraph from Sandler (2003, pp. 33–34).
74. Facts about transit in 1922 and 1940 are from American Transit Association (1943), especially charts II and IV.
75. The bicycle details come from Hugill (1982, p. 327).
76. Rae (1965, p. 1).
77. Daimler died in 1900, Benz retired in 1906, and Maybach resigned from the Daimler company in 1907 (Smil 2005, p. 115). Other details about the early Mercedes vehicles are from Hugill (1982, p. 331).
78. These registration figures are unreliable for the early years; automobile registration was not mandatory until after 1915.
79. Kaitz (1998, p. 372).
80. Monkkonen (1988, p. 172).
81. Monkkonen (1988, p. 174).
82. Moline (1971, p. 53).
83. Moline (1971, p. 26).
84. Monkkonen (1988, p. 161).
85. Dix (1904, pp. 1259–1260).
86. The quality-adjusted price index uses the coefficients on weight and horsepower for 1937 from Griliches's (1961, pp. 180–81) early and classic hedonic price study of automobiles. The calculation is based on 100 pounds of extra weight raising the quality of a car by 4 percent and an extra ten horsepower adding 8 percent to quality. We choose not to use the quality index of Raff and Trajtenberg (1997, pp. 87–88), because it implausibly states that there was no improvement in automobile quality between 1914 and 1940.
87. Volti (2004, p. 27).
88. Wells (2007, p. 520).
89. Details about Ford from Hugill (1982, p. 337).
90. Allen (1931, p. 5).
91. Georgano (1992, p. 38).
92. Hugill (1982, p. 345).
93. Moline (1971, p. 59).
94. Franz (2005, pp. 20–22).
95. Georgano (1992, p. 38).
96. Wells (2007, pp. 497, 522).
97. Franz (2005, p. 41).
98. For full disclosure, it must be admitted that the author's fondness for the 1940 Chevrolet stems in part from its role as his family's car from his year of birth (1940) until 1950; it performed without incident on a transcontinental trip in 1948 in the era of fully paved roads before the construction of limited access highways.
99. Details on the 1901 Mercedes from Hugill (1982, p. 330); it is called the "first modern" in Wells (2007, p. 508).
100. Wells (2007, p. 514).
101. The political debates over rural roads are discussed by Monkkonen (1988, p. 167).
102. Moline (1971, p. 94).
103. Hugill (1982, p. 330).
104. Greene (2008, p. 220).
105. Kaitz (1998, p. 373). This presumably refers to rural roads and excludes many miles of paved roads inside cities and nearby suburbs.
106. Moline (1971, p. 80).
107. Hugill (1982, table 1, pp. 338–39). "Good" roads are defined as macadam, brick, or concrete. Another source states that of the 2 million roads in 1912, about 160,000 were hard-surfaced, these "mainly in built-up urban areas" (Holley 2008, p. 108).

108. The railway mileage data were presented previously in figure 5–1. The highway data start with Fraumeni's (2007) measures of constant-price highway capital and interpolate mileage backward from the Federal Highway Administration number on total highway mileage as of 1995.
109. On the development of highway pavements, see Holley (2008, chapters 7 and 10).
110. Details from Hugill (1982, p. 345).
111. The map appears in Hugill (1982, figure 4, p. 345).
112. Details about the construction and design of the Merritt Parkway are provided by Radde (1993). He describes (pp. 6–9) Robert Moses's parkway systems on Long Island and in Westchester County as precursors of the limited access highways.
113. A detailed U.S. highway map dated October 23, 1940, appears in Kaszynski (2000, p. 133).
114. Greene (2008, p. 174).
115. Details about jitneys come from Miller (1941/1960, p. 150–53).
116. Details about the Fageol motor coach are in Miller (1941/1960, pp. 154–56).
117. In table 5–1, a rail trip in 1940 between Los Angeles and New York took less than half the time, two days and eight hours, plus a layover of up to ten hours in Chicago.
118. Airlines accounted for 2 percent and railroads for the remaining 70 percent.
119. Greene (2008, p. 265).
120. Monkkonen (1988, p. 168).
121. Jones (1985, table 3–6, p. 45).
122. Nye (1998, p. 178).
123. Greene (2008, p. 166) estimates that 11 percent to 12 percent of U.S. horses were in urban areas in the late nineteenth century.
124. McKee (1924, p. 13).
125. Moline (1971, p. 53).
126. Danbom (2006, pp. 166–67).
127. Data from McKee (1924, p. 12).
128. Flink (1984, p. 292).
129. Jakle (1982, p. 120).
130. Details on automobile registrations from HSUS series Df339–Df342. Percentage of automobiles financed by credit is from Flink (1972, p. 461).
131. Quotations in this paragraph from Lynd and Lynd (1929, pp. 255–56).
132. Bailey (1988, pp. 86–87).
133. Radde (1993, p. 7).
134. Welty (1984, p. 50).
135. Cohn (1944, p. 215).
136. Balderston (1928, p. 341).
137. Details on Howard Johnson's from www.hojoland.com/history.html.
138. Kaszynski (2000, pp. 77–84).
139. Nye (1998, p. 179).
140. Greene (2008, p. 78).
141. Flink (1972, p. 460).

6 FROM TELEGRAPH TO TALKIES: INFORMATION, COMMUNICATION, AND ENTERTAINMENT

1. See National Center for Education Statistics (1993) *120 Years of American Education: A Statistical Portrait*. The enrollment rate in 1870 was entirely in elementary school, with virtually no enrollment in secondary school. The enrollment rate of 57 percent for the population aged 5–17 is converted to 81 percent for the population aged 5–13 by applying the ratio of those 5–17 to those 5–13 from the same publication, table 1 (9601+4041)/9601.
2. Census data from the U.K. registrar general record for 1871 literacy rates of 80.6 percent for men and 73.2 percent for women. See richardjohnbr.blogspot.com/2011/01/literacy-revised-version.html.

3. Tebbel (1972, p. 657).
4. Facts from Hart (1950, pp. 183–84).
5. Facts in this paragraph come from Innis (1942, pp. 9–10).
6. The Lynds (1929) report that 100 percent of the blue-collar households that they surveyed in 1925 subscribed to at least one daily newspaper.
7. Newspaper circulation is the sum of daily circulation for daily newspapers and weekly circulation for Sunday-only and weekly newspapers.
8. Facts in this paragraph come from Innis (1942, p. 11).
9. Giordano (2003, p. 11).
10. www.nyu.edu/classes/keefer/ww1/byrne.html. Some historians doubt that this exchange actually happened. See Campbell (2001, p. 72).
11. Both quotations from Allen (1931, p. 76).
12. Phillips (2000, p. 271).
13. Totty (2002, p. R13).
14. Thompson (1947, pp. 90–91).
15. All three quotations in this paragraph are from DuBoff (1984, p. 571).
16. Field (1998, p. 163).
17. Field (1992, pp. 406–408).
18. Brooks (1975, p. 62).
19. http://about.usps.com/publications/pub100.pdf.
20. http://about.usps.com/who-we-are/postal-history/rates-historical-statistics.htm.
21. Fuller (1964, p. 23). Quoted by the source book from a government document, *American State Papers: Post Office.*
22. Reis also was the first to use the word "telephony." See Smil (2005, p. 228).
23. The grandfather's school is thought by many to be the inspiration for Shaw's *Pygmalion* and thus indirectly for the Lerner–Loewe musical *My Fair Lady.* See Brooks (1975, pp. 37–38).
24. Smil (2005, p. 226).
25. Bruce (1973, p. 181).
26. See Smil (2005, p. 34).
27. All quotations, as well as prices, from Glauber (1978, p. 71).
28. Fischer (1992, p. 46).
29. Gabel (1969, p. 346). See also http://techjournal.318.com/general-technology/the-origin-of-the-telephone-number/.
30. Gabel (1969, pp. 346).
31. Weiman and Levin (1994, pp. 104, 125).
32. Marvin (1988, p. 106).
33. It was not the invention of the telephone that killed letter writing, but rather the reduction in the price of a phone call. For long-distance calls, this transition took place in the United States not in the nineteenth century, but rather well after World War II. This author exchanged regular weekly letters with his parents as a college undergraduate during 1958–62, but his archival record of personal letters fades away to nothing after 1971 (although job-related letter-writing continued until the dawn of e-mail in the early 1990s).
34. From a 1903 report quoted by Glauber (1978, p. 82).
35. Brooks (1975, pp. 93–94).
36. Baumol (1967).
37. We ignore here the inconvenient fact that median wages have been increasing much slower than productivity over the past three decades owing to rising inequality and other factors. We return to these impediments to growth at the end of the book, in chapter 17.
38. The July 1877 date of discovery is from Stross (2007, pp. 29–30). Many other sources, including Schlereth (1991, p. 191), report December, 1877, as the month, because Edison later in his own accounts moved the date from July to November, ignoring the entry in his laboratory's journal.

39. Taylor, Katz, and Grajeda (2012, p. 14).
40. Edison (1878, p. 534).
41. Quotations in this paragraph are from Stross (2007, pp. 156–57).
42. It was not until 1925 that 78 rpm was adopted as the industry standard.
43. Details in this and the next paragraph are from Smil (2005, pp. 238–40).
44. Schlereth (1991, p. 193).
45. Roell (1989, p. 13).
46. www.mainspringpress.com/caruso_interview_html.
47. HSUS (1960), series P230 and P231.
48. This is estimated by taking the NIPA ratio for 1929 of nominal disposable personal income to GDP of 80.5 percent and multiplying that by nominal GDP of $31.1 billion in 1910. The number of households in 1910 was 20.5 million.
49. Sears, Roebuck catalog (1902), p. 164.
50. The phonograph data are fragmentary and extend only from 1899 to 1929. The telephone and radio series are complete but differ in concept, for the telephone series divides the number of residential telephone lines by the number of households and thus rises about 100 percent after 1960, whereas the radio series refers to the percentage of houses with at least one radio and is thus bounded at 100 percent.
51. This quotation and some of those in this and the next paragraph are from Smil (2005, pp. 241–42, 247–48).
52. The U.S. army commandeered all U.S. radio frequencies during World War I.
53. http://pabook.libraries.psu.edu/palitmap/KDKA.html.
54. Number of stations from Lewis (1992, p. 26). Sales of radio equipment from Allen (1931, p. 125).
55. These national averages must be qualified by the unequal pace of adoption of radio in particular regions. The percentage of households with radio in the 1930 census was an average of 40.3 percent, and specific figures ranged from 56.9 percent in the urban northeast to 9.2 percent in the rural south. The equivalent figures for 1940 were 82.8, 96.2, and 50.9. See Craig (2004, p. 182).
56. http://pabook.libraries.psu.edu/palitmap/KDKA.html.
57. Lewis (1992, p. 26).
58. Sears, Roebuck catalog (1927), pp. 707–712. The price on the installment plan was $29.95, implying an annual rate of interest of 30 percent. Most buyers paid much more than this, for the average nominal price of a radio purchased in 1925 was $63 and in 1930 was $78. See Craig (2004, p. 186).
59. The new RCA combined financial investment from GE with the assets of the U.S. branch of the Marconi Company and radio equipment that had been controlled during the war by the Army and Navy.
60. RCA stock prices from Lewis (1992, p. 27, 29). The stock price fell from a peak of $572 in mid-1929 to $10 in early 1931.
61. The designation "red" came from red stripes on some of the wire equipment. The government forced NBC to divest its blue network in 1943, when it was purchased by a private individual who promptly renamed it the American Broadcasting Company (ABC). The Columbia Broadcast System was established as an alternative network in 1927. Facts in this paragraph come from http://earlyradiohistory.us/sec019.htm. The fact about the fifty stations comes from Lewis (1992, p. 27).
62. A 1935 survey showed that 76 percent of rural radio owners tuned to a clear channel station as their first choice and thus were able to hear the same programming content as inhabitants of the largest cities. See Craig (2006, p. 5).
63. E. B. White, 1933, as quoted by Lewis (1992, p. 26).
64. Lewis (1992, p. 29). This quotation is supported by figure 6–4, which shows that telephones per household declined by about a quarter in the 1930s as compared to 1929.
65. Lewis (1992, p. 29).
66. Burns (1988, pp. 86–87).
67. Dickstein (2009, p. 418).

68. Fox (1984, p. 151).
69. The history and a link to the 1938 broadcast can be found at www.cbsnews.com/8301-201_162 57573836/reporting-on-history-cbs-world-news-roundup-marks-75-years/. This program has a special resonance for the author, who as a MIT graduate student in the mid-1960s picked up his Harvard graduate student wife in a 1958 VW Beetle at precisely 6:00 p.m. each night, after which they listed to CBS World News Tonight on their way home. In 1988, he listened to the fiftieth anniversary show, which rebroadcast the initial 1938 transmission.
70. Hillenbrand (2003, p. 122).
71. Greatest match race in history from http://horseracing.about.com/od/history1/1/blseabis.htm. The number of listeners and the FDR anecdote come from Hillenbrand (2003, p. 253).
72. The word "photography" was first used in 1839. This and the other facts in this paragraph come from inventors.about.com/od/pstartinventions/a/stilphotography.htm.
73. Schlereth (1991, p. 201).
74. The quotation and details about Armant and Edison are from Stross (2007, pp. 207–10). Three months before the first New York presentation of the Vitascope, the Lumière brothers in Paris developed the first projected film shows. See faculty.washington.edu/baldasty/JAN13.htm.
75. Schlereth (1991, p. 203).
76. The quotation and other facts in this paragraph come from faculty.washington.edu/baldasty/JAN13 .htm.
77. This quotation and other details in this paragraph come from Morrison (1974, p. 13).
78. Quoted by Schlereth (1991, p. 207).
79. Grossman (2012, p. 19). The Chicago Theater designed in French Beaux-Arts style still thrives today with its original 1921 decoration intact, though restored in 1986, and with its capacity reduced in the restoration from 3,880 seats to 3,600. It was the prototype for the large and lavish movie palaces of the 1920s and is the largest and oldest of those that survive. Today it regularly fills those seats for concerts by popular music acts. See www.thechicagotheatre.com/about/history.html.
80. Schlereth (1991, p. 206).
81. Data from the Toledo study are from Phelan (1919, pp. 247–48).
82. Cooper (1922, p. 242).
83. Young and Young (2002, p. 187).
84. Young and Young (2002, p. 186).
85. Personal disposable income in 1936 is from NIPA table 2.1. The movie admission of twenty-five cents is from www.picturesshowman.com/questionsandanswers4.cfm#Q19. The percentage fell from 2.4 percent in 1936 to 1.0 percent in 2012.
86. The annual TV showings of the *Wizard of Oz* were broadcast in color from the beginning, even though few households had color television sets until the late 1960s. After its initial 1956 showing, it was broadcast annually from 1959 to 1976.
87. Economists love the *Wizard of Oz,* based on the 1900 novel by L. Frank Baum, with its many oblique references to the central economic debate of the 1890s. See Rockoff (1990).
88. Young and Young (2002, p. 206).
89. Television is not treated in this chapter, even though it was demonstrated at the New York World's Fair of 1939–40. The first commercial television stations, the NBC and CBS affiliates in New York City, did not go on the air until July 1941. Wartime shortages prevented any substantial number of households from obtaining television sets until 1946.
90. www.imdb.com/title/tt0032138/quotes.
91. Lambert (1973, p. 144).
92. *Gone with the Wind* is ranked sixth on the American Film Institute's ranking of the top 100 films of all time. The excitement of its 1939 release is conveyed by its review in the *Hollywood Reporter,* December 13, 1939, p. 3. "This is more than the greatest motion picture which was ever made. It is the ultimate realization of the dreams of what might be done in every phase of film wizardry." This newspaper page is reproduced in Harmetz (1996, p. 212).

7 NASTY, BRUTISH, AND SHORT: ILLNESS AND EARLY DEATH

1. Cutler and Miller (2005, p. 1).
2. See Becker (1965).
3. Mokyr and Stein (1997, pp. 143–44).
4. A simple measure of QALYs would measure the impact of surgery as 1.0 if the patient returned to a full healthy life, as 0.0 if the patient died, and fractions between 0.0 and 1.0 if the outcome involved a decline in the quality of life, such as by loss of a limb, blindness, incontinence, or other consequences. For a critique of QALY measures together with solutions, see Prieto and Sacristan (2003).
5. Pope (1992, table 9.4, p. 282). Male life expectancy at age 20 was 44.4 in 1750–79 and 44.3 in 1870–79. Female life expectancy at age 20 was 45.6 in 1780–99 and 42.2 in 1870–79. No data are shown for life expectancy at birth.
6. Cain and Paterson (2013, p. 72).
7. Higgs (1973, p. 182).
8. Floud et al. (2011, figure 6.1, p. 299).
9. As shown by Steckel (2008, figure 7, p. 143), the average height of native-born American men declined from 68.3 to 66.5 inches between 1830 and 1890 and then increased to 70.1 inches by 1960, where the years refer to the year of birth.3
10. Meeker (1971, p. 356).
11. The Census Bureau reported that life expectancy at birth was ten years shorter for white males born in cities than in rural areas and seven years shorter for females. However, these data have been criticized for overrepresenting immigrants and underrepresenting blacks, indicating that the urban–rural difference was smaller than these estimates. See Cain and Paterson (2013, p. 85).
12. Pope (1992, p. 294).
13. Hart (1950, p. 157).
14. These annual rates of advance are calculated as natural log growth rates from the sources of figure 2.
15. Murphy and Topel (2006, p. 871).
16. Rao (1973, table 3, p. 412).
17. Troesken (2002, p. 769).
18. Higgs (1973, p. 182).
19. Both quotations are from Ewbank and Preston (1990, p. 116, 117).
20. Harris and Reid (1858, p. iv). Miasmata is a reference to miasma theory of disease, the widely accepted predecessor to modern germ theory, which proposes that epidemics spread thanks to "bad air," such as scents from rotting garbage and swamps.
21. Higgs (1973, p. 187).
22. Figure 7–4, based on the HSUS to 1998 and on selected issues of the *Statistic Abstract* from 1998 to 2007, is an update of McKinlay and McKinlay (1977, figure 3, p. 416).
23. Details on the 1918–19 pandemic are from www.flu.gov/pandemic/history/1918/the_pandemic/legacypendemic/index.html.
24. The quotation is from McKinlay and McKinlay (1977, p. 425).
25. Meeker (1971, table 6, p. 370).
26. Turneaure and Russell (1940, p. 108).
27. Turneaure and Russell (1940, p. 11).
28. 1910 percentage is from Meeker (1974, table 5, p. 411). Percentages for 1880, 1890, 1900, and 1925 are from Turneaure and Russell (1940, p. 9). Only 30,000 urban Americans were supplied with filtered water in 1880. See Condran and Crimmins-Gardner (1978, p. 40). The rapid increase from 1925 to 1940 may be caused by inconsistent data sources, although the census urban percentage of 93 percent accords with the Turneaure and Russell (1940) number of 66 million, which translates into 85 percent of the 1940 urban population of 74 million (Haines 2000, table 4.2, p. 156).
29. The quotation is from an article by Goubert, as quoted by Mokyr and Stein (1997, p. 170). The authors provide many additional details showing that clean running water and sewage disposal was not just a

one-off invention, but rather that many intermediate steps offered partial solutions that still allowed infectious diseases to fester.

30. Higgs (1973, p. 187).
31. Cosgrove (1909, pp. 87–88) and Meeker (1974, pp. 392–93).
32. Cutler and Miller (2005, p. 6).
33. Turneaure and Russell (1940, table 17, p. 132). The rate per 100,000 declined from 35.9 in 1900 to 7.8 in 1920 and then to 2.5 in 1936. The United States did not catch up to the 1912 rate of Germany or Sweden until 1934.
34. Both quotations from Green (1986, pp. 108–9).
35. The quotation is from Bettmann (1974, p. 136), as is the estimated number of deaths. Symptoms and the population of Memphis in 1870 are from www.history.com/this-day-in-history/first-victim-of-memphis-yellow-fever-epidemic-dies.
36. This contrast is suggested by Mokyr and Stein (1997, p. 156).
37. Cutler and Miller (2005, p. 2).
38. Condran and Crimmins-Gardner (1978, pp. 34).
39. Mokyr and Stein (1997, p. 158).
40. Rosen (1958, pp. 288–89).
41. Rosen (1958, p. 310).
42. Strasser (1982, p. 94).
43. Quotations in this paragraph come from Bettmann (1974, pp. 2, 10, 14).
44. Mokyr and Stein (1997, pp. 164–65).
45. Quotations are from Bettmann (1974, p. 114).
46. Ewbank and Preston (1990, p. 121).
47. Both quotations in this paragraph are from Goodwin (1999, pp. 44–45).
48. Bettmann (1974, p. 110).
49. Goodwin (1999, p. 19).
50. Poole (1940, p. 95).
51. From the *New York Times*, June 5, 1906, p. 1, as quoted by Goodwin (1999, p. 43).
52. Goodwin (1999, p. 252).
53. The FDA's current name dates back to 1930, but its predecessor organization was established by the 1906 act. See www.fda.gov/AboutFDA/WhatWeDo/History/default.htm.
54. Goodwin (1999, p. 256).
55. Goodwin (1999, p. 264); her quotations are from several sources.
56. Okun (1986, p. 10).
57. Goodwin (1999, p. 47).
58. The interaction between the roles of pharmacist and doctor is discussed in Temin (1980, pp. 24–25).
59. Quotations from Goodwin (1999, p. 75).
60. See Temin (1980, pp. 35–37).
61. "Consolidation of Professional Authority" is the title of an early chapter in Starr's magisterial book *The Social Transformation of American Medicine* (1982, p. 79).
62. Percentage for 1929 is obtained by dividing NIPA table 2.3.5, line 16, by NIPA table 1.1.5, line 1. Total expenditures for 2013 are taken from www.cms.gov, downloaded file NHEGDP12.zip.
63. Starr (1982, p. 68).
64. Steele (2005, p. 135).
65. Steele (2005, p. 140).
66. Quotations in this paragraph are from Starr (1977, pp. 594–96).
67. Rothstein (1972, p. 252).
68. This short history of medical inventions is taken from Reiser (1978, chapters 2, 3, and 5).
69. This summary comes from Starr (1982, p. 198).
70. Starr (1982, p. 232).
71. Dickie (1923, p. 31).

72. Vogel (1980, p. 1).
73. Starr (1977, p. 598).
74. Quotation from Bettmann (1974, p. 146).
75. Targetstudy.com/knowledge/invention/113/antiseptics.html.
76. Rothstein (1972, p. 258).
77. Bettmann (1974, p. 144).
78. Vogel (1980, p. 8).
79. Quoted by Vogel (1980, p. 13).
80. Vogel (1980, p. 73).
81. Wertz and Wertz (1977, pp. 121–23, p. 133).
82. Starr (1982, p. 156).
83. Stevens (1989, p. 18).
84. Stevens (1989, p. 25, pp. 48–51).
85. Vogel (1980, p. 89).
86. Moore (1927, p. 112).
87. Wertz and Wertz (1977, pp. 215–16).
88. Thompson and Goldin (1975, pp. 207–25).
89. Bonner (1991, p. 33).
90. Rothstein (1972, p. 265).
91. Starr (1982, p. 93).
92. Homeopathy was developed in the first decades of the nineteenth century. It revolves around remedies that are repeated dilutions of a specific substance in water, often repeated to the point where not a single molecule of the original substance remained in the water. See Starr (1982, pp. 96–99).
93. Marti-Ibañez (1958, pp. 112–13; pp. 126–27). The 1873 gift of $7 million by the Baltimore merchant Johns Hopkins to the medical school and hospital named after him was the largest single charitable gift in the history of the United States to that date. Johns Hopkins was the first medical school to insist that all applicants have earned college degrees, thus establishing itself as a graduate school of medicine, not just a medical school (Starr 1982, pp. 113–15).
94. Quotations and details are from Steele (2005, p. 151).
95. Rothstein (1972, pp. 291–92).
96. Additional quotations in this paragraph come from Starr (1982, pp. 118–22).
97. The author's maternal grandfather (1882–1945) was described by his mother as the "leading surgeon in Framingham, Massachusetts." His office with its several nurses and clerical employees was on the ground floor of a large Victorian house near the center of Framingham, and the family lived on the second floor. He died at age 63 of pernicious anemia, an ailment later linked to excessive exposure to X-rays.
98. Moore (1927, p. 24).
99. Moore (1927, p. 105).
100. The list of seven comes from Moore (1927, pp. 119–22).
101. Murray (2000, p. 16).
102. Starr (1982, p. 245).
103. Crossen (2007, p. B1).
104. Murray (2000, table 4.6, p. 88).
105. Starr (1982, pp. 261–62).
106. The quotation and the interpretation of the Great Depression come from Murray (2007, pp. 203–217). The verdict of "absurd" is mine.
107. Igel (2008, p. 13).
108. The origin of this phrase is Thomas Hobbes's famous 1651 treatise, *Leviathan*. Written at the end of the English Civil War, the book defends absolute political rule; without a strong leader, the resulting anarchy would cause people's lives to be, in Hobbes's opinion, "nasty, brutish, and short."
109. Brox (2010, p. 86).

110. Harrison quotation and railroad facts are from Bettmann (1974, pp. 70–71).
111. Droege (1916, p. 359).
112. Details from Aldrich (2006, pp. 124, 131).
113. Remnick (2011, pp. 21–23).
114. The annual rate of decline of the death rate was –4.6 percent per year for 1909–1939 and –3.1 percent per year for 1939–2008. The traffic fatality data come from the sources of figure 7–7.
115. The song "Our Love Is Here to Stay," by George and Ira Gershwin, was first presented in the 1938 show *The Goldwin Follies*, which ran on Broadway one year after George's death in 1937. The "slay" remark is quoted by Crossen (2008, p. B1).
116. Crossen (2008, p. B1).
117. Pinker (2011, pp. 92–95).
118. The previous two paragraphs summarize Pinker (2011, pp. 96–106).
119. Despite publicity in recent years about violence in Chicago, its 2012 murder rate of fifteen per 100,000 was substantially lower than that of New Orleans (fifty-eight), Detroit (forty-eight), or St. Louis (thirty-five). Other cities with homicide rates at least double Chicago's in that year were Baltimore, Birmingham, Newark, and Oakland, California. See www.policymic.com/articles/22686/america-s-10-deadliest-cities-2012.
120. The sources cited directly in this section acknowledge the seminal role in this literature of Usher (1973) and Rosen (1988).
121. Becker et al. (2005, p. 278).
122. In describing the contribution of his paper, Nordhaus (2003, p. 10) states, "What is radical is not the inclusion of health care but the notion advanced here that we should make a serious attempt to measure the output of the health care sector and to raise the output correctly."
123. Moore (1927, p. 59).
124. See figure 7–1.

8 WORKING CONDITIONS ON THE JOB AND AT HOME

1. The two key sources of welfare adjustments, both positive for home production and negative for costs of work such as commuting and uniforms, are Nordhaus and Tobin (1972) and Eisner (1989).
2. See the essays in the volume edited by Bresnahan and Gordon (1997).
3. A comprehensive history of retirement is provided by Costa (1998).
4. These percentages come from the data underlying figure 7–3.
5. In chapter 3, we learned that in 1870, clothing for men was largely purchased in stores, whereas clothing for women and children was largely made at home. Shoes for all members of the family were store-bought long before 1870.
6. The source for figures 8–1 to 8–4 omits data from the 1910 census, requiring that we linearly interpolate values between the 1900 and 1920 censuses.
7. Goldin (2000, figure 10.8, p. 378).
8. Goldin and Katz (2008, figure 6.1, p. 196).
9. All the percentages in table 8–1 include both those employed by a firm and also the self-employed.
10. See the documentation of higher shares of administrative workers in American than European firms in David M. Gordon (1996, chapter 2).
11. Facts from Rosenzweig (1983, p. 39). These numbers can be misleading, tending to focus on manufacturing workers, who had the highest hours of any labor group in the late nineteenth century.
12. The work week in white-collar occupations, including the office of the Northwestern economics department, has been standardized at 37.5 for many decades. The office has opened at 8:30 a.m. and closed at 5:00 p.m. for as long as anyone can remember, and this 8.5 hour day is reduced to 7.5 hours thanks to a one-hour lunch break.
13. Keynes (1931, p. 363).

14. Hours per week are available for the private nonagricultural sector back to 1900. They are extrapolated back to 1890 using hours per week for manufacturing workers, using the series that are listed in the source notes to figure 8–5.
15. Kendrick (1961, pp. 351–54).
16. Rosenzweig (1983, p. 68) reports that most blue-collar workers did not win paid vacations until the 1940s, whereas middle-class white-collar workers gained summer vacations as early as the 1880s. Some workers in company unions received paid vacations as early as the 1920s.
17. Lynd and Lynd (1929, p. 53). Michael Huberman's review of U.S. government labor market reports (Huberman, Michael. (2004). "Working Hours of the World United? New International Evidence of Worktime, 1870–1913," *Journal of Economic History 64*, no. 4 (December): 964–1001.) concludes that average hours per week on average during 1870–99 for males were 60.3 per week, very close to Costa's estimates. Further support is provided in the Lynds' survey, which found that in 1914 73 percent of industrial workers worked sixty hours per week or longer, but hours per week had declined to fifty-five by 1919 with a half-holiday on Saturday (Lynd and Lynd 1929, p. 54). It should be noted that all these numbers are averages, and laborers in some industries worked far more extreme hours.
18. These and other hypotheses to explain the decline of hours during the 1900–1920 period are provided by Hunnicutt (1988, pp. 13–22).
19. Data from Bordewich (2012, p. A15).
20. Atack, Bateman, and Parker (2000, p. 300).
21. Quotation and details from Jones (1998, p. 186).
22. The quotations and details about soil erosion come from Jones (1998, p. 163).
23. Facts in this paragraph come from Atack, Bateman, and Parker (2000, pp. 312–22).
24. Details from Green (1986, p. 44).
25. Quotations from Danbom (2006, p. 95).
26. The labor constraint is discussed in Atack, Bateman, and Parker (2000, pp. 264–65).
27. The cast-iron plow was invented in 1816, and by the 1860s, steel plows had been developed that "scoured, or shed, soil easily and held an edge." See Greene (2008, p. 190).
28. Atack, Bateman, and Parker (2000, p. 268).
29. Details about the reaper from inventors.about.com/library/inventors/blmccormick.htm.
30. Greene (2008, p. 194).
31. Teams of oxen were also used to pull the heavily loaded wagons of settlers.
32. Greene (2008, p. 198).
33. Quotations from Lears (2009, p. 144).
34. From Charles A. Siringo, *A Texas Cow Boy* (1886), as quoted by Danbom (2006, pp. 167–68).
35. Mokyr (1990, p. 139).
36. Details about combines and hybrid corn come from Green (1986, pp. 41–42). The quotation is from McWilliams (1942, p. 301).
37. Atack, Bateman, and Parker (2000, figures 7.13 and 7.14, pp. 316–17). The eight Midwestern states are Ohio, Indiana, Michigan, Illinois, Wisconsin, Minnesota, Iowa, and Missouri. The six Deep South states are South Carolina, Georgia, Alabama, Mississippi, Louisiana, and Texas.
38. The classic study of the relations between sharecroppers and merchants is provided by Ransom and Sutch (1977). Green (1986, p. 49) states that only about a quarter of the African American heads of households owned land.
39. Fite (1984, pp. 5–6).
40. Haines (2000, table 4.2, p. 156).
41. Smith (1984, p. 222).
42. Alexander (2009, p. 118).
43. Kleinberg (1989, p. 10).
44. Brody (1960, pp. 37–38).
45. Quotation and facts about steel prices are from Brody (1960, pp. 3, 28).
46. Smith (1984, p. 216).
47. Details in this paragraph come from Alexander (2009, pp. 112–13).

48. Quotations from Brody (1960, p. 33).
49. Lynd and Lynd (1929, pp. 39–40). They provide a case study of the making of glass jars: "The development of the . . . bottle-blowing machines shortly after 1900 eliminated all skill and labor and rendered a hand process that had come down largely unchanged from the early Egyptians as obsolete as the stone ax." They provide details allowing us to calculate that the number of dozen glass jars produced per worker per day grew from thirty-six in 1890 to 825 in 1925, implying an average annual growth rate of 9 percent per year.
50. David (1990, p. 359).
51. Schlereth (1991, p. 50).
52. HSUS series Ba4744, fatalities per million hours worked in coal mining, declined from 89.8 in 1931 to 42.6 in 1970. The equivalent rate for manufacturing from series Ba4742 declined between the same years from 18.9 to 15.2.
53. Alexander (2009, p. 138).
54. Death rates are from Kleinberg (1989, table 4, p. 29). The New York City analogy is mine.
55. Lynd and Lynd (1929, p. 68). There were four deaths in the recorded experience of 7,900 industrial workers in 1923, which is equivalent to a death rate of fifty per 100,000 workers.
56. Kleinberg (1989, p. 27).
57. Taft (1983, p. 135).
58. Additional details about the fire come from Alexander (2009, p. 141).
59. The NBER business cycle chronology (*see* www.nber.org) for the years between 1870 and World War I lists, in addition, less significant recessions, with trough dates reached in 1888, 1891, 1900, 1904, 1908, 1912, and 1914.
60. Brody (1960, p. 39).
61. See Kleinberg (1989, table 3, p. 21). The percentage of workers experiencing at least one month of unemployment in the year 1890 was 23.2 for carpenters, 27.5 for laborers, 38.6 for iron- and steelworkers, 41.3 for masons, and 65.4 percent for glassworkers. The volatility of iron and steel demand made overall unemployment somewhat worse in Pittsburgh than the national average.
62. Montgomery (1983, p. 92).
63. Montgomery (1983, p. 94).
64. Kesslar-Harris (1982, p. 79).
65. Kesslar-Harris (1982, p. 144).
66. Kesslar-Harris (1982, p. 119).
67. Goldin and Katz (2008, figure 6.1, p. 196).
68. Quotation attributed to Dorothy Dix from Lynd and Lynd (1929, p. 169).
69. Strasser (1982, pp. 3–4).
70. Strasser (1982, p. 49).
71. Atherton (1954, p. 200).
72. Kesslar-Harris (1982, p. 112).
73. The conquest of infant mortality was a central theme of chapter 7 in this book.
74. The 1940 percentages of housing characteristics are displayed in table 4–4, which in turn is based on the 1940 Census of Housing.
75. Lynd and Lynd (1929, pp. 168–69).
76. Lynd and Lynd (1929, p. 171). This comparison is put in perspective by a doubling in the price level from 1890 to 1925. The Lynds' survey tends to overstate the time spent in home production due to its method (recall rather than time diary). See Ramey (2009, Appendix C).
77. Ramey and Francis (2009, table 1, p. 193).
78. Ramey and Francis (2009, table 4, p. 204). The reduction for prime-age women in Ramey (2009, table 6A, p. 27) is a slightly smaller decline, from 46.8 to 29.3 hours per week of home production.
79. See Ramey (2009, table 6A, right column, average of data shown for 1920 and 1930). The similarity between the Ramey and Lynd numbers should be qualified to the extent that Ramey used the Lynds' survey as one of her numerous sources.
80. Lynd and Lynd (1929, p. 173).

81. See Mokyr (2000, p. 1). The original reference is Cowan (1983).
82. Montgomery (1983, p. 97).
83. Montgomery (1983, p, 97).
84. Shergold (1962, p. 225).
85. Rees (1961, table 10, p. 33). These averages for all manufacturing during the years 1900–1909 from Rees correspond almost exactly to the 1907–8 quoted hourly wage for steel mill ordinary laborers of 16.5 cents per hour, or between $1.67 and $1.98 per day. See Alexander (2009, pp. 109–10).
86. Ford workers had to meet certain requirements to receive this higher wage, including sobriety and family status. See Batchelor (2002, pp. 49–50).
87. Alexander (2009, pp. 106–7).
88. Quotation and details about the sociology department agent visits are from Montgomery (1987, pp. 234–36) and Snow (2013, p. B1, B4).
89. A wide variety of measurement issues is relevant to the divergence of the two series in figure 8–7 after 1980, including price index bias, the distinction between production workers and all workers, and conceptual distinctions between real wages and economy-wide productivity. See Gordon and Dew-Becker (2008). We return to these issues in chapter 15.
90. Quotation about dishwashing and anecdote about small spaces in textile mills come from Green (1986, p. 28).
91. Alexander (2009, p. 137).
92. Angus and Mirel (1985, table 1, p. 126).
93. That school completion varied with family income, and that school completion of farm children was higher than city children, come from Fuller (1983, pp. 153–54).
94. Lewis (1961, p. 66).
95. Jakle (1982, p. 85).
96. Walters and O'Connell (1988, pp. 1146–47).
97. Goldin and Katz (1999, figure 3, p. 698).
98. Smith (1984, pp. 589–90).

9 TAKING AND MITIGATING RISKS: CONSUMER CREDIT, INSURANCE, AND THE GOVERNMENT

1. Gelpi and Julien-Labruyère (2000, p. 97).
2. Gelpi and Julien-Labruyère (2000, p. 99).
3. Cronon (1991, p. 323).
4. The quotation and facts on interest rates come from Danbom (2006, p. 151).
5. Details from Calder (1999, p. 160).
6. Danbom (2006, p. 123). See also Ransom and Sutch (1977).
7. Danbom (2006, p. 123).
8. Simpson, Simpson, and Samuels (1954, p. 29).
9. Marron (2009, p. 20).
10. Cox (1948, p. 63).
11. Marron (2009, p. 22).
12. Ham (1912, p. 1).
13. Marron (2009, p. 26).
14. Quoted by Calder (1999, p. 39).
15. Calder (1999, p. 71).
16. Sears, Roebuck catalog (1902, p. 4).
17. Sears, Roebuck catalog (1908, pp. 1–2). The claim that the big 1908 book contained more than 100,000 items is stated on p. 1. The 1908 catalog contained 1,162 pages. Each individual page contained a highly variable number of items (e.g., four types of cast iron stoves or thirty types of silver teacups or fifty types of knives), and it is likely that the claimed total of 100,000 contains more than a bit of hyperbole.
18. Details from Calder (1999, pp. 178–79).

19. Kinley (1910, p. 69).
20. Facts about early installment buying for furniture and pianos are summarized from Marron (2009, pp. 38–39).
21. Ford (1989, p. 13).
22. Neifeld (1939, p. 4).
23. Facts in this paragraph come from Leach (1993, pp. 299–302).
24. Calder (1999, p. 17).
25. Olney (1991, p. 125).
26. Facts in this paragraph come from Marron (2009, pp. 56–60). Ford lagged behind General Motors not only in automobile styling and product differentiation, but also in financing. With its Ford Weekly Purchase Plan, introduced in 1923, potential purchasers were offered the chance to save $5 per week in a special interest-bearing account, obtaining the car when the purchase price had been saved up (the 1923 purchase price of a Motel T Ford was as low as $265; see chapter 5). The plan was a failure, eliciting little consumer interest when they had the alternative of obtaining the car in advance of the repayment under the installment plan favored by GMAC. Ford did not create a unit to compete with GMAC until 1928 (Calder 1999, p. 199).
27. Calder (1999, p. 195).
28. Olney (1991, p. 115).
29. The nominal consumer debt series comes from Olney (1991, table 4.1, column 1) divided by nominal GDP from Gordon (2012a, Appendix A-1. Real consumer durables spending comes from Olney (1991, table A-7), and real GDP comes from the same source as nominal GDP. The Olney data are in 1982 prices and the Gordon GDP series is in 2005 prices, so the Olney data are multiplied by 1.805, the ratio of the GDP deflator in 2005 to 1982.
30. The 1939 percentage ratio to GDP displayed in figure 9–1 was 8.6, about 17 percent higher than the 1929 ratio of 7.4.
31. The behavior of the debt-GDP ratio in figure 9–1 partly reflects price changes in the overall economy. Because a given consumer debt is fixed in nominal terms, the debt ratio naturally declined as the overall price level doubled during World War I. In fact, nominal GDP more than doubled between 1915 and 1920. Similarly, that the debt ratio declined less than the consumer durables spending ratio between 1929 and 1934 reflects the declining price ratio of those five years.
32. Olney (1991, table 4.3, p. 96).
33. Seligman (1927, vol. 1, pp. 100–108).
34. Gelpi and Julien-Labruyère (2000, p. 101).
35. Lynn (1957, p. 415).
36. Calder (1999, p. 158).
37. Facts in these two paragraphs are from Calder (1999, pp. 66–68).
38. Lynd and Lynd (1929, p. 106).
39. Radford (1992, p. 14). $10 billion was roughly 10 percent of GDP in 1928–29.
40. Details of mortgage finance come partly from Butkiewicz (2009). Data on outstanding mortgages in billions of dollars come from Wheelock (2008, figure 3, p. 136). Data on mortgage debt relative to income are from Doan (1997, Appendix table B, p. 186).
41. Wood (1931, p. 187).
42. Stone (1942, p. 12).
43. Facts in these paragraphs from Stone (1942, pp. 21–25). The term "underwriting" originated in that period, for those willing to share the risk wrote their names underneath the statement defining the particular risk.
44. The Fund kept this name until 1992, and after several mergers today is part of the Nationwide Mutual Insurance Company. See famousdaily.com/history/first-american-life-insurance-company.html.
45. Oviatt (1905b, p. 186).
46. The amount of life insurance outstanding is measured by the nominal assets of life insurance companies from HSUS series Cj741.

47. The number of policies in 1915 was 43 million, whereas the number of insured persons (allowing for multiple policies) was "25 to 30 million" (Fiske 1917, p. 317). By comparison, the number of households in 1915 was 22.5 million. This suggests that several million household members beyond the head of the household had taken out life insurance policies.
48. Life insurance in force data for 1915 comes from Fiske (1917, p. 317).
49. Life insurance in force for 1926 is reported by Knight (1927, p. 97). Assets are from the data displayed in figure 9–4.
50. Fiske (1917, p. 320).
51. Facts from Knight (1927, p. 97). Asset percentages for New York state from Nichols (1917, pp. 119–20).
52. www.usfa.fema.gov/downloads/pdf/statistics/internat.pdf.
53. Facts from disasters.albertarose.org/us_disasters.html.
54. The early history of fire insurance is provided in Oviatt (1905a).
55. Details on insurance in the 1871 Chicago fire are from Pierce (1957, pp. 12–13).
56. The GDP deflator (2005=100) was 6.4 in 1871 and 5.5 in 1906 (from Gordon 2012a, Appendix table A-1).
57. Thomas and Witts (1971, p. 271).
58. Morris (2002, p. 171).
59. Details on compulsory insurance from http://blog.esurance.com/the-surprisingly-fascinating-history-of-us-car-insurance/.
60. Sawyer (1936, pp. 24–26).
61. Facts from www.insuranceusa.com/reviews/state-farm/state-farm-timeline/.
62. The inferior status of Homestead Act lands compared to railroad land is argued by Gates (1936, pp. 655–57).
63. This interpretation of the railroad land-grants comes from Ellis (1945, p. 209).
64. Greever (1951, pp. 87–88).
65. Earl (1997, p. 1610).
66. The quotation and information in this section come from McDowell (1929, p. 250).
67. Johnson (1981, pp. 333–34).
68. Facts about degrees from Renne (1960, p. 48). The quotation is from the same book, p. 50.
69. Article I, Section 8, Clause 8 of the Constitution states the aim "to promote the Progress of Science and useful Arts by securing for limited Times to Authors and Inventors the exclusive Right in their respective Writings and Discoveries." See Nard (2010, p. 16).
70. See Tarbell (2005).
71. Lamoreaux (2010, p. 388).
72. King (2010, p. 32).
73. The standardization of nuts, bolts, screws and other fasteners, as fostered in the 1920s by Herbert Hoover, is described by Walton (1956, pp. 531–33).
74. This evaluation of Prohibition comes from the comprehensive study of its economic effects by Clark Warburton (1932, pp. 261–62).
75. As we shall see in chapter 15, the promise of universal high school graduation was never achieved in the United States. High school graduation rates reached nearly 80 percent by 1975 but then slipped back. James Heckman and others have shown that those who do not obtain high school diplomas but rather GED certificates have social and economic outcomes more similar to high-school dropouts than to high-school graduates.
76. The FDIC was created as part of the 1933 Glass-Steagall Act, which "tightened branching restrictions, created federal deposit insurance, imposed interest-rate ceilings on deposits, empowered the Federal Reserve Board to vary reserve requirements, and decoupled commercial banking from investment banking" (Vietor 2000, p. 979). This last achievement, the decoupling of commercial and investment banking, was repealed by the Clinton administration in 1999, and the repeal has been blamed in part for excess financial leverage and other aspects of the 2007–9 U.S. financial crisis and subsequent recession.

77. Cannon (2000, p. 133).
78. The author notes that the U.S. post offices of his hometown, Berkeley, California, and of his long-time residence, Evanston, Illinois, were both WPA projects built during the late 1930s.
79. Darby (1976).

ENTR'ACTE. THE MIDCENTURY SHIFT FROM REVOLUTION TO EVOLUTION

1. An easy way to date the arrival of the electric refrigerator is to refer to the Sears catalog. During the entire period 1900–1928, its section on "refrigerators" referred to what we would call "iceboxes." The first electric refrigerator was not sold by Sears until 1931, an unusual example of Sears lagging behind the market in contrast to its early lead in the 1890s in selling bicycles and sewing machines.
2. Data source is given in the data appendix, notes to the sources of figure 16–1.
3. The history of motion picture admission prices is available from http://boxofficemojo.com/about/adjuster.htm.
4. The baby boom lasted from 1946 to 1964. The oldest of the baby-boomers were eligible to retire at age 62 in 2008, whereas those of the youngest who choose to delay their retirement to age 70 will not retire until 2034.

10 FAST FOOD, SYNTHETIC FIBERS, AND SPLIT-LEVEL SUBDIVISIONS: THE SLOWING TRANSFORMATION OF FOOD, CLOTHING, AND HOUSING

1. Details in the two previous paragraphs come from Hooker (1981, pp. 310–12).
2. Large stores were first developed in Los Angeles, which, compared to most cities, was characterized by low density and a high dependence on auto transportation, which favored the building of large stores. By 1937, there were 260 supermarkets in Los Angeles, which together accounted for 35 percent of food sales in that city. Facts in this note and paragraph come from Mayo (1993, chapter 4).
3. A&P had 14,446 stores in 1936 and only 6,042 in 1941. See Mayo (1993, p. 148).
4. The list of rationed products comes from McIntosh (1995, pp. 117–19).
5. Kennedy (2003).
6. Some details in this paragraph come from Crossen (2007); the quotation is from Hooker (1981, p. 334).
7. This trend was particularly pronounced during the period 2010–14 after the data of figure 10–1 end. See Gee (2014).
8. Marsh (2008).
9. Mayo (1993, pp. 162, 189).
10. When we arrived for our first year of marriage in Oxford, England, in 1963–64, retailing was still in the Stone Age. All the markets in central Oxford, which the population accessed almost entirely by double-decked buses, required payment at each service station—a few coins for the vegetables, then a few coins for the cheese. Britain's transition to supermarkets occurred thirty to forty years after the American transition, which was typical as Europe experienced its rapid postwar growth as it discovered all that America had invented since the turn of the twentieth century.
11. The A&P economy stores were about half the typical 600 square feet area of other chain stores in the 1920s. See Mayo (1993, pp. 140, 166)
12. Baily and Gordon (1988, p. 414).
13. The 7-Eleven name referred to the initial operating hours of the stores—from 7 a.m. to 11 p.m. The first convenience store was opened by the corporate ancestor of 7-Eleven in 1927, but the growth of convenience stores began to take off after customers began economizing on gasoline after the oil price inflation of the 1970s. See Mayo (1993, p. 205).
14. Hausman and Leibtag (2007) have estimated that the arrival of a Walmart in a new location drives down the price of food by 25 percent.

15. For instance, the Dominick's chain, a major player in Chicago, was closed down by its corporate owner Safeway during the year 2013.
16. Taco Bell's goal is to deliver the food to customers in no more than two minutes and forty-four seconds. Details in this paragraph come from Greenfeld (2011, pp. 63–69).
17. Greenfeld (2011, p. 66).
18. Greenfeld (2011, p. 68) emphasizes the role of the "verification board," an electronic tool, in achieving near complete accuracy in the fulfillment of customer orders. This technique was pioneered by McDonald's in the 1990s.
19. The source of the "50 million people" fact comes from Miller (2010, p. 44).
20. Facts in this paragraph come from Brody (2013).
21. Acs and Lyles (2007, figure 2.2, p. 19).
22. Details in this paragraph are taken from Miller (2010, p. 46).
23. Lakdawalla and Phillipson (2009).
24. Lakdawalla and Phillipson (2009, abstract page).
25. Daniels (2006, p. 61).
26. Lebergott (1996, table A1, pp. 148–53).
27. The 1980 nominal imports include textiles, clothing, and footwear from SAUS 1982–83, table 1489, p. 840. The 2007 nominal imports include textiles, fabrics, apparel, and accessories from SAUS 2011, table 1311, p. 814.
28. To place this relative price change into perspective, the relative price of consumer spending on the category "Video, audio, photographic, and information processing equipment and media" declined between 1980 and 2012 change at −11.2 percent per year, and, at the other extreme, the relative price of higher education increased at a rate of 4.4 percent per year.
29. Between 2007 and 2013, the sportswear category grew at 14 percent, compared to 2.7 percent for all other types of clothing. The division of apparel imports by type of fabric classifies mixed-fabric garments by the dominant fabric; a shirt that is 60 percent cotton and 40 percent polyester would be classified in the cotton category, and vice versa. Data from Wexler (2014).
30. Details in the two previous paragraphs come from Farrell-Beck and Parsons (2007) and from Steele (1997, esp. pp. 87–88).
31. Cline (2012) cites a 1997 *Consumer Reports* article showing that a polo shirt sold by Target at $7 was of the same quality as a $75 Ralph Lauren polo shirt. Cline (2012, p. 91) explains this anomaly by the need of brands to "reduce their quality to pad their profits."
32. Cline (2012, p. 93).
33. Haines (2000, table 4.2, p. 156).
34. A qualification to this statement is that housing units are steadily being demolished in some old industrial cities of the Midwest and northeast that have suffered from major declines in population (e.g., Detroit and Buffalo).
35. The real value to unit ratio rose from 88 percent in the peak housing year of 1925 to 137 percent in the trough housing year of 1933, an increase of 56 percent. In the recent crisis the same ratio rose from 328 percent in the peak housing year of 2006 to 519 percent in the trough housing year of 2009, an almost identical increase of 58 percent compared to the 56 percent of 1925–33.
36. Podnolik (2014, section 2, p. 1).
37. The *Sunset* quotation is from Jacobs (2006, p. 71).
38. This paragraph is partly based on "Lexington: The Politics of Plenty," *Economist,* May 26, 2007.
39. As of 2011, 77 percent of the 2011 American housing stock was built since 1950, and only the remaining 23 percent was constructed before 1950. The median age of housing in 2011 was 1974. Data are from the *American Housing Survey.*
40. Isenstadt (1998, p. 311).
41. *Consumer Reports* (May 1955, p. 150).
42. This and other details about refrigerator quality come from Gordon (1990, pp. 249–70).
43. *Consumer Reports* (June 1949, p. 248)

44. *Consumer Reports* (September 1971, p. 562).
45. *Consumer Reports* (August 1960, p. 414).
46. This section on the quality of washing machines is based on Gordon (1990, pp. 282–94).
47. Details about dishwashers come from Gordon (1990, pp. 310–11).
48. Details from Gordon (1990, p. 270).
49. Quoted by Gordon (1990, p. 270) from an unnamed report issued by Consumers' Union in 1986, p. 2. This statement is obviously incorrect about submarines, for the hundreds of submarines that fought in World War II did not have air conditioning. Indeed, at Chicago's Museum of Science and Industry, where resides the only intact German submarine in the Western Hemisphere, the U-505, the guide, who leads small groups of twelve tourists through the claustrophobic interior, emphasizes the stifling uncooled air moved around only by a few small fans.
50. *Consumer Reports* (June 1965, p. 276).
51. The difference in the growth rates of price indexes with and without adjustment for energy efficiency comes from Gordon (1990, table 7.9, p. 281). Any quantity that grows at 2.6 percent per year rises by 118 percent over thirty years.
52. *Consumer Reports* (November 1985, p. 647).
53. Hayden (2002, p. 40).
54. These pairings of adjectives are suggested by Rybczynski (1995, p. 117).
55. In Chicago, its inner suburbs, and in numerous other Midwestern cities the alleys not only move the garages from facing the street to instead face the alley but also allow pickup of garbage from behind the house. They have the additional aesthetic advantage of allowing the telephone and power lines to run down the alley, freeing the streets from rows of telephone poles. Alleys have been universal in the city of Chicago since the original town plat was drawn in 1830. In 1900, fully 98 percent of residential blocks had alleys, and that figure was still more than 90 percent in 2000. See www.encyclopedia.chicagohistory.org/pages/38.html.
56. Coffey and Layden (1995, p. 139).
57. Editors of *Fortune* (1995, pp. 78–80).
58. The quotation and details in the previous paragraph are from Cohen (1996, p. 1056).
59. Cohen (1996, p. 1060).
60. This paragraph summarizes parts of Siegel (2008).
61. www.demographia.com/db-uza2000.htm.
62. www.demographia.com/db-dense-nhd.htm.
63. See Bryon et al. (2007).
64. The "mansion subsidy" phrase is used by Hayden (2000, p. 11).
65. The most important single source on the role of marketed services in explaining the difference in productivity levels and growth rates between the United States and Europe is Timmer et al. (2010, chapter 5).
66. This remark occurred at a dinner of a small group with the new British consul in Chicago in November 2012. I responded, "Yes, but haven't northern English industrial cities deteriorated in the same way?" His answer was crisp: "They are close enough so that a single plant closing does not devastate a town, and they have been saved by waves of immigration from Pakistan and India."
67. There is no mention of population loss in either of the two sources previously cited about density, Puga (2008) or Bryon et al. (2007).
68. These paragraphs summarize Lemann (1991, chapter 2).
69. See Baldassare (1992, p. 488) and Hayden (2000, p. 8). In Chicago, one of the most segregated central cities, blacks have moved primarily to southern suburbs such as Harvey and Matteson. This migration allows middle-class black families to purchase larger houses, but a universal comment is the strong desire to escape African American male gang street violence in the central city. See "Black Chicagoans Fuel Growth of South Suburbs," *New York Times*, July 3, 2011.
70. Bruegmann (2005, p. 47).

71. See Silverman and Schneider (1991, p. 193). The fifteen line items include separate assessments for county and local government, including duplicative police, fire, community college, public parks, and sewage disposal, among others.
72. See the U.S. Census Bureau, 2012 Census of Governments.
73. Silverman and Schneider (1991, p. 196).
74. Nominal median household income is from www.census.gov/prod/2012pubs/p60-243.pdf. Median nominal sales prices of new homes is from the data sources for figure 10–5.

11 SEE THE USA IN YOUR CHEVROLET OR FROM A PLANE FLYING HIGH ABOVE

1. These details are provided in chapter 16. For instance, the Willow Run plant that produced 8,000 B-24 Liberator bombers between 1942 and 1945 was converted after 1953 into a General Motors factory that produced 82 million motor vehicle transmissions until the plant was shut down in 2010.
2. The compilation of this index was a nontrivial task. The arrangement of tables in the HSUS makes it easy to include only domestically produced vehicles and to exclude imports. Not only automobiles but light trucks must be included. More subtle is the need to know that about a third of spending on automobiles in the national accounts is included not as consumer spending on vehicles, but rather as a part of business fixed investment.
3. To this day, despite having been age 9 at the time, I can remember the invoice of the 1950 Plymouth, perhaps because two days before my father arrived home with the car, the North Koreans had invaded South Korea. The price was $1,520, which stuck in my mind as being close to the year when Columbus set sail for America. There were two accessories on the invoice—$7 for directional signals and $59 for a radio. The price of $1,520 looks plausible compared to the average nominal price in 1950 of $2,300, which included higher-priced luxury cars and also pickup trucks and vans used by business firms.
4. Percentage of installation of individual items is taken from Gordon (1990, table 8.2, p. 326).
5. Ingrassia (2012, p. 345).
6. The sources of rapid productivity growth between 1920 and 1970, and especially between 1928 and 1950, are the subject of chapter 16.
7. Gordon (1990, table 8.10, p. 351).
8. The present value of fuel consumed over the first four years equaled 41 percent of the purchase price of the vehicle. See Crandall et al. (1976, p. 133).
9. This conundrum that fuel economy was influenced by a change in the mix of cars sold was solved in a research paper written in the early 1980s. If one has data on the specifications of numerous car models over a substantial period of time, one can study the relationship between fuel economy and automobile size, weight, presence of air conditioning, and other characteristics. It is also important that one use data not on "city" or "highway" gasoline mileage but rather on gasoline mileage measured at a constant speed, for the spread of the interstate highways after 1950 allowed a steady increase in travel speeds that reduced gasoline mileage. After controlling for the influence of all these factors, it is possible to measure how that relationship shifts over time. See Wilcox (1984).
10. Gordon (1990, pp. 364–65). This estimate is conservative, for it only takes into account saving on gasoline purchase costs over the first four years of the life of the car. The quality-adjusted increase of fuel economy of 66 percent between 1967 and 1984 was converted to logs and multiplied by the 31 percent initial fuel cost for 1972. Here we multiply by the 41 percent under the regime of higher fuel prices that dates back to the mid-1970s and that is more relevant for the decades since the mid-1970s.
11. This valuation is much simpler, for there is little or no need to take account of changes in automobile size, speed, or power, these having changed much less after 1984 than they did in the four decades before 1984.
12. The cumulative growth rate of 35 percent instead of 30 percent results from the effect of compound arithmetic.
13. The estimated value of higher fuel economy does not take account of the 60 percent increase in automobile horsepower that occurred between 1975 and 2013. See White (2014, p. B5).

14. Miles traveled per vehicle have changed little over the years, from 7,450 in 1929 to 9,450 in 1950 to 12,000 in 2012.
15. blogs.cars.com/kickingtires/2013/04.
16. The article is Akerlof (1970).
17. The automobile issue includes charts showing the frequency of repair for every model of domestic and imported vehicles over not just the most recent model year but also the past eight years, and until recently, repair frequencies (rated in five categories from "much better than average" to "much worse than average") were listed separately for fourteen different categories of repairs. In recent years, the annual automobile issue has dropped the listing of the separate repair categories, for they tended to be the same across categories for each model; instead, it now lists an overall rating for each model for the previous twelve years.
18. Nominal vehicle maintenance and repair expense for 1984 is taken from NIPA table 2.4.5 and is divided by the total number of registered motor vehicles in 1984. This is an understatement, for it includes only consumer expenditures, not business maintenance expenditures on business-owned vehicles.
19. I have never forgotten the sign at a gas station in Watertown, Massachusetts, where we lived in February 1965 when I was a graduate student interested in prices, selling gas for 19.9 cents per gallon.
20. The data on repair incidence are from *Consumer Reports* (April 1984, pp. 221–32).
21. This is based on a report by Michael Sivak and Brandon Schoettle at the University of Michigan Transportation Research Institute, at www.wnyc.org/286723.
22. Kay (1997, pp. 226).
23. The land area of the forty-eight contiguous United States is 2.95 million square miles, compared to a land area for interwar Germany of about 0.16 million square miles.
24. The ultimate cost was $450 billion in 2009 dollars.
25. Kaszynski (2000, pp. 166–167).
26. Nadiri and Mamuneas (1994, pp. 22–37).
27. *Economist* (February 16, 2008, p. 32).
28. Facts in this section about the interstate highway system come from www.fhwa.dot.gov/interstate/homepage.cfm.
29. Lichter and Fuguitt (1980, pp. 500–510).
30. Kaszynski (2000, pp. 156–160).
31. Coffee and Layden (1998, p. 161).
32. www.gcmap.com/mapui?P=EKO-PSC,+SFO-HNL.
33. Elko is exactly halfway between Reno and Salt Lake City, and Elko County in 2013 had a population of 18,000.
34. Garvey and Fisher (2002, pp. 27–34). By coincidence, the author flew on United Airlines from Fort Lauderdale to Chicago on April 6, 2001, the exact day of the airline's seventy-fifth anniversary.
35. The Lindbergh anecdote comes from Carryer (2007, p. 13).
36. The Philippines became an independent nation on July 4, 1946. The aircraft routing was from Honolulu to Midway (site of the famous 1942 naval battle) to Wake Island to Guam and then Manila. These legs were easy after the 2,400 distance between San Francisco and Hawaii had been bridged, and none of these flights was longer than 1,600 miles. www.gcmap.com/mapui?P=HNL-MDY-AWK-GUM-MNL.
37. Heppenheimer (1995), pp. 70–71.
38. Midway Island, 1,300 miles northwest of Honolulu, was the site of the most important single naval battle in history, where on June 4, 1942, only six months after the Japanese attack on Pearl Harbor, a single U.S. Navy squadron destroyed four large Japanese aircraft carriers.
39. United Airlines timetable, October 1, 1934.
40. The 1936 price is from the American Airlines timetable of September 1, 1937. The price level (measured by the personal consumption deflator) is 13.9 times higher than in 1937. The current price was obtained on September 15, 2014, from the American Airlines website, and is for a fully refundable first-class ticket, the modern equivalent of the fully refundable 1937 first-class ticket.
41. Cadillac details from United Airlines timetable, October 1, 1934. The price was the same in 1937.

42. The nonstop distance Honolulu to LA is 2,556 miles, slightly longer than the LA to New York distance of 2,475 miles.
43. Keeler (1972).
44. As a 40-year-old professor attending conferences in the United States and Europe, as well as taking family vacations, I had flown 53,000 miles the previous year, 1980. Not surprisingly, I signed up for AAdvantage on May 1 and with United's competing "Mileage Plus" program on May 4.
45. Only actual airline miles count for elite status, although airlines give double miles for flights to customers at certain elite levels. Miles earned by buying groceries are added to the mileage tally available for free flights but are irrelevant for elite status.
46. Prices from the United in-flight magazine, August 2014.
47. Gordon (1992, p. 396).
48. "Piketty Class," *Economist,* September 20, 2014, p. 56.

12 ENTERTAINMENT AND COMMUNICATIONS FROM MILTON BERLE TO THE IPHONE

1. Spigel (1992, p. 99).
2. Sterling and Kittross (1990, pp. 146).
3. Facts from Maclaurin (1950, pp. 147) and Sterling and Kittross (1990, pp. 147).
4. The story of Farnsworth and his epic battle with David Sarnoff is the topic of a 2007 play *The Farnsworth Invention*, written by Aaron Sorkin, who wrote the screenplay of *The Social Network*. The play is historically inaccurate in portraying Sarnoff rather than Farnsworth as the winner of the lawsuits. Instead of dying in obscurity, as claimed in the play, Farnsworth went on to a distinguished career in technology. A statue of Farnsworth stands in the U.S. Capitol building.
5. Arango (2010, pp. 17).
6. Britain was uncharacteristically ahead of the United States in the development of television. BBC went on the air in November 1936 and achieved the first outside broadcast of the coronation of King George VI in May 1937. Its audience had reached 40,000 in the London area before transmission was shut down in September 1939 for the duration of World War II.
7. Sterling and Kittross (1990, pp. 213–15).
8. Conway (2009, pp. 19).
9. Barnouw (1990, pp. 54, 93–96). Also Sterling and Kittross (1990, pp. 210).
10. Bohn and Stomgren (1975, pp. 383).
11. Sterling and Kittross (1990, pp. 254).
12. In 1949 I was age 9, and my brother was 5. We deliberately spent our late afternoons in the homes of neighbors, watching late 1940s staples such as the *Cisco Kid*, *Hopalong Cassidy*, and *Don Winslow in the Navy*. Our boycott of our parents worked, and a typical television of the day, a nine-inch RCA costing $350, arrived in our living room in March 1950.
13. Bogart (1956, pp. 87–90).
14. Sterling and Kittross (1990, pp. 263–64, 636–37).
15. Schneider (1997, pp. 23–25). Throughout the history of television, those in the Pacific time zone have seen the entire day of programming at the same hour as those in the Eastern time zone. The Central time zone has long been the anomaly, with all network broadcasts after 10 a.m. shown one hour earlier than in the Eastern or Pacific time zones. Only the morning shows between 7 a.m. and 9 a.m. are tape-delayed to be shown at the same times as in the other time zones.
16. See Spigel (1992, pp. 100).
17. Barnouw (1990, pp. 148).
18. Bogart (1956, pp. 1).
19. Van Gelder (2002).
20. Bogart (1956, pp. 106–107).
21. "TV Basics" (2012).

22. Bogart (1956, pp. 91).
23. This most famous of all TV debates took place in the studios of WBBM-TV, the CBS-owned network affiliate in downtown Chicago within two blocks of the Michigan Avenue "magnificent mile" shopping district.
24. Druckman (2003, pp. 559–71).
25. "People & Events: Selma March." www.pbs.org/wgbh/amex/wallace/peopleevents/pande08.html.
26. Spigel (1992, pp. 109).
27. "Word for Word: The Rest Is Silence," *New York Times,* February 12, 2006.
28. Bohn and Stomgren (1975, pp. 402–7).
29. Corbett (2001, pp. 25–32).
30. Bohn and Stomgren (1975, pp. 397).
31. Ganzel (2007).
32. Boddy (1985, pp. 25).
33. "All Time Box Office."
34. Daley (2010). The *Wizard of Oz* was initially shown in 1956, then annually from 1959 to 1991.
35. Bohn and Stomgren (1975, pp. 483).
36. Sterling and Kittross (1990, pp. 396–97, 638–41).
37. From Berkeley, I was able to listen to WBAP in Fort Worth and WCCO in Minneapolis, but my little radio could never stretch itself to pull in a Chicago station.
38. Millard (1995, pp. 218).
39. Bijsterveld (2010, pp. 193).
40. MacDonald (1979, pp. 88).
41. This set was located at abt.com on August 8, 2014, and the price and model number were verified by telephone with an Abt salesperson.
42. Gordon (1990, p. 303).
43. The data on real GDP are created by taking current-dollar expenditures and dividing them by a price index. Let us say that from year 1 to year 2 nominal spending on TV sets rises from 100 to 105. If the CPI determines that the price decline is –1 percent, then the price goes from 100 to 99, and the quantity of TV sets goes from 100 to 106. But if the true decline in price is –4 percent, then the second-year value of the TV component of real GDP is not 106 but 109. Consumers are receiving improved quality of TV sets that is excluded from GDP.
44. Quotations from *Consumer Reports* are from Gordon (1990, p. 308).
45. Fantel (1984).
46. The sixty-inch price quotation of $999.99 was obtained from bestbuy.com on August 8, 2014.
47. All information on 1983 nineteen-inch color TV sets comes from *Consumer Reports* (January 1984, pp. 37–41).
48. The price changes are calculated from the average price of all listed models of the designated screen size, separated between "conventional," "plasma," and "LCD," from the following issues of *Consumer Reports:* March 1992 (pp. 164–5), November 1992 (pp. 702–03), March 1997 (p. 84), December 1999 (pp. 16–17), March 2004 (p. 22), December 2004 (pp. 30–31), March 2005 (pp. 19–21), March 2010 (pp. 26–29), and December 2014 (p. 28).
49. "TV Basics."
50. Sullivan (2008) and Los Angeles Times (1993, April 1). Also see Parsons (1996, pp. 354–65) for a refutation of one of the cable television origins myths.
51. Eisenmann (2000).
52. "Television Facts and Statistics—1939 to 2000."
53. Sterling and Kittross (1990, pp. 636–37).
54. Hall (2002, pp. 336).
55. Sullivan (2008).
56. SAUS (2012), table 1142.
57. SAUS (1999), table 1440.

58. Our household bought our first VCR in 1978, when less than 1 percent of American households owned them. My recollection is that our first model required repairs at least once per year until we replaced it in the mid-1980s with a modern unit having electronic controls and programming capability.
59. This discussion of VCR prices and quality comes from Gordon (1990, pp. 313–17). See also Wickstrom (1986).
60. Secunda (1990, pp. 17–18).
61. Magoun (2002, pp. 148).
62. New York Times (1986).
63. Millard (1995, pp. 257).
64. Les Paul and Mary Ford were pioneers in using the tape recorder to achieve double-tracked harmony.
65. Millard (2002, pp. 158–67).
66. Jenish and Davies (1999).
67. Millard (1995, pp. 353–55).
68. Bergen (2011).
69. Fischer (1992, pp. 255).
70. AT&T (2014).
71. I had a job in the summer of 1961 as an intern at the Pacific Telephone Company in Oakland, California. At that time, calls from the East Bay to San Francisco were dialed, but calls from Oakland and Berkeley to Marin County across the bay still had to be connected by human operators.
72. See Joel (1984, pp. 66–67) for general discussion of developments in electronic switching. For further information on the invention and uses of the transistor see Schweber (1997, pp. 83–87) and Ganssle (2007). A more in-depth treatment of the transistor's impact will follow in chapter 13.
73. Staehler and Hayward Jr. (1979, pp. 1109–14).
74. Figure 6–3, which draws on HSUS series Dg59, Dg60, and Gordon (2012a, Appendix table A-1). All rates are adjusted to 2005 dollars.
75. See HSUS series Dg46–55, converted to per capita using HSUS Series A7, 2010–2013: The U.S. Census: "Annual Estimates of the Resident Population for the United States, April 1, 2012 to July 1, 2013."
76. Fischer (1992, pp. 255).
77. Wright (2004, pp. 31–32).
78. Agar (2013, pp. 45, 170).
79. U.S. Census (2012), table 1148, 1149.
80. Rainie (2013).
81. Quotation from Agar (2013, pp. 1). Though the author is British, this same shift has been felt in the United States.
82. Donovan and Scherer (1992, pp. 259).
83. Donovan and Scherer (1992, pp. 294).
84. Steiger (2007, pp. A8).
85. Sterling and Kittross (1990, pp. 499).
86. NY-1 is owned by the Time-Warner cable company, which provides cable service to the New York area. CLTV (Chicagoland TV) is quite different, for it is owned by Tribune Media and shares staff, weather, and news sources with Tribune-owned WGN-TV, which in turn has a nationwide presence with its national cable channel WGN America.
87. Numbers taken from circulation statistics of Newspaper Association of America (2012), converted to per household.
88. Steiger (2007, pp. A8).
89. Donovan and Scherer (1992, pp. 261–62, 270–72, 283–84).
90. Edmonds et al. (2013).
91. American Press Institute (2014).
92. Epstein (1973, pp. 247–72).
93. Jabr (2013) for an overview of findings on these subjects. See Santana et al. (2011, pp. 2–30) for a specific study on retention.

94. "Spotify" (2013). For subscription prices, see spotify.com/us.
95. Mindlin (2006). In addition to the DVD's rise, households reporting VCR ownership fell about 10 percent from 2000 to 2006.
96. Stelter (2013).
97. Nielsen Company (2014, pp. 8).
98. Auletta (2014, pp. 54–61). Though the streaming service went online in 2007, Netflix had functioned as an online DVD rental delivery service since before 2000.
99. Epstein (2010, pp. 189–94).
100. Zickhur and Rainie (2014, pp. 1).
101. Pew Research Internet Project (2014). "Mobile Technology Fact Sheet."
102. Agar (2013, pp. 177).
103. Pew Research Internet Project (2014), "Mobile Technology Fact Sheet." Because 58 percent of Americans and more than 64 percent of all cell phone owners had smartphones (the second number was reached by dividing 58 percent by the 90 percent of Americans who own cell phones of any kind), the fact that more than 60 percent of all cell owners used the Internet, 52 percent accessed e-mail, 50 percent downloaded apps, 49 percent used GPS, and 48 percent listened to music suggests that no less than 75 percent of smartphone owners use their phones for each of these reasons.
104. Agar (2013, pp. 202).
105. Twitter, Inc. (2014).

13 COMPUTERS AND THE INTERNET FROM THE MAINFRAME TO FACEBOOK

1. Source of historical information and statistics is Cray Inc. website.
2. The source of the quotation from Intel's webpage on Gordon Moore and Innovation.
3. This is a perfect example of the "rule of 70." The natural log of 2.0 is 0.693; we can use this fact to determine how many years will be required for something to double when it grows at a certain rate, or what the growth rate is if something doubles in a certain number of years. If something doubles in two years, we divide 69.3 by 2 and obtain a growth rate of 34.65 percent. Because the U.S. growth rate of per-person income between 1891 and 2007 was 2.0 per year, we know that its doubling occurred every 34.65 years.
4. The source is Intel's pressroom about Moore's Law's fortieth anniversary (2005) and Intel's pressroom about the release of Intel 15-Core Xeon microprocessor.
5. Nordhaus (2007, p. 147).
6. See Tuomi (2002). The e-mails from Varian are dated August 24 and 25, 2014.
7. Kennedy (1964).
8. Statistics and facts from Farrington (1996, p. 74).
9. Pagliery (2014).
10. Quotation from Yates (1999, p. 7).
11. Statistic from Yates (1999, p. 8).
12. Statistic from Brand, Fuller, and Watson (2011).
13. Brooker (2004).
14. Statistics from VISA, Inc. (2013).
15. Quotation from Allison (1995).
16. My first desktop computer, purchased in 1983, was a Compaq, which had a faster 8086 chip and sharper monitor resolution than the IBM PC.
17. My mother actually wrote an entire book in her late seventies during 1975–77 using a crude word processing program called "Multimate" that was almost instantly made obsolete by WordPerfect. I tried to sell her on the many advantages of WordPerfect, but she would not budge.
18. Patton (1995, p. 83).
19. Historical information and statistics from Caillau (1995).

20. As an example of the swiftness of current web searching, in writing this sentence on my desktop PC in mid-2014, I entered the search term "introduction date of Windows 95" on my adjacent laptop and within a fraction of a second, a response page appeared with "August 24, 1995" in large bold type at the top of the page.
21. O'Malley (1995, p. 80).
22. en.wikipedia.org/wiki/Wikipedia:Size_of_Wikipedia. These would be very large volumes containing 1.6 million words each, more than five times the number of words in this book.

14 ANTIBIOTICS, CT SCANS, AND THE EVOLUTION OF HEALTH AND MEDICINE

1. This refers to U.S. life expectancy at birth versus U.S. health expenditure per person, compared to those of the rest of the G7 nations. We will return to this later.
2. For these figures, see figure 7–2.
3. SAUS (2012), No. HS-13.
4. SAUS (2002), no. 93, and SAUS (2012), table 107.
5. Stevens (1989), p. 203.
6. SAUS (2012), No. HS-13.
7. CDC (2012).
8. SAUS (2012), No. HS-13.
9. CDC (2012).
10. Leaf and Burke (2004).
11. CDC (2012).
12. American Academy of Neurology (2014).
13. CDC (2011), table 9.
14. Bud (2007), p. 3.
15. SAUS (2012), No. HS-18.
16. Bud (2007), p. 99.
17. Bud (2007), pp. 25–41, and Temin (1980), p. 66. In 1943, Pfizer opened its first penicillin production plants, and by 1944 the company was producing half of America's penicillin.
18. Bud (2007), pp. 53, 98, for the information on price and consumption of penicillin. Bud (2007), p. 54, for the quotation about patients' somewhat overblown perception of the wonder drug's capabilities.
19. Bud (2007), p. 98.
20. U.S. Food and Drug Administration (2013). Part of reason for these lofty numbers in the 1940s and 1950s was that the FDA had never made drug approvals before 1938 and thus had a backlog of drugs to approve. Regulation was also more lax then. Nonetheless, the numbers fairly accurately reflect the flood of new antibiotics and other drugs onto the market during this time, never before or after equaled.
21. Temin (1980), p. 70.
22. Gellene (2009), p. A26.
23. SAUS (2012), No. HS-18.
24. Stevens (1989), p. 202.
25. CDC (2010).
26. Fordham, Skinner, et al. (2012), pp. 1–6. Though QALY is fairly widely used in Europe to assess the value and cost-effectiveness of certain treatments, it has yet to catch on in the United States. The cited study is British.
27. The information and the quotation in the previous paragraph come from Starr (1982, p. 346).
28. Blume and Geesink (2000), p. 1593.
29. SAUS (2012), No. HS-18.
30. Bud (2007), p. 3.
31. CDC (1999).

32. Stevens (1989), pp. 277–78.
33. Cheung and Menkis (1998), p. 1881.
34. Norton (2012). It is amazing that aspirin, which was discovered in 1897, has proven so effective against so many unexpected ailments. Not only do small doses significantly decrease the risk of heart attack, but recent studies have also showed that aspirin reduces the risk of dying from cancer. For more on the expanding uses of aspirin, the "2000-year-old wonder drug," read Agus (2012).
35. Jones and Greene (2013), pp. e2–e4.
36. CDC (1999).
37. Jones and Greene (2013), pp. e4–e9.
38. Acs and Lyle (2007, figure 2.2, p. 19).
39. American Cancer Society (2014).
40. Galmarini et al. (2012), p. 182.
41. Wiedemann (1994), p. 223.
42. American Cancer Society (2014).
43. Reynolds (2012), p. 2.
44. Schmidt (2012), pp. A119–A121.
45. Galmarini et al. (2012), p. 181.
46. Leaf and Burke (2004) provide both quotations and the information for most of this paragraph.
47. Life expectancy statistics from "Stages of HIV Infection," www.aids.gov/hiv-aids-basics/just-diagnosed-with-hiv-aids/hiv-in-your-body/stages-of-hiv/.
48. Facts in this paragraph from "Thirty Years of HIV/AIDS: Snapshots of an Epidemic," www.amfar.org/thirty-years-of-hiv/aids-snapshots-of-an-epidemic/.
49. https://www.aids.gov/hiv-aids-basics/hiv-aids-101/statistics/.
50. Quote from Anthony Fauci, www.cnn.com/2013/12/01/health/hiv-today/.
51. Cole and Fiore (2014), pp. 131–32.
52. Tavernise and Gebeloff (2014), pp. A1, A17.
53. Facts from Starr (1982), p. 345; the quotation comes from p. 337.
54. National Alliance on Mental Illness (2013), p. 1.
55. Gardner (2014). The "blanket of orange" description comes from an audio file on the online article page of a Judith Lyons describing her memory.
56. Pope, Ezzati, and Dockery (2009), p. 384.
57. Krewski (2009), p. 413, in reference to the Canadian study by Coyle et al. The exact estimate was that such concentrations of additional air pollution would "lead to a quality-adjusted reduction in life expectancy of 0.60 year, as compared with the unadjusted reduction of 0.80 year," suggesting that one additional year with that level of concentration would be worth only three-quarters of the unadjusted value.
58. Gardner (2014). These descriptions come from Chip Jacobs's brief audio memoir clip.
59. Pinker (2011), p. 107.
60. This paragraph summarizes Pinker (2011), pp. 399–415.
61. HSUS Series Ec190 and SAUS (2012), table 312.
62. See Pinker (2011), pp. 116–28, for a more in-depth examination of the causes behind the crime reduction of the 1990s. The *Roe v. Wade* theory comes from the economists John Donohue and Steven Levitt.
63. Light and Levine (1988), p. 22.
64. Temin (1980), p. 68, 85.
65. Starr (1982), pp. 355–59.
66. HSUS Series Bd242 and SAUS (2012), table 160.
67. Light and Levine (1988), p. 25.
68. Stevens (1989), p. 231.
69. Yount (2001), pp. 23, 40–41. While there had been a precedent for patients' consent since 1914, the emphasis on *informed* consent did not come about until the 1970s as part of the broader patients' rights movement. Since the AHA published the first Patients' Bill of Rights, several other versions have followed.

70. Starr (1982), p. 391. Some of the explanation for the growing distrust of the medical profession can be found in the rapidly growing costs of healthcare during the 1960s and 1970s, driven in part by a growing third-party payment system that incentivized maximizing services, even if they were excessive (Starr 1982, p. 385).
71. Geyman (2011).
72. Schmidt (2012), p. A121.
73. Bakalar (2011), p. D7.
74. Dotinga (2012).
75. McCarthy, McLeod, and Ginsburg (2013), pp. 1–13. The first quotation comes from page 1, the second from page 7, and the third from page 13.
76. Karanes et al. (2008), p. 8.
77. Google's Ngram Viewer is a delightful tool that allows one to look at cultural trends based on the prevalence of key words and phrases that a user can search.
78. O'Brien (2012), p. 189.
79. Munos (2009), p. 962.
80. Vijg (2011), p. 65.
81. Fuchs and Garber (2003), p. 46.
82. The previous two paragraphs summarize and quote Vijg (2011, pp. 63–75).
83. See Cohen (2013) for an account of how data-mining by artificial intelligence such as IBM's Watson could become a new diagnostic tool.
84. Stevens (1989), pp. 204–20.
85. Stevens (1989), p. 231, 296–301.
86. Starr (1982), p. 368.
87. Yount (2001), p. 9.
88. http://managedhealthcareexecutive.modernmedicine.com/managed-healthcare-executive/content/higher-costs-resulting-medical-arms-race?page=full.
89. Stevens (1989), p. 252, 306–8. The previous paragraph comes from pages 252 and 308, and the quotation comes from pages 306–7.
90. Starr (1982), p. 363.
91. Erbentraut (2014) and Thomas (2013).
92. Starr (1982), p. 434.
93. Stevens (1989), p. 288.
94. CDC (2011), table 9.
95. American Academy of Neurology (2014). The revised mortality rate was reached after seeing that total deaths from Alzheimer's according this source were just over six times higher than the CDC's figure, so we multiplied the CDC's death rate by six.
96. Fuchs (1998), p. 164.
97. Cutler and McClellan (2001, Exhibit 3).
98. SAUS (2012), No. HS-16, and Hoyert and Xu (2012), table 6. The basis for the differential in 1900 is actually of all nonwhite races, for black life expectancy was not documented on its own by the U.S. Census until 1970. However, the two figures have generally remained close together, with the life expectancy of African Americans being slightly lower.
99. Hoyert and Xu (2012), table 1.
100. CDC (1999).
101. SAUS (2012), table 182.
102. Tavernise (2013).
103. See Barreca et al. (2015).
104. www.cdc.gov/nchs/fastats/inpatient-surgery.htm.
105. Facts from time.com/3692001/birth-control-history-djerassi/.
106. Facts from www.nature.com/bdj/journal/v199/n7s/full/481.2863a.html.
107. Winship (2012), p. 17.

108. Yount (2001), pp. 5–7. In 2001, more than 160 million Americans were ensured by employer-sponsored plans.
109. Starr (1982), p. 373.
110. Stevens (1989), p. 334.
111. Starr (1982), p. 335, 380–85.
112. Stevens (1989), p. 257.
113. Quotation from Stevens (1989), pp. 325–26. Other information for previous paragraph from Stevens (1989), pp. 321–25.
114. CDC (2006), "National Hospital Discharge Survey: 2006 Annual Summary."
115. Cohn (2007), p. 78.
116. Cohn (2007), p. 64.
117. Dranove (2000), p. 67.
118. Cohn (2007), p. 68.
119. Folland et al. (2013), figure 12–1, p. 240.
120. Dranove (2000), p. 84.
121. Yount (2001), pp. 19–20, and World Bank (2014) for the 2010 data.
122. Dranove (2000), p. 88.
123. Cutler and Wise (2006), p. 64.
124. Winship (2012), p. 17.
125. Yount (2001), p. 25.
126. Facts about subsidies from obamacarefacts.com/costof-obamacare and about preventive screening from obamacarefacts.com/Obamacare-preventive-care/.
127. Details in this paragraph and the quotation are from Rosenthal (2015), p. 7.
128. Bud (2007), p. 3.
129. Some of the more recent targeted anticancer therapies include Gleevec, Avastin, rituximab, tamoxifen, and Herceptin. I am grateful to Megan McCarville for suggesting this list.

15 WORK, YOUTH, AND RETIREMENT AT HOME AND ON THE JOB

1. Full-year tuition for me at a private Ivy League college in 1958 was $1,250. The same tuition would be about $55,000 today. Because the price level has increased during this fifty-five-year interval by a factor of five, the inflation-adjusted cost of tuition has increased by a factor of ten.
2. The only two exceptions were the recession years of 1958 and 1961.
3. "Improvements in Workplace Safety—United States, 1900–1999," MMRW (1999, p. 465).
4. See Barreca et al. (2015).
5. Description from National Building Museum on pre-AC life during the 1920s, in Plumer (2012).
6. Beatty (1994, p. 64).
7. Goldin and Margo (1992, p. 3).
8. Reardon and Bischoff (2011, p. 1093).
9. Boyce, Brown, and Moore (2010, p. 474).
10. The fertility rate is the ratio of children born to the number of women of child-bearing age.
11. Ramey (2009, p. 9).
12. Ramey (2009, p. 18).
13. Harvey (2002, p. 69).
14. Coontz (2011).
15. Lamb (2011, p. 25).
16. Klenow (2012, p. 2).
17. Collins (2009, p. 20).
18. Goldin (2006, p. 8).
19. Klenow (2012, p. 1).
20. Bock (1993).

21. Hymowitz (2012, p. 56).
22. Women aged 30 or younger make more than men except in New York, Chicago, and Los Angeles, where the highest-earning men are concentrated.
23. Hymowitz (2012, p. 56).
24. Coombes (2009).
25. Goldin (2014, p. 1093).
26. Goldin (2014, p. 1118).
27. Brown, Haughwout, Lee, Mabutas, van der Klaauw (2012).
28. Wessel (2007, pp. 1–2).
29. Seburn (1991, p. 18).
30. Seburn (1991, p. 19).
31. Seburn (1991, p. 19).
32. Sass (1997, p. 99).
33. Beyer (2012, p. 3).
34. Anders and Hulse (2006, p. 2).
35. Sass (1997, p. 179).
36. Beyer (2012, p. 5).
37. *Businessweek* (March 6, 2014, p. 52).
38. Stroud (1995, p. 6).
39. Costa (1998, p. 27).
40. Brandon (2012, pp. 1–2).
41. Sahadi (2013).
42. Portman (2014, p. 2).
43. Levitz (2008, p. 2).
44. Polsky (2013, p. 2).
45. Biggs and Schieber (2014, p. 57).
46. Ghilarducci (2012, p. 5).
47. *Economist* (April 7, 2011, p. 78).
48. Levitz and Shiskin (2009, p. 3).
49. *Economist* (April 7, 2011, p. 78).
50. Hsieh, Chang-Tai et al. (2013).

ENTR'ACTE. TOWARD AN UNDERSTANDING OF SLOWER GROWTH

1. The statement that productivity growth was the slowest in the 2004–14 decade refers to cyclically adjusted productivity growth and does not apply to decades ending in recession years when the level of productivity was temporarily low—for example, 1923–33.

16 THE GREAT LEAP FORWARD FROM THE 1920S TO THE 1950S: WHAT SET OF MIRACLES CREATED IT?

1. The title of this chapter, "The Great Leap Forward," is not the first to identify the transition from the 1920s to the 1950s as a "great leap." My own attention to this puzzle began in my Ph.D. thesis, which was motivated by the doubling of the average productivity of capital in Kendrick's (1961) data between the 1920s and 1950s (Gordon, 1967, p. 3). Baumol (1986, pp. 1081–82) remarked that "it is noteworthy . . . that the great leap above historical U. S. productivity growth in the war and early postwar years were just about as great as the previous shortfalls during the Great Depression . . . . Perhaps the accumulated innovative ideas, unused because of the depression, as well as frustrated savings goals, fueled an outburst of innovations and investment when business conditions permitted." (As we shall see throughout this chapter, the great leap was far larger than the Depression shortfall, and indeed labor productivity had risen well above the pre-1928 trend by 1940–41). The phrase appears in Gordon (2000, p. 22) in the

current context: "a substantial part of the great leap in the level of multi-factor productivity had already occurred by the end of World War II." In this sense, the book title of Field (2011) repeats a phrase that had first been used decades earlier.

2. See figure 5–4. The ratio to households of total motor vehicles was 90.3 percent and of automobiles was 78.2 percent.
3. The current national accounts record real GDP in 2009 prices as $1,163 billion in 1939 and $2,237 billion in 1944.
4. The year 1928 rather than 1929 is chosen to establish the trend prior to the Great Depression and World War II. We want our log-linear trends to be drawn between years with relatively "normal" conditions of demand, and it is clear from many macroeconomic variables that the rise of output and its components from 1928 to 1929 was unsustainable, including the fact that real GDP grew by 6.4 percent from 1928 to 1929.
5. Even though the lights were "turned out" between 1929 and 1950, we nevertheless include 1941 and sometimes 1944 in the tables of this chapter to address the question, raised by Field (2003, 2011), of how much of the great leap forward occurred in the 1930s (i.e., 1928–41) versus the 1940s (1941–50).
6. TFP can also be defined as a weighted average of the ratio of output to quality-adjusted labor input and of the ratio of output to quality-adjusted capital input.
7. There is no comprehensive research study of the value of all inventions. The largest effect measured thus far is for the value of increases in life expectancy, particularly in the first half of the twentieth century. See the interpretation of Nordhaus (2003) presented in figure 7–8.
8. With a Cobb–Douglas production function and constant returns to scale, the marginal product of labor is equal to the elasticity of output to labor input multiplied by average labor productivity—e.g., output per hour. As Robert Solow showed in 1957, in principle, this elasticity should be equal to the share of labor income in total national income. See Solow (1957).
9. The real wage series combines different sources for 1870–1929, 1929–1948, and 1948–2014. See the data appendix.
10. The real wage trend grows at 1.95 percent per year and is calculated as the log growth rate between 1891 and 1928, whereas the trend for labor productivity grows at 1.89 percent per year and is based on the actual average change between 1870 and 1928. We choose not to use the real wage trend for 1870–1928, which grows at 2.15 percent per year, for if extended from 1928 to 2014, it would imply that labor's share should have risen by 25 percent between 1928 and 2014. Also, the behavior of this series on the real wage before 1891 implies an implausible increase in labor's share from 1870 to 1929.
11. Kendrick (1961, Table 31, p. 126) shows the same surge of the real wage in the 1930s. His real wage index grows at an annual rate of 3.0 percent between 1929 and 1937, much more quickly than the rates of 2.4 percent for 1919–29 and 1.8 percent for 1937–48.
12. See Denison (1962) and Jorgenson and Griliches (1967).
13. Goldin and Katz (2008, p. 33).
14. See the data appendix, where the Kendrick concept of capital is updated with data from the Bureau of Economic Analysis and is plotted as the "Official Capital" line in figure A–1.
15. Recall that TFP is a residual and includes any source of growth not captured by the measured quantity and quality of labor and capital, including not only innovation and technological change, but also such other factors as the movement of workers from the farm to the city and the shift of production from industries having low productivity to those having higher productivity.
16. The weights are based on the shares of capital and labor income in total income, an idea introduced in the seminal (1957) paper by Robert Solow. Though these shares vary somewhat over time, it makes little difference whether one takes a constant share or a variable share. The 0.7 versus 0.3 choice of shares for the twentieth century has been adopted widely, including by Goldin and Katz (2008, Table 1.3, p. 39).
17. The index is taken from Goldin and Katz (2008, Table 1.3, column 2).
18. Abramowitz and David (2000, p. 7). Their claim that technological progress was mediocre in the 1929–45 period, which is contradicted by all the evidence assembled in this chapter, is further restated (2000, p. 29). "When a combination of Great Depression and Great War produced a dramatic decline in the

growth of the private capital stock, its average age rose markedly and refined TFP, expressing the actual rate of incorporation of technological progress, was driven below the presumptive underlying rate of advance of knowledge."

19. The labor productivity ratio used to calculate TFP differs from the labor productivity series plotted in figures 16–1 and 16–2, because it incorporates an adjustment for changes in educational attainment.
20. For these and other aspects of capacity constraints in the year 1941, see Gordon and Krenn (2010).
21. The contest to build a Liberty ship in four days or less resulted in a rivalry between the son and stepson of Henry Kaiser, who were in charge of the Richmond and Portland shipyards. See Herman (2012, pp. 188–91)
22. Baime (2014, pp. 261, 277).
23. The ultimate artistic expression of reconversion after the end of World War II is the cover of *Fortune* magazine in June 1945. An artist developed a vision of a vast field perhaps three times the length of a football field. Arrayed were every item of wartime and peacetime production, neatly arranged in groups. There were tanks, military trucks, and aircraft. But there were also row after row of grand pianos, refrigerators, irons, washing machines, and automobiles. This is part of the author's framed collection of twenty-five *Fortune* covers extending from 1930 to 1947. It can be viewed at https://www.fulltable.com/vts/f/fortune/covers/aa/40.jpg.
24. These examples are among hundreds provided by Herman (2012, pp. 353–58).
25. Abramowitz and David (2000, pp. 60–61).
26. Using the current National Income and Product Accounts, real consumer expenditures per person, in 2009 dollars were, in the six years beginning in 1940, $6,912, $7,341, $7,104, $7,258, $7,419, and $7,762.
27. Higgs (1992, pp. 50–53).
28. Higgs (1992, p. 57).
29. Examples are provided in Gordon (1967, p. 100). Fully 10 percent of 1945 U.S. capacity to produce steel had been financed by the government between 1940 and 1945. The government financed 88 percent of the World War II expansion of aircraft plants. Even after the war in 1947, fully half the nation's aluminum was produced in government-owned plants. In 1951, half the rubber supply was synthetic, and all of that was produced by private firms in government-owned plants.
30. Gordon (1967).
31. corporate.ford.com/our-company/heritage/company-milestones-news-detail/680-willow-run.
32. Gordon (2012a, Appendix Table A-1).
33. The 1924 Johnson–Reed Act set tight quotas of 2 percent of the number of people from that country who were already living in the United States in 1890. Immigration of Arabs, East Asians, and those from India was prohibited outright.
34. Part of the decline in population growth was, of course, the result of delayed fertility due to the difficult economic circumstances of the Depression years and the absence of men during the war years of 1942–45.
35. For more on overbuilding in the 1920s, see R. A. Gordon (1974).
36. The classic statement of this explanation of reduced inequality during 1940–70 is presented by Goldin and Margo (1992).
37. The phrase "general-purpose technology" was introduced in Bresnahan and Trajtenberg (1995), and the role of subsidiary and complementary inventions is further examined in the introductory chapter of Bresnahan and Gordon (1997).
38. Abbot (1932, pp. 17–18).
39. The authors provide numerous examples of inventions that long preceded the commercial introduction, taking most of their dates from Mensch (1979). Dates (invention/commercial introduction) include insulin (1889/1922), neoprene (1906/1932), nylon (1927/1939), penicillin (1922/1943), Kodachrome film (1910/1935), and automatic transmission (1904/1939).
40. Alexopoulos and Cohen (2010, Figure 1, upper left frame, p. 454).
41. The required qualification is that the Chicago stockyards adopted assembly-line methods in the 1890s or even before, and Richard Garrett and Sons built steam engines on the assembly-line principle in England as early as 1843.

42. Abramowitz and David (2000, p. 48).
43. Weintraub (1939, p. 26).
44. Ristuccia and Tooze (2013, concluding section) point to both horsepower and electricity use in explaining the higher productivity of the United States compared to Germany during World War II.
45. The private equipment series displayed in table 16–2, line (1) is the same as the variable depreciation series in the data appendix, figure A–1.
46. Field (2011, p. 49) provides additional examples of the increased sizes of machinery, including an increase between the 1920s and 1930s in the size of industrial locomotives from 7.4 tons to 11.4 tons. The average capacity of a power shovel almost doubled from 1920–23 to 1932–1936.
47. Field (2011, p. 47).
48. The first centrally air-conditioned office building in the U.S. was the Milam Building in San Antonio, Texas, which was completed in 1928. See www.asme.org/about-asme/who-we-are/engineering history/landmarks/155-milam-high-rise-air-conditioned-building.
49. A detailed study of productivity growth in the electric utility industry is provided by Gordon (2004b).
50. www.tshaonline.org/handbook/online/articles/doe01. The rise of the east Texas oil fields and the personal wealth that they created has never been captured better than in Edna Ferber's 1952 novel *Giant* and the 1956 movie adaptation starring Elizabeth Taylor, Rock Hudson, and James Dean.
51. The timeline for this paragraph comes from www.inventors.about.com/od/pstartinventions/a/plastics.htm.
52. Field (2011, pp. 49–50).
53. Field (2011, pp. 74–75).
54. Bryson (2010, pp. 22–23), already quoted in chapter 2.
55. Both quotes in this paragraph are from Walton (1956, p. 532).
56. See Walton (1956, p. 533).
57. For a modern analysis of the first Industrial Revolution of the late eighteenth century, see Mokyr (2009, particularly chapters 5–12) and the many sources cited therein.
58. See table 5–2, which shows for two typical widely purchased automobiles that engine horsepower more than doubled from the forty horsepower of the 1928 Model A Ford to the eighty-five horsepower of the 1940 Chevrolet.
59. I discovered this while working on my 1967 Ph.D. thesis, and more recently, it has been documented with detailed original data by Ristuccia and Tooze (2013, Table 1). The number of machine tools was 942,000 in the *American Machinist* survey of 1940 and had grown to 1,882,841 in the same survey conducted in 1945, for an increase of 99.8 percent.
60. Government-financed, privately operated capital equipment cumulative investment is estimated in Gordon (1967, Table 24, p. 164) as $19 billion in current dollars. The total stock of privately owned equipment in the BEA fixed assets accounts for 1941 is $38.1 billion.
61. Figure 16–5 plots TFP growth rates by decade, so that the 1930s is represented by the average annual growth rate between 1930 and 1940, and the 1940's by the annual growth rate between 1940 and 1950. Field (2011) bases his conclusion that the 1930s were the most productive decade by defining the 1930s as 1929-41, which has the effect of moving the rapid growth of 1940–41 from the 1940s to the 1930s. This treatment is indeed justified by the fact that during 1940–41 the economy was still recovering from the Great Depression. However, the choice of years makes no difference in our conclusion that the 1940s registered faster TFP growth than did the 1930s. In our data, the annual average growth rate of TFP during 1929–41 was 1.78 percent per year; during 1941–50, it was 2.82 percent per year.

17 INNOVATION: CAN THE FUTURE MATCH THE GREAT INVENTIONS OF THE PAST?

1. This sentence paraphrases the exact quotation from Domar (1961, p. 712): "The magnitude of [the autonomous growth factor] is completely divorced from investment and capital accumulation. Capital merely accumulates; it does not change its quality, form or composition; *it does not serve as the*

instrument for the introduction of technical change into the production process. It is this kind of capital accumulation (wooden ploughs piled up on the top of existing wooden ploughs) that contributes so little to economic growth" [italics in original].

2. Support for this view comes from Nelson (1959, p. 102), who wrote, "Invention must usually be embodied in new plant and equipment before it yields increased productivity."
3. In Gordon (2004a), I develop a theoretical model with two economies, one with no advances in knowledge and the other with positive advances in knowledge. The result is that all inputs, even the contribution of education, grow more slowly when there is no technical change and thus no reward for extra investment and schooling. The paper shows that the critique of Solow by Jorgenson and Griliches (1967) understates the role of technical change by even more than the understatement inherent in Solow's own technique.
4. Merton (1935, p. 407).
5. Nelson (1959, p. 104).
6. Killeffer (1948, p. 1).
7. Lamoreaux (2010, pp. 368–69).
8. Describing Edison's laboratory in the 1870s, Brox (2010, p. 113) says, "But it was, for all its traditional appearance and apparent modesty, the largest private laboratory in the United States."
9. inventors.about.com/od/tstartinventions/a/transistor_history.htm.
10. The share data are from Nicholas (2010, Table 1, p. 58). The quotation is from p. 59.
11. Details about GE and AT&T Laboratories are from Lamoreaux (2010, pp. 386–87). Bell Labs was established by the merger of AT&T and Western Electric laboratories in 1925; see Gertner (2012).
12. Merton (1935, Chart III, p. 462).
13. Nelson (1959, p. 104).
14. Khan and Sokoloff (2004, p. 395).
15. Nicholas (2010, p. 61).
16. Khan and Sokoloff (2004, p. 396).
17. Khan and Sokoloff (2004, p. 395).
18. *New York Times Book Review,* July 12, 1987, p. 36.
19. www.statista.com/statistics/201182/forecast-of-smartphone-users-in-the-us/.
20. www.about.jstor.org/about.
21. This technological transition can be precisely dated. In the last stages of my writing a data-intensive book that was completed in 1988, all the computer output was delivered as huge printouts to the front porch of my home by graduate research assistants. By 1994, all computer output arrived via e-mail attachment; the piles of paper had disappeared forever.
22. For instance, in most economics departments, the revolution occurred back in the 1980s, when professors began to type their own research papers using PC word processors, and most of them, particularly the younger faculty members, reveled in the new opportunity to set their own complex equations instead of having to monitor math-illiterate secretaries. Department staffs became smaller as the need for repetitive retyping disappeared. But then progress stopped; the Northwestern economics department staff in 2014 is the same size, and carries out the same functions, as the staff of 1998.
23. Pletz (2015, p. 4).
24. Kenny (2013, p. 11).
25. The data on shares transacted for each year are the average transactions for the first complete week in January. The source is https://www.nyse.com/data/transactions-statistics-data-library.
26. Aeppel (2015, p. A10).
27. Bessen (2015, pp. 106–7). For evidence that the median number of full-time employees in the finance department at big companies declined 40 percent per billion of revenue between 2004 and 2014, see Monga (2015, p. B1).
28. Bilton (2014).
29. Entry and exit data are from Hathaway and Litan (2014, Figure 1).

30. Davis and Haltiwanger (2014, p. 14).
31. Simon and Barr (2015, p. A1).
32. Davis and Haltiwanger (2014, p. 11).
33. Decker et al. (2014, p. 22).
34. See Baily and Bosworth (2014, Table 3, p. 9). TFP growth during 1987–2011 in their data is 0.9 percent for nonfarm private business, 1.3 percent for manufacturing, 9.7 percent for ICT manufacturing, and 0.3 percent for manufacturing net of ICT manufacturing.
35. See Acemoglu, Autor, Dorn, Hanson, and Price (2014, Figure 1A, p. 3).
36. Cette, Clerc, and Bresson (2015), Chart 4, p. 87. For similar results see Bryne, Oliner, and Sichel (2013).
37. Flamm (2014, pp. 16–17).
38. This and other quotations in this section come from Mokyr (2013).
39. Details about the Verne book and its predictions come from Vijg (2011, pp. 35–36).
40. Details of the invention of electricity, the internal combustion engine, wireless transmission, and many other late-nineteenth-century innovations are contained in Smil (2005). A broader horizon of the history of invention is presented by Mokyr (1990).
41. See Watkins (1900).
42. Markoff (2013).
43. When I arrived home in Berkeley from college or graduate school near Boston, I often traveled by the SFO helicopter line, which flew frequent schedules from the SFO airport to the Berkeley marina. This company abruptly shut down in 1974 as a result of the first oil shock.
44. Roubini (2014, p. 3).
45. Brynjolfsson and McAfee (2014, p. 44).
46. See chapter 7 and Cutler and Miller (2005).
47. Vijg (2011, chapter 4).
48. These comments on mid-1990s automobile factory technology come from my membership in the NBER "pin factory group," which organized plant tours for NBER-affiliated research staff at that time.
49. Pratt (2015, pp. 53–55).
50. Quotation and details from Aeppel (2015, p. B1).
51. Autor (2015, p. 6).
52. Details on the Kiva robots in Amazon warehouses come from Autor (2014a, pp. 32–33).
53. *The Economist,* "Humanoid Robots: After the Fall," June 13, 2015, p. 77.
54. Rus (2015, pp. 4–5).
55. Aeppel (2015, p. A10).
56. Aeppel (2015, p. A1).
57. Discussion with Scott Resnick, director of revenue management of JetBlue Airlines, New York, December 6, 2013.
58. Charan (2015, p. 45).
59. Lohr (2015, p. A3).
60. *The Economist,* "Money Management: Ask the Algorithm," May 9, 2015, pp. 11–12.
61. Colvin (2014, p. 200).
62. Total economy output per hour grew at an annual rate of 0.67 percent per year between 2009:Q3 and 2014:Q3.
63. Autor (2015, p. 24).
64. Rus (2015, p. 3).
65. White (2014, p. B1).
66. The quoted title is that of Halpern (2015).
67. The 0.3 percent growth rate of productivity refers to the entire economy, not the nonfarm private sector. This concept of labor productivity is defined as real GDP divided by hours in the total economy, an unpublished series obtained from the Bureau of Labor Statistics. Growth rates of productivity for other time intervals are displayed in table 18–3.

18 INEQUALITY AND THE OTHER HEADWINDS: LONG-RUN AMERICAN ECONOMIC GROWTH SLOWS TO A CRAWL

1. The retirement of the baby boomers began in 2008, when the 1946 babies reached age 62, and will continue until 2034, when those born in 1964 reach age 70.
2. See Piketty and Saez (2003) and Piketty (2014).
3. The leading critics of the Piketty–Saez data are Philip Armour, Richard V. Burkhauser, and Jeff Larrimore. Their conclusions are similar to those of the CBO data examined in this section and show that the growth rate of incomes in the bottom half of the income distribution is much higher than in the Piketty–Saez data once allowance is made for taxes and transfers. See Armour et al. (2014).
4. The CBO's measure of before-tax income includes all cash income (including non-taxable income not reported on tax returns, such as child support), taxes paid by businesses, employee contributions to 401(k) retirement plans, and the estimated value of in-kind income received from various sources. The CBO also makes an adjustment for family size, recognizing that the living expenses of a family of four are not double those of a family of two.
5. Even though the top 1 percent pay higher taxes than the rest, they benefited from substantial reductions in income tax rates, including taxes on dividends and capital gains, that took place during the CBO interval of 1979–2011.
6. The Piketty–Saez data are inferior to the CBO data because they do not adjust for taxes, transfers, or in-kind forms of income such as employer contributions to 401K pension plans and medical insurance premia. The census data are inferior to the CBO data because "top-coding" means that the census data do not provide details on growing inequality within the top 10 percent of the income distribution; the CBO is able to provide this detail by combining census data for the lower percentiles with IRS Statistics of Income data for the top percentiles.
7. Goldin and Margo (1992).
8. Mishel et al. (2012)., Figure 4AC, p. 269.
9. As one example, Delta Airlines, which had a nonunion workforce (except for its pilots), maintained wages at the level of its unionized competitors such as American and United Airlines. Delta gained despite a parallel wage structure, because it escaped the work rules set down by labor unions at other airlines.
10. Autor, Dorn, and Hanson (2013).
11. Parts import data come from Galston (2015).
12. Schwartz and Cohen (2014).
13. Orrenius and Zavodny (2006).
14. Ottaviano and Peri (2006, p. 1).
15. Ottaviano and Peri (2006, p. 13).
16. For references on job polarization, see Autor (2014a) and Autor (2015).
17. Card and DiNardo (2002)
18. Levy and Temin (2007).
19. The 1973 number is from Mishel et al. (2012, Figure 4AH, p. 291), where the value quoted in the text are based on the "options granted" criterion. The multiple and dollar amounts for 2013 come from www.nola.com/business/index.ssf/2014/05/2013_ceo_pay.html.
20. Hymowitz and Collins (2015, p. 19).
21. Facts in this and the next paragraph come from Greenhouse (2013).
22. "Roots of the Living Wage Wave," *Wall Street Journal,* August 10, 2013.
23. www.chicagobusiness.com/article/20130517/BLOGS08/130519807/caterpillar-ceo-we-can-never-make-enough-profit.
24. Rattner (2014).
25. Rosen (1981).
26. See Bebchuk and Grinstein (2005).
27. Hall and Liebman (1998).
28. The nominal rate of return over seventeen years is 14.8 percent per year, and during the same period, the GDP deflator increased at an annual rate of 2.5 percent per year, bringing the rate of return ex-dividends

down to 12.3 percent. Including an estimated dividend return of 2.0 percent per year brings the real rate of return to 14.3 percent per year.

29. Zumbrun (2014, p. A2).
30. www.pewresearch.org/fact-tank/2014/12/17/wealth-gap-upper-middle-income/. Household incomes were adjusted by size and then sorted by income, with the top group having more than double the median income level, the middle group having between two-thirds and double the median, and the lower group having below two-thirds of the median. The lowest income that qualified a family of four for the upper group was $132,000 in 2013 dollars; the borderline income at the bottom of the middle group was $44,000.
31. The equivalent graph for females has a similar appearance and is not included here in order to simplify the discussion.
32. Irwin (2015, p. A3).
33. A time series on the share of hours worked by college graduates is presented by Autor (2014b, Figure 3A).
34. Beaudry, Green, and Sand (2013).
35. Dollar amounts are from Autor (2014b, pp. 844, 847).
36. www.pellinstitute.org/downloads/publications-Indicators_of_Higher_Education_Equity_in_the_US_45_Year_Trend_Report.pdf.
37. See Denison (1962).
38. Goldin and Katz (2008, Table 1.3, p. 39).
39. An update of high school graduation rates is provided in Murnane (2013). He concurs with Heckman that the graduation rate declined from 1970 to 2000 but presents data that there was an increase during 2000 to 2010. The 2010 graduation rate is slightly higher than in 1970 but the conclusion remains that high school completion rates have stagnated for the past forty years, particularly in comparison to the prior period, between 1900 and 1970.
40. http://globalpublicsquare.blogs.cnn.com/2011/11/03/how-u-s-graduation-rates-compare-with-the-rest-of-the-world/
41. See www.oecd.org/unitedstates/PISA-2012-results-US.pdf.
42. Kristof (2014).
43. A comparison from the detailed NIPA tables of personal consumption expenditures suggests that the rise in the relative price of the higher education deflator compared to the personal consumption deflator emerges as an increase of 3.7 times conventional PCE inflation since 1972.
44. Abel, Deitz, and Su (2014, p. 4). The non-college jobs obtained by recent college graduates are classified by the authors as good jobs in fields such as health care and skilled trades (e.g., mechanic, electrician, nurse, dental hygienist) and bad low-wage jobs such as bartender, food server, and cashier. Of the 56 percent of recent college graduates who could not find college-level jobs, 35 percent found good non-college jobs and 21 percent found bad non-college jobs.
45. Hoxby and Avery (2013).
46. Mitchell (2014).
47. Kristof (2014).
48. See Aaronson et al. (2014).
49. http://opinionator.blogs.nytimes.com/2013/08/21/hard-times-for-some/?hp.
50. This paragraph reports on a dinner conversation at the home of the British Consul-General in Chicago on November 20, 2013.
51. To simplify the discussion we ignore the likely slow decline in hours per employee and assume that it is offset by a gradual increase in the employment rate from the annual 2014 average of 93.8 percent to a steady long-run value of 95.0 percent—that is, that the unemployment rate will decline from its annual 2014 average of 6.2 percent to a steady long-run value of 5.0 percent.
52. Gordon (2014, Figure 12).
53. This paragraph is based on a Pew research study as summarized in Miller (2014, p. A23).
54. Carbone and Cahn (2014, p. 18).
55. Carbone and Cahn (2014, p. 1).
56. Results quoted in these two paragraphs come from Murray (2012, pp. 149–67).
57. Data in this paragraph come from Pettit (2012, Table 1.4).

58. Fields and Emshwiller (2014, p. A1).
59. Bushway et al. (2007, p. 3).
60. Charles, Hurst, and Notowidigdo (2013).
61. Thanks to Bill Nordhaus for correcting the numbers in this sentence. He reports that this calculation is based on the DICE-2013R model. DICE stands for "Dynamic Integrated model of Climate and the Economy."
62. Jorgenson, Ho, and Samuels (2014).
63. As shown in table 18–3, actual growth in output per hour in 2004–15 was 1.00 percent, somewhat less than the forecast of 1.20 percent growth. For the same time period, actual growth in output per member of the total population was 0.75 percent per year, slightly below the forecast of 0.80 percent growth.

POSTSCRIPT. AMERICA'S GROWTH ACHIEVEMENT AND THE PATH AHEAD

1. Saez-UStopincomes-2014.pdf downloaded from topincomes.parisschoolofeconomics.eu.
2. Mishel et al. (2012), Figure 4AH, p. 291. Income includes capital gains.
3. Upon the death of the asset holder, this tax exemption, technically called the "stepped up basis," changes the basis for calculating capital gains from the value when that asset holder purchased the asset to the value of that asset at the time of the holder's death.
4. Mishel et al. (2012), Table 4.39, p. 280. Their average value for the 1960s is expressed in 2014 dollars by taking the Mishel value in 2011 dollars and multiplying by the 2014/2011 ratio of the deflator for personal consumption expenditures. This calculation yields a real minimum wage for 1960–69 of $8.26 in 2014 dollars.
5. Labor productivity for the total economy between 1965 and 2014 increased by 125 percent; see the sources for figures 16–1 and 16–2, provided in the data appendix. Total real compensation is obtained by multiplying labor productivity by the share of employee compensation in gross domestic income, from NIPA Table 1.10.
6. Nichols and Rothstein (2015), pp. 25–26.
7. Rubin and Turner (2014).
8. The cost of prison is from https://smartasset.com/insights/the-economics-of-the-american-prison-system.
9. Miron and Waldock (2010).
10. https://www.americanprogress.org/issues/education/report/2013/05/02/62054/the-united-states-is-far-behind-other-countries-on-pre-k/
11. In addition to the Heckman source quoted in this paragraph, an extensive review of evidence on the effects of several preschool programs is provided by Cascio and Schanzenbach (2013). The discussant remarks of Caroline Hoxby and Alan Krueger provide important perspective on the issues involved in assessing the effects of expanded preschool education.
12. http://heckmanequation.org/content/resource/invest-early-childhood-development-reduce-deficits-strengthen-economy
13. The best survey of the mixed record of charter schools, providing examples of notable successes, is Epple, Romano, and Zimmer (2015).
14. Further details are provided by Norton (2013).
15. For details on changes in copyright and patent law, as well as an explanation of why these changes are undesirable, see Lindsay (2015, pp. 9–14).
16. See Kleiner (2011).
17. See Glaeser et al. (2006).
18. Details on Canadian point system from www.workpermit.com/canada/points_calculator.htm.
19. See Feldstein (2014). His paper estimates tax savings for a variety of plans besides his basic one, which allows unlimited charitable deductions and a limit of total deductions equal to 2 percent of adjusted gross income. Extra revenue would be higher if the 2 percent limit were to be set instead at zero.
20. www.cbo.gov/sites/default/files/44223_Carbon_0.pdf

DATA APPENDIX

1. All the data on structures developed in this chapter include not just private residential structures, but also residential structures. The inclusion of residential structures is required when the output concept is real GDP, for paid rent and imputed rent contribute about 10 percent of GDP. The alternative would be to exclude both residential capital and the rent portion of GDP—in other words, to consider "non-housing GDP." Either method would be consistent, but for expository purposes, it is helpful for the output concept here to refer to the familiar concept of total real GDP. A consequence of this treatment is that it substantially reduces the relative importance of adding government-financed capital to private capital input, for total private structures during 1928–50 are about twice the value of private nonresidential structures.
2. In fact it is notable how much of today's 2014 Manhattan between midtown and the downtown financial district—for example, in Soho, Greenwich Village, Little Italy, and Tribeca—contains buildings that were constructed before 1929.
3. The average investment to capital ratio for private structures during 1931–45 was 1.9 percent as compared to 4.8 percent during 1925–29.
4. Ristuccia and Tooze, Table 3.
5. The distinction between fixed and variable depreciation was first identified in my Ph.D. thesis (1967) but was not implemented there. Subsequently, I implemented it in Gordon (2000) for selected time intervals. This chapter is the first to provide an annual series going back to 1890. Subsequent to my 1967 thesis, the theoretical and empirical analysis of variable depreciation was provided by Feldstein and Rothschild (1974) and by Feldstein and Foot (1971).
6. The author lives in Evanston, Illinois, in a house built in 1889. The neighboring houses were built in 1894, 1915, 1920, and 1928. In the adjacent seventy blocks containing perhaps 800 single-family houses and a large number of multiunit condominiums and apartment buildings, fewer than 5 percent were built after 1929.
7. The current BEA Fixed Assets accounts do not provide any breakdown of the composition of government defense equipment capital for years before 1972. The decomposition for 1972 and later years shows that almost all of it consists of weapons, which must also have been true during World War II. By not including any government defense equipment in government capital input, we agree with Higgs (2004, p. 510) that government defense equipment should not be included as capital input, because it does not produce output in the usual sense.
8. GOPO capital was discovered and described in detail in Gordon (1969). For more details of war production in World War II, see Herman (2012), Baime (2014), and Walton (1956).
9. The variable depreciation adjustment is not applied to government capital, for there was no hiatus in government investment during 1930–45 as there was for private investment.
10. Kline and Moretti (2013) provide a sophisticated analysis of the effects of the TVA. Their conclusion (p. 30) is that "the TVA sped the industrialization of the Tennessee Valley and provided lasting benefits to the region in the form of high paying manufacturing jobs. Notably, the impact on manufacturing employment persisted well beyond the lapsing of the regional subsidies."

REFERENCES

Aaronson, Stephanie, Cajner, Tomas, Fallick, Bruce, Gaibis-Reig, Felix, and Wascher, William (2014). "Labor Force Participation: Recent Developments and Future Prospects," *Brookings Papers on Economic Activity,* no. 2: 197–255.

Abbot, Charles Greeley. (1932). *Great Inventions,* vol. 12 of the Smithsonian Scientific Series. Washington, DC: Smithsonian Institution.

Abel, Jaison, Richard Deitz, and Yaqin Su. (2014). "Are Recent College Graduates Finding Good Jobs?" *Federal Reserve Bank of New York* 20, no. 1: 1–8.

Abramowitz, Moses, and David, Paul A. (2000). "American Macroeconomic Growth in the Era of Knowledge-Based Progress: The Long-Run Perspective," in Engerman and Gallman (2000), pp. 1–92.

Acemoglu, Daron, Autor, David H., Dorn, David, Hanson, Gordon, and Price, Brendan. (2014). "Return of the Solow Paradox? IT, Productivity, and Employment in U.S. Manufacturing," NBER Working Paper 19837, January.

Acs, Zoltan J., and Lyles, Alan. (2007). *Obesity, Business and Public Policy.* Cheltenham, UK/Northhampton, MA: Edward Elgar.

Aeppel, Timothy. (2015). "Jobs and the Clever Robot," *Wall Street Journal*, February 25, pp. A1, A10.

Agar, Jon. (2013). *Constant Touch: A Global History of the Mobile Phone.* London: Icon.

Agus, David B. (2012). "The 2000-Year-Old Wonder Drug," *The New York Times*, December 12, p. A31.

Akerlof, George A. (1970). "The Market for 'Lemons': Quality Uncertainty and the Market Mechanism," *Quarterly Journal of Economics* 84, no. 3 (August): 488–500.

Alexander, June Granatir. (2009). *Daily Life in Immigrant America, 1870–1920: How the Second Great Wave of Immigrants Made Their Way in America.* Chicago, IL: Ivan R. Dee.

Alexopoulos, Michell, and Cohen, Jon. (2009). "Measuring Our Ignorance, One Book at a Time: New Indicators of Technological Change 1909–1949," *Journal of Monetary Economics* 56, no. 4 (May): 450–70.

Allen, Frederick Lewis. (1931). *Only Yesterday: An Informal History of the 1920's.* New York: John Wiley & Sons, Inc.

Allison, David K. (1995). "Interview with Mr. Don Wetzel, Co-Patente of the Automatic Teller Machine," conducted at the National Museum of American History, September 21.

"All Time Box Office" (2014). *IMDB.com, Inc.* http://boxofficemojo.com/alltime/adjusted.htm.

Ambrose, Stephen E. (2000). *Nothing Like It in the World: The Men Who Built the Transcontinental Railroad 1863–1869.* New York: Simon & Schuster.

American Academy of Neurology. (2014). "Study: Alzheimer's Disease Much Larger Cause of Death Than Reported [Press Release]," *AAN.com*, March 5.

American Cancer Society. (2014). "The History of Cancer," *Cancer.org.* www.cancer.org/acs/groups/cid/documents/webcontent/002048-pdf.pdf.

American Press Institute. (2014). "How Americans Get Their News," *American Press Institute,* March 17.

American Transit Association. (1943). *The Transit Industry of the United States: Basic Data and Trends, 1943 Edition.* New York: American Transit Association.

Anders, Susan, and Hulse, David. (2006). "Social Security: The Past, the Present, and Options for Reform," *CPA Journal* (May): 1–17.

Angus, David L., and Mirel, Jeffrey E. (1985). "From Spellers to Spindles: Work-Force Entry by the Children of Textile Workers, 1888–1890," *Social Science History* 9, no. 2 (spring): 123–43.

Arango, Tim. (2010). "NBC's Slide to Troubled Nightly Punchline," *The New York Times,* January 17, pp. 1, 17.

Armour, Philip, Burkhauser, Richard V., and Larrimore, Jeff. (2014). "Levels and Trends in United States Income and Its Distribution: A Crosswalk from Market Income towards a Comprehensive Haig-Simons Income Measure," *Southern Economic Journal* 81, no. 2: 271–93.

Atack, Jermey, Bateman, Fred, and Parker, William N. (2000). "The Farm, The Farmer, and the Market," and "Northern Agriculture and the Westward Movement," both in Engerman and Gallman, eds. (2000b), 245–328.

Atherton, Lewis. (1954). *Main Street on the Middle Border.* Chicago: Quadrangle Books.

AT&T. (2014). "1951: First Direct-Dial Transcontinental Telephone Call," *AT&T.* www.corp.att.com/attlabs/reputation/timeline/51trans.html.

Auletta, Ken. (2014). "Outside the Box: Netflix and the Future of Television," *The New Yorker*, February 3, pp. 54–61.

Autor, David H. (2014a). "Polanyi's Paradox and the Shape of Employment Growth," draft prepared for Federal Reserve of Kansas City economic policy symposium, September 3.

Autor, David H. (2014b). "Skills, Education, and the Rise of Earnings Inequality among the 'Other 99 Percent,'" *Science* 344 (May 23): 843–51.

Autor, David H. (2015). "Why Are There Still So Many Jobs? The History and Future of Workplace Automation," *Journal of Economic Perspectives* 26, no. 3 (summer): 3–30.

Autor, David H., Dorn, David, and Hanson, Gordon H. (2013). "The China Syndrome: Labor Market Effects of Import Competition in the United States," *American Economic Review* 103, no. 6: 2121–68.

Bailey, Beth L. (1988). *From Front Porch to Back Seat: Courtship in Twentieth-Century America.* Baltimore, MD: Johns Hopkins University Press.

Bailey, Martha J., and Collins, William J. (2011). "Did Improvements in Household Technology Cause the Baby Boom? Evidence from Electrification, Appliance Diffusion, and the Amish," *American Economic Journal: Macroeconomics* 3, no. 2 (April): 189–217.

Baily, Martin Neil, and Boswoth, Barry P. (2014). "U.S. Manufacturing: Understanding Its Past and Its Potential Future," *Journal of Economic Perspectives* 28, no. 1 (winter): 3–26.

Baily, Martin N., and Gordon, Robert J. (1988). "The Productivity Slowdown, Measurement Issues, and the Explosion of Computer Power," *Brookings Papers on Economic Activity* 19, no. 2: 347–420.

Baime, A. J. (2014). *The Arsenal of Democracy: FDR, Detroit, and an Epic Quest to Arm an America at War.* Boston, MA/New York: Houghton Mifflin Harcourt.

Bakalar, Nicholas. (2011). "M.R.I., 1974," *The New York Times*, May 17, p. D7.

Bakker, Gerben. (2012). "How Motion Pictures Industrialized Entertainment," *The Journal of Economic History* 72, no. 4 (December): 1036–63.

Baldassare, Mark. (1992). "Suburban Communities," *Annual Review of Sociology* 18: 475–94.

Balderston, Marion. (1928). "American Motor Mania," *Living Age* 15 (February): 341–43.

Balke, Nathan S., and Gordon, Robert J. (1989). "The Estimation of Prewar Gross National Product: Methodology and New Evidence," *Journal of Political Economy* 97, no. 1: 38–92.

Barnouw, E. (1990). *Tube of Plenty: The Evolution of American Television.* Oxford, UK: Oxford University Press.

Barreca, Alan, Clay, Karen, Deschenes, Olivier, Greenstone, Michael, and Shapiro, Joseph S. (2015). "Adapting to Climate Change: The Remarkable Decline in the U.S. Temperature–Mortality Relationship over the 20th Century," Yale University working paper, January.

Barron, Hal S. (1997). *Mixed Harvest: The Second Great Transformation in the Rural North 1870–1930.* Chapel Hill: The University of North Carolina Press.

Barrows, Robert. (1983). "Beyond the Tenement: Patters of American Urban Housing, 1870–1930," *Journal of Urban History* 9 (August): 395–420.

Batchelor, Bob. (2002). *The 1900s: American Popular Culture through History.* Westport, CT/London: Greenwood Press.

Bauman, John F., Biles, Roger, and Szylvian, Kristin M. (2000). *From Tenements to the Taylor Homes: In Search of an Urban Housing Policy in Twentieth-Century America.* University Park: The Pennsylvania State University Press.

Baumol, William J. (1967). "Macroeconomics of Unbalanced Growth: The Anatomy of Urban Crisis," *American Economic Review* 57, no. 3 (June): 415–26.

Baumol, William J. (1986). "Productivity Growth, Convergence, and Welfare: What the Long-Run Data Show," *American Economic Review* 76, no. 5 (December): 1072–85.

Beatty, Jack. (1994). "Who Speaks for the Middle Class?" *Atlantic Monthly* (May): 65.

Beaudry, Paul, Green, David A., and Sand, Benjamin M. (2013). "The Great Reversal in the Demand for Skill and Cognitive Tasks," NBER Working Paper 18901, March.

Bebchuk, Lucian Ayre and Grinstein, Yaniv. (2005). "The Growth of Executive Pay," *Oxford Review of Economic Policy* 21, 283–303.

Becker, Gary S. (1965). "A Theory of the Allocation of Time," *Economic Journal* 75: 493–517.

Becker, Gary S., Philipson, Tomas, and Soares, Rodrigo. (2005). "The Quantity and Quality of Life and the Evolution of World Inequality," *American Economic Review* 95, no. 1 (March): 277–91.

Bedford, Henry F. (1995). *Their Lives and Numbers: The Condition of Working People in Massachusetts, 1870–1900.* Ithaca, NY/London: Cornell University Press.

Benson, Susan Porter. (1979). "Palace of Consumption and Machine for Selling: The American Department Store, 1880–1940," *Radical History Review* 21 (fall): 199–221. http://rhr.dukejournals.org/cgi/reprint/1979/21/199.pdf.

Bergen, Jennifer. (2011). "30 Years of the Music Industry in 30 Seconds," *Geek.com*, August 23. www.geek.com/geek-cetera/30-years-of-the-music-industry-looks-like-in-30-seconds-1415243/.

Berry, Thomas S. (1988). *Production and Population since 1789: Revised GNP Series in Constant Dollars.* Richmond, VA: The Bostwick Press.

Bessen, James. (2015). *Learning by Doing: The Real Connection between Innovation, Wages, and Wealth.* New Haven, CT/London: Yale University Press.

Bettmann, Otto L. (1974). *The Good Old Days—They Were Terrible!* New York: Random House.

Beyer, Lisa. (2012). "The Rise and Fall of Employer-Sponsored Pension Plans," *Workforce* 24 (January): 1–5.

Biggs, Andrew, and Schieber, Sylvester. (2014). "Is There a Retirement Crisis?" *National Affairs* no. 20 (summer): 55–75.

Bigott, Joseph C. (2001). *From Cottage to Bungalow: Houses and the Working Class in Metropolitan Chicago, 1869–1929.* Chicago, IL: University of Chicago Press.

Bijsterveld, Karin. (2010). "Acoustic Cocooning: How the Car Became a Place to Unwind," *Senses and Society* 5, no. 2: 189–211.

Bilton, Nick. (2014). "On Big Stage of CES, Innovation Is in Background," *The New York Times*, January 13, p. B5.

Blumberg, Stephen J., and Julian V. Luke. (2013). "Wireless Substitution: Early Release of Estimates from the National Health Interview Survey, January–June 2013," *CDC*, December. www.cdc.gov/nchs/data/nhis/earlyrelease/wireless201312.pdf.

Blume, Stuart, and Geesink, Ingrid. (2000). "A Brief History of Polio Vaccines," *Science* 288, no. 5471 (June 2): 1593–94.

Bock, James. (1993). "Women Made Career Strides in 1980s: Census Data Show Marked Md. Gains," *Baltimore Sun* 29 (January).

Boddy, William. (1985). "The Studios Move into Prime Time: Hollywood and the Television Industry in the 1950s," *Cinema Journal* 24, no. 4: 23–37.

Bogart, Leo. (1956). *The Age of Television*. New York: Frederick Ungar.

Bohn, Thomas W., and Stomgren, Richard L. (1975). *Light and Shadows: A History of Motion Pictures*. Port Washington, NY: Alfred Pub. Co.

Bonner, Thomas Neville. (1991). *Medicine in Chicago 1850–1950: A Chapter in the Social and Scientific Development of a City.* Urbana/Chicago: University of Illinois Press.

Boorstin, Daniel. (1973). *The Americans: The Democratic Experience.* New York: Random House.

Bordewich, Fergus M. (2012). "How the West Was Really Won," *Wall Street Journal,* May 19–20, p. A15.

Brand, Samuel, Fuller, Frederick Lincoln, and Watson, Thomas Sr. (2011). "The Automation of Personal Banking," IBM 100: Icons of Progress. http://www-03.ibm.com/ibm/history/ibm100/us/en/icons/bankauto/

Brandon, Emily. (2012). "What Retirees Do All Day: Here's How Retirees Are Using Their Leisure Time," *U.S. News and World Report*, July 2, pp. 1–2.

Bresnahan, Timothy F., and Gordon, Robert J., eds. (1997). *The Economics of New Goods*, Studies in Income and Wealth, vol. 58. Chicago, IL: University of Chicago Press for NBER.

Bresnahan, Timothy F., and Trajtenberg, Manual. (1995). "General Purpose Technologies: 'Engines of Growth'?" *Journal of Econometrics* 65, no. 1 (January): 83–108.

Brinkley, Garland L. (1997). "The Decline in Southern Agricultural Output, 1860–1880," *Journal of Economic History* 57, no. 1 (March): 116–38.

Brody, David. (1960). *Steelworkers in America: The Nonunion Era.* New York: Harper Torchbooks.

Brody, Jane E. (2013). "Many Fronts in the Obesity War," *The New York Times*, May 21, Tuesday science section, p. D4.

Brooker, Katrina. (2004). "Just One Word: Plastic," *Fortune*, February 23.

Brooks, John. (1975). *Telephone: The First Hundred Years.* New York: Harper and Row.

Brown, Clair. (1994). *American Standards of Living: 1918–88.* Oxford, UK: Blackwell.

Brown, Meta, Andrew Haughwout, Donghoon Lee, Maricar Mabutas, and Wilbert van der Klaauw. (2012). "Grading Student Loans," *Liberty Street Economics, Federal Reserve Bank of New York* 5 (March).

Brox, Jane. (2010). *Brilliant: The Evolution of Artificial Light.* Boston, MA/New York: Houghton Mifflin Harcourt.

Bruce, Robert V. (1973). *Bell: Alexander Graham Bell and the Conquest of Solitude.* Ithaca, NY/London: Cornell University Press.

Bruegmann, Robert. (2005). *Sprawl: A Compact History.* Chicago, IL/London: University of Chicago Press.

Bryce, James. (1888/1959). *The American Commonwealth*, Louis M. Hacker, ed. New York: Capricorn Books, G. P. Putnam's Sons.

Bryne, David M., Oliner, Stephen D., and Sichel, Daniel E. (2013). "Is the Information Technology Revolution Over?" *International Productivity Monitor* no. 25 (spring): 20–36.

Brynjolfsson, Erik, and McAfee, Andrew. (2014). *The Second Machine Age: Work, Progress, and Prosperity in a Time of Brilliant Technologies.* New York: W. W. Norton & Company Inc, 80.

Bryon, Kevin A., Minton, Brian D., and Sarte, Pierre-Daniel G. (2007). "The Evolution of City Population Density in the United States," *Economic Quarterly* 93, no. 4 (fall): 341–60.

Bryson, Bill. (2010). *At Home: A Short History of Private Life.* New York: Doubleday.

Bud, Robert. (2007). *Penicillin: Triumph and Tragedy.* Oxford, UK/New York: Oxford University Press.

Burian, Steven J., Nix, Stephan J., Pitt, Robert E., and Durrans, S. Rocky. (2000). "Urban Wastewater Management in the United States: Past, Present, and Future," *Journal of Urban Technology* 7, no. 3: 33–62.

Burns, George. (1988). *Gracie: A Love Story.* New York: Putnam.

Bushway, Shawn D., and Stoll, Michael A., and Weiman, David, eds. (2007). *Barriers to Reentry? The Labor Market for Released Prisoners in Post-Industrial America.* New York: Russell Sage Foundation.

Butkiewicz, James L. (2009). "Fixing the Housing Crisis," *Forbes*, April 30, p. 26.

Caillau, Robert. (1995). "A Little History of the World Wide Web," World Wide Web Consortium, www.w3.org/History.html.

Cain, Louis P., and Paterson, Donald G. (2013). "Children of Eve: Population and Well-being in History," *Population and Development Review* 39, no. 3.

Calder, Lendol. (1999). *Financing the American Dream: A Cultural History of Consumer Credit.* Princeton, NJ: Princeton University Press.

Campbell, W. Joseph. (2001). *Yellow Journalism: Puncturing the Myths, Defining the Legacies.* Westport, CT: Praeger.

Cannon, Brian Q. (2000). "Power Relations: Western Rural Electric Cooperatives and the New Deal," *The Western Historical Quarterly* 31, no. 2 (summer): 133–60.

Carbone, June, and Cahn, Naomi. (2014). *Marriage Markets: How Inequality Is Remaking the American Family.* Oxford, UK/New York: Oxford University Press.

Card, David, and DiNardo, John E. (2002). "Skill-Biased Technological Change and Rising Wage Inequality: Some Problems and Puzzles," *Journal of Labor Economics* 20, no. 4: 733–83.

Carpenter, Rolla C. (1898). *Heating and Ventilating Buildings.* New York: John Wiley and Sons.

Carr, Clark E. (1909). *Railway Mail Service.* Chicago: A. C. McClurg & Co.

Carroll, Abigail. (2010). "The Remains of the Day," *The New York Times*, November 28.
Carryer, Edwin. (2007). "Air Transport in the 1930s," *Dying Earth*, pp. 5–23.
Cascio, Elizabeth U., and Schanzenbach, Diane Whitmore. (2013). "The Impacts of Expanding Access to High-Quality Preschool Education." Brookings Papers on Economic Activity, Fall, 127–78.
CDC. (1999). "Achievements in Public Health, 1900–1999: Decline in Deaths from Heart Disease and Stroke—United States, 1900–1999," *Morbidity and Mortality Weekly Report* 48, no. 30 (August 6): 649–56.
CDC. (2010). "National Hospital Discharge Survey: 2010 Table," *CDC.gov*. www.cdc.gov/nchs/fastats/inpatient-surgery.htm.
CDC. (2011). "Deaths: Final Data for 2011," *CDC.gov*. www.cdc.gov/nchs/data/nvsr/nvsr61/nvsr61_06.pdf.
CDC. (2012). "LCKW9_2010," *CDC.gov*. www.cdc.gov/nchs/nvss/mortality/lcwk9.htm.
Cette, Gilbert, Clerc, Christian, and Bresson, Lea. (2015). "Contribution of ICT Diffusion to Labour Productivity Growth: The United States, Canada, the Eurozone, and the United Kingdom, 1970–2013," *International Productivity Monitor* no. 28 (spring): 81–88.
Chandler, Alfred D. (1977). *The Visible Hand: The Managerial Revolution in American Business*. Cambridge, MA: Belknap Press.
Chapin, Robert Coit. (1909). *The Standard of Living among Workingmen's Families in New York City*. New York: Charities Publication Committee.
Chapman, Arthur. (1932). *The Pony Express*. New York: G.P. Putnam's Sons.
Charan, Ram. (2015). "The Algorithmic CEO," *Fortune*, January 22, pp. 45–46.
Charles, Kerwin Kofi, Hurst, Erik, and Notowidiglo, Matthew. (2013). "Manufacturing Decline, Housing Booms, and Non-Employment," NBER Working paper 18949, April.
Cheung, A., and A. H. Menkis. (1998). "Cyclosporine Heart Transplantation," *Transplantation Proceedings* 30: 1881–1884. New York: Elsevier Science Inc.
Clark, Edward Clifford. (1986). *The American Family Home, 1800–1960*. Chapel Hill: The University of North Carolina Press.
Clark, Thomas D. (1964). *Pills, Petticoats, and Plows: The Southern Country Store*. Norman: University of Oklahoma Press.
Cline, Elizabeth L. (2012). *Overdressed: The Shockingly High Cost of Cheap Fashion*. New York/London: Penguin Group.
Coffee, Frank, and Layden, Joseph. (1998). *America on Wheels: The First 100 Years—1896–1996*. Los Angeles, CA: General Publishing Group.
Cohen, Andrew. (2013). "Happy 75th Birthday, CBS World News Roundup," *The Atlantic*, March 12.
Cohen, Lizabeth. (1996). "From Town Center to Shopping Center: The Reconfiguration of Community Marketplaces in Postwar America," *The American Historical Review* 101, no. 4 (October): 1050–81.
Cohn, David L. (1940). *The Good Old Days: A History of American Morals and Manners as Seen through the Sears Roebuck Catalogs 1905 to the Present*. New York: Simon and Schuster.
Cohn, David L. (1944). *Combustion of Wheels: An Informal History of the Automobile Age*. Boston, MA: Houghton-Mifflin.
Cohn, Jonathan. (2007). *Sick: The Untold Story of America's Health Care Crisis—and the People Who Pay the Price*. New York: Harper Collins Publishers.
Cole, Helene M., and Fiore, Michael C. (2014). "The War against Tobacco, 50 Years and Counting," *The Journal of the American Medical Association* 311, no. 2 (January 8): 131–32.
Collins, Gail. (2009). *When Everything Changed: The Amazing Journey of American Women from 1960 to the Present*. New York: Hachette Book Group, Inc.
Colvin, Geoff. (2014). "In the Future, Will There Be Any Work Left for People to Do?" *Fortune*, June 16, pp. 193–201.
Condran, Gretchen A., and Crimmins-Gardner, Eileen. (1978). "Public Health Measures and Mortality in U.S. Cities in the Late Nineteenth Century," *Human Ecology* 6, no. 1: 27–54.
Conway, Mike. (2009). *The Origins of Television News in America: The Visualizers of CBS in the 1940s*. New York: Peter Lang.

Coombes, Andrea. (2009). "Men Suffer Brunt of Job Losses in Recession," *Wall Street Journal*, July 16.
Coontz, Stephanie. (2011). "Women's Equality Not Quite There Yet," *CNN*, March 7.
Cooper, J. van Cleft. (1922). "Creation of Atmosphere," *American Organist*. June, 240–42. Reprinted in Taylor et al. (2012), 196–98.
Coppin, Clayton A., and High, Jack C. (1999). *The Politics of Purity: Harvey Washington Wiley and the Origins of Federal Food Policy*. Ann Arbor: University of Michigan Press.
Corbett, Kevin J. (2001). "The Big Picture: Theatrical Moviegoing, Digital Television, and beyond the Substitution Effect," *Cinema Journal* 40, no. 2: 17–34.
Cosgrove, J. J. (1909). *History of Sanitation*. Pittsburgh, PA: Standard Sanitary Manufacturing Co.
Costa, Dora. (1998). *The Evolution of Retirement: An American Economic History, 1880–1990*. Chicago, IL/London: University of Chicago Press for NBER.
Cowan, Ruth Schwartz. (1983). *More Work for Mother: The Ironies of Household Technology from the Open Hearth to the Microwave*. New York: Basic Books.
Cox, Reavis. (1948). *The Economics of Installment Buying*. New York: Ronald Press.
Craig, Lee A., Goodwin, Barry, and Grennes, Thomas. (2004). "The Effect of Mechanical Refrigeration on Nutrition in the United States," *Social Science History* 28, no. 2: 325–36.
Craig, Steve. (2004). "How America Adopted Radio: Demographic Differences in Set Ownership Reported in the 1930–1950 U.S. Censuses," *Journal of Broadcasting & Electronic Media* 48, no. 2: 179–95.
Craig, Steve. (2006). "The More They Listen, the More They Buy: Radio and the Modernizing of Rural America," *Agricultural History* 80, no. 1 (winter): 1–16.
Crandall, Robert W., Gruenspecht, Howard K., Keeler, Theodore K, and Lave, Lester B. (1976). *Regulating the Automobile*. Washington, DC: The Brookings Institution.
Cray Inc. webpage on "Company History." www.cray.com/About/History.aspx.
Cronon, William. (1991). *Nature's Metropolis: Chicago and the Great West*. New York/London: W. W. Norton.
Crossen, Cynthia. (2007). "Before WWI Began, Universal Health Care Seemed a Sure Thing," *Wall Street Journal*, April 30, p. B1.
Crossen, Cynthia. (2008). "Unsafe at Any Speed, with Any Driver, on Any Kind of Road," *Wall Street Journal*, March 3, p. B1.
Cutler, David M. (2006). "An International Look at the Medical Care Financing Problem," in David Wise and Naohiro Yashiro, eds., *Issues in Health Care in the U.S. and Japan*. Chicago, IL: University of Chicago Press, 69–81.
Cutler, David M., and McClellan, Mark. (2001). "Productivity Change in Health Care," *American Economic Review Papers and Proceedings* 91 (May): 281–86.
Cutler, David M., and Miller, Grant. (2005). "The Role of Public Health Improvements in Health Advances: The Twentieth Century United States," *Demography* 42, no. 1 (February): 1–22.
Daley, Brian. (2010). "'The Wizard of Oz' Television Tradition Continues on TNT," *Examiner.com*, December 15.
Danbom, David B. (2006). *Born in the Country: A History of Rural America*, 2nd ed. Baltimore, MD: The Johns Hopkins Press.
Daniels, Stephen R. (2006). "The Consequences of Childhood Overweight and Obesity," *The Future of Children* 16, no. 1 (spring): 47–67.
Darby, Michael. (1976). "Three-and-a-Half Million U.S. Employees Have Been Mislaid: Or, an Explanation of Unemployment, 1934–1941." *The Journal of Political Economy*. 84, no. 1 (February): 1–16.
David, Paul A. (1990). "The Dynamo and the Computer: An Historical Perspective on the Modern Productivity Paradox," *American Economic Review Papers and Proceedings* 80, no. 2 (May): 355–61.
Davis, Steven J., and Haltiwanger, John. (2014). "Labor Market Fluidity and Economic Performance," NBER Working Paper 20479, September.
Decker, John, Haltiwanger, John, Jarmin, Ron S., and Miranda, Javier. (2014). "The Role of Entrepreneurship in U.S. Job Creation and Economic Dynamism," *Journal of Economic Perspectives* 28: 3–24.
Denison, Edward F. (1962). *The Sources of Economic Growth and the Alternatives before Us*. New York: Committee for Economic Development.

Dickstein, Morris. (2009). *Dancing in the Dark: A Cultural History of the Great Depression.* New York: W. W. Norton and Company.

Dix, W. F. (1904). "The Automobile as a Vacation Agent," *Independent* 56: 1259–60.

Doan, Mason C. (1997). *American Housing Production 1880–2000: A Concise History.* Lanham, MD/New York: University Press of America.

Domar, Evsey. (1961). "On the Measurement of Technological Change," *Economic Journal* 71, no. 284 (December): 709–29.

Donovan, Robert J., and Scherer, Ray. (1992). *Unsilent Revolution: Television News and American Public Life.* Cambridge, UK: Cambridge University Press.

Dotinga, Randy. (2012). "Huge Rise in CT, MRI, Ultrasound Scan Use: Study," *USNews.com*, June 12. http://health.usnews.com/health-news/news/articles/2012/06/12/huge-rise-in-ct-mri-ultrasound-scan-use-study.

Doucet, Michael J., and Weaver, John. (1991). *Housing the North American City.* Montreal, Canada: McGill Queen's University Press.

Droege, John A. (1916). *Passenger Terminals and Trains.* New York: McGraw-Hill.

Druckman, James N. (2003). "The Power of Television Images: The First Kennedy–Nixon Debate Revisited," *The Journal of Politics* 65, no. 2 (May): 559–71.

DuBoff, Richard B. (1984). "The Telegraph in Nineteenth-Century America: Technology and Monopoly," *Comparative Studies in Society and History* 26, no. 4 (October): 571–86.

Earl, Anthony S. (1997). "Colleges of Agriculture at the Land Grant Universities: Public Service and Public Policy," *Proceedings of the National Academy of Sciences* 94, no. 5 (March): 1610–11.

Edison, Thomas A. (1878). "The Phonograph and Its Future," *The North American Review* 126, no. 262 (May/June): 527–36.

Editors of *Fortune.* (1995). *The Changing American Market.* Garden City, NY.

Edmonds, Rick, Guskin, Emily, Mitchell, Amy, and Jurkowitz, Mark. (2013). "The State of the News Media 2013: An Annual Report on American Journalism: Newspapers: By the Numbers," Pew Research Center, May 7.

Eisner, Robert. (1989). *The Total Incomes System of Accounts.* Chicago, IL: University of Chicago Press.

Ellis, David Maldwyn. (1945). "Railroad Land Grant Rates, 1850–1945," *The Journal of Land and Public Utility Economics* 21, no. 3 (August): 207–22.

Emerson, Ralph Waldo. (1841). *The Journals of Ralph Waldo Emerson, vol. V 1838–41.* Boston: Houghton Mifflin (published in 1911).

Emmet, Boris, and Jeuck, John E. (1950). *Catalogs and Counters: A History of Sears, Roebuck and Company.* Chicago, IL: University of Chicago Press.

Engerman, Stanley L., and Gallman, Robert E., eds. (2000a). *The Cambridge Economic History of the United States*, Vol. II: *The Long Nineteenth Century.* Cambridge, UK/New York: Cambridge University Press .

Engerman, Stanley L, and Gallman, Robert E., eds. (2000b). *The Cambridge Economic History of the United States*, Vol. III: *The Twentieth Century.* Cambridge, UK/New York: Cambridge University Press.

Epple, Dennis, Romano, Richard, and Zimmer, Ron. (2015). "Charter Schools: A Survey of Research on Their Characteristics and Effectiveness," NBER Working Paper 21256, June.

Epstein, Edward J. (1973). *News from Nowhere: Television and the News.* New York: Random House.

Epstein, Edward J. (2010). *The Hollywood Economist: The Hidden Financial Reality Behind the Movies.* Brooklyn, NY: Mellville House.

Erbentraut, Joseph. (2014). "Why This Hospital Turned an 18-Year-Old Away after He Was Shot," *The Huffington Post*, May 20.

Ewbank, Douglas C., and Preston, Samuel H. (1990). "Personal Health Behavior and the Decline in Infant and Child Mortality: The United States 1900–1930," in John Caldwell et al., eds. (1990). *What We Know about Health Transition: The Cultural Social and Behavioural Determinants of Health.* Canberra: Australian National University, pp. 116–49.

Fairbanks, Robert B. (2000). "From Better Dwellings to Better Neighborhoods: The Rise and Fall of the First National Housing Movement," in Bauman et al. (2000), pp. 21–42..

Fantel, Hans. (1984). "Television 101: Basic Buying," *Fortune*, October, p. 46.

Farrell-Beck, Jane, and Parsons, Jean. (2007). *Twentieth Century Dress in the United States.* New York: Fairchild Publications.

Farrington, George C. (1996). "ENIAC: The Birth of the Information Age," *Popular Science*, March, p. 74.

Federal Communications Commission. (2010). "Trends in Telephone Service." https://apps.fcc.gov/edocs_public/attachmatch/DOC-301823A1.pdf.

Feldstein, Martin S. (2014). "Raising Revenue by Limiting Tax Expenditures," paper presented to conference on Tax Policy and the Economy, August.

Feldstein, Martin S., and Foot, David K. (1971). "The Other Half of Gross Investment: Replacement and Modernization Expenditures," *Review of Economics and Statistics* 53: 49–58.

Feldstein, Martin S., and Rothschild, Michael. (1974). "Towards an Economic Theory of Replacement Investment," *Econometrica* 42, no. 3: 393–423.

Fernandez, Manny. (2010). "Let Us Now Praise the Great Men of Junk Food," *The New York Times*, August 8.

Field, Alexander J. (1992). "The Magnetic Telegraph, Price and Quantity Data, and the New Management of Capital," *Journal of Economic History* 52, no. 2 (June): 401–13.

Field, Alexander J. (1998). "The Telegraphic Transmission of Financial Asset Prices and Orders to Trade: Implications for Economic Growth, Trading Volume, and Securities Market Regulation," *Research in Economic History* 18 (August): 145–84.

Field, Alexander J. (2003). "The Most Technologically Progressive Decade of the Century," *American Economic Review* 93 (September): 1399–1413.

Field, Alexander J. (2011). *A Great Leap Forward: 1930s Depression and U.S. Economic Growth.* New Haven, CT/London: Yale University Press.

Fields, Gary, and Emshwiller, John R. (2014). "As Arrest Records Rise, Americans Find Consequences Can Last a Lifetime," *Wall Street Journal*, August 19.

File, Thom, and Ryan, Camille. (2014). "Computer and Internet Use in the United States: 2013," *American Community Survey Reports.*

Fischer, Claude S. (1992). *America Calling: A Social History of the Telephone.* Berkeley: University of California Press.

Fishlow, Albert. (1966). "Aspects of Nineteenth-Century American Investment in Education," *The Journal of Economic History* 26, no. 4: 418–36. www.jstor.org/stable/2115900.

Fiske, Haley. (1917). "Life Insurance as a Basis of Social Economy," *Science Monthly* 4, no. 4 (April): 316–24.

Fite, Gilbert C. (1984). *Cotton Fields No More: Southern Agriculture 1865–1980.* Lexington: The University Press of Kentucky.

Fite, Gilbert C. (1987). *The Farmers' Frontier: 1865–1900.* Norman: University of Oklahoma Press.

Flamm, Kenneth. (2014). "Causes and Economic Consequences of Diminishing Rates of Technical Innovation in the Semiconductor and Computer Industries," preliminary draft manuscript.

Flink, James J. (1972). "Three Stages of American Automobile Consciousness," *American Quarterly* 24, no. 4 (October): 451–73.

Flink, James J. (1984). "The Metropolis in the Horseless Age," *Annals of the New York Academy of Sciences* 424: 289–301.

Floud, Roderick, Fogel, Robert W., Harris, Bernard, and Hong, Sok Chul. (2011). *The Changing Body: Health, Nutrition, and Human Development in the Western World since 1700.* Cambridge, MA/New York: Cambridge University Press for NBER.

Ford, Janet. (1989). *The Indebted Society: Credit and Default.* New York: Routledge.

Fordham, Richard, Skinner, Jane, Wang, Xia, Nolan, John, and the Exeter Primary Outcome Study Group. (2012). "The Economic Benefit of Hip Replacement: A 5-Year Follow-up of Costs and Outcomes in the Exeter Primary Outcomes Study," *BMJ* 2 (May 25): e1–e7.

Fox, Stephen. (1984). *The Mirror Makers: A History of American Advertising and Its Creators.* New York: William Morrow.

Franz, Kathleen. (2005). *Tinkering: Consumers Reinvent the Early Automobile.* Philadelphia: University of Pennsylvania Press.

Fuchs, Victor R. (1998). *Who Shall Live? Health, Economics, and Social Choice.* Singapore/River Edge, NJ: World Scientific.

Fuchs, Victor, and Garber, Alan M. (2003). "Medical Innovation: Promise and Pitfalls," *The Brookings Review* 21, no. 1 (winter): 44–48.

Fuller, Bruce. (1983). "Youth Job Structure and School Enrollment, 1890–1920," *Sociology of Education* 56, no. 3 (July): 145–56.

Fuller, Wayne E. (1964). *RFD: The Changing Face of Rural America.* Bloomington: Indiana University Press.

Gabel, Richard. (1969). "The Early Competitive Era in Telephone Communication, 1893–1920," *Law and Contemporary Problems* 34, no. 2 (spring): 340–59.

Galishoff, Stuart. (1980). "Triumph and Failure: The American Response to the Urban Water Supply Problem, 1880–1923," in M. Melosi, ed., *Pollution and Reform in American Cities, 1870–1930.* Austin: University of Texas Press.

Gallagher, Brian Thomas. (2012). "The Big Chill: Frozen Food Innovator Clarence Birdseye Changed the Way We Eat," *Bloomberg Business Week*, May 14, pp. 84–86.

Gallman, Robert E. (2000). "Economic Growth and Structural Change in the Long Nineteenth Century," in Engerman and Gallman, eds. (2000a), pp. 1–55.

Galmarini, Darío, Galmarini, Carlos M., and Felipe C. Galmarini. (2012). "Cancer Chemotherapy: A Critical Analysis of Its 60 Years of History," *Critical Reviews in Oncology Hematology* 84: 181–99.

Galston, William A. (2015). "How the Vise on U.S. Wages Tightened," *Wall Street Journal,* April 1.

Ganssle, J. G. (2007). "The Transistor: Sixty Years Old and Still Switching," *Embedded Systems Design* 20, no. 12 (December 1): 53.

Ganzel, Bill. (2007). "Movies and Rural America," *Farming in the 1950s and 60s.* www.livinghistoryfarm.org/farminginthe50s/life_18.html.

Gardner, Sarah. (2014). "LA Smog: The Battle against Air Pollution," *Marketplace.org*, July 14.

Garvey, William, and Fisher, David. (2002). *The Age of Flight: A History of America's Pioneering Airline.* Greensboro, NC: Pace Communications.

Gates, Paul Wallace. (1936). "The Homestead Law in an Incongruous Land System," *The American Historical Review* 41, no. 4 (July): 652–81.

Gee, Kelsey. (2014). "Butter Makes Comeback as Margarine Loses Favor," *Wall Street Journal*, June 25, p. B1.

Gellene, Denise. (2009). "Sir John Crofton, Pioneer in TB Cure, Is Dead," *The New York Times*, November 20, p. A26.

Gelpi, Rosa-Maria, and Julien-Labruyère, François. (2000). *The History of Consumer Credit: Doctrines and Practices.* New York: St. Martin's Press.

Georgano, Nick. (1992). *The American Automobile: A Centenary.* New York: Smithmark Press.

Gertner, Jon. (2012). "True Innovation," *The New York Times Sunday Review*, February 26.

Geyman, John. (2011). "The Decline of Primary Care: The Silent Crisis Undermining US Health Care," *PNHP.org*, August 9.

Ghilarducci, Teresa. (2012). "Our Ridiculous Approach to Retirement," *The New York Times*, July 22, p. 5.

Giordano, Ralph G. (2003). *Fun and Games in Twentieth-Century America: A Historical Guide to Leisure.* Westport, CT: Greenwood Press

Glaeser, Edward, Gyourko, Joseph, and Saks, Raven. (2006). "Urban Growth and Housing Supply," *Journal of Economic Geography* 6: 71–89.

Glauber, Robert H. (1978). "The Necessary Toy: The Telephone Comes to Chicago," *Chicago History* 7, no. 2 (summer): 70–86.

Goldin, Claudia. (2000). "Labor Markets in the Twentieth Century," in Easterlin and Gallman, eds. (2000b), *The Cambridge Economic History of the United States, Vol. III* (pp. 549–623). Cambridge: Cambridge University Press.

Goldin, Claudia. (2006). "The Quiet Revolution That Transformed Women's Employment, Education, and Family," *American Economic Review* 96, no. 2 (May): 1–21.

Goldin, Claudia. (2014). "A Grand Gender Convergence: Its Last Chapter," *American Economic Review* 104, no. 4 (April): 1091–1119.

Goldin, Claudia, and Katz, Lawrence F. (1999). "Human Capital and Social Capital: The Rise of Secondary Schooling in America, 1910–1940," *The Journal of Interdisciplinary History* 29, no. 4 (spring): 683–723.

Goldin, Claudia, and Katz, Lawrence F. (2008). *The Race between Education and Technology.* Cambridge, MA: The Belknap Press of the Harvard University Press.

Goldin, Claudia, and Margo, Robert A. (1992). "The Great Compression: The Wage Structure in the United States at Mid-Century," *Quarterly Journal of Economics* 107 (February): 1–34.

Goodwin, Lorine Swainston. (1999). *The Pure Food, Drink, and Drug Crusaders, 1879–1914.* Jefferson, NC: McFarland & Company.

Gordon, David M. (1996). *Fat and Mean: The Corporate Squeeze on Working Americans and the Myth of "Managerial Downsizing."* New York: Martin Kessler Books, the Free Press.

Gordon, Robert Aaron. (1974). *Economic Instability and Growth: The American Record.* New York: Harper and Row.

Gordon, Robert J. (1967). "Problems in the Measurement of Real Investment in the U. S. Economy," PhD thesis presented to the MIT Economics Department, May.

Gordon, Robert J. (1969). "$45 Billion of U.S. Private Investment Has Been Mislaid," *American Economic Review* 59, no. 3 (June): 221–38.

Gordon, Robert J. (1990). *The Measurement of Durable Goods Prices.* Chicago, IL/London: University of Chicago Press for NBER.

Gordon, Robert J. (1992). "Productivity in the Transportation Sector," in Zvi Griliches, ed., *Output Measurement in the Service Sectors.* Chicago, IL: University of Chicago Press for NBER, pp. 371–422.

Gordon, Robert J. (2000a). "Interpreting the 'One Big Wave' in U.S. Long-term Productivity Growth," in Bart van Ark, Simon Kuipers, and Gerard Kuper, eds., *Productivity, Technology, and Economic Growth.* Boston: Kluwer Publishers, pp. 19–65.

Gordon, Robert J. (2004a). "The Disappearance of Productivity Change," in *Productivity Growth, Inflation, and Unemployment: The Collected Essays of Robert J. Gordon.* Cambridge, MA/New York: Cambridge University Press, pp. 90–133.

Gordon, Robert J. (2004b). "Forward into the Past: Productivity Retrogression in the Electric Generating Industry," in *Productivity Growth, Inflation, and Unemployment: The Collected Essays of Robert J. Gordon.* Cambridge, UK/New York: Cambridge University Press, pp. 172–217.

Gordon, Robert J. (2012a). *Macroeconomics,* 12th ed. Boston, MA: Pearson/Addison-Wesley.

Gordon, Robert J. (2012b). "Is U.S. Economic Growth Over? Faltering Innovation and the Six Headwinds." NBER Working Paper 18315, August.

Gordon, Robert J. (2013). "The Phillips Curve Is Alive and Well: Inflation and the NAIRU during the Slow Recovery," NBER Working Paper 19360, September.

Gordon, Robert J. (2014b). "A New Method of Estimating Potential Real GDP Growth: Implications for the Labor Market and the Debt/GDP Ratio," NBER Working Paper 20423, August.

Gordon, Robert J., and Dew-Becker, Ian. (2008). "Controversies about the Rise of American Inequality: A Survey," NBER Working Paper 13982, May. A shorter version appeared as "Selected Issues in the Rise of Income Inequality," *Brookings Papers on Economic Activity,* 2007, no. 2: 191–215.

Gordon, Robert J., and Krenn, Robert. (2010). "The End of the Great Depression 1939–41: Fiscal Multipliers, Capacity Constraints, and Policy Contributions," NBER Working Paper 16380, September.

Gordon, Robert J., and van Goethem, Todd. (2007). "A Century of Downward Bias in the Most Important CPI Component: The Case of Rental Shelter, 1914–2003," in E. Berndt and C. Hulten, eds., *Hard-to-Measure Goods and Services: Essays in Honor of Zvi Griliches,* Conference on Research in Income and Wealth. Chicago, IL: University of Chicago Press for NBER, pp. 153–96.

Grebler, Leo, Blank, David M., and Winnick, Louis. (1956). *Capital Formation in Residential Real Estate: Trends and Prospects.* Princeton, NJ: Princeton University Press for NBER.

Green, Harvey. (1986). *Fit for America: Health, Fitness, Sport, and American Society.* New York: Pantheon Books.

Green, Harvey. (2000). *The Uncertainty of Everyday Life 1915–1945.* Fayetteville: University of Arkansas Press.

Greene, Ann Norton. (2008). *Horses at Work: Harnessing Power in Industrial America.* Cambridge, MA: Harvard University Press.

Greenfeld, Karl Taro. (2011). "Fast and Furious: The Drive-Thru Isn't Just a Convenient Way to Fill Your Car with Fries; It's a Supreme Achievement in American Manufacturing," *Bloomberg Business Week*, May 9, pp. 63–69.
Greever, William S. (1951). "A Comparison of Railroad Land Grant Policies," *Agricultural History* 25, no. 2 (April): 83–90.
Greenhouse, Steven. (2013). "Fighting Back against Wretched Wages," *The New York Times*, July 28.
Gries, Jon M. (1925). "Housing in the United States," *The Journal of Land and Public Utility Economics* 1, no. 1 (January): 23–35.
Griliches, Zvi. (1961). "Hedonic Price Indexes for Automobiles: An Econometric Analysis of Quality Change," in *The Price Statistics of the Federal Government*. General Series 73. New York: National Bureau of Economic Research, pp. 173–96.
Grossman, Ron. (2012). "Humble Theaters Became Movie Palaces," *Chicago Tribune* February 26, p. 19.
Haines, Michael R. (2000). "The Population of the United States, 1790–1920," in Engerman and Gallman, eds. (2000a), pp. 143–206.
Hall, Brian J., and Liebman, Jeffrey B. (1998). "Are CEOs Really Paid Like Bureaucrats?" *Quarterly Journal of Economics* 113 (August): 653–91.
Hall, Robert Trevor. (2002). *Stretching the Peacock: From Color Television to High Definition Television (HDTV), an Historical Analysis of Innovation, Regulation and Standardization*. (Doctoral dissertation). ProQuest/UMI. (UMI Number: 3071648).
Halpern, Sue. (2015). "How Robots and Algorithms Are Taking Over," *New York Review of Books,* April 2, pp. 24–28.
Ham, Arthur H. (1912). *The Campaign against the Loan Shark.* New York: Russell Sage.
Harmetz, Aljean. (1996). *On the Road to Tara: The Making of* Gone with the Wind. New York: Harry N. Abrams.
Hart, James D. (1950). *The Popular Book: A History of America's Literary Taste.* New York: Oxford University Press.
Harvey, Brett. (2002). *The Fifties: A Women's Oral History*. Lincoln, NE: ASJA Press.
Hathaway, Ian, and Litan, Robert E. (2014). "What's Driving the Decline in the Firm Formation Rate? A Partial Explanation," *Economic Studies at Brookings,* November.
Hausman, Jerry, and Leibtag, Ephraim. (2007). "Consumer Benefits from Increased Competition in Shopping Outlets: Measuring the Effect of Wal-Mart," *Journal of Applied Econometrics* 22, no. 7: 1157–77.
Hayden, Dolores. (2000). "Model Houses for the Millions," Lincoln Institute of Land Policy Working Paper WP00DH2.
Hayden, Dolores. (2002). "Revisiting the Sitcom Suburbs," *Race, Poverty, and the Environment* 9, no. 1: 39–41.
Hayden, Dolores. (2003). *Building Suburbia: Green Fields and Urban Growth, 1820–2000.* New York: Vintage Books.
Henderson, J. Lloyd. (1956). "Market Milk Operations, 1906 versus 1956," *Journal of Dietary Science* 39, no. 6: 812–18. http://download.journals.elsevierhealth.com/pdfs/journals/0022–302/PIIS0022030256912061.pdf
Hendrickson, Robert. (1979). *The Grand Emporiums: The Illustrated History of America's Great Department Stores.* New York: Stein and Day.
Heppenheimer, T. A. (1995). *Turbulent Skies: The History of Commercial Aviation.* New York: John Wiley and Sons.
Herman, Arthur. (2012). *Freedom's Forge: How American Business Produced Victory in World War II.* New York: Random House.
Higgs, Robert. (1973). "Mortality in Rural America, 1870–1920: Estimates and Conjectures," *Explorations in Economic History* 10, no. 2: 177–95.
Higgs, Robert. (1992). "Wartime Prosperity? A Reassessment of the U.S. Economy in the 1940s," *Journal of Economic History* 52, no. 1 (March): 41–60.
Higgs, Robert. (2004). "Wartime Socialization of Investment: A Reassessment of U.S. Capital Formation in the 1940s," *Journal of Economic History* 64, no 2 (June): 500–520.

Hillenbrand, Laura. (2003). *Seabiscuit: An American Legend (Special Illustrated Collector's Edition).* New York: Ballantine Books.

Hilton, George W. (1982). *The Cable Car in America.* San Diego, CA: Howell-North books.

Holbrook, Stewart H. (1947). *The Story of American Railroads.* New York: American Legacy Press.

Holley, I. B. (2008). *The Highway Revolution, 1895–1925.* Durham, NC: Carolina Academic Press.

Holohan, Dan. (1992). *The Lost Art of Steam Heating.* Bethpage, NY: Dan Holohan Associates.

Hood, Clifton. (1993). *722 Miles: The Building of the Subways and How They Transformed New York.* New York: Simon and Schuster.

Hooker, Richard J. (1981). *Food and Drink in America: A History.* Indianapolis, IN/New York: The Bobbs-Merrill Company.

Hortaçsu, Ali, and Syverson, Chad. (2015). "The Ongoing Evolution of US Retail: A Format Tug-of-War." NBER Working Paper 21464, August.

Hounshell, David A. (1984). *From the American System to Mass Production, 1800–1932.* Baltimore, MD/London: The Johns Hopkins University Press.

Hoxby, Carolyn, and Avery, Christopher. (2013). "The Missing 'One-Offs': The Hidden Supply of High-Achieving Low-Income Students," *Brookings Papers on Economic Activity* (spring): 1–50.

Hoyert, Donna L., and Xu, Jiaquan. (2012). "Deaths: Preliminary Data for 2011," *National Vital Statistics Reports* 61, no. 6 (October 10): 1–51.

Hsieh, Chang-Tai, Hurst, Erik, Jones, Chad, and Klenow, Peter J. (2013). "The Allocation of Talent and U.S. Economic Growth," Stanford University Working Paper, January.

HSUS. (1960). *Historical Statistics of the United States, Colonial Times to 1957.* Washington, DC: Bureau of the Census.

HSUS. (2006). *Historical Statistics of the United States*, Millennial Edition Online, Susan B. Carter, Scott Sigmund Gartner, Michael R. Haines, Alan L. Olmstead, Richard Sutch, and Gavin Wright, eds. Cambridge, UK: Cambridge University Press 2006. http://hsus.cambridge.org/HSUSWeb/HSUS EntryServlet.

Huberman, Michael. (2004). "Working Hours of the World United? New International Evidence of Worktime, 1870–1913," *Journal of Economic History* 64, no. 4 (December): 964–1001.

Hughes, Thomas Parke. (1983). *Networks of Power: Electrification in Western Society, 1880–1930.* Baltimore, MD: Johns Hopkins University Press.

Hugill, Peter J. (1982). "Good Roads and the Automobile in the United States 1880–1929," *Geographical Review* 72, no. 3 (July): 327–49.

Hunnicutt, Benjamin Kline. (1988). *Work without End: Abandoning Shorter Hours for the Right to Work.* Philadelphia, PA: The Temple University Press.

Hymowitz, Carol. (2012). "Behind Every Great Woman: The Rise of the CEO Mom Has Created a New Kind of Trophy Husband," *Bloomberg Businessweek*, January 9–15, pp. 55–59.

Hymowitz, Carol, and Collins, Margaret. (2015). "A Retirement Toast," *Bloomberg Business Week*, January 12–18, pp. 19–20.

Igel, Lee. (2008). "A History of Health Care as a Campaign Issue," *The Physician Executive* (May–June): 12–15.

Ingrassia, Paul. (2012). *Engines of Change: A History of the American Dream in Fifteen Cars.* New York/London: Simon and Schuster.

Innis, Harold A. (1942). "The Newspaper in Economic Development," *The Journal of Economic History* 2 supplement (December): 1–33.

International Motion Picture Almanac. (2006). New York: Quigley Publications.

Irwin, Neil. (2015). "Why Less Educated Workers Are Losing Ground on Wages," *The New York Times*, April 23, p. A3.

Isenstadt, Sandy. (1998). "Visions of Plenty: Refrigerators in America around 1950," *Journal of Design History* 11, no. 4: 311–21.

Jabr, Ferris. (2013). "The Reading Brain in the Digital Age: The Science of Paper versus Screens," *Scientific American*, April 11.

Jackson, Kenneth T. (1985). *Crabgrass Frontier: The Suburbanization of the United States.* New York/Oxford, UK: Oxford University Press.

Jacobs, Eva E., ed. (2003). *Handbook of Labor Statistics*, 6th ed. Lanham, MD: Bernan Publishers.
Jacobs, James A. (2006). "Social and Spatial Change in the Postwar Family Room," *Perspectives in Vernacular Architecture* 13, no. 1: 70–85.
Jakle, John A. (1982). *The American Small Town: Twentieth-Century Place Images.* Hamden, CT: Archon Books.
Jenish, D'Arcy, and Davies, Tanya. (1999). "The Walkman at 20," *Maclean's* 112, no. 35 (August 30): 10.
Jerome, Harry. (1934). *Mechanization in Industry.* New York: National Bureau of Economic Research.
Joel, Amos E. Jr. (1984). "The Past 100 Years in Telecommunications Switching," *IEEE Communications Magazine* 22, no. 5 (May): 64–83.
Johnson, Eldon L. (1981). "Misconceptions about the Early Land-Grant Colleges," *The Journal of Higher Education* 52, no 4 (July–August): 331–51.
Jones, David S., and Greene, Jeremy A. (2013). "The Decline and Rise of Coronary Heart Disease: Understanding Public Health Catastrophism," *American Journal of Public Health* (May 16): e1–e12.
Jones, David W., Jr. (1985). *Urban Transit Policy: An Economic and Political History.* Englewood Cliffs, NJ: Prentice-Hall.
Jones, Mary Ellen. (1998). *Daily Life on the Nineteenth Century American Frontier.* Westport, CT: The Greenwood Press.
Jonnes, Jill. (2003). *Empires of Light: Edison, Tesla, Westinghouse, and the Race to Electrify the World.* New York: Random House.
Jorgenson, Dale W., and Griliches, Zvi. (1967). "The Explanation of Productivity Change," *Review of Economic Studies* 34, no. 3 (July): 249–84.
Jorgenson, Dale W., Ho, Mun S., and Samuels, Jon D. (2014). "What Will Revive U.S. Economic Growth?" *Journal of Policy Modeling* 36, no. 4 (July–August): 674–91.
Kaitz, Karl. (1998). "American Roads, Roadside America," *Geographical Review* 88, no. 3 (July): 363–87.
Karanes, Chatchada, Nelson, Gene O., Chitphakdithai, Pintip, Agura, Edward, Ballen, Karen K., Bolan, Charles D., Porter, David L., Uberti, Joseph P., King, Roberta J., and Confer, Dennis L. (2008). "Twenty Years of Unrelated Donor Hematopoietic Cell Transplantation for Adult Recipients Facilitated by the National Marrow Donor Program," *Biology of Blood and Marrow Transplant* 14: 8–15.
Kaszynski, William. (2000). *The American Highway: The History and Culture of Roads in the United States.* Jefferson, NC/London: McFarland Publishers.
Katz, Michael B., Michael J. Doucet, and Mark J. Stern. (1982). *The Social Organization of Early Industrial Capitalism.* Cambridge, MA: Harvard University Press.
Kay, Jane Holtz. (1997). *Asphalt Nation: How the Automobile Took Over America, and How We Can Take It Back.* New York: Crown Publishers.
Keating, Ann Durkin. (2004). *Chicagoland: City and Suburbs in the Railroad Age.* Chicago, IL/London: The University of Chicago Press.
Keeler, Theodore E. (1972). "Airline Regulation and Market Performance," *Bell Journal of Economics* 3, no. 2 (autumn): 399–424.
Kendrick, John W. (1961). *Productivity Trends in the United States.* Princeton, NJ: Princeton University Press for NBER.
Kennedy, David M. (2003). "What Is Patriotism without Sacrifice?" *The New York Times*, February 16.
Kennedy, T. R. Jr. (1964). "Electronic Computer Flashes Answers, May Speed Engineering," *The New York Times*, February 15.
Kenny, Charles. (2013). "What the Web Didn't Deliver," *Bloomberg Business Week*, June 20, pp. 10–11.
Kesslar-Harris, Alice. (1982). *Out to Work: A History of Wage-Earning Women in the United States.* New York/Oxford, UK: Oxford University Press.
Keynes, John Maynard. (1931). "Economic Possibilities for Our Grandchildren," in *Essays in Persuasion.* London: MacMillan, pp. 358–74.
Khan, B. Zorina, and Sokoloff, Kenneth L. (2004). "Institutions and Technological Innovation During Early Economic Growth: Evidence from the Great Inventors of the United States, 1790–1930," NBER Working Paper 10966.
Kidwell, Claudia B. (1979). *Cutting a Fashionable Fit.* Washington, DC: Smithsonian Institution Press.

Killeffer, David H. (1948). *The Genius of Industrial Research.* New York: Reinhold Publishing Corporation.

Kimes, Beverly Rae, and Clark, Henry Austin Jr. (1996). *Standard Catalog of American Cars: 1805–1942.* Iola, WI: Krause Publications.

King, David C. (2010). *Presidents and Their Times: Herbert Hoover.* Tarrytown, NY: Marshall Cavendish.

Kinley, David. (1910). *The Use of Credit Instruments in Payments in the United States.* Washington, DC: National Monetary Commission.

Kipling, Rudyard. (2003). *Kipling's America Travel Letters, 1889–1895* (D. H. Stewart, ed.) Greensboro, NC: ELT Press.

Klein, Maury. (2007). *The Genesis of Industrial America, 1870–1920.* Cambridge, UK/New York: Cambridge University Press.

Kleinberg, S. J. (1989). *The Shadow of the Mills: Working-Class Families in Pittsburgh, 1870–1907.* Pittsburgh, PA: University of Pittsburgh Press.

Kleiner, Morris M. (2011). "Occupational Licensing: Protecting the Public Interest or Protectionism?" W. E. Upjohn Institute for Employment Research Policy Paper no. 2011-009, July. http://research.upjohn.org/up..policypapers/9/.

Klenow, Pete. (2012). "The Allocation of Talent and U.S. Economic Growth," *SIEPR Policy Brief,* July.

Kline, Patrick M., and Moretti, Enrico. (2013). "Local Economic Development, Agglomeration Economies, and the Big Push: 100 Years of Evidence from the Tennessee Valley Authority," NBER Working Paper 19293, August.

Knight, Charles K. (1927). "Fraternal Life Insurance," *Annals of the American Academy of Political and Social Science* 130 (March): 97–102.

Krewski, Daniel. (2009). "Evaluating the Effects of Ambient Air Pollution on Life Expectancy," *The New England Journal of Medicine* 360, no. 4 (January 22): 413–15.

Kristof, Nicholas. (2014). "The American Dream Is Leaving America," *The New York Times,* October 26.

Laermans, Rudi. (1993). "Learning to Consume: Early Department Stores and the Shaping of the Modern Consumer Culture (1860–1914)," *Theory, Culture & Society* 10, no. 4 (November): 79–102. http://tcs.sagepub.com/content/10/4/79.

Lakdawalla, D, and Phillipson, T. (2009). "The Growth of Obesity and Technological Change," *Economics and Human Biology* 7, no. 3 (December): 283–93.

Lamb, Vanessa Martins. (2011). "The 1950's and 1960's and the American Woman: The Transition from the 'Housewife' to the Feminist," *University of Toulon* (June): 1–106.

Lambert, Gavin. (1973). *GWTW: The Making of* Gone with the Wind. Boston, MA: An Atlantic Monthly Press Book, Little, Brown and Company.

Lamoreaux, Naomi R. (2010). "Entrepreneurship in the United States, 1865–1920," in David S. Landes, Joel Mokyr, and William J. Baumol, eds., *The Invention of Enterprise: Entrepreneurship from Ancient Mesopotamia to Modern Times.* Princeton, NJ: Princeton University Press, pp. 367–400.

Landsberg, Steven. (2007). "A Brief History of Economic Time," *Wall Street Journal,* June 9.

Lane, Rose Wilder. (1935). *Old Home Town.* New York: Longmans, Green.

Larsen, Lawrence H. (1990). *The Urban South: A History*. Lexington: The University Press of Kentucky.

Leach, Willam R. (1993). *Land of Desire: Merchants, Power, and the Rise of a New American Culture.* New York: Random House.

Leaf, Clifton, and Burke, Doris. (2004). "Why We're Losing the War on Cancer (and How to Win It)," *Fortune* 149, no. 6 (March 22): 76–97.

Lears, Jackson. (2009). *Rebirth of a Nation, The Making of Modern America, 1877–1920.* New York: HarperCollins.

Lebergott, Stanley. (1976). *The American Economy: Income, Wealth and Want.* Princeton, NJ: Princeton University Press.

Lebergott, Stanley. (1996). *Consumer Expenditure: New Measures and Old Motives.* Princeton, NJ: Princeton University Press.

Lebhar, Godfrey M. (1952). *Chain Stores in America.* New York: Chain Store Publishing Company.

Lemann, Nicholas. (1991). *The Promised Land: The Great Black Migration and How It Changed America.* New York: Alfred A. Knopf.

Levenstein, Harvey A. (1988). *Revolution at the Table: The Transformation of the American Diet.* New York: Oxford University Press.
Levinson, Marc. (2011). *The Great A&P and the Struggle for Small Business in America.* New York: Hill and Wang.
Levitz, Jennifer. (2008). "Investors Pull Money out of Their 401(K)s: Hardship Withdrawals Rose in Recent Months, Plans Say; Concerns about Tax Penalty," *Wall Street Journal*, September 23, pp. 1–3.
Levitz, Jennifer, and Shishkin, Philip. (2009). "More Workers Cite Age Bias after Layoffs," *Wall Street Journal*, March 11, pp. 1–3.
Levy, Frank, and Temin, Peter. (2007). "Inequality and Institutions in 20th Century America." NBER Working Paper 13106, April.
Lewis, Sinclair. (1961). *Main Street.* New York: New American Library.
Lewis, Tom. (1992). "'A Godlike Presence': The Impact of Radio on the 1920s and 1930s," *OAH (Organization of American Historians) Magazine of History* 6, no. 4 (spring): 26–33.
Lichter, Daniel, and Fuguitt, Glenn. (1980). "Response to Transportation Innovation: The Case of the Interstate Highway," *Social Forces* 59, no. 2 (December): 492–512.
Life Insurers Fact Book. (2013). Washington, DC: American Council of Life Insurers.
Light, Donald, and Levine, Sol. (1988). "The Changing Character of the Medical Profession: A Theoretical Overview," *The Milbank Quarterly* 66 (supplement 2): 10–32.
Lindsey, Brink (2015). *Low-Hanging Fruit Guarded by Dragons: Reforming Regressive Regulation to Boost U.S. Economic Growth.* Washington, DC: The Cato Institute.
Lohr, Steve. (2015). "Maintaining a Human Touch as the Algorithms Get to Work," *The New York Times*, April 7, p. A3.
Los Angeles Times. (1993). "John Walson Sr.; Built First Cable TV System," April 1.
Lubove, Roy. (1962). "The Tenement Comes of Age," *The Progressives and the Slums: House Reform in New York City.* Pittsburgh, PA: University of Pittsburgh Press.
Lynd, Robert S., and Lynd, Helen Merrell. (1929). *Middletown: A Study in Contemporary American Culture.* New York. Harcourt, Brace and Company.
Lynn, Robert A. (1957). "Installment Credit before 1870," *Business History Review* 31, no. 4: 414–24.
MacDonald, J. Fred. (1979). *Don't Touch That Dial! Radio Programming in American Life, 1920–1960.* Chicago, IL: Nelson-Hall.
Maclaurin, Rupert W. (1950). "Patents and Technical Progress—A Study of Television," *Journal of Political Economy* 58, no. 2: 142–57.
Maddison, Angus. (1995). *Monitoring the World Economy 1820–1992.* Paris: OECD, Development Centre.
Maddison, Angus. (1999). "Poor until 1820," *Wall Street Journal*, January 11.
Magoun, Alexander B. (2002). "The Origins of the 45-RPM Record at RCA Victor, 1939-1948," in Hans-Joachim-Braun (ed.), *Music and Technology in the Twentieth Century*. Baltimore, MD: Johns Hopkins University Press, pp. 148–57.
Markoff, John. (2013). "In 1949, He Imagined an Age of Robots," *The New York Times,* May 21, p. D8.
Marron, Donncha. (2009). *Consumer Credit in the United States: A Sociological Perspective from the 19th Century to the Present.* New York: Palgrave MacMillan.
Marsh, Bill. (2008). "The Overflowing American Dinner Plate," *The New York Times,* August 3, Sunday business section, p. 7.
Martí-Ibañez, Félix. (1958). *Centaur: Essays on the History of Medical Ideas*. New York: MD Publications.
Marvin, Caroline. (1988). *When Old Technologies Were New: Thinking about Electric Communication in the Late Nineteenth Century.* New York/Oxford, UK: Oxford University Press.
Mayo, James M. (1993). *The American Grocery Store: The Business Evolution of an Architectural Space.* Westport, CT/London: Greenwood Press.
McCarthy, Jeanette J., McLeod, Howard L., and Ginsburg, Geoffrey S. (2013). "Genomic Medicine: A Decade of Successes, Challenges, and Opportunities," *Science Translational Medicine* 5, no. 189: 189sr4.
McCloskey, Deidre. (2014). "Measured, Unmeasured, Mismeasured, and Unjustified Pessimism: A Review Essay of Thomas Piketty's *Capital in the Twenty-First Century*," *Erasmus Journal of Philosophy and Economics* 7, no. 2: 73–115.

McDowell, M. S. (1929). "What the Agricultural Extension Service Has Done for Agriculture," *Annals of the American Academy of Political and Social Science* 142 (March): 250–56.

McIntosh, Elaine N. (1995). *American Food Habits in Historical Perspective.* Westport, CT/London: Praeger.

McKee, John M. (1924). "The Automobile and American Agriculture," *Annals of the American Academy of Political and Social Science* 115 (November): 12–17.

McKinlay, John B., and McKinlay, Sonja M. (1977). "The Questionable Contribution of Medical Measures to the Decline in Mortality in the United States in the Twentieth Century," *Health and Society* 55, no. 3: 405–28.

McShane, Clay, and Tarr, Joel A. (2007). *The Horse in the City: Living Machines in the Nineteenth Century.* Baltimore, MD: The Johns Hopkins University Press.

McWilliams, Carey. (1942). *Ill Fares the Land: Migrants and Migratory Labor in the United States.* Boston, MA: Little, Brown.

Meeker, Edward. (1971). "Improving Health of the United States, 1850–1915." *Explorations in Economic History* 9, no. 1: 353–73.

Meeker, Edward. (1974). "The Social Rate of Return on Investment in Public Health, 1880–1910," *The Journal of Economic History* 34, no. 2 (June): 397–421.

Melosi, Martin V. (2000). *The Sanitary City: Urban Infrastructure in American from Colonial Times to Present.* Baltimore, MD: Johns Hopkins University Press.

Mensch, Gerhard. (1979). *Stalemate in Technology: Innovations Overcome the Depression.* Cambridge, MA: Ballinger.

Merton, Robert K. (1935). "Fluctuations in the Rate of Industrial Invention," *Quarterly Journal of Economics* 49, no. 3 (May): 454–74.

Millard, Andre. (1995). *America on Record: A History of Recorded Sound.* Cambridge, MA: Cambridge University Press.

Millard, Andre. (2002). "Tape Recording and Music Making," in Hans-Joachim Braun, ed., *Music and Technology in the Twentieth Century.* Baltimore, MD: Johns Hopkins University Press, 158–67.

Miller, Claire Cain. (2014). "Financial Security Is Increasingly Trumping Marriage, Report Says," *The New York Times*, September 24, p. A23.

Miller, John Anderson. (1941/1960). *Fares Please! A Popular History of Trolleys, Horse-Cars, Street-Cars, Buses, Elevateds, and Subways.* 1941 edition New York: Appleton-Century-Crofts, reprinted in a 1960 Dover edition with identical content but a new preface and photos.

Miller, Lisa. (2010). "Divided We Eat," *Newsweek.* November 29, pp. 42–48.

Mindlin, Alex. (2006). "DVD Player Tops VCR as Household Item," *The New York Times*, December 25, p. C3.

Miron, Jeffrey, and Waldock, Katherine. (2010). *The Budgetary Impact of Ending Drug Prohibition.* Washington, CATO Institute.

Mishel, Lawrence, Bivens, Josh, Gould, Elise, and Shierholz, Heidi. (2012). *The State of Working America*, 12th ed. Ithaca, NY/London: ILR Press, an imprint of Cornell University Press.

Mitchell, Josh. (2014). "Remedial 101: Call for Reform," *Wall Street Journal*, November 18, p. A3.

Mokyr, Joel. (1990). *The Lever of Riches: Technological Creativity and Economic Progress.* New York/Oxford, UK: Oxford University Press.

Mokyr, Joel. (2000). "Why Was There More Work for Mother? Technological Change and the Household, 1880–1930." *Journal of Economic History* 60, no. 1 (March): 1–40.

Mokyr, Joel. (2009). *The Enlightened Economy: An Economic History of Britain, 1700–1850.* New Haven, CT: Yale University Press.

Mokyr, Joel. (2013). "Is Technological Progress a Thing of the Past?" EU-Vox essay posted September 8, www.voxeu.org/article/technological-progress-thing-past.

Mokyr, Joel, and Stein, Rebecca. (1997). "Science Health, and Household Technology: The Effect of the Pasteur Revolution on Consumer Demand," in Bresnahan and Gordon, eds., pp. 143–206.

Moline, Norman T. (1971). *Mobility and the Small Town 1900–1930.* Chicago, IL: The University of Chicago Department of Geography, Research Paper no. 132.

Monga, Vipal. (2015). "The New Bookkeeper Is a Robot," *Wall Street Journal*, May 5, B1.

Monkkonen, Eric H. (1988). *America Becomes Urban: The Development of U.S. Cities and Towns 1780–1980.* Berkeley/Los Angeles: University of California Press.
Montgomery, David. (1983). "Labor in the Industrial Era," in Richard B. Morris, ed., *A History of the American Worker.* Princeton, NJ: Princeton University Press, pp. 79–114.
Montgomery, David. (1987). *The Fall of the House of Labor.* Cambridge, UK/New York: The Cambridge University Press.
Moore, Harry H. (1927). *American Medicine and the People's Health.* New York/London: D. Appleton and Co.
Morris, Charles. (2002). *The San Francisco Calamity by Earthquake and Fire.* Urbana/Chicago: The University of Illinois Press.
Morrison, Craig. (1974). "Nickelodeon to Picture Palace and Back," *Design Quarterly* 93: 6–17.
Mumford, Lewis. (1961). *The City in History: Its Origins, Its Transformations, Its Prospects.* New York: Harcourt, Brace and Company.
Munn, Orson D. (1915). *Trade Marks, Trade Names, and Unfair Competition in Trade.* New York: Munn & Co.
Munos, Bernard. (2009). "Lessons from 60 Years of Pharmaceutical Innovation," *Nature Reviews* 8 (December): 959–68.
Murnane, Richard J. (2013). "U.S. High School Graduation Rates: Patterns and Explanations," *Journal of Economic Literature* 51, no. 2 (June): 370–422.
Murphy, Kevin M., and Topel, Robert H., eds. (2003). *Measuring the Gains from Medical Research: An Economic Approach.* Chicago, IL: University of Chicago Press for NBER.
Murphy, Kevin M., and Topel, Robert H. (2006). "The Value of Health and Longevity," *Journal of Political Economy* 114, no. 5 (October): 871–904.
Murray, Charles. (2012). *Coming Apart: The State of White America 1960–2010.* New York: Crown Forum.
Murray, John E. (2007). *Origins of American Health Insurance: A History of Industrial Sickness Funds.* New Haven, CT/London: Yale University Press.
Nadiri, Ishaq, and Mamuneas, Theofanis. (1994). "The Effects of Public Infrastructure and R&D Capital on the Cost Structure and Performance of U.S. Manufacturing Industries," *The Review of Economics and Statistics* 76 (February): 22–37.
Nard, Craig Allen. (2010). *The Law of Patents*, 2nd ed. New York: Aspen Publishers.
National Alliance on Mental Illness. (2013). "Mental Illness: Facts and Numbers," *NAMI.org* (March 5), pp. 1–3. www.nami.org/factsheets/mentalillness_factsheet.pdf.
Neifeld, Morris R. (1939). *Personal Finance Comes of Age.* New York: Harper & Bros.
Nelson, Richard R. (1959). "The Economics of Innovation: A Survey of the Literature," *The Journal of Business* 32, no. 2 (April): 101–27.
Newman, Bernard J. (1928). "Rural Housing in the United States of America," presented at the International Housing and Town Planning Conference, Paris, July, published in part I of the conference proceedings.
Newspaper Association of America. (2012). "Trends and Numbers: Newspaper Circulation Volume," *Newspaper Association of America*, September 4.
The New York Times. (1986). "Growing Up, in Three Minute Segments," *The New York Times*, November 5.
Nicholas, Tom. (2010). "The Role of Independent Invention in U.S. Technological Development, 1880–1930," *The Journal of Economic History* 70, no. 1 (March): 57–81.
Nichols, Austin, and Rothstein, Jesse. (2015). "The Earned Income Tax Credit (EITC)," NBER Working Paper 21211, May.
Nichols, Walter S. (1917). "Fraternal Insurance in the United States: Its Origin, Development, Character and Existing Status," *The Annals of the American Academy of Polical and Social Science* 70, no. 1 (January): 109–22.
The Nielsen Company. (2014). "More of What We Want: The Cross-Platform Report," *The Nielsen Company*, June. www.tvb.org/media/file/Nielsen-Cross-Platform-Report_Q1-2014.pdf.
Nordhaus, William D. (1997). "Do Real-Output and Real-Wage Measures Capture Reality? The History of Lighting Suggests Not," in Bresnahan and Gordon, eds. (1997), pp. 29–70.
Nordhaus, William D. (2003). "The Health of Nations: The Contribution of Improved Health to Living Standards," in Murphy and Topel, eds. (2003), pp. 9–40.

Nordhaus, William D. (2007). "Two Centuries of Productivity Growth in Computing," *The Journal of Economic History* 67, no. 1 (March): 147–52.
Nordhaus, William D., and Tobin, James. (1972). "Is Growth Obsolete?" in William D. Nordhaus and James Tobin, eds., *Economic Research: Retrospect and Prospect*, vol 5: *Economic Growth*. New York: National Bureau of Economic Research, pp. 1–80.
Norton, Amy. (2012). "More Americans Getting Pacemakers," *Reuters.com*, September 26.
Norton, Andrew. (2013). "Australian College Plan Has Helped Students, at a Cost," *New York Times*, July 11.
Nye, David E. (1998). *Consuming Power: A Social History of American Energies*. Cambridge, MA/London. The MIT Press.
O'Brien, Jeffrey M. (2012). "The Great Stem Cell Dilemma," *Fortune*, October 8, pp. 186–95.
Officer, Lawrence H. (2011). "The Annual Consumer Price Index for the United States, 1774–2010," MeasuringWorth, 2011. www.measuringworth.com/uscpi/.
Ogle, Maureen. (1996). *All the Modern Conveniences: American Household Plumbing, 1840–1890*. Baltimore, MD: Johns Hopkins University Press.
Okun, Mitchell. (1986). *Fair Play in the Marketplace: The First Battle for Pure Food and Drugs*. DeKalb: Northern Illinois University Press.
Olney, Martha. (1991). *Buy Now Pay Later: Advertising, Credit, and Consumer Durables in the 1920s*. Chapel Hill/London: University of North Carolina Press.
O'Malley, Chris. (1995). "Drowning in the Net," *Popular Science*, June, pp. 78–80.
Orrenius, Pia M., and Zavodny, Madeline. (2006). "Does Immigration Affect Wages? A Look at Occupation-Level Evidence," Federal Reserve of Dallas Research Paper 302, March.
Ottaviano, Gianmarco I. P., and Peri, Giovanni. (2006). "Rethinking the Effects of Immigration on Wages." NBER Working Paper 12497, August.
Oviatt, F. C. (1905a). "Historical Study of Fire Insurance in the United States," *Annals of the American Academy of Political and Social Science* 26, no. 1: 155–78.
Oviatt, F. C. (1905b). "Économic Place of Life Insurance and Its Relation to Society," *Annals of the American Academy of Political and Social Science* 26, no. 1: 181–91.
Pacyga, Dominic A., and Shanabruch, Charles, eds. (2003). *The Chicago Bungalow*. Chicago, IL: Arcadia Publishing for the Chicago Architecture Foundation.
Pagliery, Jose. (2014). "JetBlue's Weird Password Rule: No Q or Z," *CNN Money*, May 15.
Panschar, William G., and Slater, Charles C. (1956). *Baking in America*. Evanston, IL: Northwestern University Press.
Parsons, Patrick R. (1996). "Two Tales of a City: John Walson, Sr., Mahanoy City, and the 'Founding' of Cable TV," *Journal of Broadcasting & Electronic Media* 40, no. 3: 354–65.
Patton, Phil. (1995). "How the Internet Began," *Popular Science*, June, p. 85.
"People & Events: Selma March" (2000). *PBS Online*. www.pbs.org/wgbh/amex/wallace/peopleevents/pande08.html.
Pettit, Becky. (2012). *Invisible Men: Mass Incarceration and the Myth of Black Progress*. New York: Russell Sage Foundation.
Pew Research Center. (2013). "Home Internet Access." http://www.pewresearch.org/data-trend/media-and-technology/internet-penetration/.
Pew Research Internet Project. (2014). "Mobile Technology Fact Sheet," Pew Research Internet Project. www.pewinternet.org/fact-sheets/mobile-technology-fact-sheet/.
Phelan, Rev. J. J. (1919). "Motion Pictures as a Phase of Commercialized Amusements in Toledo, Ohio," *Film History* 13, no. 3: 234–328.
Phillips, Ronnie J. (2000). "Digital Technology and Institutional Change from the Gilded Age to Modern Times: The Impact of the Telegraph and the Internet," *Journal of Economic Issues* 34, no. 2 (June): 266–89.
Pierce, Bessie Louise. (1957). *A History of Chicago*, vol. III: *The Rise of a Modern City 1871–1893*. Chicago, IL/London: University of Chicago Press.
Piketty, Thomas. (2014). *Capital in the Twenty-First Century*. Cambridge, MA/London: Belknap Press of Harvard University Press.

Piketty, Thomas, and Emmanuel Saez. (2003). "Income Inequality in the United States, 1913–1998," *Quarterly Journal of Economics* 118, no. 1 (February): 1–39.
Pinker, Steven. (2011). *The Better Angels of Our Nature: The Decline of Violence in History and Its Causes.* London: Allen Lane.
Pletz, John. (2015). "No More Pens, No More Books," *Crain's Chicago Business*, April 20, p. 4.
Plumer, David. (2012). "How Air Conditioning Transformed the U.S. Economy," *Washington Post*, July 7.
Podnolik, Mary Ellen. (2014). "Big Times: Home Size Hits Record," *Chicago Tribune*, June 3.
Polsky, Carol. (2013). "Many Older Workers Can't Afford to Retire," *Newsday*, March 31, pp. 1–4.
Pope, C. Arden III, Ezzati, Majid, and Dockery, Douglas W. (2009). "Fine Particulate Air Pollution and Life Expectancy in the United States," *The New England Journal of Medicine* 360, no. 4 (January 22): 376–86.
Pope, Clayne L. (1992). "Adult Mortality in America before 1900: A View from Family Histories," in Claudia Goldin and Hugh Rockoff, eds., *Strategic Factors in Nineteenth Century American Economic Growth: A Volume to Honor Robert W. Fogel.* Chicago, IL: University of Chicago Press for NBER, pp. 267–296.
Portman, Rob. (2014). "Heading Off the Entitlement Meltdown; Demography Is Destiny: The Retirement of 77 Million Baby Boomers Is Not a Theoretical Projection," *Wall Street Journal*, July 21, pp. 1–2.
Pratt, Gill A. (2015). "Is a Cambrian Explosion Coming for Robotics?" *Journal of Economic Perspectives* 29, no. 3 (summer): 51–60.
Prieto, Luis, and Sacristan, Jose A. (2003). "Problems and Solutions in Calculating Quality-Adjusted Life Years (QALYs)," *Health Qual Life Outcomes*, December 19. www.ricbi.nim.nih.gov/pmc/articles/PMC317370/.
Puga, Diego. (2008). "Urban Sprawl: Causes and Consequences," *Eis Opuscles del CREI,* no. 18 (January).
Pursell, Carroll. (2007). *The Machine in America: A Social History of Technology*, 2nd ed. Baltimore, MD: The Johns Hopkins Press.
Radde, Bruce. (1993). *The Merritt Parkway*. New Haven, CT/London: Yale University Press.
Radford, Gail. (1992). "New Building and Investment Patterns in 1920s Chicago," *Social Science History* 16, no. 1: 1–21.
Rae, John B. (1966). *The American Automobile: A Brief History.* Chicago, IL: University of Chicago Press.
Raff, Daniel M. G., and Manuel Trajtenberg. (1997). "Quality-Adjusted Prices for the American Automobile Industry: 1906–1940," in Bresnahan and Gordon, eds. (1997), pp. 71–101.
Rainie, Lee. (2013). "Cell Phone Ownership Hits 91% of Adults," Pew Research Center, June 6.
Ramey, Valerie. (2009). "Time Spent in Home Production in the 20th Century United States," *The Journal of Economic History* 69 (March): 1–47.
Ramey, Valerie, and Francis, Neville. (2009). "A Century of Work and Leisure," *American Economic Journal: Macroeconomics* 1 (July): 189–224.
Ransom, Roger L., and Sutch, Richard. (1977). *One Kind of Freedom: The Economic Consequences of Emancipation.* New York/Cambridge, UK: Cambridge University Press.
Rao, S. L. N. (1973). "On Long-Term Mortality Trends in the United States, 1850–1968." *Demography* 10, no. 3: 405–19.
Rattner, Steven. (2014). "The Myth of Industrial Rebound," *The New York Times Sunday Review*, January 26, p. 1.
Reardon, Sean, and Bischoff, Kendra. (2011). "Income Inequality and Income Segregation," *American Journal of Sociology* 116, no. 4 (January): 1092–1153.
Reed, Robert C. (1968). *Train Wrecks: A Pictorial History of Accidents on the Main Line.* Seattle, WA: Superior Publishing Company.
Rees, Albert. (1961). *Real Wages in Manufacturing: 1890–1914.* Princeton, NJ: Princeton University Press for NBER.
Reiser, Stanley Joel. (1978). *Medicine and the Reign of Technology.* Cambridge, UK/New York: Cambridge University Press.
Remnick, David. (2011). "When the Towers Fell," *The New Yorker,* September 18, pp. 21–23.
Renne, Roland R. (1960). "Land-Grant Instituions, the Public, and the Public Interest," *Annals of the American Academy of Political and Social Science* 331 (September): 46–51.

Reynolds, Handel. (2012). *The Big Squeeze: A Social and Political History of the Controversial Mammogram.* Ithaca, NY: Cornell University Press.
Riis, Jacob August. (1890/1970). *How the Other Half Lives; Studies among the Tenements of New York.* Cambridge, MA: Belknap Press of Harvard University Press, 1970.
Ristuccia, Christiano Andrea, and Tooze, Adam. (2013). "Machine Tools and Mass Production in the Armaments Boom: Germany and the United States, 1929–44," *Economic History Review* 66, iss. 4 (November): 953–74.
Rockoff, Hugh. (1990). "The Wizard of Oz as a Monetary Allegory," *Journal of Political Economy* 98 (August): 739–60.
Roell, Craig H. (1989). *The Piano in America, 1890–1940.* Chapel Hill: University of North Carolina Press.
Root, Waverly, and de Rochemont, Richard. (1981). *Eating in America: A History.* Hopewell, NJ: The Ecco Press.
Rosen, George. (1958). *A History of Public Health.* Baltimore, MD: The Johns Hopkins University Press.
Rosen, Sherwin. (1981). "The Economics of Superstars," *American Economic Review* 71, no. 5: 845–58.
Rosen, Sherwin. (1988). "The Value of Changes in Life Expectancy," *Journal of Risk and Uncertainty* 1: 285–304.
Rosenzweig, Roy. (1983). *Eight Hours for What We Will: Workers and Leisure in an Industrial City, 1870–1920.* New York: Cambridge University Press, 1983.
Rothstein, William G. (1972). *American Physicians in the Nineteenth Century: From Sects to Science.* Baltimore, MD/London: The Johns Hopkins University Press.
Roubini, Nouriel. (2014). "Rise of the Machines: Downfall of the Economy?" *Nouriel Unplugged: Economic Insights of a Global Nomad,* blog post, December 8.
Rubin, Robert E. and Turner, Nicholas. (2014). "The Steep Cost of America's High Incarceration Rate," *Wall Street Journal,* December 26.
Rus, Daniela. (2015). "The Robots Are Coming: How Technological Breakthroughs Will Transform Everyday Life," *Foreign Affairs* (July/August): 2–7.
Rybczynski, Witold. (1995). "How to Build a Suburb," *The Wilson Quarterly* 19, no. 3 (summer): 114–26.
Sahadi, Jeanne. (2013). "America's Debt: The Real Medicare Spending Problem," *CNN* 7 (February).
Sandler, Martin W. (2003). *Straphanging in the USA: Trolleys and Subways in American Life.* New York/Oxford, UK: Oxford University Press.
Santana, Arthur D., Livingstone, Randall, and Yoon Cho. (2011). *Medium Matters: Newsreaders' Recall and Engagement with Online and Print Newspapers.* Unpublished doctoral dissertation. Eugene: University of Oregon.
Sass, Steven. (1997). *The Promise of Private Pensions.* Cambridge, MA: Harvard University Press.
Sawyer, E. W. (1936). *Automobile Liability Insurance: An Analysis of National Standard Policy Provisions.* New York/London: McGraw-Hill.
Schlereth, Thomas J. (1991). *Victorian America: Transformations in Everyday Life, 1876–1915.* New York: HarperCollins Publishers.
Schmidt, Charles W. (2012). "CT Scans: Balancing Health Risks and Medical Benefits," *Environmental Health Perspectives* 120, no. 3 (March): A118–A121.
Schneider, Arthur. (1997). *Jump Cut! Memoirs of a Pioneer Television Editor.* Jefferson, NC: McFarland.
Schwartz, Nelson D., and Cohen, Patricia. (2014). "Falling Wages at Factories Squeeze the Middle Class," *The New York Times,* November 21, p. 1.
Schweber, Bill. (1997). "The Transistor at 50: Not Even Considering Retirement," *EDN* 42, no. 26 (December 18): 83–86.
Sears, Roebuck Catalogue. (1902). Introduction by Cleveland Amory. New York: Bounty Books.
Sears, Roebuck Catalogue. (1908). Joseph J. Schroeder Jr., ed. Chicago, IL: Follett Publishing.
Sears, Roebuck Catalogue. (1927). Alan Mirken, ed. New York: Bounty Books.
Seburn, Patrick. (1991). "Evolution of Employer-Provided Defined Benefit Pensions," *Monthly Labor Review* (December): 16–23.

Secunda, Eugene. (1990). "VCRs and Viewer Control Over Programming: An Historical Perspective," in Julia R. Dobrow, ed., *Social and Cultural Aspects of VCR Use*. Hillsdale, NJ: Lawrence Erlbaum Associates, Inc.

Seligman, Edwin R. A. (1927). *The Economics of Installment Selling: A Study in Consumer Credit with Special Reference to the Automobile.* 2 vols. New York: Harper and Brothers.

Severson, Robert F. Jr. (1960). "The American Manufacturing Frontier, 1870–1940." *The Business History Review* 34, no. 3: 356–72. www.jstor.org/stable/3111880.

Shanabruch, Charles. (2003). "Building and Selling Chicago's Bungalow Belt," in Pacyga and Shanabruch, eds. (2003), pp. 53–74.

Shaw, William H. (1947). *Value of Commodity Output since 1869.* New York: National Bureau of Economic Research.

Shergold, Peter R. (1962). *Working Class Life: The "American Standard" in Comparative Perspective, 1899–1913.* Pittsburgh, PA: University of Pittsburgh Press.

Sichel, Daniel. (2011). "What Happened to Prices of Simple, General-Purpose Products over the Centuries: Nails and Screws since about 1700." Federal Reserve Board working paper, September.

Siegel, Lee. (2008). "Why Does Hollywood Hate the Suburbs?" *Wall Street Journal*, December 27–28, p. W4.

Silverman, Arnold, and Schneider, Linda. (1991). "Suburban Localism and Long Island's Regional Crisis," in *Built Environment* 17, nos. 3/4: 191–204.

Simon, Ruth, and Barr, Caelainn. (2015). "Endangered Species: Young U.S. Entrepreneurs," *Wall Street Journal*, January 2, A1.

Simpson, William R., Simpson, Florence K, and Samuels, Charles. (1954). *Hockshop.* New York: Random House.

Sinclair, Upton. (1906). *The Jungle.* New York: Doubleday, Page & Co.

Smil, Vaclav. (2005). *Creating the Twentieth Century: Technical Innovations of 1867–1914 and Their Lasting Impact.* New York/Oxford, UK: Oxford University Press.

Smith, Page. (1984). *The Rise of Industrial America: A People's History of the Post-Reconstruction Era.* New York: McGraw-Hill.

Snow, Richard. (2013). "Henry Ford's Experiment to Build a Better Worker," *Wall Street Journal*, May 10, p. B1.

Snyder, T. D., and Dillow, S. A. (2013). *Digest of Education Statistics.* Washington, DC: National Center for Education Statistics.

Solow, Robert M. (1957). "Technical Change and the Aggregate Production Function," *Review of Economics and Statistics* 39: 312–20.

Solow, Robert M. (1987). "We'd Better Watch Out," *The New York Times*, July 22.

Soltow, Lee and Edward Stevens. (1981). *The Rise of Literacy and the Common School in the United States: A Socioeconomic Analysis to 1870.* Chicago, IL: University of Chicago Press.

Sonoc, Scott. (2003). "Defining the Chicago Bungalow," in Pacyga and Shanabruch (2003), pp. 8–30.

Span, Christopher. (2009). *From Cotton Field to Schoolhouse.* Chapel Hill: The University of North Carolina Press.

Spigel, Lynn. (1992). *Make Room for TV: Television and the Family Ideal in Postwar America.* Chicago, IL: University of Chicago Press.

"Spotify." (2013). *Music Week* 4 (March 1).

Staehler, R. E., and Hayward Jr., W. S. (1979). "Traffic Service Position System No. 1 Recent Developments: An Overview," *Bell System Technical Journal* 58, no. 6: 1109–18.

Starr, Paul. (1977). "Medicine, Economy and Society in Nineteenth-Century America," *Journal of Social History* 10, no. 4 (summer): 588–607.

Starr, Paul. (1982). *The Social Transformation of American Medicine.* New York: Basic Books.

Steckel, Richard H. (2008). "Biological Measures of the Standard of Living," *Journal of Economic Perspectives* 22, no. 1 (winter): 129–52.

Steckel, Richard H., and White, William J. (2012). "Engines of Growth: Farm Tractors and Twentieth-Century U.S. Economic Welfare." Northwestern University working paper, February 9.

Steele, Valerie. (1997). *Fifty Years of Fashion: New Look to Now.* New Haven, CT/London: Yale University Press.

Steele, Volnay. (2005). *Bleed, Blister, and Purge: A History of Medicine on the American Frontier.* Missoula, MT: Mountain Press Publishing Company.

Steiger, Paul E. (2007). "Read All about It: How Newspapers Got into Such a Fix, and Where They Go from Here," *The Wall Street Journal*, December 29, pp. A1, A8.

Stelter, Brian. (2013). "As DVRs Shift TV Habits, Ratings Calculations Follow," *The New York Times*, October 6.

Sterling, Christopher H., and Kittross, John M. (1990). *Stay Tuned: A Concise History of American Broadcasting.* Belmont, CA: Wadsworth Publishing Company.

Stevens, Rosemary. (1989). *In Sickness and in Wealth: American Hospitals in the Twentieth Century.* New York: Basic Books.

Stevenson, Robert Louis. (1892). *Across the Plains with Other Memories and Essays.* New York: C. Scribner's Sons.

Stilgoe, John R. (2007). *Train Time: Railroads and the Imminent Reshaping of the United States Landscape.* Charlottesville/London: University of Virginia Press.

Stone, Mildred F. (1942). *A Short History of Life Insurance.* Indianapolis, IN: The Insurance Research and Review Service.

Stotz, Louis. (1938). *History of the Gas Industry.* New York: Stettiner Bros.

Strasser, Susan. (1982). *Never Done: A History of American Housework.* New York: Pantheon.

Streightoff, Frank Hatch. (1911). *The Standard of Living among the Industrial People of America.* Boston, MA: Houghton Mifflin, 1911.

Stross, Randall. (2007). *The Wizard of Menlo Park: How Thomas Alva Edison Invented the Modern World.* New York: Crown Publisher

Stroud, Hubert. (1995). *The Promise of Paradise: Recreational and Retirement Communities in the United States since 1950.* Baltimore, MD: Johns Hopkins University Press.

Sullivan, Bob. (2008). "Cable TV: King of Misleading Come-ons," *MSNBC.com*, January 28.

Taft, Philip. (1983). "Workers of a New Cenury," in Richard B. Morris, ed., *A History of the American Worker.* Princeton, NJ: Princeton University Press, pp. 115–50.

Tarbell, Ida M. (2005). *The History of the Standard Oil Company.* New York: McClure, Phillips & Company.

Tavernise, Sabrina. (2013). "Joblessness Shortens Lifespan of Least Educated White Women, Research Says," *The New York Times*, May 30.

Tavernise, Sabrina, and Gebeloff, Robert. (2014). "Smoking Proves Hard to Shake among the Poor," *The New York Times*, March 25, pp. A1, A17.

Taylor, Timothy D., Katz, Mark, and Grajeda, Tony. (2012). *Music, Sound, and Technology in America: A Documentary History of Early Phonograph, Cinema, and Radio.* Durham, NC/London: Duke University Press.

Tebbel, John William. (1972). *History of Book Publishing in the United States.* New York: R. R. Bowker and Co.

"Television Facts and Statistics—1939 to 2000" (2001). *TVHistory.tv.* http://tvhistory.tv/facts-stats.htm.

Temin, Peter. (1980). *Taking Your Medicine: Drug Regulation in the United States.* Cambridge, MA/London: Harvard University Press.

Thernstrom, Stephan. (1964). *Poverty and Progress: Social Mobility in a Nineteenth Century City.* Cambridge, MA: Harvard University Press.

Thomas, Gordon, and Witts, Max Morgan. (1971). *The San Francisco Earthquake.* New York: Stein and Day.

Thomas, Monifa. (2013). "Renewed Call for a Level 1 Trauma Center at University of Chicago Hospital," *Chicago Sun-Times.com*, May 28.

Thompson, John D., and Goldin, Grace. (1975). *The Hospital: A Social and Architectural History.* New Haven, CT: Yale University Press.

Thompson, Robert L. (1947). *Wiring a Continent: The History of the Telegraph Industry in the United States, 1832–1866.* Princeton, NJ: Princeton University Press.

Totty, Michael. (2002). "Have We Been Here Before? A Look at How the Internet Is Similar to—and Different from—Landmark Inventions of the Past," *Wall Street Journal* (July 15), R13–R14.

Towne, Mavin, and Rasmussen, Wayne. (1960), "Farm Gross Product and Gross Investment in the Nineteenth Century," in Trends in the American Economy in the Nineteenth Century, The Conference on Research in Income and Wealth. Princeton, NJ: Princeton University Press for NBER.

Troesken, Werner. (2002). "The Limits of Jim Crow: Race and the Provision of Water and Sewerage Services in American Cities, 1880–1925." *The Journal of Economic History* 62, no. 3: 734–72.

Tuomi, Ilika. (2002). *Networks of Innovation: Change and Meaning in the Age of the Internet.* Oxford, UK/ New York: Oxford University Press.

Turneaure, F. E., and Russell, H. L. (1940). *Public Water Supplies.* New York: John Wiley & Sons.

"TV Basics: A Report on the Growth and Scope of Television" (2012). *Television Bureau of Advertising, Inc*, June.

Twitter, Inc. (2014). "About: Company." *Twitter.com.* https://about.twitter.com/company.

U.S. Census Bureau. (2012/2013). "Computer and Internet Access in the United States."

U.S. Food and Drug Administration. (2013). "Summary of NDA Approvals & Receipts, 1938 to the Present," *FDA.gov.* www.fda.gov/AboutFDA/WhatWeDo/History/ProductRegulation/SummaryofNDAApprovalsReceipts19.

Usher, Dan. (1973). "An Imputation of the Measure of Economic Growth for Changes in Life Expectancy," in Milton Moss, ed., *The Measurement of Economic and Social Performance,* Studies in Income and Wealth, vol. 38. New York: Columbia University Press for NBER, 193–225.

Van Gelder, Lawrence. (2002). "Milton Berle, TV's First Star as 'Uncle Miltie,' Dies at 93," *The New York Times*, March 28.

Vietor, Richard H. K. (2000), "Government Regulation of Business," in Engerman and Gallman, eds. (2000b), pp. 969–1012.

Vijg, Jan. (2011). *The American Technological Challenge: Stagnation and Decline in the 21st Century.* New York: Algora Publishing.

VISA, Inc. (2013). "VisaNet: The Technology behind Visa."

Vogel, Morris J. (1980). *The Invention of the Modern Hospital: Boston 1870–1930.* Chicago, IL: The University of Chicago Press.

Volti, Rudi. (2004). *Cars and Culture: The Life Story of a Technology.* Westport, CT: Greenwood Press.

Walters, Pamela Bernhouse, and O'Connell, Philip J. (1988). "The Family Economy: Work and Educational Participation in the United States, 1890–1940." *American Journal of Sociology* 93, no. 5 (March): 1116–52.

Walton, Francis. (1956). *Miracle of World War II: How American Industry Made Victory Possible.* New York: The Macmillan Company.

Warburton, Clark. (1932). *The Economic Results of Prohibition.* New York: Columbia University Press.

Watkins, John Elfreth Jr. (1900). "What May Happen in the Next Hundred Years," *Ladies Home Journal*, November, p. 8.

Weaver, William W. (2010). *Culinary Ephemera: An Illustrated History.* Berkeley: University of California Press.

Weiman, David F., and Levin, Richard C. (1994). "Preying for Monopoly? The Case of the Southern Bell Telephone Company, 1894–1912," *Journal of Political Economy* 102, no. 1 (February): 103–26.

Weintraub, David. (1939). "Effects of Current and Prospective Technological Developments upon Capital Formation," *American Economic Review* 29 (March): 15–32.

Wells, Christopher. (2007). "The Road to the Model T: Culture, Road Conditions, and Innovation at the Dawn of the American Motor Age," *Technology and Culture* 48, no. 3 (July): 497–523.

Welty, Eudora. (1984). *One Writer's Beginnings.* Cambridge, MA/London: Harvard University Press.

Wertz, Richard W., and Dorothy C. (1977). *Lying-In: A History of Childbirth in America.* New York: The Free Press.

Wessel, David. (2007). "Lack of Well-Educated Workers Has Lots of Roots, No Quick Fix," *The Wall Street Journal*, April 19, pp. 1–2.

Wexler, Alexandra. (2014). "Cotton's Crown Threatened by Manmade Fibers," *Wall Street Journal*, April 25, p. B1.

White, Joseph B. (2014). "Detroit Gallops Again," *Wall Street Journal*, p. B5.

White, Richard. (2011). *Railroaded: The Transcontinentals and the Making of Modern America.* New York: Norton.

Wiedemann, H. R. (1994). "Sidney Farber," *European Journal of Pediatrics* 153, no. 4 (April): 223.

Wickstrom, Andy. (1986). "Statistics Support the Love Affair with the VCR," *Philadelphia Inquirer*, May 11.

Wilcox, James A. (1984). "Automobile Fuel Efficiency: Measurement and Explanation," *Economic Inquiry* 22 (July): 375–85.

Winnick, Louis. (1957). *American Housing and Its Use: The Demand for Shelter Space.* New York: John Wiley & Sons, inc.

Winship, Scott. (2012). "Bogeyman Economics," *National Affair* no. 10 (winter): 3–21.

Wood, Edith Elmer. (1919). *The Housing of the Unskilled Wage Earner: America's Next Problem.* New York: MacMillan.

Wood, Edith Elmer. (1931). *Recent Trends in American Housing.* New York: MacMillan.

Wright, Russell O. (2004). *Chronology of Communications in the United States.* Jefferson, NC: McFarland.

Yates, JoAnne. (1999). "The Structuring of Early Computer Use in Life Insurance," *Journal of Design History* 12, no. 1: 7–20.

Young, David M. (1998). *Chicago Transit: An Illustrated History.* DeKalb: North Illinois University Press.

Young, William H, with Young, Nancy K. (2002). *The 1930s.* Westport, CT/London: The Greenwood Press.

Yount, Lisa. (2001). *Patients' Rights in the Age of Managed Health Care.* New York: Facts on File, Inc.

Zickhur, Kathryn, and Rainie, Lee. (2014). "e-Reading Rises as Device Ownership Jumps," Pew Research Internet Project, January 16.

Zumbrun, Josh. (2014). "Market Missteps Fuel Inequality," *Wall Street Journal,* October 27, p. A2.

CREDITS

Chapter 1: Introduction

Excerpt from THE AMERICANS: THE DEMOCRATIC EXPERIENCE (V3) by Daniel J. Boorstin, copyright © 1973 by Daniel J. Boorstin. Used by permission of Random House, an imprint and division of Penguin Random House LLC. All rights reserved.

Chapter 2: The Starting Point

Horace Greeley, "To Aspiring Young Men," *New York Tribune* editorial, 1846.

Chapter 3: What They Ate and Wore and Where They Bought It

Excerpt from THE GOOD OLD DAYS—THEY WERE TERRIBLE! By Otto L. Bettmann, copyright 1974 by Otto Bettmann. Used by permission of Random House, an imprint and division of Penguin Random House LLC. All rights reserved.

Chapter 4: The American Home

Mark H. Rose, one sentence from page 2, in Cities of Light and Heat: Domesticating Gas and Electricity in Urban America. Copyright © 1995 by The Pennsylvania State University Press. Reprinted by permission of The Pennsylvania State University Press.

Chapter 5: Motors Overtake Horses and Rail

CREATING THE TWENTIETH CENTURY: TECHNICAL INNOVATIONS OF 1867-1914 AND THEIR LASTING IMPACT by Smil (2005). By permission of Oxford University Press, USA.

Chapter 6: From Telegraph to Talkies

"How Motion Pictures Industrialized Entertainment," *Journal of Economic History* 72 (Dec. 2012, no. 4), 1036–63. Used with permission.

Chapter 7: Nasty, Brutish, and Short

Rosen, George. Foreword by Pascal James Imperato, MD, MPH&TM. Introduction by Elizabeth Fee. Biographical Essay and New Bibliography by Edward T. Morman. A History of Public Health, Revised Expanded Edition. p. 169. © Copyright 1958 by MD Publications, Inc., New York, New York © 1993, 2015 Johns Hopkins University Press. Reprinted with permission of Johns Hopkins University Press.

Chapter 8: Working Conditions on the Job and at Home

Harvey Greene, excerpts from *The Uncertainty of Everyday Life, 1915-1945*. Copyright © 1992 by Harvey Green. Reprinted with the permission of The Permissions Company, Inc., on behalf of the Univeristy of Arkansas Press, www.uapress.com.

Chapter 9: Taking and Mitigating Risks

Emerson, Ralph Waldo. (1841). *The Journals of Ralph Waldo Emerson, vol. V 1838–41*. Boston: Houghton Mifflin (published in 1911).

Chapter 10: Fast Food, Synthetic Fibers, and Split-Level Subdivisions

Rybczynski, Witold. (1995). "How to Build a Suburb," *The Wilson Quarterly* 19, no. 3 (summer): 114–26.

Chapter 11: See the USA in Your Chevrolet or from a Plane Flying High Above

Music by Leon Carr, Words by Leo Corday, Copyright © 1948 (Renewed) by Music Sales Corporation and Fred Ahlert Music Corp., International Copyright Secured. All Rights Reserved. Used by Permission. Warning: Unauthorized reproduction of this publication is prohibited by Federal Law and is subject to criminal prosecution.

Excerpt from TURBULENT SKIES by T. A. Heppenheimer, copyright © 1995 by T. A. Heppenheimer. Published by John Wiley and Sons, Inc.

Chapter 12: Entertainment and Communications from Milton Berle to the iPhone

Spigel, Lynn. (1992). *Make Room for TV: Television and the Family Ideal in Postwar America*. Chicago, IL: University of Chicago Press. Used with permission.

Chapter 13: Computers and the Internet from the Mainframe to Facebook

Used with permission of InfoWorld Copyright© 2015. All rights reserved.

Chapter 14: Antibiotics, CT Scans, and the Evolution of Health and Medicine

Copyright © Jun 5, 1984 Paul Starr. Reprinted by permission of Basic Books, a member of the Perseus Books Group.

Chapter 15: Work, Youth, and Retirement at Home and on the Job

From *The New York Times*, April 20 © 2008 *The New York Times*. All rights reserved. Used by permission and protected by the Copyright Laws of the United States. The printing, copying, redistribution, or retransmission of this Content without express written permission is prohibited.

Chapter 16: The Great Leap Forward from the 1920s to the 1950s

Ford, Henry. (1922). *My Life and Work*. Garden City, NY: Doubleday, Page & Co.

Chapter 17: Innovation

Peter Theil, credo of his venture-capital firm, Founders Fund.

Page 591: Watkins, John Elfreth Jr. (1900). "What May Happen in the Next Hundred Years," *Ladies Home Journal*, November, p. 8.

Chapter 18: Inequality and the Other Headwinds

MARRIAGE MARKETS by Carbone, Cahn (2014) 57 words as an epigraph from p. 18. By permission of Oxford University Press, USA.

INDEX

THE PRINCETON ECONOMIC HISTORY OF THE WESTERN WORLD

Joel Mokyr, Series Editor

Growth in a Traditional Society: The French Countryside, 1450–1815
by Philip T. Hoffman

The Vanishing Irish: Households, Migration, and the Rural Economy in Ireland, 1850–1914
by Timothy W. Guinnane

Black '47 and Beyond: The Great Irish Famine in History, Economy, and Memory
by Cormac Ó Gráda

The Great Divergence: China, Europe, and the Making of the Modern World Economy
by Kenneth Pomeranz

The Big Problem of Small Change
by Thomas J. Sargent and François R. Velde

Farm to Factory: A Reinterpretation of the Soviet Industrial Revolution
by Robert C. Allen

Quarter Notes and Bank Notes: The Economics of Music Composition in the Eighteenth and Nineteenth Centuries
by F. M. Scherer

The Strictures of Inheritance: The Dutch Economy in the Nineteenth Century
by Jan Luiten van Zanden and Arthur van Riel

Understanding the Process of Economic Change
by Douglass C. North

Feeding the World: An Economic History of Agriculture, 1800–2000
by Giovanni Federico

Cultures Merging: A Historical and Economic Critique of Culture
by Eric L. Jones

The European Economy since 1945: Coordinated Capitalism and Beyond
by Barry Eichengreen

War, Wine, and Taxes: The Political Economy of Anglo-French Trade, 1689–1900
by John V. C. Nye

A Farewell to Alms: A Brief Economic History of the World
by Gregory Clark

Power and Plenty: Trade, War, and the World Economy in the Second Millennium
by Ronald Findlay and Kevin O'Rourke

Power over Peoples: Technology, Environments, and Western Imperialism, 1400 to the Present
by Daniel R. Headrick

Unsettled Account: The Evolution of Banking in the Industrialized World since 1800
by Richard S. Grossman

States of Credit: Size, Power, and the Development of European Polities
by David Stasavage

Creating Wine: The Emergence of a World Industry, 1840–1914
by James Simpson

The Evolution of a Nation: How Geography and Law Shaped the American States
by Daniel Berkowitz and Karen B. Clay

Distant Tyranny: Markets, Power, and Backwardness in Spain, 1650–1800
by Regina Grafe

The Chosen Few: How Education Shaped Jewish History, 70–1492
by Maristella Botticini and Zvi Eckstein

Why Australia Prospered: The Shifting Sources of Economic Growth
by Ian W. McLean

Cities of Commerce: The Institutional Foundations of International Trade in the Low Countries, 1250–1650
by Oscar Gelderblom

Lending to the Borrower from Hell: Debt, Taxes, and Default in the Age of Philip II
by Mauricio Drelichman and Hans-Joachim Voth

Power to the People: Energy in Europe over the Last Five Centuries
by Astrid Kander, Paolo Malanima, and Paul Warde

Fragile by Design: The Political Origins of Banking Crises and Scarce Credit
by Charles W. Calomiris and Stephen H. Haber

The Son Also Rises: Surnames and the History of Social Mobility
by Gregory Clark

Why Did Europe Conquer the World
by Philip T. Hoffman

The Rise and Fall of American Growth: The U.S. Standard of Living since the Civil War
by Robert J. Gordon

Unequal Gains: American Growth and Inequality since the 1600s
by Peter H. Lindert and Jeffrey G. Williamson

Brazil in Transition: Beliefs, Leadership, and Institutional Change
by Lee J. Alston, Marcus André Melo, Bernardo Mueller, and Carlos Pereira